Praise for
Zen and the Art of Making a Living

Comments from Career Professionals

"*Zen and the Art of Making a Living* is one hell of a book. I [feel] that [it] really challenges *What Color Is Your Parachute?* for leadership in the career field. Nice job!"
— Daniel Lauber, author of *Non-Profit and Education Job Finder* President, Planning Communications, River Forest, IL

"After fifteen years, four thousand clients and authorship of my own career counseling program, this is simply the best book in its field that I have ever seen! I have reviewed almost all career counseling books, programs and strategies available. None is better than *Zen and the Art of Making a Living*."
— Jim Fritz, V.P. Program Development, Access Influential, Inc., Denver, CO

"Over the past six weeks, I have read and digested your book *Zen and the Art of Making a Living*. As a therapist and educator, I found your writing very readable and informative. More importantly, on a personal level I was struck by the depth at which many of the ideas resonated in my psyche. I was impressed with the scholarly yet deceivingly simple marriage of the ideas you presented. Your succinct, clear melding of Archetypes, Zen, and Career seemed so appropriate in dealing with the 'Fallen heroes' I travel with daily. I see your work as a source of inspiration for many men and women."
— Larry Dick, L-M Dick and Associates, Alberta, Canada

"[Our staff enjoys] your book, and, of course, we share the book with our students. Your ideas about meaningful livelihood are important to me and to my students. Your book with its basic principle of choosing to be in control of one's career is very valuable to these people. It helps us to help them to create their new reality."
— Lou Smith, Re-Creating Your Future, Dallas, TX

"First I would like to say thank you in a very large way! I was given your book, *Zen and the Art of Making a Living*, last March. I am an outplacement consultant . . . and also have a private practice working with people in career and life transition. It is the best book and most aligned material I have ever come across. . . . Since receiving the book, I have been recommending it, not only to my clients, but to other consultants, career centers, and friends. I have probably recommended it to several hundred people so far. I acknowledge you for an epic and powerful piece of work. It makes my life a lot easier and is a great way for me to support my clients. . . . Again, thank you. Your work is very important at this time."
— R. B., outplacement consultant, Colorado Springs, CO

"Thank you. Thank you graciously, passionately, joyously. I had lost purpose . . . and your book provided a mirror, a process, a background, chunks of wisdom, assurance. . . . My 'work' has just begun, of course, but your book really reaches me. It sings to me. I wanted to say thank you for your work, for putting me back on the Way, for re-awakening me."

— E. J.,
Haverhill, MA

"Just had to tell you—I've had the 'ultimate' Zen experience with your book, *Zen and the Art of Making a Living*. I was thoroughly 'stuck' in regard to career decisions. . . . I bought the book and immersed myself in it, vowing to 'do' the book as quickly and as thoroughly as possible so that I could get myself to decide upon a direction and get on with my life. . . . I am busily doing the next step I need to take, career-wise. I do not know exactly how and where this step will lead me, but my next step is obvious, and I have finally admitted that that sort of clearness is all that matters to me."

— C. B. I.,
Worthington, OH

"I have just ordered from a favorite local bookstore ten copies of your book, *Zen and the Art of Making a Living*. What a wonderful out-of-the-blue gift to friends and not-so-friends alike. This is a WORK! . . . What a work! For both the spiritual life/philosophies AND [as] a practical workbook . . . There ain't none—not like this! Thank you."

— C. K. L.,
Perrysburg, NY

"I picked up a copy of your book, *Zen and the Art of Making a Living*: by page ten, I was on the phone trying to locate your phone number. Thank you for writing this most wonderful expression of love. I have always considered work as a person's primary art form; your book is the first time I've run across the idea put forth so totally and helpfully. . . . Thank you so much for giving and sharing." — R. S.,
Marion, IA

"Thank you for your time and energy in writing *Zen and the Art of Making a Living*. Of the books I have read, yours will be listed as one of the most influential in changing the way I think and live." — S. P.,
Silver Spring, MD

"I am amazed at the talent of Mr. Boldt in so many ways. Certainly, his ability to organize a very lengthy publication in a way that takes each individual through the process so they can understand it and actually achieve the desired outcome, in itself is a tremendous accomplishment. . . . His talent in writing effectively, clearly, yet [in a way that can be] understood by people of various educational backgrounds is a beautiful talent. Most importantly, his eloquent style, his words come from a place within himself that is truly real. I thank him from the bottom of my heart and soul for helping me and many others to change their lives. . . . Words cannot express the thanks for the gift he has given so many."

— C. M.,
Westport, CT

"Your Zen guide to creative life was a lifesaver. It was the Zen wisdom and the myths and your love beaming from every page that took me back to my real home. Thank you for existing, Laurence. Thank you for the book."

— I. G.,
St. Jean-Gonville, France

"I recently finished reading your book, *Zen and the Art of Making a Living,* and wanted to thank you for writing such a fine piece of work. . . . Your book has given me inspiration on using my diverse skills within my life instead of trying to conform to somebody else's set of ideals for my career. . . . Since reading your book, I've had the opportunity to express the artist in me. I recently landed the lead role in a music video. In addition, I am currently writing a script based on true life experiences. . . . Again, thanks for writing *Zen and the Art of Making a Living.*"
— T. H.,
Boston, MA

"Before graduating from college, I wasn't quite sure what occupation I would choose for my life's work. Fortunately, I read your book, *Zen and the Art of Making a Living.* As a result of the insights I gained from your book, I've chosen the path of an entrepreneur and have come to discover my purpose in life."
— B. K.,
Mishawaka, IN

"I love your book *Zen and the Art of Making a Living*! The view it shares resonates deeply in me, and also the spiritual dimensions it addresses hit home. . . . Thank you. Thank you."
— C. J.,
Brooklyn, NY

"I am a forty-eight-year-old white male who is coming to the end of his primary professional career. About a month ago, I found your book. I have found your work fascinating. It has changed my life. . . . I have bought three copies of the book (only because the store didn't have more) and given them to friends. Without exception, everyone feels that your book is outstanding and enlightening. They all say it is changing their lives for the better, as well. This is a long-winded way of saying 'Thank you. Thank you more than you will ever know.' Your book is nothing short of a miracle."
— T. W.,
Gaithersburg, MD

"Your *Zen and the Art of Making a Living* created an eye-opening impact with me. I've found what's calling me. . . . I'm pursuing it, and I'm at the point of catching it and riding it home. Thanks for your dedication. It helps."
— D. L.,
Los Angeles, CA

"Thank you for your excellent book, *Zen and the Art of Making a Living.* I find it thoughtful and thought provoking, helpful and insightful. . . . I have a great pleasure in recommending your book to my clients."
— D. G.,
Los Angeles, CA

"I just wanted to tell you how very much I have enjoyed your book, *Zen and the Art of Making a Living.* All the time and caring, effort and excellence that have been crafted into your work have made it a trusted and very useful companion."
— J. M.,
Aptos, CA

"Your book *Zen and the Art of Making a Living* is brilliant and inspiring. It is a major breakthrough in the usually very dry realm of career-seeking. I am honestly in awe of the amount of time and hard work you have put into creating it."
— A. H.,
Port Orchard, WA

"I have been a career counselor . . . for the past ten years. In all of this time, I have not found a book that is as effective and well rounded. . . . Your book has become a fixture in my career center. But beyond its appeal to me, I think it finally takes career education in the many directions necessary to establish, not only one's identity, but an assessment of what makes work meaningful to an individual. Few, if any, texts I've worked with in the past have accomplished this."

— M. R. H., career counselor,
Seattle, WA

"I am writing this letter while enthusiastically making my way through *Zen and the Art of Making a Living* and wanted to express my reaction and thanks. For three years, I have run the Women's Outreach Program for a community college in New Jersey, guiding women towards careers through empowerment, education, and support. I am grateful that there are career counselor/authors out there, like yourself, who affirm and give flesh to the things we try to do on a daily basis. . . . Your work reminds me what the path means and [of] the necessity for tending my own psychic garden so that the fruits of a value-laden life will be mine. Thank you."

— A. F., career educator,
New York, NY

"I am a career/placement counselor located in New York City. I wanted to thank you for writing such a wonderful book. It seems . . . the unfortunate trend is for people to keep their work and emotional/spiritual lives separate. I believe the integration of the two is the very essence of happiness in one's work life, and I was glad to learn that someone [had] elaborated so eloquently on the topic. I also loved the way your book was laid out—it is very user friendly and interactive, without losing its deeper meaning. Thank you."

— A. S., career counselor,
Brooklyn, NY

Comments from Readers

"How can I possibly express the life-transforming realizations your book has helped me to see? I truly feel blessed to have found it. It's given me a whole new perspective on work and couldn't have come along at a better time in my life. I've been longing to make a career change for many years, and your book has inspired me to go for it."

— Dave Powell,
Newman, GA

"I am writing to you to let you know how much I enjoyed and benefited from your book, *Zen and the Art of Making a Living*. I found it fascinating, stimulating, meaningful, and helpful. You truly helped me to resolve to take the first steps on a new path (my quest) for which my heart and my mind have been yearning for years. It has served not only as an invaluable resource for information and ideas but also as a source of wisdom and a jumping-off place for discovery. I thank you for writing it."

— Jeffrey R. Kastin,
La Jolla, CA

"I recently discovered your book, *Zen and the Art of Making a Living*. It's the best career planning book I've ever read, and I've read quite a few. Unlike most career planning books, your book deals with the deeper issues of what work (and life) is all about."

— D. S.,
San Francisco, CA

ARKANA

ZEN AND THE ART OF MAKING A LIVING

Laurence G. Boldt is a nationally known writer and career consultant based in the San Francisco Bay area. He has given speeches and conducted workshops across the country and been featured in such publications as *New Age Journal* and *Newsweek*. His previous books include *How to Find the Work You Love* (Arkana, 1996) and *Zen Soup* (Arkana, 1997).

From my client, Laurence...
To my friend, Laine.
May it ring true to the
symphony already playing
In Your Heart....

Friends Forever,

2004

ZEN

and the Art of Making a Living

A Practical Guide to Creative Career Design

LAURENCE G. BOLDT

PENGUIN/ARKANA

ARKANA
Published by the Penguin Group
Penguin Putnam Inc., 375 Hudson Street, New York, New York 10014, U.S.A.
Penguin Books Ltd, 27 Wrights Lane, London W8 5TZ, England
Penguin Books Australia Ltd, Ringwood, Victoria, Australia
Penguin Books Canada Ltd, 10 Alcorn Avenue, Toronto, Ontario, Canada M4V 3B2
Penguin Books (N.Z.) Ltd, 182–190 Wairau Road, Auckland 10, New Zealand

Penguin Books Ltd, Registered Offices: Harmondsworth, Middlesex, England

First published in the United States of America by Lightning Press 1992
Revised edition published in Arkana 1993
This second revised edition published in Arkana 1999

1 3 5 7 9 10 8 6 4 2

Illustrations used with permission of Suzuki, Daisetz T., *Zen and Japanese Culture,* Bolligen Series LXIV. Copyright © 1959 by Princeton University Press. Illustrations from *Zen Painting and Calligraphy* by Jan Fontein and Money L. Hickman. Copyright © 1970 by Museum of Fine Arts, Boston, Massachusetts. Used by permission. Illustrations from *The Art of Zen* by Stephen Addiss used with permission of Stephen Addiss. Copyright © 1989 by Harry N. Abrams. Lu K'uan Yu (Charles Luk), *Taoist Yoga,* © Lu K'uan Yu, 1973 (York Beach, ME: Samuel Weiser, Inc., 1973), p. 150. Used by permission. Lu K'uan Yu (Charles Luk), *The Secrets of Chinese Meditation* © Charles Luk, 1964 (York Beach, ME: Samuel Weiser, Inc., 1964), p. 16. Used by permission. Illustrations from *Pelican History of Art. Art and Architecture of India,* by Benjamin Rowland. © 1953 by Yale University Press. Used by permission. #28—Yantra of Krsna, courtesy of John Stevens; #32—The six chakra, courtesy of John Stevens; #145a—"Katsujinken," "The sword that gives life" by Gempo, courtesy of John Stevens; #203b—"Namu amida butsu" by Ryokan, courtesy of the Kimura Collection; and #207—"Dai birushanabutsu," "Mahavairocana Buddha" by Juin, courtesy of the Kinami Collection from *Sacred Calligraphy of the East* by John Stevens, © 1981. By arrangement with Shambhala Publications Inc., Boston. Excerpts from *Foundations of Tibetan Mysticism* by Lama Anagarka Govinda, copyright © 1969, 1991, Samuel Weiser, Inc., York Beach, ME. Used by permission. Excerpts from *The Tao of Power* by R. L. Wing. Copyright © 1986 by Immedia. Used by permission of Doubleday, a division of Bantam, Doubleday, & Dell Publishing Group, Inc. Excerpts from *Winning the Marketing War: A Field Manual for Business Leaders* by Gerald A. Michaelson. Published by Madison Books/Abt Books. Copyright © 1987 by Abt Books. Reprinted by permission of the publishers. Excerpts from *Getting Funded: A Complete Guide to Proposal Writing* by Mary S. Hall used with permission of author. Copyright © 1988 by Mary S. Hall. Continuing Education Publications. Excerpts from *The California Nonprofit Corporation Handbook* by Anthony Mancuso. Published by Nolo Press. Copyright © 1991 by Anthony Mancuso. Reprinted by permission of publishers.

LIBRARY OF CONGRESS CATALOGING IN PUBLICATION DATA
Boldt, Laurence G.
Zen and the art of making a living: a practical guide to creative
career design/Laurence G. Boldt.—Rev. ed.
p. cm.
Includes bibliographical references and index.
ISBN 0 14 01.9599 8
1. Religious life—Zen Buddhism.   2. Career development.
I. Title.
BQ9286.B65   1999
650.14—dc20   98–55070

Printed in the United States of America

*When one happens on a book of this kind, he is
well advised to throw it away.*
                        Shū-an

CONTENTS

Acknowledgments

To John Panama

I t is no exaggeration to say that this book would not have been possible without the help of many. To all who have contributed, my heartfelt thanks. I am especially grateful for the input of consulting clients and of seminar and classroom participants. The program was originally developed as a response to your interests and desires. Your input has been critical at every stage. Additionally, your kind words have been a tremendous encouragement along the way. Many thanks.

Further thanks is due several dedicated volunteers for their excellent work. Kim Grant is a capable editor whose enthusiasm for the book has been a large part of making it happen. Susan Shapiro's assistance in typesetting and layout has been indispensable. Sonny King's persistent and tenacious proofing has saved me from incomprehensibility too many times to count.

I also want to thank several people for making possible the Penguin edition of this book. Thanks to my agent, Peter Beren and to Michael Jacobs for seeing the potential of the book. Thanks also to my editor at Penguin, David Stanford, for his careful handling of the book and his easy manner and good humor throughout.

While I am most grateful to these and others for their efforts, responsibility for the book and all of its shortcomings and errors remains mine. A project of this size is bound to have errors and need revision to stay up to date. We encourage you to write us with corrections, updates, and information you think might be of interest to readers of future editions of this book. Feedback of all kinds is most welcome. Please be advised that, for the sake of time, we may not be able to respond to all correspondence. Thank you for your understanding and cooperation.

Preface to the
Revised Edition

In looking back over the nearly ten years since the first edition of this book was published, I am happy to say the career field has come a long way. It is no exaggeration to say that in its philosophical approach and methodology, the field has advanced more in the last ten years than in the previous fifty. There were times in the early 1980s, when I began my career consulting work and the development of the program on which this book is based, that I felt like a voice crying in the wilderness.

At the time, upwards of 95 percent of all career professionals were committed to what I call the "best fit" or "match game" model of vocational guidance. The ol' "tell me your interests and/or skills and I'll tell you what you are supposed to be" approach to vocational guidance. ("Better yet, I'll give you a battery of tests and let my computer tell me what you are supposed to be.") A process whose dominant, and in many cases only, guidance tool consisted of a mechanistic matching of test results to occupational fields left many cold. My belief that there was a more humane way of doing things, one that would celebrate the human spirit and embrace the innate dignity and creativity within all people, inspired a journey that ultimately led to the writing of this book.

Happily, today there are many more career counselors, consultants, and "coaches" committed to the threefold process of providing a context that: (1) encourages individuals to get in touch with who they really are and what they really want, (2) assists them in formulating career goals based on these insights, and (3) aids them in developing definite plans for the realization of these goals. Many career professionals have told me that this book has played a significant role in helping them to adapt their approach. They've told me that it provided them with an alternative methodology that freed them from a philosophical model with which they had long felt at odds.

If we search more deeply for the causes of the dramatic shift in philosophy and methodology of the career field in the past few years, three major ones stand out. First, a creative approach to career development is more engaging, fun, and rewarding not only for the client but for the career professional as well. While the old way of doing things was, in a sense, easier for both the client and the career counselor, it left a lot to be desired for each. Being treated as if he or she could be plugged, like an interchangeable part, into some kind of mammoth job machine was not exactly a spiritually uplifting experience for the client. For the career professional, running people through the same mill day after day, month after month, year after year was not a particularly challenging or fulfilling way to go through life. It was probably not surprising that career counselors working in this fashion were not encouraging people to pursue work *they* would love!

As better materials have become available, more and more career professionals have adapted their approach. Moreover, in recent years, the career field has been the beneficiary of an influx of talented and highly motivated new professionals—attracted to the field in the first instance by the prospect of making a life out of assisting others in fulfilling their hearts' desires. Increasingly, this approach to career development is becoming the standard among a large and growing segment of the field.

The remaining two factors driving change in the career field come as a response to changes in the broader society. These are, first, a shift in values among a large and growing segment of the population away from narrow economic definitions of success and, second, the dramatic changes in the workplace brought about by a historic restructuring of the economy. These are themes we will take up at length in a new section entitled "Doing the Work You Love: A Social Movement for the Twenty-first Century" (see page xxxvi).

Like its methodology, the career literature has also improved markedly in the last few years. In updating the bibliography for the current edition of this book, I've had the opportunity to review virtually every new publication that has come on the scene in the career field in the last five years. I am happy to report that there are many good ones, most of which are included in the bibliographies throughout this book. While on the whole, the career literature remains rather dry and soulless, more books are being written with heart and intelligence. Moreover, there are a great many more well-organized, informational resources available today for the career changer. In addition to better materials for those deciding on a career or looking for employment opportunities, more books can be found with down-to-earth advice for those looking to escape the nine-to-five job routine. Incidentally, the revised edition of this book includes a new section on the booming field of home-based business, which, as many are finding, can provide a ticket to a new life (see pages 404–409).

When this book first came out, the World Wide Web did not even exist. Today, it offers a variety of informational tools, networking resources, and professional services for the career-changer. We've included Internet resources throughout this revised edition. Whether you are interested in finding an internship or a place to volunteer, whether you want to start your own business, work freelance, start a nonprofit, do background research on companies, or find out about specific job openings, you will find ways to tap into resources available on the Internet. Those of you with online capabilities will be able to begin immediate research on ideas that occur to you as you are reading this book.

Many people who read this book become excited about the ideas contained within as well as the possibilities it suggests to them for transforming their own lives. They want opportunities to dive more deeply into the material and to share this experience with like-minded people in a supportive setting. This edition includes a section on starting a life work development group (see pages xxx–xxxiii). I would to encourage those of you who feel so inclined to begin groups of your own.

There are also an increasing number of personal growth and life's work development courses available through a variety of adult education vehicles. Classes and seminars have sprung up all over the country for finding one's purpose and for starting home or freelance businesses, as well as other types of entrepreneurial enterprises. A host of educational opportunities is available for those who want to beat the nine-to-five routine or improve their job-hunting and personal marketing skills. In short, the support materials, systems, and networks available to people who are seeking a way to do the work they love have greatly expanded in number and quality in recent years. There has never been a better time to take up the quest for a truly fulfilling experience of work.

A Personal Note

On a more personal note, I want to thank the many people who have taken the time to write to me. Your letters and the stories of courage, compassion, and commitment that fill them are an inspiration and blessing to me. Writing this book was truly a labor of love. I am happy that it has been so well received and gratified to know that it touched so many, so deeply. People have asked me many times if I was surprised by the success of what is admittedly a long, and in certain respects, demanding book. While I never doubted the value of the material in this book, nor that it had an audience, there were times when I did have doubts about how large that audience might be. One day, not long before the book was finished, while taking a break from writing, I was strolling down a city street near my office when a thought of this kind entered my head. Perhaps, I thought, certain parts should be omitted to make the book more accessible to a wider audience. Just then, I noticed a crude sign that someone had taken the trouble to paste onto a street corner mailbox. It read simply: QUALITY IS FOR EVERYONE. I laughed at myself and the play of the universe and went back to work.

Preface

As you've probably guessed by now, this is not your usual career planning guide. Many of those books seem to have been written for automatons. This is a career guide for human beings. It's really a book about love in action, about joy, about beauty, about caring. It's for people who want to express their talents in meaningful ways that serve others. Its purpose is not to cram you into some category or stuff you into a gray flannel box. Its aim is to assist you in developing what you need to express what's in you in the outer world. In other words, it's designed to help you do your thing. If you don't know what your thing is, it will even help you find it. That's the good news; and no question about it, this program works.

Now here comes the bad news. Well, sort of . . . It takes a lot of work. Yes, that's right, w-o-r-k. It takes "outer work" like research, learning, outreach, and follow-through, and it takes "inner work" like soul-searching, thought, and decision-making. The information in, and the structure of this book will help, but in the end, you are the one making all the decisions. If you don't like decision-making, you'd probably be better off reading one of those "put you into a gray flannel box" career guides. They have all kinds of neat little tests that tell you what you should be. I don't know what you should be, and to tell you the truth, neither does any other career consultant—no matter how impressive their tests. Fortunately, you do know.

You may not think so, but you really do know what you are here to do. Many of you are carrying around a great secret that you have yet to let yourself in on. One purpose of this book is to get the part of you that knows to start talking to the part of you that thinks it doesn't know. Of course, it's really up to you; you are the active ingredient. Your sincerity, intensity, and desire are what will make this process work for you. If you're the kind of person who enjoys adventure, you'll find most of the work in this process challenging and fun. In fact, once you get into it, you will start getting really turned on by the discoveries you make about yourself and the strategies and plans you develop to realize your visions of life at its best.

That's the action of this book—designing creative strategies for realizing your life's work. This *is* a comprehensive career guide. You'll find many of the same subjects that are discussed in the gray flannel career books. You'll find information on how to write a résumé, how to assess your skills, how to take a job interview—all the basics. In addition, you'll find a wealth of information not generally found in career planning guides, information on: starting your own business, working as a freelance, founding a nonprofit corporation, managing multiple careers, boosting your self-esteem, and much, much more.

Most importantly, all of this information will be presented within the context of viewing work as your creative expression of love in action. Right along, we'll be reminding you of the pitfalls and challenges that face those who have the audacity and the courage to be themselves in their work lives. Traditionally, career success has been defined by externals like salary, benefits, recognition, status in the community, and long-term security. From the standpoint of *Zen and the Art of Making a Living*, these parameters are entirely inadequate. External rewards may dazzle others, but only your heart can tell you whether you have found fool's gold or the real McCoy. Being true to yourself is what counts in the end.

Some of you may be judging yourselves for not already knowing what your life's work is. Some of you may feel like kicking yourselves for spending year after year working at something that wasn't really you. Look, there is nobody here but you and me, and just between the two of us, I'm not perfect either. So take a load off. Relax. Kick off your shoes, loosen your belt. On this journey, it doesn't matter where you have been. This journey is about where you are going and digging on the process of getting there—one step at a time. . .

For my part, I promise not to bore you on purpose. I want you to come along for the entire ride, and I know that for that to happen, you've got to be having fun along the way. True, some parts of this book may not be as exciting as surfing Waikiki. I'm not going to tell you that writing a résumé is more fun than a night on the town, but it can be more fun than peeling onions, and we all know that if we want onions in the soup, somebody's got to peel them. It's the same with writing a business plan or a grant proposal or doing some of the other work in this book. There are times when somebody's got to do it, and that somebody usually ought to be you. These things may not be intrinsically thrilling, but on the other hand, if you have the right attitude, you *can* have fun doing them. Most of all, you'll feel good about yourself for having done what's good for you.

Why This Book Was Written

I first got into the career field because I recognized how central work is to the happiness of the individual and the character of any society. Work offers the individual the opportunity to share acts of love and beauty, to see himself reflected in the image of his work. By the work that a society chooses to do or *not* to do, it defines its values and shapes its future. Since work is what we do with most of our waking lives, we must, if we count life valuable, consider what we are working for.

I also realized that today, for all too many, work is drudgery, the thing to do to pay the bills, or a mad chase for material wealth and social status. I saw how bored, alienated, under-challenged, or over-stressed so many are in their work and how their unhappiness at work affects their families, friends, and communities. It seemed to me that the popular conception of work as principally a matter of economics and social status was at the heart of the matter. Many individual tragedies of alienation, emptiness, and despair, as well as community, national, and global problems seemed to be aggravated, if not in fact caused, by this conception of work.

For many who came to me seeking career guidance, a "better

job" (as defined by pay and benefits alone) was not enough. There was a real desire for a broader conception of work—one that would reflect the spiritual as well as the material life of man. My search for such a vision of work led me finally to the notion of work as art, the unique creative expression of the individual. (I cannot begin to acknowledge all the influences in shaping this view, though the work of Joseph Campbell, Ananda K. Coomaraswamy, and Alan W. Watts must be mentioned.) The essence of a vision of work as art is inspiration and excellence. Work, inspired in conception and spirited in performance, is art. We will discuss this vision of work in some detail in the section we call "Prologue: The Art of Life's Work." As time goes by, I become ever more convinced that this vision contains the seed of a cultural transformation of considerable magnitude.

Even as the conventional notion of work was failing many, so too, the conventional career-planning methodologies that had arisen out of this conception were, for many, inadequate. Many people who were looking for more fulfilling work were completely turned off by the conventional career-planning process. It isn't hard to understand why. "Vocational guidance" programs were originally designed to help employers "better fit" employees into positions within their organizational structures. They were never intended as a means of helping individuals realize their creative potential or achieve their own best work.

Over the years, career planning and vocational guidance evolved, but this notion of "finding the fit" was carried over as an integral part of conventional career-planning theory. Programs cut from this cloth tended to reduce human beings to collections of personality traits or skills that could be matched with pre-existing job slots. They focused on developing ever more elaborate tests and measures to find the perfect fit. Yet no matter how logical and systematic these programs might have seemed, they often failed to reach people where they lived. Like painting by numbers or dating by computer, something seemed to be missing from these programs—the LIFE of spontaneous engagement. The "best fit" model, after all, tends to view people as static, interchangeable parts in a grand machine, not as living, growing, and conscious beings.

On the other hand, there were books that, while long on metaphysics and ideals, were short on the practical nitty-gritty of making things happen in the real world. People would read these books and get inspired for a time but take no action. It all seemed so overwhelming. They didn't know where to begin. I saw the need for a program that would speak to people's hearts and souls, yet be practical enough to help them take definite action.

Over a number of years, I worked to develop such a program. Its purpose is to enhance human creativity in work, and in so doing, to assist people to experience the full joy of living. It has three key ingredients: a spiritual or mythic approach to life in general and work in particular, an emphasis on service, and freedom of choice—a wide range of options with which to construct a viable life's work.

An Integrated Approach to Work

Why is this one book and not two? What is all this stuff about Zen and mythic archetypes doing in a career book loaded with practical, mundane material about finding a job and all the rest? This *is* the Zen of it—the spirit in the everyday. Zen is the integration of the spiritual and material—the shattering of any artificial separation we might impose. In the words of Kakuzo Okakura, author of *The Book of Tea*, "A special contribution of Zen to Eastern thought was its recognition of the mundane as of equal importance with the spiritual."[1] It seems to me that in our alienated, fractured modern life, this is a contribution *we* desperately need—an awareness of the sacred in the ordinary.

But why the archetypes? The purpose of injecting the archetypes is to provide a tool with which we can begin to experience the power of myth and symbol in our lives—to put everyday life in a context that's mythically and imaginatively involved. How can we do that unless we can do it in our work? We cannot simply skirt around the edges of life; we must honor the spirit of life in all, even in the most practical or seemingly mundane aspects.

The grayness of the gray flannel life is the lack of imaginative or spiritual involvement. By beginning to recognize and consciously work with the archetypes presented in this book—the Poet, the Hero, the Magician, the Warrior, and the Student-Sage—one may begin to experience his entire life in a mythic or spiritual context. Everyday life is experienced as a heroic quest and played as a game. In it, we fight for what we believe in, and we learn eagerly as students, and wisely, patiently as sages. All of this is framed within a poetic view of life—a view guided by the heart, alive with the spirit, and nourished in love.

A Service Orientation

It is a fundamental premise of this book that to attempt to make a career choice, apart from an examination of our values and apart from a consideration of the impact that our doing has upon society, is to make an immature choice. It is immature because it lacks the confidence to face up to one's responsibility to mankind. "They" are never going to make the world a better place. It's up to you and me, and we *can* do it—if we have the love, the courage, and the patience.

We must have the love to go for what we know is right, even if it means paying a price. We who love life must work with life for life, while celebrating the mystery that is life. In short, we must be actively engaged in making the world the best it can be, while loving it exactly as it is. We must have the courage to believe that the world we have dreamed will one day be made manifest and that what we do as individuals makes a difference. We must have the courage to reject the idea of settling for work that is destructive to human happiness, or even indifferent to it. We must have the patience to view the movement toward life's work as a lifelong unfolding process—not something we can do in a week, a month, a year, or even several years but something that takes a deep commitment and the patience to see it through.

Freedom of Choice

Those who take up their work as a creative pursuit, those who are really working from "the inside out" in a spirit of service, need a wider range of alternatives than the conventional nine-to-five job format alone. While we do offer a complete section on "Landing the Right Job," we have included a larger palette of colors from which to choose in painting the picture of your life's work. These include starting your own business, working freelance, and even preliminary information for starting a nonprofit organization. We have sections on creating multiple careers and on obtaining grants, sections on volunteering and on networking, sections on negotiating and on obtaining publicity. We encourage you, at every point, to consider and take advantage of the wide range of available options.

This book is, of course, a transition resource book and hardly the last word. It provides a technology for applying a love-inspired orientation toward work within the existing economic, educational, and social structures. We might add that these structures do not, for the most part, encourage one to be oneself or to serve one's fellow man in a spirit of love and beauty.

At a later point, a new technology will be required, but this can only gain wide currency when society's emphasis on economics is broadened to include spiritual and social values, when education has become more a matter of developing the individual than of filling his head, when the organization of work is less centralized, and when the individual members of the society participate more fully in its decision-making at all levels—in short, when we are more spiritually evolved. While this book contains some suggestions for how things might be, it is written to be used with things as they are now. It's an imperfect book for an imperfect world.

About the Title

This work is an attempt to apply the spirit of Zen to the human activity of living and working in the postmodern world. I am not a Buddhist or any "ist," but as D. T. Suzuki says, "Zen professes itself to be the spirit of Buddhism, but in fact, it is the spirit of all religions and philosophies." It is in this transcendent sense that I use the word *Zen*. I am not talking about a particular religion or dogma, or even a historical or cultural point of view, but of awareness and spirit applied to everyday life and work.

To remain caught up in ideas and words about Zen is, as the old masters say, to "stink of Zen."
Alan Watts

The "Zen lessons" in this book can be applied as easily by Christians, Jews, Hindus, Moslems, Universalists, agnostics, and atheists as by Buddhists. I trust that the monastic purists will not take offense at my use of "Zen words" but will see the moon I'm pointing at. Still, I will use a minimum of Zen terminology. This is intended to be a popular book, not a book for scholastics or monastics. Where I can find a Western word or metaphor that fits the feel, I will prefer it.

Even as Bodhidharma brought Zen from India to China, so have the likes of D. T. Suzuki, Reginald Blyth, Alan Watts, and more recently, a flood of Zen monastics, brought Zen to the Western world. The Chinese culture into which Bodhidharma planted the Zen seed was significantly different from his native India. In China, Zen (Ch'an) teachings evolved to integrate and express Taoist and Confucian elements. Zen further adapted when Eisai brought the Ch'an teachings to Japan, incorporating the native Samurai and Shinto traditions. As D. T. Suzuki puts it, Zen "is extremely flexible in adapting to almost any philosophy or moral doctrine . . ."[2]

> *For wayfarers of all times, the right strategy for skillfully spreading the Way essentially lies in adapting to communicate. Those who do not know how to adapt stick to the letter and cling to doctrines, get stuck on forms and mired in sentiments—none of them succeed in strategic adaptation.*
>
> *Zhantang*

Now that Zen has reached the West, with its radically different cultural milieu, we can expect still further adaptation. The Western culture has a tradition of social action, particularly among religious or "spiritually attuned" individuals. One might expect Western Zen to adapt in this direction. Additionally, today we are in an urgent situation unlike that faced by the Ch'an patriarchs. Today our world is in peril, both from the threat of immediate death by nuclear, chemical, and biological warfare and from the slow death of environmental degradation, overcrowding, and the destruction of the integrity of the biosphere. This too is, no doubt, bringing a further adaptation of Zen.

When points within this book do not appear to parallel the teachings of Rinzai, Dogen, or even Bodhidharma, remember that they did not live in our time and place. Additionally, and perhaps more fundamentally, every man or woman expresses his own experience of Zen. For me, Zen says simply and emphatically: *We are one. This is it.* If we have realized this, then to act otherwise is lunacy. Sane or loony, we are all here together, and like it or not, this is it.

*A Note about Language and Grammar

Like the content of this book, the use of language and grammar is at times unconventional. The occasional use of slang or nontraditional punctuation is intended to enhance a conversational tone. Further, since the content varies greatly throughout the book, the style varies accordingly. As for gender-specific pronouns, I use both he and she, not in clumsy combination, but by shuffling back and forth between the two.

How to Use This Book

*Change and growth take place when a person has
risked himself and dares to become involved with
experimenting with his own life.*

Herbert Otto

This is a big book, and it may, at first, seem a little overwhelming. The purpose of this section is to give you an overview of what's in it—so that you can begin to think about how to get the most out of it. The first step in determining how to use this book is to decide what you are looking for from it. We have found that there are at least five distinct ways in which people enjoy using this book. You may gain benefit from any of these ways or from some combination. We list them below according to the amount of effort required—starting with the most and moving to the least. (The highlights on page xxvii will help you find your way around the book.)

Five Ways to Use This Book

1. **A Life Work Planning Book:** The first way to use this book is as a life work planning book. You certainly don't have to start from the beginning and work through all the processes to the end. We know from experience that relatively few of you will use it in this way. You can still gain considerable benefit by working at it on a piecemeal basis.

2. **A General Interest Book on "The Way" or "Art" of Life's Work:** A second way to use this book is to draw on the practical philosophy of creative work presented herein. We have endeavored to present an integrated vision of a postmodern view of work—one consistent with advancing the spiritual life of the individual and the survivability of life on this planet. This vision invites us to view life's work as an Art, a Quest, a Game, a Battle, and a School. To get a quick overview of these elements and how they work together into a coherent paradigm, see the diagram on page xxv. At times, it may seem that we are drifting a bit from the subject of work, but this is entirely consistent with the theme of this book—the integration of life and work, sacred and ordinary, beautiful and practical.

3. **A "How-to" Career Guide:** A third way to use the book is as a "how-to" book of specific information. If, for example, you would like specific information on how to research a particular career that interests you, how you might go about setting yourself up as a freelance, how to conduct an effective job search, or how to gain publicity for yourself, your business, or nonprofit foundation—you can simply look up this information in the appropriate sections.

4. **A Quote Book:** A fourth way to use this book is as a compendium of inspiring quotes. Many people find that they enjoy browsing through the book from time to time, finding inspiration and stimulation in a wealth of carefully selected quotations.

5. **A Career Resource Reference:** You can look up additional information sources in the specific sections that you are interested in or in the complete bibliography at the end of the book.

6. **A Focus for Life's Work Support Groups:** Once you have read the book, you may want to start a life's work support group to assist you in completing the exercises and to provide moral support on your journey to meaningful life's work. See pages xxx-xxxiii for some tips to help get you started.

Zen and the Art of Making a Living

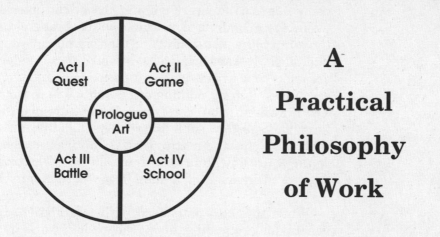

A

Practical

Philosophy

of Work

Prologue: The Art of Life's Work: Your life's work is an Art in the sense of expressing your essential self in the world of forms. The inspiration and the discipline of the artist provide a metaphor for a new vision of work. Lessons from mythology can help us to approach a creative psychology of work. (See chapters 1–4, pages 36-123.)

Act I: The Quest for Life's Work: Your life's work is a Quest, in the sense that through it, you discover yourself. Like the heroes of old, those who follow the path of life's work make of their lives a quest for the shining apparition of their own best selves. (See "The Quest for Your Best," pages 126-142.)

Act II: The Game of Life's Work: Your life's work is a Game, in the sense that to fulfill it, you must play roles—such as a career role. Working from a strong sense of a purpose allows you to approach the game with a sense of play. We invite you to choose a "career game" you can get into—then play on purpose. (See "Playing the Game: Winners, Losers, and Choosers," pages 250-269.)

Act III: The Battle for Life's Work: Your life's work is a Battle, in the sense that the effort to execute it takes place within socio-economic and temporal-spatial limitations. No matter how good our intentions, how loving our motives, without aggressive action and a knowledge of the marketplace, we may abandon our grand intentions to the realm of mere dreams. (See "Winning in the Marketplace," pages 328-345.)

Act IV: The School of Life's Work: Your life's work is a School, in the sense that it is a constant learning process. Learning is essential, both in creating the changes you intend and in responding well to the changes happening all around you. (See "Learning to Change: The Old Boy and the Student-Sage," pages 508-532.)

Life's Work Planning

Since the other ways of using this book are rather straightforward and conventional, we will concentrate our remaining discussion on using this as a life's work planning book. The process of life's work planning can be defined, in a general sense, as creating a picture of the world you want to live in and then organizing your energies into building it. It takes being part dreamer, part builder. If we are not dreamers, our aspirations will be too low, and we will sink into emptiness, leaving nothing of lasting value to those who follow. Yet, if we are not builders, if our dreams are not given the shape, form, and substance of living reality, then they are nothing more than phantoms and platitudes, the mirages we chase to escape a world we are unwilling to confront and love. The true idealist is no dewy-eyed dreamer but a committed foot soldier in the cause of his vision.

While this book is packed with information, resources, and general understandings about the world of work, it is essentially a book of questions. One way or another, you'll need to answer many of these questions on the road to your life's work. You may answer them formally in this book, or you may grapple with them some other way, perhaps without even realizing that you are. The important thing is not the form but the quest, the journey, and your commitment to it.

No book can tell you how to find your way; it can at best catalyze and awaken the way within you. You can paint by numbers, but you'll never produce a masterpiece like that. A masterpiece requires the soul and inspiration of an artist. To paint the masterpiece of your life, you need more than forms and systems. You need a heroic commitment to your best self. Born in your heart, tempered by your head, shaped with your hands, and walked with your own two feet, your life's work is your special gift for mankind.

What follows is an attempt to point at some of the significant landmarks along the way to your life's work. It is not the only way. It is not even a way, per se. It is simply a description of some of the important scenery along the way. You must find your own way, the road to your Self and its expression in the world. This process should be approached with a spirit of introspection, adventure, and fun. You must rely upon yourself over any form, system, or structure. Having said all this, here's the plan in a nutshell:

Zen and the Art of Making a Living
Life's Work Planning Program in a Nutshell

Act I: The Quest for Life's Work: In this unit, you will consider your vision for the world. You'll go on to identify your work purpose, your part in the grand play of life, your key talents, and the specific objectives you would like to accomplish in this life. This unit includes a special section on breaking through the fear barriers to unleashing your full potential. See page 143 for a more complete overview of the process work in "Act I."

Act II: The Game of Life's Work: You begin by mentally projecting yourself into the career roles that will best enable you to express your mission in life. Next, you are guided through the sometimes difficult process of conducting research on the careers you have envisioned. Finally, you have a chance to make a thorough and critical evaluation of the careers you have selected to help you determine what's really right for you. See page 270 for a more complete overview of the process work in "Act II."

Act III: The Battle for Life's Work: In this unit, you will develop your personal marketing strategy. Whether you decide to build your own organization or work for an existing one, this unit is packed with the kind of practical information you need to move ahead. With the information in this unit and the additional resources referred to, you will be able to assemble what you need to capture your market share or make the job interviewer sit up in his chair. See pages 345-346 for a more complete overview of the process work in "Act III."

Act IV: The School of Life's Work: In this unit, you will develop a strategy for making the transition from what you are doing now into your new career. You'll find sections devoted to increasing your ability, credibility, and marketability. You'll learn how to improve your self-image, enlist the support of friends and loved ones, and how to love what you are doing 'til you are doing what you love. See pages 532-533 for a more complete overview of the process work in "Act IV."

Working through the Time, Space, and Stuff

The beginning is the most important part of the work.

Plato

The biggest difficulty in any work is getting started. Consequently, we'd like to encourage you to begin as soon as possible. Make a conscious decision that you're going to work through the program until you are satisfied you have gotten all you can from it. Consistent attention to the questions presented in this book will yield exciting, even life-transforming, results. The following are some tips that will help you to get the most of your life's work planning efforts.

The Time

Schedule your life's work planning sessions. Determine in advance how long each session will be and when they will be. We recommend an hour to an hour and a half once a week. Try to work at the same time each week if at all possible—for example, eight o'clock on Wednesday evenings. This will enlist the aid of your subconscious mind in working on the process in the interim. In other words, when your mind knows that at eight o'clock on Wednesdays you'll be concentrating and writing about your life's work, it will provide you with ideas throughout the week. You'll wake up in the morning with ideas. In the shower or driving home from work or in the middle of a conversation, ideas will come to you. When you work on a regular basis, you can incorporate these moments of inspiration into your scheduled work.

It is helpful to review your work. If you're working on a weekly basis, take the time at the end of each month to look over all you've written, your discoveries and decisions. Do this in a leisurely and relaxed fashion. You might take a Sunday afternoon and just look over everything you've written. Let it sort of synthesize and coalesce in your mind. Look at what your answers are telling you; let new ideas come to you.

The Space

If at all possible, establish a regular place where you can work in an uninterrupted fashion. If you don't have an office or study in your home, we recommend that you set up a special table or desk in a designated area as free from distractions as possible. You'll want to do a good deal of concentrated thinking and reflecting, and a quiet workspace helps a lot. Be sure that your family or the people you live with understand that you require their cooperation in giving you the space you need to work on the program. Let them know you're not to be interrupted during this time. Arrange to have someone watching the children, and hold the telephone calls. Additionally, a designated work place will help you keep all of your work in one place. This becomes especially important as you get into the research phase of your process.

The Stuff

At times, you might be stuck, but if you persevere, you will get through the blocks. Awareness of your emotional responses throughout this process will help you to stay on course. You may experience feeling sad or depressed, angry or frustrated from time to time. The Chinese say even a hurricane doesn't last a day. So don't worry, it will pass. The parts of our subconscious minds that are hooked into negativity and limitation may begin to create certain problems or symptoms. These may include feeling sleepy or fatigued, even having a bit of an upset stomach or a headache. Of course, these symptoms have nothing to do with the program. They are a part of the emotional process of getting to clarity and commitment. We have to understand that this is a process. After all, if we were there now, we would be doing it, and we would have no need to do anything except to carry on in our life's work.

> *Our demons are our own limitations, which shut us off from the realization of the ubiquity of the spirit… each of these demons is conquered in a vision quest.*
>
> *Joseph Campbell*

Understand that up to now we have kept ourselves from our work. Our subconscious beliefs have kept us from either the discovery of our life's work or from taking the necessary action to make it manifest. What's held us back is ourselves. If we are going to transcend our old limitations, we're going to have to deal with things we have avoided in the past. For example, some people have difficulty answering probing questions that require self-examination. Others have difficulty doing the necessary research and goal-setting work. Persist through the difficulties, whatever they may be, and you will open doors to a deeper, richer experience of yourself and your work.

How to Start Your Own Life's Work Support Group

In the first few years of my career consulting practice, I worked with clients exclusively on a one-to-one basis. When I began doing seminars, I was immediately struck by the power that group dynamics can add to this work. I soon discovered that by providing a minimum of structure, information, and motivation, a powerful wave of energy—one with a distinct life its own—could be tapped and made to serve the process of finding and creating a meaningful life's work. A tremendous wellspring of suppressed energy would come bubbling to the surface as people began sharing their deepest desires with a group of like-minded and supportive individuals.

Many people feel isolated with respect to their career issues, having no place in their daily lives in which to explore their dreams. Seeing others from all walks of life and a diverse range of ages and socio-economic levels engaged in the same process is both reassuring and highly motivating to them. Listening to and sharing with others makes the whole process seem more real to many. Those who would tend to be more timid or self-doubting on their own gain confidence from the example provided by more confident and self-aware participants. In a variety of ways, people in this kind of supportive group setting feed off of one another's energy, enthusiasm, knowledge, and insights.

The basic structure to all my career work involves asking the client questions (a number of which are contained in the exercises within in this book). The key is getting people to confront and answer these questions in a sincere and honest way—which is to say—from their hearts. The group dynamic adds momentum to the process, an intangible but palpable energy, which individuals can access to move more quickly through areas that might otherwise bog them down.

Because of my own experience in working with groups, I was delighted to learn that people were beginning to form support groups on their own. Providing this kind of context can be a valuable service to others that, at the same time, gives added support to one's own quest. Toward that end, *you* may want to create a life's work development group of your own. Below are some tips that have proved helpful to those who have set up successful groups in the past.

Membership

Your group should have a minimum of four, and no more than twenty, people. Optimal group size ranges between ten and fourteen members. It's best to have an even number of participants so that each group member will have a partner to work with. Participants might include friends and acquaintances, coworkers, or members of organizations you belong to. Some people post flyers or run ads in their local newspapers to fill out their groups. Restrict membership to those who are seriously committed to the process of creating a new life's work. Don't allow hangers-on at your meetings—for example, group members' spouses who are not themselves seeking a new experience of work. You're much better off with a small group of sincere and dedicated seekers than a larger group with a lot of dead weight.

Discuss the issue of membership at your first meeting and establish clear policies about adding new members. Because this is a step-by-step process in which each new element depends upon what has come before, you will probably want to close the group to new members after the second or third meeting. Group members should be expected to attend all meetings, complete homework, and participate in group exercises and discussions. If it is impossible for a group member to attend a particular meeting, the meeting facilitator should be notified (see below).

Leadership

Without clear direction and a well-focused agenda, your life's work gatherings run the risk of degenerating into chat, gossip, or gripe sessions, where energy and time are spent but little is accomplished. For this reason, we strongly recommend that your group designate a facilitator or discussion leader for your meetings. It will become the facilitator's responsibility to set the meeting's agenda and to keep the group focused and moving forward. Facilitating a group of this kind can be a great way for those who feel they might want to someday work in the career field to get firsthand experience of some of the issues involved.

Your group may choose to elect a single leader or a leadership team that takes turns in facilitating the meetings. Group leadership might rotate from person to person, with each member taking a turn leading a meeting in his or her home. However your group chooses to resolve the leadership issue, make sure *someone* takes responsibility for each meeting. The facilitator should participate in all of the activities and not dominate the group. At the same time, he or she should make sure that the group stays focused on fulfilling its objectives for the week.

Structure

Of course, the structure of the meeting will vary from session to session, depending on the topic under discussion. Generally though, meetings should include focused discussion of reading material and the completion of exercises from the book. When moving through the exercises, instruct participants to write down their responses to all the questions in a given exercise (they will have a record of their responses which they can take home), then have them share their answers with a partner, a break-out group, or the group as a whole. One of the principal values that many receive from the group experience is that it supports them in doing the exercise work they might otherwise avoid. In addition, sharing their answers with a partner or in a small group context enables them to affirm their answers and receive feedback on them.

This process can bring up a host of related ideas and issues that participants may want to discuss. Nevertheless, it's best to stick to the agenda. Don't allow the group to get sidetracked with chit-chat or the personal concerns of a single individual. Leaders should encourage those who would like to talk about other issues to carry on their dialog outside designated meeting times—over coffee after the meetings or at other times throughout the week. Offering light refreshments after meetings can provide group members with opportunities to socialize and make arrangements to carry on their discussions. Often, individuals attempt to anticipate problems, mentally projecting ahead to areas of personal concern that have the effect of steering the group off course. The exercise work contained within this book is designed to take you step by step through the process of discovering and ultimately realizing your life's work. Encourage participants to trust the process and remind them that their concerns will most likely be addressed at a later point in the work.

Guidelines

Establish and agree upon clear operating guidelines at the first meeting. Take notes and distribute copies to all the members. Basic guidelines might include: agreeing to create a supportive environment in which people feel free to share their dreams without fear of condemnation, giving full attention and respect to whomever is speaking, keeping sharings brief enough to allow all members a turn to speak, and staying within the time limits specified by the facilitator.

Time

At your first meeting, agree upon a regular and unchanging time for all future meetings. While flexibility is nice in theory, a regular meeting time greatly increases the likelihood of holding your group intact. Weekday evenings early in the week tend to work best for most people. Allow a minimum of two hours per meeting—more if you have a large group. Plan to meet once a week for eight to twelve weeks. At your final meeting, evaluate your group's progress and determine where to go from there.

Place

You can hold meetings in your home, at a public venue, or in various group members' homes on a rotating basis. In any case, make sure the room you use is clean, comfortable, and inviting. Anticipate potential interruptions and distractions, and do your best to eliminate them. Unplug telephones, mute pagers, and turn down the volume on answering machines. Make child-care arrangements for the little ones. Keep household pets outside or confined to areas away from the designated meeting area.

Materials

Each participant will need a copy of *Zen and the Art of Making a Living*, a notebook for exercises and group processes, and a writing implement. If the meetings are being held at your home, you may want to supply extra pens, pencils, and note pads for those who forget them.

Final Thoughts

Each group is an organic entity with a personality and intelligence all its own. The guidelines above are offered as a basic structure upon which you can build. Starting a life's work development group can provide a fun way to begin the process of taking creative control of your work life, while at the same time assisting others to do the same. If this appeals you, by all means go for it!

How This Book Is Organized

The Essays: The essays that precede each unit (act) and many of the sections provide you with general understandings that can save you time, energy, and frustration in the long run. It is not necessary that you read these before you do the process work. Still, we think that you will find them helpful in bringing clarity to some of the complex issues of work. These include essays that make up the "Prologue" unit, as well as essays on the Quest, the Game, the Battle, and the School of life's work, a series on discovering life's work, and one on the new economics. Just so you'll know how to find or skip over them, we'll tell you that the essays are formatted with quotations and Zen art in the margins.

Specific How-to's: Where you see a two-column format, you'll know you are looking at specific how-to information. For the most part, this is information of a kind more typically found in career-planning books. Topics include: informational interviews, skill assessment, formulating a training strategy, enhancing self-esteem, building and utilizing contact networks, writing a résumé, landing an interview, interview techniques, job-hunting techniques, fundamentals to starting a business, basic steps to founding a nonprofit organization, enlisting support from friends and relatives, volunteering, long-term life's work planning, and much more.

Process Work: This is the meat. It is the "work" of this workbook. You do not have to do all of the processes. Look over all of the material, and do the ones best suited to your purpose. To get an overview of the process work within each "Act," see the "What's Ahead" information on pages 143, 270, 345–346, and 532–533. Worksheets are provided at the end of most of the sections.

Resources: While this is a comprehensive career-planning book, no single book can possibly contain all that each individual needs for success. Consequently, we have included over four hundred bibliographical entries on everything from global issues to writing a résumé, from starting a nonprofit organization to creating a success image, from education and training resources and financial aid to entrepreneurship and marketing. For your convenience, you will find the bulk of these resources listed within the text immediately following a discussion of the subject matter to which they apply. The remaining sources are in the bibliography at the end of the book.

Affirmations: At each step along the way, we have provided affirmative thoughts to complement the material. Repeated exposure to these affirmations will help keep you in the right frame of mind throughout the process of discovering and realizing your life's work.

The Road to Your Life's Work

The road to your life's work is the ongoing process of taking the best of what's in you and expressing it fully in the outer world. It's a never-ending journey filled with challenges and obstacles. These obstacles we call "roadblocks," or "detours." The challenges and their potential detours represent the inner as well as the outer terrain you must traverse in pursuit of your work. Following the introduction to each "Act," you will find a detour indicating a place where you might get off track. Awareness of the detours and the challenges they represent can help you stay the course.

Challenge I: Know who you are. The first challenge is to know who you are and why you are here on this earth. Unless you are up to this challenge, you have no chance of realizing your life's work. You'll be left taking a reactive rather than a creative approach to your work. The first roadblock is denial—an unwillingness to deeply examine your life and to discover your unique visions, talents, and gifts. **Detour #1—The Denial Trap (see page 144).**

Challenge II: Be yourself in this world. The second challenge is to shape your life's work, or vocation, into a viable career role or set of careers. Unless you are up to this challenge, you may allow your creative visions to languish in the realm of might-have-beens. It is important that you select a career role that gives you the freedom to be yourself at work. The second roadblock is that of approval—of compromising your visions or values for the sake of gaining approval. **Detour #2—The Approval Trap (see page 271).**

Challenge III: Organize your efforts for maximum results. The third challenge is that of finding a vehicle (or vehicles) through which you can effectively advance your life's work in the marketplace. Being up to this challenge means persisting until you can either find the right organization to work for, or you create your own. The third roadblock, or detour, is to settle for taking what is easily available rather than to persist until you get what you really want. **Detour #3—The Availability Trap (see page 347).**

Challenge IV: Make the changes necessary to make it happen. The final challenge is to make the changes necessary to realize your life's work. You'll want to develop a plan for making the transition from what you are doing now to what you ultimately want to do. You'll want to acquire the knowledge, skill, and experience you need to succeed. The final roadblock is lack of confidence in yourself, that is, in your ability to learn and remain patient through all of the tests. **Detour #4—The Lack of Self-Confidence Trap (see page 534).**

Doing the Work You Love:
A Social Movement for the Twenty-First Century

Every great movement must experience three stages:
ridicule, discussion, adoption.

John Stuart Mill

 powerful new social movement is transforming the way people live and work. For years, virtually invisible to those not directly involved, this movement has been quietly building momentum. Today its impact is no longer in doubt. In recent years, it has become the subject of a spate of newspaper and magazine articles and has been featured in a variety of television and radio programs. Truly grass-roots, this is a social movement without political action committees, paid lobbyists, or effective national or international organization. It is a bottoms-up movement in which people are transforming society not by mass political action but by reorienting their own lives. It is a broad-based movement affecting men and women of all ages, races, and socio-economic backgrounds in many nations.

At the heart of this emerging social movement is a fundamental redefinition of work and success. For a variety of reasons, people's expectations of what their work life can and should be have been dramatically and irrevocably altered in recent years. While throughout most of the twentieth century, work was viewed principally as a means to an end—be it survival, security, status, or power—today it is increasingly being valued on its own terms. More and more people are coming to expect that their experience of work should include meaning, challenge, self-expression, and joy. More and more, people are looking for ways to integrate their values and talents into their everyday experience of work. And more and more, they are finding them—discovering that it really is possible to earn their way in the world without compromising, indeed by celebrating, the promptings of their hearts and souls. The cat is out of the bag and there is no putting it back. The "work-for-love" movement has caught on.

For all of its possibilities and promise, we should recognize that this is a social movement in its infancy. Moreover, it would be a mistake to minimize the significant ideological, psychological, and institutional barriers that impede its further development. Nevertheless, this is clearly an idea whose time has come. The encounter between this idea and the barriers blocking its further expansion will undoubtedly be one of the great dramas in the social history of the twenty-first century.

The impact of this social transformation on the daily lives of individuals and on society as a whole will be on a scale comparable to that wrought by the shift from family-arranged to love-based marriage. In the stories of Tristan and Iseult and Romeo and Juliet, we are reminded of the price paid by early trailblazers who broke the social convention of their day. These are romantic stories, to be sure. Yet we ought not dismiss the pain they portray as the mere hyperbole of fiction, nor forget that in real life, those who dared to defy tradition and follow their own hearts faced banishment, ostracism, even death. Nevertheless, despite tremendous ideological, psychological, and institutional resistance, in the relatively brief span of a few hundred years, the ideal of love-based marriage had become the prevailing social standard.

Though these things take time, there is every reason to believe the work-for-love ideal will take hold even more rapidly than the marriage-for-love ideal did centuries ago. Despite the difficulties, people are breaking through every day, finding their way to an integrated and meaningful experience of work. Each person doing work she truly loves serves as an example to the people closest to her as well as to those she encounters in the course of her work. She inspires the people in her life to take a fresh look at their own dreams and to question the assumption that they can't make them real. Each and every time someone finds his or her way, he or she helps pave the way for others, giving this movement its self-renewing vitality and sustaining its momentum. Yet until this new ideal of work becomes the dominant one, it will continue to take uncommon courage, strength, and perseverance for individuals to realize it in their daily experience.

As important as an ideological shift is, it is only one aspect of genuine transformation. For instance, the fact that most people today expect to marry for love doesn't guarantee that any given individual actually will. Even marrying the right person for the right reason is no guarantee that one will be able to create a happy and enduring relationship. This takes much more than the belief in "true love." Again, the analogy holds for our experience of work. Many who believe that their work ought to be a fully integrated experience, reflecting their values, talents, and deepest desires are, for a variety of reasons, unable to realize this ideal in their own lives.

Making the translation from idea to reality can be a difficult process, often taking many years and consistent, determined effort. Let's say that for a particular individual, doing the work she loves requires that she go into business for herself. She may lack the self-confidence to get started, the openness to learn and grow, or the discipline to see it through. Her progress may be impeded by the fact that she was inadequately prepared by the educational system to face the challenges of self-employment. It may be slowed by difficulties in gaining access to the capital she needs to launch or expand her business, or by the often excessive regulations and heavy taxes that governments impose on those who venture forth on their own.

Of all potential barriers, the psychological factor is undoubtedly the most significant. I agree with Lincoln that "your own resolution to succeed is more important than any other one thing" and have seen it proved too many times to believe otherwise. The individual with sufficient desire, dedication, and perseverance will find a way to make it work. If she lacks knowledge and skills, she will acquire them. If she lacks capital, she will find a way to get it or begin on a shoestring budget; if she is met with excessive regulation and taxes, she will overcome these obstacles as well. Having said this, we ought not minimize the difficulties nor dismiss those who lack the inner strength or who, for a variety of reasons, may be unwilling or unable to make the sacrifices that are often necessary to realize an integrated experience of life.

Creative Empowerment: An Educational Agenda for the Twenty-First Century

While as individuals we have to work with things as they are, collectively we have the power to change them, to create in society more fertile ground for the germination of the creative seeds that lie dormant in all its members. Toward this end, we should realize that even the factor of psychological resistance is not without an institutional component, and to some degree, institutional remedies. For example, I have heard college and university career center staff recount time and again how difficult it is for them to get college students to take a serious interest in planning their careers, let alone discovering their unique purposes or missions in life. In the broader society, young people are often dismissed as cynical, apathetic, or lazy. Yet we can hardly blame them, when nothing in their formative education has encouraged them to assume responsibility for the direction of their own lives or given them the practical skills they need to follow their own paths.

I have seen firsthand how the attitudes and skills necessary to succeed can be readily acquired by even so-called "troubled" or "difficult" high school students. I have seen as well the transforming effect this kind of training can have on a student's outlook on life and belief in his or her own possibilities. I have developed such programs myself and am aware of a number of excellent programs designed by others. It is a great failing of our current educational system that programs of this kind are exceptional and not an integral part of modern education. Many more could join the ranks of those doing what they love if our educational system were committed to preparing young people to do so.

Of course, it will always be up to the individual to realize his or her own destiny. As Walt Whitman said, "NOT I—NOT ANYONE else, can travel that road for you,/You must travel it for yourself." Yet we can create a context in which young people are encouraged to take up the quest and are armed with the spiritual, mental, and emotional resources to conquer whatever inner demons or outer obstacles lie between them and their creative self-expression.

Today, we often hear political and educational leaders lament students' low math and science scores, but we hear precious little about the need for programs that will help them develop their own creative capacities. Excelling in math and science are worthy goals and particularly so for those who are naturally suited to these kinds of pursuits. But what about schooling young people in the fundamentals of the creative process? What about preparing them to function independently in the market society in which they live? If we are honest, we have to admit that the implicit goal of virtually all public (and most private) education for many years now has been to equip students with skills and attitudes that will make them more valuable as workers for those whose agendas they will spend their lives serving. It has not been to help students discover their own purposes and construct and realize goals based on these.

A person who can survive or even thrive without a job, may *choose* to take one. On the other hand, what real choice has a person who needs a job to live? The best he can hope for is a "good job," with "good" generally defined in economic terms alone. More and more people are seeing through the illusion that a "good job" as conventionally defined is synonymous with a fulfilling life. As one reader of this book wrote to me: "For too long, I have taken jobs or career paths that have carried prestige or security or remunerative rewards but have had little if any spirit in them. No one ever told me before that it is essential to my own well-being, as well as that of the world, for me to be doing work that I love and for which I am naturally gifted. Comments such as 'It's only your job, it's not your life' have been only too common. No one ever understood me when I have insisted that to me work is not just a job, that it must have a spiritual component."

"No one ever told me before" is a comment I have heard time and again in consultations, classes, and seminars as well as in letters from men and women of all ages from all over the world. While it is gratifying to know that readers got that message from this book and that it played a part in helping them turn their lives around, it is also sad and unfortunate that many had to wait for mid-life to hear it and suffer years of needless pain as a result. Why, we might ask, are people not being told from the time of their earliest encounter with the educational system? Why must they wait to be told or to figure it out for themselves after years of trial and error? We could do much better by giving the creative empowerment of the individual the place it deserves among our educational priorities.

The innate creativity within all human beings can be fostered and developed. Risk-taking can be encouraged. Self-confidence can be enhanced by giving students the tools they need to recognize and overcome limiting beliefs, by instructing them in the elements of the creative process, by providing opportunities to create, and validating their efforts to do so. Students can be encouraged to identify and develop their unique talents and gifts. A sense of community responsibility and a spirit of service can be nurtured from an early age. It is my hope that in this new century, goals of this kind will become integrated into public education—that in practice, *to educate* will come to reflect the true meaning of the word's origin "to draw out." If we will commit ourselves to nurturing and drawing out the creative best within each and every individual, our society will reap benefits we can hardly imagine today.

While the educational issue and other areas of institutional resistance remain in critical need of attention, the work-for-love movement goes on gathering ever greater momentum. All over the world, people are responding to the call for a more conscious and joyous experience of work. While the primary impetus springs from universal promptings deep within the human soul, there are a number of reasons why these promptings are finding greater resonance today than twenty or thirty years ago. We will explore some of these reasons below.

Waking to the Call of Conscious Work

We have called this book *Zen and the Art of Making a Living*. If *Zen* means anything, it means to be awake, to bring full presence and consciousness to what we are and what we do. In fact, the word *Buddha* itself means "An Awakened One" or "One who is Awake." To be awake with respect to work means to be conscious in the choices we make about the work we do and conscious in the way we actually do the work. If we want to think about the process of awakening, we can think about how people wake up each morning. Some people awaken naturally. It's as if an internal alarm clock goes off, telling them that the time for sleep has come to an end. Others require an external alarm clock to wake them, and still others require an alarm clock with a delay or snooze-control function. Yet, in a certain sense, waking up is waking up —no matter how you get there.

Today, many people are waking up to the need for a new, more conscious approach to work and career. For some, this awakening is coming principally from their internal alarm, from a deep yearning to express their inborn talents, gifts, and abilities. Others are motivated primarily by an external alarm. They feel called to serve humanity, to make a meaningful difference by spreading joy and/or eliminating suffering in the world. For still others, the awakening is coming from the irritating buzz of the snooze alarm— the recognition that the workplace has fundamentally changed and that, as a result, they must assert greater control over their own destinies. We will explore each of these wake-up calls next. Of course in reality, it's usually a combination of these factors rather than any single one that prompts an individual to begin the quest for a new, more conscious, experience of work.

The Internal Alarm:
A Desire for Creative Self-Expression

Your internal alarm is going off if you feel stuck, stifled, or bored with your current work situation. If your primary experience of work is a "have to" and not a "want to," your internal alarm is going off. If you feel as though you have to be someone else on the job, your internal alarm is ringing. If you feel like only part of you is showing up at work every day, your internal alarm is trying to rouse you from your slumber. If you feel that all the thrill, joy, or challenge has gone out of your experience of work—or that they were never there to begin with—your internal alarm is sounding loud and clear. Your internal alarm is going off if you know you have talents or abilities that are being ignored or could be more fully developed. Now if this alarm is sounding and we choose to ignore it, there can be considerable consequences to our self-esteem, our relationships with our mates and children, our physical health, and our spiritual and emotional well-being.

As long as you are trying to be something other than what you actually are, your mind wears itself out.

J. Krishnamurti

While there have always been consequences associated with an unfulfilling experience of work, today there is a growing awareness of them. Revelations from the health, personal growth, and psycho-therapy fields have heightened public awareness of the costs of suppressing creative self-expression at work. Recent studies have found that unhappiness at work is the number one risk factor for heart disease—greater than smoking, high cholesterol, or hyper-tension. In psychotherapy, many have come to realize that the pain and frustration they felt about their work situation and their failure to confront it directly, was a factor leading to a divorce or to alcohol or drug abuse. Others have come to recognize the toll an unhappy experience of work took on their parents and how this came to affect their own lives. In short, more and more people are coming to recognize that while there may indeed be difficulties attending the process of creative self-expression, the costs of self-denial or self-suppression can be devastating to human happiness.

For many, the spiritual quest (and the awareness gained on it) becomes the impetus to seek an experience of work more in line with the deepest aspirations of their souls. In recent years, as a survey of the lists of best-selling books will confirm, there has been a growing interest in all things spiritual. Perhaps even more important is the mounting interest people are showing in practical strategies for integrating spiritual awareness into all aspects of daily life, including work. All of these factors are prompting people to pay greater attention to the internal alarm when they feel it rousing them from their slumber.

The vocation of every man and woman is to serve people.

Leo Tolstoy

The External Alarm: A Call to Service

There is as well an external alarm trying to wake us up to a more meaningful experience of work. We hear this alarm in the situations in the world around us that cry out for our love and attention. You're hearing the external alarm if you feel you could be making a more meaningful difference in the world. You're hearing the external alarm if you feel that you were born for some high purpose or calling, even if you're not sure what it is. You're hearing this wake-up call if the sufferings of others are as real to you as your own. You're hearing this alarm if you feel you have love to give and a desire to help others that is going unfulfilled. If you are more interested in confronting the problems of the world than in escaping from them, the external alarm is tolling for you.

There are costs to ignoring this alarm as well. For the individual, the cost is a kind of deadening of the soul. We cannot be fully awake, fully alive, fully human—and remain indifferent to the world in which we live. We all want to make the world a better place for having been here; to deny this desire is to deny our very selves. From the standpoint of society, we lose the gifts and contributions of those who hear the call and refuse to embrace it. It is certainly true that the problems of our communities and nations, let alone the world, often seem overwhelming. Yet if we know that we are doing our best in our own unique way to make the world a better place, we can feel at peace, no matter how minuscule our individual efforts may seem in the grand scheme of things.

Like the internal alarm, the external wake-up call is being heard with a new urgency today. Many of the world's problems have reached a critical point of crisis. Issues such as the environment and global population cry out for immediate attention. Moreover, many today recognize the spiritual and cultural crisis that besets modern civilization. They see the need for an alternative vision of life to that given us by the dominant and increasingly global commercial culture that seems hell-bent on turning everything and everyone into a product for sale. The social and political movements of the sixties and seventies (the civil rights, anti-war, and feminist movements) instilled the baby boom generation with a belief that their lives ought to include a commitment to social responsibility. Many who had become distracted by or preoccupied with other concerns are returning to these roots. People of all ages yearn for a meaningful and rewarding experience of work. And yet, to paraphrase Albert Schweitzer, the only ones who will find real happiness are those who find a way to serve.

These two alarms, or wake up calls—the desire to express and the desire to serve—provide the essential keys to creating the work you love. Without self-expression, life lacks spontaneity and joy. Without service to others, it lacks meaning and purpose. I have spent fifteen years helping people to discover and pursue their true vocations or callings in life. In that time, I have read, thought, meditated, written, and lectured extensively on the subject. I know of no better nutshell statement of the path to finding one's true calling in life than the simple formula given by Aristotle: "Where your talents and the needs of the world cross, there lies your vocation." These two, talents and the needs of the world, are the great wake-up calls to your true vocation in life. To ignore either is, in some sense, to lose your soul.

The Snooze Alarm: Waking Up to a New Reality

Many hear these wake-up calls and start out on the quest for a new, more integrated and fulfilling life. Many more ignore them, hit the snooze button and to go back to sleep. They hear, however faintly, the alarms, but are not roused to wake or to act. Sometimes it just seems like too much trouble to wake up. Paralyzed by fear, unable to shake off the mesmerizing effects of routine and the inertia of the status quo, they roll over to catch a few more ZZZs. Fear whispers: "Go back to sleep, you won't be able to make it work financially." It tells you that you don't have the heart, talent, discipline, or chutzpah to make it work, that doing work you love is reserved for rare individuals, people more gifted or advantaged than you. Fear says: "Forget these quixotic dreams; you're lucky to have any job at all." Yet just when you are ready to forget the whole thing, that darn snooze alarm starts ringing.

Even if we manage to mute the voice of our hearts, suppressing our desires to express ourselves and to make a more meaningful contribution, the work environment we find ourselves in today will not let us drift along in complacency. In the final two decades of the twentieth century, the entire landscape of work and career changed dramatically. As the president of a leading executive recruiting firm put it, "The way people approached their careers in the past is history. It will never, never, never return." These historic changes in the job environment represent the snooze alarm, the final wake-up call to take responsibility and begin shaping your own career destiny. For today's worker, this alarm is ignored at great peril. The chime of the snooze alarm is loud and clear, ringing out: THE WORKPLACE IS CHANGING . . . THE WORKPLACE IS CHANG-

ING . . . THE WORKPLACE IS CHANGING. There are a number of factors driving these changes. We will explore some of the more important ones below.

Globalization: The global marketplace means different things to and for different people. What it means for American workers is that they are in direct competition with data processors in India and Ireland, with manufacturing labor in Mexico and Indonesia, and with technical experts in Korea and Taiwan. To date, those working in low-skilled manufacturing jobs and in related support industries have borne the brunt of the pain associated with the globalization of trade. Whole sectors of manufacturing have been eliminated in the U.S. and other technologically advanced countries. According to the Economic Policy Institute, "Trade accounted for fully 83% of the total 2.7 million jobs lost in [U.S.] manufacturing employment between 1979 and 1994 . . . Although the trade deficit eliminated more employment opportunities for the non-college educated, . . . [there] was a net loss of 290,000 jobs for the college educated." As the workforce in the developing world continues to become better educated and as technology continues to break down the barriers of distance, college-educated white collar workers can expect to experience in this new century the kinds of job losses that their less-educated blue collar counterparts did in the last two decades of the twentieth.

Merger Mania: Today, big business is more concentrated than ever. In the last twenty years, the banking, insurance, pharmaceutical, media, publishing, transportation, healthcare, utility, and retail industries—to name only a few of the more visible ones—have seen merger on top of merger. Many of these mergers have united companies across international boundaries. For workers, mergers and acquisitions are virtually synonymous with layoffs. Moreover, mergers spark more mergers, which in turn, bring even more layoffs. Even companies that manage to avoid being gobbled up by bigger ones feel increased pressure to slash labor costs in order to remain competitive. Merger mania has induced corporate management to look more and more to their short-term stock price and less to long-term profitability when making investment and cost-cutting decisions. Indeed, in the 1990s, for the first time, we began to see large-scale layoffs among companies that were simultaneously reporting strong, and in some cases, record profits. These layoffs were intended to boost the perceived value of company shares in the stock market. Merger mania shows no signs of abating. Barring an extremely unlikely reversal, consolidation will continue apace and will continue to exert pressure on corporate

management to reduce labor costs. We can expect merger-related job layoffs to continue well into the twenty-first century.

The Electronic Revolution: The new electronic technologies are significantly less labor-intensive in manufacturing, management, data collection, and processing than were the old technologies of the industrial era. In some fields, one person with a computer can do the work formerly done by half a dozen. In other fields, new technologies are on their way to replacing some positions altogether. Bank tellers are being replaced with automated tellers; receptionists, with voice mail; gas station attendants, with self-serve and electronic pay-at-the-pump sites. Manufacturing companies that remain within the technologically advanced nations are increasingly turning to computers and robots in their efforts to cut labor costs. Yet the impact of the new technologies on the workplace has not been confined to low-skilled or blue collar jobs. In the early years of the twenty-first century, the electronic revolution is expected to make an even greater impact on middle-management white collar workers.

Out-sourcing: Another trend reshaping the workplace is the rise in temporary, part-time, and independent contractor work. By the early 1990s, Manpower Inc., a temporary services company, had become the nation's largest employer, eclipsing long-time leader General Motors. Today, nearly 25 percent of the U.S. workforce, or one in four American workers, is a temporary, part-time, or contract worker. Many companies are hiring independent contractors for a variety of functions once done exclusively in-house. From accounting to janitorial services, from employee training to manufacturing itself, large companies are hiring out. For example, at this writing, Microsoft has not a single full-time employee engaged in manufacturing in the U.S. While it does have a relatively small number of full-time employees devoted to manufacturing in Ireland and Puerto Rico, the bulk of the work is contracted out.[1] Providing a variety of services to large organizations has been one of the major growth areas for new small business. At the same time, the out-sourcing phenomenon has displaced thousands from once secure jobs within large corporations and will likely continue to do so.

Mass Retail: In many small towns across America, factory outlets and discount superstores have all but eliminated local retailing. In urban centers and small towns throughout America and Europe, independent bookstores, hardware stores, office supply stores, grocery stores, barbershops, restaurants, and locally-owned de-

People wish to be settled. Only as far as they are unsettled is there any hope for them.

Emerson

partment stores have been replaced by large superstores, factory outlets, or franchise chain stores. In many sectors, the small independent retailer is going the way of the small independent farmer. In the healthcare industry, the changed status of doctors from independent entrepreneurs to employees of large HMOs can be seen as another example of this trend. While mass retail has eliminated many small businesses, it has also been a major source of new jobs. Unfortunately, many of these are jobs are part-time, low-paying, and not particularly challenging or rewarding.

The New Work Environment: Dangers and Opportunities

Coming all at once, the trends discussed above have in a few short years radically and inexorably transformed the American workplace. Though most who have lost their jobs as a result of these changes have found new ones, the lion's share have had to do so at a lower skill level and for less pay than they enjoyed in their previous positions.[2] In response to these and other changes, many are turning to a variety of self-employment options. In recent years, the number of people working freelance and/or in home-based businesses has risen sharply. Whether they choose to strike out on their own or work for others, people find themselves in a new work environment, one that requires them to take greater responsibility for shaping their career destinies. In this respect, the message of the snooze alarm is no different from that of the other two wake-up calls.

It's obvious to most workers today that the old ways of doing things just don't work any more. Workers know that qualities like company loyalty and a nose-to-the-grindstone attitude no longer pay off the way they once did. They understand that they can no longer rely on their employers to provide them with secure jobs. Whether workers respond creatively and decisively, or get tangled up in denial or distracted by outrage and anger, will spell the difference between taking advantage of the new situation and becoming a victim of it.

The job environment of today is not only less secure than it was twenty years ago, it is also more demanding. It is more demanding in three key respects. First, full-time workers are working more hours per week than at any time since the second World War. Americans work more hours per year than the people of any major industrialized nation.[3] Downsizing usually means that remaining workers carry a heavier workload. Employers are not only asking workers to work longer hours for less real pay—in many cases they are asking them to give up benefits as well, including overtime pay.

Second, more is being demanded from workers in terms of the responsibilities they are being asked to assume and in terms of the pace at which they are expected to learn new skills and incorporate new knowledge on the job. The era of mindless pencil pushing or monotonous factory work is over. Gone forever is a time when "just showing up" was enough. Today, even factory workers are expected to bring their brains to work. On the job, performance pressure in all fields is becoming increasingly intense. Productivity is being monitored as never before and is often measured in terms of team rather than individual performance. The pace of technological change demands that workers continually incorporate new knowledge and skills on the job. Fewer and fewer jobs today, especially better-paying ones, can be learned once or mastered for life. Workers must be prepared to keep learning for as long as they are on the job.

Finally, since it now takes the combined efforts of both adult members of a household to make the same amount of money (actually less in real dollars) than just one earned thirty years ago, people have less time to spend with their families or to do a variety of other things they enjoy.[4] As noted economist Robert Heilbroner puts it, "Lack of time is the new poverty." Many today feel that their lives have come to revolve around work. Now, if these people don't value and enjoy what they are doing every day and if they feel as though they could lose their jobs at any time, they are likely to ask themselves, What's the point?

In the face of the changes sweeping through the workplace in the developed world, it simply seems less risky and more inviting for people to take the leap into doing something they really love. In fact, many have told me that what motivated them to begin reexamining their lives and to choose career paths more suited to their values and talents were job layoffs (or the threat of them). The ringing of the snooze alarm forced them to finally pay attention to the other two wake-up calls, which had been ringing in the background all along. In time, they came to view the loss of a job as a blessing in disguise, providing the impetus to make a change that they might otherwise have put off indefinitely. The loss of a job or the threat of one provided the wake-up call they needed to create a more fulfilling experience of work. "After all," they reasoned, "if I have to go through the effort of changing careers or perhaps become self-employed, why not make it about something I care about and enjoy?"

While echoes from the snooze alarm are sending waves of anxiety and fear throughout the modern workplace, they are also providing the impetus for a variety of creative responses. Fifteen or

Always bear in mind that your own resolution to succeed is more important than any other one thing.

Abraham Lincoln

twenty years ago, the individual with the dream of pursuing a more independent career path looked at the risks involved versus the security of his corporate job and decided that he was better off staying where he was. Today, many people are recognizing that it is at least as risky *not* to follow their dreams and begin charting their own destinies. The fact is that the current work environment provides greater reinforcement to follow your dreams and fewer enticements not to. Whether we choose to work for ourselves or for the small business organizations that are providing most of the new jobs, the qualities necessary for success are precisely those that the person doing the work he loves is likely to posses, namely: self-motivation, a high level of energy, a willingness to learn and grow, and perseverance.

Another trend affecting today's workplace is what is often called the "down-shifting" or "voluntary simplicity" movement. Growing numbers of people are refusing to define themselves or the value of their lives by the financial criteria of the dominant commercial culture. They are seeking ways to reduce their living costs and are placing time above money in their priorities. *The Trends Journal* published by the Trends Research Institute estimates that by the year 2005, 15 percent of the population in the developed world will be in some way practicing voluntary simplicity.[5] Running parallel to this trend has been the shift in population away from urban centers toward small town America, where living costs are cheaper and the pace of life is slower. People today are looking for ways out of the rat race. They are discovering that the less invested they are in the pursuit of material acquisition, the more latitude they have in the choices they make about their work and about what to do with the all the time of their lives.

The new electronic technologies that are costing many people their jobs are, at the same time, making it easier for people to create their own work. E-mail and the World Wide Web have made it possible for anyone with a phone line, a computer, and a modem to conduct business from anywhere in the world. By 1998, thirty million Americans were using e-mail, and Internet sales for the year 2000 were projected to reach twenty billion dollars.[6] The Internet offers small start-up companies a way to successfully compete with much larger and well-established firms. Those offering specialized products and services are no longer limited to the demographics of their immediate area but can reach the entire world in an efficient and relatively inexpensive way. Moreover, informational resources that just a few years ago were hard to find in the best libraries in the world are today available to anyone anywhere with access to a computer and modem. Mission-oriented nonprofit organizations are also taking advantage of the Internet to promote and fund their causes. The Internet is not the pancea is it so often hyped up to be, but it does offer real opportunities for restructuring the way we work.

One of the exciting things about this movement is the way it brings together people with disparate social backgrounds, experience, and points of view. Many who have developed great discipline, strength, and ability on their way up the corporate ladder are coming to realize that work without heart is meaningless, dry, and empty. They are seeking a greater sense of meaning and purpose than can be realized through the pursuit of goals that revolve around money, status, or power alone. On the other hand, there are those who have developed a spiritual awareness but who have allowed themselves to be marginalized by their unwillingness to confront things as they are and develop the discipline and strength necessary to bring their inner realizations into manifestation in the outer world. They are coming to realize that a spiritual life includes a sense of social responsibility and that in order for them to make a difference in the direction of society, they must match sensitivity with the strength to persevere.

In the past, people with these differing perspectives on life seemed like polar opposites, who could never really understand or relate to one another. The more disciplined would tend to dismiss the more sensitive as impractical idealists, at best, or hopeless flakes at worst. On the other hand, those who had developed inner awareness and perhaps saw themselves as sojourners on the spiritual path would tend to dismiss successful corporate executives as selfish jerks. Today, a dialog has begun, and people in each camp are realizing that they have things to learn from those in the other. In truth, love *and* power, heart *and* discipline, compassion *and* strength are needed in equal measure. It is wisdom that unites the two. The dialog between those that hold these two perspectives and the synthesis it is spawning are vital components pushing the pace of social transformation.

While we cannot predict with any certainty how the nature of work will change in the coming century, it seems at this point inevitable that the work-for-love movement will continue to grow. Certainly the three wake-up calls discussed above will go on sounding, and there is every reason to believe that people will go on listening to them. This is truly an exciting time to be alive and one pregnant with possibilities. By making the commitment to follow your heart and do the work you love, you are part of a truly historic social transformation, one that has the potential to make the world a more just, humane, and beautiful place. Best of luck on your quest!

The Art of Life's Work

Wherein we consider the spirit at work
and meet our hero

Where the spirit does not work with the hand, there is no art.

Leonardo da Vinci

In "Prologue: The Art of Life's Work," we set the stage for the four-act play that follows. The theme of this unit is to consider how we can express our full creative potential and aliveness through work. In the introduction, we begin our discussion of the "Art of Life's Work" by contrasting the prevailing myth of the "little king" with the philosophy of work as art. Chapter 1 explores approaching work as creative self-expression and contrasts this with the more traditional problem-solving approach to work. Chapter 2 draws on lessons from Zen and the creative arts in an attempt to discover how each of us can make our work poetry in motion—love in action. Chapter 3 considers how we can enhance our experience of work through a conscious and creative encounter with universal, mythic, or archetypal energies. Chapter 4 speaks to awakening the heroic consciousness in our lives and work and explores the potential for greatness and heroic action within us all.

The Grail Quest or the Bourgeois Nest?

If you follow your bliss, you put yourself on a kind of track, which has been there all the while waiting for you, and the life that you ought to be living is the one you are living.

Joseph Campbell

Work is one of the great topics of humankind. We can know no people—their culture, history, art, or religion—without understanding their approach to work. In seeking to understand a historically distant culture, the anthropologist is interested, not only in the work these people did and how they did it, but *why* they did it. It is not enough for the anthropologist to know of a people's artifacts and technologies; she must know something of their myths if she would understand them. In the same way, we cannot understand ourselves without a knowledge of the myths we live and work by. In this introduction, we will briefly explore a central myth that has shaped our attitudes toward work in the modern age. We will then suggest an alternative vision of work for the postmodern era.

Myths shape our attitudes and aspirations in ways we scarcely recognize, grabbing hold of our imaginations and channeling our energies into prescribed patterns of behavior. Today, our dominant myth about work is the myth of "a world of little kings." This myth provides a social ideal, a measure for judging the relative worth of various activities and members of society. It is a view of life that many today are finding to be personally empty and socially ruinous. They, perhaps like you, are questing for another way.

Modern Times: Man in the Machine Age

It all began—not with the water wheel or the steam engine, the railroad or mass production—the modern world was born with the ticking of a clock. We don't really know when the first clock appeared in Europe. We do know that by 1335, the people of Milan could hear their all-mechanical town clock strike out the hours. Later in the same century, domestic versions of the clock became available throughout Europe. By the sixteenth century, we had personal time in the form of the watch. These early "time machines" were harbingers of a profound shift in the world view—one that would touch virtually every aspect of human life—the dawn of the machine age.

> *The hours of folly are measured by the clock; but of wisdom, no clock can measure.*
> *William Blake*

We have been gearing up ever since. Time has become more precise and more "valuable" as the years have rolled by. Today time *is* money, as every child in day care knows. We save, borrow, and spend time until our bodily gears are exhausted. If we could travel back in time, we would, no doubt, have a difficult time explaining to a thirteenth-century peasant that today we "have no time," that we feel under time "pressure," that time is "getting away from us," that we are in a "time crunch."

Gears, clocks, and hourly wages just weren't known in the Middle Ages. Man lived by the calendar, the sacred holidays and festivals marking the passage of cyclical time, recounting an endless drama of life, death, and regeneration. While calendarial time is based on nature's seasons and the earth's place in the universe, clock time is an abstraction of the mind. The shift from calendar to clock time took natural man into an abstract, linear world, sectioned off into minute particles. Life was no longer to be

organized around the rhythms of nature but around a machine—
the clock.

Today the clock has become an almost trite symbol of the
Industrial Revolution, where the gears of industry turned on the
labor of the punch-clock worker. In compensation for his labors, the
worker became "geared" toward the pursuit of the "good life." Why,
it was only a matter of time before the marvels of science would
allow the common man to enjoy the good life, once known only to the
aristocracy.

The Little King's Paradise:
A Promise Unfulfilled

About the time the Industrial Revolution was really getting into
gear, political revolutions were everywhere replacing kings with
parliaments, presidents, and promises. The key promise was that
the common man would one day soon be king. He would possess for
his own the kingly prerogatives of power, leisure, and security—
power over his station in life, the liberty of leisure, and the security
of property.

Mass education would destroy class distinction and give every
man the power over his station. Science would give him leisure:
washing machines, refrigerators, plumbing, automobiles. Government would guarantee his security through old age benefits and
either state assignment of housing or governmental support and
incentives for home ownership.

Every man would be king, enjoying the goods of life made
possible through machines and mass production. There would soon
arise whole nations of little kings, each at home in his castle; if not
a palace, then perhaps a country estate; if not a country estate, then
a home in the suburbs; if not a home in the suburbs, then perhaps
a condo, an apartment, a mobile home—any kingdom, no matter
how small. This is what we worked for. *We labored for a kingdom
and the promise of the leisure to enjoy it.*

---

*Too many people spend money they haven't
earned, to buy things they don't want, to impress
people they don't like.*

Will Rogers

We aspired to the kingly life of leisure, a life of ease, a life to do
with whatever we pleased, to be as irresponsible as we imagined

Of Cabbage and Kings:
Power, Leisure, and Security

Power through Technology: The Corporate Society. We put our faith in the power of technology and the technical sciences to solve all of our problems. As the production of atomic and chemical weapons demonstrates, technology has the potential for tremendous power, but it is not necessarily good. The danger is not with technology per se but in either elevating it to a religion—science as savior—or allowing it to be used solely as a tool for profit. The "free market" doctrine of the inherently benign nature of "competing technologies" fuels a global arms race which endangers us all. Just because we can do something (have the power) doesn't mean we should do it. Power does not necessarily corrupt, but power for power's sake is the road to disaster.

Individualism through Leisure: The Consumer Society. The advance of the philosophy of individualism has strangely failed to include individual expression in work. It has not meant better craftsmanship or fuller individual participation in the purpose and goals of work. It has rather come to mean "pleasure in leisure" or, in short, consumption. We claim to be an individualistic society, yet we reside in cracker-box houses and scurry about in cookie-cutter cars. We live in suburbs that look so much alike it requires a road map to tell them apart. We toil away at dull or meaningless jobs and suppress our individuality and creative zest in hopes of acquiring the status symbols which Madison Avenue tells us we need to be *individuals*. Today people in third-world countries want in on the act. Irreplaceable resources dwindle, but still we try to consume our way into heaven. Perhaps if we were happier, we wouldn't *need* so much stuff.

Security through Secularism: The Bureaucratic State Society. Secularism has developed into reliance upon the state, the government. Big Brother will take care of us in old age, solve all of our social ills, and create the Great Society. The sum of our duty to our fellow man, to nature, and to the environment is to be a good "citizen" and vote for the best candidates. We have relied on political solutions rather than individual spiritual development and social cooperation. Bureaucracies abound, but they have not reduced anxiety, nor produced lasting security.

the aristocracy to be. Labor unions advocated less work for more benefits—never challenging the nature or objectives of the work, only demanding more leisure and security *away* from work. Golf and tennis, the games of the aristocrats, became the staples (with the stables) of the country club set, where the new upper middle class could play the part of landed gentry on a subscription basis.

The more ambitious were not content with little kingdoms and playing weekend gentry. They would be empire builders. They would rule whole industries and employ thousands, have their own armies, and crush all opposition. While these industrial giants set out to conquer ever larger domains, the less ambitious or advantaged had to content themselves with whatever leisure and security they could manage.

Kingly life (at least that of the better kings) was, no doubt, more than power, leisure, and security, but these were what we coveted. Duty, responsibility, wisdom, honor, courage, magnanimity—these kingly virtues might be admired in passing, but they were not envied like the others. Like a young sibling, jealous of the privileges of an older brother, we viewed the king from afar and ogled the privileges we would one day have for ourselves. *We would be kings and take for ourselves as much power, leisure, and security as we thought we deserved and could get away with.*

The promise of a future kingdom kept the wage worker toiling away. If he wasn't enjoying what he was doing, well, the age of leisure was just around the corner. It is amusing today, at the beginning of the twenty-first century, to read the predictions made as late as the mid-1970s about the life of leisure that was just around the corner for the common man. Today, children of the two-career family, who seldom see either parent, scoff at the notion that they will grow up to a life of leisure. Still, we rush to get our share of the goods of life, before our time runs out. We cling to the hope that, if not by the miracles of science, then perhaps by the miracle of the credit card, we can live the life of kings. (Increasingly, leisure has become associated, not with rest, refinement, or a contemplative life—but with consumption. *Leisure,* which we get from the Latin *licere,* "to be permitted," has come to mean permission to consume as much as we want, without consideration for others or the environment.)[1]

By now, many realize that the promise was empty, indeed. We were promised that we would be little kings, and yet it seems we have so little control over the direction of our lives. The little king is a prisoner of his own "freedom"—from responsibility and conscience. His inner life is barren and hollow; his humanity, atrophied; his creativity, flat. Not surprisingly, some of the most telling criticism of modern society has come from some of our most

Come out of the circle of time, and into the circle of love.

Rumi

insightful psychiatrists, people who see first-hand the psychological anguish of "the little king." Erich Fromm described modern life as producing men "who feel free and independent, not subject to any authority or principle of conscience—yet willing to be commanded, to do what is expected of them, to fit into the social machine without friction; who can be guided without force, led without leaders, prompted without aim—except the one to make good, to be on the move, to function, to go ahead."[2] To be obsessed with control, yet unable to direct his own life, to consume without satisfaction, to seek security in isolating conformity—such is the lot of the little king—such, his "freedom."

Victor Frankl, author of *Man's Search for Meaning,* put it like this: "For too long we have been dreaming a dream from which we are now waking up; the dream that if we improve the socio-economic situation of people, everything will be okay, people will become happy. The truth is that as the struggle for survival has subsided, the question has emerged: Survival for what?"[3] While the struggle for survival remains paramount for a large part of the human population, those of us who have the luxury of asking this question have a responsibility, not only to ourselves, but to those who don't.

It is preoccupation with possessions, more than anything else, that prevents us from living freely and nobly.

                            Bertrand Russell

The dream from which we are now awakening is what we have called the myth of the little king. Now some would say that today we have no myth to live by, and in the strictest, or archaic, sense of the term, this is so. (We will discuss myth in this context in chapter 3.) Yet, as much as nature, the mind of man—his imagination— abhors a vacuum. If we have no genuine myth to show us the way of life, then a counter- or pseudo-myth arises to fill the void. Today we live by the pseudo-myth of the little king.

Of course, most of us don't actually live like kings; yet most are still caught up in the myth. We wish it were so. So high school kids rent limousines on prom night; we dream of the "lifestyles of the rich and famous" and hope to win the lottery. To wish for something is to believe in it (the *lief* in belief originally meant wish). If you believe in the myth, not intellectually, but deeply—subconsciously, you accept it as the standard by which you judge yourself and others.

The little-king myth is today at once a practical anachronism and a widely popular view that holds great currency in the imaginative life of the global culture. While most of us in the West still believe in the myth (and we are busy exporting it to the far reaches of the globe), many are coming to see it for the empty fiction that it is. Working for security, status, and consumer items is simply not enough for many today. We have a sense that work ought to nurture and uplift us spiritually and psychologically. The little-king myth and the values it promotes are increasingly seen as inadequate. Two major factors are peeling away the scales from our eyes.

1. The growing recognition of the importance of nonmaterial, psychological, and spiritual factors to happiness and fulfillment in life, generally, and at work in particular.

2. The achievement of the global village and the critical state of environmental, economic, and peace issues . . . Increasingly, we are coming to recognize that we are all together in this thing called life on earth.

These are really flip sides of the same coin. We cannot address the needs of the community, the nation, or the world apart from consideration of the psychological and spiritual needs of the individual, or vice versa. The great fallacy of the little king myth is its suggestion that the individual ego is a thing apart—apart from nature, from the spirit of life, from his fellows, and even from his own psyche. To conceive of ourselves as separate is to create an artificial boundary between "me" (the ego) and "them" (everything and everyone else). Our separate kingdoms become our prisons. We can't lock "them" out without locking ourselves in. Individual alienation and social and environmental conflict must result from this separative consciousness.

> *This time, like all times, is a very good one, if we but know what to do with it.*
>
> *Emerson*

In the remainder of this introduction, we will step back from our over-simple historical narrative and examine some of the deeper issues involved in transforming our relationship to work. We will see that the way we view work is fundamentally shaped by the way we view life and ourselves, that is, our image of man, and that we cannot transform our relationship to work without transforming our image of who we are.

For the Bold: Breaking with the Mold

The myth of the little king and the values that it inculcates—ambition (power), consumerism (leisure), and security in conformity—give us a prescription for how we are supposed to live our lives. To want something different from this is to enter the dark forest of uncharted experience. As Joseph Campbell put it, "You don't have to go very far off the interpreted path to find yourself in very difficult situations. The courage to face the trials and to bring a whole new body of possibilities into the field of interpreted experience for other people to experience—that is the hero's deed."[4] The hero, in living her own life, in being true to herself—radiates a light by which others may see their own way.

> *What each must seek in his life never was on land or sea. It is something out of his own unique potentiality for experience, something that never has been and never could have been experienced by anyone else.*
>
> *Joseph Campbell*

This is no easy task but one demanding the greatest integrity, courage, and skill. As Colin Wilson has written, "modern civilisation, with its mechanised rigidity is producing more outsiders than ever before—people who are too intelligent to do some repetitive job, but not intelligent enough to make their own terms with society."[5] Those "intelligent enough" to make their own terms with society are what we will later refer to as "artists of life." The outsider views himself as a product of a culture he rejects—the artist views himself as a culture-builder. As would-be artists, we begin with the right attitudes or, as the Buddhists might say, "right views"—taking a mature approach beyond mere protest and complaint—accepting the responsibility to *create* the life we would live. Everything we will say in the remainder of this book is there to assist you in this creative process. Clearly, if we are to accomplish this, we will require a new image of what work is and what work is for.

Life shrinks or expands in proportion to one's courage.

Anaïs Nin

A Question of Balance

On our way to developing a new image of work, we can take a lesson from Jungian psychology. According to Jung, the individual psyche (of both men and women) has feminine and masculine aspects or values. Roughly speaking, the feminine values are concerned with *being*; the masculine, with *doing*. In the Jungian conception, the masculine aspect of self is concerned with *controlling* the external world. Technology is the pre-eminent means of achieving control. In a society where masculine values dominate, technology is highly valued and advanced. The feminine aspect of self is concerned with enlarging the individual's *experience* of the world as it is—that is, with being. In a society where masculine values dominate, people have little experience with being; they lose touch with what Joseph Campbell called "the rapture of being alive." The key to psychological maturity, Jung would tell us, is balance.[6]

The balanced individual is free, in the words of Joseph Campbell, "to pass back and forth across the world division, from the perspective of the apparitions of *time* [the world of doing] to that of the causal deep [the world of being] and back—not contaminating the principles of the one with those of the other, yet permitting the mind to know the one by virtue of the other."[7] Modern man is a prisoner of time—so involved in his doings that he has lost touch with his being. As individuals and as a society, we have lost our balance. We might ask with Anne Morrow Lindbergh, "Why have we been seduced into abandoning this timeless inner strength of woman [the feminine values] for the temporal outer strength of man [the masculine values]?"[8]

Only those who will risk going too far can possibly find out how far one can go.

T. S. Eliot

The effects of this cultural bias are not merely academic. They are everyday life, where good has become synonymous with expensive; practical, with commercial; science, with technology. The good doctor or lawyer is the one who costs the most money. Practical decisions are ones that make the largest short-term profit, regardless of long-term costs. Science is no longer the pursuit of knowledge, but the pursuit of technological "solutions." The problem is we accept all of this as though it were the only way. The starving artist is cliché, but we seldom hear of the starving engineer.

Today, even art has become commercialized. It has become a tool for profit and, therefore, a means for better controlling the environment, rather than the revelation of deep inner experience. The same can be said of much of religion, which is often nothing more than a social club. Religion is used as a means of abating the loneliness and isolation of an existence lived without an experience of spirit. It has, to a large degree, lost its fire, its bliss. Philosophy has been left to the technical specialists, and wisdom, especially in high places, runs in short supply.

The feminine values are the fountain of bliss.

Certainly our common-man-as-king myth, with its exclusive emphasis on controlling the environment, produces a half-formed individual, alienated from the life-vivifying powers of nature and spirit—cut off from his own conscience. Without the balance of feminine values, the sanctioned drives for power, leisure, and security are more apt to produce little tyrants than philosopher-kings. The feminine values are the wellspring of life, the fountain of bliss, the ocean of life eternal. Without the regeneration of these living waters, life becomes the barren *Waste Land* of T. S. Eliot. We become slaves to time and technology. The more enslaved and stuck in time we feel, the more desperately we try to control our time and our lives. Yet the more we attempt to gain control through our mechanical creations (both mental machinations and material gadgetry), the more controlled by them we feel. Today the mechanical gear is being replaced by the electronic chip, and the pace of time becomes a frantic clip.

We miss the bliss, the touch of the eternal. We are stuck in time, stuck in trying to control, stuck with a sense of missing something. We miss the bliss, and so we try to drown time in a bottle of wine, a flood of sex, or a warm jacuzzi. Imitation bliss comes and goes, and too soon, time again comes marching in. Bliss is rest, but we are restless.

> Know the masculine,
> Keep to the feminine.
> Lao Tzu

The women's movement to date has provided little challenge to our overly masculine value structure. It has been more concerned with finding a place for women within the existing structure than with challenging the assumptions upon which it is based. (If the common man can be king, why not the common woman?) In its wake, we have not become a more feminine (that is, a more spiritual/artistic) society. The introduction of women en masse into the workplace means women, as well as men, feel the pressure to conform to the existing masculine-dominated value structure.

The Whole 'n' Parting

In his effort to control his world, modern man rejected all he could not understand through reason or experiment. He accepted that "such knowledge as is not empirical is meaningless." He denied the great Mystery of life and put his faith in ratio-nality. A ratio is a portion, a part. In rationality, we divide life into parts, but in endless fragmentation, we miss the experience of the whole. Life is simultaneously the ratio (the part) and the whole—at once the same and different. A stream is the same stream, yet each moment the water is different. Starting from the ratio, life is an endless series of problems to be solved. Starting from the whole, life is a mystery to be revealed.

The rational scientific point of view tells us that life is a problem to be solved. Through analysis, problems can be solved, but always new problems take their place. This is the endless tail chase of Q and A—the Hydra who sprouts new heads every time you cut one off. The poet, the sage, the scriptures, the mythologies of the world suggest that life is not a problem to be solved but a mystery to be revealed. But alas, toward these we turned a deaf ear.

We rejected the Mystery of the whole and came to rely on rational conscious attention as the sole means of experiencing the universe. This gave us a one-at-a-time (abstract, linear) sense of reality—a world of separate things. Our way of dealing with a world conceived of in separate parts was to attempt to exercise ever greater control over it. A world of separate parts (without a unitive whole) was perceived as a jumbled mess. It was up to us to impose law and order on this chaos. We put our faith in political laws to control the wills of others and natural laws to regulate nature. Politics and science became the religions of the modern era. Little king religion is concerned with controlling the parts, not with opening to the whole. The felt need for control and the emphasis on fragmentary, rational knowledge arise together—head and tail of the same dragon.

> *Nothing divides one so much as thought.*
> *Reginald Blyth*

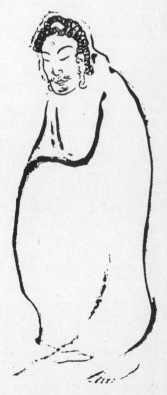

Today, many of us see the "problem of life" as a matter of addition. Our whole effort is to gain and hold, acquire and defend. We fear to let go. The cry of the little king is, "More, more, more!" The answer to our social problems is ever greater economic growth (a good unto itself) and more and better technological solutions. On the personal level, the answer is more stuff of one kind or another: knowledge, money, fame, recognition, admiration, etc. Perhaps, we dream, if we get enough parts, they will add up to a whole. But alas, all the king's horses and all the king's men can't put poor ole Humpty Dumpty back together again.

Society tells us the only thing that matters is matter—the only things that count are the things that can be counted. We start

O, Heart, remember thee That Man is none, Save One.

Coventry Patmore

counting with toys, then grades, then friends, then bank accounts, then years to retirement. What is there to life that can't be counted? That can't be measured? That can't be dissected or analyzed? What is this, that when you try to reduce it—it wiggles away? The moment you try to grab it—it escapes. No matter how we try to comprehend it, life itself remains an indefinable mystery.

Our science can record similarities or differences in nature, but it can't touch the Mystery. Below, Isaac Newton states the difficulty of trying to understand any whole from a series of parts.

> The orbit of any one planet depends on the combined motion of all the planets, not to mention the action of all these on each other. But to consider simultaneously all these causes of motion and to define these motions by exact laws allowing of convenient calculation exceeds, unless I am mistaken, the force of the entire human intellect.[9]

The difficulty he describes is not a matter of a backward seventeenth century technology but a fundamental limitation of analysis for ever comprehending the whole. There are mysteries that simply defy analysis. If we limit our knowledge to that which can be quantified, we miss, not only the wonder of the Mystery, but the possibility of its revelation.

It has been said that Mystery is revealed through purification. Zen tells us that we must purify even the idea of purification; we must enter into the Mystery direct. All can approach the Mystery in nature. The Taoist and transcendental English and American poets contemplated the Mystery this way—in landscape and rain, in birdsong and nightfall. Looking in nature, we catch glimpses of an order—patterns within a leaf, rings on a tree, cycles of seasons, migrations of birds. These glimpses hint at an incomprehensible, transcendent Mystery. The more of the Mystery we glimpse, the more we are struck by its incomprehensibility, and the more deeply we are moved to purify our sense of separation, our fixation on ourselves as little parts.

The Art of Life's Work: The Mystery of Being in Action

The new image of work we will call "The Art of Life's Work." Life's work is not machine work obsessed with control—negating the Mystery of Life. It is an integrated expression of Being and doing— what Zen calls the "infinite way of doing finite things." It is a celebration of the Mystery of Life. We needn't be desperate prisoners of the time machine, struggling to lord it over our separate little kingdoms. We can live in cognizance of the Eternal and in harmony with life, nature, and one another. We can dedicate ourselves to loving and serving our fellow man in the realization that he and we are a part of the great eternity of existence, the great Mystery of Life. This is what is meant by "follow your bliss"—do from *being*. Act in time from the ecstasy of the timeless.

A life's work comes out of the Living Mystery. It moves into the limited world of time and forms; this is the work, hence, life's work. Life and work are not things apart. Work is more than gaining privileges and possessions; it is ongoing, ecstatic, LIVING experience. When we tap into living experience, we no longer feel as though we must be king. We can just be ALIVE at work! *When we live in the bliss, there is no difficulty that is insurmountable. If we miss the bliss, there is no compensation that is adequate.*

We are kept out of the Garden by our own fear and desire in relation to what we think to be the goods of our life.

Joseph Campbell

The highest order of duty to self is to follow your bliss. To thine own self be true. The highest order of duty to society is to make your fullest contribution to its well-being. These duties meet in life's work. They may appear (especially in the short-term) to be in conflict, but in the long run of a life span, they can be seen to be threads interwoven so tightly as to be almost indistinguishable. It cannot be said where one begins and the other ends.

Freud said the basic requirements of human existence are love and work.[10] A genuine life's work breaks down any barriers we might impose to separate the two. Love is not a category, a compartment of life separate from work. It is pervasive. When we are in love, we feel boundless life. We touch the timeless. Work is simply the forms into which we pour this living substance of love. In life's work, we honor both our timeless love and the time-bound world of form we live in. Freud was correct: Love (and through it, the timeless pulse of life) and work (and through it, the world of time and forms) are the basic stuff of human life. Work without love is dry and empty. Love without work is incomplete. Our task is to tap into the eternal ocean of bliss and somehow express that energy in the world of forms and time. This is the art of creative living. While engaged in life's work, we can be said to be practicing artists—motivated, not by external rewards, but by the intrinsic joys of self-expression and service to humanity.

Artists in each of the arts seek after and care for nothing but love.

Marsilio Ficino

A Postmodern Vision: Everyone an Artist

(The discussion that immediately follows draws on the work of Ananda K. Coomaraswamy, an exceptionally gifted philosopher and art historian of the twentieth century. See especially *Christian and Oriental Philosophy of Art* and *The Transformation of Nature in Art,* both published by Dover. This discussion is necessarily brief; I will explore these themes in greater depth in a future book, *The Way of the Artist.*)

Art is the proper task of life.
Friedrich Nietzsche

Some may find it hard to accept that Nietzsche's statement (above) applies to them, yet we will insist throughout this book that every man or woman is, in potential, an artist and, when living authentically, one indeed. Ananda K. Coomaraswamy wrote: "However broad or narrow, noble or ignoble, the subject of the art, however elegant or crude the language, art is always recognizable as art. *All that we demand of an artist is that he should offer us living water:* for this water has a miraculous quality, and even though it be offered in a thimble it will fill a bowl . . ." (Emphasis added.)[11]

An experience I had many years ago shaped my own views of work as art. I had arrived in Europe for the first time, there to study the art and architecture of the Old World. After traveling all night, I arrived early in the morning and went straightway to a downtown hotel to check in. There was no one at the desk, but I heard the most incredible singing ringing through the building. A voice of such spirit, beauty, and joy as I had never heard. It was "not the tongue, but our very life singing." Following the voice, I went upstairs. There, in the third-floor hallway was the origin of the voice—a young woman on her hands and knees pushing a bristle brush with both hands. In this woman, I had encountered a genuine artist of life. Her art echoed in me long after the noise of so many museum images had faded.

This little story illustrates a couple of important points: that we not mistake art for artifact, or again, that we not mistake the art with the craft. As Coomaraswamy wrote, "the thing is a work *of* art, made *by* art, but it is not art itself; the art remains in the artist…"[12] If we can enter into what Coomaraswamy is suggesting here (and he is by no means alone in this view; see pages 48 and 75.), we can understand that, not only can we all be artists, but indeed, it is our

The Whole Business of Man Is The Arts, & All Things Common.

William Blake

duty, for artists are what we naturally are. The art is in the man or woman—in their consciousness. The Zen saying, "How wondrous this, how mysterious! I carry fuel, I draw water,"[13] gives this perfectly. Again emphasizing consciousness over craft, Blake said, "Jesus & his Apostles & Disciples were all Artists."[14] If you cannot find art in your consciousness, you will never find it at all.

The most awkward means are adequate to the communication of authentic experience, and the finest words no compensation for lack of it. It is for this reason that we are moved by the true Primitives and that the most accomplished art craftsmanship leaves us cold.

Ananda K. Coomaraswamy

The artist's craft may be a "fine" or "applied" art. We are not suggesting that all of us can or should be "fine" artists but that we err if we assume "that there is one kind of man that can imagine, and another that cannot; or to speak more honestly, another kind whom we cannot afford to imagine without doing hurt to business…"[15] Of course, there are greater and lesser artists, whatever the craft. The test of greatness is the depth of the artist's vision, and only secondarily, the skill of her technique. As Coomaraswamy would say, it is the artist's vision (love) from which the "living waters" spring. "It is not by an intellectual or categorical activity that we can judge the intensity of an artist's vision. We cannot judge except by our response and whether or not we *can* respond will depend on our own state of grace."(Emphasis added.)[16]

The First Work of the Artist Is Herself

The purpose of the whole (work) is to remove those who are living in this life from a state of wretchedness and lead them to the state of blessedness.

Dante

The artist must be a developed individual—an authentic hero and never a mere product of society. The hero, as Dorthea Dooling so aptly expressed it, "may be you or me, but only at the highest reaches of our most impossible possibility."[17] Her role is to release

Industry without art is brutality.

Ananda K. Coomaraswamy

the active powers of nature, soul, and spirit into the lives of men. The intensity of her vision is reflected in her capacity to fuse these three into a radiant, harmonious, whole. Nature provides the medium and energy of the work—the dancer's body, the painter's colors, the sculptor's stone, the composer's instruments, the poet's paper and ink or computer chip—as well as the body's transformation of these. The musician trains her ear; the painter, his eye and hand; the dancer, her body. The soul provides the symbols, the mythic forms, the archetypal energies through which a universally human art is made intelligible. The spirit arrests the mind—projecting the experiencer out of himself into the realm of the infinite, the transcendent Mystery.

Before she can express them in art, the artist must deeply encounter these energies in life. Modern life is so configured as to negate the powers of nature, soul, and spirit—to encourage you to put all of your eggs (faith and aspirations) into society's basket. Society tries to make you think that it is your only source of nourishment and protection, power and refreshment. And who is this society? None other than our little king—the adolescent ego.

Traditional cultures understood that society is always essentially adolescent and sought to honor, celebrate, and make conscious the greater powers of nature, soul, and spirit through communally shared myths, rituals, and initiations, and in the higher religions, through individual transformation. Here we must distinguish between society and culture. A society can be interested in a man or woman only as a political or economic entity; a culture is interested in more. Culture means literally "to cultivate" or "to care for."[18] Cultures care for their peoples as natural, spiritual beings and not simply as workers or consumers. Cultures cultivate an awareness of the deep energies of life and of the particular gifts of the individual, and so naturally produce art. Modern society (the little king with his machines) has usurped the role of the greater powers in seeking to make itself the Alpha and Omega of human experience.

The trick of society is to make you think it is the whole banana of life. For your physical food, you are to depend, not on the bounty of Mother Nature but on supermarket chains, chemical conglomerates, and giant agribusiness firms. Western man has become increasingly alienated from his body and nature. You are to depend on society for its evaluation of your sanity—measured, not in terms of the ancient wisdom or sacred psychologies but in terms of "normality"—the sharing of the society-dominant world view. Western man has become alienated from his conscience and the universally human. You are to depend upon social religion to tell you what God is or upon social science to tell you that God isn't.

Western man stands alienated from his divinity and from Ultimate Reality. (By Western man we mean, not simply those who live in the West but all who embrace its vision of life.) All of this puts extreme pressure on the social dimension to fulfill all of man's needs and puts pressure on him to conform; for unlike in other cultures, he has no other concept of power, no other source of protection.

> For, in order to turn the individual into a function of the State, his dependence on anything beside the State must be taken from him.
>
> *Carl Jung*

Again, our task is to re-energize the living powers of nature, spirit, and psyche into society. This is always the work of the artist—opening, as Blake said, "the immortal Eyes of man" to the reality beyond and beneath his mental abstractions. Having come to recognize and trust the energies which support it, we may come at last to develop a relationship of trust with society, not in unexamined innocence, but in the full acceptance of our responsibilities to it. We can only trust society when we are no longer exclusively dependent upon it—when we can live as natural, human beings in touch with the deeply spiritual within. The first work of the artist, then, is not the transformation of matter into some artifact, but the transformation of his own consciousness, or put another way, transforming his relationships to nature, spirit, psyche, and society.

The key to the transformations lies in developing relationships of trust with each of these aspects. Trust is not arrived at through an effort of will or conscious intention; it comes in the simple recognition that we are not separate from, but one with, nature, spirit, the universally human, and our unique historical and cultural context. All of these are forces greater than our little personality kingdoms. All may be trusted on their own terms, but these terms must be understood and not confused. We will encourage you to trust each of these powers by acknowledging or acting-in-the-knowledge-of them. Act-in-the-knowledge-of nature—its spontaneous growth and its inherent polarity. Act-in-the-knowledge-of spirit and its transcendent Mystery. Act-in-the-knowledge-of the psyche and its archetypal energies. Act-in-the-knowledge-of society and serve it as a *culture-builder,* and not simply as a *cultural product.* Together these energies will guide you on your journey to life's work.

When Nations grow Old,
The Arts grow Cold
And Commerce
settles on every Tree.

William Blake

The Little-King Model

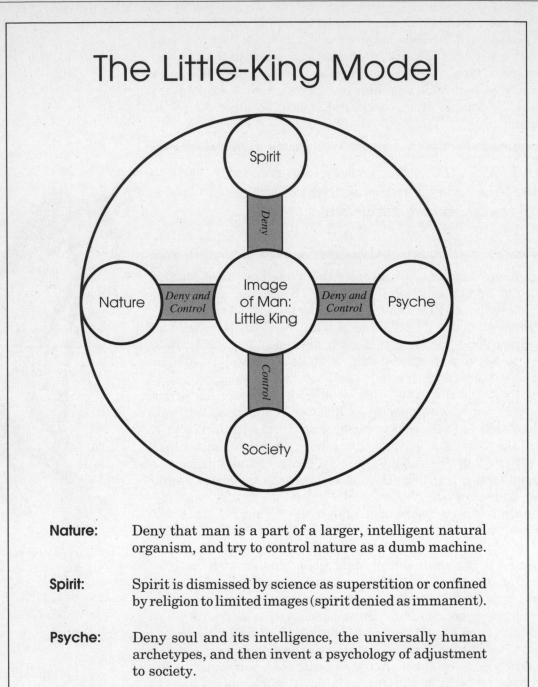

Nature: Deny that man is a part of a larger, intelligent natural organism, and try to control nature as a dumb machine.

Spirit: Spirit is dismissed by science as superstition or confined by religion to limited images (spirit denied as immanent).

Psyche: Deny soul and its intelligence, the universally human archetypes, and then invent a psychology of adjustment to society.

Society: Society dominates as the axis of control—man's whole life is defined in terms of society.

The Way of the Artist

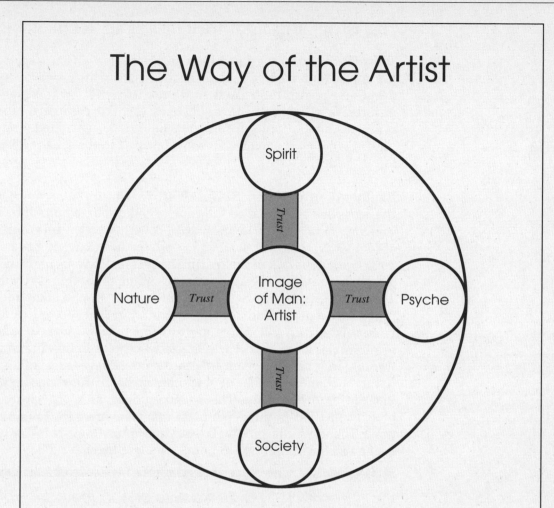

Nature: Transform relationship to nature: trust nature's sponta-neous growth from the inside out and its polarity, black and white, birth and death.

Spirit: Transform relationship to spirit from king, judge, or dead God image to the living spirit—immanent in all things, yet transcendent to them.

Psyche: Transform relationship to psyche by opening to its intui-tions and taking instruction from the myths and ancient wisdom teachings.

Society: Transform relationship to society by viewing it in terms of the responsibility to one's fellow man and in openness to higher powers.

Transforming Our Relationship to Nature

Transforming our relationship to nature begins with understanding how we approach it. Today, most of us have little experience of nature (or so we think), and so we are left with our ideas about nature. We will examine three big ones: (1) nature is inferior to the conscious mind, (2) nature is a machine to be controlled, and (3) nature is not good enough (here *good* is used in the sense of "being fair or ethical").

Eradicate Inferior (or Sinful) Nature: Nature is not inferior to the conscious mind, but to the contrary, the source of its life. The conscious mind requires a brain to think with, which it gets courtesy of Mother Nature. Yet somehow (perhaps from our old-time religion?) we got the notion that nature has got it all wrong, and it is the job of man, with his superior conscious mind, to set things straight. This is the wild and woolly view of nature so prevalent in the nineteenth century, and carrying over into our own. *Modern* came to be associated with man-made, and all things natural came to be seen as dirty, messy, or heathen. Traditional peoples living "in nature" were inferior races; women, who are more closely associated with nature, became "the inferior sex;" natural bodily functions became unclean or unwholesome. The modern notion was to put nature out of sight and out of mind—to attack it. Of course, we couldn't go around blindly bulldozing and cementing nature "out there" without losing touch with nature "in here." And lose touch we did.

> . . . technology is destructive only in the hands of people who do not realize that they are one and the same process as the universe.
> Alan Watts

Control the Machine, Nature: Where we could not eradicate nature, we attempted to control it as if it were a machine—a kind of giant clockwork. As much as possible, we attempted to make natural functions into social, mechanical ones. We start with childbirth, where life is not given by the mother as the embodiment of Mother Nature but by a socially licensed doctor and his marvelous machines. We are fed, not mother's milk, but a product of a mechanized factory. We try to act as though we are the boss of nature—that through our marvelous science, we can piecemeal manipulate it—without bothering to respect, much less to understand it. Often our attempts at control only make a bigger mess of things. Nature *can* be improved upon, as in a Japanese tea garden or a beautiful city park. Yet this is best accomplished when we work with nature and by our own nature—so that the city park is as natural a human action as a beaver's dam or an eagle's nest.

Nature is not a dead machine but a living miracle. Your conscious mind is not required to digest your food or beat your heart. Nor can it direct the movements of the stars, the orbiting of planets, the migration of birds, the sprouting of seeds. If one stops to contemplate this, she recognizes that this great natural intelligence lives within. Right now, you are sitting in the midst of a miracle. Acknowledge it. Honor it. Nature is neither a wild creature to be tamed, nor a machine that can be adroitly controlled by pushing all the right levers. Nothing you can do from conscious intention can in any way rival the mystery of the life happening spontaneously within you—right now.

Thus, those who say they would have right without its correlate, wrong; or good government without its correlate, misrule, do not apprehend the great principles of the universe, nor the nature of all creation.

Chuang Tzu

Avoid the Polarity of Nature: Nature is not the one-sided affair that we seem to wish it were. Having attempted to eradicate and control nature, to discount its blessings, we are all the more shocked by its destruction. For most of us, nature is not the birth of a child, the bounty of food, a gentle summer day, or health—nature is a hurricane, an earthquake, a flood, or an illness. Traditional peoples living in nature, as a part of nature, are naturally attuned to its ways. They know the lesson of nature is polarity: life/death, black/white, gain/loss—that the way of nature is the way of sacrifice. Creation *is* suffering. The image is there in childbirth—for you to enter life, your mother must suffer. It is there every time you take a meal—some sentient being (plant or animal) has died to give you life.

Traditional peoples love the animal while stalking, killing, and carving it. We buy our meat prepackaged in cellophane—we don't want to be reminded of death or sacrifice. We want good without bad, happiness without suffering, beginnings without ends, life without death. We try to sugarcoat or avoid the pains of life. The sick, the old, and the dying are shunned. They remind us of our own mortality. Whether we like it or not, nature's way is our way. We

A man is related to all nature.

Emerson

must come into accord with it, not as an intellectual understanding, but deeply felt in the depths of our being—opening our hearts to the sorrows as well as the joys of life. Nature's way is only shocking for someone who lives in an artificial world of his own imagining, where everything is at right angles, and nothing is crooked.

Nature in Art: Ananda K. Coomaraswamy defined art as "the involuntary dramatisation of subjective experience."[19] Involuntary here means spontaneous; even as love cannot be coerced or willed, neither can creativity be forced. The art of creative living is not the execution of some intentional program for life, but a natural, evolving expression. In chapter 1, we will explore how we might learn to trust nature, growing spontaneously, as nature does, from the inside out.

Transforming Our Relationship to Spirit

At least since the Council of Constantinople in 869, the spirit has been denied as essential in man. Both our traditional religion and modern science dismiss the spirit as irrelevant to daily life. Religion does admit of the soul and the Holy Spirit (which comes to man from without but is not innate to him), yet the *emphasis* is on the ethical—good vs. bad, right vs. wrong. As Joseph Campbell said, contemporary "religious life is ethical; it is not mystical."[20]

For modern science, "mystical" is a kind of dirty word. The spirit is a childish superstition from a bygone era. The word *science* originally meant simply "knowledge," and as the quote by Plotinus (below) indicates, it was considered that there could be knowledges of different kinds, including spiritual. (Plotinus is hardly original but following Pythagoras, Socrates, and Plato in this matter.) Modern science is only interested in that knowledge perceivable through the senses, either directly or through augmenting instrumentation (empirical knowledge).

This bias rejects knowledge of the realm of ideas as well as the realm of spirit. That ideas cannot be sensibly perceived does not make them unreal (e.g., mathematics are proved by logic, not by measurement). Neither is the spiritual unreal because it cannot be measured by the senses or their instruments, nor proved by logic. (Immanuel Kant dealt definitively with this last point.)[21] So much of our modern disdain for the spiritual or mystical results from a confused understanding of the word *science*. We retain its original meaning, *knowledge,* in other words, that which is intelligible; yet we graft on it a new meaning, one that limits all knowledge to the empirical.

*Know Ye not . . .
that the spirit of God
dwelleth within you?*

I Corinthians 3:16

Knowledge has three degrees—opinion, science, illumination. The means or instrument of the first is sense; of the second, dialectic; of the third, intuition.   Plotinus

The Man who never in his Mind and Thoughts travel'd to Heaven Is No Artist.

William Blake

This fashion of the denial of spiritual knowledge runs contrary to the great mystical and philosophical teachings of the world. The term *Philosophia Perennis* or Perennial Philosophy was apparently first used by Leibnitz and developed in modern times by Ananda K. Coomaraswamy and Aldous Huxley. The Perennial Philosophy is what Huxley called "the Highest Common Good" in all traditions—cutting across religious traditions, historical epochs, ethnic inflectives—Hindu, Taoist, Buddhist, Greek, Jewish, Christian, Islamic. It belongs to no religion but is the essence of them all. Huxley renders the crux of the Perennial Philosophy thus:

> *First: the phenomenal world of matter and of individual consciousness . . . is the manifestation of a Divine Ground within which all partial realities have their being, and apart from which they would be nonexistent.*

> *Second: human beings are capable not merely of knowing about the Divine Ground by inference; they can also realize its existence by a direct intuition . . . [uniting] the knower with that which is known.*

> *Third: man possesses a double nature, a phenomenal ego and an eternal Self, which is the inner man, the spirit, the spark of divinity within the soul. It is possible for a man, if he desires, to identify himself with the spirit and therefore the Divine Ground, which is of the same or like nature with the spirit.*[22]

Even if one has not fully identified with this spirit and, thereby, had direct experience, he can in some way intuit that the spirit within him is one with the Divine Ground out of which all things have arisen and into which they will again return. This cannot be proved by evidence of the senses nor understood by logic or deduction, and is therefore called Mystery. There is no genuine art that does not in some way acknowledge (act-in-the-knowledge-of) this Mystery. That the Perennial Philosophy is currently out of fashion or that it "makes no sense" (again, it is transcendent or trans-senseable) in no way reflects on its efficacy or veracity. For in these matters, as Joseph Campbell said, the majority is always wrong.

"The majority's function in relation to spirit is to try to listen and open up to someone who's had an experience beyond that of food, shelter, progeny, and wealth."[23] These "someones" are the genuine artists, mystics, sages. The consistency of their revelations across time and culture lead the open-minded individual to recognize in the Perennial Philosophy inherent truth about the Reality of who we are. (See *The Perennial Philosophy,* by Aldous Huxley, Perennial Library, 1944, *The Transcendent Unity of Religions,* by Frithjof Schoun, Quest, 1984.)

If we are to learn to trust spirit, we in the West must venture beyond these primitive images of God as king, judge, or dead man. The Roman Catholic tradition epitomizes the king model. Early Roman Catholic churches were called "Basilicas," or "royal houses." The Pope wears a crown and carries a staff; you kneel to kiss his ring. I once saw the Pope entering Saint Peter's at the Vatican. There he was with all of his attendants—being carried slowly down the aisle on a palanquin—the Swiss Guards standing sharply at attention. When at last he sat upon the throne, the entire congregation broke into applause. This is a king. The Pope is standing in for King God. The accent in this model is on authority and decrees issued from on high.

The religious idea of God cannot do full duty for the metaphysical infinity.

Alan Watts

From the Jewish tradition, we get the judge model. Read the Book of Judges: this is how the Hebrews organized society. Even when they took a king in Saul, this was recognized as adopting something foreign—the judge was the homegrown model. In this model, you get a heavy emphasis on judging by the letter of the law. The accent is on collective righteousness enforced, not by the king, but by the group—everyone is checking up on you to make sure you are doing it right. This is picked up again in the Protestant religions. The Protestant church typically resembles, not a throne room, but a courtroom. You have the minister in the black robe, who comes out to the pulpit like a kind of prosecuting attorney and throws the book at you—with the rest of the congregation playing the role of jury.

Of course, you have heard that God is dead. You probably have an image of an old guy with a grey beard who just died one day. The old codger got so tired of being the boss and the judge that he just up and croaked.

Thou shalt know God without image and without means.

Meister Eckhart

We might not want to admit it, but these are our images of God—way back there in our subconscious minds. They shape the way we approach the world. If you imagine God as the big king, then you want to be the little king—the boss of your little world. If you think God is the judge, then you think, I'll be a good little judge and go around making sure *they* are doing things right. If you think God is dead, you feel yourself to be an orphan, forsaken and adrift in a sea of meaninglessness—a kind of Sartrian existentialist. Most likely you have a combination of the three. (God is there in the back of your mind bossing and judging you but dead when you need Him.) We have called the controlling pseudo-myth "the little-king model," yet we can see elements of the Judge and the dead God within it. From the king, we get our ambition; from the judge, our hyper-conformity; and from the dead God, our insatiable consumerism and focus on entertainment. A genuine experience of spirit requires that we move beyond these primitive images of God. For this reason, we will, when we speak of spirit, do so in terms of Zen—though we could have just as easily used Plato or the Western mystics; for in matters of spirit, there are no contradictions.

Spirit in Art: In chapter 2, we will explore the Zen spirit at work. We will say nothing here of the role of spirit in art except to quote two great artists and two great philosophers:

> *Where the spirit does not work with the hand there is no art.*
> *Leonardo da Vinci*

> *The greatest productions of art, whether painting, music, sculpture or poetry, have invariably this quality—something approaching the work of God.*
> *D. T. Suzuki*

> *The human mind cannot go beyond the gift of God, the Holy Ghost. To suppose that art can go beyond the finest specimens of art that are now in the world is not knowing what art is; it is being blind to the gifts of the spirit.*
> *William Blake*

> *All that is true, by whomsoever it has been said has its origin in the Spirit.*
> *Thomas Aquinas*

One comes to be of just such stuff as that on which the mind is set.

Upanishads

Transforming Our Relationship to Psyche

Can it really be said that before the day of our pretentious science, humanity was composed solely of imbeciles and the superstitious?

R. A. Schwaller de Lubicz

We know ourselves as human beings through the psyche, the human imagination. The Chinese say that in man (the human soul), Heaven (spirit) and Earth (nature) unite. Through man, nature makes love to (becomes fully conscious of) spirit. The human psyche (literally, soul) is universal in its nature and individual in its expression.

To say that there is a universal human soul or imagination may be out of fashion, and yet how else can we account for the amazing correspondences in the art and mythologies of the world? How else can we account for human compassion, the readiness of one human being to *suffer with* another? For, as Arthur Schopenhauer suggested, when we act in compassion at the risk of our own lives, it is because we recognize the other to be, in fact, our very own self.[24] Careful examination will bear up what we intuitively know. After fifty years of studying diverse cultures, the great American anthropologist Franz Boas concluded that "in the main the mental characteristics of man are the same all over the world."[25]

The psyche is the realm where the universal human imagination meets the individual conscience. A man or woman in touch with conscience (literally, "together with" *(con)* "knowledge" *(science)* or "the inner Knower") and the potent properties of soul is an authentic human being and not easily controlled by the pressure to conform to social norms.[26] He knows where he is in the universe, in the stages of life, and in relation to the archetypal energies. Mythology speaks to the Knower within us all. It tells us what it is to be human and how to live in accord with the energies of life. Carl Jung wrote that man is "a being operated and manoevred by archetypal forces instead of his 'free will,' that is, his arbitrary egoism and his limited consciousness. He should learn that he is not the master in his own house and that he should carefully study the other side of his psychical world [the shadow], which seems to be the true ruler of his fate."[27]

Jung's statement echoes the lessons of the world's great mythologies: there are archetypal forces inherent in man, which he must recognize and come into accord with before he can be thought of as a mature individual. The role of mythology and genuine psychology is to guide the individual in this "inner work." Today, our notion of psychology rejects the soul and its inner work, reducing "psychology" to a means of effecting, with the aid of academically trained specialists, social "adjustment" or behavior "modification." The genuine psychology of the "inner work" is not the domain of the specialist but of every living human being.

We must get beyond the simple-minded notion that psychology is something "invented" in the nineteenth century by Doctor Freud or William James or Alexander Bain. Psychology, as the word itself indicates, is properly the study of the soul. Thousands of years of wisdom precede the good Viennese doctor. To toss this treasure overboard in favor of a narrow "scientific" psychology is a crime no less heinous than the burning of the library of Alexandria. (Jung, for example, recognized that one could not properly call himself a student of psychology and dismiss the wisdom of ancient China, India, Egypt, or Tibet, much less Greece and the folktales of Europe—and fortunately for us, he didn't.)

Mythology is the womb of man's initiation to life and death.

Joseph Campbell

In many fields today, overspecialization is a positively dangerous trend. Buckminster Fuller wrote: "The more specialized society becomes, the less attention does it pay to the discoveries of the mind, which are intuitively beamed to the brain, there to be received only if the switches are on. Specialization tends to shut off the wide-band tuning searches and thus to preclude further discovery of all-powerful generalized principles."[28] More than this, overspecialization tends to separate from us the pearls of wisdom already pulled from the depths of the human psyche.

In our overly specialized culture, we've lost the value of the universalist, the generalist. The universalist is a humanist in the best sense of the word. Her subject is man, not in any particular historical or cultural context, not in narrow specialization, but man whole, as he is. Especially in our time of great transition and upheaval, it is vital that we integrate the lessons of those who have made it their task to study what is constant in the human experience. In the century now ending, we have had great universalists, among them: Carl Jung in Psychology, Joseph Campbell in Mythology, Ananda K. Coomaraswamy in Art, Aldous Huxley and Frithjof Schuon in Religion, Buckminster Fuller in the study of the structure of the universe. All have had their difficulties with academic narrow-mindedness, and yet all have left legacies well worth mining. They themselves have made it their task to extract the diamonds from the coal of human knowledge.

In discovering the universally human, in other words, the human soul, you recognize your own soul and its unique life's work. The only way one is capable of original work is to work in unoriginal themes—the universal human themes. Only in this is there the

I am in you and you in me, mutual in love divine.

William Blake

possibility of art. One's true work is never merely "my work," but humanity's work. It's not really self-expression, unless by "self" we mean it with a capital S, and that Self is the Self within all mankind.

Psyche in Art: In chapter 3, we will explore the role of the psyche in work. We will consider how we can come to trust our psyche by developing a constructive relationship with conscience, by learning to face our own shadow, or dark side, and by accessing mythic archetypes, the creative energies of the soul. Joseph Campbell said, "The artist is the one who communicates myth for today. But he has to be an artist who understands mythology and humanity..."[29]

Transforming Our Relationship to Society

Society *is* a source of power and a protection for the individual. It teaches and protects us through our many years of dependence. As human beings, we are born into a long period of dependency and incompleteness. The moment the umbilical chord is cut, we are helpless. We are biologically incomplete and dependent upon others for our survival. This physiological fact has a profound effect on our psychology. We develop a psychology of approval-seeking as a reaction to our biological helplessness. This *is* an effective strategy. First, in seeking the approval of our parents, we win their affection and support: they take care of us. Second, seeking approval becomes the motivating force to learn and thereby to complete ourselves as full members of adult society. We learn to walk, talk, and all the rest we need to function as members of our society.

Even as approval motivates, disapproval has tremendous power to limit or correct our behavior. Because we associate winning approval with survival, signs of disapproval are experienced as threats to our survival and become effective tools for social conditioning. While efficacious in our youth, the psychology of approval is a positive drag on our development as mature adults. Traditional cultures helped individuals through this transition or transformation of consciousness with rites of initiation. In the modern world, we are left to ourselves to make this transformation—each one for herself.

Society and Art: In chapter 4, we will consider how we can develop toward society a relationship of trust—not as a conformist who takes its model hook, line, and sinker but in knowing that to be fully one's self requires that one take responsibility for his fellow man. Increasingly, we recognize the need for this transformation.

In the seventeenth and eighteenth centuries, a revolution in thinking turned the existing social order on its head. It was the realization of "the rights of man." The next great revolution in thinking has already begun. It is the realization of "the responsibilities of man." While continuing to protect and enlarge human rights, we must, if we are going to make a world worth living in, be equally concerned with human responsibilities. This includes the responsibility to make a meaningful contribution through our work. After all, most of us spend more of our waking adult lives working than doing anything else.

What we choose to do as individuals, taken together, becomes what we as a society choose to do. As responsible individuals, we cannot make our career choices as if oblivious to this fact. Even if we wanted to, we could not bury our heads in the sand. The evidences of our responsibility are all around us. It is fair to say that collectively we have, up to now, made some rather poor choices. For currently, as a global society, we are choosing to live under the threat of nuclear terror; we are choosing to live in a world of vast inequities in the distribution of wealth and resources; we are choosing to pollute and abuse our environment, fouling air and water, forcing the extinction of thousands of species of plants and animals. We are choosing to crowd into urban centers that foster the breakup of the family, breed disease (in the undeveloped world) and drug use (in the developed), and destroy community and cultural values.

Of course, we are also collectively choosing to do many good and noble things. Still, the enormity of our difficulties requires that each of us consider our responsibilities to the world we live in when making our individual career choices. Most of our problems are man-made. They are a result of the way we think and the way we do, and we can change these—one individual at a time.

We begin from the recognition that all beings cherish happiness and do not want suffering. It then becomes both morally wrong and pragmatically unwise to pursue only one's own happiness oblivious to the feelings and aspirations of all others who surround us as members of the same human family. The wiser course is to think of others when pursuing our own happiness.

The Fourteenth Dalai Lama

Today we stand at a crossroads in human history. We have the opportunity to create a new image of ourselves at work, one which will surely trigger a revolution as profound, as shocking, as transforming as the Industrial Revolution. Even as the Industrial Revolution could not occur until there was a massive shift in society's view of work and wealth, so must an equally profound change in thinking regarding work and wealth occur before the next quantum leap in man's social evolution can flourish. We can no more conceptualize the impact of such a change than a pre-industrial miller in the hills of England or New Hampshire could have conceptualized the impact of the Industrial Revolution he was helping to foster. We are charting new ground. We must.

Humanity: A Multidimensional Phenomenon

The "work-as-art" or "man-as-artist" paradigm we have outlined above provides a new tool for choosing and evaluating your work as an individual. (We will explore this at some length in "Prologue: The Art of Life's Work.") In the remainder of this discussion, we will briefly sketch some of the social and cultural ramifications of this view of work. Of course, a work-as-art view *does* imply an entirely different set of values around which to organize society. However, these values cannot take hold in society by imposing or proselytizing some abstract utopian theory but will "arise mutually" with individually transformed artists. In this, we can distinguish the work-as-art paradigm from prevailing theories of social transformation. Prevailing oppositions to the current structure of society focus on the need for change within the conventional view of man as a one-dimensional creature—that is, as an exclusively social (i.e., economic and political) being. They argue for economic and social justice within the confines of a view of man as a mechanistic, soulless, and unnatural creature.

The work-as-art conception is interested in man as a multi-dimensional being. It does not suggest that if "everything were equal" or that if "the playing field were level," everyone would be happy. It does not put its faith in the free market, in democracy, in social welfare programs, in economic growth, in the redistribution of wealth, etc. (Neither, by the way, is it inherently opposed to any of these.) Owning the means of production without having some sense of what to do with them will hardly "save the masses."

The work-as-art conception views one-dimensionality itself as the source of the alienation of modern man. Again, this alienation is *not* an economic, political, or social problem, and therefore, its

If all men lead mechanical, unpoetical lives, this is the real nihilism, the real undoing of the world.

Reginald Blyth

"solution" will always evade economic, political, and social theorists. Prevailing political theories (radical to conservative) accept the narrow (one-dimensional) little-king model of man. They differ in their analysis of the problem (e.g., "class conflict," "patriarchal power," or "lack of economic growth") and, therefore, in their prescriptions (e.g., dictatorship of the proletariat, women in the board rooms, greater economic incentives for capital investment), but all accept a narrow view of humankind.

> *I think the person who takes a job in order to live—that is to say, (just) for the money—has turned himself into a slave.*
>
> Joseph Campbell

A craft can only have meaning when it serves a spiritual way.

Titus Burkhardt

When the individual (consciously or tacitly) accepts the narrow, one-dimensional view of man in his approach to work, he degrades his humanity on two counts—regardless of the monetary compensation he receives. First, he degrades himself in his choice of work, choosing that which he considers the best trade for his labor; second, he surrenders all responsibility for his work (to his employer). In this, the corporate vice president may be as degraded as the factory worker. If each is doing soulless work, shaped by values not his own, then each is equally degraded. All little-king analysis, radical to conservative, views the corporate vice president as "advantaged" and the factory worker or secretary as relatively "disadvantaged." This sets up a false conflict (rich against poor, men against women, labor against management) that denies the essential brotherhood, or humanhood, of all humanity.

It assumes a "them," that has what "we" (or "me") need(s), that is, economic or political power, without ever pausing to consider whether the acquisition of this power would be, really, the panacea one hopes for. For the unionist, feminist, or Marxist who sincerely believes that the white, male corporate executive has "all the power" or a life to be envied, we recommend *Quiet Desperation: The Truth about Successful Men,* by Jan Halper.[30] To be sure, the executive possesses more creature comforts, but he is not necessarily a happier creature. (His unhappiness is often compounded because he feels guilty for feeling unhappy, while possessing what others so desperately seem to want, and has no idea of what else to do—beyond achieving still more power and possessions.) For the "less fortunate," a one-dimensional perspective, not only produces envy and resentment, but more importantly, it distracts the individual from the pursuit of his or her own happiness through

Thoroughly to know oneself, is above all art, for it is the highest art.

Theologia Germanica

growth—that is, from contacting the deeper energies within and discovering his or her unique purpose in life.

Honoring one's own, and insisting on the humanity of all people, is the natural outcome of a work-as-art perspective. The little-king perspective sets up a master/slave or victim vs. oppressor dichotomy that fosters division, conflict, and hatred. We have been conditioned to see all human relationships from this narrow and destructive context. For those who insist on some type of dualistic means of comparison, "the degraded" vs. "the fully human" seems a more useful measuring stick. *Degraded* here does not indicate a failure to adhere to some set of moral rules but the diminution or confinement of consciousness (to the narrow realm of the political and economic). *Fully human* suggests acting in consciousness of the various levels of human awareness, especially those at the "higher" end of the spectrum. Where the little-king model views growth and wealth in terms of ever greater economic and political power, growth from the way of art is the expansion of consciousness into nature, spirit, and soul—the richness of life that results from a multidimensional consciousness.

While trapped in the box of one-dimensional consciousness, we feel constrained. We are like the man whose pants are too tight—he can "neither sit, nor stand, nor lie." He is anxious and ill at ease. He knows or senses that something must change. This "something" is not a rearrangement of the furniture within the box but an expansion of consciousness into areas he has heretofore ignored. As Plato said, "philosophy [literally the love of wisdom] begins with wonder." It is with wonder and humility that we approach the unknown. We expand into new ways of seeing, into new modes of being. We learn to approach nature, and through it, the mystery of that which is *tzu-jan* (of itself so) whose action is *wu wei* (nonstriving). We learn to approach the mystery of spirit in its immanent and transcendent qualities. We learn to approach the mystery of the human soul with its individual destiny and universal harmony.

There are signs that many today are ready for this expansion in consciousness—ready to grow and expand, as all nature does, from the inside out. As E. F. Schumacher wrote, "Some people are no longer angry when told that *restoration must come from within:* the belief that everything is 'politics' and that radical rearrangements of the 'system' will suffice to save civilisation is no longer held with the same fanaticism [that it once was.]"[31] In this there is great promise. If we can learn to redirect anger at "them" into the dynamic transformation of ourselves—we may yet discover the art of creative living.

"Art-quality" for All

Some may object that the image of man as artist is elitist—that the common man or woman cannot attain to art, either in consciousness or in the execution of their craft. It could be argued in reply that many so-called primitive cultures did, in fact, achieve a "society of artists." Yet this is not a wholly adequate response, for they did so while operating within fixed traditional systems, having limited vocational choice and a shared mythic and symbolic vocabulary—neither of which apply to our situation today. Our task, then, is a new and more difficult one. There is no model we can imitate or "get back to." Yet today we recognize that the underlying truths that the great art of the world sought to represent are universal and not limited to any particular ethnic inflection. They belong, finally, to all humanity.

The way of the artist is a universally human way, not dependent upon a shared religion, myth, geography, or even technology. It works as well in Bali as in New York City, in China as in the Middle East. Ultimately, quality is for everyone—both in terms of aspirations and end results. We all benefit from quality workmanship, from the products of men and women who know themselves as total beings and not simply as workers or "job-holders." Were all to aspire to be artists, all would benefit from more beautiful meals, clothing, parks, homes, schools, etc. We would benefit further from living with people, not alienated from—but happy in—their work. Those capable of the greatest art would not waste their talents in a vain struggle to be king of the hill but would release the gifts they hold deep within their souls.

The little-king view of life is no less elitist in theory, yet far more destructive in its effect. Everyone cannot be king, and while this image dominates our imaginations, we view life in terms of separation and competition, and therefore, conflict. On the other hand, the way of the artist is inclusive—respecting and celebrating the wonders of nature, the dignity of humanity, and the radiance of the Transcendent Mystery. No genuine artist views himself as superior in essence to others.

Still, aren't we just substituting one ideal or image for another, and doesn't the truth stand behind any image? Of course, words or any symbolic images are always only maps of the territory of truth, never reality itself. No map, no matter how excellent, is ever to be confused with the territory that it indicates. Yet, since few know the territory directly, most are left dealing with maps—and, to be sure, there are better and worse maps. At the dawn of the third millennium c.e., the little-king map has us totally lost and utterly confused. The map we are here suggesting can help us find our way again. The way of the artist, as we have laid it out, offers us an image of man in harmony with nature, the deep rhythms of the human soul, and the Transcendent Mystery. In the end, it may produce, if not an enlightened society, at least a happier and more humane one.

The Art of Everyday Living

You can experience your everyday life as art by bringing to it the qualities of the artist—inspiration and absorption, creativity and resourcefulness, play and delight. But first, unwind. No one can live as an artist who feels anxious, knotted up in fear. Fortunately, there are only two great fears—the fear that life is going to end and the fear that it isn't. It is easy to see that the fear of death arises from attachment to the temporal—from holding on to what must be let go of. But why should we fear living?

We fear living because we don't believe we are adequate to life. Tangled in the mumbo-jumbo of conditioned beliefs, we get so hung up on limitation that we fail to recognize our basic adequacy as human beings. Denying limitation or obsessing on it keeps us knotted up in fear. Artists play with limitation. They neither deny it, nor are they overwhelmed by it. There are only so many words in any language, but that doesn't keep the poet from writing. There is only a certain range of color the eye can see, but this doesn't keep the painter from painting. There are a limited number of notes that we can hear, but that doesn't keep the composer from composing. The artist accepts the limitations of form, not with fear and dread, but as the starting point of creation.

You can be the artist of your life by recognizing that, for all of your limitations, you are basically adequate to life. For all of its difficulties, life is basically adequate for you. Accept that, while it may not fit some imaginary conception of perfection, the world is basically adequate; and you are basically adequate to the world. Be here now with what is, and play with the stuff of your life. If you have twelve crayons in your box, use your creativity and resourcefulness to make the best picture you can with these. Don't spend your time worrying that someone else has forty-eight or sixty-four crayons. As you are, you are basically adequate to life.

Your basic adequacy is not won or done. It is not because you own a home or because you have a good job, not because you have a big bank balance or because you have a certain relationship, not because you are American or politically correct. Your basic adequacy is in your breath, in your beating heart—in your life. You are adequate to life because you *are* life. You have all you need—a heart, a body, an imaginative mind, a basic connection with all of life. You have an earth to walk on. It has gravity to hold you. It has water and fire, plants and trees, mountains and valleys. It's an adequate earth. The sky is adequate. It has sun and moon. It has stars—not too many, not too few. As you begin to attune to the adequacy of life all around and within you, you will see ever more opportunities for creative play. Even as the artist accepts the tools of his craft and creates with these, accept all the stuff of your life and creatively play with it.

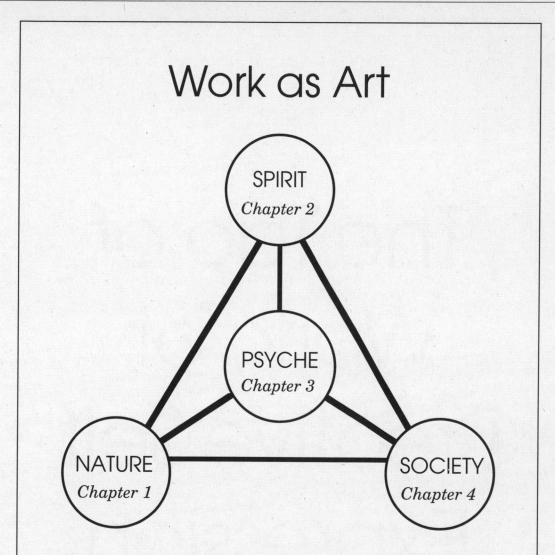

Work as Art

SPIRIT
Chapter 2

PSYCHE
Chapter 3

NATURE
Chapter 1

SOCIETY
Chapter 4

This is a book about work. Work can be most simply and broadly defined as human action—our doing. In the West, we have separated our doing from our Being. This separation, or alienation, has profound consequences on the quality of our lives. It is for precisely this reason that we have, as Ananda K. Coomaraswamy said, "for the first time in history created an industry without art."[32] Everything that we will say in the remainder of "Prologue: The Art of Life's Work"—the lessons we will draw from Taoism, from Zen, from art and myth, and from the great humanitarian activists—will be with a view toward discovering how we might unite our Being with our doing.

CHAPTER 1

The Tao of Work; or, Creative Self-Expression

Let everything be allowed to do what it naturally does,
so that its nature will be satisfied.
                                        Chuang Tzu

How can we make of work a genuine art—an expression of our deepest selves? We begin by asking, What are we working for? Is the purpose of work to solve problems or to creatively express oneself? The way each of us answers this question shapes our lives as individuals and our world. It affects our psychology as well as our activities—the way we feel about the world and the things we do in it. We can't really get too far into this without at least a brief consideration of world view, of the way we approach the world. After a consideration of the metaphysics underlying conventional attitudes toward work, we will go on to explore how our approach to career design differs from more traditional career-planning models.

Follow that will and that way which experience confirms to be your own.

Carl Jung

The Western view of life, inherited from Middle Eastern mythology, tends to view man as a stranger in a strange land. Thrust out of the Garden into a hostile world, he is condemned to toil and sweat, to eke out his existence in a perpetual struggle against nature and his fellow man. The ancient "man as stranger" element of the religious world view remained implicit in the "scientific" world view developed over the last few centuries. Briefly stated, the common sense of the scientific world view goes something like this: Quite by accident, man has arisen out of a dead and dumb universe. He has every reason to fear that he may fall back into it. Consequently, he makes it his business to distinguish himself from nature at every turn. This is his dirty little secret: He is a sort of bastard child of stones and slime, of animal violence and lust. Since he is embarrassed by his connection with the natural world, he insists upon his respectableness through a righteous quest to establish a rational order.

Nature is a mess he will put right. He will straighten it out, figure it out, reason this insane chaos into a predictable set of rules that he can deal with. His one great tool in this noble endeavor is his rational mind and the technologies he can construct with it. It will save him from the ravages of wild and cruel nature. Though it cannot beat his heart, digest his food, or maintain other vital functions, that part of his brain responsible for conscious attention, he considers the *summum bonum* of the human species. It's as if one portion of his brain (that responsible for conscious attention) refuses to admit that it is connected to the rest of his brain, let alone the rest of his body or the rest of the natural world. It alone is "intelligent."

The world view of traditional Taoist China (and many other traditional cultures) begins with a different set of assumptions.[1] Man was not thrust into a strange world; he came out of it as naturally as water comes out of a bubbling brook. He is not against nature; he cannot be separated from it—he is in nature, and nature in him. Nature is not dead and dumb; all of nature is alive and intelligent. It is not hostile and wild but friendly and ordered. Man's purpose is not to conquer and lord it over nature but to come into accord with it. The Taoist understands that there is in nature a profound intelligence that the rational mind can never comprehend. Even as a horse cannot run beyond the borders of its corral, so the rational mind cannot venture beyond the limits of language and the categories of thought.

While the Taoist view trusts nature, including what it calls Self Nature, our Western approach puts all its faith in the rational mind. As we discussed in the introduction, a solely rational orientation gives a problem-solving approach to life, one that denies the Mystery of life, the indefinable, unexplainable fount of creative living. A society at odds with nature will be at odds with the creative. For where are the mysterious creative powers more evident than in nature—from the miracle of the seed to the genesis of the galaxies?

Creativity is a function of the nature within us; call it intuition, native intelligence, or the subconscious mind. The rational conscious mind can intend, but it cannot, of itself, create. A conscious mind can intend a child, but it cannot create one. A conscious mind can intend a work of art, but cannot, of itself, create it. If we are to live a creative life, we must learn to trust nature within and without. The venerable Taoist Chuang Tzu told the following story: Once a one-legged dragon named Hui asked a centipede, "How do you manage all those legs? I can hardly manage one!" "As a matter of fact," replied the centipede, "I do not manage them." The centipede that doesn't trust nature can hardly walk; the human being that doesn't trust nature can hardly live his own life. Creativity bubbles up from within when we open to trust what the Taoist calls our "original nature."

From the hostile-world, problem-solving approach, we seek to barricade ourselves into static, defensive positions. We don't trust nature—in the environment, in others, or in ourselves; we don't trust our innate creativity. From the natural-world approach, we open to life and its infinite creative possibilities. We can easily see how the differences in these world views affect our attitudes toward work. In the simplest terms, work can be defined as human activity. So we are back to the question we started with, namely: Is work, is human activity, principally for problem solving or self-expression?

The approach of traditional career models is to help people defend against problems. The implicit assumption is a notion of work as a means of defending against the problems of poverty, ridicule, boredom, and the like. A problem-solving approach to work puts us in a defensive posture, from which we hope for escape—ultimately, from work itself. (Defending, after all, is a rather tiresome business.) Since work is something we are forced to do to solve our problems, the implication is that no problems equals no work. So, many dream of winning the lottery and "solving all their problems" and not "having to" work.

Our approach is to assist people in creating their life's work, their full self-expression. We view work, not as a means of achieving *freedom from problems*, but as the vehicle for expressing the *freedom to create*. Creating your life's work is not solving the occupation problem. It *is* the art of creative living. From this perspective, you are not a problem but a creative, living being. Work is not a problem but a natural, ongoing, creative process. We are not interested in coming up with a good solution to the career problem but in the full creative expression of the individual.

Art always has something of the Unconscious about it.

D. T. Suzuki

The Tao is near and people seek it far away.

Menicus

Your life's work does not exist "out there" in a world apart. You can't order up the perfect career or set of careers the way you might order a lawn mower from the Sears catalogue. Being too concerned with what is "out there" before you know what you want "in here" puts you in a position of powerlessness. We encourage you to begin by identifying the results you want, and then to move confidently and deliberately in that direction, no matter how small your steps may seem. In this way, you move from strength and remain in creative control.

If it's truly creative, the direction of your life's work is "from the inside out." We will provide tools you can use in this process—tools to help you tap the creative vision and power within—and tools to help you better understand what's "out there" and how you can make it work for you. Traditional career models tend to view your creativity, energy, and zest for life as rough edges that must be shaved off to effectuate a better fit with what is "out there." Exactly what doesn't fit (the rough edges of the old model) is what will drive the process of creating a life's work—your creativity, energy, and zest for life.

We have been told that we must face the facts of life; but we must also, if we are really going to live, face the spirit and the emotional power of life. To describe Michelangelo's *David* as a marble statue of a Hebrew king in his youth gives you the facts but none of the spirit or emotional power of the work. To say that *Don Quixote* is the story of a madman wandering about in hallucination strips it of the power, spirit, and art of its message. It is no less ridiculous to reduce your life to a set of facts. You are not your place of birth, your height, weight, or degrees, your résumé, or credit history. You are a being of spirit, emotional power, and intelligence.

Traditional career models are only interested in the facts of your life, for example, your education, skills, training, and experience. We will consider the facts but also the all-important creative intangibles. From the perspective of life as art, the facts of your life are the media with which you will create. Color is not painting. Notes are not music. Words are not poetry. For color to become painting; notes, music; or words, poetry, there must be knowledge of technique, emotional power, and the radiance of spirit. To view your life as art is likewise to recognize that the facts only become significant, and really interesting, through the application of technique, emotional power, and the radiance of the spirit. We are not negating the importance of facts. You require technical skill and knowledge of the marketplace the way a painter requires color—these are essential. But remember, as the French painter Chardin said, "One uses color, but *paints* with feeling." (Emphasis added.)

An exclusive emphasis on facts limits creativity. While a hard-headed, nothing-but-the-facts approach is often touted as an objective or scientific approach to reality, modern physics understands the limitations and fallacy of this view. As physicist Werner Hiesenberg put it, "the mere act of observing something changes the nature of the thing observed."[2] This statement, called the uncertainty principle, means, in essence, that there is no objective reality we can discern with our senses. In our relationship to reality, a hard head is of less use than an open mind. The truly creative people, whether in science or art, would agree with Albert Einstein's assertion that "imagination is more important than knowledge" or that "the only really valuable thing is intuition." Intuitions, and not facts—imaginations, and not data banks, are the beginnings of creations.

> *It is the natural instinct of a child to work from within outwards; "First I think, and then I draw my think." What wasted efforts we make to teach the child to stop thinking, and only to observe!*
> *Ananda K. Coomaraswamy*

The problem-solving approach to life generates feelings of fear and anxiety. But, as Rollo May put it, "what the artist or creative scientist feels is not anxiety or fear; it is joy. The artist, at the moment of creating, does not experience gratification or satisfaction [as one might at solving a problem] but . . . joy." He defines joy as "the emotion that goes with heightened consciousness, the mood that accompanies the experience of actualizing one's own potentialities."[3] This gets to the crux of it—creating the joyous life or struggling from fear and powerlessness.

Since our problem-solving efforts are always tail-chasing and do not resolve, we soon tire of them and seek relief in escape. From a problem-solving approach, escape is what passes for joy. It is not the true joy of "heightened consciousness," but the limited pleasure of diminished awareness. Many social critics have pointed out the escapism of modern life and its many manifestations. There are the individual manifestations seen in narcissism, alcohol and drug abuse, compulsive consumption, and addiction to television and entertainments. There are the collective manifestations of war, environmental destruction, national debt, and the like. As long as we seek to defend against problems, we try to escape from them. As long as we view work as a means of solving problems, we "live for the weekends."

Escapism generates still more problems, which in turn we seek to defend against and ultimately to escape from. This is the vicious

Facts, to become poetic, must be fused with being.

Gerald Sykes

To be properly expressed a thing must proceed from within, moved by its form.

Meister Eckhart

cycle of modern life. Of course, the tendency to escape from life is hardly a modern invention. (The Buddha gave his Four Noble Truths over two thousand years ago as a strategy for creative living beyond escape.) Yet our modern world view encourages a problem-solving approach that leads inevitably to escapism.

Learning to approach life creatively is the challenge before us as individuals and as the human race. Man's innate creativity holds a powerful key to the transformation of reality. Lewis Mumford wrote, "Every transformation of man . . . has rested on a new image of the cosmos and the nature of man." Indeed, these images are how we mark history into eras: The Classical Era, the Middle Ages, the Renaissance, the Modern Age, etc. Our hostile-world, rational, problem-solving approach evolved over time into an image of the world, indeed of the universe, as a giant machine. The conception of the universe as a machine marks the Modern Age.

Ironically, science, the pride of the Modern Age, has been at the forefront in exposing the limitations of the machine model. Quantum physics and ecology, for example, have demonstrated that an image of a universe of separate, isolated parts is not a terribly useful way of conceiving of reality. While increasingly outdated, even from a scientific point of view, the legacy of the machine model affects the way we think in a range of subject areas, including our topic, work.

The mechanistic view of the world gave us a set of terms that still affect how we think about work. Work as a concept is "the treadmill" or "the old grind." Work as action is "cranked out" and "geared up." One's relationship to work is a matter of "fitting in" or of "meshing with." Economies are machines for making jobs. (Incidentally, our word *job* originates from the Middle English *jobbe,* meaning "mouthful," and clearly comes from the notion of work as a solution to the feeding problem.)[4] From this perspective, work is a very serious affair, a boring routine, a dull drill. Since this is what people think work is, it's no wonder they want to escape from it.

World View	Life Approach	Attitude	Outcome
Mechanical	Problem-solving	Defensiveness	Escape
Organic	Creativity	Openness	Creative Confrontation

From an organic view of the world, we get an image of work as living, growing, evolving, creative action. Work comes out of life the way grass grows, the way apple trees "apple." Because human beings are active creatures, they naturally work. That is exactly the point— naturally work—not work like machines but work as integral parts of nature. Yet human beings are not plants or animals. Our creating is not simply a matter of reproduction. Human beings can ask: "Why to create?" "What to create?" "How to create?" That human beings ask these questions is no less natural than pear trees "pearing" or monkeys "monkeying around." We are naturally creative, questioning creatures and must be unnaturally molded into mindless machine workers. Where spontaneity is the enemy of the machine society, it is the essence of natural action and, therefore, of work.

We view work first and foremost as a vehicle of self-expression. This expression naturally gives a life of integrity, service, enjoyment, and excellence. (See highlight on page 51.) Your natural self-expression comes out of you and is therefore integral, an expression of "thine own self." It is naturally your highest and best service, since the best thing you can do for others is to be yourself. Self-expression is naturally joyous and exciting and naturally prompts one to work with excellence. When you are doing something integral to yourself, something you love, you naturally want to make it the best you can—the way you want to give a friend a lovely present. Your self-expression is your gift to the world. Discovering your life's work is not a mechanical process of assembling facts; it is more a matter of trusting yourself. Realizing it is a matter of trusting yourself *and* gaining specific knowledge, taking definite action, and persevering.

Going with the Flow and Creating What You Want

The great challenges of life are to BE and to EXPRESS. These are the lessons of "Zen" and of "the Art of . . ." Lose your spontaneity, your ability to sense and move with the flow of your deepest being, and you become stiff, numb, out of sync with life. Lack the ability to create structure, and you risk remaining socially marginal and/or psychologically alienated—unable to express yourself in a full and enlivening way. In either case, you risk an inauthentic life. Spontaneity and structure—these two have a creative tension, recalling the notion of life, the authentic life, as a razor's edge.

In certain circles, there is a long-standing argument about whether 'tis nobler to "go with the flow" or to "create what you want." There is really no conflict between the two. In fact, "creating what you want" is a natural extension of "going with the flow." This is so if by "going with the flow" you mean "following your bliss," moving with the flow—the energy—of your deepest desires. Your deepest desires are at one with the universe, a natural expression of it. Your deepest desires (not commercially manufactured ones) are as organic as any towering tree, roaring stream, or flowering

To know oneself, one should assert oneself.

Albert Camus

The Tao's principle is spontaniety.

Lao Tzu

bush. To resist their flow is to block your own natural growth and, collectively, our natural evolution. Desire, deep desire, is the sap of the tree of life.

Going with the flow is, then, the first step to creating what you want. Yet in itself, it is not complete. To get into a truly positive, creative relationship with life, we must confront structure. Structure is necessary to every creative work. The composition of a musical score requires the creation of a structure; the writing of a book requires the creation of a structure; the scripting of a comedy act requires the creation of a structure. So, too, starting a business, a nonprofit foundation, or even creating the job you want—all require that you create a structure. The simple truth is this: Structure cannot be avoided. If you don't create your own structure, you have to deal with someone else's.

I must Create a System or be enslav'd by another Man's.

William Blake

Creating a full-blown job search, the kind we will discuss in "Act III," requires you to create a more structured job-hunting effort than merely answering want ads or firing out scores of résumés. Starting your own business, setting yourself up as a freelance, or founding a nonprofit foundation require the creation of still more structure, as well as the creation of additional structures for their maintenance and growth. The more involved you are in creating the structures of your life, the greater the sense of freedom and self-expression you will experience in your work. This is true, so long as the original impulse, the creative vision that generates these structures, comes out of your own being, out of your desire, and not from some abstract idea of what you "should do," and so long as you continue to remain responsive to additional creative intuitions.

The most effective structures naturally present themselves when we move out of creative openness—out of spontaneity—going with the flow of our hearts. In this way, structure is intuitively perceived in principle before it is realized in practice, and it is continuously evolving. When creating structure, we don't want to get locked into some dead end but remain open to spontaneous evolution. As artist Julia Jones puts it, "This is the way I approach the creation of art: I always have a plan [structure], but I allow things to happen." In this way, structure serves our creative vision; we are not blindly serving structure.

Perhaps because we in modern life feel ourselves to be prisoners of structures we have not created—structures which, however inspired in origin, have hardened into lifeless, grinding machines—many of us resist structure altogether. In this, we miss the possibility of realizing our own fullest creative potential. We can create structure without getting stuck in it. Yet to do this, we must continue to "go with the flow," never imagining that we have achieved the ultimate structure, or indeed that one even exists. Structures are built for the expression of creative desire and must not be taken as ends in themselves.

"Going with the flow" requires that you be here now, that you not allow yourself to drift automatically into a lackadaisical conformity to structure. It also requires respecting your humanity and holding it inviolate. Work doesn't have to be a dehumanizing experience and should not be accepted as such. One of the main tenets of Mahatma Gandhi's theory and practice of nonviolence is noncooperation with anything that diminishes human dignity. Of course, noncooperation means not engaging in anything that is blatantly oppressive or abusive to others. It also means avoiding that which is oppressive to one's own soul—to one's innate sense of humanity.

For example, when people are treated as machine-like workers and not taken seriously as human beings, tremendous emotional suffering results. Resentment and self-loathing are sure to build in those who remain in these situations. If we are to become a humane society, we must recognize that this emotional suffering is every bit as real as physical suffering—and put an end to it. This pain is mother to an army of social and psychological ills, which we desperately try to solve piecemeal, only to find new manifestations. Humane work has to take into account the fact that people are emotional and spiritual, as well as intellectual and physical, beings.

So often today, white-collar workers are hired for their brains alone; blue-collar and service workers, for their bodies only, as though these could be detached from the beings who possess them. As a consequence, there is so much emotional pain around work in our culture. This pain spills over into virtually every aspect of life. Families, relationships, and communities are deeply affected by it. We can't really blame anyone for this, or at least, it does us no good to do so. Freedom can't be demanded from others—it must be created for ourselves. In his essay "Self-Reliance," Emerson writes: "But now we are a mob. Man does not stand in awe of man, nor is his genius admonished to stay at home, to put itself in communication with the *internal* ocean, but it goes abroad to beg a cup of water of the urns of other men." (Emphasis added.)[5]

We must first become self-reliant; while we are still begging, pointing the finger serves no purpose. We can only learn to relax more deeply into the now eternal moment of our being and learn to create, like artists, structures that have definite use and meaning

Is not the core of nature in the heart of man?

Goethe

The Natural Art of Human Living

The great German author Thomas Mann wrote, "Art is the spirit in matter, the natural instinct toward humanization, that is, toward the spiritualization of life..."[6] Mann's conception of art as *the natural instinct toward humanization, or spiritualization,* provides a bridge uniting the fine and the practical arts, the spiritual life with the art of creative living. The understanding is that the *impulse to humanity*, the movement "toward the spiritualization of life" is the origin of art, the progenitor of all that is noble in the creative arts, in science, in humanitarian service, indeed, in all fields of endeavor.

This conception unites the work of Gandhi with the Japanese tea ceremony, the mission work of Albert Schweitzer with Mozart's *Magic Flute*, Navaho sand painting with the great cathedrals of Europe, the work of Mother Teresa with that of Goethe, the poetry of the Troubadours with the scriptures of India, the work of Albert Einstein with that of the anonymous but devoted local elementary school teacher. All of these are art because they spring from what Mann calls the *natural instinct to humanization.* Setting aside for the moment the issue of the relative merit of these or of any other works of art, we can recognize this natural impulse as their common origin.

Following your natural instinct to humanity is the road to your art, your life's work. This is another way of saying, "Follow your bliss." While we tend to think of art as something for a privileged few, Mann's conception recognizes art as the natural expression of our humanity. As such, art is not exceptional, but ordinary. In many traditional cultures, it was expected that all people were, or ought to be, artists. (We can see remnants of such a culture today in Bali.) In regaining our naturalness, we regain our humanity and our art.

There *are* significant differences in the relative value of the arts and in the quality of their execution. (We err if we fail to take these into account.) Still, there is something to be gained in the recognition of the one impulse that gives rise to all the arts. *Major or minor, epic or commonplace, the arts are the works of the spirit.* They are acts of love that unite and "spiritualize" our lives. On the other hand, as Leonardo da Vinci said, "where the spirit does not work with the hand, there is no art,"[7] no matter the virtuosity of the technique employed. All true art ought be celebrated for the sake of the impulse to humanity that gives it birth. This impulse is itself the art; it is what makes life worth living and, more than that, a thing of wonder, glory, and splendor.

The fine arts, especially, evoke our humanity in their contemplation. If we study these arts with a view toward the underlying patterns, the ever-recurring Universal archetypes, we cannot help but recognize, we cannot help but convince our minds, that the ground from which these images emanate is the universal ground of Being in which man, the earth, the universe, and all things reside. The Ever-Becoming of this Being, the grand play of creation in which we are privileged to participate, is itself the Great Art to which all of the lesser arts point. As the sunlight reflects and recalls the Sun, so the radiance of the arts reflects and recalls the Great Art of Infinite Being, Ever-Becoming. Naturally.

in our lives. We can learn to be truly self-reliant, trusting in our innate humanity and in our ability to create, maintain, and dissolve structures as appropriate.

Gandhi also emphasized the importance of self-reliance. Self-reliance is critical to creating structures we can live with and for remaining free of confining structures imposed by others (or even those of our own making). Self-reliance is a matter of spiritual and emotional maturity. It doesn't mean everyone out for him- or herself. Many of the most important things to be done in this world require that we work together. The critical points are that those working in a structure have some part in creating it—that it be useful and meaningful in their lives—and that structure never become "just the way it is." Structures, even at their best, are never "the way it is" but only limited vehicles for the expression of use and meaning. When they outlive either their use or their meaning, structures ought to be dissolved. The sad truth is that today, far too many have little, if any, input on the structures they work with; they experience their work as neither useful nor meaningful but "just the way it is."

When we lack self-reliance, when we depend upon someone else's structure for direction and support, we never know when it is going to shrink, collapse, or simply replace the part that we play in it. The corporation, the federal, state, or local government, can suddenly and unilaterally decide that what you are doing, and may have been doing for many years, is no longer necessary. This is often experienced as painful and disheartening. Perhaps it is all the more painful because we, at least obliquely, realize that all along our work was not principally a means of self-expression but of problem-solving, and damn it anyway, now we are right back to the problem—and know nothing more of our self-expression in the bargain.

Being is thoughtless—beyond and beneath all categories of thought. Expression is the realization of creative thought. Being is still; expression, moving.

The freedom to create, then, means that we can, to whatever degree, BE in touch with the essential core of Self and Life, and that we can EXPRESS through structures that we have some part in creating. We can say that the maximum experience of freedom in work requires the ability to freely and deliberately create structure, the ability to maintain structure through adaptation, the ability to freely let go of structure, and the ability to know when each is appropriate.

But then if I do not strive, who will?

Chuang Tzu

For one who has conquered the mind,
The mind is the best of friends,
But for one who has failed to do so,
His very mind will be the greatest enemy.
Bhagavad-Gita[8]

Many Westerners think of Eastern religion as seeking to induce a mindless, negative, trance-like consciousness, which they call Nirvana. As the quote above clearly indicates, the enlightened man is not a tranced-out dope. His mind is his friend. He uses it creatively to express. He can think—and think clearly. And he can simply Be. He can rest, and he can move to express. His thinking is not the random chatter of self-consciousness that most of us call thinking. It is deliberate—holding and developing the thought of some creative vision or idea for the accomplishment of some human purpose.

One way or another, we all have to find what best fosters the flowering of our humanity in this contemporary life, and dedicate ourselves to that.
Joseph Campbell

To express is to take an idea, not of what one is, but of what one can make or express, and to make or express it. In this sense, creative expression always has an impersonal quality to it. For example, we have a sense of the world's great art as belonging to humanity and not to the individuals who created it. Unique self-expression turns out to resonate with all of humanity, while conformist work seems strangely alienated and isolating. The deeper we go within ourselves, the closer we are to everyone. In regard to work, the question, What do you want to be? throws us off track. Better questions are: What do you want to make? What do you want to express? What do you want to create?

Many today are seeking a wholistic approach to life and work, one that integrates the spiritual and material. Too often these seem separated by a wide chasm bounded by steep cliffs. Our lives take on a schizophrenic quality—spiritual here, practical there. We require a bridge or bridges—effective ways of uniting the spiritual and material, the sacred and the ordinary. We offer here, not a bridge, but some principles of creative design and some materials with which you can build *your* bridge. To bridge the sacred and the ordinary, we must tap the spirit and emotional power of creative living and gain knowledge of how things are and how they work. In this way, we can create the life of our inborn nature.

Don't listen to friends
when the Friend
inside you says
"Do this."

Gandhi

I.S.E.E. My Life's Work

While we cannot tell you what your life's work is in any detail, we can suggest a few terms to serve as a frame of reference while you are making your search. In your life's work, you will find a mix of integrity, service, enjoyment, and excellence.

Integrity: Your life's work is something you deeply care about. In line with your values and ideals, it's something you can be proud to work for. Of course, it is important that your work not conflict with your values and ideals. More than this, a life's work is born out of your visions, values, and ideals. It's giving life to your ideals, anchoring them in the everyday world of action. **Key Words:** Purposeful, meaningful, responsible, honest, truthful. **Essential Question: Who Am I?**

Service: Your life's work is your way of making this world a better place. It's something you can make an important contribution to. We all want to give, to know that what we do is benefitting others. Your life's work is an opportunity to put your love in action. It's your way of taking a stand to help your fellow man. **Key Words:** Helping, caring, loving, giving, contributing. **Essential Question: How can I make this world a better place?**

Enjoyment: Your life's work is something you love to do, something your talents can find full expression through. If we enjoy our work, we are sure to bring our creativity and enthusiasm to it. If we do not, we are sure to get burnt out, frustrated, resentful, or indifferent. No matter how noble the ideal or seemingly valuable your service, you must bring joy to it if you are to be truly successful. Work without joy is a chore or a bore. Channel your creative powers into meaningful contributions. **Key Words:** Talents, creating, feedback, joy, gratitude. **Essential Question: What do I love to do?**

Excellence: Your life's work is something you can give your all to. Something you can dedicate yourself to. The dancer has his body pain, the writer struggles and racks his brain, the craftsman sweats every detail, the musician has his endless scales. Always quality has its price. It takes extra effort to make it nice. **Key Words:** Dedication, persistence, determination, quality. **Essential Question: What can I dedicate to enough to persist to excellence?**

CHAPTER 2

Zen at Work; or, Poetry in Motion

The truth of Zen, just a little bit of it, is what turns one's hum drum life, a life of monotonous, uninspiring commonplaceness, into one of art, full of genuine inner creativity.

D. T. Suzuki

We have called this book *Zen and the Art of Making a Living,* and you may well ask, What is Zen? A Sufi was once asked, "What is a Sufi?" He replied, "A Sufi is a Sufi." What is Zen? Zen is Zen.[1] Big help, you may say. Ask a Zen master, and he might choke you, or hit you with a stick, or laugh, or insult you, or spit in your face.

If you're still asking, What is Zen?, look at the question—it's all words. Words are symbols. Symbols are not what they stand for. Water is not these five letters *w-a-t-e-r*. Only an idiot would confuse the fluid reality with the letter symbols. You can't drink letters on a hot day. The reality behind all symbols has been called the *Mystery*, the *Unnameable*, the *Unexplainable*, the *Tao*, *God*, many names. Whatever you name it, you can't name it; whatever symbol you invent, it cannot hold the reality it represents. Since it can't be named, Zen is as good a name as any. But Zen is not about knowing about this reality. Zen is drinking it in everyday life.

I was first introduced to Zen through my interest in poetry. Poetry is our best (though entirely inadequate) attempt to reveal and express the Great Mystery of life in mere words. Zen poets seem to have an uncanny knack for providing awakening glimpses of the Mystery in the ordinary. Their poems are slices of ordinary life, lived with extraordinary vigor, insight, grace, and humor. The attentive reader can't help but feel refreshed and amused, ready to meet the situations of his own life with new energy and detachment.

> . . . Zen makes use, to a great extent, of poetical expressions; Zen is wedded to poetry.
>
> D. T. Suzuki

Of course, Zen poems are not alone in this. East or West, inspired poetry has been called scripture, or sacred verse. Writing about the Old Testament prophets, David Ben-Gurion notes that "it is a strange but significant fact that all the prophets were poets, so much so that any prose passages in the prophetic writings must be suspected of being later additions."[2] In *Mahayana Buddhism,* author Paul Williams instructs that "the Mahayana *sutras* were not the words of the Buddha but rather the works of poets."[3] We will not belabor the point beyond restating Aldous Huxley's general assertion that "the original scriptures of *most* religions are poetical and unsystematic." (Emphasis added.)[4]

Poetry is not to be thought of as mere words upon a printed page. A poem is an interactive relationship of word and consciousness. It is the act of hearing that makes the poem come alive. Indeed, *sruti,* the Sanskrit word for the scriptures, means "hearing."[5] Scriptures are not scriptures, poems are not poems, until they are heard. Rightly heard, poetry can be a gateway to Mystery.

Likewise, poetry can serve as a metaphor for a vision of work as art. From the Western vantage point, the notion of equating poetry with work may seem peculiar. We are used to thinking of work as a necessary drudgery or a moral responsibility, as a means to economic gain or ego gratification, but hardly as poetry. Work is what you have to do when you grow up, or it's a way of paying the bills, relieving boredom, achieving status, exercising power, or getting rich. This is life and work as "prose"—driven by the fears and ambitions of the mind, haunted by the necessities of the body—functional but soulless.

"Poetic" work comes from the heart. Where "prosaic" work struggles to satisfy the material demands of the body and the ego demands of the mind, poetic work delights in the spirit of living.

Spirit led and fed, there isn't a trace of other-worldliness, moral superiority, or retreat about it. Not a matter of engaging in superior occupations, poetic work intensifies and exalts human experience in whatever it finds itself engaged. While it goes without saying that it does not become involved in that which would violate its source (the heart), poetic work differs from the prosaic, not so much in content as in its approach.

Perhaps the best way to give a sense of the difference between these two approaches is to look at two phrases: "have to" and "want to." "Have to's" have a bit of grudge to them, a holding back, an inner struggle. "Want to's" move ahead directly. I *have to* work. I *have to* pay the bills. I *have to* impress people. I *have to* get rich. I *have to* beat the competition. I *have to* save the world. I *want to* work. I *want to* buy things. I *want to* be myself. I *want to* make money. I *want to* win. I *want to* share love. Feel the difference?

The things you have done because you truly wanted to—you experienced. The things you have done because you thought you had to—you missed. Zen says, This is it! Don't miss it with a lot of "have to" concepts. Dig on life! Zen embraces life; necessities, it calls *desires.* Since it lives, it "wants to" live. Since it works, it "wants to" work. Zen is not fighting with itself.

Everywhere I go I find a poet has been there before me.

Sigmund Freud.

Desires that are just are termed Truth.
Without desires, Truth cannot be understood.
    Hung Tzu Ch'eng
    (Discourse on Vegetable Roots)

How can we bring to work the spirit of Zen—of poetry in motion? We can start by listening to the "want to's" of our hearts, of our original nature. Poetry, after all, is all in the hearing. As a poem depends upon the "hearer" to make it Poetry, a life depends on the "liver" to make it Living. Inspired poetic works can be analyzed, but that is so much nonsense if they are not heard. Lives can be planned, controlled, and organized, but that is so much nonsense if they are not lived. Zen says LIVE! Be what you are!

Dare to Be the Poet of Your Life's Song

A poet is one who hears and one who *makes.* In fact, our word *poet* comes from the Greek *poietes*—one who makes.[6] To make is to bring into form. The poet brings into form what she hears in the depth of her heart—the echo of her life's destiny. Oh, maybe she can only make out a couple of notes. They roam around in the back of her mind and won't let go. Maybe she hears only a refrain or a simple tune. Perhaps she hears a glorious symphony in full orchestration. Whatever music she hears, she plays it with intense energy. She makes the song of her heart sing through her life.

A poem is the realization of love . . .
Rene Char

Again, poetic work is not limited to stanzas on a printed page. Mother Teresa was a poet, as was Einstein. St. Francis was a poet and Martin Luther King. Michelangelo was a poet, and so was Mozart. All who hear a voice calling them to a mighty purpose and labor to give it expression are poets. Still, all poems are not epics. There are farmer poets and cleaning poets, healing poets and sewing poets, cooking poets and building poets. Some hear better than others, and some are better at making, but all can be the poets of their own lives by joining the hearing and making—the inspiration and the action.

We can carry our metaphor of work as poetry (hearing and making) a step further by introducing two terms, one from the Western tradition, one from the Eastern. The Western term is *vocation;* the Eastern, *Dō.* The word *vocation* means "calling." Your vocation is the work you are called to perform. From the Japanese, we take the word *Dō. Dō* has been translated "way" or "art of," as in the art of flower arrangement or the art of archery. *Dō* is a mindful attitude and manner of performance. It has been called "the infinite way of doing finite things."

In the Supreme Presence of Mind
there is total absence of "mine."

Your life's work is a matter of the *use* that you are called to make of your life (vocation) and the *way* (*Dō*) in which you execute it. The *use* is the function served; the *way,* the manner in which it is served. The use of a meal is to eat. The way that the food is selected, prepared, served, and eaten will spell the difference between enjoyment and a lot of gas. The right vocation and the right way of executing it—this is life's work.

Vocation: Hearing the Call

Everyone has been made for some particular work, and the desire for that work has been put in every heart.

Rumi

We have said that vocation means calling. To get the call, you have to be listening. It's hard to listen when you have a lot of preconceived notions about what you should do, or fears of inadequacy, or prejudices about how one kind of work is better or more worthy than another, or vested interests (like having trained and worked so long at something that isn't really you). If you want to find your true calling, you have to forget all of that and follow your Bliss.

Dive deeply into being, beyond identity and form. Encompass all around you. Penetrate into absorption—absorb into bliss—sail on bliss—into complete quietness. Enter into emptiness—where "self" is no more. Silence the noise of fear and craving, the static of social obligation. Have no fear; in silence the image or form of your life's natural expression will become clear. It is in your heart; it has been there all along. As the great poet Rumi has written, "Everyone has been made for some particular work, and the desire for that work has been put in every heart."[7]

Can you hear it? Can you silence the confusion of the mind and its conflicts and listen for your Bliss—the voice of your heart? Listen now for the voice out of the Silence. Listen for what moves or draws you the most. Listen for what you can dedicate yourself to. Listen to what you love. If many things attract your attention, you're still on the surface. Go deeper. A relative few will speak powerfully to you. When you hear this call, what will it say? Make this—bring this into being. A poet is one who hears and one who makes.

Look with thine ears.

Shakespeare

If you ask him: "What is silence?" he will answer, "It is the Great Mystery! The holy silence is His voice!" If you ask: "What are the fruits of silence?" he will say: "They are self-control, true courage or endurance, patience, dignity, and reverence. Silence is the cornerstone of character."

Ohiyesa (Charles Eastman)

We All Have It: The Desire to Be Useful

Have you ever noticed what energetic creatures we humans are? Most of us appear happier when we are busy than when we are not. We seem to feel the need to do something. Many of the other animals seem to have this as well. But we humans have this other thing—this notion of being useful. We don't want to do just anything. We want to do something meaningful, something useful. George Bernard Shaw put it like this: "This is the true joy in life, the being used for a purpose recognized by yourself as a mighty one."[8]

> *The vocation, whether it be that of the farmer or the architect, is a function; the exercise of this function as regards the man himself is the most indispensable means of spiritual development, and as regards his relation to society the measure of his worth.*   Ananda K. Coomaraswamy

The words of truth are always paradoxical.

Lao Tzu

Now some may protest that none of us are terribly useful, but that doesn't keep us from trying. The Chinese sage Lao Tzu (or the poets writing in his name) wrote that those who know do not speak, and those who speak do not know.[9] One wonders why he bothers to break his own silence to tell us this. Perhaps there is something in our nature that is bound and determined to be useful—even if it knows better.

The modern Indian philosopher and teacher J. Krishnamurti would often say: "Do not accept it [what he was saying] because the speaker is telling you. The speaker is not important." Still he went on speaking right to the end. Even after there were dozens of books, tapes, and films, he kept talking on into his nineties. If the speaker was altogether unimportant, and everyone knew what he had to say, why keep saying it? Maybe next time someone would hear! Maybe he just loved to talk. Or maybe he just couldn't help making himself useful.

Your calling is your natural way of being useful, the way it was natural for Lao Tzu to be useful in speaking to remind us that those who speak do not know. Apparently, he just couldn't help himself from sharing—naturally. Just as naturally, you have a calling, a unique way of being useful. Struggling and straining to find your calling is a good way to miss it. It's natural, after all.

You have heard that life is a dance. And if you have seen cells dividing, or the sun on the water, or birds before the mate, you can see that it *is* a dance. If you think too much when you're dancing, you trip over your feet. In the same way, if you miss the rhythm of your life (with too much self-conscious "have to" thinking), you'll stumble through it a bit awkward and out of place. The graceful dancer listens for the music and trusts her feet to respond.

> *Consciously or unconsciously, every one of us does render some service or other. If we cultivate the habit of doing this service deliberately, our desire for service will steadily grow stronger, and will make, not only for our own happiness, but that of the world at large.*
>
> *Mahatma Gandhi*

Follow Your Native Compassion and Bliss

In listening for the song of your life's work, the notes to follow are your native compassion and bliss, or *karuna* and *ananda*.[10] We will call *compassion* the desire to act for the benefit of others—to eliminate their suffering or increase their happiness. *Bliss* we can call the Transcendent Joy of Consciousness, Life Ecstatic.

The Buddha, like all the great sages, tells us that it is the craving desire to act for self-interest that binds us to suffering. Jesus said, to save yourself, lose yourself—lose these self-interested cravings. Yet how can we eliminate desire? Desire is the very stuff of life—to kill it would be to destroy life itself. We cannot destroy desire, but we can begin to recognize that beyond the transient desires of ego there lie deeper desires for love and service to all mankind. We can "lose ourselves" in our desire to give of our love and talent. This, we have been told by all the great teachers, is the road to happiness.

Why, then, is this road so little traveled? Most of us are too busy running down approval alley. Our years of dependency, from infancy through adolescence, condition us to try to *please* others in order to get from them what we need (or think we need) to survive. The conditioned drive to please, to get approval, is a learned mental process based on the memory of past experience and the hope or threat of future consequences. It moves us out of the now-present-moment of spontaneous giving into concern for gaining approval or avoiding disapproval in the future. Where pleasing is a calculated mental process, compassion comes straight from the heart. Out of a here-and-now feeling of identity arises a spontaneous urge to act for the benefit of others.

> *The art of life, of a poet's life, is, not having anything to do, to do something.*
>
> *Henry David Thoreau*

Many of us find the please-for-approval habit a hard one to break. Doing so means accepting full responsibility for our own lives—breaking our chains of emotional dependence, letting go of our unending approval demands. Only then can we hear the compassion note echoing from within. Only then can we move in the direction it wants to take us. As we accept responsibility for our own lives, our desire to serve others increases. It seems we have more energy to give. Energy once tied up in the infantile desire to please can now find release in the compassion of universal love.

To the mind that is still, the whole universe surrenders.

Lieh Tzu

To love is to transform; to be a poet.
Norman O. Brown

Zen finds in *trshna*, selfish ego-centered love, the seed of *karuna*, universal compassion. Melting ice changes in form, not in essence. All the while, the ice of selfish love contains the water of universal compassion. Rearranging the letters in the word *please*, we get the word *ASLEEP*. The "please" mode is simply sleeping compassion. Awakening genuine compassion leads you to the best use of your life—"a purpose recognized by yourself as a mighty one."

The Buddha has further told us that our fundamental nature is constant Ecstatic Bliss. Yet, paradoxically, we miss the Bliss in our desperate attempts to find happiness. When we stake our happiness on other people, places, things, or circumstances, we are sure to come up wanting. This brings to life the sense of a roller coaster ride of elation and depression, an endless cycle of ups and downs.

Of course, gains and losses, advances and reversals are inevitable in life, but they neither *cause* us to be happy nor to be unhappy. In our attachment to and investment in these turns of events, we miss the ecstatic pulse of life, its radiant Bliss. Bliss is not pleasure without pain. Genuine Bliss holds infinite sorrow as space holds the earth, without effort or weariness. Our adolescent and unrealistic craving for pleasure without pain is simply "sleeping Bliss" (pleasure = ASLEEP-U-R). Even as we miss Compassion in trying to please, so we miss Bliss in trying to find happiness.

The Perfect Way is only difficult for those who pick and choose; Do not like, do not dislike: all will then be clear.

Seng-ts'an

The Buddha enjoins us to hold to the middle—recognize that pleasure and pain (like and dislike) are but two sides of the same coin. Sometimes it comes up heads; sometimes, tails. Aware of pleasure and pain, but neither attached to the one nor repulsed by the other, the Buddha resides in the center of Bliss.

Zen masters laugh at our vain attempts to find happiness in outer circumstances. In this, we are like a man standing in a clear stream while dying of thirst, or as the Polynesians say, we are "standing on a whale fishing, for minnows." Bliss, the sages tell us, is not a thing to be acquired, conquered, or possessed by outer means; rather, it is an ongoing experience to relax into. Ever-abiding and without cause—Bliss simply Is. To recognize this, to know it in the gut, is to awaken the sleeper. The Zen masters call this the recognition of one's own "original [blissful] nature."

Now, getting back to work, whatever gets you really turned on, enough to work for with dedication, sacrifice, and excellence, has the quality of this blissful, original nature in it and is moving you toward your life's work. If you both find great joy in your work and are ready to sacrifice for it, you are on the right track. You are following your bliss—beyond the pairs of opposites.

To be willing to suffer in order to create is one thing; to realize that one's creation necessitates one's suffering, that suffering is one of the greatest of God's gifts, is almost to reach a mystical solution to the problem of evil.

J. W. Sullivan

The compassion and bliss notes are usually drowned out by all the "have to" static over the security, approval (status), and power needs that occupy so much of society's time and interest. Money is usually mixed up with all three. Joseph Campbell said that "social pressure is the enemy!"[11] Society gives us preconceived, abstract notions of how our lives are supposed to be and puts on tremendous pressure to see that we conform.

Then, of course, there is our own weakness and rigidity. We fear change. We try to create a predictable life that is as unthreatening as possible. Yet it's not knowing what's coming around the corner that makes life interesting. Look at nature; it's full of surprises. It curves, zigzags, wiggles, and bends. Its forms grow, expand, decay, and die. Change is everywhere, ongoing. Yet for all its changes, nature has an order, an intelligence.

Take thy Bliss O Man!

William Blake

As the innocent infant relies upon the mother for sustenance, so the innocent wanderer, following his native compassion and bliss, relies upon the natural intelligence of life to sustain him.

So it is with compassion and bliss. Follow them; they know where to take you. Don't interfere with growth; yield to it. There is an intelligence in this. Often it can only be understood in retrospect. Though we may not have understood at the time, something was guiding us all the while. When we yield to our compassionate, blissful nature, its intelligence takes the lead. We are moved by something at once intrinsically a part of ourselves, and yet, infinitely larger.

Allow your natural compassion and bliss to ripen, and you are sure to find your vocation sooner or later. It may not come out like you thought, but that's part of the adventure of life—and the fun! Pay attention to where compassion and bliss take you, and watch the thing unfold. Even if you miss the *heart* promptings of compassion and bliss, you can still *mentally* recognize your desire to be useful. (Watch how children naturally want to help.) Since we can't help trying to be useful, we may as well decide to be useful at things that foster harmony, increase beauty, and generally make life more palatable. Certainly we can decide not to be useful at things that are destructive, dull, or drab.

If the notion of following your compassion and bliss to your vocation seems too vague or nebulous, don't worry. Later on, we will put it to you in more concrete terms. For now, simply recognize your desire to be useful, and see where it wants to take you.

Dō: Making the Art of Zen

So far, much of what we have said may sound a bit mystical. Were Zen to stop here, it would be all but useless in daily life. But Zen is as much at home with the practical business of everyday living as with the transcendent realization of Bliss. It is every bit as much concerned with "form" as with "emptiness." Indeed, the Zen insight is that form is emptiness, emptiness form. Zen doesn't ask us to be something that we are not but to be more fully what we are. At work Zen discovers "the infinite way of doing finite things." Its actions, however ordinary, are exaltations. Performed without hesitation or doubt, they reveal the ordinary greatness of man.

Whatever your calling, your vocation, your way of being useful, how you go about it is as much "your work" as what you do. If *use* is purpose, *Dō,* or *way,* is purposefulness, acting without waste or haste, in a spirit of play. Zen influence on Japanese culture gave rise to many *Dō's,* or ways. Anyone who has ever experienced a Japanese tea ceremony has some idea what purposeful action is. Here, in the simple act of serving and taking tea, life is artistry. Human dignity, strength, and grace are honored in purposeful, present action.

> *There are various Ways. There is the Way of salvation by the law of Buddha, the Way of Confucius governing the Way of learning, the Way of healing as a doctor, as a poet teaching the Way of Waka, tea, archery, and many arts and skills. Each man practices as he feels inclined.*
>
> Miyamoto Musashi

Every man or woman is a potential poet or artist. Everyone has the capacity to bring to their work the dignity, purposefulness, and presence of the artist. Like art, work holds up a mirror to life. The work reflects the creator, his strengths and flaws, his skill and resolve. An individual encounters human society, physical nature, and the particular medium, tools, or objects of his work, and shapes these in the image of his consciousness. The melding of creator and creation is the artistry of work.

The dictionary defines art as "the disposition or modification of things by human skill, to answer the purpose intended." Our word *art* comes from the Greek *artunein*—to arrange.[12] We arrange by sight. We *see* how to arrange things to answer the purpose intended. Where *vocation* is a matter of hearing what to do, *making* is a matter of seeing how to do it. We will use the metaphor of *art* and *sight* in discussing *Dō*—the making of a life's work. It is important to remember that while we will frame this discussion of *making* in terms of the formal arts, everything that will be said applies as well to the art of living, generally. Whether our making is in humanitarian service, the production and distribution of beneficial products or services, the transmission of some special knowledge or wisdom or whatever else—art has lessons for all of us.

In giving form to her vision, the creative artist measures her efforts against the inner vision she holds. The final product is always inadequate. Yet, as Michelangelo said, it's in striving for perfection that the artist touches the divine. This striving for perfection, for the fullest realization of the thing imagined, elevates ordinary life to the level of sublime, transcendent experience. Striving for perfection is the passion of art—the ready sacrifice of

You wish to see; Listen. Hearing is a step toward Vision.

St. Bernard

the artist. The word *sacrifice* literally means "to make sacred,"[13] and, as we shall see, the sense of the sacred is of utmost importance to the artist.

> *The way of the mystic and the way of the artist are related, except that the mystic doesn't have the craft.*
>
> Jean Erdman

While it is this striving for perfection that gives art its passion, imagination gives it its play. Both in the sense of enjoyment and in the sense of the dramatic, art is play. The revelations of imagination, the *satori* of every genuine artistic inspiration are sublime delight. Art is magical or, in Zen terms, *marvelous*, when vision, content, design, and technique form an inseparable unity. Today we rely heavily upon technique, but as D. T. Suzuki put it, "technical knowledge is not enough. One must transcend techniques so that the art becomes the artless art . . ."

"Artless art" has the quality of revelation. One feels that in beholding it, he has received a precious gift; a conscious spirit has moved over this form, in turn evoking the spirit of the beholder. This sense of the gift is equally present in the practical and the contemplative arts—as much in entering a well-made home or sitting down to a well-prepared meal as in enjoying a fine piece of music or poetry. It is the essence of the experience of any work as art. The all-embracing humanity of Zen tells us that there is no sphere of human life exempt from the display of this gift-giving spirit.

> *Although profoundly "inconsequential," the Zen experience has consequences in the sense that it may be applied in any direction, to any conceivable human activity, and that wherever it is so applied it lends an unmistakable quality to the work.*
>
> Alan Watts

It is easier and more useful to talk about what art does than what it is. Art communicates awareness—consciousness. All art reflects some *theory* (in the original sense of the word, i.e., "a way of seeing").[14] This is true whether or not the theory is ever understood or articulated by the artist. A way of seeing, or *theory,* of art is expressed through a work's *content* and *design* language. Of course, the language of art is not limited to words. Movement, sound, light, shape, color—all design elements are a kind of artistic language. Additionally, every art has a *technique,* a way of "modifying things by human skill." We will discuss the theory, content, design, and technique of art below. As we will see, we can draw on these elements in shaping any life's work.

Vision or Theory of Art: To quote art critic and historian Herbert Read: "Any general theory of art must *begin* with the supposition that man responds to the shape and surface and mass of things present to his senses, and that certain arrangements in the proportion of the shape and surface and mass of things result in pleasurable sensations whilst the lack of such arrangement leads to indifference or even positive discomfort and revulsion."[15]

Read's essential point, what he calls the starting place for any theory of art, is that "certain arrangements" evoke pleasurable responses, while other arrangements provoke less favorable responses. The origin of the word *art,* as we have already discussed, is "to arrange." So we can say that the true artist is a master arranger or master of arrangements. He may "arrange" in any field of action—in any of the making or doing arts. Whatever his field, he knows how to evoke "pleasurable sensations."

Be still and cool in thy own mind and spirit.
George Fox

Now what are these pleasurable sensations? It is important that we not be confused in this matter. To bring this out, we will draw on James Joyce's theory of art as expressed in *Portrait of the Artist as a Young Man.*[16] Joyce distinguishes between what he terms "proper" and "improper" art. The pleasure of proper art, he calls "aesthetic arrest." (We will get to this.) The "pleasures" of improper art are not the genuine pleasures appropriate to art but rather impostors. These impostors, Joyce calls the "pornographic" and the "didactic." The "pleasure" of pornographic art is the excitement of the *desire to possess* the object represented. Pornographic art is seen in the advertising barrage to which most of us are daily subjected. "Make the thing look sexy, alluring, sensually enticing, so they will want to possess it."

The "pleasure," if you could call it that, of didactic art is the excitement of a sense of *fear and loathing* in relation to the object represented (not unlike the "pleasure" many seem to get from watching horror films). We see this represented in art used as a tool

There is no patriotic art and no patriotic science.

Goethe

The productions of all arts are kinds of poetry and their craftsmen are all poets.

Plato

for social criticism or as propaganda for some political or cultural agenda. "Political" and "confessional" art and much of "women's art" or "gay art" is didactic. Of course, this is not to say there are not great artists who are women or gay, only that genuine art transcends these labels. Georgia O'Keefe put it emphatically: "There is no man's art or woman's art; there is just Art."

This capital *A* Art that Georgia O'Keefe is referring to above is what Joyce calls "proper art." Joyce tells us that while improper art has a *kinetic,* or moving, quality, proper art has a *static,* or still, quality. Improper art excites the mind to move toward or away from its object. Proper art brings the mind to rest. In the symbolic language of Western poetry and art, the changeable moon often represents the moving or kinetic aspect of consciousness, while the sun represents the changeless or static dimension. In Zen, the kinetic (moving or moon dimension) is sometimes called "mind"— and the static (still or sun dimension), "No-Mind."[17] So we can say, proper art radiates the still sun of eternal No-Mind, or that in proper art, the motions of the mind are arrested in the rest of No-Mind.

The motions of the mind excited by improper art (its "pleasures") are, as we already discussed, desire and loathing. Joyce says that the pleasure of proper art is "aesthetic arrest," stopping or arresting the motions of the mind. In contemplation of the work of art, "the mind is arrested and raised above desire and loathing."[18] This is exactly the goal of meditation—to arrest the mind—transcending attachment (desire) and repulsion (loathing). And so now we can see that art, proper art, in both its contemplation and in its practice, is indeed meditation—mind arresting. And this is Zen. The word *Zen* itself is Japanese for the Indian *dhyana,* usually translated "meditation."[19]

In Zen the important thing is to stop the course of the mind.

Saying of "an Ancient"
quoted by Takashina Rosen

The motive of proper art is neither "for" or "against," but to bring out what Joyce calls "the radiance." The *radiance* of a work of art shows in its ability to arrest the mind in joyous contemplation. We want to linger and enjoy the beauty of the work. The Buddha said that the contemplation of beauty eliminates selfish desire. For Rodin, "art is contemplation. It is the joy of the intelligence." Blissful serenity, intense stillness, this is radiance. While Joyce's theory of art was intended for the contemplation of the fine arts, we can see in it keys to *Dō,* or working in the way of art, in any field of human endeavor. In action, in the doing arts, radiance comes through in what Zen would call *wu wei,* or effortless action. Acting from the center, moving from the stillness, action is radiant.

We have then come, in a somewhat roundabout way, to the essential point: *The pleasure in art, both in its practice and in its contemplation is meditation, that is, the arresting of the mind.* We lose ourselves in art. As Arthur Schopenhauer noted, the contemplation of great art switches off the sense of "other." As we merge our consciousness with the art object, we lose the sense of ourselves as a thing apart.[20] This "loss of self" is extremely pleasurable—echoing the transcendent bliss of the mystics. Likewise, in the practice of art, the sense of self is lost in ecstatic absorbtion. One loses oneself and gains eternity. Moving safely between the twin whirlwinds of desire and repulsion, the artist enters into paradise. While here on earth, attending to the most practical of affairs (his daily work), the artist, as Blake would say, "travels in his mind to Heaven." This is Zen at work, the essence of work as art—self-liberation.

If you realize what the real problem is—losing your-self—you realize that this itself is the ultimate trial.
Joseph Campbell

The heart has its reasons that the mind knows nothing of.

Blaise Pascal

Dō is active contemplation or meditation—moving or doing in aesthetic arrest. Or we could say moving without moving—moving without the motions of the mind. Lao Tzu wrote, "The secret of the magic of life is in using action to attain non-action."[21] For St. Augustine, "our whole business in this life is to restore the health of the eye of the heart whereby God (the Infinite) may be seen."[22] Our business (work life) ought not and need not keep us from "our business in this life." Indeed, working in the way of the artist does not impede but enhances and expresses spiritual life. The practice of art, or *Dō,* purifies "the personal system so that it moves over into the universal."[23] In the making of the art, we are remaking ourselves; we are developing confidence in what Zen calls our "original nature."

Having now perhaps some inkling of how we might approach work as *Dō* or "way" or "the art of," we will briefly examine how we can recognize a work of art, be it our own life's work or the art of another. Of course, there is no simple formula—of artists it may properly be said that it takes one to know one. Still, we give four essential characteristics to look for—comprising a kind of practical theory of art. Note that the elements of this theory apply equally to the "fine" or "common" arts.

1. **The work of art is inspired.** It is conceived of the spirit, born of the Buddha nature, whispered by the muse—however you want to say it—the work of art in some way echoes the transcendent Mystery. It suggests something more than itself. What Joseph Campbell said of myth—that it is a "metaphor transparent to transcendence"—applies to the work of art. Both in the making arts and in the doing arts, the radiance of spirit shines through. We recognize a Beauty that transcends the beautiful and the ugly. This is the **integrity** of the work of art—that it arises from the essential self of the artist. *The secret of art lies in the artist himself.* (Kuo Jo Hsu)[24]

2. **The work of art is useful.** The artist has a sense of his responsibility to the community of mankind, and therefore, he makes that which can be put to good use. The use intended may be for the practical life of the body, the refreshment of the mind, or the awakening of the soul. In every case, the artist has in mind the use of his work. It comes out of compassion for humanity. "The secret of art," as the sculptor Antoine Bourdelle put it, "is love."[25] This is the quality of **service** in the work of art—that the artist makes the work, not simply for himself, but for all mankind. *The general end of art is the good of man.* (Aristotle)[26]

3. **The work of art is natural.** The artist is naturally suited to his work. Be he a carpenter, an orator, a doctor, or a poet, his work is what he naturally does, that is, loves. This is what gives work the quality of play. While working at what is naturally his to do, the artist enters into the work so completely—he loses himself in it. This is the **enjoyment** of the work of art—the natural, spontaneous, self-abandonment of the artist in what he loves. *It is certain that the secret of all art . . . lies in self-oblivion.* (Riciotto Canudo)[27]

4. **The work of art is beautiful.** Beauty is not an end in itself, but the by-product of making or doing things well. Beauty results from the aspiration to perfection. Yet it accepts and allows that natural imperfection which is human. Beauty is not found in mechanical correctness but in human aspiration—in making and doing with love. If in-spiration is the call of Heaven, a-spiration is the desire to realize Heaven on Earth. The artist knows that, as Michelangelo said, "trifles make perfection and perfection is no trifle." This is what gives the work of art the quality of **excellence**—the artist's striving for perfection in making the work beautifully. *O Excellence! how narrow are thy paths, how arduous thy ways! Happy the man who can climb thy paths and tread thy ways!* (Gottfried von Strassburg)[28]

* The "Vision Questing" and "Clarifying Values" sections of "Act I: The Quest for Life's Work" are designed to help you explore and develop a *theory* for the art of your life.

Content: The content of "proper art" may be the "super-ordinary sacred" or the "ordinary sacred." The sacred art of India or medieval Europe reflects the sacred in the super-ordinary aspect. The subject is theistic—God in splendor, majesty, and miraculous exploits. Zen art more typically represents the sacred in the ordinary aspect: the rock gardens, the calligraphy, the tea ceremony, the martial arts. Ordinary things like rocks and trees, ordinary activities like writing, taking tea, and fighting are approached with a presence and a sense of wonder that can only be called sacred.

> *What is particularly intriguing, in fact, is that whereas many peoples tend to locate this experience (of the sacred) in certain unusual, if not 'supernatural' moments and circumstances. . . the Oriental focus is upon mystery in the most obvious, ordinary, mundane—the most natural—situations of life.*
>
> Conrad Hyers

In the West, this sacred-in-the-ordinary aspect can be seen in works such as Cezanne's still lifes or his paintings of Mont Saint Victoire, in van Gogh's *Boots with Laces* or *Starry Night,* or even in T. S. Eliot's *Cocktail Party.* Of course, the two (super-ordinary and ordinary) are not mutually exclusive. Blake, Rembrandt, Mozart, and many others have revealed the sacred in both super-ordinary and ordinary content.

The work will teach you how to do it.

Estonian Proverb

* The "Pointing to Purpose," "Targeting Talents," and "Marking Mission Objectives" sections of "Act I: The Quest for Life's Work" are designed to help you discover the *content* of your life's work.

Design: We have seen that "proper art" is a kind of meditation and that its content may be any work approached in a sacred manner. Approached in this way, the work becomes a vehicle for an *epiphany*—a revelation of the infinite in the finite. Now, we will briefly consider design. Our word *design* originates in the Latin *designare,* "to mark out."[29] Through her design, the artist marks out the time and space boundaries or forms through which she will reveal the infinite. In approaching your work as art, your first design choice is your choice of career. Every career has its own unique boundaries, limitations, and patterns, and as Joseph Campbell put it, "When you choose a vocation, you have actually chosen a model, and it will fit you in a little while."[30]

William Blake said, "Eternity is in love with the productions of time."[31] Design is in time, both in the sense that a poem, a painting, a song, a humanitarian service live in the finite world of form and in the sense that every design reflects the historical and cultural context in which it is produced. The Infinite in Shakespeare speaks through the design forms of Elizabethan sonnets, comedies, histories, and tragedies. The Infinite in Michelangelo shines forth through the forms of "High Renaissance" sculpture, painting, and architecture. The Infinite in Bach echoes through Baroque musical forms—e.g., fugues, masses, and concertos. The Japanese poet Matsuo Basho revealed the Infinite in the seventeen syllable *haiku* form. One feels that these great souls would have somehow expressed the Infinite, no matter the time, place, or form of their work.

Love is love's reward.
John Dryden

The design forms these artists selected reflect the historical and cultural contexts in which they lived, as well as their own unique style. Similarly, your life's work will be shaped by the time you live in, yet your own unique expression. The design of your work, the career you choose, ought to be a natural vehicle for your unique talents and temperament so that you will be able to say with Henri Matisse, "I am unable to distinguish between the feeling I have for life and my way of expressing it." This is the essence of vocation.

✳ You will have the opportunity to shape the *design* (i.e., select your career role) of your life's work in "Act II: The Game of Life's Work."

Technique: The true artist is always a master of technique. His compassion and bliss drive him to excel in his art. The artist is so stimulated by these "that he naturally possesses a sustained interest strong enough to impel and guide him through a lifetime of searching for an adequate. . . vocabulary, with which to objectify his subjective impulses in translatable traditional symbols."[32] Strive to be the best you can at what you do, to expand your vocabulary in the language of your art.

The essence of technique is discipline. Even as Zen embraces the necessities of physical survival, so it embraces the necessities of the *Dō* (the discipline of the work). Without regret, second thought, or self-pity, it plunges in. What must be done to perfect oneself in one's craft *is* done, without pausing to consider, Do I like to do it? In this way, the artist becomes first master of himself and then of his art.

Again, the execution of art is meditation—self-collected, mindful, deliberate action. Its deliberateness is not that of imposing an abstract form but of unself-conscious, spontaneous action. Zen trusts "the original nature" to act of its own accord. In one deliberate Zen brush stroke, a world of images is born. Again, D. T. Suzuki: "Zen wants to act, and the most effective act is, once the mind is made up, to go on without looking backward."[33]

All labor that uplifts humanity has dignity and importance and should be undertaken with painstaking excellence.

Martin Luther King, Jr.

Work on New York's Saint John the Divine cathedral has been going on for over a hundred years. The people who are working on it now will most likely be dead when it is finished. Yet the work calls for the finest craftsmanship. How does one stay motivated working at building something he will never see finished? Zen responds: by concentrating on the process—working for the sake of the work, losing yourself in the now moment of action. Work without attachment.

✳ You will have the opportunity to consider how you can improve your capacity to excel in your career field by improving your *technique* in "Act IV: The School of Life's Work."

The Poetic Work Is Hearing and Making

Hearing	Making
Inspiration	Action
Idea	Form
Reception	Creation
Vocation	*Dō*
Use	Way
Substance	Style
Imagination	Discipline
Inflow	Outflow
Subjective	Objective

The Life of Beauty

Modern life has altogether too much ugliness. This is doubly so since most of it is so unnecessary. The ugliness of poverty may be excused, but the ugliness of the mediocre, the bland, and the lifeless is an appalling waste. Beauty sensitizes the soul—evoking the finer, subtler feelings and inspiring noble thoughts. Ugliness depresses and diminishes life—sapping the creative spirit of the individual and weakening the character of society.

> We have come to think of art and work as incompatible, or at least independent categories and have for the first time in history created an industry without art.   Ananda K. Coomaraswamy

There is unnecessary ugliness, not only in the things we make, but in the way we make them. Mass production ensures that quantity dominates quality, and profit rules beauty. White collar or blue, the worker is taken to be a machine. Engaged, not as a whole person, but as a tool of production, he becomes alienated from his work and himself. No wonder the worker is more interested in sports or gossip than in his or her work. No wonder, in the words of popular bumper talk, he "would rather be fishing" or she "would rather be shopping." Work devoid of meaning and spirit, work without the discipline and satisfaction of a job well done, is work without joy. So work has gotten a bad name, and we live for the weekends. Art curator and philosopher Ananda K. Coomaraswamy put it like this: "It is taken for granted that while at work we are doing what we like least, and at play what we should wish to be doing all the time."[34]

Zen and art can teach us how to work beautifully. From Zen, we can learn to embrace work, to accept responsibility for ourselves and our world, without seeking to escape. From art we can draw lessons—the lessons of the spirit at work (the inspiration of the artist) and the lessons of dedication to and sacrifice for the vision one sees. Zen says: No sense waiting for Heaven. This very life on earth is the Buddha Realm. Therefore, let it be a beautiful life. The Buddha nature is within all things; therefore, treat them with love and kindness, care and understanding.

Conceiving of ourselves as artists in whatever work we do gives us a metaphor for a life of integrity, service, enjoyment, and excellence. We can draw strength from the lives of the great artists and cultivate an appreciation of their works. Really, there is no

...a first-rate soup is more creative than a second-rate painting.

Abraham Maslow

significant transformation of our increasingly global culture without changing our ideas about what work is and what work is for. Conceiving of ourselves as artists and injecting the spirit of beauty into our work from beginning to end can play an important role in this transformation. Cultivating an appreciation of art and the artistic life fosters a desire to serve humanity in a spirit of beauty—no matter one's calling.

Learning to appreciate the art of others is as much a part of building a beautiful world as developing the artist within ourselves. Real art appreciation will produce, not only more and better contemplative or "fine" artists, it can also produce better carpenters, managers, and tailors, and most importantly, better human beings. Art is for the sake of the living everywhere. Its lessons, traditions, and revelations belong to us all.

Many today would have us believe that art is for the cultured few—the museum hounds and the wine and cheese set. The implication is that art is too good to be contaminated with the vulgar business of living. While art is safely locked away from the soiling hands of the common man, the greatest vulgarity of all is perpetuated. Art is reduced to an investment commodity. In the name of protection (from the masses), art has become a favorite form of capital speculation.

Beauty is truth, truth beauty,—that is all Ye know on earth, and all ye need to know.

John Keats

To have great poets, there must be great audiences.

Walt Whitman

It is clear that even without cultivating a deep appreciation or understanding, art speaks to us all. One doesn't have to understand a cathedral to appreciate its beauty or comprehend a musical composition to be moved by it. You certainly don't have to be a poet, playwright, director, or scholar to appreciate a Shakespearean play. Something within us recognizes art. Perhaps it is because we ourselves are artists at heart. Even as we all share in a spiritual life, whether we are "enlightened" or not, so we are all artists—whether masters, journeymen, apprentices, or hacks. Cultivating an awareness of the art we are called to perform and of the manner in which we perform it can only improve our craft.

In saying that everyone can be an artist, we in no way mean to denigrate the arts—to cheapen or to lessen the standards of excellence in any of the arts. It is not that we all take dance classes and are suddenly "dancers" or that we take creative writing classes and are now "poets." It is rather that in whatever our craft, we lift ourselves to the highest standards of excellence in that field. This

For man is by nature an artist.

Tagore

doesn't mean that we cannot as amateurs enjoy dancing or writing or singing; indeed, these brighten our lives (and what we practice as amateurs may enrich our art). It is simply to recognize the difference between being an amateur and being an artist in any field.

Of course, all arts or artists are not equal. It is absurd to compare a well-cooked meal with Mozart's *Requiem* or the local home architect with Michelangelo; it is even more absurd to eat tasteless meals or live in cracker-box houses because their makers aren't Mozarts or Michelangelos. If we are called to be cooks, or architects, or whatever, we can be the finest we can be at our professions. Beautiful clothing, lovely meals, well-designed homes, parks, and cities uplift the spirit of man. They reveal a vision of beauty, of the mystery of life, and in this they are art.

In Japan, the place where "the art" is practiced is called the *"Dō-Jo,"* or "house of enlightenment." There is a popular saying: "The *Dō-Jo* is everywhere." Wherever work is done in a present, conscious way, there is the house of enlightenment. Transformation is the action of both spiritual liberation and art. Zen sees, in the stuff of suffering, the tools for liberation. For the artist, the physical world provides the raw materials for revealing a higher consciousness of Beauty.

The only lasting beauty is the beauty of the heart.
Rumi

It is, of course, in the imagination that all art begins. In the words of Jacob Bronowski: "The characteristic gift that makes us human is . . . the gift of imagination. The power that man has over nature and himself lies in his command of imaginary experience."[35] The art of life is facing that awful power and then leading it in the way of Beauty, until it learns to find its way naturally. Dostoyevsky said, "Beauty will save the world." Beauty rightly understood and widely practiced *will* save the world. It is not too farfetched to imagine a civilization of artists working in love and joy to reveal a world of Beauty. Though it may take a thousand years, we can begin at once.

To believe that what has not occurred in history will not occur at all, is to argue disbelief in the dignity of man.
Mahatma Gandhi

Modern Artists on Spirit

Everything passes, and what remains of former times, what remains of life, is the spiritual. In everything we do, the claim of the Absolute is unchanging.

Paul Klee

Whoever does not detach himself from the ego never attains the Absolute and never deciphers life.

Constantin Brancusi

If the universal is the essential, then it is the basis of all life and art. Recognizing and uniting with the universal therefore gives us the greatest aesthetic satisfaction, the greatest emotion of beauty. The more this union with the universal is felt, the more individual subjectivity declines.

Piet Mondrian

Construction on a purely spiritual basis is a slow business. . . The artist must train not only his eye but also his soul. . .

Wassily Kandinsky

Something sacred, that's it. We ought to be able to say that such and such a painting is as it is, with its capacity for power, because it is "touched by God."

Pablo Picasso

Firmament and planets both disappeared, but the mighty breath which gives life to all things and in which all is bound up remained.

Vincent van Gogh
(*Describing* Starry Night)

CHAPTER 3

Myth at Work; or, Crafting the Story of Your Life

The role of the artist I now understood as that of revealing through the world-surfaces the implicit forms of the soul, and the great agent to assist the artist was the myth.
Joseph Campbell

The word *myth* means story. But a genuine myth is not just any story. It is a story of an encounter with universal human energies and experience. It is, as Joseph Campbell said in his final and most refined definition, "a metaphor transparent to transcendence."[1] If we approach myth as fact, it is clearly ridiculous. We don't really think that a god named Zeus had a splitting headache from which (with the help of an ax) Athena sprang or that a guy named Ulysses went around in a boat encountering sirens and cyclopes. It is not as fact but as metaphor that the mythic stories speak to us. To approach myth as fact is to miss the point. Similarly, to view your life as "nothing but the facts" is to miss an opportunity for a marvelous adventure, a conscious encounter with the universal energies and dilemmas of the human drama. In this encounter, we take the hero's journey; we experience life as art; we put "soul" into our work.

The one thing in the world, of value, is the active soul.

Emerson

Think of a work of art, a fine piece of literature, for example. A great work of art *is* a great work of art because it reveals the universal in the particular—so that across time, place, and culture we experience the works of Homer or Virgil, Dante or Shakespeare speaking directly to us. To view your life as a mythic story, to approach it as a work of art, is to recognize the play of the universal in the particulars of your life. In this chapter, we will identify some of these "universal energies" and how you might consciously, constructively, and artistically engage them on the way to creating your life's work.

The myths hold keys to a timeless psychology of creativity. Clearly, if we are to be artists of life, it is useful for us to have some understanding of the psychology of the creative process. But what does myth have to do with psychology? To begin with, in its life-instructing function—in what it can tell us about how to live—myth *is* psychology, in the literal meaning of the word *psycho* (soul) and *logos* (description). As the word itself implies, the work of any genuine psychology is to describe the landscape of the soul. This landscape comes to life in vivid, rich, and haunting detail in the world's great mythology.

> *Myths are clues to the spiritual potentialities of the human life.*   *Joseph Campbell*

Where the Zen poetry of work is in the now, immediate experience of *being*, the psychology or mythology of work considers the process of *becoming*. It describes the soul's journey, the pilgrim's progress, if you will, and the inner territory one encounters on this journey of becoming. Through the ages and across cultures, there have been many psychologies (soul descriptions). They were traditionally expressed in the intuitive language of myth and symbol, a language we have largely forgotten. As a result, much of the wisdom of these ancient psychologies remains a mystery to us. Recently, Jungian psychology (the only widely popular modern psychology that, in fact, *is* one, i.e., the only one concerned with describing the landscape of the soul) has begun to provide a framework through which we can begin to approach some of these soul mysteries. We will briefly consider the relation of three basic elements of this framework: myth, archetype, and symbol, then go on to consider four universal or archetypal energies that we can play with in creating life's work.

Myth and Archetype: For Joseph Campbell, "myth is the secret opening through which the inexhaustible energies of the cosmos pour into human cultural manifestation."[2] These "inexhaustible energies" of the cosmos are what Carl Jung referred to as *archetypes*. Archetypes, as Jung defined them, are the primordial energies that underlie human consciousness. How these energies got there is not entirely clear. Yet whether they are a sort of a human microcosm of the great macrocosmic energies of the universe, an intrinsic part of human biology, or dispositions acquired through common human experience is not the central point for Jung. The point is that they *exist* as a fundamental part of human experience and that we are better off for learning to recognize and come to terms with them.

The archetypes provide the cosmic or psychic raw material of myth. Across cultures and time, we see this same basic psychic stuff or raw material worked and reworked in great variety. The mythic stories, their heroes, friends, and foes, their deeds and adventures are particular representations of these archetypal energies. No matter how the stories of world mythology differ in detail, one can always recognize common themes. These common themes arise from the universality of the archetypes.

Symbol: If the archetypes are the raw material of myth, then symbols are its vocabulary. Symbols are the language of the imagination—the active ingredients of mythology and psychology. As Carl Jung said, "The psychological mechanism that transforms energy is the symbol."[3] He elsewhere tells us what this "transformation" is all about: "The symbols act as transformers, their function is to convert libido from a 'lower' into a 'higher' form."[4]

> . . . *the degradation of the sense of symbol in modern society is one of its many signs of spiritual decay.*
>
> Thomas Merton

Symbols transform the energy of the individual and collective psyche. The power of symbol lies in its capacity to transcend the limits of reason—to penetrate the conscious mind and communicate directly with the subconscious. While this power is enormous, it is not always well used. Allowing, as Jung suggests, that the *true function* of symbol is to "convert" "lower" libido energies into a "higher" form, we mustn't get the idea that the power of symbol (or sign) can't be used for more malevolent aims. The mass hysteria of the Nazis, for example, relied upon a peculiar brand of mythic interpretation and the very deliberate, effective, and perverse use of symbol and ritual.

The secret of art is love.

Antoine Bourdelle

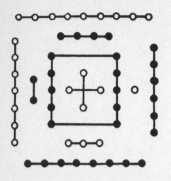

Whoever controls the media—the images— controls the culture.

Allen Ginsberg

The power of symbol should hardly surprise us. We need not be students of mythology or history to understand its effect. Advertisers use symbols every day to try to transform our energy—prompting action to buy their products. The logical connections between cowboys and cigarettes, half-naked women and beer, babies and tires may be dubious, but the power of these images is not in dispute. Today, the power of symbol is wielded with greatest effect, not by its traditional keepers in religion and art, but by Madison Avenue and political image-makers, Hollywood and commercial television, MTV and the recording "industry." We are everywhere surrounded by what Joyce called pornographic art, the use of symbols as tools of manipulation. (See chapter 2.)

While dictators and advertisers certainly know and use the power of symbols as psychological tools of transformation, the scientific view of life and "scientific psychology" in particular tend to downplay their power in the inner life of the individual. This has important consequences. As Jung says: "Modern man does not understand how much his 'rationalism' (which has destroyed his capacity to respond to numinous symbols and ideas) has put him at the mercy of the psychic underworld. He has freed himself from 'superstition' (or so he believes), but in the process, he has lost his spiritual values to a positively dangerous degree."[5]

Through the centuries, religion and art used the power of symbol *as an end in itself* for the transformation of consciousness, to uplift and awaken. Today their influence is minimal. Instead, politicians use this power *as a means* to gain and maintain control; commercialists use it to sell products. If we are to take control of our own destinies, we must reclaim this power for ourselves as individuals. We must consciously develop our own relationships to myth, archetype, and symbol.

Symbolism is no mere idle fancy or corrupt degeneration: it is inherent in the very texture of human life.

Alfred North Whitehead

That's what this chapter is all about—encouraging you: first, to experience your life as myth, as a story of the individual encounter with the universal; second, and as a part of the first, to learn to recognize the universal or archetypal energies; third, to develop your own creative relationship to these archetypes through symbol. In this way, the "inexhaustible energies" of the cosmos can pour into your life and, in so doing, transform you and the world around you.

We will present four archetypes that we hope you will recognize and work with on your journey to life's work. These are the Hero, the Magician, the Warrior, and the Scholar (or Student-Sage). Developing your own symbolic relationship with these archetypes can transform your experience of work (and life). These four archetypes can help us to begin to approach a psychology of work—work as a means of soul development, as well as providing deep insight into the creative process. These archetypes show up all over the place in mythic stories and adventures. Are they the only ones? Of course not. I have found these particular archetypes to be especially useful in creating and executing a life's work. While we might note that they do in some way parallel the four wisdoms of Zen Buddhism (The Great Perfect Mirror Wisdom, The Marvelous Observing Wisdom, The Perfecting-of-Action Wisdom, and The Universal Nature Wisdom),[6] they do not belong to any one tradition but arise, as it were, from life itself. Names for these universal energies vary and are less important than the energies themselves.

Around the world, teachings relating to the four directions or four wisdoms abound. We might mention the four directions of the Native American medicine wheel, the four rivers of the Garden of Eden, the four gardens of the Islamic Paradise, the four sons of Horus in Egyptian mythology, and the four Holy Living Creatures of Ezekiel's vision (eagle, lion, man, bull), often portrayed as the four authors of the gospels in Christian sacred art. Of course, this list is hardly complete; our purpose here is a practical, not a scholarly one. Still, we would be remiss if we did not point out that our presentation only hints at the profound wisdom of the world-wide teachings of the sacred four. Our aim here is to show how we might engage these universal energies in the specific and ongoing process of creating and maintaining a life's work.

Before we look at each of the archetypes in greater detail, we want to emphasize that archetypal energies are simply that—energies. Like the four elements to which they, in some essential way, correspond, these energies may take positive or negative expression. We can experience water as refreshing spring or raging flood, fire, as light and heat or as hellish holocaust. Air can kiss with a cool, gentle breeze or ravage with a mighty cyclone; earth can give the joy of beauty, the bounty of food, or quake with terror and spit molten rock. The value of working deliberately with the archetypes is to move into a conscious and constructive experience of the vital energies they represent. Whether we are aware of it or not, we are all dealing with archetypal energies. In Jungian terms, negative manifestations of archetypal energies result from their denial or suppression and are called shadow aspects. (We will briefly consider the shadow aspects of the four archetypes below under the

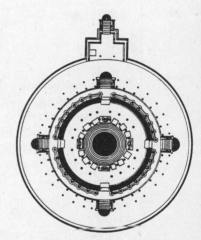

The Universal is always the same, the specifics are always different.

Robert Aitken

Symbols of the Archetypes

Perhaps the best or easiest way to understand the action or function of the archetypes we are referring to is to consider the symbols with which they are often associated.

The Hero

The Seeker of the Grail—The Decider of Roads: Two of the strongest symbols of the Hero are the cup, or Grail, and the road, or path of adventure. The Grail represents the Quest, the Hero as Seeker. It signifies the fullest potential of life, the yearning for one's true life. The road represents choice, the crossroads of decision, the Hero as Decider. What will you give your life for? Whom does the Grail serve? The key for the Hero is consecration to service to humanity. The test is the choice between creative problems and neurotic problems.

The Magician

The Showman—The Shaman: Two of the strongest symbols of the Magician are the mask and the wand. The mask represents the play in illusion, the Showman Magician donning costume and role. The wand represents the mastery of the forces of nature, the Shaman or Master Magician consciously invoking the cosmic powers of Light. The key for the Magician is developing detachment and clear perception. The test is: Are you psyched up or psyched out for the game of life?

The Warrior

The Horseman—The Swordsman: Prime symbols of the Warrior are the horse and the sword. Riding the horse signifies the mastery of the animal nature, or aggressive energy. The Warrior can mount the magic horse of creative aggression and ride like the wind. The Warrior's sword, spear, lance, or arrow is that which penetrates. Penetration is achieved through concentration. The Warrior has developed the power of single-minded concentration. The key for the Warrior is endurance. The test is: Will you persist or give up?

The Scholar (Student-Sage)

The Child—The Old Wise Ones: Two of the strongest symbols for this aspect are the child and the old wise ones or grandparents. The Nativity is a kind of veneration of the child. All hope, potential, growth and learning capacity are there in the child. All the suffering of humanity, and the compassion we feel for all mankind are there in the child. (One who can't feel compassion for children can't feel at all.) The veneration of the old wise ones or grandparents signifies respect for the wisdom tradition. Myths and stories represent the wisdom and knowledge of the old, the continuity of human experience. The key for the Scholar is the heart of intuition. The test is: Are you a steward or owner of knowledge?

headings "Shadow Play.") To help you better understand how these energies are universally active, whether for good or for ill, and to put all of this in a practical context specifically related to your work life, we will briefly (and somewhat oversimply) describe these energies below.

Hero—The Creative Power of Decision: Decision-making is an essential part of human life; no matter what you do, you will always make decisions. The power to decide what to focus on, in other words, the power to decide what is important and the power to decide what you want to create, are basic to the creative life. The decisions you make about your work life are especially important, since most people spend more of their waking lives working than doing anything else. Your choices will affect, not only yourself and those closest to you, but in some way the whole world. The Hero energy is about claiming the decision-making power, being conscious of the decisions you make, and accepting responsibility for them.

Magician—The Creative Power of Imagination: Imagination is an essential part of human life; no matter what you do, your imagination is operative. If imagination is not set to the task of building a creative life, it busies itself with weaving a web of inner fears and doubts, blame, and excuse. How well you use your imagination can be the difference between succeeding and failing in your work. The power to effectively and deliberately activate imagination and the power to receive and interpret the spontaneous promptings of imagination are basic to the creative life. The Magician energy is about embracing imaginative power, being conscious of what your imagination is doing in shaping and responding to the events of your life, and accepting responsibility for how you use this power.

Warrior—The Creative Power of Aggressive Action: Aggressive energy is an essential part of human life; no matter what you do, you will always have aggressive energy. You can use it for good or for ill or deny it altogether in a self-destructive self-abdication—nevertheless, aggressive energy will always be a part of your life. The power to tap the vital pool of aggressive energy and the power to direct this energy towards the accomplishment of constructive purposes is basic to the creative life. It will take the disciplined and concentrated use of aggressive energy to accomplish your life's work. Wimping out or getting bitter or hostile will limit your creative capacity. The Warrior energy is about fully embracing the aggressive power, being conscious of how you are channeling your

aggressive energy, and accepting responsibility for how you use this power.

Scholar—The Creative Power of Learning and Teaching: Learning and teaching are essential to human life; no matter what you do, you will always be learning and teaching something. You can learn about sports or celebrity gossip, about what time various television shows come on, or you can learn about that which, in some way, makes your world a better place. You can, by your example, teach about greed and indifference, derision and confusion, or you can, by example, teach how we can all live together in healthy and beautiful ways. To succeed in the emerging new economy, you will need to become a lifelong learner, and we trust you will want to exemplify whatever is, to you, constructive and uplifting. The Scholar energy is about claiming the learning/teaching power, being fully conscious of what you are learning and teaching, and fully accepting responsibility for how you use this power.

Look within. Within is the fountain of good, and it will ever bubble up, if thou wilt ever dig.
Marcus Aurelius

We can think of the artist of life as the Self, wielding the awesome creative powers of decision-making and imagination, of aggressive action, and the learning/teaching dimension—building a life of beauty on these four pillars. The key is consciousness. As Jung put it, "In the history of the collective, as in the history of the individual, everything depends on the development of consciousness."[7] We encourage you to become conscious of these inner powers and engage them creatively in your own life.

The Hero (The Quest for Life's Work)

Imagine, for example, that in approaching the Quest for life's work, you view, consider, and experience yourself as a hero or heroine tracking a great treasure which, having won, you will bring back for all to see and enjoy. This is an altogether, qualitatively different experience from "looking for a good job" or "finding a niche" or "discovering how to have it all." You are a Parzival or Dante, a Psyche or Penelope. However you frame it or name it, you are a hero—moving into the field of questing—following your bliss. You frame your experience, in this case your searching and questioning, not as that of a confused and pathetic groper who doesn't know what to do but as a Hero on a Quest.

The Seeker of the Grail

You can tell when people are just going through the motions in their work and when they are putting their whole selves into it. The people who can put their whole selves into their work are the ones who have put their whole selves into the Quest to find it—and who keep questing the whole of their lives. It's an unfolding process, a marvelous, never-ending path of discovery. One reason people remain in untenable work situations (or any untenable situation, for that matter) is because they put a negative frame around the process of questioning, of seeking, of looking for a better way. They view self-questioning as a sign of weakness, rather than as an essential element of the creative life.

The Hero is comfortable with not knowing, and yet he is not willing to tolerate confusion. His comfort with not knowing gets him going on the Quest; his unwillingness to tolerate confusion keeps him going until he has answers that ring true *for him*. In every invention, every creative work of art, every advancement in scientific understanding, there is experienced, at some point, the tension between not knowing and not accepting confusion. This creative discontent is beautifully expressed in the following quote from Einstein: "The years of searching in the dark for a truth that one feels but cannot express, the intense desire and the alternations of confidence and misgiving, until one breaks through to clarity and understanding, are only known to him who has himself experienced them." This is hero stuff—seeking and searching for a better way.

Think of how embarrassed the average person, especially male, is with not knowing what he is going to do next. While the artist of life is comfortable with "I don't know yet; I am still seeking, probing, searching," the average Joe thinks he must have all the answers right away, even before he has seriously asked the questions. He dreads the uncomfortable space of not knowing and seeking and so clings to something pat—in other words, to something he has been told and has accepted without examination.

Of course, in addition to the "know-it-alls" with the quick answers, there are those who have simply given up on seeking, and accept confusion or muddling as a sort of "natural order of things." They have resigned themselves to not knowing and have given up the Quest. Their "not knowing" isn't a matter of having yet to find an answer. Indeed, they shape no question. Confusion hangs over them, an amorphous and ubiquitous black cloud of doubt and

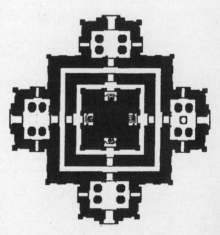

Be patient toward all that is unresolved in your heart And try to love the questions themselves.

Rainer Maria Rilke

The hero's will is not that of his ancestors nor of his society, but his own. This will to be oneself is heroism.

Ortega y Gassett

despair. The "know-it-all" tends toward defensiveness; the resigned, toward depression. The true Hero (or Heroine, if you prefer) has the gonads to ask the really big questions, questions like: Who am I? and What in the world am I doing here?—and to stay with them.

The Hero as seeker decides what to focus on, in other words, what is important. He is the philosopher or contemplative, exercising judgment in making value choices. George Bernard Shaw said of the creative process, "You imagine what you desire; you will what you imagine; and at last you create what you will." Desire begins the creative process, setting imagination and will to work. The Hero's seeking informs desire—before he wants, he asks what to want. He recognizes that we tend to desire what we focus our attention on, and that what we focus on is often more someone else's doing than our own. Parents, teachers, television programmers, movie producers, newspaper editors, etc., select what we focus on, and in so doing, shape our desires. The Hero decides for himself what to focus his attention on (what is important), and in so doing, what the story of his life will be about.

Man's activity consists in either a making or doing. Both of these aspects of the active life depend for their correction upon the contemplative life (that is, the Hero).

Ananda K. Coomaraswamy

Many of us first contact this seeking aspect of the Hero in our youth. Sometime in our late high school or early college years, a lot of us begin to reflect on the values and philosophies that our society represents and the directions we would like to take in our own lives. We are young and idealistic and not yet heavily invested in the status quo. Exposure to history, anthropology, sociology, art, mythology, literature, and philosophy, etc., teaches us that ours is not the only way to organize this thing called human society. We begin to see more clearly the nature of our particular culture from the reference point of others.

The realization of choice and the potential for change hit us like a bolt of lightning—the way we do it in this society is *not* the only way. There are many ways. There is nothing sacrosanct about the choices we have made—as individuals or collectively. We understand that many options are open to us now, and they always will be. We are exposed to so many ideas, values, choices. We become more sophisticated. We may even come to realize that "social reality" exists only because people agree to it and only for as long as they agree to it. Likewise, we may realize our individual "reality" is plastic stuff, shaped by the questions we make important. We realize we have choice.

About the time we are really getting into all this, we are faced with the fact that our college days will soon be history. Now it's time to go out into the "real world." "Real" here, of course, means sanctioned, socially approved of, conventional, having no more or less reality than any other social order—past, present, or possible. The "real" world of today's Western society may not adequately represent values you identified with in your youthful philosophical search or may emphasize others that you would not choose. But now, all of a sudden: *Nobody's asking what you think, Buster.*

It's time to get a job. Time to forget all that stuff about choices. Don't think about visions or values. Don't concern yourself with whys. Just be responsible (sic) and concentrate on how you can get the "best" job. Suppress your awareness of yourself as an observer and creator of social reality and plunge into playing the game as it is already defined, with your eyes closed. We have seen other ways. We are aware of choice, and yet if we are to be "respectable" citizens, we must try to forget. Be a good kid now and get yourself heavily involved in the game of winning social approval—anything else and you risk the label "irresponsible." That's enough to keep most of us in line for a long time. We still think about these things—now and then. We may talk about it late at night, some weekend over a few beers. We may bore our children with repeated tellings of stories about the good old days of our freedom (of choice). What was questing, searching, evaluating now gets stuffed, shelved, and compartmentalized—but make no mistake; it is not dead. It is only sleeping.

Once we see the light of choice, we must put on blinders in order to go back to sleep. The trouble is, we put these blinders on by choice and in awareness of the choice. We will go along, though we know the emperor has no clothes. This makes it difficult to fall into a really deep sleep. It is more of a waking trance. We may struggle to keep our eyes closed, but from time to time, the light gets in anyhow. Its perception reminds us of how alienated we feel, mostly from ourselves. Whatever happened to all those choices, all those possibilities? Now everything seems set in stone, and we are quickly turning into stone. Of course, whether you've gotten off the trail a bit or are just taking it up for the first time, it's never too late for questing.

Awaken the Hero. Don't be afraid to seek, to ask questions, or to stay with it until you have answers that really work for you. In Norse mythology, the first human was named *Ask*. Asking ques-

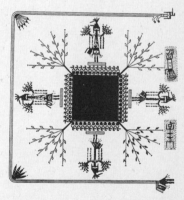

I was so full of sleep at the time that I left the true way.

Dante

*Questions are the
creative acts
of intelligence.*

Frank Kingdon

tions is the first distinction between humans and the rest of life. Humans ask. Most only ask what they are told to ask. The Hero asks his or her own questions. We will invite you to embody the Hero as Quester as you move through the self-examining questions in "Act I: The Quest for Life's Work."

The Decider or Chooser of Roads

As well as the quester or questioner, the Hero is the inner King or Queen, the chooser, the decider, the one who gives directions, who sets the life course. This is the aspect of Hero as the conscience, deciding the right things to do; in the Buddhist tradition, it is called *buddhi*, or discriminative will. The Hero bravely ventures into the dark forest of the unknown, and once, through great effort, he comes to see the light, he is determined to live by the light he sees. Because his vision, or clarity, is hard won, he is not easily dissuaded from his insights. Homer describes the Hero when he says, "What he greatly thought he nobly dared."

Life is either a daring adventure or it is nothing.
Helen Keller

The Hero is the chooser at the crossroads of life. He admits that he and we together always have a choice and that he and we are always responsible for what is chosen. The first choice of the Hero is the choice to be one, to live a life dedicated to full consciousness and responsibility. The Hero exercises the judgment that selects out what is worthy of his or her time, attention, and energy, that is, worthy of his or her life. *To choose a life direction is the Hero's greatest choice.* Even those who claim not to be making decisions but living according to the intuitions of poetic or Divine grace made a choice at some point to seek the intuitive life and must continually decide to act upon or ignore the promptings of intuition. In any case, the Hero's life course is never merely random or automatic. He chooses to be conscious of the choices he makes and accepts full responsibility for the same. He knows that the greater his awareness, the better the choices he will make.

While our culture honors the executive function (Warrior), we hardly recognize, let alone honor, the Hero as seeker and decider of roads. We have so many rushing about—busy doing this and that, but few who have deeply considered the direction they want to move in, either as individuals or as humankind. Together we crash about like a giant headless horseman, hardly aware of where we are going or the effect we are having on the world around us. The Hero is the one who sets the direction for the Warrior (and the rest). The warrior energy of the unprincipled and undirected nowhere man is ripe for the plucking and can be, and so often is, manipulated for all kinds of foolishness. In this, we can wonder with Shakespeare at "what men do daily not knowing what they do." We have been told over and again that it takes courage to be a warrior, and surely it is so, but it takes even more courage to be a Hero—to, as Thales said, "Know thyself."

The Hero's motivation is love, compassion—something bigger than him- or herself. Inspired and nourished by the great mythic themes, his life is transformed so fundamentally, so radically, that without anything changing—everything seems to have changed. The suffering he experiences is no longer personal suffering but human suffering. The work that he does is no longer personal work but humanity's work. The energies that he employs are no longer mere personality traits but aspects of great mythological archetypes.

When we quit thinking primarily about ourselves and our own self-preservation, we undergo a truly heroic transformation of consciousness.
                                    Joseph Campbell

The Hero as chooser is the one who decides what to create, to build, to make. The Hero is the inner king or queen setting the agenda for the other creative powers, commanding them to work his visions into reality. In relation to the other archetypes, the Hero is first among equals. We cannot be artists of life without the courage to seek and the courage to stand by our insights. Likewise, the Magician, the Warrior, and the Scholar all serve the life directions set forth by the Hero. For this reason, we will discuss the Hero at length in the next chapter.

Shadow Play: The shadow hero is the nowhere man, without conscience, direction, or personal integrity, "the little king." The Hero is decided, and the first decision, as we will discuss, is to live, to say yes to life. The nowhere man is indecisive. He doesn't know who he is, what he wants, or where he is going. The nowhere man thinks: It's a beautiful day, someone paid me a compliment, it's payday, I like to live. Life is good. But the next day, it's raining, he feels his aches and pains a little more acutely, the dog does doo on his morning newspaper, and the boss is upset. So he thinks: I hate

All truth is an achievement. If you would have truth at its value, go win it.

T. T. Munger

life; it's a terrible thing that I'm being forced to endure. His days go on like this, a virtual rollercoaster of elation and depression. That is why he's called the nowhere man.

The Magician (The Game of Life's Work)

Once the Hero has, through searching and self-examination, determined a direction or outcome he would like to pursue, he hands the project over to the Magician. The inner Hero says, Imagine this! and the inner Magician goes to work making a mental mock-up of the result. The Magician is the ruler of the i•Magi•Nation. The true Magi, or Magicians, are those who have mastered the creative powers of the imagination. Of course, the inner Magician, or imagination, is active, whether it is under the directorship of the conscious Hero or in the muddled command of the nowhere man. Depending on who is in charge, the magician is a powerful, creative ally, a pesky nuisance, or a positively dangerous foe.

The true Magician makes her magic in accord with the Hero's directions and as a reflection of the poetic view of life. She plays out the ritual game of career, puts on costume and mask, and wields the secret knowledge of her craft. She knows there is magic in making, in creating. In ancient times, gods or magical rites were associated with all the crafts: cooking, weaving, metallurgy, healing, writing, dance, theater, leadership, farming, architecture, carpentry, music, oratory, history, etc. In ancient Hawaii, the craft masters were called *Kahunas* and were honored as spirit masters of their arts.

Artist! You are a magician: Art is the great miracle.
Péladan

Cosmic Theater: The Great Magic Show

Theater and stagecraft have a kind of magic in their capacity to create and pull us into a world of illusion. East Indian cosmology views the world, indeed the entire material creation, as a kind of giant cosmic theater—the *lila,* or play, of creation in the realm of *maya* or illusion.[8] Shakespeare gives us a similar notion in his "All the world's a stage, and all the men and women merely players." Our word *illusion* originates from the Latin *illudere*, literally "to play on."[9] Illusion is what we play on and in.

If you go to a Hollywood set and see the illusion of a town created by a series of storefronts, you know it is not a "real" town, yet the storefronts are made of "real" stuff—boards and nails. The appearance of a town is an illusion, but that with which the illusion is built is real. Likewise, Hindu cosmology tells us that the appearance of the world around us is an illusion, a stage set, but that this set is made of real stuff. We individually and collectively shape the real stuff of the universe into its many appearances through the power of imagination. The inner life of the imagination holds a power we must face and learn to use constructively or risk individual and collective destruction.

> *We are what we think. All that we are arises with our thoughts. With our thoughts we make the world.*
> *Buddha*

The Showman and His Box of Magic Props

The Magician is always dealing with illusion and perception. The showman Magician knows how the illusion of magic is created. If you do a sleight of hand trick with me and I say, "Wow, that's magic!" you don't think to yourself, I really made the ball or quarter disappear. You know how the trick is done. For one not to be fooled by illusion, he must first be disillusioned; that is, he must see how the trick is done. This is when, as Alan Watts said, the life of Zen begins.[10] If you need to be somebody special or always on top, if it matters too much to you what people think or you're ashamed of this or that, then you're ready to be tricked. Before you can be a real Magician, you must first become disillusioned with all of that. (See "Playing the Game: Winners, Losers, and Choosers," page 250.) When we understand that we are not these egos or *persona* masks that we pretend to be, we are freer to play with the illusion stuff of ego and personality—freer to play the Magician.

Where we encounter ceremony, rituals, secrets, the psychic—be it the psyche-up or the psyche-out—this is the realm of the Magician. We may think of magic as a bygone relic from an ancient time, dominated by superstition and the fear of ghosts. Still, we can recognize magical elements in a host of rituals that populate modern life. For example, why does the judge still wear the black robe? (Or in England or South Africa, the robe and the wig?) What practical purpose do these serve? Perhaps the donning of the ceremonial costume is meant to impress upon the minds of the participants that this is no mere mortal but one possessed of some supernatural wisdom, one sanctioned with the power to determine the fates of other's lives. Why do we still wear the cap and gown at

> *Men are so simple and yield so readily to the desires of the moment that he who will trick will always find another who will suffer himself to be tricked.*
>
> *Machiavelli*

graduation, white at weddings, or black at funerals? We have some sense of these events as magic rituals.

The Magician uses tools such as ritual, costume, space, language, number, symbol, suggestion, and visualization to make his art. Below we will consider how a few of these elements of magic affect our lives today. Space requires that we be brief. The purpose of this discussion is simply to stimulate an awareness of the magic all around us, and how we might perhaps better use this magic for the good of all.

The Magic of Ritual: In business, the "power lunch" is a ritual. The handshake is said to have developed as a means of showing no weapon; the wine-tasting ritual, as a means of discovering whether or not the vino was poisoned. Why do we still carry our important papers about in animal skins or wear hides on our feet and around our waists? Surely there is some old animal magic in this. The animal trophies that hang in the men's club, the bar, or the executive's office or "den" are supposed to confer some magic power to their owners.

The Magic of Costume: Today men wear the suit and tie uniform. Prior to the French Revolution, men's dress was more varied and, certainly amongst the well-to-do, much more colorful, ornate, and elegant. The infatuation with Roman law, custom, and culture that attended the French Revolution produced the stoic military-like costume of the suit and tie. Putting on the suit and tie is a ritual that affects body carriage, speech, and ways of relating. When a group of men in this attire change to, say, tennis clothes at a resort or country club, different manners of speech, movement, and interaction are immediately apparent. To appreciate the real power of this magic, imagine men the world over forsaking the suit for more comfortable or colorful clothing. This alone would change the world.

The Magic of Space: Territorial boundaries—the corner office, the physical and people barriers that separate the "big man" from the rest—these are the magic of space. In the fifties, the key to the executive washroom was a status symbol. For the lower echelons, a reserved parking space indicates that they have "arrived." The perquisites of limousine rides, private yachts, and Lear jets all reflect a kind of magic in one's ability to use and control space. Certainly one hundred years ago, flying across oceans would have been considered magic. Any physical space that impresses people to the point where they forget themselves is magical use of space. Bankers, for example, use this magic when they give their buildings the appearance of imposing temples. The Chinese practiced an ancient art known as *Feng Shui*. Its purpose was to use and arrange space so as to effect a harmonious environment. They knew that use of space could create good or bad magic.

The Magic of Language: Most professions have their own secret language. Why do doctors still write prescriptions in Latin? Why are legal terms loaded with French and Latin? Why are fraternities "Greek"? Some special terms are necessary to distinguish fine points of difference; most are simply code words designed to make the initiated unintelligible to the masses. The plaques, diplomas, or certifications on the wall usually indicate initiation into some secret society and its language.

The Magic of Number: The magic squares and formulas of the alchemist may seem foolish to some today, and yet how are skyscrapers, nuclear bombs, or ocean tankers designed? With magical lines and numbers, geometry and mathematics, the great buildings, machines, and implements of war and peace take shape in this world.

The Magic of Symbol: Corporations spend millions in designing and projecting a corporate logo because they understand the power of symbol. Reebok's use of the Union Jack, Chrysler's use of the five-pointed star, or Safeway's use of the *Tai Chi* (Supreme Ultimate) are hardly accidental. The Great Seal of the United States of America is a kind of super symbol loaded with ancient symbols. The swastika, ancient symbol of life, has come to be so closely associated with the Nazis that today many cannot look at it without feeling fear, horror, and dread.

The Magic of Suggestion: Advertising uses the magic of suggestion in the barrage of commercials that we are all subjected to. Those who fear the influence on society of violent television and movies fear their suggestive power. The news media are using a kind of suggestive power in what they select out as the important issues of life. Peer pressure and association have suggestive power. It is well known that people tend to become like the people they associate with. Parents who tell their children that they are stupid or will never amount to anything, or the individual who tells himself, "I will succeed"—each is using the power of suggestion.

The Magic of Visualization: In recent years, the dramatic results achieved by top flight athletes and by health practitioners have convinced all but the most closed-minded skeptics of the power of visualization to effect results. A growing list of books, such

You can't depend on your judgment when your imagination is out of focus.

Mark Twain

as *Mental Training for Peak Performance* by Steven Ungerleider,[11] detail the improvements in performance achieved by Olympic athletes and others who practice visualization. Dr. Bernie Siegel and others in the medical field have reported on scores of seemingly miraculous recoveries effected by those who use visualization as a major component of their healing process.[12] If the power of visualization can actually increase the weight Olympic weight-lifters can lift or reduce the size of cancerous tumors, it can certainly be a powerful tool in creating the results you want to effect in your life. (See page 568.)

So many elements of the magic show are designed to psyche people out. The business man wooing a major client takes him out on his private yacht, into his field of magic power. He romances the client with the banquet, the music, the lights on the water, the powerful or beautiful people he surrounds himself with. He impresses him with the power expressed in his wealth and retinue. The client negotiates away the store and the next day wonders what happened. If you can be impressed, you can be psyched out. Weakness in your magic shows in the ways you can be impressed. When you are impressed, you lose your center, your self. You move into someone else's field—they have and take the power. This is why the Zen *bushido* master says, "Don't show weakness," or the Jedi Warrior Obi-Wan Kenobi says, "Hide your feelings, Luke."[13] Don't let them see you sweat—or too impressed.

Whatever you do to psyche yourself up for the game of life is also a part of your magic. The essence of the psyche-up is to project personal power, magnetic, dynamic energy—in other words, confidence. This confidence, or self-esteem, is conveyed through energy level, strength and tone of voice, posture, and body language.

The Genius, The Shaman, and the Creative Womb of Emptiness

The Chinese sage Lao Tzu tells us that the usefulness of things is in their emptiness. The useful part of the wheel is the hub; the useful part of a pot is the empty space within.[14] Consider the mystery of the seed; throw it in the seemingly empty earth and watch life spring forth from the emptiness. There is mystery, magic, and creative power in the emptiness. Think of the creative artist. She knows that for all her searching, concentrating, and disciplined effort, the really exciting breakthroughs will come as inspirations from the emptiness.

The goal, the Hero's direction, is a seed, a potential; throw it on the emptiness of the imagination. Let imagination show you the way. Learn to trust in its magic subconscious power. Walk in expectancy, looking for signs of its revelations along the way. If we only move into what we are sure we know how to do and are not willing to let imagination show the way, we block our creative potential. The creative life, like the growing of a plant, is a mystery, a surprising unfoldment.

From What-is all the world of things was born
But What-is sprang in turn from What-is-not.
Lao Tzu

In the Indian Vedas, the creative principle of life is imaged as a golden embryo.[15] It is said that the entire manifest universe arises out of the living emptiness of this cosmic womb energy. Every kid in science class is told that nature abhors a vacuum. The Magi creates a magic empty space by drawing a magic circle. Within this vacuum, or empty space, he creates his magic. You can think of your goals as providing the boundaries of a magic circle. Within the empty space of this circle, your imagination or inner magician works to create the outcomes you desire.

The two-headed Janus was the Roman god of doors and gates.[16] Like Janus, the Magician is a two-headed gatekeeper. She looks within and without, guarding the gate between the conscious and subconscious mind. In traditional cultures, a shaman was one who had learned to deliberately and intentionally pass through the gate into the awesome realm of the subconscious and come back again.

A shaman, as defined by Michael Harner in *The Way of the Shaman*, is one who can "contact and utilize an ordinarily hidden reality in order to acquire knowledge, power, and to help other persons."[17] While perhaps not to the same degree or in the same way as the shaman, we can all develop the capacity to contact an "ordinarily hidden reality" and draw from it what will be useful to our daily lives. We're not talking about performing any kind of strange rites, but simply developing the capacity to see that there may be more or less to things than immediately meets the eye. We can learn to, as Plotinus said, "close our eyes and invoke a new manner of seeing."[18]

For example, many Jungians make use of "dream therapy." Through this practice, one learns to read the signs and symbols of the hidden world of dreams with the aim of discovering what the individual subconscious, or even the collective unconscious, might be "saying" at a particular time. Dreams can be a rich source of creative and life-instructing information, insight, and inspiration. To gain real value from our dreams, we must develop the capacity

The faculty of imagination is both the rudder and the bridle of the senses.

Leonardo da Vinci

All poetic inspiration is but dream interpretation.

Hans Sachs

to clearly see and recall our dreams and to consciously interpret their importance.

In the Biblical stories of Nebuchadnezzar and Daniel and of Joseph and the Pharaoh, we see the importance of the interpretative function of dreams. In each case, the King or ruler recalled a dream in precise and graphic detail; yet until he found someone with the insight to interpret the dream for him, the information transmitted through it remained a mystery. This process applies to all information arising from the emptiness of the subconscious mind. Inspiration and insights must be interpreted by the conscious mind to gain full value. This brings us back to the image of Janus looking within the subconscious mind and looking without, interpreting with the conscious mind.

The power to receive and interpret knowledge from the emptiness also recalls the image of the great oracles of Delphi. Like the tribal chiefs and their shamans, the great kings of old relied on Magi, oracles, and astrologers to give them knowledge from the hidden reality. Throughout the stories of world mythology, we see the archetypal Hero receiving aid from the archetypal Magician.

The final aspect of magic that we will consider is the one we are engaged in here, that is, the conscious invocation of the archetypal energies. Every traditional culture uses masks and ritual drama for this purpose. One puts on the masks and becomes the archetypal Warrior or Magician; one moves as the archetypal energy, transcendent to egoic limitation. The great Magicians of old did not view themselves as making magic but rather as evoking natural and metaphysical laws.

Shadow Play: A Magician can be a Magus, a sorcerer, a charlatan, or shyster, depending on the depth of his knowledge and the purity of his motive. The shadow magician is the manipulator, the liar, the conman, the devious scoundrel. If you don't have the Quest, that is, a purpose larger than yourself, you are left with using your magic, your imagination, for less than constructive purposes.

The Warrior (The Battle for Life's Work)

The Hero makes the decision; the Magician develops a plan; the Warrior's job is to carry it out. King Arthur makes a decision, gains magical help from Merlin, and sends his knights out to do his bidding. Without his knights, without his warriors, the King's decisions are meaningless. A king or a queen without warriors to enforce his or her decisions is useless indeed, as King Lear so poignantly learned in Shakespeare's tragedy. The Warrior is the one who gets things done.

As a Warrior, you have a sense of yourself as a champion of your vision, the larger-than-self purpose to which your inner Hero has committed. This becomes your banner, and with it held high, you ride out to slay the dragons of doubt and fear, to defeat the view of life that holds nothing dear. The Warrior starts down this road, inspired and full of optimism—and runs smack into obstacles, blocks, and opposition. These test his character and resolve. They tempt him to forsake his duty (to himself and others) and abandon the vision of his Quest. He battles his own inner doubts as well as the external resistance to making things happen in the real world. Some obstacles threaten, intimidate, or coerce; others seduce, entice, and charm him from his duty. In any case, they prey upon his weakness and tempt him to relent, to give in to the belief that life doesn't make a difference and that choice is not. The Warrior battles the whole of his life, within and without, against the notion that life doesn't make a difference.

Has fear ever held a man back from anything he really wanted, or a woman either?
George Bernard Shaw

The Warrior perseveres in the face of difficulties and doubts. Study the myths of the world, and you will see these things portrayed symbolically. As soon as the Hero gets the call, the obstacles arise, and there's something difficult to do. There are dragons to slay, raging seas to cross, wicked stepmothers to outwit. In other words, there is uncomfortable stuff to do. The minute you answer the Hero's call, the Warrior's tests begin. How you handle these tests will determine whether you will live as a free man, a free woman—or cower in slavish bondage to circumstance.

Riding the Windhorse of Creative Aggression

Now all the Hero wants to do is fulfill his duty; all the Poet wants to do is express her vision of beauty in the world—which are nice things to do. The problem is, if he's too much of a nice guy or she too much of a nice gal, they'll never do them. They start with grand intentions and run smack into obstacles to penetrate, hurdles to jump over, hoops to jump through. He starts to think, Do I really want to do this? She thinks, Is this really important? Good intentions are not enough; commitment and sacrifice are necessary.

Let me not pray to be sheltered from dangers
but to be fearless in facing them.
Let me not beg for the stilling of my pain
but for the heart to conquer it.
Tagore

Warriors actually enjoy discipline, not as something imposed from without, but as an opportunity to live life to the fullest. While the nice guy (wimp) hopes that if he kisses enough rear, somebody will do it for him, the Warrior knows he must rely on himself. Warriors succeed because they have to—because they put themselves in situations that demand their all. True Warriors have the dignity that comes from self-reliance and from having been tested and proven under the fire. Much of the world's great literature and drama have as their action the transformation of the youth (or, if older, the wimp or thug) into the Warrior. A heroic motive, a purpose larger than self, gives the individual the impetus to rely on himself as never before. It is for others that he becomes a stronger, more self-reliant individual and acquires the dignity that all people crave. He rides what the Tibetans call the *windhorse* of dignity, self-respect, and power. He no longer doubts his basic goodness as a human being.

Anyone who proposes to do good must not expect people to roll stones out of his way, but must accept his lot calmly, even if they roll a few more upon it.
Albert Schweitzer

We can think of Warrior energy as penetrating and protecting, piercing barriers and defending boundaries. The Warrior protects life and pierces the boundaries of limitation and stagnation. Both require creative aggression. The Warrior is master of aggressive energy. People with a lot of aggressive energy determine the sociocultural landscape: Those who work for the good make this power serve the heart; those who work for ill, whether consciously or unconsciously, use this power to serve their lower instincts. One way or another, aggression is a part of the human experience.

For many, *aggression* is a bad word. They associate it with violence, cruelty, tyranny, and oppression. Yet aggression—the assertion of power—is required for every creative as well as every destructive act. Concentration is the assertion of a single idea, image, or train of thought to the exclusion of all else. That exclusion is aggressive. Great artists through history have been known for aggressive concentration on their work. One had better not interrupt Beethoven while he is composing or Michelangelo while he is carving. In Tibetan Buddhism, they call this creative tenacity *all-accomplishing wisdom*.

Life is a fight. You must remain concentrated and not reveal your defects; through continuous training and self-control, gradually you discard them.
Taisen Deshimaru

Zen masters have been known to be extremely aggressive in their teaching techniques—hitting, kicking, spitting, throwing things—shocking the student out of his slumber. Jesus was aggressive while confronting the money changers in the temple. Elsewhere he called men vipers, hypocrites, and serpents—aggressive terms, to be sure. Mahatma Gandhi's use of fasting was an aggressive act. He held his own body hostage and threatened to destroy it unless the changes he wanted were adopted. Mother Teresa was aggressive in the demands she made upon the sisters in her order and in fighting for those in her care. If her followers could not accept the strict discipline she imposed—and cheerfully—they were dropped. Martin Luther King, Jr.'s March on Washington was an aggressive act. The point of these examples is simply to demonstrate that Warrior aggression is necessary for positive, creative action and that aggression is not necessarily violent.

The Sword of Present Concentration

From Japanese *bushido*, or "way of the warrior," we can learn three keys for making aggressive energy serve our creative visions: *be present, be concentrated*, and *be strong*.

Be Present: The Warrior is totally alive. He accepts his life and his death. Most people accept neither. They live in terror of death and muddle through life half asleep, scarcely aware of the dangers and opportunities that lie all around them. Native American warriors cried on their way to battle, "Today is a good day to die!" Mohammed said, "Die before ye die."[19] Japanese *bushido* teaches the warrior to be internally dead, meaning *still*. Being dead within, the samurai is completely free to respond—immediately and in all directions—without. The aliveness of the Warrior, his conscious, alert presence, arises from his inner deadness. In Japanese *bushido*, this consciousness is called the *shin,* or "spirit" aspect.

Those who reach greatness on earth reach it through concentration.

Upanishads

Be Concentrated: Then there is the aspect of technique or *wasa*. The essence of technique is concentration. One way of considering the Japanese *Dō's*, e.g., *Aikido, Judo, Kendo* (sword), *Kyudo* (archery), *Chado* (Tea), is as a means of concentrating on a single act. If you can do a single act with total presence, be it wielding a sword, arranging flowers, or serving tea, then this concentrated presence will carry over to other aspects of your life. The person who does things in a sloppy fashion never develops concentration, that is, his or her expression of the Warrior.

Technique is never merely mental. It must become instinctive, immediate, total. The warrior who has to think about what he is doing in combat will soon be dead. If one thinks of his motions in calligraphy, it will come out stiff. If one thinks before he releases the bow, the arrow will miss. Training and technique must become total, must involve the body as well as the mind.

Be Strong: The final aspect is that of strength of body. The Warrior must have a strong body, because he will ask it to do what is contrary, that is, uncomfortable stuff. If your body is weak, it becomes boss. When your body is strong, it obeys the commands of mind and spirit.

It is said, Good technique defeats body strength. Good *shin*, or consciousness, defeats good technique. This is why the old *dō-jo* master in his eighties will whip the strong, young buck every time. The old master has the patience to look for weakness—in Japanese, *suki*, or opportunity. When he sees it, he strikes. The young buck, too eager to attack or too self-conscious, leaves himself open.

Courage is not the absence of fear, but rather the judgment that something else is more important than fear.

Ambrose Redmoon

From the European tradition of the knight, we can learn something about the Warrior's relation to the Poet. Many of the great knights of old practiced what has come to be called "The Art of Courtly Love." Poetry and song were the means through which the knight expressed his love for and dedication to his Lady. Recently, scholars (for example, Frances Gies, *The Knight in History*,)[20] have provided rather convincing evidence that the etiquette of Courtly Love was, in fact, an elaborate ritual filled with spiritual significance—a vehicle for honoring the spirit in the ordinary. In this ritual, both the knight and the lady were playing prescribed, symbolic roles.

The Lady (standing for the knight's True Self) says, "Kill me some dragons." The knight goes out and slays the dragons or defeats the opponents. He comes back all full of himself and thinks, "Ah, what a fine thing I have done." And the Lady says, "Is that all? That's not much. The heroes of old who really loved their Lady did truly great and heroic deeds. Go out and do something really great, and then I'll consider if you're really serious." Even as the knight's Lady taunted her suitor to ever greater heroism, so today we can be inspired by the literature of spirit (mythic and poetic)—spurred and egged on to the Avalon of our Quest. True Warriors endure for Love.

There is nothing stronger in the world than gentleness.

Han Suyin

Shadow Play: The shadow warrior is a mercenary. He might be a hired gun, selling his aggressive energy for the highest ransom or an accommodating lackey, harboring aggression in hopes of ingratiating himself with the powers-that-be. Both the bully and wimp have sold out. The discipline of the Warrior comes in learning to use aggressive energy to serve the inner Hero—that is, a consciously and freely chosen, larger-than-self purpose.

The Scholar (The School of Life's Work)

What we mean by Scholar is not necessarily a bookish fellow with a grey beard. The archetypal Scholars might appear in various cultures as the grandfathers or the grandmothers, the keepers of the knowledge and the wisdom of the people.

I once saw a film about an African family in an arid climate. The grandfather knew the old ways of his people, which had been passed on for thousands of years. His son had a few years of elementary school and began to lose the old ways. The old man's grandson, in turn, went off to the university and knew virtually nothing of the traditional teachings. One day, the grandson arrived at the village with a strange and noisy machine. He was very excited—telling everyone that with this contraption he could find water. There he was bumbling about with this noisy machine, looking quite ridiculous and having little luck besides, when the old grandfather happened onto the scene. "What are you doing?" asked the old man. "Looking for water," came the reply. The old man laughed. He walked out into the desert, and where he saw certain plants, he began to dig. Sure enough, he found water. Now if finding water is important, the old man, who never had a day of schooling in his life, is a better scholar than the university-trained grandson.[21]

This story gives a sense of what we mean by the archetypal Scholar. The Scholars are the knowledge and wisdom keepers of a people, a culture, and of humanity as a whole. *Scholar* is not really a satisfactory word to describe this aspect. In "Act IV," we coin the term *Student-Sage*, which gets closer to the meaning but is a bit clumsy to use. We will use the terms Scholar and Student-Sage interchangeably throughout.

The Hero sets the direction, determining what to create; the Magician develops the plan; the Warrior executes it; the Scholar is the course-correcter. In the learning and teaching or exemplifying capacities, the Scholar keeps one on track. The Scholar learns that which is necessary to advance and keeps an awareness of where one is in the process of creation. The Scholar looks at the situations of life as opportunities to learn and as opportunities to exemplify what she believes in. Recognizing the Scholar in your life comes in the realization that you are learning and teaching twenty-four hours a day.

Of course, true learning is more than collecting and storing data; it is an organic process of self-expansion and discovery. While learning, we grow naturally, as trees expand—in circles of knowledge, wisdom, and ability. To live is to learn. With apologies to Bob Dylan, we can say, "He not busy learning that which betters himself and his world is busy dying."

Likewise, teaching isn't simply passing on a certain body of knowledge—a formal operation we do apart from the rest of our lives. First and foremost, we teach by example. In the way we live our lives, we are teaching about what we think is important and valuable. Whether we choose to exemplify the selfish, the mediocre, or the indifferent or to take a creative approach to life, we are constantly teaching. The Scholar recognizes that just as she is teaching others, others are teaching her. As a wise friend of mine often says, "Some people are teaching you where it's at; some are teaching you where it's not at."

The Scholar includes both what Blake called "The Wisdom of Innocence" and "The Wisdom of Experience." In myth, this archetype presents itself in images such as the Divine Child, or Innocent, and as the Old Wise Man, the Crone, or the Wise Old Grandmothers. (The two in one nature of this archetype is expressed in mythic figures such as Pluto, who is represented as a bearded, wise old man or as a playful youth.) The special relationship of children and grandparents represents the two aspects of this learning-teaching archetype we call the Student-Sage. The child represents the learning or growth potential within us, the grandparent, the tested wisdom of experience. In traditional cultures, the older people pass their knowledge to the younger through a kind of hands-on apprenticeship and through storytelling. We will first consider apprenticeship and then the storytelling aspect.

Your motive in working should be to set others, by your example, on the path of duty.

Bhagavad-Gita

The Student: Child Apprentice, Beginner's Mind

Apprenticeship is the way of learning with love. Think of times when you learned something one-on-one: your mother taught you how to cook, or your father taught you how to play baseball or to do some kind of handiwork, or maybe a friend taught you how to play jacks or do a new dance step. Recall the sweetness of this. Learning in the physical presence of the one who teaches you to do the thing— this is a tender and beautiful experience. You always feel sort of like a child when you are learning from someone who loves you. Now imagine if someone taught you to do your work in this way, not hovering over you constantly, but from time to time being there, physically present, showing you. The important thing is that learning come with love, in a spirit of goodwill and rapport.

If you go to work for a corporation and they give you a "video orientation," then perhaps someone to watch over you, you don't experience this sense of the apprenticeship. You're probably a bit suspicious of the watcher's motives. You may think of them (and perhaps with good reason) not as a friendly and supportive *mentor* but as a sort of *monitor,* sent to keep you in line or to catch you screwing up. The difference between a monitor and a mentor is the human element, caring for the person as a person and not simply as a "worker." Corporations, bureaucracies of every kind, encourage people to act as monitors, not mentors. Of course, there are outstanding exceptions, but mentoring is not standard practice.

...Without love the acquisition of knowledge only increases confusion and leads to self-destruction.

J. Krishnamurti

Beyond encouraging people to act like machines, bureaucratic systems tend to reduce knowledge to bits of information with all the humanity blanched out. This reductionism has gone hand in hand with the move in recent years toward automated instruction. We will miss something profound if we attempt to teach people solely from computers, video screens, or audio tapes. Something about the human presence itself is vital to passing on the wisdom-knowledge of humankind. People taught only by machines will become machines. People taught by loving humans will become loving humans.

In addition to the move from mentoring to monitoring and automated instruction, there is pervasive emphasis in our society on the cramming-to-learn method of instruction. Of course, this is hardly new. Followers of Confucius stressed the importance of an exacting study of the Confucian and earlier Chinese classics. Systems of examination were eventually established to recognize those who excelled in such study. Since the successful completion of the examinations was necessary to virtually every position of responsibility or standing, students became more concerned with passing tests than with penetrating to the essence of the knowledge.

*Is not indeed every
man a student, and
do not all things
exist for the
student's behoof?*

Emerson

Systems of examination, originally designed to foster understanding, became perverted from a means to an end. Finding people more concerned with passing tests than with penetrating to understanding should not surprise us today. It has been around for at least a thousand years.[22]

The reductionist approach and emphasis on testing tends further to select out those knowledges that admit to objective examination and to ignore more subjective subjects—the kind that involve value choices, for example. Wisdom cannot be reduced to informational bits and bytes that can be programmed into people or scored according to nationally standardized measures. In the time-honored tradition of the crafts, even the most practical knowledges of weaving or stone masonry, candle making or cloth spinning were taught in a spirit of love and wisdom. When teaching is happening with love, more than knowledge is being shared. Something indescribable, yet immensely important, transfers from the one to the other. If we are to be good Student-Sages, then this is our way through life: receiving this "human substance," along with knowledge, as students and giving it, along with knowledge, as teachers or sages.

The Sage: Grandmother and Grandfather Story

In addition to, and often as a part of, apprenticeship, traditional cultures transmitted wisdom-knowledge through storytelling, song, dance, theater, visual art, etc.—but principally, storytelling. Dance, art, and music, as much as the spoken word, were means of telling a story, the story of a particular people, the story of their god, the story of their origin, the way they came to be the way they are. The Sage knows stories: her own story, the story of her people, the story of humanity, perhaps even the story of life itself. She has a sense of being a trustee, a steward, and a record keeper, part of an unbroken line extending back and forward, honoring those who have gone before and feeling profound responsibility for those yet to come.

The world is our school for spiritual discovery.
Paul Brunton

Today we are story starved, hungry for stories that will feed our souls. Oh, we have plenty of stories. We consume more stories than any people in human history. Television sitcoms, cops and robbers "dramas," formula movies full of violence, and escapist fantasies, romance, and spy novels are cranked out by their respective "industries" like so many widgets at the factory. But it's a hollow diet. Most of these stories lack spiritual nutrition—confidence, direction, insight, and inspiration. It isn't just pop culture—the stories of many of our "serious writers" are equally devoid of soul food. As with junk foods, we can consume these stories in great quantities and remain malnourished. The Scholar respects the art of story telling. She knows that stories, from children's nursery rhymes to the most serious novels and everything in between, make a profound difference in the lives of individuals and in the character of a society. Whether we want to admit it or not, stories, all stories, teach values in a uniquely powerful way—by giving them life in our imaginations.

Myth, legend, drama, ritual, dance, art, in addition to whatever else they may be, are vehicles for carrying profound knowledge about the human experience. They can teach us about what it means to be human and about the wide range of creative living strategies humankind has developed over many thousands of years. The Chinese poet Lu Chi, in his classic *Wen Fu (The Art of Writing)*, instructs on the importance of honoring the old wise ones. "Learn to recite the classics, sing in the clear virtue of ancient masters," and "There are no new ideas, only those which rhyme with certain classics."[23] In the West we have, "There is nothing new under the sun." The new that doesn't rhyme with the best of the old cannot be said to be wise. As Aquinas said, "All that is true, by whomsoever it has been said, has its origin in the Spirit."[24]

We began this chapter with a discussion of a mythic approach to life—viewing your life as a story of an encounter of the universal in the everyday. The Sage aspect of the Scholar is that which has a sense of where you are in the story of your life. Her insight gives continuity and meaning to the events of your life. Her long-term perspective and detachment encourage the Scholar as student to learn that which will enrich and better her own life and that of all mankind. In this we have a kind of closure, the completing of a cycle begun by the Hero as seeker or Quester. The Hero is shaking things up, questing, seeking, moving into the unknown, until direction is found. The Sage aspect of the Scholar brings the opportunity to examine whether or not one is, in fact, exemplifying what she determined to do as the Hero. She considers the lessons learned and yet to be learned on the journey through life.

Shadow Play: The shadow scholar uses knowledge for his own ego and sense gratification. He is an opportunist who, without conscience or compassion, sells his knowledge to the highest bidder. He reasons that the labors of his studies have earned him an expertise that he now "owns" as a kind of personal commodity to trade as he

逢磨元来觀自在

Education is not filling a bucket but lighting a fire.

William Butler Yeats

wills. The ramifications that this "trading" has on the world at large don't concern him. Further, he lacks a sense of story in his life—and the wisdom and the patience that this engenders.

Working with the Archetypes

Jung repeatedly emphasized that for the individual to gain real value in working with the archetypes—emotional involvement is critical. Archetypes are not merely dead images. "They are living pieces of life itself—images that are integrally connected to the individual by the bridge of the emotions." He stresses that it is "by being charged with emotion [that] the image gains numinosity (or psychic energy)…"[25] Active engagement with the archetypes intensifies our experience of life—moving us out of the mundane, drab, half-asleep life, into the wide awake intensity of life lived full on. Nothing is as intense as play. Constructively engaging the archetypes in a spirit of play energizes and intensifies life to a surprising degree. It's as though you plugged yourself into a great psychic energy amplifier.

> *It is a myth, not a mandate, a fable not a logic, and symbol rather than a reason by which men are moved.*
> *Irwin Edman*

You might, in reading myth or in seeing plays or films that draw on mythic images, experience yourself embodying these energies. Recently a friend remarked, "I studied psychology for years, but I get more uplift and inspiration from a movie like *Star Wars*—more applied, effective psychology than I ever got at school." While her study of psychology dealt in dry theories and "controlled experiments," the images from the film touched her emotions. The imaginative power of her subconscious mind was effectively and powerfully engaged. Joseph Campbell said of myth, "Once this subject catches you, there is such a *feeling* . . . of information of a deep, rich, *life-vivifying* sort that you don't want to give it up."[26] [Emphasis added.] As my friend sourced on these images (for example, the archetypal warrior battling the dehumanizing forces of darkness), she began to feel herself embodying that archetypal energy. She was, in effect, playing, moving, experiencing in a different world, a world of her own creation. It was no longer life as television, something to passively observe and critique, but an interactive experience of the inner world of the imagination and the outer world of events.

I think that what we're seeking is an experience of being alive, so that our life experiences on the purely physical plane will have resonances within our own innermost being and reality, so that we actually feel the rapture of being alive.

Joseph Campbell

In the experience of life as television, one is a passive *tabula rasa* on which things happen. He is not living in a world of his own creation but a world made and controlled by ambivalent or even hostile forces beyond his reach. He feels alienated from and overwhelmed by this world. The artist of life is imaginatively engaged in the world around him. He accepts it as the setting, the backdrop on which the story of his life is being played out. He is creatively engaged in his life—using imagination to shape events and imaginatively responding to events. The victories and the obstacles, the angels and devils of his inner and outer life—all are elements of the story of his life—a story he is simultaneously writing and acting in.

History is a nightmare from which I am trying to awake.

James Joyce

Around the Wheel

The Poet doesn't tell his story. He tells The Story. The Story is the encounter of the individual with the universal. Great literature, whether intended or not, has a mythic or poetic dimension. We understand that it is not a story about an individual, that is, a history; it is a story of an encounter of the individual with the universal, that is, a poetry. If the spiritual or poetic life is the capstone of human experience, then the foundation on which this capstone rests is the four wisdoms. Similarly, if the poetic center is the source of all great inspiration, then these four aspects are the vehicles through which the inspiration becomes manifest.

Around the world, all who teach the sacred four indicate that we must pass through all four directions—that we must develop ourselves in all four aspects if we are to be complete and balanced human beings. Ask yourself: What kind of Hero am I? What kind of Magician? What kind of a Warrior am I? What kind of Scholar? By the strength of your Hero, your Magician, your Warrior, and your Scholar, you are able to do or not.

Even if we cannot yet hear the voice of the heart, the direct intuition of the Poet, we can, in the meantime, be developing as Heroes, Magicians, Warriors, and Scholars. We can, as Heroes, learn to respect the dictates of our conscience and develop our

All wrong-doing arises because of mind. If mind is transformed can wrong-doing remain?

Buddha

volitional will, the capacity to decide without vacillation. We can, as Magicians, creatively direct imaginative power and develop the ability to see the soul or inner meaning of things. We can, as Warriors, develop the alertness, concentration, and strength of endurance we will require, should we ever be fortunate enough to hear the voice of the Muse. We can, as Scholars, grow in learning and teaching that which is life-preserving and affirming. By consciously making all we make—we make ourselves ready to hear the voice of the heart.

Light on the Shadows

It is clear to many of us that the world is in critical need of change if we are even to survive on this planet. But how to change? Jung points out that our typical idea of change is to blame others or the "system." He goes on, "It would be much more to the point for us to make a serious attempt to recognize our own shadow and its nefarious doings. If we could see our shadow (the dark side of our nature), we should be immune to any moral and mental infection and insinuation."[27] In other words, learning to recognize our own shadow inoculates us from the destructive elements of the collective unconscious and mass culture. It is an individual process, indeed an individuating process: it takes the courage to face one's dark side.

He then learns that in going down into the secrets of his own mind he has descended into the secrets of all minds.

Emerson

As I become more aware of these archetypal energies, I must be willing to admit that I am largely an effect of life-controlling decisions which I have made and for which I am responsible but of which I am now hardly aware. I must be willing to recognize that much of my imagined freedom is not conscious choice but slavish obedience to the compulsions and constraints of repressed memory, collective and individual. I must be willing to recognize where I am using the creative powers of my imagination, not as an artist creating a life of beauty, but as a kind of black magician—conjuring demons and monsters in thoughts of fear and guilt, jealousy and revenge, destruction and injury. I must be willing to recognize within myself the dark warrior whose undisciplined and unfocused aggression wreaks havoc and destruction, turning green fields to barren wastelands. I must be willing to face that I may be using the knowledge of my craft, or any knowledge for that matter, for destructive or indifferent aims.

Only if I am willing to conceive of myself as a slave to conditioned habit, to infantile and unexamined choice, will the possibility of acting as a true Hero, a conscious quester and chooser, become a viable option. Only as I am willing to conceive of myself as having an imagination populated, and even dominated, by forces from the psychic underworld does the possibility of being a true Magician arise. Only if I am willing to conceive of myself as a destructive warrior, abusing the aggressive energy of life or bottling it up in self-destructive and world-polluting stagnation, can I possibly become a true Warrior—a brave and gentle knight. Only if I am willing to conceive of myself as playing the whore with the knowledge I possess, selling it for destructive or indifferent aims, can I become a true Scholar.

- Right now, are my choices conscious or automatic? Do I accept my responsibility for life, that is, my choices, or do I seek to escape?

- Right now, in this instant, is my imagination creating beauty or destruction?

- Right now, in this moment, is my aggressive energy serving a higher purpose, or is it stagnating or openly destructive?

- Right now, in this instant, is my knowledge serving the greater good, or is it unused or abused?

In earlier times, working with these energies was something that was done in community. Today we are left to work these things out on our own. As we said earlier, part of your magic lies in your capacity to consciously invoke these energies into your life. In the process, you might create your own dramas, rituals, and creative relationships to symbol. If you enjoy writing, you might write your autobiography—your life journey or story—from the standpoint of your relationships with these energies. This can be an illuminating process and is only one example of the many ways you can begin to creatively engage these energies.

We have organized the remainder of this book around the themes of the Quest, the Game, the Battle, and the School of Life's Work. The four archetypes (Hero, Magician, Warrior, Scholar) correspond to these four "Acts" of Life's Work. Of course, these energies do not fit into neat little compartments or categories; they show up all over the place. The point of suggesting correspondences

"What is the path?" the Zen Master Nan-sen was asked. *"Everyday life is the path,"* he answered.

is simply to show which energies predominate at each point. We promised a book on life's work, and we can easily see that these are energies that we will, in one way or another, work with for the rest of our lives. In the next chapter, we will look more closely at the Hero. Remember, the Hero is first among equals, the inner director, or chooser of roads.

It doesn't happen all at once . . . You become. It takes a long time.

Margery Williams

Zen, Myth, and Symbol

The Zen insight was historically and is today—directness. The Indian pantheon of innumerable Gods, demons, demigods, titans, and celestial beings was rejected by Buddhism generally, and especially Zen, in favor of direct pointing. Zen Buddhism is extremely sparse in its use of images and icons. Zen is always reminding us that *the finger is not the moon;* the symbol is not the reality it points at.

While perhaps not as elaborately as the Indian, the Western tradition also relies heavily upon symbolic representations. A Western artist might use the sun to represent immortality, divine light, the logos, etc. A tree might represent fulfillment, the fruits of labor, the paradisiacal realm, the fall, etc. For Zen, sun is sun, tree is tree, rain is rain, flower is flower. The emphasis is not on the thing as a stand-for-symbol but on its "suchness."

Koans are the folk stories of Zen Buddhism, metaphorical narratives that particularize essential nature.
Robert Aitken

Yet even anti-symbolic, anti-mythological Zen is stuck with symbols and a mythological tradition. The Zen tradition is communicated through the sutras and through stories about Zen masters and their encounters with students, ordinary people, and everyday life. The primary symbol employed is the word: the sutras, the stories, the *koans*, the *mondo* (questions and answers). There are stories of Zen masters tearing up the scriptures, but to be sure, they missed a few, for many have survived. Zen texts and stories often remind one to regard the ancients and the sutras. Apparently it's best not to tear up the sutras until you see the moon.

When Buddha was enlightened, the first thing that he reportedly said was, "This cannot be taught." In other words, "This cannot be communicated through symbol." Yet pointing at the moon is not altogether a futile activity. For without this pointing, we might never know that there is something to experience. The scriptures and the sages in their communications, the artists in their representations, are all saying: There is something to EXPERIENCE! Anyone interested in the welfare of humanity must be interested in symbols and myths, for it is by these that we communicate and by these that the world and its social reality are shaped.

CHAPTER 4

The World Calls for the Postmodern (Blissful) Hero

*Have we not come to such an impasse in the modern
world that we must love our enemies—or else?
The chain reaction of evil—hate begetting hate,
wars producing more wars—must be broken, or else we
shall be plunged into the dark abyss of annihilation.*
                                        Martin Luther King, Jr.

I f ever there was a time that called for heroic action, it is the one we live in today. Never in our history have we possessed the awesome capacities for self-destruction that we now hold. From the immediate destructive power of nuclear holocaust to the slow death of environmental decay, we live in dangerous times. We simply cannot go on with business as usual. Perilous times call for heroic action. It is time that we suspend our preoccupation with economic life to the exclusion of all other values and put love into action in every sphere of life.

Today heroic action is not a matter of conquering new lands, slaying dragons, or crossing uncharted seas. The heroic life awaits all who are ready to take up the challenge of making this world the best it can be. Even as the hero of old had to confront the unknown, today we must confront the known. We must confront the world we find ourselves in while keeping before us the image of the world that could be. We must face our conditions and "breathe into them the breath recuperative of sane and heroic life" (Walt Whitman).

I believe in life after birth!

Maxie Dunham

> *After the final no there comes a yes and on that yes the future of the world depends.*
> *Wallace Stevens*

Perhaps inspired by Hamlet, Albert Camus said that the fundamental choice is suicide or life.[1] The intellectually honest person must square up to the choice: To be or to not be. Among the living, there are but two kinds of people, those who have said YES to life and those who have ducked the question. Those who have honestly decided that life is not worth living are no longer with us.

That which says YES to life, we call the heroic view of life. That which ducks the question, we call the anti-heroic view of life. The heroic YES must be total, unequivocal—the affirmation of a love that completely embraces human life exactly as it is. Anti-heroic avoidance is born of fear. It gives rise to a deep guilt, a gnawing self-contempt. It endeavors to build an abstract ideational world that emphasizes either the "good" or the "bad," but as we shall see, neither Pollyanna positivism nor cynical resignation are intellectually honest.

The Heroic View of Life: Love for Existence

The intellectually honest person must face the fact that his own existence is dependent upon the destruction of other sentient beings. Whether it is plants or animals that I kill to sustain my life in this world, I'm a murderer. I can try to rationalize, prepackage, or otherwise avoid it, but I live on destruction. This alone is enough to make a person feel guilt and repulsion. After all, how can I justify my existence when it depends upon the destruction of others? I cannot. I can only accept that it's the way of life, that death, decay, and destruction are as much a part of life as birth, growth, and regeneration. Life is full of pairs of opposites. Night and day, winter and summer, man and woman, on and on. ***Heroic love transcends the opposites in its embrace of them.***

I exist as I am, that is enough.
Walt Whitman

In life's work, bliss and sacrifice are two sides of the same coin, complementary opposites. It takes disciplined effort to produce beauty in art, music, fashion, or even the presentation of an evening meal. What is most pleasing to our senses often comes, not from sensual pursuit, but from meticulous effort. George Bernard Shaw said, "This is the true joy in life, the being used for a purpose recognized by yourself as a mighty one . . ."[2] The joy is the bliss, the being used, the sacrifice. Shaw is saying that if we want to know the greatest joy in life, we ought to dedicate ourselves to a purpose which we conceive of as a mighty-heroic-valuable-meaningful one and give our very all to it.

We in the West, with our tradition of glorifying the rights of the individual, find it repugnant to speak in terms of sacrifice or "being used." We are told we must assert ourselves and "look out for number one." To "be used" is to lose, and we who idolize material success are loathe to lose, to sacrifice. And so we miss the bliss. We may be materially comfortable, but we miss bliss. We tranquilize, aerobicize, fantasize, and gluttonize in the hope of awakening our zest for life or of deadening the pain that we feel from its loss.

Today we seek quick happiness, not lasting bliss. We want to have it all. Though we have been told of agony and ecstasy, of losing oneself to save oneself, we run from the pain of the world. We build isolating idealistic bubbles around ourselves, thick shells designed to keep out the pain of the world. In our effort to block out the pain, we miss the bliss.

Back to Bliss: Unzipping the Ego

How then do we get back to bliss? The better question might be, "How did we lose it?" Every child knows the joy of living. His bliss is innocent. He has not yet felt the weight his culture will soon hoist upon him, the weight of thought, of conflicting roles and obligations, of social manners, habits, and customs, of being right and proving himself make him a socialized individual capable of functioning in his society. However useful all this may be in "socializing" him, it robs him of his bliss.

He is wrapped in mental cellophane and shipped off to become a useful member of society. What is the wrapping about? Mental cellophane is protection from the direct experience of life. It's an

You can and you must expect suffering.

Mother Teresa

idealistic insulation from pain. It's endless categories and types; it's prejudices, should-be's, and hypes. Every society has its own distinctive wrap. Oh, the shape and the hues are individual, but just the same, you can spot Russian cellophane or French or American.

> *We're so engaged in doing things to achieve purposes of outer value that we forget the inner value, the rapture that is associated with being alive, is what it is all about.*
>
> Joseph Campbell

The older we get, the more difficult it is to keep out the pain of the world, so we add layer after layer of cellophane. By middle age, a lot of us can hardly breathe. Wrapped up in mental cellophane, we are awkward and stiff, slowly suffocating talking heads, devoid of direct experience.

Reclaim the bliss! Split the seam of your cellophane wrap! Step out of thought and convention. Leave your mind behind. Feel the breeze, dance naked in the moonlight, move freely, spontaneously, blissfully. It feels good out here. Don't worry, you will be able to handle pain when it comes. You are strong now.

How do we split the seam once and for all? How can we live naked and unwrapped? By learning to live with pain. Not in spite of it, not in hope of its end, not crushed by it, but with it. As a tree must anchor its roots deep in the earth in order to stretch forth to the skies, so must we who would reach the greatest heights of human experience be ready to meet the pain of this world square on. The innocent child in his bliss will one day, like Buddha, discover that this world is full of pain and that if he is to live, fully live, he must live with it.

Heroic love is not something that can be hyped, pep-talked, or adroitly argued into someone. It must be felt by each alone. It is not a matter of majority vote or popular consensus. *Each must conquer for him- or herself the desire to run away from life*. There's no escaping from life, really. You are here. There is no denying it. Maybe you don't know why or how, but you are here. You may as well decide to love it like you find it. Life, after all, is for living.

Either you think that life should not exist, that it's all a big mistake—or you affirm its basic goodness. You say yes to life, with all of its pain and beauty, horror and majesty, sorrow and bliss. It is good that life exists. It's as simple as that. **Oh yes, do all you can**

Is not life a thousand times too short for us to bore ourselves?

Friedrich Nietzsche

to make the world a better place, but remember—that comes out of acceptance, not out of rejection. Love in its truest form is without condition. It accepts life exactly as it is. Yet paradoxically, love is also the strongest force of change.

Zen wants us to be the Mother of All Things, to embrace everything exactly as it is—to see all that is as "my will being done on earth." Total acceptance. Zen also asks us to be the Father of Creative Movement—to exert the will to transform, to change, to improve, to evolve. So, in this understanding, we can say with Lao Tzu, "Know the masculine, but keep to the feminine"—act for change from the embrace of things as they are. This is the only action or creative movement. All else is reaction.

Humanity: One of a Kind

All people share in a state and relationship we call the human condition. In this we are one; we are of a kind. You are human; I am human; they are human—we are all human. Since we're all of a kind, we might as well act that way. Really, aren't we all doing everything we do to gain happiness or avoid suffering? Of course, many of our efforts are misguided in that they do not bring the results we seek. Still, we are all, in our own ways, trying to be happy.

> Today . . . we know that all living beings who strive to maintain life and who long to be spared pain— all living beings on earth are our neighbors.
> *Albert Schweitzer*

Through the ages, various religions and philosophies have offered formulas for happiness. Perhaps the simplest is: Be kind— treat all people as being of your kind. We can say that to see *kind* is to be kind—for who would want to injure oneself or those of one's kind? Beyond sex, race, religion, nationality, talent, social or economic status, or political power, we share our humanity. Differences, of course, exist, and it is well to recognize and honor these but never at the expense of forgetting our essential "kindness" as humans—not, at least, if we would be happy. Of course, kindness doesn't have to look any particular way. It is a recognition, not a set of prescribed actions. In this recognition, you can trust—remember your "kindness" and act.

We cannot be more sensitive to pleasure without being more sensitive to pain.

Alan Watts

Anti-Heroic View of Life: Self-Contempt

The anti-heroic life is based, not on love, but on self-contempt, or shame. Where love comes out of an identification of kind, contempt sets up a need for separation. The need to be separate comes out of the belief that mankind is a low level of life. You must separate yourself from that lot. What makes you different is what makes you good. Your difference might be that you are an American, or Jewish, or Christian, or rich, or intellectual, or conservative, or liberal, or whatever.

> *No work of love will flourish out of guilt, fear, or hollowness of heart, just as no valid plans for the future can be made by those who have no capacity for living now.*
>
> *Alan Watts*

It is only when we realize that life is taking us nowhere that it begins to have meaning.

P. D. Ouspensky

Although few "respectable" people would dare to say it so bluntly, the internal rationalization goes something like this: "The normal run of people are a sort of contemptuous mob. I would be in that mob were it not for my trendiness, causiness, wealthiness, holiness (whatever it is that separates me from the masses)." We hate ourselves as we are, because we don't believe we are what "we should be," because we are constantly making demands.

We make demands upon life, demands upon ourselves, demands upon others. We will love it when our demands are met and not a minute before. If life were more to my liking, I would love it; if I were more to my liking, I would love me; if others were more to my liking, I would love them. In the meantime, I will hold back, and I will hold on to what I think distinguishes me from the rest of the rabble.

> *There is nothing with which every man is so afraid as getting to know how enormously much he is capable of doing and becoming.*
>
> *Sören Kierkegaard*

When one tries to prove his identity through distinctive possession, he is on insecure ground. It matters not whether the possession be a title, a position, a social status, a marriage partner, an accumulation of wealth, or a cause—it is sure to bring him anxiety. The owner becomes anxious about losing his possession, for its loss translates in his mind as a loss of separate identity. Once more he is confronted with the spectre of finding himself indistinguishable from the mob he so deplores.

"Doing good" can become a distinctive possession that separates you from the masses. That is why the motive of the hero must be love, first, foremost, and always, love. Love for existence—your own and that of others. If you secretly hate yourself but you're "trying to do good," your hatred will color the water. You can only give to others what you experience yourself.

The hero must first be a lover. Then he may attempt to heal others: their minds with high ideals, their emotions with loving feelings, their bodies with nourishment and touch. But these things are secondary. It is the existence that he loves, and it is the love that makes the difference.

Mother Teresa's work with the poor and the dying was certainly a heroic work. She emphasized to those in her order the importance of doing their work with a spirit of joy and a feeling of love. She said, "If you can't do it with love and cheerfulness, don't do it at all, go home."[3] She understood that you can't hate the existence and heal the particular need.

The miracle is not that we do this work, but that we are happy to do it.

Mother Teresa

Understanding contempt for life helps us to understand how so many wars have been fought in the name of religion, how so many good ideals have been used in destructive ways. The fault is not with the religion or the ideal but with the practitioner's hatred of himself and of life. In the Crusades, the Christians marched into battle crying, "God is mighty!" The Muslims cried, "God is all!" But because they each "possessed" God, they couldn't comprehend their own slogans.

Cynics are fond of pointing out these atrocities as an excuse to discount any basis for a moral or ethical life. Surely hypocrisy does exist, but that is no justification for excusing ourselves from a moral responsibility to our fellow man. It is contempt for humanity that must be overcome, not our desire to serve. If we are to survive and flourish as a race, we must remake, not only our society, but ourselves as individuals. Ironically, we cannot succeed in remaking ourselves until we accept ourselves as we are. We must say yes to life. Yes to life with all of its beauty and terror. Yes to life with all of its brilliance and depravity. Yes to life with all of its sorrow and bliss.

One cannot always be a hero, but one can always be a (hu) man.

Goethe

Love Makes a World of Difference

Love until it hurts. Real love is always painful and hurts: then it is real and pure.

Mother Teresa

My life is an indivisible whole, and all my activities run into one another; and they have their rise in my insatiable love of mankind.

Mahatma Gandhi

It's easy to imagine that making the world a better place is simply a matter of throwing money at its problems. Of course, money helps make things happen, but it is secondary to love and character. As Albert Einstein put it, "I am absolutely convinced that no wealth in the world can help humanity forward, even in the hands of the most devoted worker in this cause. The example of great and pure individuals is the only thing that can lead us to noble thoughts and deeds. Money only appeals to selfishness, and irresistibly invites abuse. Can anyone imagine Moses, Jesus, or Gandhi armed with… money bags…?"[4]

The fear of pain and death makes most of us but shadows of what we might be. Yet even suffering, mixed with love, with purpose, with joy, becomes heroic—an exaltation of the human spirit. And what of death? Listen to the speech Dr. Martin Luther King made days before he was shot. You can tell, somehow, he knew it was coming. Still, he went ahead undaunted, unbowed. Like a thousand heroes before him, he held on to a vision of man mightier than fear. Heroic action cuts the bounds of fear and triumphantly asserts that there is a spirit in us that is noble and mighty. This loving spirit exists within all life, including yours. *The heroic life lives in dormancy in all and in active expression in the great men and women.*

The heroic life is a beautiful life. You cannot hear Martin Luther King's "I Have a Dream" speech and miss hearing the beauty. You cannot see Mother Teresa and miss seeing the beauty. You cannot study Gandhi's life and miss sensing the beauty. You just can't. I think everyone sees it. But what does it take to transfer that beauty into an active force in our own lives?

Identification. We must be able to identify with the hero as being fundamentally like ourselves. Otherwise, heroic action is dismissed as the peculiar behavior of some peculiarly great individual. This behavior is worthy of admiration, to be sure, but not capable of imitation by the ordinary man and woman. Heroes, whether living or dead legends, are seen as fundamentally different from the rest of us. Of course, we are not all equally gifted or talented, but we are all capable of heroic action.

How then do we create identification with heroic models?

1. **By realizing that the greats of history were human beings, cut from the same cloth as we.** They put their pants on one leg at a time. They had to deal with the same emotions and inner doubts, the same outside pressures and concerns.

2. **By seeing that they are all around us.** Thousands of so-called ordinary people are every day involved in heroic service to their fellow man. Most of this service goes unrecognized and unnoticed by the wider public because it does not fit with the conventional view of what is valuable and important.

Everybody can be great. Because anybody can serve. You don't have to have a college degree to serve. You don't have to make your subject and verb agree to serve. You don't have to know about Plato and Aristotle . . . (or) Einstein's Theory of Relativity . . . (or) the Second Theory of Thermodynamics in physics to serve. You only need a heart full of grace. A soul generated by love.
Martin Luther King, Jr.

The Way is not far from man; if we take the Way as something superhuman, beyond man, this is not the real Way.

Confucius

The point of telling the hero's story is that our identification with the hero allows us, at least for a time, to move beyond the fear and defensive hesitation that hold us back from full participation in life. We experience what the Greeks call *catharsis*.[5] Catharsis doesn't mean rant and rave and scream and yell and then there is catharsis. The cathartic experience is the release experienced in the cessation of the emotions that ordinarily dominate life, namely fear and guilt. Catharsis happens when we identify with the character and move along his emotional track until he and we are free of guilt and fear.

That's why the stories from ages old have been told—so that you might feel, if only for an instant, what it is to be so bold. So ALIVE. In that, you find life. You find bliss. You find courage. You can feel it. Where did it come from? It was there all along, beneath the clouds of shame and fear. Cathartic identification has temporarily blown the clouds away. Now you feel the pure brilliance of your being. Courage isn't something you've put on. Fear is something you've taken off. You feel the power and grace of your naked Self.

We all have the capacity to inspire and uplift one another. When you see someone heroically facing a tragedy of some kind or heroically working to express his vision of love in action—it's an inspiration. That person could be black, white, yellow, red, rich, or poor, Protestant, Catholic, or Jew; it doesn't matter. *It's the spirit that you identify with.* It lifts your spirit to see someone exalting his. Each of us can approach our daily lives in a way that exalts the human spirit. We can be living examples of human dignity, love, and brotherhood. We can create a society based on love for one another and respect for the mystery of life.

I have not the shadow of a doubt that any man or woman can achieve what I have, if he or she would make the same effort and cultivate the same hope and faith.

Mahatma Gandhi

You have seen the earth from space. Maybe it was only a photograph, but you have seen it. All over the world, people have seen themselves from another reference point. Having seen ourselves from somewhere else, we can no longer be so much in the dark about where we are. We are on earth, together with the great oceans and land masses, together with six billion of our fellow humans, we are on earth. For the first time, we have a perspective of ourselves as one world. For the first time, that image is a part of our psyche, and for the first time, we have a global culture. We can decry this culture and its banality. We can try to stop the push toward universality by emphasizing ethnic or cultural differences, but inevitably we are moving to one world. Our efforts are better spent in attempting to elevate this culture than in reverting to separation.

How can we elevate this culture we live in? How can we make it more human, more sane? What kind of values do we want represented in the images that bounce around the world in an instant? What will we televise? What will we glorify? What will we fax? What will we compute? Will it be about love or loot? We are deciding.

I cry: Love! Love! happy happy Love!
free as the mountain wind!
William Blake [6]

Living on the Edge

Look at Bodhidharma's fierce scowl. Strong as an ox, he won't take any bull. He's a radical, a rebel, a revolutionary. He knows that it's society's job to tame the individual and the individual's job to get free.

Society's propaganda will tell you that you are inadequate, that it's your fate to live in fear and beg for the approval of others, that things are just the way they are, and there's nothing you can do about it. You must resign yourself to a gray existence; you must go along to get along.

But there is Bodhidharma, fiery eyes, teeth showing, intent and determined, a free spirit who will not buy the propaganda of mediocrity. He challenges you to be free enough of society to actually help transform it for the better.

That's what this book is about. It's about being personally free and socially active. It is not for wimps. It takes the courage to say no to every attempt to fit you into a category and make you a carbon copy of your next door neighbor. It takes the courage to say no to every attempt to turn you into a beggar, pleading for the approval of others. It takes courage to say no to the needless suffering of your fellow man. No to becoming hypnotized and tranquilized. No to becoming greedy and indifferent. No to becoming clay in somebody else's hand.

Things were no different in Bodhidharma's day. Society has always been the free man's greatest enemy. And the free man has always been society's greatest friend. How did society treat Jesus or Socrates, Galileo or Martin Luther King? Yet look what they have left mankind.

Bodhidharma, if we could get him to talk, would tell us that it's our wanting to be somebody special that turns us into slaves of approval. He is a nobody who works for everybody, who kow-tows to none, condemns none, loves all in his rascal way. I'm not your leader, he might say. Don't follow me. Be your own leader. Watch your parking meter.

This book says: What is in you, let it out. What you really want to do, do it. Don't yield to doubt. Love is the greatest religion, the greatest philosophy, the guiding light of the free man. Love is what it's all about.

The Quest for Life's Work

Wherein our hero asks:
What in the world am I doing here?

NOT I—NOT ANYONE else, can travel that road for you,
You must travel it for yourself.

Walt Whitman

A lifelong adventure awaits those who are ready to take up the quest for their life's work. The first step on this journey is to determine the direction you want your life to take. In "Act I: The Quest for Life's Work," we invite you to examine several key landmarks to help you get your bearings. These include: your vision for the kind of world you want to live in, your values, your purpose in life, your talents, and specific objectives you would like to accomplish while on this earth. With your commitment and these landmarks, you will be able to determine, at least in a general sense, what your life's work is.

The Quest
for Your Best

"Each entered the forest at a point he, himself, had chosen, where it was darkest and there was no path."

These lines come from an ancient story we have come to call *The Quest of the Holy Grail*.[1] It is a story rich in inner meaning and significance. When the knights of King Arthur's court had seen an apparition of the Grail through a veil, they determined to go on a quest to find it. And they thought, "We should go out together to find the Grail." But then they realized that this would be "a disgrace." No, each must go alone into the forest and enter at the point he himself would choose, "where it was darkest and there was no path."

Entering the forest alone at the darkest spot, this is the road less traveled. To walk this pathless path is to take the hero's journey. This book is for those who, like the mythic heroes of old, are ready to make of their lives a quest for the shining apparition of their own best self—ready to take the hero's journey. The word *hero* is etymologically related to *heresy* and *heretic*. All three are derived from the Greek *hairétikos,* meaning "able to choose."[2] A hero is a chooser. A hero chooses the questions of his or her life and thereby, his quest.

If a man does not keep pace with his companions perhaps it is because he hears a different drummer. Let him step to the music he hears, however measured or far away.

Henry David Thoreau

For all of us, *the question is the quest-I-on.* In other words, the questions we ask or fail to ask shape the journeys of our lives. What distinguishes the hero from the rest is that he or she chooses the questions and earnestly seeks them; the rest blindly, and often half-heartedly, follow the conventional questions of their society. As Joseph Campbell puts it, "The usual person is more than content, he is even proud, to remain within the indicated bounds, and popular belief gives him every reason to fear so much as the first step into the unexplored."[3] Will you live your life spontaneously from the heart and its pathless call or conventionally from prescribed role? Will you take the path less traveled or the well-trodden road? This is the dilemma that Zen and the Grail myth put to us, each in its own inimitable way.

The Grail myths of the West and the Zen insights of the East inform and instruct one another. Both say loud and clear: Be yourself—be done with fear. Both say: Trust your original nature. Both say: Beware the conventional and its deadening influence. Both instruct us to walk the pathless path, and both remind us that only in trusting our original, spontaneous, loving nature are we authentic—or even safe.

For both, the Question is imperative. In Zen, the *koan,* or question, is the vehicle for *kensho*—seeing into one's own real nature. Zen has long used the *koan,* or impossible question, as a means of awakening one to what Sören Kierkegaard calls "the supreme paradox." "The supreme paradox of all thought is the attempt to discover something that thought cannot think." Likewise, the Question is central to the Grail stories. As Grail scholar John Matthews writes: "Many, if not all, of the Grail mysteries are

If you observe well your own heart will answer.

R. A. Schwaller de Lubicz

about self-discovery, hence, the emphasis on questions. The Quest is a journey inward as well as through the lands of the Grail."[4]

Man is not the creature of circumstances.
Circumstances are the creatures of men.
          Benjamin Disraeli

Wisdom asks the right questions. Many of the world's myths, legends, even children's fairy stories revolve around questions—How was the world created? When and how did man first appear? What should one ask for when given three wishes? Likewise, many of the world's scriptures revolve around questions. In the stories of the Zen masters and in much of the Buddhist writings, in the Sufi stories and in much of the Upanishads, we find a question/answer format. The whole of the Bhagavad-Gita is in this style. Jesus questions his disciples and answers their questions. The Book of Job is an extended "What if?" question. Plato's *Dialogues* are full of questions, and philosophy (literally, the love of wisdom) generally is concerned with questions. Scientific discoveries are driven by questions. These are just a few examples.

Where wisdom asks the right questions, Enlightenment is getting back behind the questioner, the hungry, restless mind. Zen calls this "seeing into your own self-nature," into the loving, blissful consciousness that is before question, attention, or mind and out of which these seem to arise. As the Sixth Cha'n patriarch Hui Neng puts it, "From the first not a thing is." Where nothing is, there is nothing to get or to ask. This is called the Zen doctrine of No Mind.

What is this place where thought is useless?
Knowledge and emotion can not fathom it!
     Yumen's reply to the question of a certain monk

Questions are also central to creative work. In his wonderful book, *The Craft of Novel Writing,* author Colin Wilson writes: "Go to the heart of most novels and you will find a question mark. This applies also, of course, to stories, which are simply novels on a smaller scale."[5] Literature is not alone. In every creative medium, we find creative work formed, fired, and glazed by questions. For example, da Vinci's *Last Supper* was shaped by the question: How to render this scene so that "the movements of the figures represent the passions of their souls"?[6]

In considering the relative merit of several centuries of novels, Wilson suggests as a criteria for judgment the expanse of their world view. At the bottom are the novels that reflect what he calls a "Communal [Conventional] Life World." Toward the middle are those with an "Individual Life World." At the top are those that approach the universal realm, which he calls "Purely Objective Vision."[7] These three exactly correspond to one's psychological development on the path of awakening or enlightenment—moving out of the *conformity* of convention into the *individuation* of self and then transcending the individual self in *universalization*— what in the East is referred to as *mukta* or "liberation." The Self that is not self. The hero, literary or actual, must individuate from the mass of automatic conformity—become himself—and then begin to discover the relationship of this self to all of life.

Wilson suggests that "the novel is a form of thought experiment . . . The aim of all these thought experiments is the exploration of human freedom."[8] Again the parallels are exact. The spiritual path through "universalization" and the artistic path through "Purely Objective Vision" are probing the outer boundaries of human freedom. The Zen *koan* is a thought experiment—penetrating through thought, finally, into no thought. The story of the Holy Grail is a thought experiment, taking us through the psychological terrain of the hero's journey. (We will explore it later.)

We can make our own lives creative thought experiments. Ask more expansive questions than convention dictates, and you widen your consciousness. Stay with these questions, and you deepen it. In exploring the range of human freedom, we can benefit from those who have gone before. We can learn from those who have, through spiritual and/or artistic "thought experiments," explored the boundaries of human limitation and gone beyond. George Bernard Shaw said, "You use a glass mirror to see your face; you use works of art to see your soul."[9] Scriptures and mythology likewise have this soul-reflective quality. Midas asks for gold; Solomon, for wisdom; Arjuna, for understanding—What are you asking for?

*The only journey is
the one within.*

Rainer Maria Rilke

*Ask and it shall be given unto you.
Seek and ye shall find.*
Luke 11:9

We have already suggested viewing your life as a story—call it a poem, a novel, a play. Colin Wilson observes that "you can't write a really effective play—or a novel—about someone who doesn't know what he wants."[10] So it is with the story of your life; it doesn't get really interesting until you know what you want. The first step to knowing what you want is to choose the questions you want to explore and to determine, like a good novelist, to work them through. (The process work in "Act I" can help with this.)

Wilson notes that among novel writers, there are high fliers and low fliers. We can think of these as degrees of difficulty. In gymnastics, one may execute a simple exercise perfectly or a very difficult one imperfectly. A novelist can write a nice little story about achieving "Communal Life World" objectives, or she can attempt to take on bigger questions. Obviously, the more difficult the questions, the bigger the challenges and the greater the possibility of failure. As with novelists and their stories, so with all of us and our lives. We can take our questions from the "Communal Life World" (What do they want me to do?) or from the "Individual Life World" (What do I want to do?), or we can ask, "What does humanity, the human soul, want me to do?" We can be high fliers or low fliers. Heroes are high fliers. Sometimes they crash and sometimes they succeed brilliantly—but they are always after the big questions.

Nurture your minds with great thoughts. To believe in the heroic makes heroes.

Benjamin Disraeli

The mind runs on questions. Questions ignite the mind the way spark plugs ignite your automobile engine. All imaginative journeys are prompted by questions, be they the mundane questions of moving the body about (Is it time to rise? What shall I wear? What shall I have for breakfast? What is my schedule for today?) or the psychological need questions (Will she make me happy? Will he be faithful? Will my children fail or succeed? What will people think?) or the deeper attitudinal questions (How can I defend myself? How can I get by? How can I be approved of by others? How can I avoid losing? How can I get ahead of people or back at them?). Most of this questioning is so automatic that we hardly notice it. Conventionally, we call it subconscious and either dismiss it altogether or try to psychoanalyze it into "normality," whatever that is.

Your conscious or subconscious imaginative life, then, is just a matter of questions, or rather, of chasing after answers to questions. Everything you've thought, everything you've imagined, came from a question that your imagination followed. When you find your mind drifting in fantasy, some question sent it on that journey. When you imagine a better world, some question sent you on that journey. Becoming mindful is becoming aware of the questions you are asking. Moving toward your life's work is coming to ask the questions appropriate to it and persisting with them.

Human beings can alter their lives by altering their attitudes of mind.

William James

Your Book of Questions

What are the dominant questions of your life? Your dominant questions determine its direction and shape. They form a kind of skeletal structure in relation to which the action and circumstances of your life are but the material coverings. No matter what materials you use to cover the skeletal structure of a geodesic dome, you can't, by the covering alone, change it into the form of a forty story skyscraper, the Statue of Liberty, or a canoe. So it is in our lives; we can put a fresh coat of paint on things, new sidings or roofings, but these will not change their fundamental shape. New questions deeply asked will shape a new life. Further, in the process of tearing down one structure and building another, we may happen upon the mystery behind all structures and see the true nature of the raw materials used to build them.

You can't make a silk purse out of a sow's ear, and you can't follow the bliss of your life's work by asking the conventional questions of the day. As Emerson said, "Whoso would be a man [or woman] must be a nonconformist."[11] Think of the automatic conventional questions, questions like: How can I get by? How can I be approved of by others? How can I avoid losing? How can I be the big cheese? How can I defend myself? Then consider questions like: Who am I? What in the world am I doing here? How can I serve? and even, What is the meaning of life? Clearly these two sets of questions lead to fundamentally different lives.

> *Live the questions now.*
> *Rainer Maria Rilke*

The latter set of questions held with sincerity and tenacity are as much *koans* as the well-known, "What is the sound of one hand clapping?" If you think that the question: "Who am I?" is any less a *koan* or any less difficult to answer, then you haven't ever really asked it, not deeply, as a *koan* is to be examined. To take these questions as *koans* is to awaken to an experience which those who pass by these questions, because they are simple or obvious on the one hand or obtuse or unanswerable on the other, will never know. What will be the *koans* of your life and work? Whatever they be, your questions will shape your journey.

The road to individuation, the way to live as king of your own life, is the way of asking questions. This is the Zen way of the *koan*. Zen historian Heinrich Dumoulin notes that, while today the Zen master usually chooses the student's *koan*, "in former times, the

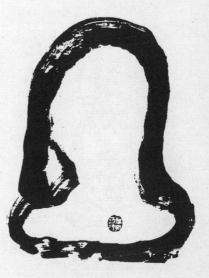

How can I be useful, of what service can I be? There is something inside me, what can it be?

Vincent van Gogh

disciple chose the *koan* himself."[12] Choose your questions, your *koans*—make your start. If and when you are ready for a teacher, this will occur of its own. Find a way to quiet your mind—as the Zen master said, "Solving *koans* in action is a billion times harder than solving them in *zazen* (sitting meditation)." One needn't do *zazen*, but it helps if, in whatever way works for you, you get still.

It is said that there are three essentials to the Zen practice of the *koan* (quoted by Zen master Hakuin): the great root of faith, the great ball of doubt, and tenacity of purpose.[13] The faith is in one's original nature, in the ultimate reality of the Buddha (literally, Awakened) experience. The great ball of doubt means applying "concentrated doubt" to the *koans*. Tenacity of purpose is the intensity of commitment, the firm resolve that ultimately "shatters" doubt. These (faith, doubt, and tenacity of purpose) are just the same qualities of all the great mythic heroes. Certainly they are the qualities of Parzival, the hero of the Grail myth, whom we will consider below.

They are also essential qualities for those who would seek the call of their life's work. The great root of faith shows in your confidence in your vision for a better world and in your own part in it. The great ball of doubt represents the inner fears, doubts, vagaries, and the outer obstacles and adversities en route. The tenacity of purpose is the dogged determination to see it through. Take a *koan* for your life's work: What am I doing here? What is my destiny? How can I serve? What is my real life? Whatever your question, however you phrase it, enter into it with an intensive imaginative exploration.

Underlying great doubt there is great satori, where there is thorough questioning there will be thoroughgoing experience of awakening.
Zen Saying Quoted by Hakuin

Lacking this imaginative questing, life becomes the mechanical, dry, empty wasteland. To reawaken it, we "must become as little children." We must allow our imaginations the freedom to explore in humility and openness. We must have what Zen calls a beginner's mind. All the great explorers have this childlike humility and openness. Isaac Newton wrote, "I do not know what I may appear to the world; but to myself I seem to have been only like a boy playing on the seashore, and diverting myself in now and then finding a smoother pebble or a prettier shell than the ordinary, whilst the great ocean of truth lay all undiscovered before me."

And his own thoughts, along that rugged way, Pursued, like raging hounds, their father and their prey.

Shelley

Einstein said, "The more I learn, the more I realize I don't know." In every field, the "big" people have little pretension.

Now let's return to the Grail myth. Who is the hero of the Grail myth? Called variously Parzival, Perceval, Gallahad, or Bors in different versions of the story, he is the one adequate to "Grail Quest." His adequacy is not a matter of big muscles or intellectual refinement but of a simple, childlike heart. Parzival (from here on, we discuss the Grail story in terms of the Wolfram von Eschenbach version)[14] often seems something of a fool. The line between the hero and the fool is always thin indeed.

The greatest obstacle to being heroic is the doubt whether one may not be going to prove one's self a fool; the truest heroism is, to resist the doubt; and the profoundest wisdom, to know when it ought to be resisted, and when to be obeyed.

Nathaniel Hawthorne

Parzival is raised by his mother. His father was a knight and came to his end in the way knights often do. Mother would that the same not happen to her fair-haired boy. She secludes him from knightly things and stories as insurance, but of course this fails, for no one can be kept from his destiny. One day, three knights show up in bright and shining armor, and the boy is enchanted. Mother then hopes to have him ridiculed out of his quest, for as she observes, people are usually ready to "turn away from mockery."

Within our impure mind the pure one is to be found.

Hui Neng

She wants him to give up this foolish business of grand and heroic intentions. (Many young men do give up their dreams to please mother, or the "mother" projected onto their wives.) So she gives him a pitiful old nag of a horse and a ridiculous costume, one that Wolfram tells us makes him look exactly like a fool.[15] The lesson is clear: Every Quester must be prepared to face ridicule. One who accepts the prescribed role seems sure of himself. He knows what to do even if he is just doing what he is told. The one who breaks out of the conventional mold must figure out for himself what he is about. It is not only his desire for "something different" but his searching after he-knows-not-what that makes him seem a fool.

This is precisely where one requires what Zen calls "the root of faith." It has been said that the meanest form of atheism is to not believe in oneself. This kind of atheist, if he takes up the quest at all, is soon ridiculed out of it. The following quote from Dag Hammarskjöld gives the sense of the kind of faith required of the heroic Quester.

He broke fresh ground—because, and only because, he had the courage to go ahead without asking whether others were following or even understood. He had no need for the divided responsibility in which others seek to be safe from ridicule, because he had been granted a faith which required no confirmation—a contact with reality, light and intense like the touch of a loved hand: a union in self-surrender without self-destruction, where his heart was lucid and his mind was loving.[16]

The crux of the story of Parzival and his quest for the Grail is suggested in his first encounter in the Grail castle. After various adventures, Parzival has sort of stumbled into the Grail castle. This is the wisdom of innocence. The purity of the simple fellow gets him into the Grail castle. In the castle lives a king who is sorely wounded. The king's illness has brought devastation to the kingdom—it has become the Wasteland.

> The theme of the Grail is the bringing of life into what is known as 'the wasteland.' The wasteland is the preliminary theme to which the Grail is the answer... It's the world of people living inauthentic lives— doing what they are supposed to do.
> Joseph Campbell

Parzival can redeem the king and kingdom by asking a simple question. The wounded king is brought before him, and Parzival wants to ask, "What ails thee, brother?" But he has been told good knights don't ask a lot of questions. The decisive moment for him is the choice between acting spontaneously from his heart or conventionally from his role as a knight. He fails; innocence is not enough, for he has already been socially indoctrinated. It has caused him to doubt the promptings of his heart, and as Wolfram says in the very first line of his Parzival, "If vacillation dwell with the heart the soul will rue it."[17]

He chose to act conventionally, the way he thought he was supposed to. He muffed his opportunity for the Grail because he was trying so hard to be a good boy. He goes to bed that night, and when he gets up in the morning, the castle is empty. As he leaves the castle, he hears a voice shouting, "You silly goose. Why didn't you open your gob and ask the lord the Question?"[18] Though a little dense, he soon enough comes to realize that he has missed his chance. He is sorely bummed out. As Wolfram says, "It was a cause of great remorse to the warrior that he had been so slow to ask the Question as he sat beside the sorrowing king."[19] Now for five long

Life's most urgent question is, what are you doing for others?

Martin Luther King, Jr.

years he tries desperately to find his way back to the castle. He is booed and jeered. Everyone knows he has failed, and everywhere is the desolation of the Wasteland.

He is gaining now the wisdom of experience, of commitment, loyalty, and dedication. He must face the great ball of doubt. His journey now weaves through a maze-like set of experiences through which he comes to redeem and understand his past. Holding to his quest, his question, his *koan,* provides him with the ball of string which he can, like Theseus in his encounter with the Minotaur, unwind and thus find his way out of this labyrinth of a wasteland and back to the Grail castle. Of course, he eventually triumphs and, in fact, becomes the Grail King. Through his tenacity of purpose, his loyalty to the Quest, he is told he has changed God's law. "A greater marvel never occurred. . . . you have wrung the concession from God."[20] Just so, all who take up the great Quest-I-ons of life and hold tenaciously to them will enter into a marvelous life, the life of their destiny.

For Parzival, the basic issue is compassion. In other words, "What ails thee, brother?" In the Buddhist Bodhisattva tradition, this compassion is called "joyful participation in the sorrows of others"—the consecration of action in service to humanity. Without compassion, without the heart of spontaneous action, all one has is conventionality in one form or another. Of course, we can be conventionally spiritual, intellectual, yuppie, hippie, "revolutionary," or whatever. It's still the wasteland. You can recognize it right away. It lacks spontaneity, freshness, energy—life. Zen.

The way out is through the heart. The heart is the heart of things, the center of life. If the heart is not the center of your life, you are not really living; you are inauthentic—this is what the Grail myth is telling us. You're stuck with the wasteland of the conventional. Again, as Wolfram says, "If vacillation dwell with the heart the soul will rue it." The victory of the Grail Quest is the assertion of the spontaneous impulse of the heart over the automated, conventional monotony of uninspired, unimaginative life.

A joyful heart is the inevitable result of a heart burning with love.

Mother Teresa

In another and older version of the Grail story, the one told by Chrétien de Troyes, the critical Question on which the story turns is: "Whom does the Grail serve?"[21] While the phrasing of the Question is different, the issue remains essentially the same. Is life for the endless desires, fears, and hostilities of the ego or for something

A person starts to live when he can live outside of himself.

Albert Einstein

larger than this? Not only the Grail story but many of the great souls from various ages and places have told us reality and authentic living transcend the barren life of narcissistic ego entrapment.

In the World of Reality there is no self,
There is no other-than-self.
                              Seng-ts'an

What is reality?
Selflessness.
                   Sufi saying

Love . . . is a living reality.
                   Albert Schweitzer

I believe that unarmed truth and unconditional love will have the final word in reality.
                   Martin Luther King, Jr.

The spontaneous, loving heart is the reality of human life. The mechanical, fortressed, inauthentic life of the ego is a transitory, dreamlike phase we seem to pass through on an apparent journey from innocence to experience and beyond. The desire to be what you are, to know the reality of love beyond self and other, begins to awaken the sleeper from his slumber.

You may have experienced that when before you awaken from a dream, you sometimes incorporate events of the "real world" into your dream, for example, the sound of an alarm clock or a dog barking. When this happens, you are still in the dreaming state, but the "real world" is moving into your awareness, and if its sound is loud enough or persistent enough, it will soon wake you up. In the same way, the "desire to serve" bridges the dream world of the inauthentic life with the real life. While we think, "I have a desire to serve," we are still dreaming but hearing a sound from the real world. When we awaken, we know that we do not possess love as a thing apart but that we *are* that love; we do not have a desire to serve—we *are* service and cannot be otherwise.

Focusing on your desire to serve is asking to be roused into your real life. Mahatma Gandhi said: "Consciously or unconsciously, every one of us does render some service or other. If we cultivate the habit of doing this service deliberately, our desire for service will steadily grow stronger, and make, not only for our own happiness, but that of the world at large."[22] We can think, "I have this mind, and I'll put it in the service of humanity. I have emotions, and I want to put those in service to humanity. I have these abilities; I want to put them to service to humanity." And out of this will come the particular manifestations of our work—the entree is the desire to serve. Hear the call from the real world waking you to the way of happiness. Scattered through these pages in various quotations are many voices calling us to heed the desire to serve. Below are just a few:

*I don't know what your destiny will be, but one thing I
know: the only ones among you who will be really happy
are those who have sought and found how to serve.*
                                    Albert Schweitzer

Get beyond love and grief; exist for the good of man.
                                    Ha Gakure

The sole meaning of life is to serve humanity.
                                    Tolstoy

*Mankind's role is to fulfill his heaven-sent purpose through
a sincere heart that is in harmony with all creation and loves
all things.   Morihei Ueshiba (Founder of Aikido)*

Of course, it only makes sense that, as all of these (and so many
more wise ones) have said, your mission in life is to serve humanity.
You can't get to your life's work from a point of view of: What's going
to make me hot, rich, or let me get off easy? These questions won't
give you your life's work, because they are not asking for it. If you
want the seed thought that's going to give you your life's work, this
is it: How is humanity to be served by this existence? or, expressed
another way: What is my real life? The specific forms of your life's
work arise out of this deep desire to serve humanity—to know your
real life. Compassion moves us to serve, to ask, "What ails thee,
brother?" Wisdom wants us to ask, Whom does the Grail serve?—
in other words, What is my real life? or Who am I? Following these
questions is living the Quest.

---

*Innate Ideas are in Every Man, Born with him; they
are truly Himself. The Man who says that we have No
Innate Ideas must be a Fool & Knave, Having No
Conscience or Innate Science.*
                                    William Blake

*The concept of
an individual with
a conscience is
one whose highest
allegiance is to his
fellow man.*

Ralph Nader

Right now, in this moment, you contain everything you need.
Zen says, let go of the conception of yourself as a lack walking
around waiting for fulfillment. The seed is within. It is not something that needs to be added or invented. All you can do is create the
right circumstances for its germination. The questions that we will
present you with in the pages that follow are not there so that you
can come up with brilliant answers (though you may), but rather
that through the process of questioning (questing) you might put a
new light on the seed or add just a tad more water and suddenly—
germination.

What Gets You Going and Keeps You Going on the Quest?

What gets the hero going on the quest? What sustains her in her seeking? The beautiful and the sublime. Art and life, through the Beautiful and the Sublime, call us to the Quest and nourish us along the way. To the sensitive heart, Beauty, the radiance of the veiled Grail, calls one out of the world of convention. Stop and think of it. What are the world's great scriptures, poetry, mythology, music, paintings, etc.? Beauty! Beauty is, as Plato said, "the splendor of truth"—not truth itself—only its reflection. Beauty is the transcendent made transparent in the world of form and time. The perception of beauty in nature and art stimulates the sensitive beholder to seek its source. It starts the hero on the Grail Quest, and if he achieves it, then he too will make things of Beauty which will call the next generation of heroes to the questing life.

> *The most beautiful thing we can experience is the mysterious. It is the source of all true art and all science. He to whom this emotion is a stranger, who can no longer pause to wonder and stand rapt in awe, is as good as dead: his eyes are closed.*
>
> *Albert Einstein*

There is another way, the way of the terrible or as it is sometimes called, "the sublime." Edmund Burke describes the sublime thus: "Whatever is fitted in any sort to excite the ideas of pain and danger, that is to say, whatever is in any sort terrible, or is conversant about terrible objects, or operates in a manner analogous to terror, is a source of the sublime..."[23] Confrontation with death and death at its most terrible, war, can open one up to a new experience of life.

War is an extreme example, but we confront the sublime at every turn. We face the sublime in encountering the sheer horror of life—destruction, suffering, pain, war, and tragedy of every kind. Religious experience and ritual attempt in some way to come to terms with the sublime. In the Christian communion, we drink the blood of Christ; in Tibetan Buddhism, instruments of sacred music are crafted from human skulls and thighbones; in the Hindu religion, the goddess Kali stands with a garland of skulls drinking the blood of her victims. In primitive or traditional cultures, ritual animal and even human sacrifice and painful initiatory rites are an attempt to reconcile the human psyche with the sublime.

Compared to what we ought to be, we are half awake.

William James

Much of the art and literature of the modern era deals especially with the sublime. The awakening of Pierre, one of the main characters in Tolstoy's *War and Peace*, involves his encounter with the sublime. Like Parzival, he too is troubled by questions. Pierre is a thoughtful fellow earnestly seeking meaning. He travels up on this philosophy and down on that disillusionment, until finally the shock, the overwhelming horror of war, gives him release from his quest for meaning. "What had worried him in the old days, what he had always been seeking to solve, the question of the object of life, did not exist for him now. That seeking for an object in life was over for him now; and it was not fortuitously or temporarily that it was over. . . And it was just the absence of an object that gave him that complete and joyful sense of freedom that at this time made his happiness."[24] He had, as Zen would say, awakened his mind without fixing it anywhere.

> *Man is unhappy because he doesn't know he's happy. . . If anyone finds out he'll become happy at once.*
>
> Dostoyevsky (The Possessed)

This release gave him a kind of, from the conventional perspective, madness. "Pierre's madness showed itself in his not waiting, as in the old days, for those personal grounds, which he called good qualities in people, in order to love them; but as love was brimming over in his heart he loved men without cause . . ."[25]

Of course, this experience sounds good, like something many of us would like to know for ourselves. The difficulty is—we must cross the wasteland to get there—the barren, empty, dry, and desolate places of our inner lives—the great ball of doubt. We can not pretend to have put an end to the questions until they are, in fact and forever, silenced by the quest itself. We can only be where we are now, while keeping in view the reality of our destiny (and awakening). The heroic spirit carries on in the quest for real life and work, in spite of inner doubts and outer obstacles.

Driven on by creative discontent, refusing to settle for less, he stays the course, she keeps on keeping on. This is the theme of Goethe's masterpiece, *Faust*. If Faust becomes satisfied, Mephistopheles gets him. The "devil" and his hellish wasteland gets the man or woman who becomes self-satisfied. With reference to work, Peter Drucker has put it like this: "No matter what job it is, it ain't final. The first few years are trials. The probability that the first choice you make is right for you is roughly one in a million.

You ask me for a motto. Here it is: SERVICE.

Albert Schweitzer

All the fish needs
Is to get lost
in the water
All man needs
is to get lost
In Tao.

Chuang Tzu

If you decide your first choice is the right one, chances are you are just plain lazy...”[26]

Keep away from people who try to belittle your ambitions. Small people always do that, but the really great make you feel that you, too, can become great.

Mark Twain

And what becomes of those who hear the call and refuse? Joseph Campbell writes: “Refusal of the summons converts the adventure into its negative . . . the subject loses the power of significant affirmative action and becomes a victim to be saved. His flowering world becomes a wasteland of dry stones and his life feels meaningless . . . All he can do is create new problems for himself [and others] and await the gradual approach of his disintegration.”[27] All *we* can do is encourage you to go on the quest—invite you to consecrate yourself to your best for the sake of all mankind.

The *Koan* of Creativity

In his early essays, Zen writer D. T. Suzuki discussed the process through which the student of Zen moves in consideration of the *koan* to the *satori* of enlightenment. He said that the process was marked by stages of *accumulation, saturation*, and *explosion*.[28] These three exactly parallel the creative process known to creative artists and scientists. We will briefly consider this process first with reference to the *koan* and then in terms of creative work.

In consideration of the *koan* the first stage begins with the accumulation of energy and focus, developing mental concentration, moving confidently into the *koan*. One tries to answer from memory or intellect and is foiled. Initial confidence is followed by doubt, the stage of saturation. We have already quoted Zen Master Hakuin’s assertion that the greater the doubt, the greater the eventual *satori*. We can also say, the greater the doubt, the greater the saturation.

Achieving total saturation may take more or less time—time is not as important as intensity. Imagine that you are trying to melt a certain metal with a melting temperature of two thousand degrees Fahrenheit. You could keep this metal in a low temperature fire for a very long time without getting anywhere. To get the transformation, you have to reach the critical point of intensity—in this case, two thousand degrees. It doesn’t matter whether it takes a day or a week, one year or twenty; you have to reach the critical point of intensity before you have the melt, the transformation. So it is with the *koan*; extreme intensity of doubt, total saturation, brings the explosion of awakening. Now let's consider the role of *accumulation, saturation*, and *explosion* in the creative process.

Accumulation: This is the initial phase of the creative process. We might call it "great beginnings." This is the stage when the idea first occurs and generates the initial action. For this stage to come to its fullest development, one must do everything she can to accumulate that which supports the initial revelation. She might accumulate knowledge or materials, the support of other people, or her own energy through the scheduling of time. Her love for the vision she has seen sets her in motion, collecting the technical, material, intellectual, and human resources she requires to manifest it. She moves with confidence, trusting that, as George Herbert said, "Love makes one fit for any work."[29]

Saturation: This is the second phase of the creative process. We might call this stage "great absorption" or "magnificent obsession." It's the one that separates the men from the boys, the women from the girls. At this point, we find out that there is a world of difference between being *interested by* something and being *interested in* something. You might be *interested by* an attractive person walking down the street, but to create a relationship with someone, you have to be consistently *interested in* them—warts and all. The original creative idea might have seemed interesting to you, but are you ready to stay with it—to keep creating interest in it, even when you're not sure of what you're doing? This is the test of saturation.

In the first stage, the creative idea comes to you; in the last stage, it takes on its own life; in the middle, the saturation stage, it takes your life. It temporarily embodies in you. Because of your love for this vision, you freely give yourself over to it. Think of a creative idea as a living entity that exists on another plane of existence. This entity wants to live on the physical plane. The problem is, it doesn't have a physical body; so it will borrow yours while you make one for it. The entity will tell you how to construct its new body and will work through you to do it. Time and again, creative artists report on this process.

Often labor pains are associated with the body-building process. This is why the lives of creative artists sometimes take on a tragic quality. Until they have set the idea free, they hang suspended, as it were, between two worlds (the idea realm of the creative vision and the physical world of manifestation). Saturation in the creative

The excellency of every art is its intensity, capable of making all disagreeables evaporate.

John Keats

vision may cause them to neglect other areas of their lives. The artist lives for the work even more than for himself. One biographer of Mozart has written of the great composer: "Artistically he succeeded, though he died penniless. Throughout [he was] . . . a creative artist with a goal that had to be achieved. No matter what, he adhered to his vision."[30] This is creative saturation—that no matter what, you adhere to your vision.

Intensity is the essence of saturation. Sometimes the work comes out all at once. Mozart was said to have written many of his compositions as if taking dictation. On the other hand, many reworkings are often necessary to realize the original vision. Beethoven reworked the theme of the *adagio* movement of his Fifth Symphony at least a dozen times; James Joyce spent nineteen years on *Finnegan's Wake;* Cezanne, at least eight years on his great *Women Bathers*.[31] Often the artist is forced by the demands of the vision to grow—to develop in ways that make him better able to express the creative image. After many years of work, part one of Goethe's *Faust* was published in 1808. Twenty-four years later, part two was published. Goethe was still at work on his masterpiece in the last months of his life. One can say without question that the man who wrote part one was not the same man who wrote part two. He grew with the work. He remained intensely saturated in it throughout.[32]

Explosion: This is the final stage of the creative process. We might call it "happy endings." In this stage, the work becomes a thing in itself, whole and complete. A tremendous explosive relief often accompanies the completion of a creative work. The thing has its own life now and is done with you (though something of you is in it). There may be a sense of loss. If we hold too tightly to that which now has its own life, if after the high voltage of saturation we find our energy dropping to a more mundane level, if we no longer feel useful, or if we are struck at how far the creation seems to stand from the original vision, we may feel a sense of loss or let down.

On the other hand, we might experience great joy on completion. One may feel as though a great burden has been lifted from his shoulders. He may feel free to pursue other creative endeavors that were not possible while he was saturated in the previous creative work. Even as a pregnant woman cannot conceive, we are not free to begin great new projects while in the midst of building the body for a great idea. The joy of the completion is in the total release of saturated energy. As we can see, each stage of the creative process has its own joy. There is the enthusiastic joy of the new idea, the concentrated joy of absorption or saturation, and the explosive joy of completion.

What is Art? It is the response of man's creative soul to the call of the Real.

Tagore

What's Ahead in Act I

There are a number of ways to slice a cake. There are, likewise, a number of ways to find your life's work. No matter how you slice it, cake is cake. No matter how you find it, your life's work is your life's work. In "The Quest for Life's Work," we present several methods, or approaches, to help you tap into your life's work. Each approach stands on its own as a means of discovery. Yet combining all of these methods will help you to see your work with a clarity and breadth not possible through any single method. Each method can be thought of as tapping into a different level of awareness. Some of these approaches may resonate with you more than others. Whatever method you use, the key ingredient in finding your life's work is your desire. With enough desire and commitment, any of these methods or others will work for you. Lacking sufficient desire, all methods are inadequate.

"Scene I: Vision Questing" invites you to consider your world view (the way you see the world) and the effect that it has in shaping the world. Further, it asks you to consider what world, national, or community problems you might like to work toward solving. Finally, it asks you to use your imagination in seeing the world as it could be and to recognize and honor the inspirations that have already come to you.

"Scene II: Clarifying Values" asks you to answer questions like: What values are most important to me? What is my basic philosophy of life? What are the most important lessons I have learned in life? What seemed most important to me as a child?

"Scene III: Pointing to Purpose" invites you to answer questions like: What am I doing here? What is my part in this grand play of life? How can I make a difference? What do I want to do?

"Scene IV: Targeting Talents" asks you to answer questions like: What do I love to do? What am I naturally good at? What are my natural strengths and abilities? Further, it asks you to consider how you can best put your talents to work in service to your vision, values, and purpose.

"Scene V: Marking Mission Objectives" This section invites you to answer questions like: What specific outcomes do I want to effect? What can I realistically achieve in the span of my life? What *must* I do?

It is the first of all problems for a man (or woman) to find out what kind of work he (or she) is to do in this universe.

Thomas Carlyle

Detour #1: The Denial Trap

Man is a social animal. This statement is a truism, one we all accept and pass by without contemplating the meaning. If man is a social animal, then his existence and action cannot but affect his fellows. Man, fully conscious of himself as a social being (regardless of whatever else he may be), recognizes that he affects and creates social reality in his individual choices and actions. If he is a social animal, he cannot do otherwise. Therefore, to say that he has a responsibility to the social order he is creating and perpetuating is almost too clumsy an expression, for that responsibility is no different from the responsibility to himself. It is simply a matter of being what he is.

The denial of the social aspect of man is a denial of self. It is a denial of one's own nature. This denial takes two forms: "Don't Care" and "Don't Know." "Don't care about others" equals "Don't care about self." "Don't know what I can contribute to others" means "I don't know myself." It is in hiding behind "Don't Care" and "Don't Know" that we perpetuate folly. For to act without self-knowledge (self-awareness) is to make action itself a denial of self. By self-knowledge here, we do not mean some mystical apparition; we mean the simple realization of the basic truism we began with, i.e., man is a social animal.

One can now begin to understand how we have come to make such a mess of our world. We have been acting without basic self-awareness. We have been acting as if we were not social. Precisely because this denial has been so strong, we are now beginning to break free of it. Our denial has produced weapons of destruction and environmental consequences that put in jeopardy the entire human species.

The individual's denial of social nature has come at last to put the individual at risk. We are being forced to face the fact that we are all in this together, that indeed man is a social animal.

Don't Care: "Social responsibility" is not an afterthought of an "enlightened person"; it is a fundamental part of being true to what one is. The pursuit of so-called "self-interest" apart from the realization of the social nature of self is immature because it is unaware. The mature individual cares, not out of largess, but because he cares about himself.

Don't Know: "Don't know what to do" is the last hiding place from awareness. (We discuss this on pages 237–244.) Here we will simply say: Do something that needs to be done. Don't do things that are better left undone. Support those who are doing things that need to be done. Find what needs to be done that goes undone and do it.

Crafting the Story of Your Life

Throughout this book, we will be asking you to think of your life as a story. When most novelists sit down to write, they don't know everything that is going to happen in their story. They start with an idea, a compelling central question that they work out through the plot and characters. We invite you to approach the story of your life in this way—to start with the life questions you want most to explore, and shape these into a rough outline. Don't worry about the details or about how you will accomplish your objectives. We will get to that later. Start by letting your imagination follow the track of the questions or issues that grab you.

Of course, you are the main character of your life's story as well as the author. In a good novel, the main character grows and develops, so too in a good life. A good novel has an interesting plot, so does a good life. An author must be able to step back and see her story from a distance—to objectively consider whether or not it achieves her purpose. Ask yourself, "If I could look at it objectively, would I want to read the story of my life? Does it grab and hold my attention? Does it have the elements of a good story: challenges to overcome, growth, direction, confidence, a larger-than-self purpose?" If the answer is no, then perhaps the main character needs development; the plot needs to be clarified, expanded, sharpened; or excitement needs to be generated by increasing the tension between what could be and what is. If the answer is yes, then—where is the next chapter going?

Your Story's Elements

You can conceive of the action of life's work planning in terms of the elements that go into crafting a story.

Act I—The Quest for Life's Work: **Fixing the Central Questions.** Finding voice. Outlining the Plot.

Act II—The Game of Life's Work: **Developing the Characters and Their Roles.** Particularly the main character.

Act III—The Battle for Life's Work: **Clarifying the Conflicts.** Tension between what could be and what is.

Act IV—The School of Life's Work: **Identifying Character Growth.** How is the main character (you) to become a better, more capable person?

The Quest for Life's Work Affirmations

1. I am now willing to see the vision of my life's work.

2. Whatever fears or blocks may have kept me from seeing my work in the past are now dissolved by my desire to know and be my very best.

3. I am open to receiving the vision of my life's work easily and with joy. I now receive it.

4. I am willing to accept this vision and promise to be responsible to and for it.

5. Having seen the vision of my life's work, I trust that it will continue to reveal itself more fully to me as time goes by.

6. I am confident of my ability to manifest the vision I see.

7. I boldly take each and every step necessary to make this vision manifest.

8. My strongest talents and abilities are now made clear to me. I accept and embrace them with gratitude.

9. I am happy that I am a unique individual, endowed with unique talents and abilities. I never spend my precious time and energy comparing my talents with those of others.

10. I like me, and I like being who I am. I am glad I have the talents that I have, and I use them wisely in service to others.

11. Each and every day, it becomes more clear to me how I can best apply my talents to my life's work.

12. The more I focus on my desire to achieve the vision of my life's work, the more my talents become clear to me and the more effectively I use them.

Vision Questing

If we want to make something really superb of this planet, there is nothing whatever that can stop us.

Shepherd Mead

I dentifying your visions of and for the world starts you on the quest for your best. You project your vision beyond the myopic, self-centered concerns that often block the perception of a life's work. As you deeply consider what you would like to see for mankind and the world, your own part in that process will begin to come into view. In this section, you will have the opportunity to consider your world view (the way you see the world), the clarity of your perception, and the depth of your imagination. You will be challenged to love the world as it is, while holding an image of the world that could be.

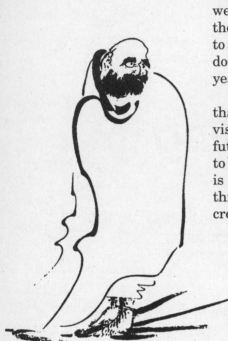

As we enter the twenty-first century, the era of global consciousness is upon us. We have come to recognize that we are drifting through space on a circular life raft. Our vision of the world and of our place on it have changed dramatically in the last several decades. This change in vision portends a similarly dramatic change in the reality of life on this planet, provided, of course, that we can integrate it in time. A vision that recognizes our place within the universe and the interdependence of all life on earth is coming to supplant the independent "man against nature" view, which has dominated Western thinking for at least the last three hundred years, and by now, has been exported to every corner of the globe.

In the discussion that follows, we consider: vision as *world view,* that is, as a way of seeing; vision as *a process of perception;* and vision as *an imaginative, or creative, process*. Your vision for the future is expressed in the way you see the world today. This applies to both your world view and your ability to accurately perceive what is going on in it. Vision as an imaginative process means simply this: everything that has ever been created began as an idea—we create what we imagine.

Vision in Three Aspects

1. World View: Vision As a Way of Seeing
2. Perception: The Vision to See What Is Going On
3. Imagination: The Vision to See What Could Be

World View: Vision As a Way of Seeing

Without vision the people perish.
Proverbs 29:18

The way you look at the world—the Germans call it *Weltanshauung* or *world view*. A world view is a "general perspective from which one sees and interprets the world."[1] Put another way, your world view is your metaphysical window to the world. *Metaphysic* means, simply: beyond (*meta*) the physical (*physic*). A metaphysic is a view that cannot be accounted for on the basis of empirical evidence; it can neither be proved nor disproved by fact or argument. It's an overarching way of seeing that colors all our so-called objective observations and "logical" interpretations. The old metaphysical debate in the West was: Does God exist or not? Today the question is: Is life sacred or not?

In the most general terms, there are but two world views. One can take the view that life is sacred or the view that life is a commodity. A sacred view of life gives birth to feelings of duty, protection, and love. It emphasizes values of joy, beauty, happiness, and caring and sets up an *internal* constraint against the exploitation of other individuals, groups, or species. Our word *sacred* comes from the Latin *sacer* "from the root seen also in *sanus*, sane."[2] A sacred view of life, then, is a sane view of life. A commodity view is interested in profit, domination, and control. It seeks to "gain the world" and subjugate it to the will of man (and only "the fittest" men at that). At the core of the commodity view of life are two seeds: *individual self-interest economics* and *man-against-nature technology*. Planet earth is choking on these seeds.

An entirely new system of thought is needed, a system based on attention to people, and not primarily attention to goods. . .

E. F. Schumacher

You needn't be religious in the conventional sense to hold a sacred view of life. There are those who claim no personal God, yet have a sense of the sacredness of life. On the other hand, there are those who profess belief in God and yet seem to view life as a commodity. Christian or Jew, Moslem or Buddhist, Hindu or humanist, atheist or agnostic, pantheist or shamanist, if life is sacred to you, you may have more in common than you think. While there are endless differences in the interpretation and emphasis made by those who hold a sacred, or sane, view of life, a few essentials are commonly accepted. These include *wholeness*, *harmony*, and *radiance*. (These terms are from Joyce's theory of art. Notice the parallels with the Eastern *sat, cit, ananda*—or being, consciousness, and bliss; the Christian Father, Son, and Holy Spirit; or the Greek three graces—Thalia, Euphrosyne, and Agalia; etc.)

The Wholeness of Life: *There is an intelligent life order that is beyond human understanding.* This life order may be called divine or natural intelligence, cosmic or scientific law, or a host of other names, but anyhow, it exists. This life order is an integrated whole. It is more than a sum of its parts. In fact, the idea of considering static "parts" as having existence beyond language is anachronistic to modern physics. In the words of Fritjof Capra, "...the constituents of matter and the basic phenomena involving them are all interconnected; they cannot be understood as isolated entities but only as integral parts of a unified whole."[3]

The universe is made of one kind of what-ever-it-is, which cannot be defined.

Thaddeus Golas

The Harmony of Life: *Call it the web of life, ecological interdependence, gaia, or the noosphere, we are all in relationship with one another.* The universe is better understood as a living organism than as a machine. Events in one part of the organism affect the whole of the organism. Since every change affects the entire system, we ought to seek harmony in the system rather than the advantage of any individual, group, or species over others. As Martin Luther King, Jr. wrote: "It really boils down to this: that all life is interrelated. We are all caught in an inescapable network of mutuality, tied into a single garment of destiny. Whatever affects one directly, affects all indirectly."

Everything in Nature contains all the powers of Nature. Everything is made of hidden stuff.
Emerson

The Radiance of Life: *Life itself has value.* Beyond any purpose we can imagine, life itself is valuable and ought to be celebrated, preserved, and protected. Save the whales or rain forests, whether profitable or not; avoid war; uphold human dignity, because life is valuable. Life is a Mystery. In the words of Albert Schweitzer: "We can no longer say that there is a senseless existence with which we can do as we please. We recognize that all existence is a mystery like our own existence."[4]

Again, these terms of the sacred do not belong to any particular religion or even to religion per se. The following from Albert Einstein has all the elements of a sacred view of life: "[The scientist's] religious feeling takes the form of a rapturous amazement [radiance] at the harmony [harmony] of natural law, which reveals an intelligence of such superiority [wholeness] that, compared with it, all systematic thinking and acting of human beings is utterly insignificant."[5]

For the purposes of this discussion, we will assume that you hold a sacred view of life. While the facts and logic that support a sacred view are, to those who hold it, overwhelmingly persuasive; for those who don't, they're not. We will not try to convince those who are not already so inclined or make a lengthy restatement of the argument for those who are. For those who need convincing, *Small Is Beautiful: Economics As If People Mattered*, by E. F. Schumacher and *The Tao of Physics*, by Fritjof Capra state the case well, not to mention the Bible, the Talmud, the Upanishads, the Bhagavad-Gita, the Koran, the Dhammapada, etc.

Out of the sacred view, ethics flow naturally. From a commodity point of view, efforts at moral or ethical restraints must rely on reward and punishment. Holding to a sacred view, we can let ethics take care of themselves. Losing a sacred view, ethics are always artificial, inadequate, and bound to create resistance and opposition.

Commodity ethics: *Everything is for sale, and the one with the gold rules . . .*

Sacred ethics: *Do unto others as you would have them do unto you . . .* Love your neighbor as yourself. What goes around comes around, etc.

Again, sacred or not, a world view is a metaphysic, and metaphysics are indeed *meta* (beyond) the physical. They are essentially choices. While a metaphysic can never be proved or disproved by facts, a metaphysic does select out the facts that support it and ignore those that do not. For example, happiness is not a matter of fact but of attitude. If one is unhappy, he finds the facts to substantiate his unhappiness; if happy, he finds the facts to support his happiness. Happiness, while independent of facts as a cause, can itself become a fact. We all can recognize the fact of a happy man or woman. Occasionally such a recognition of fact can even trigger a spontaneous change of attitude. This is the effect that an example can have on us. He has not proved the efficacy of his view by logic; rather, by example, he has demonstrated it.

Nothing is so contagious as an example. We never do great good or great evil without bringing about more of the same on the part of others.
François de La Rochefoucauld

If we're going to change the quality of life in any appreciable way, we must begin, not with facts, but with attitudes. Outer changes always begin with an inner change of attitude. Albert Einstein called this change of attitude "a new level of thinking." He said, "The world we have made as a result of a level of thinking we have done thus far creates problems we cannot solve at the same level at which we created them."[6] Acting from the attitude of a sacred view of life creates a new set of facts, as well as a different perception of the existing facts. It represents a "new level of thinking."

Many do not know that we are here in this world to live in harmony.

Dhammapada

Continue to soil your bed and you will one night suffocate in your own waste.

Chief Seattle 1844

It is less important that we change the minds of others than that we have the courage to put our sacred vision into practice. Those who are caught up in the commodity world view will probably remain unconvinced, at least in the near term. They may try to involve you in "proving" the viability of your vision or discount it as unrealistic or even simple-minded. Remember, from a commodity world view, economic profit is what is real and valuable. All other values are secondary, even superfluous: "It's nice to do good, but what REALLY matters is the bottom line." The commodity world view is not fundamentally interested in what is right or necessary, valuable or serving, beautiful or wise but in what will sell. Its important facts are dollar signs and profit potentials and often only short-term ones at that. Other facts may not register through the filter of the commodity metaphysic.

Apart from business, economic profitability has become the sole, or at least dominant, criteria by which projects in science, art, and the humanities are judged. In considering whether a project is "worthy of support," its purpose or quality is less important than its bottom-line potential. The term *viable*, which originally meant "able to live," has come to mean "economically profitable." This redefinition has meant the extinction of thousands of species of plants and animals, not to mention the elimination of many human pursuits that are seen as superfluous to profit. All this, it is argued, is a necessary part of the high standard of living we enjoy. But, as E. F. Schumacher has noted, high standards of living do not necessarily mean high standards of life.[7]

Those with a commodity view may have difficulty seeing, let alone supporting, what you are trying to do. (Unless, of course, you frame it in commodity terms, for example, "green profits.") "Good works" are agreeable from the commodity standpoint, so long as their advocacy does not challenge the legitimacy of the commodity view itself. For example, it is worthwhile to educate and train the inner city poor *because* we have a labor shortage and need more skilled workers to "stay competitive." This is an acceptable commodity argument. On the other hand, asserting the dignity and value of all human life as sacred and worthy of a decent and even a beautiful life may not be heard by those with a commodity perspective.

Make a profit coming and going; this is progress from a commodity approach. The commodity metaphysic, which has been the ruin of the environment, is now ready to turn "saving" the environment into a commodity. Today the business magazines are trumpeting the big profits waiting to be made on the environment. Water polluted and loaded down with chemicals from industrial waste and agricultural run-off? Don't ask fundamental questions about the ethics of the commodity world view; delight in the fact that bottled water is now the fastest growing part of the "beverage industry." The commodity world view that gave us preserved, processed, and "enriched" foods will now give us the original "all natural" foods as high-priced specialty items.

The commodity world view holds that the creation of life itself is a commodity to be owned and sold for profit. For years we have had patents on "grain food commodities." (Meanwhile the genetic diversity of the planet's food grains has dwindled.) Now, genetic strains of animals have been patented. What's next? While all of the above are taken as signs of progress from the commodity view, they are clearly dangerous from any sane perspective interested in the long-term quality of life on this planet.

Every great movement must experience three stages: ridicule, discussion, adoption.
                                    John Stuart Mill

The purpose of this discussion is not to condemn or complain but simply to demonstrate that so much of the insanity of this world makes perfect sense (is understandable) from the commodity metaphysic. If we are going to change the world in any fundamental way, we must collectively change the way we see the world and ourselves in it. This, of course, can only happen one individual at a time. The writer who gives up his art to strike it rich in advertising or the manager who takes less pay and more hours to work for a nonprofit foundation engaged in a service he believes in—each is deciding in his own way the future of the world. The victories and defeats are one at a time—not a matter of "them" but of you and me. Gandhi put it eloquently: "I believe that if one man gains spiritually, the whole world gains with him, and if one man falls, the whole world falls to that extent."[8]

Of course, the sacred view of life is still the minority view in the developed world. From the standpoint of the commodity metaphysic, it is a dangerous heresy. If you put your sacred world view into practice, you may be ridiculed or scorned, not because your view is unsubstantiated by the facts, but because it is not yet the prevailing one. (All minority views are considered stupid until they gain acceptance.) You may be told to "grow up" or to "get with it." Certainly we can all grow more mature. Yet it is lunacy to imagine that the rejection of the sacredness of life is a necessary element of the maturation process. If it is, we will shortly mature our species out of existence. "Get with it" may mean: "Get into step. March your way

The more I study physics, the more I am drawn to metaphysics.

Albert Einstein

into consumer heaven. Never mind the larger social perspective or the deeper spiritual one—just get what you can while you can."

Whoso would be a man must be a nonconformist.
Ralph Waldo Emerson

If you are out of step because you are taking the time to reflect upon your direction or because you are already acting out of a sacred view, be undaunted in the face of the pressure to conform. You cannot prove the validity of a sacred view of life, but you can over time create and leave behind something that others can recognize. See life as sacred, and work to make it so. From the context of a sacred view of life, we create from perceiving a need or directly from inspiration. Later we will consider creating from inspiration. For now, let's consider how we create from perception.

Perception: The Vision to See What Is Going On

Nothing has such power to broaden the mind as the ability to investigate systematically and truly all that comes under thy observation in life.
Marcus Aurelius

The second aspect of vision is *perception*. Even as we create the world by our attitudes toward it, so do we create the world by our perceptions of it. It is one of the great marvels of consciousness that whatever situation we clearly perceive, we improve. To see is to see a better way; to perceive any problem clearly is to begin to create its solution. All we need is the wisdom and patience to keep looking and the love to hold what we see up to the light of understanding. Only when we doubt our capacity to create (love) do we begin to block and distort our perceptions of the world. Only then do we fear to look at it square on. From the love and confidence of clear perception, the world must become a better place. It is a necessity.

Again, whatever we give our loving attention to naturally improves. We all know, for example, that plants respond to loving kindness and attention. *The Secret Life of Plants,* by Peter Tomkins and Christopher Bird, gives incredible testimony to the power of loving attention to affect plant growth and well-being.[9] What is true for plants is certainly true for the "higher" forms of life. We all have had practical experience with this; areas of our lives that we avoid and neglect become problem areas. Once we begin to give these areas loving attention, they start to improve.

We usually move from avoidance and confusion to attention and clarity only when we perceive that it is necessary. It was Plato who gave us that wonderful saying: Necessity is the mother of invention. Necessity is simply the perception that something must be improved (i.e., given more attention) and that the perceiver is the one to do something about it. Once we deem it necessary, we begin to look over what we had previously overlooked, until we see a better way. Necessity often forces us out of the prejudices and conceptual limitations that have heretofore blocked our perception. Necessity has an intensity, an urgency to it. Without this intensity, there is no drive to keep looking for a better way.

For example, well over 50 percent of all employed Americans consistently report that they are dissatisfied in their work.[10] Most, however, never allow their dissatisfaction to reach the point where action becomes a necessity. They never know the kind of necessity that would compel them to thoroughly examine themselves and their environments until they perceive a truer vision of their life's work.

Of course, necessity, like beauty, is in the eye of the beholder. No matter how deplorable a situation may seem to an outsider, the individual involved finds no reason to look for a better way until, for him, it becomes a necessity. When discontent reaches the point of necessity, we demand of ourselves and our world that a better way be shown. Until then we put up with less. Because we fear and hate the problems that seem to trap us, we find no way out. It is often necessary that we find more confidence and love before things can start to improve.

I clearly see how the Eternal Light
*   Shines in your mind,*
*   So that upon its mere sight, love is enkindled.*
*   Dante*

Joyously participate
in the sorrows
of others.

This applies to the bigger picture of planetary and community problems as well as to our individual concerns. We are stuck in these problems until we have the confidence and strength to look at them with love. The gift of the innovator is his ability to keep his attention on what most of us avoid. He makes it a necessity to find a better way. She keeps looking until she does. We can say that it was a necessity for Jonas Salk to discover the cure for polio, for Maria Montessori to design a better way of educating children, or

The soul . . .
Never thinks
without a picture.

Aristotle

for Gandhi to devise an effective means of nonviolent social change. Creative discontent was driving them all.

Where is creative discontent taking you? What is the better way you see for the world as a whole or in some particular arena? Perhaps it's the cure for some contagious disease or a means of more efficient energy use. Perhaps it's a way of improving communication within families. Maybe it's a necessity for you to create a better way of dealing with drug addiction or a better way of coordinating nonprofit resources and activities. Maybe it's a necessity to create a better way of utilizing the knowledge, skill, and energy of the elderly. Perhaps it's a necessity for you to bring about an advance in whatever field you work in or want to work in. What are your necessary discoveries? If you don't know yet, keep looking. Sharpen your observation skills.

There is nothing so difficult but that it may be found out by seeking.

Terence

Leonardo da Vinci kept extensive notebooks. Hundreds of detailed drawings of everything from the flight of cannonballs to the structure of plants, from human anatomy to fish eggs, honed his observation skills. What he learned from these detailed observations was of great benefit to him in his later inventions and artistic creations.[11]

Buckminster Fuller kept detailed diaries in what he called his "Chronofile." Fuller viewed himself as a guinea pig and the world as his laboratory. Careful observation of both led him to an important discovery. In his words: "Chronofile observation showed that the larger the number for whom I worked, the more positively effective I became. Thus it became obvious that if I worked always and only for humanity, I would be optimally effective." It was on the basis of these observations that he determined to commit all of his ". . . productivity potentials to dealing with our whole planet Earth . . ."[12] His discovery of optimal effectiveness in world service was probably his single most important discovery, since all later discoveries depended upon his fixing his attention on global problems.

A man of science doesn't discover in order to know,
he wants to know in order to discover.
Alfred North Whitehead

Careful observation helps to keep the mind in shape. In the words of da Vinci, "Iron rusts from disuse; water loses its purity from stagnation, and in cold weather becomes frozen; even so does inaction sap the vigors of the mind."[13] All the great minds seem to be saying: "Don't be afraid of problems. Take a creative look at them." Creative solutions arise spontaneously upon the clear perception of particular personal, community, or planetary problems. Whatever level you are working on, get clear on exactly what the problems are. Penetrate to the essence. According to Einstein, "The formulation of a problem is far more essential than its solution."

Seeing with the Eyes of Patience: Unmasking the Ignorance Blinder

Often our ignorance blocks us from creative solutions. We cannot see a solution until we have sufficient data. We must have the patience to persist until we see a problem clearly enough for a solution to occur. Many times the solutions are right in front of our noses, but we don't see them. For example, Buckminster Fuller was able to demonstrate that we have all the energy we need on the planet to exist in a high standard of living, without having to destroy nonreplenishable resources.

Don't listen to what they say. Go see.
Chinese Proverb

Most of us accept the conventional assumptions of lack because we are ignorant of the facts and lack the patience to investigate. But Fuller and the "World Game" he founded ". . . demonstrated beyond any argument that humanity can carry on handsomely and adequately when advantaged only by its daily energy income from the Sun-gravity system." As with energy supply, so too, food, ". . . we can take ample care of all human food needs."[14] (Those interested in more on this are directed to *Critical Path* [St. Martin's Press, 1982] by R. Buckminster Fuller.)

Time and again, we accept limitations simply because we don't know any better. We must exert the confidence and maintain the patience to investigate until we see a better way. Two hundred years ago, Alexander Hamilton described this kind of confident patience when he said: "Men give me credit for some genius. All the genius I have lies in this; when I have a subject in hand, I study it profoundly. Day and night it is before me. My mind becomes

For ignorance is in reality the Buddha nature.

Cheng-Dao Ke

For the contemplative is the path of knowledge; For the active is the path of selfless action.

Bhagavad-Gita

pervaded by it. Then the effort I have made is what people are pleased to call the fruit of genius. It is the fruit of labor and thought."

It is our duty as men and women to proceed as though the limits of our abilities do not exist.
Pierre Teilhard de Chardin

Remember, people were once told that bleeding was the best cure for disease and that slavery was an economic necessity. We have been told we must sell out to get along and that many of the world's problems are insurmountable. Always we can yield to the blinder of ignorance or make resolute our determination to look until we see a better way. It has been wisely said that there is nothing that will not reveal its secrets to you if you love it enough. All things improve with loving attention.

Seeing with the Eyes of Strength: Unmasking the Fear Blinder

It is not ignorance alone that keeps us from perceiving our personal, community, and planetary problems or from acting to

---

Buddha's Enlightenment Begins by Seeing Suffering

While most of us in this culture are seeking the lifestyles of the rich and famous, Gautama Buddha, who grew up in a life of tremendous luxury, sought the imperishable. Gautama Buddha was born Prince Siddhartha. It had been prophesied that he might one day become a great renunciate. His father, the king, wanted very much to avoid this. He tried to keep the prince from ever seeing any suffering, lest it prompt him to renounce the princely life. He kept young Siddhartha safely closeted in beautiful palaces. Around him were only beautiful people, beautiful things, and beautiful goings-on. He never saw old age or sickness, ugliness or death. He lived a comfortable life with his wife Yasodhara and son Rahula.

By the time he was twenty-nine, the prince was getting bored with hanging around the palace all day. He asked his abate them. For example, we daily see scenes of war, injustice, indignity, and violence flashed before us on our television screens. Yet many of us have insulated and isolated ourselves from the suffering of the world. The need seems so great, the hunger so vast as to be almost overwhelming. In fear of being overwhelmed, we dull our senses.

All the world is full of suffering, it is also full of overcoming it.

Helen Keller

It *is* a hungry world we live in. This world is hungry, not just in material terms, not just because over 20 percent of its population faces chronic malnourishment or starvation. It's hungry in so many ways—hungry for knowledge, hungry for wisdom, hungry for caring, hungry for justice, hungry for beauty, hungry for peace, hungry for joy, hungry for love, your love. Rather than to fear the enormity of world problems, we can act with courage, responding to the particular hungers we are called to feed. Mother Teresa put it like this: "What we do is nothing but a drop in the ocean, but if we didn't do it, the ocean would be one drop less." Mahatma Gandhi said, "Whatever you do may seem insignificant, but it is very important that you do it."

father if he could go out and look around and see how the other folks lived. His father said yes, but in advance of the prince's visit, sent out his men to clear the streets of anyone who was poor, old, sick, or suffering in any way. Everything was given a fresh coat of paint and spruced up nicely.

In full regalia, the young Siddhartha sallied forth to see the world for himself. Alas, all of his father's efforts were in vain. The prince encountered an old senile man, a man wracked by disease, and a corpse on its way to the funeral pyre, with grieving friends and relatives in tow. He also saw an ascetic who had renounced the world.

After seeing all this suffering, Siddhartha thought his life of material comfort had been a waste. He became an ascetic, seeking to discover what there is that is beyond sickness, old age, and death . . . *So it was that seeing the sufferings of the world was the beginning of the Buddha's quest for enlightenment.*[15]

> *Alas! the fearful Unbelief is unbelief in yourself.*
> *Thomas Carlyle*

The hunger of the world cries out for the food of your loving attention. Listen and discover what kind of food you have; then distribute it where it is most needed and wanted. Do you have spiritual food or the food of laughter? Do you have wisdom food or affection food? Do you have beauty food or confidence food? Whatever food you have, share it. We can all feed each other our best food, and in so doing, nourish all life. Remember, there are so many ways to serve. It needn't look any particular way. It is up to you to see clearly—to find your way.

Of course, to see suffering is to feel suffering. Many fear that they won't be able to handle the suffering of the world and its people. Many of us have dedicated our lives to feeling good, to avoiding suffering at all costs. We want day without night, beauty without ugliness, comedy without tragedy. Sooner or later, we must find a love big enough and strong enough to love life exactly as it is.

> *Man was made for Joy and Woe;*
> *And when this we rightly know,*
> *Thro' the World we safely go,*
> *Joy and woe are woven fine,*
> *A clothing for the soul divine.*
> *William Blake*[16]

If it hurts to see the suffering of the world, it also hurts to avoid it. Avoidance has its pain, no matter how we try to deaden it. In America, 120 million prescriptions for psychiatric drugs are written each year. Thirty million people take sedatives on a regular basis. Fifteen percent of the American population are alcoholics. Each year, we spend approximately fifty billion dollars on illicit drugs. Suicide rates among our young have skyrocketed in the last two decades. These are problems that know no ethnic, racial, or class boundaries.

Clearly we cannot run from the pain of the world. Rather, we can learn to look with eyes of strength into the darkest abyss and not flinch. We can gain confidence in the knowledge that only that which we avoid as individuals and as a species will, in the long run, hurt us. What we refuse to be aware of does not go away. If anything, it only becomes more pronounced. Below are a few facts that we must not be afraid to be aware of. Information about the state of the world is available, but you may have to dig a little to find it. (See list of sources on pages 177–178.)

No one must shut his eyes and regard as non-existent the sufferings of which he spares himself the sight. Let no one regard as light the burden of his responsibility.

Albert Schweitzer

- In the world economy, weapons and drugs are the number one and two industries, respectively.

- The largest killer of children worldwide is diarrhea (for which there is an inexpensive and easily administered cure).

- The average American consumes fifteen times as much of the world's resources as the average Indian.

- More grain goes to feeding American cows than to feeding all the people of India and China (approximately two billion people).

- The difference in income between the rich and poor is greater in America than in any of the other top twenty industrialized nations.

- Sixty-six percent of the world's population take in roughly 10 percent of the world's income.

- One percent of the U.S. population owns as much wealth as the lower 80 percent.

- According to a recent study reported by the Food Research and Action Center, 5.5 million children in America are hungry. One in eight American children under the age of twelve go to bed hungry.

> *Can I see another's woe*
> *And not be in sorrow too?*
> *Can I see another's grief*
> *And not seek for kind relief?*
> *William Blake*[17]

*Bless relaxes,
damn braces.*

William Blake

Seeing with the Eyes of Beauty: Unmasking the Hatred Blinder

There is some soul of goodness in things evil, Would men observingly distill it out.

Shakespeare

It is easy to hate and often difficult to love. With clear perception, we see the weakness of man, his greed, folly, and capacity for cruelty. It seems that everywhere we look, we see man's inhumanity to man. We are tempted to hate—to be angry and bitter at "them"—for making such a mess of the world. Or we hate the people we have known whom we perceive as hurting or blocking us as individuals. It seems we have a thousand reasons to hate.

Yet to do so is to violate the basic necessity of our being—love. Without love, we cannot be what we are. We may think we have every right to hate or that we are hating for the right reasons, but all the while, hatred is shaping us in the image of the thing we detest. In our efforts to rid the world of evil, we can ourselves become caught up in the evil of hatred. Once tricked into returning hate for hate, we become locked in a vicious circle. Hatred disables our creative capacities and sucks all the beauty out of life. This brings us no advantage but only increases the chance that we will suffer more injury—so then, more hate. On and on it can go . . . Surely we can accomplish no great good nor have lasting happiness with hatred in our hearts.

I hold myself to be incapable of hating any being on earth. By a long course of prayerful discipline, I have ceased for over forty years to hate anybody. I know this is a big claim. Nevertheless, I make it in all humility.

Mahatma Gandhi

When we see people acting in ways that seem to injure us or others, we feel an impulse to condemn the insanity of their actions and to hate them as people. Of course, with a bit of detachment, we see that the problem is simply ignorance and weakness. To hate people for their ignorance or weakness is to become a part of the problem. The solution can only come with the understanding of wisdom and the strength of love. The Buddha said: *Never has hatred ended by hatred. Only by love does hatred cease.*[18]

From a sacred point of view, life is not merely random combinations of inert matter; life is conscious, and consciousness is life! The more conscious we are, the more alive we are, the less conscious, the less alive. "Aliveness" gives us the energy to experience and handle the situations of life. *The more we are willing to be aware of, the more energy we have to create with.* Love is the energy of accepting awareness (life). Hatred is the energy of resisting (or avoiding) awareness. When we resist awareness of something (hate it), we put a damper on our consciousness. We tie up, in denial and defensive reactions, energy that we need to enjoy and handle the situations of life. The greater our avoidance and denial, the less energy we have to create with and the more we will tend to feel like victims—at effect of life.

We all seek safety. We could say that everything we do is an attempt to *make safe*. This is true no matter how dangerous the action appears. It applies to the heroic risk-takers attempting to make their group or humanity as a whole safer (e.g., Gandhi, King) or to make safe the integrity of their own souls (e.g., Socrates, Sir Thomas More). It also applies to the miser, addict, and criminal attempting to make safe their bodies or egos. While the hero acts out of love and furthers life, the others act from hate and diminish it. All are attempting to make safe; the difference is that, while love creates a better way, hatred can only destroy.

Our wisdom (or its lack) is reflected in what we believe will gain us the safety we seek. Hatred is only a misguided attempt at creating safety. The miser, addict, and criminal are all trying to be safe (right) while feeling desperately unsafe (wrong). They are attempting to make safe within a context of avoidance. *While in avoidance, the greater the effort to make safe, the greater actual danger we place ourselves in.* Love is the only safe way. This is so since only in love do we enjoy full consciousness—the full aliveness to enjoy and handle life.

If I keep a green bough in my heart, the singing bird will come.

Chinese Proverb

Of course, the examples above are extreme, but the principle applies to all of us: ***while we hate, we block our capacity to create.*** While in the spell of hatred, the world seems dark and gloomy, bleak and hopeless. Love restores the eyes of beauty, the eyes of the artist. Only with the eyes of beauty can we see the way to a better world. To have a sense of the right without being self-righteous, to have the strength to see the evil of the world and yet to give back love and understanding—is to retain the ability to create a better life for yourself and others.

> *There is a comfort in the strength of love;*
> *'Twill make a thing endurable, which else*
> *Would overset the brain, or break the heart.*
>   *William Wordsworth*

Imagination: The Vision to See What Could Be

The third aspect of vision is *imagination.* Even as we can open our physical eyes to the problems and opportunities of the world as it is, so we can open our mind's eye to the possibilities of as yet unseen realities. To open our physical eyes fully, we must learn to trust that whatever we see, we can look at with eyes of love. To open our mind's eye, we must learn to trust that in some way we will make manifest what we see in our imaginations in the world of form.

Though it is crude to do so, we can say that the vision of perception is the vision of the scientist, and the vision of imagination is the vision of the artist. *Perception,* of course, involves seeing clearly what exists in the outer world; *imagination* means "the act or power of forming mental images of what is not actually present."[19] Of course, these classifications are meant to describe differences in methodologies, not to classify individuals. (Many of the truly great geniuses in both art and science have been well developed in both imagination and keen observation.) Both types of vision are creative. In the former, we give our attention to some situation until we see a better way; in the latter, the creative image seems to come from nowhere. It comes all at once as a bug in the ear, the whispering of the muse.

. . . when your thinking rises above concern for your own welfare, wisdom which is independent of thought appears.

Ha Gakure (Hidden Leaves)

In a seventeenth century samurai text called *Ha Gakure (Hidden Leaves)*, we find this distinction in vision described thus: "Some men are prone to having sudden inspirations. Some . . . arrive at the answer after slow consideration."[20] Usually, we are best at one type of vision or the other. Of course, we all use both, and we all can learn to use each better. However we arrive at our creative visions, it is most important that we claim them and commit ourselves to their realization. As each of us acts on our visions for the world, we better ourselves, almost without trying. Confucius said, "He who wishes to secure the good of others has already secured his own."[21]

The vision of imagination, since it is a pictorial, right brain process, doesn't lend itself well to systematic, left brain discussion. Let's just say that if necessity is the mother of invention, then playfulness is the father. Playfulness is the dew-fresh, childlike spirit of wonder. A roving, wandering, wondering, "what if" kind of a rascal. Unconventional, lightning flash, sailing through the cracks, images come, free and unattached.

The right brain process we are hinting at here is not logical and measured. It is intuitive and spontaneous. If it sounds a little silly, it is important to recognize that it works. Michael Faraday imagined living the life of an atom. He went on to discover the electromagnetic theory. Albert Einstein imagined himself flying through space at light speed. Such play as this was significant in the development of the general theory of relativity. It is said that in the beginning, the telescope was just a toy for Galileo.

Without this playing with fantasy no creative work has ever yet come to birth. The debt we owe to the play of the imagination is incalculable.
                                    C. G. Jung

Go on a vision quest. Consecrate yourself to a high purpose—then let go—when inspirations come—make them manifest in a form that can be enjoyed by others. Remember that the process of imaginative vision has more to do with receptivity than concentrated effort. Struggling and straining don't help; they actually impede the process. Start by relaxing, playing, keeping an open mind. After all, ideas are all around us. Like radio waves, they fill the air. We have simply to open to receive them.

You enhance your receptivity as you relax into stillness and play. Meditation eliminates the mental clutter and clatter that block inspirations. Play gives your mind the freedom to wander where it will. Alfred Benit said, "I find that images appear only if we give our minds uncontrolled freedom . . ." Just let yourself be in a state of reverie. Inspirations come to a mind that is relaxed and alert. The Zen saying is: "Awaken the mind without fixing it anywhere."

When open, our minds have tremendous power to receive ideas. Yet much of the time, we jam our creative imaginations with the static of negativity and limiting beliefs. We are so sure of how

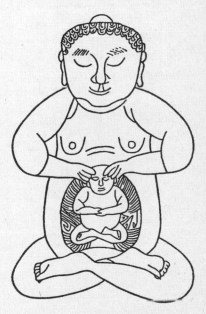

Awaken the mind without fixing it anywhere.

Kungo Kyo

things are that we lose all perspective on how things could be. We have lost the wonder of the childlike mind. We tend to think alike. This conformity of thought maintains society's traditions on the one hand and perpetuates its misconceptions on the other.

What is now proved was once only imagin'd.

William Blake

> *An original concept . . . prefers the mind imbued with the love of Nature, untainted with hidden plans for Her exploitation.*
>
> R. G. H. Sui, (Tao of Science)

Artistic revelation for the artist and artistic perception for the beholder come as "Aha!!!" The artist is as surprised (or more) at his discovery as anyone. From the reference of his conscious mind, it is coming from somewhere else. Call it "the muse," "the mind that is no mind," or "Dionysian ecstasy," a power greater than himself is working itself through him. Intense love has shattered the conscious control barrier, revealing something of the greater-than-self mind and its awful majesty. Less mystically, we can say that love relaxes the stranglehold of the conscious over the subconscious and allows the artist to tap a far deeper and richer well of inspiration.

Where *do* creative visions come from? When it comes to ideas, there is nothing new under the sun. In a sense, all ideas already exist. Newton's discovery of the law of gravity illustrates the point; if the law of gravity is operative, then it was always so, even before the fateful day that the apple came his way (or so they say). He didn't invent or make up gravity; he simply discovered an already existing idea. Before man began to use fire to warm himself and cook his food, the capacity of fire to do these things existed. In a sense, these uses were latent within the idea of fire. The property and action of the law of displacement was operative long before Archimedes took his famous bath.

> *I invent nothing; I rediscover.*
> Rodin

All creative ideas are discovered. The new world called America existed before Columbus or Leif Erickson (or whoever else had dibs on it) bumped their boats on its shores. They did not create America from nothing. They simply made it known to people (including themselves) who were previously ignorant of its existence. So it is with all discoveries. Every discovery, whether through observation or direct inspiration, opens a new world to the discoverer. Further, if the discoverer can somehow communicate her discovery, it becomes a boon she bestows on her society.

To help us understand how all ideas exist now, imagine a universe of ideas, a vast, timeless realm that contains all ideas. Now imagine within this broad universe a smaller subset of all known ideas. These are the ideas that have been discovered. Their time has come. Voltaire said, "There is one thing stronger than all the armies in the world, and that is an idea whose time has come."[22] How it is that an idea's time comes, we cannot say. But when it does, it transforms the world.

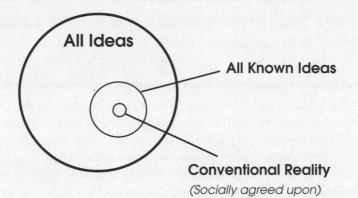

All Ideas

All Known Ideas

Conventional Reality
(Socially agreed upon)

There is often a significant lag between the discovery of an idea and its manifestation. Leonardo Da Vinci envisioned the modern submarine and helicopter four hundred years before their actual manifestation. In 1690, Denis Papin, inventor of the pressure cooker, first proposed the idea of a piston-driven automobile. Yet it was not until 1896 that the first auto was built. This lag principle applies to social and spiritual ideas as well as to physical inventions. Some have suggested the notion of a critical mass or a "hundredth monkey theory" to explain the lag. These theories suggest that when a certain portion (by no means a majority) of the population adopt a new idea, it becomes a part of the conventional, socially agreed upon reality. (See *The Hundredth Monkey* by Ken Keyes.)[23]

Enlighten the people generally, and tyranny and oppressions of body and mind will vanish like evil spirits at the dawn of day.
                                        Thomas Jefferson

If all ideas already exist, what is the role of the genius? Geniuses are those whose receptivity or keen observation allows them to discover previously unexplored or long forgotten sectors of the universe of ideas. A great genius explores sectors that lie beyond the reach of ordinary awareness and brings the ideas she finds there "down to earth" by expressing them in a way that the rest of us can comprehend. Much like Jack in "Jack and the Beanstalk," she climbs the ladder of consciousness and returns with the gold-laying goose of newly discovered or rediscovered ideas, often with the giant of entrenched mediocrity hot on her trail.

I call intuition cosmic fishing. You feel the nibble, and then you have to hook the fish.
                                        Buckminster Fuller

The genius serves as a conduit for ideas, expanding the subset of all known ideas to include a greater portion of the universe of all ideas. Einstein's genius lies, not in the difficulty of his ideas (his theory of relativity is taught to many high school students), but in their potential to enlarge our understanding of the universe we live in. You too have the potential for genius, the potential to expand your known universe.

We are familiar with the great discoveries of history. Those of Copernicus, Gutenberg, Newton, Edison, and Einstein are just a few examples. Yet equally important is the process through which each one of us comes to discover for ourselves the answers to the age-old questions: Who am I? and What am I doing here?

Thoreau said, "Man's capacities have never been measured, nor are we to judge of what he can do by any precedent, so little has been tried."[24] Imagine what wonderful new worlds of ideas are yet to be discovered. They exist now and await discovery, even as the light bulb waited for Edison; relativity, for Einstein; *The Magic Flute,* for Mozart. Like all ideas, your creative visions already exist, whether you have discovered them or not. You may be the next Einstein; yet even if you are not, the way in which you live your life is of great importance to yourself, your loved ones, and in some significant way, to the world as a whole. At this point, you may be asking yourself, But how do I go about discovering the important visions of my life?

When an inspiration hits you, *pay attention*. This is how you develop confidence in your imagination—one step at a time, by acting on your inspirations. As you continue in this, you may gain the confidence to tap into ever higher realms of thought and take

Image creates desire. You will want what you imagine.

J. G. Gallimore

responsibility for ever greater visions. Often we ignore our inspirations and then wonder why our lives seem to lack the marvelous or magical quality we felt as children. Children trust their imaginations and are not afraid of seeming ridiculous. We really needn't fear; we all *are* a little ridiculous.

A genuine vision is a pregnant idea, teeming with life and possibilities. Visionary ideas give birth to other ideas, as well as to the actions that materialize them. Even with ideas that come directly from inspiration, we often have to keep looking for ways to apply them or for other ideas that support them. When asked how he got his ideas, Einstein replied that he only had one. According to Einstein, the rest of his work was merely the development of a single visionary idea. Imagine that.

Francis Bacon said: "A man would do well to carry a pencil in his pocket, and write down the thoughts of the moment. Those that come unsought for are commonly the most valuable, and should be secured, because they seldom return." That's good advice even today. Keep a notebook or journal with you and near your bed. Catch the ideas as they come pouring in. Your dreams can be an important source of creative visions. Your mind is a maker of models. Seeing the image of your vision builds the first model. Getting it down on paper builds the second and so on. Don't expect complete perfection on the first attempt to make this vision manifest. Just begin your sketch, no matter how blind or foolish you may feel. Remember: A journey of a thousand miles begins with the first step, no matter how awkward or tenuous that step may be.

Everything around you—this book, the room you are in, the clothes you are wearing, the political and economic systems you live in—began as an idea in someone's head. Come to think of it, every created thing began as an idea in some fertile mind. In the words of Robert Collier, "The source and center of all man's creative power . . . is his power of making images, or the power of imagination."

Your imagination is your preview of life's coming attractions.

Albert Einstein

You must be the change you wish to see in the world.

Mahatma Gandhi

You have probably had inspirations that you have discounted. Perhaps you have a vision of a better way in art, in science, in education, in child care, in health care, in nutrition, in farming, in social philosophy, in politics. Whatever your vision, recognize it and work to give it expression. *Recollecting your creative inspirations will reconnect you with a potent energy source in your life which you may have been neglecting.* Tune in again, and watch the very thought of the vision charge you with positive feelings and set you in motion.

The visionary artist sees and gives expression to the deeper inner reality that we all experience. Through his art, we are able to experience more deeply our humanity, the mysteries of existence, and the god-like beauty of the human spirit. The poet gives voice to what we all know but cannot express. The artist shapes, forms, and colors the sublime radiance of life. Let them speak:

> *I am the poet of the body and I am the poet of the Soul.*
> *The pleasures of Heaven are with me and the pains of Hell are with me.*
> *The first I graft and increase upon myself, the latter I translate into a new tongue.*
> *Walt Whitman*[25]

> *In every block of marble I see a statue as plain as though it stood before me, shaped and perfect in attitude and action. I have only to hew away the rough walls that imprison the lovely apparition to reveal it to the other eyes as mine see it.*
> *Michelangelo*

But I am no artist, you may protest. Yet is your life any less a canvas because you do not paint? Is your voice any less potent because you do not give it pen? Is your soul barren of song because you compose no notes? No, a thousand times! Life well lived is the greatest art of all. The art of your life is not a matter of talent. It is a matter of MOUNTING THE COURAGE TO LIVE.

It's mounting the courage to SEE what you really are, to be dazzled by the Radiance that is You. Mounting the courage to imagine what this world could be. Mounting the courage to die a thousand deaths to LIVE one life to the fullest. Translate the pains of hell into a new song. Lovely apparitions of possibilities as yet undreamed await those whose hands are strong and steady enough to hew away the rough walls and make their creative vision a manifest reality.

No one knows what he can do until he tries.
Publilius Syrus

Making visible the glorious inner life in the everyday world of form is the creative process. Neurosis is but expression denied. We can't hide and express at the same time any more than we can move forward and backward at once. We hide because we do not accept ourselves as we are. We will not admit the pains of hell, fearing we have not the courage to translate them into a new song. We hide in shame outside the Gates of Eden, invisible to ourselves, blind to others.

Fear not: Your hands are worthy to chisel out the divine image. Live in openness to the possibilities. The muse will visit without call, but she abides only with those who make works of her inspirations. None but yourself can tell you that you are worthy to be her scribe, her errand boy, or handmaiden. Seek her out. Serve well the images she inspires. O noble son, O noble daughter, you are worthy of her divine touch. Consecrate yourself to the sacred vision you see.

Fear not: You can bear the pains of hell and translate them into a new song. As all heroes before you, you must conquer the pains of hell. Open eyes will shed tears, for this world is full of sorrow. The flames of hell reflected in wet pools of tender eyes blaze brilliant the light of love. The sorrow of the world humbles and purifies all idle vanities. Look upon the world, stripped bare, not in a blank stare, but gently with eyes that care. Mother Teresa, who had reason to know, has said, "Sorrow shared becomes joy." What sorrows in this world do we not share, you and I, my brother, my sister?

A man's value to the community primarily depends on how far his feelings, thoughts, and actions are directed towards promoting the good of his fellows.
Albert Einstein[26]

Creating from Vision

All that is is a result of what we have thought.
                    Suttapitaka

Man is what he believes.
                    Anton Chekhov

Imagination rules the world.
                    Napoleon I

The idea that is not dangerous is unworthy of being called an idea at all.
                    Elbert Hubbard

The only real valuable thing is intuition.
                    Albert Einstein

A man's dreams are an index to his greatness.
                    Zadok Rabinowitz

Look within. Within is the fountain of good, and it will ever bubble up, if thou wilt ever dig.
                    Marcus Aurelius

There will be a decrease in the desire for individual advancement, and an increase in the desire for the advancement of the race as a whole.
                    Eugene E. Thomas

What in the World Could Be?

In the space below, write your vision of the world you would like to live in. Do not concern yourself with how realistic your vision is, how it would be implemented, or what your part in creating it might be. Simply write your vision as though you could wave a magic wand and have it manifest in one fell swoop. This is your opportunity to create your utopia. Use additional sheets of paper if necessary.

_____

_____

_____

_____

_____

_____

_____

Now do the same for your nation.

_____

_____

_____

_____

_____

_____

Now do likewise for your community.

_____

_____

_____

_____

_____

_____

_____

 Attitudes are more important than facts.
Carl Menninger

Your World Needs Your Love

This process provides you with the opportunity to assess the needs of your world, nation, and community. We have found that one of the key components to a satisfying and fulfilling life's work is the sense that you are making a contribution to the world you live in. This exercise is a problem-solving approach to your world that will help you determine what you can do to make it better.

In your estimation, what are the most critical needs on the planet that are going unmet, or what are the greatest sources of pain and suffering in the world?

_____
_____
_____
_____
_____
_____
_____
_____

In your nation?

_____
_____
_____
_____
_____

In your community?

_____
_____
_____
_____
_____

 No one is useless in this world who lightens the burdens of another.

Charles Dickens

Perceiving the Need

What situation or need in your community, nation, or world moves you most to want to act? *"More than anything I really want to do something about . . ."*

_____

_____

_____

_____

_____

_____

What situation in the world, your nation, or your community do you complain about the most? *"Somebody really ought to do something about . . ."*

_____

_____

_____

_____

_____

_____

How could you ultimately be most effective in working on these problems? *"If I were to take responsibility to do something about this, I would . . ."*

_____

_____

_____

_____

What is the most cynical reason you can come up with for not acting?

_____

_____

Are you going to let that stop you from doing your part?

_____

 In nothing do men approach so nearly to the gods as in doing good to men.
Marcus Cicero

Why Not?

Like George Bernard Shaw (see below), ask yourself, Why not? Here are a few of my "why nots." Now write yours.

1. Why not love each other?
2. Why not live in peace?
3. Why not value happiness more and consume less?
4. Why not feed the world's hungry?
5. Why not develop safe, efficient, nonpolluting, replenishable energy systems?
6. Why not develop and implement educational models that encourage the development of both creative and critical thinking as well as a sense of personal and global responsibility?
7. Why not encourage individuals to become aware of their gifts and how they can use them to better the world?

Why not: _____

_____

Why not: _____

_____

Why not: _____

_____

Why not: _____

_____

Why not: _____

_____

Why not: _____

_____

Why not: _____

_____

You see things and say, "why?" but I dream things that never were and say, "why not?"
George Bernard Shaw

"Your World Needs Your Love" Sources

For those interested in a more systematic study of global problems and opportunities, we suggest reading from the following:

Artful Work: Awakening Joy, Meaning, and Commitment in the Workplace. Richards, Dick. New York: Berkeley Books, 1997.

Beyond Growth: The Economics of Sustainable Development. Daly, Herman E. Boston: Beacon Press, 1997.

Building a Win-Win World: Life Beyond Global Economic Warfare. Henderson, Hazel. San Francisco: Berrett-Koehler Publishers, Inc., 1996.

The Corporate Planet: Ecology and Politics in the Age of Globalization. Karliner, Joshua. San Francisco: Sierra Club Books, 1997.

For the Common Good: Redirecting the Economy Toward Community, the Environment, and a Sustainable Future. Daly, Herman E., and John B. Cobb Jr. Boston: Beacon Press, 1994.

*   *Gaia Atlas of Green Economics.* Ekins, Paul et al. New York: Anchor Books, 1992.

*   *Gaia: An Atlas of Planet Management.* Myers, Norman, and Nancy J. Myers. New York: Anchor Press, Doubleday, 1993.

Gaviotas: A Village to Reinvent the World. Weisman, Alan. White River Junction, Vt.: Chelsea Green Publishers, 1998.

The Global 2000 Report to the President: Entering the Twenty-First Century, Vol. I. Council on Environmental Quality Staff. New York: Penguin USA, 1982.

Global Dreams: Imperial Corporations in the New World Order. Barnet, Richard J. New York: Simon and Schuster, 1995.

*   *Hammond Atlas of the World.* Hammond Incorporated. New York: Random House. Updated Reglarly.

The Illustrated Book of World Rankings. Kurian, George T. Armonk, N.Y.: M.E. Sharpe, 1996.

In Earth's Company: Business, Environment, and the Challenge of Sustainability (Conscientious Commerce). Frankel, Carl. New Haven, Conn.: New Society Publishers, 1998.

*   *The New Book of World Rankings.* Kurian, George T. New York: Facts on File. Published annually in September.

Newsletters in Print. Detroit: Gale Research Co. Published annually.

One World, Ready or Not: The Manic Logic of Global Capitalism. Greider, William. New York: Touchstone Books, 1998.

Our Ecological Footprint: Reducing Human Impact on the Earth. Testemale, Phil. New Haven, Conn.: New Society Publishers, 1995.

Path of Compassion: Writings on Socially Engaged Buddhism. Eppsteiner, Fred. Berkeley: Parallax Press, 1988.

The Peace Corps and More: 175 Ways to Work, Study and Travel at Home and Abroad. Benjamin, Medea, and Miya Rodolfo-Sioson. Santa Ana, Calif.: Seven Locks Press, 1997.

Planethood: The Key to Your Future. Ferencz, Benjamin B., Ken Keyes Jr., and Robert Muller. Coos Bay, Ore.: Love Line Books, 1991.

The Public Issues Handbook: A Guide for the Concerned Citizen. Rosenbaum, Robert A. Westport, Conn.: Greenwood Press, Inc., 1983.

Small Is Beautiful: Economics as if People Mattered. Schumacher, E. F. New York: HarperCollins, 1989.

* *The State of the World Atlas: A Unique Visual Survey of Global Political, Economic and Social Trends.* Kidron, Michael, Ronald Segal, and Angela Wilson. New York: Penguin USA, 1995.

State of the World: A Worldwatch Institute Report on Progress Toward a Sustainable Society. Brown, Lester R. New York: W.W. Norton & Co. Published annually in January.

Stewardship: Choosing Service Over Self-Interest. Block, Peter. San Francisco: Berrett-Koehler Publishers, Inc., 1996.

Vital Signs: The Environmental Trends That Are Shaping Our Future. Brown, Lester R., Michael Renner, Christopher Flavin, and Linda Starke. New York: W.W. Norton and Company, 1997.

Waging Peace II: Vision and Hope for the 21st Century. Krieger, David, and Frank Kelly, eds. San Bernardino, Calif.: Noble Press, 1988.

What You Need to Know about Business, Money, and Power. Kidron, Michael, and Ronald Segal. New York: Simon & Schuster, 1987.

When Corporations Rule the World. Korten, David C. San Francisco: Berrett-Koehler Publishers/Kumarian Press, 1996.

* *World Development Report.* The World Bank. New York: Oxford University Press. Published annually.

Asterisks (*) indicate sources that provide broad surveys or information at a glance.

 To work for the common good is the greatest creed.
Albert Schweitzer

Clarifying Values

Why not spend some time determining what is right for us, and then go after that?

William Ross

Thomas Jefferson gave us a worthy maxim for sorting out the importances of life. He said: "In matters of principle, stand like a rock. In matters of taste, swim with the current."[1] What principles do you want to stand for? What values are central to your life? The choices you make will determine your future and with the choices of others, the future of life on our planet. The objective of this section is to assist you in identifying and clarifying your values.

"Know thyself," said Thales. Knowing oneself is no less important today than it was in the sixth century B.C. Yet modern life runs at such a pace that we seldom take the time to examine our lives. We become strangers to ourselves—so caught up in seeking the approval of others or in oiling the great machinery of society that we take little time to pause and reflect upon the deeper issues of our existence.

For the secret of man's being is not only to live but to have something to live for.
                                                                        Dostoyevsky

Our educational system is of little help. We aren't trained to be critical thinkers, to perceive the fundamental principles or values behind a given political, economic, social, or interpersonal agenda. The mass media tell us their version of current events with little debate about the fundamental value choices involved in major policy decisions. It is up to each of us to discern the cornerstone principles upon which our society stands and determine for ourselves their merit or fallacy. It's up to each of us to determine the kind of future society we will create by deciding on the kind of values we will emphasize today.

For good or for ill, ideas and the values they reflect have tremendous power to shape our world. The great debate of ideas must not be left to a few academics in ivory towers or "experts" on talk shows. It must become an integral part of everyday life if we are to create a sane and healthy society. We owe it to ourselves and our society to consciously examine and make explicit our values.

The individual who takes the time and makes the effort to discover for him- or herself what is valuable and what is peripheral in life has internal guideposts to live by. Of course, in practice, making value choices is not as easy as it sounds. At times, values conflict. One esteemed value or principle seems to run against another. Much of the great literature of the world—from Abraham and Isaac to Arjuna and Krishna, from the plays of Sophocles to the death of Socrates, from Hamlet to Huck Finn—turns on how individuals resolve their moral dilemmas.

Moral dilemmas are only possible for those with strongly held principles. The pressure of value conflict provides the strongest test of character. Often today we take the convenience store approach to values; whatever one we need, we will just run in and get it. We take whatever value seems expedient in the moment to justify our actions. We then sanctimoniously elevate moral neglect into high duty by invoking the doctrine that all value assertions are unscien-

Know Thyself.

Thales

tific and relative. In our efforts to rid ourselves of the responsibilities (and anguish) of moral dilemmas, we have thrown out our best chance to develop character. However trying moral dilemmas may be, they are more healthy for the individual and the society than eliminating all value conflict by eliminating all conviction.

The Ch'an masters who carried Zen to Japan brought with them Confucian ethics. They advocated the adoption of Confucian values as a means of promoting the welfare of the society and providing a cultural environment favorable to Zen realization.[2] In discussing the role of fundamental values in guiding individual behavior, Confucius said, "If a man will *carefully cultivate* these in his conduct, he may still err a little, but he won't be far from the standard of truth."[3] We seldom err when we make explicit our core convictions and endeavor to align our behavior with them.

Below, we invite you to consider three categories of values in human life: universal (or archetypal) values, cultural (or ethnic) values, and individual (or personal) values.

Universal Values

Freedom consists not in refusing to recognize anything above us, but in respecting something which is above us; for by respecting it, we raise ourselves to it, and, by our very acknowledgement, prove that we bear within ourselves what is higher, and are worthy to be on a level with it.

Goethe

Be still, and know that I am God.

Psalms 46:10

Who am I? What is there of me that is not simply the forces of socialization and heredity? What is the essential? Who am I, stripped of the particular social and cultural milieu into which I was born? Is there anything of me that cannot be explained away by genes or social means?

Universal values reveal and inform the essence of the human condition. Through the universal values, we link our individual experience with the rest of humanity and the cosmos. In the universal values, the barriers of time and place, language and culture crumble before the eternal dance of life. Universal values are experienced, not comprehended. Can you comprehend a sunrise? Fathom a flower? Translate a smile?

That the Upanishads, the Bible, or the plays of Sophocles can speak with relevance to our lives today tells us that there are, at the core, certain timeless constants to the human condition. That we feel wonder at the Sphinx, awe at the cathedrals of Notre Dame or Chartres, or serenity at the Taj Mahal tells us that these values can not be contained by words. That we can be moved by Beethoven, soothed by Mozart, identified with Hamlet or Faust speaks tomes on the mystery of universal values and the laugh they have on time, place, and death.

Universal values are not the exclusive domain of the poet, artist, mystic, or monk. No fair-minded reader of Carl Jung, Joseph Campbell, or Erich Neumann can dispute the presence of universal values in the myths and legends by which all peoples have sought meaning and direction. Today, we are so occupied in material and economic pursuits that universal values receive little attention. Still, when we deny them in our waking lives, they haunt us in our dreams, as Jung has shown. Universal values move us out of our separate roles and identities into the vast expanse of timeless reality.

Universal values can be experienced as: life, joy, brotherhood, love, peace, unity, sacrifice, service, God, eternity, bliss, etc.

Cultural Values

Society is a necessary condition of life in this world and a necessary medium of personal self-realization through community; that is why we hold it to be a part of the order of creation.

Will Herberg

Cultural values are the generally agreed-upon social values of the day. They serve to establish and maintain social order. They are peculiar to time and place and can be extremely volatile. Cultural values are concerned with ethics, with right and wrong, good and bad, with manners and customs. We see cultural values reflected in the ideas and behaviors a society rewards as well as those it punishes. Cultural values are a mixed bag for the individual. Especially in a highly complex society like the late twentieth century Western culture, there is likely to be much with which the individual resonates and much with which he does not.

Man has speculated for centuries on the best ways to organize human society: from Plato's *Republic* to More's *Utopia,* from Bacon's *New Atlantis* to Wells' *Anticipations.* The society in which we live is itself a speculation. It is man's attempt, with his limited knowledge and psychological and spiritual development, to construct the best world he can imagine.

The world is his who can see through its pretension. What deafness, what stone-blind custom, what overgrown error you behold, is there only by sufferance–your sufferance. See it to be a lie, and you have already dealt it its mortal blow.
                    Ralph Waldo Emerson

Of course, there is nothing wrong with speculating, but it is dangerous to forget that we are. When speculation becomes "truth," opinion "fact," and prejudice a "holy cause," demagoguery is not far behind. When we mistake cultural values for universal ones and proclaim them as doctrine, we risk intolerance, chauvinism, oppression, and every form of brutality and stupidity. While cultural values may be (as Claude Levi Strauss and others have suggested) functional, they are, nevertheless, essentially arbitrary. There is no contradiction here. A shovel serves the function of turning over earth, but so can a grader, a bulldozer, a plough, a shoe horn, a coin, or a bare hand. The fact that a cultural value or custom serves a given function does not necessarily imply that it is the only, or even the best, way of doing so. In certain primitive cultures, human sacrifice no doubt served a function, but in other cultures, that same function was served by animal sacrifice and, in still others, without any loss of life.

That we in this culture have chosen the automobile as the dominant mode of transportation has ramifications on virtually every aspect of social life. The suburb, the supermarket, the freeway rush, the shopping mall, the parking lots, the drive-in banks and restaurants owe their lives to the auto. Yet if one were asked to specify exactly what caused, and continues to cause, reliance on the automobile, one would be hard put to come up with a definitive, rational explanation.

The engineer has his explanation; the sociologist, hers; the management professor, his; the historian, hers; the cultural anthropologist, his; the economist, hers. Each considers important those factors peculiar to their specialization. Some pontificate, but all speculate. Rational attempts to comprehend causes for the peculiarities in various social orders are always approximations.

While attempts to trace the origins and development of cultural patterns rely upon speculation, they can, nevertheless, help us better understand ourselves and our world. Speculation will al-

Economics and politics are the governing powers of life today, and that's why everything is screwy.

Joseph Campbell

The good man is the friend of all living things.

Mahatma Gandhi

ways be incomplete. In this sense, history *is* bunk. Still, speculating on the history of ideas, the origins and propagation of cultural values, is more than entertainment. With careful execution, it becomes a source of insight into our psyche, time, and society. It provides an opportunity to step out of our cultural skins and observe our common prejudices, taboos, and superstitions, as well as our cultural strengths.

In a sense, every culture is a person. As with people, when cultures meet, there is the potential for conflict and for creative interaction. We are too familiar with cultural conflicts and the destruction these have wrought. Yet, it is well to remember that the meetings of cultures have also triggered tremendous creative explosions. Zen was born in a meeting of Chinese and Indian cultures. The Renaissance sprang from a meeting of the ancient Greek and medieval European cultures. A number of scholars have recognized a Buddhist influence in Neoplatonic thought. Jazz is African meets European music. Some have said that the great medieval romance poetry (including the Grail and Tristan traditions) evolved out of a meeting of the Islamic (Sufi) and European cultures.[4] American Transcendentalists studied the Indian Vedas and Upanishads. Many of the German philosophers of the nineteenth century (e.g., Schopenhauer and Nietzsche) were influenced by the philosophy of China and India.

Modern writers including: Hermann Hesse, E. M. Forster, Somerset Maugham, Aldous Huxley, Alan Watts, Carl Jung, Joseph Campbell, and the Beat poets, to name only a few, were heavily influenced by the East. Van Gogh shows Japanese influence. Gandhi drew heavily from Tolstoy, and Martin Luther King, in turn, from Gandhi. Modern dance began by cross-pollinating ballet with aboriginal dance. These are only a few illustrations; much of what we find exciting and interesting has come from a meeting of cultures.

If you see in any given situation only what everybody else can see, you can be said to be so much a representative of your culture that you are a victim of it.

S. I. Hayakawa

If all one knows is one's own culture, one has only met one person. Those who know no culture but their own tend to be narcissistic, simply because they've never known anyone else to have a relationship with. Much of what we understand as unique personality is simply the mask *(persona)* of culture. The field of psychology since Freud has placed great importance on childhood experience and particularly the role that parents play in shaping personality. Of course, parents do not fall from the skies and are themselves the products of culture.

The study of other cultures helps you to see yourself as both *a spectator* and *a participant* in your personal life drama. It gives you a frame of reference. Of course, moving to Japan to live in a high-rise, commute by subway, and work for a large corporation is not necessarily meeting another culture. (One tea ceremony will teach you more about Japanese culture than weeks in Tokyo nightclubs.) Oswald Spengler suggested that the key to understanding any culture is the study of its sacred (poetic, mythic, religious) tradition, which he calls "culture forming."[5] A century before, William Blake put it like this:

> *It is not Arts that follow & attend upon Empire,*
> *but Empire that attends upon & follows the Arts.*
> *William Blake*[6]

We see our silly cultural ethnocentricity in books and indeed entire academic departments that purport to be world history, when they are in fact European or, at best, Western history. We are told that the history of Western art is "THE HISTORY OF ART," that Western philosophy is "PHILOSOPHY." We teach world literature without the Mahabharata or the Ramayana. Of late, there has been a trend to incorporate snippets from other cultures into "world courses," but these are, for the most part, merely token. Of course, we are not alone in this. The Chinese thought Western-ers barbarians and made no attempt to learn from them, until it was too late. When Gandhi was asked what he thought of Western civilization, he reportedly said that he thought it would be a good idea.

Cultural Values are seen reflected in: language, ethics, status systems, aesthetics, education, government, law, economics, philosophy, social conventions (of every kind), social institutions (of every kind), etc.

Individual Values

Individual values are our private meanings. These result from individual temperament and experience. Individual meanings can be a source of individual strength (as in a marriage vow or the

Scatter Joy.

Emerson

consecration of a knight) or weakness (as in idiosyncratic fears). Personal role models, parents, teachers, and childhood chums shape individual values. Biology and physical environment also play a role.

Two men respond to war wounds in different ways. One remains cheerful, buoyant, and productive; the other becomes bitter, morose, and difficult. No doubt the injury means something different to each. The proverbial straw that breaks the camel's back does so because of the weight of individual meaning given to it.

Moral courage and character go hand in hand . . . a man of real character is consistently courageous, being imbued with a basic integrity and a firm sense of principle.

Martha Boaz

The concept of a life script has been suggested to account for the individual differences in attributing meaning to experience. We tend to project early personal relationships onto the present and replay the issues of these relationships over and over again. We distort perception and impute personal meanings resurrected from images of the past. A client's decision not to buy one's product is taken as a personal rejection, unconsciously recalling a negative and critical father who withheld the support one craved. A friend's pain or bad mood becomes a personal affront, unconsciously recalling a cold and emotionally distant mother.

An earlier experience of pain can lead us to hold associated stimuli with disdain. Embarrassment or ridicule at school can, by association, lead one to reject learning *in toto*. Others may have difficulty understanding how strongly these private meanings affect us.

Any object, event, or idea can take on individual meaning. What others find the odd piece is, to the sentimental owner, a cherished treasure. Personal "power spots," a special piece of ribbon, a baseball player's favorite number, these have personal meaning. Even objects that hold cultural significance may represent, to the individual, values and feelings beyond those culturally assigned to them. For example, a marriage ring may represent more than a social contract of fidelity. For one person, it may symbolize inspiration, joy, and the strength to do one's best. For another, it might represent bondage to an unhappy existence. The difference in meaning is individual.

Individual Values are reflected in: individual goals, humor, vows, relationships, commitments, personal objects (of every kind), personal preferences (of every kind), etc.

In addition to determining which universal, cultural, and individual values are most meaningful for you, consider the relative priority of each of the categories of values. For me, the universal values are at the top of the list. Each of the categories of meaning has its place, but it is through the universal values that we experience a sense of oneness with the entire human race and, indeed, the cosmos. Encountering universal values gives an experience so rich and profound as to make the others seem shallow by comparison.

Today, in the midst of writing this, I took a stroll past the county courthouse. There, a photographer, quite intently engaged in his craft, asked me for the time. Nothing peculiar in this, except that he was standing beneath an enormous clock on the side of the building. I thought of how often we are like this photographer, so focused on a narrow part of the landscape that we miss the wider view. Our personal and cultural biases limit and distort our perception of the universal wonder that is life.

Even as the hands of a clock are powered from the center, which remains ever still, so the universal values remain ever at the center of human life, no matter where the hands of time are pointing—past, present, or future.

Of course, all three categories of meaning overlap. An artist may use his *personal* experience to express *universals* in a *culturally* relevant motif. On a universal level, the image of Jesus on the cross may symbolize the conquering of the lower selfish aspect of man in his sacrifice for others, dying to the old self to be born to the new, or the love of the creator for creation. Culturally, the image may represent the Christian church and its impact on the Western psyche and society or a popular subject of Western art. Personally, it may represent the abhorrence one has for those aspects of the Christian legacy one rejects, or it might represent a personal relationship with a living God-Man. Of course, on every level, the possibilities are rich. As Goethe said, "Everything transitory is but a reference."[7]

That civilization perishes in which the individual thwarts the revelation of the universal.

Tagore

Values

Cowardice asks the question, Is it safe? Expediency asks the question, Is it politic? Vanity asks the question, Is it popular? But conscience asks the question, Is it right? And there comes a time when one must take a position that is neither safe, nor politic, nor popular, but he must take it because his conscience tells him it is right . . .
                                                        Martin Luther

Thus to be independent of public opinion is the first formal condition of achieving anything great . . .
                                                        G. W. F. Hegel

Think nothing profitable to you which compels you to break a promise, to lose your self-respect, to hate any person, to suspect, to curse, to act the hypocrite, to desire anything that needs walls and curtains about it.
                                                        Marcus Aurelius

We are prone to judge success by the index of our salaries or the size of our automobiles rather than by the quality of our service and relationship to mankind.
                                                        Martin Luther King, Jr.

We cannot live only for ourselves. A thousand fibers connect us with our fellow-men; and along those fibers, as sympathetic threads, our actions run as causes, and they come back to us as effects.
                                                        Herman Melville

The more a man lays stress on false possessions, and the less sensitivity he has for what is essential, the less satisfying is his life.
                                                        Carl Jung

Know Thy Values

After you have read the preceding discussion, answer the questions below. (Refer to the examples given in the discussion if you are unclear as to the nature of each kind of value.)

What universal values speak most powerfully to you? Why? _____

_____

_____

_____

_____

What cultural values speak most powerfully to you? Why? _____

_____

_____

_____

_____

What individual values speak most powerfully to you? Why? _____

_____

_____

_____

_____

Overall, what values are most important to you? (Name at least five.) _____

_____

_____

_____

_____

Now prioritize your top five values and list them below:

1. _____

2. _____

3. _____

4. _____

5. _____

What You Value Most

Alternative exercise: Take fifteen three-by-five cards or tear off fifteen card-sized sheets of paper. Next, label each of the cards with one of the values listed in the preceding discussion or other values that are of primary importance to you. When you have labeled all fifteen cards, go through and rank them from the most important to the least. Next, eliminate five of the least important values, so you're now down to ten cards. This will be difficult but important. Next, drop one more card. You may find that you will rearrange your original order. In any case, drop another card until you have eight, then seven, then six, and finally (and this will be especially hard), drop one more. Now you are left with your top five values. Check them against the ones you have omitted and against any other values that may have occurred to you in this process, until you are satisfied that you are holding in your hands the cards that represent your top five values.

Whether you used the "Know Thy Values" process from the previous page or the alternative exercise above to select your top five values, we invite you to further differentiate these and briefly explain why each is of such importance to you.

My number-one priority value: _____

Why? _____

_____

My number-two priority value: _____

Why? _____

_____

My number-three priority value: _____

Why? _____

_____

My number-four priority value: _____

Why? _____

_____

My number-five priority value: _____

Why? _____

_____

 Back of every noble life there are principles that have fashioned it.
George Horace Lorimer

Instant Recall

Reviewing highlights from your past may reveal clues to your life's work. Additionally, the questions may help you get *a feeling* for what it would be like to actually be engaged in your life's work. When giving your answers to the questions below, do not limit yourself to previous work experience. Draw upon your entire life experience.

Recall times when you have been most creative. These are times when you created something (an event, a thing, a product, a system).

_____
_____
_____

Recall times when you have been most committed. These are times when you were deeply involved, emotionally committed, and determined to persist in spite of all obstacles. _____
_____
_____

Recall times when you were most decisive. These are times when you knew exactly what to do. You knew you were right, and you acted deliberately and confidently, perhaps even in spite of the doubt and objections of others. _____
_____
_____

Recall a time when everyone said you couldn't do it, but you knew you could, and you did it anyway. What was it? How did it feel? _____
_____
_____

Recall times when you have been so absorbed in what you were doing that you hardly noticed the time. What were you doing?_____
_____
_____

 You will find as you look back upon your life that the moments when you have really lived are the moments when you have done things in a spirit of love. Henry Drummond

Highlights from the Past

What do you consider to be the greatest accomplishment of your life? Why?

_____

_____

_____

_____

_____

What is the most exciting thing you have done in your life? Why?

_____

_____

_____

_____

_____

When have you taken the strongest stand in your life? What were you standing for?

_____

_____

_____

_____

_____

Review your answers to the questions above with a view toward what they might suggest to you about your life's work. Look for patterns, redundancies, events that you repeatedly recalled. What insights do your answers suggest? Write these in the space below.

_____

_____

_____

_____

_____

 Work to become, not to acquire.
Elbert Hubbard

You Have Always Known

The premise behind this set of questions is that somewhere in the back of your mind, you have always known what you are here to do. Recalling your childhood may help you unlock this knowing. Children are more readily aware of "knowing" because they have yet to inculcate either the limiting beliefs or the sense of defeat that often cloud the issue for adults.

What did you most want to give to the world when you were a child?

_____
_____
_____
_____
_____
_____

As a child, what situation in the world hurt you the most, and how did you respond to that? (Recognize that the pain as well as the joy of life may be a clue to your life's work.)

_____
_____
_____
_____
_____
_____

What insights do the answers to these questions give you?

_____
_____
_____
_____
_____

Until Death Do You Play Your Part

Imagine that you have just passed on. You have devoted yourself to your life's work and have been successful in its execution. What is the legacy that you have left behind? What contribution did you make to a better world? What is your epitaph? When all is said and done, what statement did your life make? What will you be remembered for? Write it below.

𝔥𝔢𝔯𝔢 𝔩𝔦𝔢𝔰

_____

𝔅𝔬𝔯𝔫 _____ 𝔇𝔦𝔢𝔡 _____

 That action is best which provides the greatest happiness for the greatest number.
Francis Hutcheson

Your Philosophy of Life

If you could share one bit of wisdom with the whole world, what would it be?

_____
_____
_____
_____
_____

Is there anything you'd be willing to put it all on the line for? If so, what?

_____
_____
_____
_____
_____

What has been the most important lesson you have learned in your life? Why?

_____
_____
_____
_____
_____

Briefly, what is the basic philosophy of your life?

_____
_____
_____
_____
_____
_____

 Few men ever drop dead from overwork, but many quietly curl up and die because of un-dersatisfaction.

Sidney J. Harris

Personal Bill of Rights and Responsibilities

Take the opportunity to declare your "Personal Bill of Rights and Responsibilities." Your "Personal Bill of Rights and Responsibilities" is what's right for you, your personal standard of behavior. It includes what you expect of yourself, what you view as your responsibility to others, and what you will and will not tolerate from them.

1. _____

2. _____

3. _____

4. _____

5. _____

6. _____

7. _____

8. _____

9. _____

10. _____

It is the chiefest point of happiness that a man is willing to be what he is.

Desiderius Erasmus

Your Mission Statement

Review all of your answers to the "Vision Questing" and "Clarifying Values" sections; then write out your life's mission in the space below. Your Mission Statement answers the question, What am I here to do on this earth?

_____
_____
_____
_____
_____
_____
_____
_____
_____
_____
_____
_____
_____
_____
_____
_____
_____
_____
_____
_____
_____
_____
_____

Now review what you have written, and write a condensed Mission Statement. State the mission of your life in no more than two sentences.

_____
_____
_____
_____
_____
_____

Pointing to Purpose

All the world's a stage,
And all the men and women merely players.
Shakespeare

All the world's a stage, and all of us are players. We have our time upon the stage of life and then depart. While on the stage, we play our parts, however poorly or well. Each character in this grand play has lines to deliver and action to make while he "struts and frets" upon the stage. What is the message you want your life to proclaim? Is it about beauty or cooperation, wisdom or inspiration, peace or enlightenment? What is it that you want your life to say when it is all said and done? Answering these kinds of questions is what this section is all about.

It's motive alone that gives character to the actions of men.

Jean de la Bruyere

Think of your "purpose" in life as your message. Every life has something to say. Find the voice, the message of your life. Ask yourself, Why has this character made his entrance? What is the purpose of the action of her life? In a well-staged play, there is no thing or action without purpose. Every word, movement, lighting effect, costume, prop, or its absence—delivers a message. What is the message you want an audience of six billion to get from the action of your life? What is your part in *this* Globe Theater?

In an essay entitled "The Basis of Artistic Creation in Literature," playwright Maxwell Anderson articulated several key elements that he found essential in all great plays. In his words: "A play can't be written without them—or at least it can't be a success . . ." He found that these elements applied as much to modern as to Elizabethan or ancient plays. Below we explore a few of these elements and consider how they apply to the grand play of life. (Quotes below from *The Bases of Artistic Creation* by Maxwell Anderson et. al.)[1]

1) "The story of a play must be the story of what happens within . . . the heart of a man or woman. It cannot deal primarily with external events. The external events are only symbolic of what goes on within." This is the poetic sense of life—external events are symbolic of what goes on within. To be authentic, the play, or action of your life, must come from within, must flow from your heart. The spiritual or inner life cannot be separated from work—or from anything else, for that matter. All action is self-reflecting.

2) "The story of a play must be a conflict—and specifically, a conflict between the forces of good and evil within a single individual." This inner conflict gives your life its drama and creative tension. The good of your best self is engaged in an ongoing conflict with the evil of settling for less. In the great plays, Anderson notes that ultimately "the forces of good . . . must win" (or evil must fail). This does not mean there are not setbacks or failings along the way.

3) Indeed, as Anderson puts it: "The protagonist of a play cannot be a perfect person. If he were, he could not improve, and he must come out at the end of the play a more admirable human being than he went in." Surely, all of us hope to come out of this play of life more admirable people for having lived it. It is not that the protagonist never falls but that each time he does—he rises again—now stronger, now truer.

4) "Excellence on the stage is always moral excellence. A struggle on the part of the hero to better his material circumstances is of no interest unless his character is somehow tried in the fire, unless he

comes out of the trial a better man." This moral excellence gives the character a heroic quality. A hero is, in the words of Joseph Campbell, "someone who has given his or her life to something bigger than oneself."[2] This is what makes a character "interesting." This is why we root for him. Heroic action can come from any of us. In Campbell's words, "When we stop thinking primarily about ourselves and our own self-preservation we undergo a truly heroic transformation of consciousness."[3] In this transformation, we take on, not only the hero's character, but his voice. A weak, selfish character has a halting, confused, or muddled voice, while a strong, heroic character speaks with dignity, assurance, and upliftment. "Moral excellence" rings through his voice.

To Find Your Part: Don't Exaggerate, Deny, or Minimize Your Importance

Many people fall into patterns that limit their capacity to recognize their part in the play of life. There are those who *exaggerate* their importance in the overall scheme of things. There are those who *deny* that they have any effect on the world. Still others admit their effect but *minimize* their abilities. Any of these extremes impedes the process of discovering your purpose, or part, in the play of life. (From here on, we will use the terms *purpose* and *part* interchangeably.)

It's easy to *exaggerate* our importance in the overall scheme of things. Many are blocked from tapping into their purpose in life by their insistence that it come with a personalized name tag. They expect the sky to open and a deep bass voice from on high to say, "Well, my son (or daughter), this is your purpose . . ." Choirs of angels, lightning, and thunder are optional, but the bass voice is a must.

> *The importance and unimportance of the self cannot be exaggerated.*
> *Reginald Blyth*

Don't overpersonalize; great purposes are not individual. They have historical continuity. They were begun before you and will continue after you. Rome was not built in a day; neither was science, art, or culture. We stand on the shoulders of those who have come before and owe our best to those who will follow. No great purpose relies upon any single individual. It is always a group effort. This may be a little difficult for our egos to accept, but it will make finding our purpose less difficult.

Wherefore by their fruits ye shall know them.

Matthew 7:20

Many *deny* that there is any purpose or message to what they do. For example, some screenwriters, playwrights, and authors claim that there is no purpose or point to their work—beyond, of course, making them money. It's just a movie, a play, a book. It has no "message." Of course, this is silly. Everything we do is a message, a communication. Every action has a message in the way that every musical note has a sound. There are no soundless notes any more than there are "messageless" actions or characters. Every message has a tone, creating ripples that uplift or diminish life. Think of the Zen gardens. The careful attention given to the placement of each opbject speaks to us. It says everything counts.

Where any purpose is denied, look for dollar signs—a sense of life as a commodity. Underlying so much of the work of the twentieth century is this notion that life is a cheap commodity. Human beings should feel lucky if they are employed, never mind at what. Animal life is to be exploited as long as profitable and exterminated when it gets in the way. Water, which scientists claim as the origin of life, is for washing away our messes. Air is the dumping ground for toxic gases and particulate matter. Land is to be cleared, stripped, rented, and cemented.

I will act as if what I do makes a difference.
William James

If life is cheap, its only value is what someone will pay for it. But ask yourself, Does the life of a man have less value because he is paid little for his service? Is a field or marsh worthless until it is "developed" into a profitable property? Are clear streams and blue skies worthless because they do not put money in someone's pocket? Those who defend the value of life are often reduced to arguing that "saving the environment is good business," that "helping people in the inner cities is good for the economy." They must justify life on economic terms, rather than on the basis of its own intrinsic value.

In the era we call the Middle Ages, Zen (Cha'n) Master Zhenjing said, "It is hard to find anyone who is willing to say that what is right is right and what is wrong is wrong . . ."[4] These types are no easier to find today. In our era, to speak directly of what is right is often viewed as a heretic challenge to the prevailing creed of value relativity. This "religion" stands on the doctrine that all value judgments are "unscientific." It's unscientific to say that anything is any better than anything else. It's all relative; it doesn't make a difference. While the advocacy of values is out of bounds, the wheels of profit turn without restraint. The doctrine of "no values" is the intellectual or moral license for greed, exploitation, and abuse. (That is why we ask you to consider and make explicit your visions and values before considering your work purpose.)

Remember that you are an actor in a play and the Playwright chooses the manner of it . . . your business is to act the character that is given you and act it well; the choice of the cast is Another's.
                                                        Epictetus

Of course, it does make a difference what we do or don't do. Human beings and their labor, the animals, the atmosphere, the water, the earth, its food and minerals are not mere commodities to be bought and sold; they are the stuff of life. Whether you spend your life making bombs or doing community service, you are making a point about what you think is important. *The life spent in doing what you love is a different life indeed from putting yourself out for hire to the highest bidder.* The only way you can say it makes no difference is to say life makes no difference.

While some *exaggerate* their importance and others *deny* having any effect, still others *minimize* the importance of their contribution. They do not deny that it makes a difference what we do. They simply claim that they themselves cannot do much. No doubt they underestimate their abilities, as we will discuss below. Still, if you think you are in this camp, remember the advice that great actors give to their protégés: Better to have a small part in a great play than a large part in a bad play. The ages-old drama of love, brotherhood, and human advancement is a great play. A small role in this epic, played with sincerity, dignity, and strength adds immeasurably to the play. Everyone cannot be a star, and yet where would the stars be without the supporting cast? In the end, the important point is not that you have a large role but that you accept your part and play it well.

It is better to do your own duty, however imperfectly, than to assume the duties of another person, however successfully. Prefer to die doing your own duties: the duties of another will bring you into great spiritual danger.
                                        Bhagavad-Gita

It's not enough to say, "I'm earning enough to live and support my family. I do my work well. I'm a good father. I'm a good churchgoer." That's all very well BUT YOU MUST DO SOMETHING MORE.
Albert Schweitzer

Your work is to discover your work and then with all your heart to give yourself to it.

Buddha

Most of us tend to underestimate the contributions we can make. We hold ourselves hostage to our pasts. We erect boundaries around our creative imaginations, lest they venture too far beyond what we have already achieved. Blast the boundaries. Go beyond. When you raise your expectations of yourself, you create a space to grow into. At first, it may seem like an empty space, but over time you will fill that space with new responsibilities and skills. You are far better to overestimate what you can do and come up short than you are to underestimate and settle for less than your best.

Push out your limits; stretch the envelope of your imagination. We call the difference between what you imagine yourself capable of doing and what you are actually doing now, your "creative gap." The size of the creative gap in your life represents your personal commitment to the pursuit of excellence. Stretch it by expanding your vision of what you can contribute. Remember, when the distance between your current performance and your ultimate vision is too small, you will feel confined and stagnant. When the distance is right, you will feel alive, challenged, and creatively stimulated. In helping you to define your work purpose, we ask you to consider: What moves you the most? Whom do you want to serve? and How many do you want to reach?

What Moves You the Most?

Perhaps there is some situation in your community, nation, or world that moves you so strongly, so irresistibly, that you have to act. It is so out of alignment with your vision of the world you want to live in that you feel compelled to do something about it. Perhaps you want to see to the material comfort of humanity. You feel moved to see that everyone has adequate food, shelter, and clothing. Perhaps you are moved by the neglect or abuse of children, and you want to make a difference in this area. Perhaps it's ignorance or illiteracy that moves you to act. Perhaps you are moved to protect the animals or the environment. Maybe you are moved to write beautiful music or to share your vision for the world through art or dance.

You might work against poverty, injustice, indignity, ill health, or mental deprivation. Martin Luther King and Mahatma Gandhi were moved by the lack of dignity and justice with which man treated his fellow man. You might work for beauty and truth, joy and understanding. Einstein was touched by a desire to know where we stand in the universe. Mozart was moved by music that still inspires today. Luther Burbank was moved to discover how plants and man could better care for one another.

When people are serving, life is no longer meaning-less.

John Gardner

Whether you are working to end suffering or to spread joy, you are part of building the world you want to live in. In any case, you must be powerfully moved, personally inspired. You will need that inspiration later on, when you begin to confront the problems of manifesting your vision. Respond to a need or build from an inspiration, but go with what moves you the most. Trust the voice of your heart—it will lead you to your life's work. In the end, your desire to serve and your faithfulness to your highest ideal will guide you to its recognition and realization.

What thou lovest well remains, the rest is dross
What thou lov'st well shall not be reft from thee
What thou lov'st well is thy true heritage.
Ezra Pound

Whom Do You Want to Serve?

Is there any particular group or sector of the population that you feel particularly drawn to serve? Perhaps you grew up in a rural area, and you have decided that you want to provide health-care services for folks in your community. You know these people. You know their needs, wants, and aspirations. Perhaps you feel particularly drawn to working with children or the elderly. Maybe you are a member of a particular ethnic or racial group, and you want to help people in your group. Perhaps you feel a particular tug on your heart strings when you encounter a certain group or kind of people. Follow that tug.

How Many Do You Want to Reach and How Deeply?

When contemplating your life's work, give some consideration to the scope of the impact you want to make. Is the change or benefit you want to make at the level of the individual, family, community, nation, or planet? How many lives do you want to reach and at what level of depth? The quality or depth of the impact that you make upon others can be as important as the breadth of your impact. For example, an elementary teacher may profoundly impact the twenty-five students that she teaches each day for a year. Her students will grow up to be better people and to give more to the world because of her effort and love.

You have probably heard it said that effectiveness is a matter of doing the right things, and efficiency is doing things right. *Your work purpose reflects what you think are the right things to do.* It is the why-you-do that precedes the what-you-do. Find your purpose, your part—and you will be effective in life. When we concentrate on purpose, the results take care of themselves, even as when we care for a tree, the fruit takes care of itself.

Thoreau said, "Be not simply good—be good for something." Discover what you are good for! Look within your heart and out upon the world. Look at how much the world needs your love and at how much you want to give it. Then determine to live your life on purpose, to play your part as it was meant to be played.

And whosoever of you will be the chiefest, shall be the servant of all.
Mark 10:44

Your Mission Statement (See page 196.) was a general statement about why you are here on this earth. Now we're going to step that down a bit and begin to focus on what your work here is. You will construct what we call a "Work Purpose Statement." The objective of this section is to help you to identify your work purpose. To do this, we will look at work in terms of the service rendered. We will examine your potential service in three parts: first, "What: The Way You Want to Serve"; second, "Who: The People You Want to Serve"; and finally, "How Many: The Scope of the Impact You Want to Make."

Living on Purpose

The way to be happy is to make others so.
Robert Ingersoll

Live your life as though every act were to become a universal law.
Henry David Thoreau

Live as you will have wished to have lived when you are dying.
Christian Furchtegott Gellert

Nothing comes from nothing.
Shakespeare

Here is the test to find whether your mission on earth is finished: If you're alive, it isn't.
Richard Bach

A man has to live with himself, and he should see to it that he always has good company.
Charles Hughes

The most sublime act is to set another before you.
William Blake

What: The Way You Want to Serve

The first step to developing your work purpose statement is to identify what you would like to do by identifying the fields you would most like to make a contribution to. Below are examples of "I want to" statements that express work purposes. You may be able to take one of these as a skeleton of your work purpose statement and amend or adjust it to suit your purpose. You may want to start entirely from scratch, using the statements that follow as guides in constructing your own work purpose statement. However you arrive at it, your work purpose statement should be your own, reflecting what you most want to express or accomplish.

You may realize that you have more than one work purpose. In that case, pick the one that represents the area you want to focus on most over the next seven to ten years. If you still end up with several areas of focus, rank them and pick one major area of focus. The alphabetical list below is not intended to be complete or exhaustive. It represents just a few of the more common areas in which people with whom we have worked have expressed interest.

Agriculture: I want to produce or advance the production of the foodstuffs that will provide people sustenance and nourishment in a manner that is environmentally sound.

Animal Care: I want to see to it that the animals are protected and treated with care, compassion, and dignity.

Architecture: I want to design structures that are at once functional and uplifting to the spirit.

Art: I want to portray, through artistic media, universal truths that uplift and inspire.

Business: I want to provide valuable products and services including: _____

Clothing: I want to design, manufacture, or distribute quality clothing that is aesthetically pleasing, comfortable, and healthful.

Communication: I want to provide communication technologies and/or services that will help people to achieve their goals.

 In the long run you hit only what you aim at. Therefore, though you should fail immediately, you had better aim at something high.
Henry David Thoreau

Culinary Arts: I want to design, prepare, and/or produce delicious, nutritious foods. I want to provide an atmosphere that will make eating a fulfilling, even spiritual experience.

Defense: I want to provide for national security and defense. I want to see to it that people are safe, protected, and free to pursue happiness in their own way.

Economic Development: I want to assist people in developing a higher standard of living. I want to do so in a manner that respects values of human dignity and ecological balance. I want to ensure that economic growth is based on the production of useful goods and services.

Education: I want to train and develop people's minds, character, knowledge, and skills. I want to help people to broaden their horizons and deepen their understanding.

Energy: I want to design, develop, or promote safe, efficient, nonpolluting, and replenishable energy systems. I want to increase the efficiency of existing energy systems until new ones are in place.

Engineering: I want to design, construct, or manage road works, water works, building, machinery, etc., which will serve to improve people's quality of life.

Entertainment: I want to provide laughter, drama, song, or dance to lighten and enlighten people's lives.

Environment: I want to clean up and protect the environment and to do all I can to see that it is kept as safe and as pure as possible.

Family: I want to provide services that will strengthen and support family units and family happiness.

Government: I want to work with government institutions to ensure that government remains responsive to the people and provides them with the best possible services.

Health: I want to share with people the skill, knowledge, love, and energy necessary to care for their health and physical well-being.

History: I want to help people to better understand their past, to see how things have come to be as they are, and to understand the great historical processes of change and their consequences.

Industry: I want to manufacture materials that will make people's lives more fulfilling, free, and productive.

Information Services: I want to provide people, in an easy-to-use and readily available form, the information they need to make informed and effective decisions.

Men must find and feel and represent in all of their creative works Man the Eternal, the creator.

Tagore

Interior Design: I want to create the kinds of interior spaces that elevate people's spirits and bring out the very best in them.

Journalism: I want to inform people about current events and issues. I want to help them to be aware of the people and events that shape their lives.

Justice: I want to protect people's rights and ensure that they are treated fairly and with human dignity.

Landscaping: I want to create exterior environments that provide people with upliftment and joy.

Law: I want to write, interpret, or practice legal remedies for human problems, conflicts, or grievances.

Life Sciences: I want to help people better understand and utilize the biological and organic processes of life to further their well-being and minimize the dangers to their health.

Management: I want to manage organizations that serve people's needs and aspirations.

Music: I want to share beauty, joy, understanding, and harmony through the vehicle of music.

Organization: I want to help people to be more effective by organizing personnel, material, ideas, and financial resources that will facilitate the achievement of their goals.

Peace: I want to promote world peace. I want to further international cooperation, understanding, and harmony. I want to exemplify and promote universal love and brotherhood.

Performing Arts: I want to take an active role in portraying the wonder, poignancy, beauty, and drama of the human experience before live audiences.

Philosophy: I want to challenge people to think of the deep and fundamental issues of life. I want to encourage them to examine their beliefs and the effect that holding these ideas has upon themselves and others. I want to share with them the wisdom of the ages.

Physical Education: I want to teach people how to utilize their bodies to maximize efficiency, promote health and longevity, and reduce physical stress and tension.

Physical Science: I want to help people understand the physical world in which they live and how it can be made to serve them even better.

 Maturing adults . . . would want . . . each on his own or in fellowship with others, to undertake some project for human betterment.
H. A. Overstreet

Politics: I want to help people to gain a voice in the decisions that affect their lives.

Psychology: I want to help people better understand their minds and emotions, their motivations, drives, and desires. I want to help them unlock the power of their minds and emotions to achieve their highest potential.

Recreation: I want to help people relax, play, and rejuvenate. I want to facilitate the relaxation of their bodies, minds, and spirits.

Religion: I want to minister to people's spiritual needs. I want to help them to discover who they are, what it is to be, and how to be free.

Sports: I want to help people discover the joys of effort, persistence, cooperation, teamwork, and physical development that sports provide.

Technology: I want to design, manufacture, or promote technological advances that will help people to achieve a happier, richer, more productive lifestyle.

Trade: I want to promote goodwill and cultural interaction by helping people to trade their products and services with others.

Transportation: I want to help people to get from place to place in a clean, economical, and safe manner and in a way that makes the most efficient and least destructive use of natural resources.

What: Summary

In the space below, construct your own statement indicating how you want to serve in the areas you most want to make a contribution. If you have more than one work purpose, indicate the one that you most want.

Example: I want to assist people in developing higher self-esteem.

_____

_____

_____

_____

_____

_____

_____

_____

_____

_____

_____

_____

_____

_____

_____

_____

_____

_____

_____

_____

Whom: The People You Want to Serve

The next step in writing your work purpose statement is to identify the people you want to serve. These people are your constituency, the people for whom you are responsible in your work. Most career programs consider the people that you will be serving, if they consider them at all, much later in the career-planning process. We think this is a mistake. After all, the purpose of work is to serve, to contribute to others. We are all serving someone, however poorly or expertly, however appropriately or inappropriately. Identify the primary beneficiaries of your work.

Age	Income	Race
_____Prenatals	_____Destitute	_____White
_____Infants	_____Economically	_____African
_____Preschoolers	deprived	American
_____Children	_____Lower middle	_____Hispanic
_____Adolescents	_____Middle income	_____Asian
_____Young adults	_____Upper middle	American
_____Middle age	_____Wealthy	_____Native
_____Elderly	_____Extremely	American
_____All ages	wealthy	_____Other
	_____All incomes	_____All races

Sex

_____Males

_____Females

_____Both sexes

I feel the capacity to care is the thing which gives life its deepest significance and meaning.

Pablo Casals

Ability

_____Extremely gifted

_____Gifted

_____Above average

_____Average

_____Below average

_____Disadvantaged

_____Extremely disadvantaged

_____All levels of ability

Special Cases

_____Prisoners

_____Homeless

_____Pregnant

_____Disabled (physically)

_____Disabled (mentally)

_____Disabled (emotionally)

_____Victims of specific diseases

_____People of other countries

_____Disaster victims

_____Armed forces

_____Orphans

_____Illiterate

_____Animals

_____Delinquents

_____Hungry

_____Sick

_____Veterans

_____Immigrants

_____Dying

_____Other

Who: Summary

In the space below, construct a statement indicating who you want to serve.
Example: I want to serve adolescent females from economically deprived areas who
are above average in academic ability.

_____

_____

_____

_____

_____

_____

How Many: The Scope of the Impact You Want to Make

The final step in writing your work purpose statement is to determine the scope of the impact or the size of the playing field on which you choose to operate. For example:

_____Individuals	_____Statewide
_____Small groups	_____National region
_____Neighborhood	_____Nationwide
_____Community	_____Multinational
_____Citywide	_____Worldwide (Global)
_____Countywide	

How Many: Summary

Now write the scope or the scale of service that you primarily want to operate on. Example: I want to begin working on a citywide basis and eventually move to a statewide program.

_____

_____

_____

_____

_____

_____

_____

_____

_____

_____

_____

_____

_____

_____

 One person with a belief is a social power equal to ninety-nine who have only interests.
John Stuart Mill

Your Work Purpose Statement

Review your answers to the three preceding exercises, and restate them in the spaces provided below.

What: The way I want to contribute is...

_____
_____
_____
_____
_____
_____

Who: I want to serve...

_____
_____
_____
_____
_____
_____

How Many: The scale I want to work at is...

_____
_____
_____
_____

Now write a work purpose statement that includes who you want to serve, the way you want to serve them, and the scope of the impact you want to make.

My Work Purpose Statement:

_____
_____
_____
_____
_____
_____
_____

Food for Thought

This country has more problems than it should tolerate, and more solutions than it uses . . . Our society has the resources and the skills to keep injustice at bay and to elevate the human condition to a state of enduring compassion and creative fulfillment. How we go about using resources and skills has consequences which extend well beyond our national borders to all the earth's people.

Ralph Nader

Many of the same conditions that produce today's greatest perils also open fascinating new potentials.

Alvin Toffler

. . . if existing agricultural knowledge were everywhere applied, the planet could feed twice its present population.

Will and Ariel Durant

While it is true that an inherently free and scrupulous individual may be destroyed, such an individual can never be enslaved or used as a blind tool.

Albert Einstein

Since wars begin in the minds of men, it is in the minds of men that we have to erect the ramparts of peace.

UNESCO Charter

1. Be discoverers. 2. Be ready helpers. 3. Be friend makers.
The Brownie "B's"
(Girl Scouts)

Targeting Talents

Every man has his own vocation,
talent is the call.

Emerson

Your talents provide a window that opens into the discovery of your life's work. The purpose of this section is to help you identify your talents and start thinking about how you can put them to work building the kind of world you want to live in. What are your gifts to the world? What is it that you have to share with the rest of us that will make our lives richer, more fulfilling, and more enjoyable? Many of us think of talents in relation to writing, music, or dance—as artistic, dramatic, or entertainment skills. But talents are more than these; they include a wide range of natural abilities. We invite you to follow your talents and follow your bliss.

Talent Is More Than Skill

Every man's leading propensity ought to be call'd his leading Virtue & his good Angel.

William Blake

Don't confuse talents with skills. Talent is natural; skill, learned. Skills are acquired abilities, learned through study, imitation, training, and practice. We can think of talents as our genetic endowment. While skills are important (we will consider skills at length in "Act II"), talents provide an open door into the discovery of your life's work. Talent is not simply what you're good at. You can have an undeveloped or undiscovered talent or be reasonably proficient in areas where you have no special talent. Your talents are found in the things you truly love to do.

While your talents are unique to you, your skills are often as much the result of someone else's doing as your own. Your mother decides you will learn to play the piano; your father starts you in the family business; grandma reminds you, "There are three generations of lawyers in this family," and so on. Much of what we have become skilled at is simply what was in front of us—hodgepodge collections of geographic, social, economic, and political influences that, to borrow from Shakespeare, "signify nothing." The often random and haphazard way that skills are acquired makes them unreliable indicators for life's work.

Beyond this, it is a mistake to draw conclusions about potential ability solely from past experience. No one would look at a healthy infant and say he will never walk or talk, simply because he hasn't done so before. While it is important to value what you have already learned to do, it is equally important to recognize that you are still in the process of growing. You may have undiscovered talents. With a relatively small degree of talent and considerable training and technical skill, you may achieve competency, perhaps even a high degree of commercial success, but if you pursue what you have real talent in, you will experience the joy of being fully alive in your work.

Often we have so much invested in training and developing our skills that we are unwilling to admit we have little real talent for the area. When we do admit it, we feel a sense of relief, for now we can go on to discover our genuine talents and pursue them with a passion. Developing talent is the road to your creative best. Don't let a poor investment (of your time and energy) continue to rob you of what could be the greatest joy in your life. If you've made a poor investment, cut your losses, and begin at once to exploit your talents to the ultimate!

Your talents can hardly wait to express. They are itching to get out and about. To go through life without releasing your strongest talents leads to feelings of frustration, resentment, even depression. You feel bottled up, envious, and discouraged. You may even question if you should exist at all. It's as if you were damming a great river of energy. The release of talent is one of the great joys in life. The moment of expression is timeless, effortless, fluid, and vivifying. You feel a deep harmony—self, humanity, and the physical world are one. You feel right with the world.

Focusing on Purpose Releases Talent

More talent has been squandered by the low expectations that result from lack of purpose than from any other cause. Purpose marshals talent. You can spend your time analyzing your talents, comparing yours with those of others, wishing you had more, or feeling superior for those you do possess, but you will never tap into the deepest well of your own talent until you set yourself to some great purpose.

> *When you are inspired by some great purpose, some extraordinary project, all your thoughts break their bounds: Your mind transcends limitations, your consciousness expands in every direction and you find yourself in a new, great and wonderful world. Dormant forces, faculties and talents become alive, and you discover yourself to be a greater person by far than you ever dreamed yourself to be.*
>
> *Patanjali*

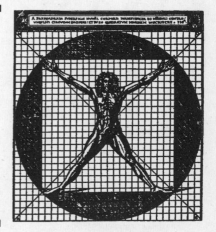

If you are dedicated to your purpose, you will find a way to express your talents through it. We are not drawn to areas where we have no talent or latent ability. On the contrary, we are drawn to a particular field because we know we have an important contribution to make to it. Talent is said to be raw when it is undeveloped. Talent is incomplete, however developed, when it is not aligned with your vision, values, and purpose. When it is integrated with these, there is no telling how far you can go.

You may currently be a "two" on a one-to-ten scale of competency in the area that best reflects your vision, purpose, and talents and a "nine and a half" in another area. Work at what you love the most, even if you're only a "two." Trust that your love for what you are doing will see you through. That's not easy, but better to grow into what you love than to pretend you're satisfied with a developmental dead end.

If people knew how hard I worked to get my mastery, it wouldn't seem so wonderful after all.

Michelangelo

Talents Are a Sacred Trust

From the commodity view of life (see "Scene I: Vision Questing"), talents are possessions, tools for personal gratification. From a sacred view of life, talents are gifts that we hold in trust. After Michelangelo completed his first *Pietà*, he heard rumors that another artist was getting credit for having done this work. One night, he stole into the cathedral and carved his name on the back of the *Pietà*. Later he called this act an abomination and a desecration. This *Pietà* was the only work he ever signed. Michelangelo recognized that the sacred gift of talent cannot be possessed.[1] One has a responsibility to share his talents without trying to own them.

When one is engaged in a favorite pursuit or a subject absorbingly interesting, the normal conception of labor or time and artificial social distinctions disappear from the mind. In fact, life itself is absorbed in the engagement, or it may be said that one's life is tuned in harmony with eternal life.
G. Koizumi (Judo Master)

Jesus told the parable of the talents.[2] In the story, the faithful stewards have risked and invested their talents and doubled their worth. They are given greater responsibility. The unfaithful steward buried his talent out of fear of taking a risk. His little responsibility was taken away. The story applies to discovering and utilizing your natural abilities. Risk investing yourself fully into the talents you now recognize, and you may discover others that you never knew you had.

You won't discover or express your talents while playing defense, while seeking the safe and sure, the tried and secure. You have to risk, take chances, fully invest yourself if you want to discover and express your talents. We needn't get bogged down in either false modesty or arrogant pride. Talents are natural gifts, developed through the discipline and concentration that come from caring.

It is your work in life that is the ultimate seduction.

Pablo Picasso

Talents Are What You Enjoy

What great joy it is to work and to see how we can effect change in the world, how we can build, shape, and make it better. We love feedback. Consider a child playing in the water. He seems fascinated by the effect he is having. He splashes in the water—it strikes him in the face—he laughs. What fun is feedback! How wonderful it is to build something of value, to give your love and understanding and see the effect you are having. Joy and play expand as you put your talents to work. Your talents are the way you can make the biggest splash and have the biggest laugh. As a practical matter, when you are looking for your talents look for:

1. What you enjoy doing
2. What you enjoy thinking about
3. What you enjoy learning about
4. What you enjoy as a process

What You Enjoy Doing

What do you have the most fun doing? This is the first tip-off to your talents. Talent is the kind of thing you can lose yourself in while you are doing it. Yet, because it is so much a part of you, its pursuit brings you to an ever deeper experience of yourself. We enjoy doing what we are naturally good at.

> *A musician must make his music, an artist must paint, a poet must write if he is to ultimately be at peace with himself.*
>
> Abraham Maslow

What do you most enjoy doing? Writing or hiking, discussing politics or playing with children, making things with your hands or dancing? Do you enjoy gardening or reading, painting or public speaking? If you especially enjoy doing some activity and you want to discover if you have real talent in this area, ask yourself if you also enjoy thinking about it, learning about it, and if you enjoy it as a process. These additional questions may help you to discover talent in areas where, up 'til now, you have had little experience.

What You Enjoy Thinking About

Do you find yourself pondering the nature of the universe or thinking about the varieties of social organization and their effects? Do you spend a good deal of time ruminating about the psychological or physical makeup of man? Do you spend time thinking about mythological stories or international relations? Do you compose songs or music in your head? What do you enjoy thinking and talking about? Your idea of a fascinating conversation would be a discussion about . . . ?

What You Enjoy Learning About

One of the best tip-offs to talent comes in observing what you most enjoy learning about. Since talent seeks expression, you naturally enjoy learning that which makes possible the fuller expression of your talents. You will learn quickly and develop rapidly in areas where you have real talent. You can even enjoy learning about the more mundane aspects because they move you toward the full release of talent. The joy that you experience in stretching out the envelope of your abilities inspires you to ever greater heights. The strength you gain in honing your talent translates into every aspect of your life. You are not only a happier person for pursuing your talent but a stronger and more resilient one, as well.

What You Enjoy As a Process

There is a difference between what you might enjoy as a simple event and what you enjoy as a process. Process is a better tip-off to talent. Let's suppose you enjoy writing letters. This "doing of writing" is a tip-off, but it is an entirely different process from writing books or even articles. These involve problems of organization, style, research, logic, concentration, and persistence, which generally do not apply in writing personal letters. Greater self-confidence is also required, simply because one is taking on a much larger task. You might enjoy "doing singing" in the car or the shower or with a group of friends; but this is altogether different from enjoying the process of rigorous voice training, the scales, the breathing exercises, and the endless hours of practice required of the professional.

Having talent in an area does not mean that you are necessarily going to be thrilled or in wild ecstasy over every part of the process. It doesn't mean you won't have difficulties and frustrations. It doesn't mean that there won't be things to do that you would (in the short-term) rather not do. Still, you must in some measure enjoy the process as a totality.

The musician, the architect, the teacher, the philosopher, the dancer, the poet, the government leader, those who protect the earth and the animals, those who protect the children and the poor, those true scientists who seek to know, those who make things grow—it takes all kinds. Identify your talents, and begin to think about how you can put them to work building the kind of world you want to live in.

We know what we are, not what we may become.

Shakespeare

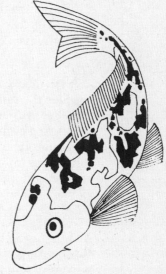

Releasing Talent

We never know how high we are
Till we are called to rise.
And then, if we are true to plan
Our statures touch the skies.
   Emily Dickinson

Man's capacities have never been measured, nor are we to judge of what he can do by any precedent, so little has been tried.
   Henry David Thoreau

Do what you can with what you have, where you are.
   Theodore Roosevelt

[One] who is naturally and constitutionally adapted to and trained in some one or another kind of making, even though he earns his living by this making, is really doing what he likes most, and if he is forced by circumstances to do some other kind of work, even though more highly paid, is actually unhappy.
   Ananda K. Coomaraswamy

A.C.T. to Release Your Talents

Don't worry if you can't get at your talents right off. There are things you can do to create a climate favorable for their recognition and ultimate expression. We suggest that you cultivate talent by practicing *attitude* and *creativity* in all you do. Recognize that the expression of talent is simply the greatest pleasure in work. You can develop your capacity for this pleasure. With attitude and creativity, you can act your way to the full release of talent.

Attitude: Cultivating a constructive attitude gives you the energy you will need for the full release of talent. The essence of a Zen attitude can be put like this—No self-pity! Suffering in the material world is inevitable; therefore, do not be shocked or upset by it. Bring to your work a spirit of gratitude. Be glad to be alive and happy to have the opportunity to work, to give in any capacity. In cultivating this attitude, you become more active in your inner life—quickening your imagination. Zen tells us to practice attitude while doing any work, however menial, monotonous, or mundane it may seem. Do not resent work—embrace it. *When you have finished your rice, wash your bowl.*

Creativity: The practice of creativity gives you the confidence you will need to express your talent. The first level of enjoyment in work is attitude. Next comes creativity. Creativity requires still greater inner aliveness—a more active imagination, and so, is more pleasurable. From the standpoint of Zen, we can say that creativity shows in applying *upaya*—"skillful means," or resourcefulness— to your work. To be resourceful, you must first accept things as they are, then go on to make a masterful arrangement of them. For example, because one is poor, he needn't live in an ugly way. The creative, resourceful one will make of his clothing and home beautiful arrangements that show his love and humanity. Creative resourcefulness is bold and confident, unafraid of obstacles or difficulties, using them as catalysts to spark ever greater creative achievement.

Talent: Talent is the final expression of joy in work. Attitude says: Don't resent. Creativity says: Invent, arrange, play. Talent is silent—bliss. While practicing your talent, your art, you are not. You have forgotten yourself. To forget oneself is the greatest of all pleasures—the ultimate joy. For it means destroying time—the greatest of all barriers. One who has not developed attitude is frustrated: time and self-remembrance weigh heavy on him. Attitude frees, creativity, still more, but in the expression of talent, one becomes the slayer of time. He enters into the time-less. When you are fully expressing your strongest talents, your joy is complete. "Do I then strive after *happiness?* I strive after my work!" (Nietzsche)[3]

Tapping into What You Enjoy

What do you enjoy most about your current work? (Even if you dislike most of it, there may be one feature that you enjoy.)

_____
_____
_____
_____

What do you most enjoy doing when you're not working? (Hobbies, recreational interests, etc.)

_____
_____
_____
_____

What do you most enjoy learning about?

_____
_____
_____
_____

What do you most enjoy making? (What do you enjoy as a beginning-to-end process?)

_____
_____
_____
_____

If you were financially independent and money was not a factor, what kind of work would you do?

_____
_____
_____
_____

It sometimes seems that intense desire creates not only its own opportunities, but its own talents.
Eric Hoffer

Taking the Talent Quiz

Rank each of the following talents on a one-to-ten scale, with a ten representing an extraordinary level of talent; a five, an average level of talent; a one, an extremely small amount of talent.

	Rating
1. An ability to organize	4
2. An ability to motivate	7
3. An ability to mediate	8
4. An ability to instruct	~~8~~9 X
5. An ability to manage	6
6. An ability to execute	4
7. An ability to lead	7
8. An ability to inspire	10
9. An ability to counsel	9
10. An ability to make things work (like mechanical ability)	7
11. An ability to build things	6
12. An ability to design things	7
13. An ability to heal	7
14. An ability to put people at ease (diplomacy)	9 X
15. An ability to contemplate (philosophize)	9
16. An ability to arrange things beautifully	~~8~~7
17. An ability to make beautiful things	7
18. An ability to perform (entertain)	9 X
19. An ability to communicate through speech	10
20. An ability to tell stories that instruct	9
21. An ability to be playful	8
22. An ability to persist	8
23. An ability to perceive the essential	9
24. An ability to juggle many responsibilities or activities at once	6
25. An ability for efficiency	6
26. An ability to be loyal	~~6~~8
27. An ability to be appropriate	6
28. An ability to be self-disciplined	5
29. An ability to be tolerant	5
30. An ability to concentrate	2
31. An ability to love	6
32. An ability to be happy	9 X
33. An ability to be balanced	8
34. An ability to be generous	7

35. An ability to be compassionate — 6
36. An ability to be dignified — 8
37. An ability to be tender — 6
38. An ability to be strong — 8
39. An ability to be impeccable — 7
40. An ability to be popular — 9 x
41. An ability to be enthusiastic — 8
42. An ability to express through the written word (writing) — 8
43. An ability to express through movement (dance) — 4
44. An ability to express through the visual arts — 4
45. An ability to express through music — 4
46. An ability to analyze — 8
47. An ability to be persuasive — 9
48. An ability to synthesize ideas — 8
49. An ability for logical or abstract thought — 9
50. An ability for imagination and vision — 9
51. An ability for athletics — 7
52. An ability for tactics — 8
53. An ability to strategize — 87
54. An ability to interpret or translate languages — 4
55. An ability to make things grow (plants) — 2
56. An ability to negotiate — 6
57. An ability to protect or defend — 7
58. An ability to invent things — 7
59. An ability to evaluate or judge — 8
60. An ability to explore or discover — 9
61. An ability to experiment — 7
62. An ability to nurture — 4
63. An ability to invest — 4
64. An ability to cooperate — 86
65. An ability to inspect — 87
66. An ability to investigate — 8
67. An ability to plan — 9
68. An ability to discern — 9
69. An ability to perceive opportunities — 7
70. An ability to clarify — 9
71. An ability to harmonize — 7
72. An ability to establish rapport — 8
73. An ability to be decisive — 7
74. An ability to initiate or begin — 2
75. An ability to complete or conclude — 3

Top Ten Talents

Now, having ranked yourself on each of the talents indicated in the "Talent Quiz," go back and review your answers. From the talents that received the highest scores, construct a list of your top ten talents. For those of you who have many high-rated talents, it may take a good deal of thought to winnow it down to ten. Continue until you are satisfied that you have identified your top ten talents.

1. _inspire_
2. _comm. thru speech_
3. _councel_
4. _comtemplate_
5. _stories that instruct_
6. _perceive essential_
7. _persuasive_
8. _abstract thought_
9. _vision/imag._
10. _explore/discover_

Talent Feedback

Now give your list to at least five people who know you in different ways (e.g., your spouse, a friend, coworkers, boss, or mentor, etc.) Ask them to examine your list and give you feedback on how well you have evaluated your talents. Tell them their honest opinion will be greatly appreciated. Ask them to indicate to you if perhaps you've overrated yourself in a certain area, or if there are any obvious omissions, or areas where you have a strong ability that you may have overlooked. Write what you learn in the space below.

_____

_____

_____

_____

_____

_____

_____

_____

_____

_____

Many individuals have, like uncut diamonds,
shining qualities beneath a rough exterior.
Juvenal

Integrating Your Talents and Purpose

How will you employ your talents in the furtherance of your life's work? Review your work purpose statement and your major talents, and think of how you can put your talents to work in pursuit of your life's work.

I will use my ability to: _____

to further my work purpose by: _____

_____

_____

_____

_____

_____

_____

_____

_____

I will use my ability to: _____

to further my work purpose by: _____

_____

_____

_____

_____

_____

_____

_____

_____

I will use my ability to: _____

to further my work purpose by: _____

_____

_____

_____

_____

_____

_____

_____

Your Mission: Give Birth
to the Great Idea of Your Life

Everyone has a great idea for their life. For many it remains unfertilized, unrecognized. Some abort the idea before it ever has a chance to grow. Some abandon it in its infancy. Still others chain the idea to themselves and make it twisted and distorted. And some set it free. Discover the great idea of your life, and set it free. But don't kid yourself. It will take every ounce of you. No weak, half-hearted effort will raise this child. Only a mother's love will get the job done.

In raising an idea, as in raising a child, there are joys and sorrows, frustrations and victories, agony and ecstasy. A child can get you up at three o'clock in the morning; so can an idea. A child can keep you up all night because it's sick and in need of care; so can an idea. Child or idea, you thrill when it says its first word or takes its first step, when it has its first day at school, when it first falls in love, and when, finally, it is free of you and yet full of you. The work of the creative person is to make her idea independent of her, just as the work of a parent is to make her child independent.

He who wants to do good knocks at the gate; he who loves finds the gate open.
                                                                Tagore

Many times people are afraid to embrace their idea, their vision, because deep down they know that they will become responsible for it, and it will hold them, like a child holds a mother, until it is free of them. Just as a mother becomes a servant of the child, so the creator becomes the servant of her creation. Like any parent, she is both happy and sad the day she sets it free. It's a labor of love. What we mean by "giving your best" is taking on the great idea of your life and carrying it, nurturing it, loving it until it can stand on its own two feet, and you are free. Take an idea that will grab hold of you and not let you go until it has squeezed the very best from you.

That idea is your life's mission. Your mission is your special gift to mankind. It is the most appropriate vehicle through which to express your unique talents, interests, and abilities. A life's mission is not simply an occupation. Rather, it's a steady application of effort to the lifelong challenge of remaining true to your best. It's the love of your life in action.

Marking Mission Objectives

If you only care enough for a result, you will almost certainly attain it.

William James

The next step is to lay out some of your *mission objectives*. A mission objective is a statement of a specific outcome you want to effect in your lifetime, in other words, a lifelong work goal. Unlike a work purpose, a mission objective is limited in time; that is, it is either done or it isn't. To build an orphanage, to create a foundation, to publish a book, to produce a film—these are all possible mission objectives. They are either done or not. The purpose of this section is to give you an opportunity to mark out your mission objectives.

Establishing long-term goals, or mission objectives, gives you a point of focus. In a sea of constant change and turmoil, you have an anchor for your attention and a direction for your life. The Japanese have a saying: "The focused mind can pierce through stone." When you lack focus, your energy is scattered and dispersed. Focus pulls your energy together and magnifies its impact. A laser can cut through a sheet of solid steel with the amount of energy required to light an ordinary light bulb. The quantity of energy is the same, yet focus intensifies its power.

Imagine shooting an arrow into the air. The arrow soars for a time and then falls limply to the ground. Now imagine taking aim upon a definite target. Your sight clearly fixed on the bull's eye, you let go the arrow. You hear the satisfying thud as the arrow slams into the target. Without a target, you have nothing to aim at, and without aim, you have virtually no chance of hitting the target. Focus, then, requires a target and concentrated aim. Long-term goals serve as your targets, and repeated concentration on these targets helps you hit the mark.

If you do not look at things on a large scale it will be difficult for you to master strategy . . .
Miyamoto Musashi

It's clear that a great many personal, social, environmental, and global problems have resulted from short-sighted thinking. Adopting a long-term perspective helps us improve the quality of the decisions we make. For example, if we thought more about those who will follow, we would no doubt take better care of our environment. As nations, we would balance our national budgets and not throw our children and grandchildren into debt. As companies, we would think less in terms of short-term profits and more in terms of bringing long-term benefits to others, and in so doing, to ourselves. Our educational institutions would concentrate on developing individuals who can think for themselves and on arming them with the tools they need to succeed in the twenty-first century, rather than pushing endless standardized tests on them. In short, if we are to take seriously our responsibility to future generations, we must make choices with the long view in mind.

In the same way that taking into account our responsibility to those who follow influences our choice of work, it influences the quality of our performance—our commitment to excellence. Do we write books, produce films, or compose music that will be enjoyed by those of as yet unborn generations, or do we go for the quick

If you have love you will do all things well.

Thomas Merton

buck? Do we build beautiful, quality buildings that will stand for centuries, or do we slap together bland boxes and cubes? Do we raise the next generation on healthy, nourishing food, or do we feed them microwaved, processed fare? Do we create organizations that build harmony and understanding, protect the environment, and promote world peace, or do we leave it to someone else? The good things you really want to do and accomplish—*do* them. It's an important part of being true to yourself.

But don't you have to be realistic? Don't you have to compromise? Never compromise your deepest desires. Never give up on your desire to be your best, or on doing your best to make it manifest. Don't sell out your ideals—easy to say, I know—but hard to live up to. It can sometimes seem like a battle. Something within us is urging us on to our best; yet something seems to pull us down to settling for less. All I can say is: *stand strong*. Do the best you can. If you fall (and we all do), get back up, and focus on that which seems to pull the good out from you. Give your attention to that which, when you focus on it, makes you feel strength, dignity, self-respect, and a sense of being destined to achieve your best life—whatever that means to you.

Ideas must work through the brains and the arms of good and brave men, or they are no better than dreams.

Ralph Waldo Emerson

Of course, you may have to compromise in the way your objectives take shape. It is often necessary to start small. As you gain confidence, knowledge, and experience, you move closer to the objectives you have set for yourself. Perhaps even in the end, your accomplishments will fall short of your original vision. Perhaps others who follow will complete what you begin. Still, holding the vision, the ideal, out in front of you will encourage you to give more than you might ever have dreamed possible. We can rise only as high as our aspirations; we can only achieve what we intend. Set your sights high.

We all want to give our best. Giving is as natural as breathing and, if we are *really* to live, just as necessary. When expression of the desire to give is somehow blocked, trouble starts. Energy that would naturally go into making constructive contributions gets diverted into less healthy pursuits. The most common ways in which these diversions manifest are confessing unimportance and pulling for the pity of others (passive hostility) or feigning exagger-

For what profit a man, if he gain the whole world and lose his own soul? Or what shall a man give in exchange for his soul?

Mark 8:36,37

ated importance and demanding their admiration (aggressive hostility). Variations on these two themes are virtually endless. History is replete with examples. *As a practical matter, we have simply to remember that a blocked expression of the desire to contribute produces anger, frustration, and resentment.* Whether we turn the anger inward in the form of self-sabotage or outward in the form of verbal or physical violence, it eats up our lives. Held over time, this anger can destroy relationships, weaken health, and sap creativity.

*Resolve to be thyself, and know that he
Who finds himself, loses his misery.*
　　　　　　　　　　　Coventry Patmore

Many a good relationship has been destroyed when one or both parties in that relationship have failed to achieve a clear sense of direction, or purpose, in their lives. The aimless party feels bad about him- or herself and so begins to find fault with the other and makes excessive demands on the other. The aimless one demands attention, wanting the other to constantly reassure him that he is lovable and okay. This becomes a horribly destructive and draining game.

Another equally destructive game is to play off many different "lovers." The object of this game is to fill with admirers the void left by your failure to adequately express your desire to contribute. Its object is, again, to reassure you that you are okay. You may create great anxiety for yourself and your loved ones by living far beyond your means. Again, this is an attempt to impress upon yourself and others that you have made it, that you are okay. The point is that you are not here to *be* someone else or just to be *with* someone else. You're here to be yourself, to make your unique contribution to the world. In the end, giving your best is the best you can do for your relationships and yourself.

For years, it has been known that stress is a contributing factor to many types of illness. Recently, researchers at Columbia University have made the link between illness and an individual's sense of control in his or her life. For example, people who work in jobs where they have little control (e.g., cooks and assembly line workers, etc.) are more likely to suffer heart attacks than those who have greater control. Apparently, as you increase control in your life, you reduce negative stress. Overeating, drug abuse, smoking, and alcoholism are frequently the result of the stress associated with not having taken responsibility to create a meaningful life's work, a work that gives you a sense of direction and control. Committing yourself to giving your best fosters good health by reducing negative stress.

It is hard to feel creative in a job that you are doing just to get by. Creativity is a way of life, not a matter of chance or a mysterious force to be summoned out of the ethers. If what you are doing most of the day requires no creative skill, chances are, your creativity is on the way downhill. You're not going to walk in the door and suddenly be creative at home if all day you've been vegetating at your work. Your creative powers grow and develop through use. The more you are challenged, the more you grow. The point is: Don't settle for less; follow your desire, and work to make it manifest.

Our plans miscarry because they have no aim. When a man does not know what harbor he is making for, no wind is the right wind.

Seneca

There is no getting away from problems in this life. You're either going to have the creative problems that come with realizing this vision of yours, or the neurotic problems that arise from the suppression of desire. Creative problems, or challenges, test you and spur you to your best. Neurotic problems are simply the murky water of suppressed desire. Let's face it, your deepest desires aren't going away. Talk to people in nursing homes. See if many don't still have the idea of the thing they always wanted to do but didn't. They are haunted by regret. Their desires didn't go away just because they didn't act on them. Your desire isn't going away either. Honor it, and do your best to give it expression. Keep coming back to it; feed it more and more attention. Let your desire become so strong that no fear from within or obstacle from without can stop your commitment to give your best.

Sooner murder an infant in its cradle than nurse unacted desires.

William Blake

In the exercise that follows, we encourage you to list your mission objectives, things you would most like to accomplish in your life. We don't expect that your list is necessarily going to be complete, or even accurate. Don't worry; you're not setting anything in stone. There may be omissions. Your list may not reflect the full range of all you want to accomplish. Once you get your feet wet, you may discover a host of additional possibilities that you haven't even considered. There may be inaccuracies. Once you begin, you may discover that you no longer want to accomplish things that were your original objectives. Again, you are not setting anything in stone. You are beginning to mark out the territory of your life's work with specific targets that you can use as reference points along the way.

Transforming Visions into Goals

Let's be honest. For a lot of us, writing goals just isn't as much fun as dreaming about visions. A vision is, in a sense, complete within itself, while a goal represents a great deal of effort for only a fraction of the vision. In your imagination, you can experience the totality of the vision now, with practically no effort, while working toward goals demands effort and the capacity to overcome resistance. Resistance results from the physical limitations of the natural world—time, space, energy, and matter. Resistance is overcome by concentrating and focusing energy. Writing definite goals is a powerful step to concentrating your energy.

Written Goals Are Best: A goal is a measurable written statement of a definite next step toward the realization of a vision you want to see manifest. If it's not written down, it's not really a goal. It's a wish, a dream, a vision, a hope but not a goal. Writing your goals down forces you to clarify and refine them. Several studies have shown that a written goal is more likely to be achieved than one that is merely thought or talked about. For example, in 1954 a survey was made of individuals graduating from Yale University. It was found that only 3 percent had definite written financial goals; 10 percent had a clear idea but had not written it down; 87 percent had no idea of their goals. Twenty years later, these Yale graduates were again interviewed. The 3 percent who had written goals had made more money than all the rest combined. Leaders in business, industry, and finance have long known the power of written goals in achieving success. Today, more and more individuals are writing personally meaningful goals in all areas of their lives, including career.

Goals Can Promote Well-Being: There are indications that identifying goals reduces stress and improve one's sense of psychological well-being. In his book, *A Strategy for Daily Living,* Dr. Ari Kiev writes, "In my practice as a psychiatrist, I have found that helping people to develop personal goals has proved to be *the most effective way* to help them cope with problems."(Emphasis added.) Many psychological problems are the result of an abundance of unchanneled or unfocused psychic energy. When we lack direction or creative challenge, life seems alternatively dull and boring or overwhelming and confusing. Establishing clear goals puts you in charge of your life. You're not at the whim of changing circumstances or opinions of others. You know exactly what you want. You look forward to the coming years because you know that you will progress and how you will progress.

Goals Increase Motivation: Once a goal is clearly fixed in your mind and written down on paper, you can begin to measure progress toward that goal. Psychologists studying motivation in the workplace have identified clear and consistent feedback as the most effective means of improving motivation and increasing performance. Feedback is only meaningful to the extent that it is the measurement of progress toward clear, definite goals. We encourage you to take the time to identify long-range career goals—your mission objectives.

Mission Objectives

He who would accomplish little must sacrifice little; he who would achieve much must sacrifice much; he who would attain highly must sacrifice greatly.
James Allen

Do not turn back when you are just at the goal.
Syrus

There's no substitute for hard work.
Thomas Edison

Life always gets harder toward the summit—the cold increases, the responsibility increases.
Friedrich Nietzsche

I want to be thoroughly used up when I die, for the harder I work, the more I live. I rejoice in life for its own sake.
George Bernard Shaw

Thinking is the hardest work there is, which is the probable reason why so few people engage in it.
Henry Ford

It takes a long time to bring excellence to maturity.
Syrus

Mission Objectives

In the space below, lay out some of your mission objectives.

Mission Objective 1: _____
_____
_____
_____
_____
_____

Mission Objective 2: _____
_____
_____
_____
_____
_____

Mission Objective 3: _____
_____
_____
_____
_____
_____

Mission Objective 4: _____
_____
_____
_____
_____
_____

Mission Objective 5: _____
_____
_____
_____
_____
_____

What If You Still Don't Know?

Most ignorance is vincible ignorance: We don't know because we don't want to know.
                                        Aldous Huxley

What if, after doing the exercises in "Act I" and contemplating on your own, you still don't know what your life's work is? In my work with clients, I always assume that they *do* know, and I tell them so. I simply don't believe their "not knowing." I ask them to consider *why they might not want to know.* I suggest to them that they may not want to be aware of knowing because of the responsibility for action that knowledge brings. If I profess not to know what my work is, then I can't be blamed for not having achieved it. If I do know, then how can I justify not taking action, either to myself or to others? How could I justify not making a sincere effort to develop myself so that I would be better able to work in this area? Again, knowledge brings responsibility.

In this program, you started with your vision of the world, your assessment of its needs, your values, and a consideration of what you have to give to it. If, after sincerely attempting to answer the questions, you still don't know what your life's work is, we suggest that you:

1. Continue to put your attention on the kind of world you want to live in, on what the world needs, and on what you have to give. (See "Act I: Action Steps" on page 245.)

2. Understand why you might not want to know. Below are a few of the more popular "reasons" why people "do not know" what they want to do.

"Reasons" Why You Might Not Want to Know What Your Life's Work Is

1. Fear of failure
2. Fear of rejection
3. Fear of reality
4. Fear of losing identity (face)
5. Fear of pain (and sacrifice)
6. Fear of commitment
7. Fear of making the "wrong choice"
8. Fear of not being in control
9. Fear that it will never work

Fear of Failure

Fear of failure often results from a false definition of what failure is, and by extension, of what success is. If failure is defined only in terms of ends, outcomes, and completions, then the possibility of failure is a real one. Likewise, if failure is measured by the standards and judgments of others, it is a very real possibility. If, on the other hand, you measure your success in terms of doing your best to realize your highest potential and make your maximum contribution, failure is only a failure of effort, the failure to fully apply yourself. To overcome fear of failure: (1) Value your process as well as your finished product, (2) Don't make comparisons, except with yourself, and (3) Don't be lazy. Make your best effort. *Since we as individuals are completely in control of any effort that we make, we are better advised to make our best efforts than to involve ourselves in fear and worry, which after all, can only hamper our performance.*

Fear of Rejection

Our society is extremely approval oriented. There's tremendous pressure to conform to narrowly defined images of success. People, by and large, understand static positions and finished products far better than dynamic creative processes. *A great inventor is a silly tinkerer until his invention is perfected and accepted.* The process of pursuing your life's work may not bring immediately obvious results. It may appear to others as though you are "doing nothing" while you're going through the process of self-examination, research, learning, training, or developing products or services.

> *Our doubts are traitors and make us lose the good we oft might win by fearing to attempt.*
> *Shakespeare*

While this kind of work is absolutely vital to attaining your life's work, it is not currently highly valued in society. This is especially true if it means loss of income or social status in the process. While a temporary loss of income and status may be a necessary and constructive step toward the achievement of your life's work, it is often viewed by others, whose opinion one values, as a step backward. They may think that you are slipping or "losing it" and may pressure you to "give up this foolishness" and return to a more "secure" position. If we are overly dependent upon the approval of others, its withdrawal may seem like the end of the world. Happily, the end of one world is often the beginning of a new, far richer and more fulfilling one.

Additionally, you may risk social rejection for taking controversial stands or for attempting to do things that haven't been done before. If you are particularly sensitive to the fear of rejection, you may view the pursuit of your life's work as threatening the approval of friends and loved ones as well as more general social approval. ***Recognize that while approval comes and goes, we ultimately have to live with what we think of ourselves: remaining true to your conscience is the safest possible course.***

Fear of Reality

This fear arises in those who have consistently denied reality and have constructed fantasy worlds. In their fantasy worlds, they're always good, accomplished, beautiful. They are, in a word—perfect. In the real world, none of us is perfect. People who tend to be

perfectionists dread the thought of being evaluated on their performance. After all, performance always has a measure of imperfection in it. We can maintain our perfect dream of ourselves in our heads and never have to confront our limitations. In my mind, I can imagine a perfect book. But the one you are reading, as I am well aware, is imperfect. Its imperfection reflects, not only the limitations of the material world, but those of its author. Still, I offer it to you, imperfect as it is, in hope that it may be of value to you. Your offerings will likewise be imperfect, but they nevertheless can be valuable.

I believe that anyone can conquer fear by doing the things he fears to do . . .
Eleanor Roosevelt

While the fears of failure and rejection are largely concerned with how others perceive us, the fear of reality is concerned with how we perceive ourselves. Are we willing to leave our mental ivory towers and face our imperfection, our smallness in the grand scheme of things, our frailness and humanity? In the imaginary fantasy world, I am not only perfect, I am omnipotent. In the real world, I am neither. It's hard to venture forth and risk much when you live inside of a protective bubble designed to preserve your cherished illusions. In pursuing your life's work, you will burst the bubble of your fantasy world. ***Your caring and desire to give will push you to risk facing the reality of your shortcomings as well as the limitations of this world.***

Fear of Losing Identity

Individuals who do not have a strong sense of their own identity attach a great deal of significance to titles and positions. A focus on title or position is static and, as such, perceived as secure (at least as long as one maintains the title or position). The pursuit of a life's work, on the other hand, is dynamic. Its success is measured, not in terms of positions or titles achieved, but in terms of the degree to which one makes the greatest contribution possible. The pursuit of a life's work may require the abandonment of a certain title or position which, even though unfulfilling, gives one some sense of security. ***When you know you are more than the positions or titles you hold, you are free to do your best without being afraid of the tests.***

Fear of Pain (and Sacrifice)

The fear of pain could also be called the reluctance to make the necessary sacrifices. If, when you meet resistance or encounter obstacles, you habitually retreat into your protective bubble, you probably suffer from this fear. For some, contemplation of their life's work requires a quantity and depth of thought to which they are unaccustomed. They have resistance to thinking about or concentrating on this subject because it forces them to confront their values and beliefs, to answer the age-old questions: Who am I? and What am I doing here? Many people find these questions painful.

This is particularly true since they recognize that once they have been successful in discovering their life's work, they may be setting up a course of even more self-sacrifice. A cartoon appearing some years ago in a popular magazine depicted two well-dressed men seated in armchairs by a blazing fire with one saying to the other, "I used to ask myself, 'What can I do to help my fellow man?' but I couldn't think of anything that wouldn't have put me to considerable inconvenience." ***You must be willing to put yourself to "considerable inconvenience."***

Fear of Commitment

Today, while commitment is widely touted, it is rarely practiced. People are particularly sensitive about making commitments. This is true in areas beyond work, for example, in marriage and relationships. Our popular concept of freedom is freedom from commitment, or obligation. Given this, it is not surprising that we tend to avoid voluntarily committing ourselves. The fault in this kind of thinking lies in our ideas of what freedom is and how best to achieve it. If we view freedom as a hedonistic lack of restraint, we are unlikely to equate it with the discipline necessary to achieve a life's work. Discipline must be embraced as the road to freedom. ***We pursue our life's work, not to diminish our freedom, but rather to expand it; we expand our freedom by leading lives that are fully integrated, by doing our best to practice what we preach, by putting our ideals to work.***

Fear always springs from ignorance.
Ralph Waldo Emerson

Fear of Making the "Wrong Choice"

Decision-making requires, not only that we accept definite limitations, but that we, in fact, impose them on ourselves. There is a certain aspect of human nature that resists limits of any kind. Yet, if we are to fully embrace life as a creative adventure, we must learn to put limits on our activities (not our potentials). Every truly creative person does so. Classical art, poetry, music, and drama all operate within the definite limits of form. These limits do not impede creativity, but rather challenge the composer to make his message fit the formal structure. Limits force him to make every line, every note, every scene count.

> *Nothing is terrible except fear itself.*
> *Francis Bacon*

When making decisions, you must leave behind the billowy clouds of vision and confront the practical limitations of space, time, energy, and matter. In other words, you have to make your visions work for you in the world in which you live. In this world, you can't do all things at once; you can't be all things to all people. You have to choose what you are about as an individual and establish the priorities of your life. Recognize that when you decide to focus on a particular vision, you may have to let go of one or several others, at least for a time. You have to make a choice.

The important thing is that you make the best choice possible for you at this time. If it is not your ultimate choice, don't be concerned. You will have plenty of opportunities to refine and reconsider your course, once you have begun it. The important thing is to begin. The worst choice is no choice. The best choice is choosing what you love the best. ***Choosing your priorities and values makes the strongest possible statement about who you are in this life.***

Fear of Not Being in Control

The fear of losing control is the fear that you will get in over your head. There will be too much to learn, too much information to process, too much to do. The remedy to this fear is simply the recognition that creating life's work is a step-by-step process that you control from beginning to end. Establish the parameters of your area of expertise. Continued focus and study in this area will bring added knowledge and, with it, increased confidence. What we cannot control is the fact that we have a limited time on this earth, and therefore, we must choose how we will use it. *Make the most of the time you have. Be deliberate. Take it step by step. Control what you can; forget the rest.*

Fear That It Will Never Work

People who have this fear have decided that "it" simply won't work for them. They believe their lives cannot really be the way they want them to be. They feel beaten down—defeated by life. They suffer from chronic low self-esteem. They've lost belief in themselves and, with it, the power to dream. If you fall into this group, identify when it was that you decided it was over, that it couldn't work—the point where you stopped believing in yourself. What were the events that precipitated this decision?

> *There are costs and risks to a program of action, but they are far less than the long range risks and costs of comfortable inaction.*
>
> John F. Kennedy

Objectively analyze the situation and the reasons for your failure to achieve the results you wanted. Perhaps you didn't have adequate information. Perhaps you didn't make enough effort. Perhaps you listened to those who said you would fail. Whatever the reasons, objectively identify them. A great high jumper may miss a height that is well within his reach. But he *does not* conclude that he is a failure as an athlete. He says, "My approach was too slow. My hip was too low . . ." He identifies specifics that he can correct. *Understand specific reasons for past failures and you free yourself to try again.*

Fear can be a factor at any step of the process of moving toward your life's work. We focus on it at the beginning because if you don't get past your initial fears, you're not even in the ball park. If you do get past them initially, you can apply what you learn along the way to overcome later difficulties.

Putting Fear on the Run

If you are having difficulty identifying your life's work, review the nine fears above. Indicate the top three that slow you down and what you plan to do to overcome them. Keep acting into fear until it is no more.

Fear 1: _____

What I will do to overcome this: _____

_____

_____

_____

_____

_____

Act into Fear and Watch It Disappear

Fear 2: _____

What I will do to overcome this: _____

_____

_____

_____

_____

_____

Act into Fear and Watch It Disappear

Fear 3: _____

What I will do to overcome this: _____

_____

_____

_____

_____

_____

Act into Fear and Watch It Disappear

Act I: Action Steps

If you still don't know what your life's work is, do and learn until you do.

1. Volunteer your time working for causes you believe in.

2. Study global, national, and/or community problems, first-hand if possible. See bibliography on pages 177–178.

3. Study philosophy, religion, mythology, sociology, history, anthropology, science, art, etc., with a view toward developing personally meaningful values.

4. Read the biographies of great individuals with a view toward learning effective strategies and raising your expectations.

5. Study success principles generally, and develop or strengthen a positive mental and emotional attitude toward life.

6. Develop skills that will stand you in good stead, regardless of your later career choices. For example:

a. Speaking	g. Performing well
b. Writing	under pressure
c. Negotiating	h. Planning
d. Managing	i. Critical thinking
e. Teaching	j. Creative thinking
f. Mentoring	k. Public relations

7. Learn techniques such as speed-reading, superlearning, and meditation, which will help you to keep up with all you will need to learn and remain relatively unburdened by it.

Act I Review

My Mission Statement: *(page 196)*

My Work Purpose Statement: *(page 213)*

My Top Ten Talents: *(page 226)*

My Integration Strategy: *(page 227)*

I will use my ability to:

in order to:

I will use my ability to:

in order to:

I will use my ability to:

in order to:

My Mission Objectives: *(page 236)*

The Game of Life's Work

Wherein our hero makes a career choice

Is the system going to flatten you out and deny you your humanity, or are you going to be able to make use of the system to the attainment of human purposes?
Joseph Campbell

We assume that by now you have some sense of what your life's work is. It's time to begin thinking of the career roles that will serve as the best vehicles for expressing it. Up to now, virtually everything we have asked you to consider is about what you want to create in the abstract. In "Act II: The Game of Life's Work," we are going to begin dealing with the real world environment in which you will create your work. We will be talking about playing the career game and about how to play it consciously, without letting it beat or trap you. We will suggest how you might make of your career a dynamic vehicle for expressing your purpose and realizing your best.

Playing the Game:
Winners, Losers, and Choosers

The play's the thing.
Shakespeare

Earlier (chapter 3), we noted the correspondence of the Magician archetype with the Game of Life's Work. The Magician's realm is the realm of imagination, of theater. The magic of the theater comes to life on an empty stage. A few painted scenes, a few simple props, a few scraps of material fashioned into costumes, a few effects of light—and an entire world is created. The magic of theater convinces you, the viewer, that you have entered into something that isn't. Under its spell, the once empty stage seems transformed into a tropical island or a medieval kingdom, a Roman courtyard or a modern courtroom. Yet, when the show is over and the lights come back up, you look at this place and say, "Oh, this was just a little stage."

In the discussion that follows, we are going to take you on a backstage tour. We're going to endeavor to show you how society's theater, or game, is created. We're going to let you in on the secret of its stagecraft. Now we should warn you that this may be somewhat disillusioning. For what had once seemed enduring and concrete will look far more ephemeral with the house lights turned up. You will still be able to enjoy the play, in fact, all the more. Yet its effects will never charm or frighten you to the same degree, once you know how the magic is made. In addition to considering the game of society, we will focus on the game of career and how to play it. We will even touch on the cosmological dimensions of game.

The game of society plays tricks with our imaginations. Like Dorothy and her companions, we are seduced by the apparent majesty of a Great Wizard of Oz. We venture far out of our way to seek his blessing, only to find ourselves quaking before the awful images he projects. Yet once we see how these images are constructed, we no longer fear or fetch for them. No longer do we imagine that the Great Oz can do for us what we can only do for ourselves. Now we are free to unleash the full creative power of our hearts and minds, right where we are, in our own backyards. Yet first, we must gather the courage to peek behind the veil—to see how this silly little man projects the fearful image of the Magnificent Oz. To our shock or delight, we will discover that we are that funny little man. We, alone and together, have projected the Great Oz of social convention out of our own imaginations.

The theater of the mind, the magic realm of imagination, is perhaps most easily approached through the study of dreams. In the twentieth century, the once strange and remote world of dreams began to come under scientific scrutiny. Researchers recognized a phenomenon referred to as "lucid" or "creative dreaming." It was noted that for lucid dreamers, dreams do not simply "happen" as they do for most of us. Lucid dreamers are actually able to consciously create and direct the course of their dreams. It was further discovered that the capacity for creative, or lucid, dreaming could be developed through a deliberate training.[1] The critical stage in this development comes when the individual recognizes that he ultimately controls the images of his dreams. He becomes, as it were, awake while dreaming. He awakens to, or becomes aware of, the choice that he has in creating, directing, and editing the images that play on the stage of his mental theater—the imagination.

Turning up the house lights, peeking behind the veil, awakening within the dream, we become conscious of the choices that make up society's game. We get behind its images and see that they are, finally, nothing (but our own imaginations) and therefore, nothing to fear. And now, the tour begins . . .

Nothing can bring you peace but yourself.

Emerson

Society has a game going. Like it or not, you were recruited into this game. Every game needs ends, goals, outcomes, prizes. In other words, it needs a way of separating winners from losers. Winners are those who get the prizes and titles. Losers are those who don't. In society, the game is based on *winning-models* and title acquisition. Conforming to the winning-models and proper title acquisitions makes you a "winner." Deviating from the winning-models and the lack of proper titles makes you a "loser."

Of course, no one invites you to choose the winning-model by which you will be judged and by which, most likely, you will come to judge yourself. Society does, however, entice you with rewards and chasten you with ridicule into accepting the winning-model as the only game in town. Though individuals are not invited to choose the model, the model's continuance depends on most people choosing to play for its prizes. This is the irony of the game—the key to its drama. *We choose to forget that we have a choice, that we have chosen the game that runs our lives.*

The beater and the beaten: Mere players of a game ephemeral as a dream.

Muso

Society's game is rather like a giant lotto. Everyone buys a ticket and plays along in the hope of being one of the lucky few who strike it rich. Everyone starts out trying to win, yet in order for the model to maintain its glamour, most people can't win. Who would strive to win a prize everyone has? Societies arrange their games to give the appearance that things have to be a certain way—the way they are. Below we will discuss the ways this is done in our society: through *envy for rank and property titles* and *the shame of social ridicule.*

Rank Titles: A Position of Power

In 1989, the dictator of Rumania called out the army to quash an uprising of the people. Instead, the army chose to side with the people, and the dictator was executed. The dictator's power, or lack of it, was based on what individuals in the army chose to do. This illustrates a basic point: *A person's power within society depends upon the deference that others choose to give to their title.* The all-powerful king or dictator is virtually powerless after the revolution.

We seek titles with the expectation that once we possess them, others will have to give us deference. It's the title that gets the deference, not the person holding the title. It's not Joan Smith who gets deference, but Dr. Joan Smith, M.D. Richard Nixon's deference level plummeted the day he resigned the title "President."

Titles win us deference, and though we attempt to hold them for perpetuity, they are subject to the slings and arrows of outrageous fortune. Marketing Vice President, Robert L. Doe can one day find himself without the corner office or the morning limo ride that go with the title. Dr. Joan Smith can (heaven forbid!) lose her license to practice. General Douglas MacArthur can find himself without an army to command. Even popes have lost their titles. Most people find the deference that accompanies titles gratifying to their egos and their pocketbooks. They will fight, scratch, and kiss the proverbial rear to keep a T.I.T.L.E. they hold dear.

Still, despite our best efforts, titles remain insecure. The higher the rank, the bigger the fall, and the better the gunslingers ready for a showdown. The hot star in business, sports, entertainment, or politics quickly becomes yesterday's news when they "fail to produce." What, then, can we hold on to? Better than rank titles are property titles. Through convention, we have come to give more permanence to property titles than rank titles.

Property Titles: King of the Hill

Rank is rarely held for life and can't be passed on. Where it appears to be passed on, as in the case of the chairman or president of the firm passing his title on to his son, the authority to do so is based on ownership, not on rank. Hostile takeovers demonstrate the priority of property titles over rank titles. The founder and chairman can find himself without a company if a corporate raider is able to acquire a controlling interest in the stock property of the company.

Realizing the insecurity of rank, rank-holders try to convert rank advantage into property holdings. The *Mexico City chief of police* builds the multimillion dollar home on a hill high atop the city. The *Communist party boss* buys a palatial villa in the forest hills—the *rock star,* a Beverly Hills mansion. The function these properties serve is not merely the enjoyment of beautiful surroundings. They are a statement. "I have made it." "I have won what cannot be taken away." "I'm king of the hill." "I'm above it all."

Property, then, is the ultimate form of legitimacy in our society. It's the big prize. With enough property, you can control many rank titles in many spheres of influence, without possessing any rank title yourself. While you must continue to prove (with few notable exceptions) that you are worthy of rank, you seldom have to prove that you are worthy of property. Another name for "serious prop-

Once the game is over, the king and the pawn go back into the same box.

Italian Proverb

erty holdings" is financial independence. For most, it is only a dream.

Most people don't own much property. They are dependent upon rank for deference and status. That's why companies have ten vice presidents and garbage collectors are called "sanitary engineers." People work for rank titles today (even if the title is Assistant to the Assistant of the Assistant of the Chief for Miscellaneous Services) and the hope of big-time property tomorrow.

The powers-that-be, meaning those who hold the most property and the "best" titles, have the most to lose by people not taking all this seriously. It becomes their interest to perpetuate the notion that all rankings are real, important, and just. First, they earned or deserve the property title, and second, it is more or less their inalienable right to keep it forever—through their offspring. It's a tough break for losers, but that's the way it is. Besides, with enough pluck and luck, they too could become winners. Of course, we shouldn't give the impression that this is a one-sided affair. As William James said, "Lives based on having are less free than lives based on either doing or being."[2] "Winners" often end up psychologically chained to their possessions, property, or rank.

He who possesses most must be most afraid of loss.

Leonardo da Vinci

Because of the role property plays as the ultimate prize in the social game, there is great ceremony around the legitimacy of its possession. Traditionally, the king's role as the ultimate property-holder in the realm was confirmed in elaborate ceremonies blessed by the pontiff or his emissaries. Today, major property-holders buy and collect works of art to confer a certain spiritual legitimacy to their status. They support the status quo by endowing, often in their own names, important rank-conferring institutions, such as the prestigious universities.

The role of ceremony is to make the status quo seem a kind of divine, or at least natural, order. I live in California, where it was okay for the Spaniards to take land from the Indians, and the Mexicans from the Spaniards, and the Americans from the Mexicans. Yet it's not okay for you to take it from the guy who owns it now. Why? Well, the first and most obvious answer is force. If you did, the police would come arrest you.

But how is any law enforced? With the consent of those it is enforced on. When most people decide to break laws, they become unenforceable. The highway patrol doesn't enforce fifty-five miles

The trouble with the rat race is that even if you win you're still a rat.

Lily Tomlin

per hour because most people go sixty-five. There's no way they can catch them all. It's the same way with any law, written or unwritten. Most enforcement is self-enforcement. A society that needs zillions of police is on shaky ground.

Social Ridicule: Shame on You

Life must be lived as play.

Plato

How, then, do you get people to take the game seriously? With juicy, alluring prizes, to be sure, but remember, only a few people can win the big prizes or they won't mean much. The primary means of getting people to take the game seriously is social ridicule. Social ridicule is based upon shame, the shame of being a loser. To the degree that you can be shamed, you will be manipulated by ridicule. *Every society uses ridicule as a means of social control.* Look at societies from a standpoint of what they ridicule and you can understand their winning-models and why they have developed the way they have.

Ridicule triggers the individual's sense of shame or guilt. It says, "Get back in line, you loser, you." And it's very effective. *Remember, most of us are losers.* We are losers for two reasons. First, we do not fit the winning-model (serious property), and second, we choose to accept the model as a guide to our worth. Losers have self-contempt; they feel shame. Losers accept themselves as losers and feel defeated. Still, they do not want to be EXPOSED as losers. Being ridiculed is being exposed. Once you decide that you can't win, the next step is to play defense against the ridicule of being exposed as a loser.

Humour is the only test of gravity, and gravity of humour. For a subject which will not bear raillery is suspicious; and a jest which will not bear a serious examination is certainly false wit.
(Quoted by Aristotle)

So we go along and act extra nice, hoping no one will expose us. Our motto becomes: Don't rock the boat. We put down others (who obviously are bigger losers than we are). We put down people of other races, people who are poor, people who are "stupid," people who "talk funny," people who have physical or mental disabilities. We make up reasons for losing—extenuating circumstances. We had a deprived childhood, or our parents didn't love us, or we were jilted by a lover or treated unfairly by a boss, or we have chronic aches and pains.

We try extra hard to look like winners, living beyond our means. Or we try to deaden the pain of losing by becoming addicted to things that take us mentally or emotionally away. Drugs, alcohol, television, affairs—any convincing escape will do. We get into attacking the model or calling the "winners" cheaters, scoundrels, and wife beaters. Or we get into destroying the game as terrorists or violent revolutionaries. If you don't think you can get good titles, you may go for bad titles. Something distinguishing. If you don't think you can be the world's greatest X and you're still into having titles, then you possibly could be the world's worst something. The idea is to call yourself a loser before anyone else does.

Remember, all of this presupposes that we choose to accept the game and its winning-models and define ourselves as losers. What if we observe the game and come to the conclusion that we are not particularly delighted about the prizes being offered? What if we think that the whole lotto concept of a few winners and many losers is fallacious? What if we come to see either the particular game or this kind of gaming process as destructive?

When you observe people playing a destructive game, you have a number of options: You can try to oppose them. You can start another game and try to get them interested in playing. You can remind them of the infinite game possibilities and the fact that they are always the choosers, and that in this sense, there are no winners and losers. Let's explore these options.

Opposing the Game Ranking System; or, Fighting the System

Fighting the game ranking system tends to actually maintain the system, with minor adjustments. The game remains essentially the same, but the winners and losers trade places. *It is for this reason that political revolutions don't work.* During the Cold War years, the Soviets fought the capitalists and ended up more capitalistic. The Americans fought the socialists and ended up more socialistic. (There is an old Hebrew saying: *Don't hate your enemy, or you become like him.)*

If Men were Wise; the Most arbitrary Princes could not hurt them. If they are not wise, the Freest Government is compelled to be a Tyranny.
William Blake

A fighting force is easy to co-opt. Its interest is not in changing the game but in changing the status of in- and out-groups. I call these "pie fights," fighting over who gets what piece of the pie. Today, the powers-that-be employ armies of bright people who are especially trained to co-opt or discredit opposition groups. They are usually successful. Often the leadership of the pie fighters are bought off, threatened, or "otherwise silenced." Occasionally, they are successful at recutting the pie. It's usually a very messy process.

Changing the Rules of the Game: New Models, New Ridicule

Fighting the ranking system is about political revolution. Changing the rules of the game is about social revolution. This has happened more rarely, and the effects have been more profound. To effect social change, the winning-model has to change, as well as what is ridiculed.

Changing the rules of the game means changing ideas about what it means to be a winner and a loser. For example, in our society, hoarding is a rewarded activity. The "biggest men" are the ones with the largest hoards. The "littlest men" are those homeless, with but tiny hoards. They are ridiculed for their paltry possessions, not their lack of industry. A lazy man with many possessions is not a bum; he leads a "charmed life." In many societies, the "big man" is the one who gives away the most to others. The "littlest men" are the possessive ones who are ridiculed for their hoarding. In both cases, there is a winning-model, and deviates are ridiculed. In both cases, the model and the ridicule are means of social control, but the resulting societies and the values they emphasize are fundamentally different.

People who view the current game as placing human survival in jeopardy are attempting to rewrite the game rules. They see the current consumption-and-hoarding-model as a dead end, leading to the end of all play on earth. Increased population and the fact that more and more people from traditional cultures are playing this game every year puts tremendous pressure on the earth's life support system.

Some who are engaged in trying to change the rules of the game attempt to set up model communities based on game rules different from those prescribed by the broader society. Others attempt to communicate their point of view through various forms of media in hopes of convincing a sizeable sector of the population to agree to a new social game. They propose new models and new types of social ridicule. The environmental movement is one of the more visible

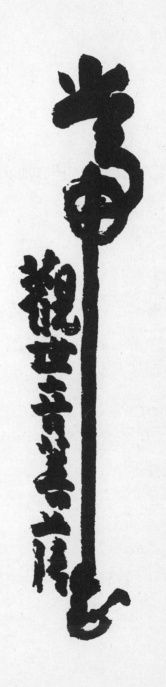

examples. It holds up the model of ecology-minded individuals and groups and ridicules polluters.

Ironically, efforts at social change are most effective when those making them are not attached to winning, in other words—when they are willing to allow others the freedom to change or not. When we need others to change, we often evoke resistance from them. They resent us forcing our point of view down their throats; they resent holier-than-thou self-righteousness. People who might otherwise be ready to change will recoil against the effort to push them into it.

Choosers Playing Games: Not Taking Any Game Seriously

Is there any other possibility besides striving to win, defending against losing, fighting the ranking system, or attempting to change the rules of the game? BE AWAKE TO CHOICE. Remember you are the chooser, and play. *Playing doesn't mean indifference.* You can play with commitment and intensity. You can play heroically and passionately. You can play with determination and perseverance. In fact, you can't play halfheartedly. You can go through the motions, but that ain't playing. It really is true that it's not about winning or losing but how you play the game.

Dilige et quod vis fac.
(Love, and do as you please.)

Playing begins with contemplating the game. Our word *contemplation* comes from the Latin *contemplari,* "to see things as they really are." See the game for what it really is and you are free to play. Recognize that the trick of the game is to seduce, manipulate, or intimidate you into feeling inferior and/or into attempting to gain that which you believe will give you a sense of superiority. When you honor all people for their humanity and don't see anyone as essentially better, worse, or different from yourself, you can no longer be tricked. You no longer need submit to projections of inferiority or try to achieve an enviable position so you can lord it over others. You can concentrate on expressing your creative best without being unduly concerned about social approval. Hold your own, and the dignity of all human beings, inviolate and you are free to play.

Put another way, the trick of the game is to capture your imagination. Images supplied by the social game enter your imagination and become animated to larger-than-life size by your emotional investment in them. These two, image and emotion, work together to draw you into the life prescribed by society. The creative power of your imagination becomes involved in building a defensive ego fortress, complete with watchtowers that scan the surrounding territory for possible threats (social ridicule) or possible new areas of conquest (titles).

Contemplating—seeing through the game—allows you to reclaim your imaginative power. You are free to use your imagination to build a life born out of the impulses of your own creative center. You put your faith in your creative intuitions and capacities rather than in the hope of some future reward or fear of some future punishment. You see your happiness in expressing what you are, not in gaining approval or avoiding its loss.

Emotional reactions (like envy and shame) keep you from playing precisely because they keep you from contemplating—seeing things as they really are. They stir up and muddy the water. When the water is still, you can see all the way to the bottom of things. Zen tells us that if we want to be free to play, we must be done with the agitation of envy and shame. Otherwise, we can be triggered, through prizes and ridicule, into performing like trained monkeys—without ever knowing how or why.

Zen is the game of insight, the game of discovering who you are beneath the social masks.
Reginald Blyth

Zen encourages us to recognize the transitory nature of reward and loss and remain awake to choice. It reminds us that we are not pushed around by society as much as we are by our own emotions. After all, through the ages, there have been many political and economic systems. None have yet, nor ever will, give man his freedom. It is not the system that enslaves man but himself. As the Hindu classic, the Bhagavad-Gita instructs: "All living creatures are led astray as soon as they are born, by the delusion that this relative world is permanent. This delusion arises from their own desire and hatred." (We might equate *desire* with envy, and *hatred*, really self-hatred, with shame.)

From the perspective of Hindu cosmology, we could say that, ultimately, the game is simply the play of *maya* and that our (or any) society's game is but a little game within this great game of *maya*. Careers (social roles and duties), in turn, are games played within the games of *maya* and society. This goes on and on like a Chinese box; inside one game is another and another and another. Zen would say that since we find ourselves in all these games, we might as well accept that we have chosen to play.

Human affairs are like a chess game: Only those who do not take it seriously can be called good players.

Hung Tzu Ch'eng

At any level where you have denied choice, you have serious-ness, unfunness, stuckness. You've gotten involved in a game and the idea of needing an outcome—a prize, title, or reward. You desire to become the chosen (one of the chosen few) and to forget you are the chooser. If you are into forgetting, then you think life is FOR-GETTING titles and rewards. More, more, more. The more ad-dicted you are to getting titles, the more stuck you become on the idea that you aren't good enough without them. It's only your attachment to (conventionally defined) winning that can make you feel like a loser. *Trust that you are good enough, and you don't have to spend your life proving that you are.*

Remember, titles are abstract, but life is living. Titles were won in the past in the hope of exercising the power they grant in the future. Life is here and now. Titles focus on differentiation. Life is a unified field. While titles can be extended, they cannot grow. Life grows. Life is FOR-GIVING Life. Life gives naturally, endlessly, the way a plant gives its bounty of food, and yet in the seed, nothing is lost.

If you realize that it's a game AND CHOOSE TO BE AWAKE, you can be in the world and not of it, with or without titles or ridicule. You can play "winning" or "changing the social game" without getting serious, without losing your playfulness. The truth is, we always have a choice. As Albert Einstein said, "While it is true that the inherently free and scrupulous individual may be de-stroyed, such an individual can never be enslaved or used as a blind tool." It's always up to the individual to choose his destiny.

Never for a moment do we lay aside our mistrust of the ideals established by society, and of the con-victions which are kept by it in circulation. We always know that society is full of folly and will deceive us in the matter of humanity. It is an unre-liable horse, and blind into the bargain. Woe to the driver if he falls asleep.

Albert Schweitzer

It may occur to you that a lot of people aren't going to get free of envy and shame or get hip to choice any time soon. They will be pretty serious and probably not much into *playing* with you. In the meantime, you may want to work on changing the rules of the game, or on taking care of people who get lost in the shuffle. You may decide to acquire a particular title so that you can use the accompanying power and deference towards these ends or others.

Remember, it doesn't have to be a certain way. It can be any way you want to play.

From awareness, there are lots of ways to play. Here are a few:

Game 1: You can play "Win the Game," without taking it seriously.

Game 2: You can play "Retreating from the World," without taking yourself too seriously.

Game 3: You can play "Taking Care of Others," without getting maudlin, uptight, burnt-out, or serious.

Game 4: You can play "Making Social Change," without getting maudlin, uptight, burnt-out, or serious.

Game 5: You can play "Professional Waker-Upper," the true poet, artist, mystic, without taking yourself too seriously.

Wanted: Life Beyond Rewards

The hook is your desire to be approved of by others. The bait is any kind of reward. The minute you go for the bait, the game is playing you. You are no longer playing the game. You get serious.

Can you work long term, without the bait of future reward? Of course—if you are playing. In this moment, as I write this, I have been working on this book off and on for the better part of three years. I don't have an agent, an advance, or a publisher, and I am having great fun. If I thought I *had to* write this book to get approval or the reward of money or fame (or had to finish it because I started it), it would quickly get serious.

I am playing writing a book because I want to say something—a lot of things actually. The world has gotten on quite nicely without my having said them and will get along just fine without ever hearing them. Still, when I have said what I want to say, I will play the game of promoting this book. Because I am playing, writing this book is teaching me many things. I trust that playing promoting this book will teach me even more.

I tell you this, not because it is any big deal, but only to communicate that I *know* there is, what for lack of a better term, is usually called "motivation," without the hope of future reward or

The reward of all action is to be found in enlightenment.

Bhagavad-Gita

recognition. The doing is the reward; the reward, the doing. That takes being here now with what you are doing.

More about rewards. Can you take them without getting hooked? Yes. But you must not need them. That is, you must not take them too seriously. Society tries to arrange itself so as to convince you that you *need* its rewards. Take learning. The Saracenes had centers of learning open to all. Everyone could come and play the game of learning from the wise and knowledgeable there assembled. They did not, however, grant degrees or titles. They thought the granting of titles anathema to learning which, after all, was the purpose of these universities. They reasoned that if they began to grant degree titles, people would become more concerned with winning their titles than with learning for its own sake. They also thought giving a title suggested some kind of finish, or completion, as though someone was now certifiably learned and needn't bother with keeping an open mind.[3]

The life of Zen begins, therefore, in a disillusion with the pursuit of goals which do not really exist—the good without the bad, the gratification of a self which is no more than an idea, and the morrow which never comes.

Alan Watts

In our society, the prevailing agreement is that the title is more important than the learning. Never mind if the man is speaking gibberish, he is, after all, "Grade-A Learned" and has the papers to prove it. Checking up on credentials is less taxing than paying attention in the moment to find out if the speaker has anything worthwhile to say.

Today, it is quite possible to "earn" a degree without doing much thinking, or even learning how to think, much less having any real experience of the subject matter. A sociology professor once told me most emphatically that there were no hungry people in America. Apparently, he had read that and had no experience of hungry people on campus or on the academic seminar circuit. This was not some crackpot assistant professor but a distinguished full professor at one of our top five sociology graduate schools.

However little degrees may relate to knowledge, let alone wisdom, they are, like all titles, taken very seriously. Parents fret over their children's entrance into the proper certifying institutions. You want to tell me what you are learning? Oh, that's nice dear. What I really want to know is HOW ARE YOUR GRADES? It's in striving for grades, in the grades, to make the grade that most

The superior man loves his soul, the inferior man loves his property.

Confucius

of us start really getting hooked into working for future rewards rather than living in the now-present moment. This striving for future rewards becomes a habit as addictive as any narcotic.

Like any narcotic, it requires a period of withdrawal. This is sometimes referred to as "dropping out," "burning out," or "taking time out." Joseph Campbell wrote, "The hero is today running up against a hard world that is in no way responsive to his spiritual need."[4] A period of withdrawal allows the individual to begin paying attention to his long-neglected spiritual needs and aspirations. Withdrawal, of course, has symptoms and can be quite painful. Recovery begins by taking one day at a time—finding one's own center and integrating its impulses with the world of work and society.

Playing the Career Game

Above, we briefly discussed the game of society in the Western world at the dawn of the third millennium C.E. Now we will focus on the game of career. Every career field is a society within the larger society. Every field has its own game, its peculiar rules and conventions, its winning-models and objects of ridicule. A given career game may parallel the game of the broader society and its values or emphasize an entirely different set of values. In choosing your career roles, consider the game in that field and how disposed you are to play it—disposed from the standpoint of skills, yes, but perhaps more importantly, disposed from the standpoint of intention. If you find that you will be railing against the absurdities of a particular game field, or that a lot of your energy is likely to be consumed in protesting the game rules, you should probably choose another field.

> *First you must find your trajectory, and then comes the social coordination.*
> *Joseph Campbell*

The key to selecting an appropriate career game is to understand your purpose—what you are working for. A clear sense of purpose helps you coordinate your inner promptings (visions, values, and talents) with the social demands of work. Once in a given career, staying focused on purpose will help you to play the career game without taking it seriously. Lack of purpose (or lack of attention to purpose) is responsible for the two big problems in work. The first is alienation, lack of direction—getting lost in the game, letting the game play you. The second is disaffection—unwillingness to play the game at all. When we learn how to work on purpose, we can play the career game, without becoming consumed by it, on the one hand, or isolating ourselves by refusing to play, on the other.

Work on Purpose

Some of us become so consumed by the game that we lose sight of our purpose. We become obsessed with having the right accessories, compulsive about the way we are perceived. We lose our balance and perspective and fall into the traps of one-upmanship, jealousy, and competition. We become so intent on what we are trying to be that we forget what we have set out to do.

But do your thing and I shall know you.

Emerson

> *Many a businessman feels himself the prisoner of the commodities he sells; he has a feeling of fraudulency about his product and a secret contempt for it. Most important of all, he hates himself, because he sees his life passing him by without making any sense beyond the momentary intoxication of success.*
>
> *Erich Fromm*

Understanding that career is a game doesn't mean we are to take it as something trivial or unimportant. It *is* important, but only in reference to our purpose, that is, only in terms of doing what we have set out to do. For example, the purpose of medicine is health and healing. Anything doctors do to further health and healing is important. Everything else is not. The fact that they went through many years of training, or spent long and arduous hours of internship, or that they are up to date with the latest technologies is only important to the degree that these now aid the doctor in "doing" health and healing. A doctor may become so distracted by technologies, drugs, prestige, income, etc., that he "forgets" or makes secondary his purpose, that is, doing health and healing.

There is nothing sinister in this: technologies are fascinating; drugs are quick and easy; prestige boosts the ego; and money is power in our society. Yet it serves to illustrate a fundamental axiom of careers: *In the game of careers, peripherals move in to fill the void left by lack of purpose.* It is impossible, as things currently stand, to eliminate all of the peripherals. (Many are social demands with which we simply must comply.) Still, we can keep the peripherals under control by keeping our purpose in mind.

The happiness of the individual worker and the beauty and humanity of a society diminish to the degree that peripherals replace purpose in work. Much of our personal alienation and global waste is simply a matter of peripherals dominating. Even benign peripherals can become malignant when they get out of hand. Career, then, can be a dangerous game if we attempt to play it without a clear, constructive purpose. Playing it effectively requires an ability to distinguish between purposeful and peripheral matters and to act on the purposeful ones.

The greater part of all the mischief in the world arises from the fact that men do not sufficiently understand their own aims.

Goethe

Once you have identified your work purpose, it's easy to see yourself playing in any one of a number of career games. Your field is open and your choices, many. If you lack purpose, you are left with only the game. This limits your playing field and increases your sense of insecurity. You come to believe that you must play a particular game, or else. Putting purpose first gets you focused on the why first and then the how. It gives you something to hold on to when circumstances, economies, or careers change. You have a constant reference point in a sea of change. A clear sense of purpose helps you understand and direct the events of your life.

Accepting the Game

While some of us become consumed by the game, others of us resent it with a passion! We are rebels without a cause (purpose). We rail against the unfairness, the futility, or the silliness of the game. We're out to show the world how ridiculous all these games are, and so we play the game of pointing out how ridiculous all the games are. We see so clearly the blindness of those who get lost in the game, but we may not see the problems we cause by our refusal to play. Francis Bacon said, "For good thoughts . . . towards men, are little better than dreams, except they be put into action; and that cannot be, without power and place."[5] We who refuse the game leave power and place to others and complain about the way they are handling things.

To be contented is noble, but to be lethargic does not enable one to benefit men or to utilize things.

Hung Tzu Ch'eng

> *The simple truth is that playing a game that you have chosen in order to demonstrate values, express purposes, or effect results that you have chosen is a very different process from having to play the game to win approval.*

Working on purpose allows you to approach the game with a spirit of play. You concentrate on your purpose and choose a career game appropriate to its expression. You don't get overwhelmed by fighting the system or trying to escape from it. You choose a game you can work with and stay focused on purpose. You don't spend your emotional energy in minor (or major) skirmishes over trifles. You don't isolate yourself on the sidelines. You choose a humane game and play.

Make Sure Your Choice Is Your Own

When we play the career game without a personally meaningful purpose, we leave our sense of success and failure to the assessment of others. In our culture, others will generally define your success by the money (property) and status (rank) rewards you have acquired. Many believe that these (wealth and status) comprise the sum and substance of career. They have no larger purpose than to survive or acquire.

Much has been made about the materialistic trends in modern society, the yuppie on the fast track to wealth and success, regardless of the costs. On the face of it, it may seem that our friend the yuppie is chasing after dollars; if we look a little deeper, we see that what he really wants is approval. If he can buy approved-of things, he will be more approved of. As a practical matter, the desire for approval dominates the career choices of many. What is it that is most approved of, most valued in our society? These kinds of questions pervade our unconscious, if not our conscious, career choices. For most, money is secondary to approval.

When we say that we have to have a certain standard of living, most of us (at least for the middle class in the developed world) are talking about a standard of living necessary to gain the approval we think we need. The great machine of the consumer society is fueled by our desire for approval. We seek our parents' approval. Men seek the approval of women—their wives or lovers. Women seek the approval of men—their husbands or boyfriends. Success in work is often measured in terms of the approval we receive from family, friends, and society in general.

Even while we chase after the approval of others, we are smart enough to know (at least subconsciously) that the minute we stop playing this game, we will be confronted with a more difficult problem, a problem called: What do I want? What do I believe in? What do I stand for? What am I all about? It's not only that we fear the disapproval of others, we doubt our own ability to find answers.

The courage to risk the disapproval of others, while at the same time going through the doubt of self-examination, is rare. When we begin to examine ourselves, we feel most insecure. It is then that we most look for approval. Finding none, many abandon the quest. This is the time for courage and perseverance.

Abraham Maslow articulated a hierarchy of values with security at the base, followed by belonging, ego-fulfillment, and finally, self-actualization. The most striking difference between the self-actualized individual and others is the degree to which he creates his life out of his own values. Self-actualized people are not dependent upon the approval of others when making major life decisions. They rely on their intuitions, values, and principles. Again, make sure your choice is your own. You are the one who is going to have to live with it.

---

to be nobody-but-yourself—in a world which is doing its best, night and day, to make you everybody else—means to fight the hardest battle which any human being can fight; and never stop fighting.

e. e. cummings

A happy life is one which is in accordance with its own nature.

Seneca

There are two general categories of information necessary to making good career choices. The first category has to do with what people in this career role typically do. This includes the kinds of things you might find in a job description: the skills, knowledge, experience, and training required to actually do the work. The second category of information considers the social dynamics or unwritten rules by which a particular career game is typically played. This takes into account all aspects of the career that are not directly tied to work performance. Later, you will have an opportunity to assess job description type stuff, the component skills, knowledge, experience, and training necessary to the performance of this career role (see "Scene II: Reality Testing"). For now, let's consider how the game is played in various career fields.

Choose a Game You Can Get Into

I'm not at all contemptuous of comforts, but they have their place, and it is not first.

E. F. Schumacher

One of the problems with traditional career-planning models is that they ignore this whole aspect of game playing, as though a job or a career involved simply those skills that might be listed on a job description. Job descriptions reflect what's really happening on the job about as accurately as formal organizational charts reflect the power dynamics within large organizations. Job descriptions and organizational charts are more theory than reality. In many career fields, you will be judged on your ability to play the game at least as much as on your work performance.

If you don't think so, try showing up to work at the office in your bathrobe. Try speaking in slang or obscenities at a formal business meeting. Try missing a bath or shower for a few days or weeks, and you will realize that there are games you have to play. You probably won't find the ability to tie a tie or make up your face on your job description but don't do these things and you will soon discover how important they are to certain career games. They may not directly affect your ability to do the actual work (many people working at home do quite nicely in their bathrobes), but they do affect the way you play the game.

Robert was a professor at a small, high-profile private college in the east. He was an excellent teacher who consistently received high marks for his classroom performance in university staff evaluations. His students also rated him highly. There was only one problem. Robert didn't go to informal faculty social gatherings. These meetings were not part of his job per se. He attended formal departmental meetings and the like, but he couldn't get into the game of socializing with the school faculty in his free time. Needless to say, Robert is no longer working at this school. Understand the rules of the game before you decide to play.

Cocktail parties, teas, weekends entertaining for the boss, the clients, the staff—these too may be a part of the career game in your field. If you wouldn't pick these people solely for the interesting and pleasant companionship they provide, then your "entertaining" is work. There are so many aspects to the career game. Let's say that you out-produce your coworker who gets the promotion, the raise, the added responsibility. You know you are doing more; still, they are getting more. Before you decide that life is totally unfair, stop to consider that they may be playing the game better than you. Remember, when you choose a career game, you are choosing to abide by rules you have not made and will probably have little impact on changing. Choose a game that works for you.

Intention is the starting place for learning. (More on this in "Act IV.") If you really "can't get into" the game in your field, you probably won't have an intention strong enough to learn to play it well. If your intention is strong, you can get into a game, even if you've never played it before and even if it runs a little counter to your personality. If your intention is lacking, trying to force yourself is not a good idea.

There is nothing so easy but that it becomes difficult when you do it reluctantly.
                                        Terence

Enjoy the Game You Are Playing

The best way to enjoy the game is to remember that it is one. Playing the career game can be distinguished from taking it seriously. If you take it seriously, you're not playing, and if you're playing, you can't take it seriously. Taking it seriously means taking yourself as a role. If you stand back and look, you can easily see how silly this is. When you are concentrating on purpose, you needn't exaggerate the importance of your role. You can enjoy the game. While playing, you can be smiling on the inside. You know it's theater, and so you concentrate on acting on purpose. As a conscious player on the stage of life, play your career role; don't let it play you.

Viewing yourself as a role not only diminishes your enjoyment but actually impairs your ability to play the role well. It puts you on the defensive. Defensiveness comes with the effort to brace oneself against the social ridicule that might trigger shame. A great deal of energy gets wrapped up in playing defense—in trying to control other people and circumstances so as to avoid social ridicule. This tends to make one rather awkward and stiff, impairing his ability to relax and concentrate on performance. To play, we must let go of the defensive posture of role and give our imaginations room to explore. Zen suggests an inner invulnerability to shame in the free play of the game as game. The fear of being exposed as a loser or a phony falls away in the realization that all roles *are* phony. They are but stagecraft, so much costume and paint.

A career role is a vehicle through which to express and fulfill your life's work. It is a tool to be used consciously and deliberately in the furtherance of your work purpose and toward the accomplishment of your objectives. A career role is not an end; it is a means. It is not an achievement; it's a means of achieving. Not merely something to be, it's a way to do (*dō*).

What's Ahead in Act II

Now let's briefly discuss the territory we will be covering in "Act II." We begin with **"Scene I: Your New Career: Getting a Picture."** The purpose of this section is to give you a chance to pre-experience both the doing and the gaming of a given field. By mentally projecting yourself into the career role you are considering, you will have a chance to get a sense of how well you resonate with the game in that field. This will allow you to eliminate inappropriate career roles before you begin the lengthy and time-consuming research process.

In **"Scene II: Reality Testing,"** you will test what you have mentally projected in the previous section against reality. In other words, you will do research and find out what the real deal is. Where you are now in your work life is a direct result of the decisions you have made or decided not to make. These decisions were based upon your awareness at the time. The quality of our decisions is no better or worse than the quality of our awareness. We see so much better with hindsight because of the additional awareness we have gained. The exercises and worksheets in this section will help you improve your *foresight* by increasing your awareness before you make a major career decision.

In **"Scene III: Evaluation: No or Go?"** you will have an opportunity to assess your research. You will then be able to determine if the career role you initially selected is one you want to dedicate yourself to. If not, you can start the process all over again.

Life Is a Game

Life is a game full of games. There is no getting around the games of life. The question is not whether we will play games but rather: What games will we play? and How well will we play them? The more we accept and understand any game, the better we are able to play it. This unit is designed to improve your general understanding of the game called "career." Additionally, and perhaps more importantly, answering the questions in the process work that follows will help you better understand the career game within the specific fields you are considering. You will have a framework for determining whether or not a particular career role is the best means for expressing your life's work at this time.

Detour #2: The Approval Trap

Every child has a desire to please, to be approved of. That desire for approval becomes linked to whatever goals, values, and behaviors are most highly esteemed by his family and society. This is a fundamental component of the process social psychologists call socialization. It is a cross-cultural phenomenon that applies equally to Eskimos and Bushmen, Europeans and Americans. Of course, the sanctioned values and behaviors vary from culture to culture, but the process operates in all.

Our Western culture is extremely materialistic. Acquisition of material resources is highly valued as an end in itself. Materialism shapes our thinking in such fundamental and pervasive ways that our perception of its impact on our lives and on the decisions we make is often obscured. Often we are not aware of being caught up in materialism; we only have a desperate sense of wanting approval.

There are two basic ways that we can sell out for approval. We can actively go after what's approved of (money), and/or we can suppress our talents because we fear to risk disapproval. We sell out when we pursue a career course primarily for the sake of money. "I really want to work in this area, but there is more demand (or pay) for that." On the other hand, we can sell short our talents to make it easier to sell our wares. "My heart and talent are really into this, but it looks safer or easier to do that." In either case, we risk our conscience. When we compromise our values in order to fit in, we mute the voice of conscience. It will be easier to sell out next time. Each time we sell out, it becomes a bit more difficult to hear the voice of the conscience, until finally it is all but silent and we have become alienated from ourselves.

Materialism: Fascination with material gain distracts us from purpose. Time and again we are confronted with tests of character. These tests often put material gain at odds with purpose. In our desire to please our fellow man, we may compromise our desire to serve him. Only firm resolve and constant attention to purpose can keep us on a steady course.

Anti-materialism: Anti-materialism rejects the resources necessary to implement purpose. It is an immature fear of power that keeps us from acquiring the resources necessary to achieve our objectives and express our talent. In fact, it is a kind of materialism, for it places concern for material resources (their denial) above purpose and talent. If you require resources to fulfill your purpose or express your talent and you deny yourself these because of an anti-material bias, you have sold out. Get what you need to succeed.

Zen Play

Zen talks out of both sides of its mouth. Out of one side it tells you what you think is you is a fiction, a joke, a nothing. Out of the other side: Take care about what you are doing. Do it with precision, excellence, and grace.

Most of us are consistent. If we comprehend the absurdity of our personal drama, we are often lazy and inattentive to life. If, on the other hand, we are passionately involved in the activities of the world, we come to take ourselves too seriously, imagining that our egos have some reality beyond our thoughts. Zen is singularly two-faced.

When the mind is still, you feel the love. The Buddhists call it "Karuna." *Karuna* is compassion: not sentimental, not maudlin, not condescending—just love for your fellow man and awareness of his suffering. Zen all of a sudden, you are the Buddha, and everyone is the Buddha, including the pesky neighborhood cat.

Compassion says, "Serve, love, be helpful." Buddhahood says: "Who are you helping with your helping? Everyone is already the Buddha. Getting serious about helping and 'saving' people is very silly." To walk the way of Zen is to walk a tightrope of active involvement without attachment.

To act without acting, to do without doing, to work without working, this is the Zen way. This is making life a play.

There is nothing left to you at this moment but to have a good laugh.

Zen master

Honoring the One behind the Mask

Life is a masquerade ball. We all are wearing costumes and masks. These help us mark the roles we are playing at any particular time. While we keep in mind their purpose, role masks serve us well. When we confuse ourselves with our roles or forget that we are choosing to play a game, roles become oppressive— capable of turning even young men and women into cardboard stiffs. In *The Art of Loving,* Erich Fromm describes the condition of the modern man—caught up in a game he has forgotten he chose to play. Fromm describes a "nowhere man" who has become so attached to his masks that he has forgotten how to play—and to love. Fromm calls this "nowhere man" an automaton. Read his description below, and see if perhaps you have met this man.

> Modern man is alienated from himself, from his fellow men, and from nature. He has been transformed into a commodity, experiences his life forces as invest- ments which must bring him the maximum profit obtainable within existing market conditions. Human relations are essentially those of alienated automa- tons, each basing his security on staying close to the herd, and not being different in thought, feeling, or action. While everybody tries to be as close as possible to the rest, everybody remains utterly alone, pervaded by a deep sense of insecurity, anxiety and guilt which always results when human separateness cannot be overcome. . . Automatons cannot love; they exchange their "personality pack- ages" and hope for a fair bargain.[6]

The postmodern man (or woman) is not an automaton but an alive and loving player in the game of life. He or she is a gamesman, not in the sense of being a shrewd manipulator, but in the sense of one who is game for life and ready to play. *The automaton struggles for ends*. He wants to *have something* that is fixed in time, for example, a title, a position, rewards of every kind. *The gamesman plays an open-ended game*. The gamesman wants to *do something,* and that changes. An automaton becomes habituated to a role. A gamesman never confuses himself with his role.

Now that you are about to frame your life's work in terms of a career role, we want to remind you to stay loose. The career game that you choose to play ought to attract you and be fun for you. Even so, beware of the trap of hiding in it, of losing your spontaneity and humanity for the sake of the role. Gamesmen remember that they have put on masks and can take them off, and every now and again, even while they are wearing them, they lift them just a bit, and peek through.

The gamesman knows that she can fall into the automaton habit, not only by concretizing into her role but also by taking the roles of others too seriously. Often we forget that the policeman or doctor, the university professor or boss, the secretary or waitress is so much more than the role each plays in our lives. Gamesmen relate to people first and foremost as human beings and only secondarily as their roles. Gamesmen see, honor, and love the one behind the mask.

The Career Game

When making career choices, we are in a general sense choosing our playing field, our teammates, the rules and regulations by which we will play, the goal lines, and (yes, Mathilda) our opponents.

Playing Field: Where will you be playing this career game of yours? Indoors or out? In a skyscraper or a storefront? Is it a static field, like an office desk—or a moving one, like a Lear jet?

Teammates: What kind of people will you be playing with, and in what type of formations do they generally play? In some fields, you have to run tight with the pack. In others, you can plan on being the lone wolf most of the time. In some fields, teammates will play like opponents. In others, they will be very supportive. In many careers, you have to be a member of the "club" in order to play, or to play effectively. Some clubs are very traditional, formal, and obvious. Others are more spontaneous, informal, and insidious.

Rules and Regs: Some of the rules and regs are designed to expedite the work function. Some are designed to protect the organization against legal, market, or political injury. Some are designed to protect the community against the excesses of the organization or its players. Some are simply social conventions that attempt to make a given work environment predictable and understandable. Some are accepted matters of taste, e.g., in writing, it is considered bad form to start every sentence in the same paragraph with the same word. (No, Mrs. Eckhart, I haven't forgotten.) Some career fields are more into rules and regs than others.

Goal Lines: Every field has its goal lines. The goal lines are the commonly agreed upon standards of success. As we have seen above, these may have little or nothing to do with the stated work purpose. For example, at most universities, professors are more likely to be judged on the basis of what they do or do not write, than on how well they teach. Even when the "goal lines" do not match your work purpose, you will be expected to pursue them or risk disapproval, anything from slight annoyance to major hostility. Peer pressure in many career fields is enormous. Try to choose a career where the peer pressure will push you in the direction you want to go.

Opponents: An opponent can be anyone who is holding a purpose counter to your consciously stated work purpose. This, of course, could include even yourself or your teammates from time to time. The career game itself can be an opponent when your purpose differs greatly from the accepted goals in your field.

What to Look for in a Career Game

Choose the game that best allows you to fulfill your purpose.
Purpose is the engine that drives your life's work. Choose a career, not because you want to be something, but because you want to do something. If you take a career as something to be, you will get distracted by the game and forget your purpose. You may find the ideal career role for the full expression of your purpose, or you may find that it will require several career roles. These you might pursue concurrently or one after the other.

Choose a game that allows you to fully express your talents. Even as your career role must allow you to fully express your purpose, so must it allow you to fully express your talents. You can think of your talents as your built-in tool kit. Let's say that your tool kit is full of wrenches and your career role calls almost exclusively for hammers. You are not fully utilizing your talents if you're only using your wrenches for hammering. Wrenches will hammer, but they do something else better and more naturally. If you can accept this somewhat silly metaphor, you can see that it is important to know what is in your tool kit and the best way to use it.

Choose a game that is compatible with your personality. You must be ready to agree with the game in your field. In other words, the game must be agreeable to you. You ought to enjoy playing it. Of course, you may not enjoy every aspect of it, but generally it should be pleasurable to you. If you detest the game, it will be hard for you to concentrate on purpose. A fair number of the requirements of the game ought to be things you enjoy doing.

Choose a game you can commit yourself to. Choose a game you can get into playing long enough and intensely enough to excel at. Choose a game you can respect and feel a sense of honor in playing, one with a tradition you can take pride in.

 By honors, medals, titles no true man is elated. To realize that which we are, this is the honor for which we are created.   Angelus Silesius

A Work Purpose May Be Expressed through Any One of a Number of Career Roles

Below we will examine how several individuals have put their talents and work purposes together in the process of envisioning various career roles. Remember, there is always more than one way to make it work. Find the best way for you.

Ron loves the great outdoors. He feels most serene and yet alive when he is in the woods. He loves the forest and feels protective of it. His work purpose is involved with protecting and preserving our environmental resources. He might work as a forest ranger, an ecologist, an environmental lawyer, or in any of a number of other capacities depending upon his visions, talents, and the specific objectives he wants to accomplish.

Judy loves music. Singing, playing, or listening, music is an important part of all that she does. She has the talent and the inclination. Her work purpose involves bringing joy and beauty to the world through music. Judy might work as a performer, a composer, a producer of music, or in a variety of other roles related to music.

Dan is a communicating man. His thoughtful words always seem to lend a hand. He is at his best sharing with people about things he deeply believes in. His work purpose is tied to teaching people how to get along better in this world. Dan could pursue his work as a professor, a diplomat, a psychologist, or in many other related fields.

Kim is a take charge kind of person. She's a leader. She feels most like herself when organizing teams of people toward the accomplishment of constructive objectives. Her work purpose involves organizing and leading people to achieve their best. Kim might work as a politician, a business executive, a community organizer, or any of a number of leadership capacities, again depending upon her visions, talents, and the specific objectives she wants to accomplish.

As the examples above illustrate, a life's work is more comprehensive than a specific career or occupation. Each of the individuals cited above could pursue their life's work through any career or combination of careers. The examples given represent just a few of the ways that each of these people could pursue their life's work. We encourage you to take the time to generate a number of career approaches to your life's work. Be creative and think of as many ways as you possibly can of putting your vision, purpose, talents, and objectives to work in specific career roles.

Selecting Your Career Roles

Write your work purpose statement below (see page 213). Next, generate a list of possible career roles that you could employ in the pursuit of this work purpose.

Work Purpose Statement

_____

_____

_____

Career Roles

1. _____
2. _____
3. _____
4. _____
5. _____
6. _____
7. _____
8. _____
9. _____
10. _____
11. _____
12. _____
13. _____
14. _____
15. _____

Now select the three that you feel most attracted to, and list these below:

1. _____
2. _____
3. _____

When a man does not know what harbor he is making for, no wind is the right wind.
                                            Seneca

278 Act II • The Game of Life's Work

The Game of Life's Work Affirmations

1. I now see the career or combination of careers that best expresses my life's work.

2. Because I choose my career with full awareness, I am able to play with intensity without getting serious.

3. I have the will, energy, and persistence to investigate the career I have chosen and find out all pertinent information.

4. I am totally honest and realistic in my appraisal of myself and my abilities.

5. I remain confident that I can flourish in the career or combination of careers that best support my life's mission.

6. I trust myself. I know that if a career is right for me, even if I do not now possess the skills and knowledge that I need to excel in this career, I will acquire all that I need and more.

7. Nothing can stop me from achieving my purpose in life. Every step that I take gives me new confidence that I will succeed in making manifest my vision for myself and others.

The process that follows is a scientific approach to career decision-making. It is scientific in the sense that it applies the scientific method: developing a hypothesis, testing the hypothesis, evaluating the results of the test, then determining the validity of the hypothesis. Here, you will develop a hypothesis about which career role will best allow you to take advantage of your talents and purpose. Next, you will conduct research to test your hypothesis. Then, you will evaluate the results and determine if the original hypothesis was indeed correct or if you need a new one. The exercise that immediately follows will save you time by helping you to make sure your working hypothesis is reasonably sound before you conduct your research.

Your New Career:
Getting a Picture

I have learned this at least by my experiment: that if one advances confidently in the direction of his dreams, and endeavors to live the life which he has imagined, he will meet with a success unexpected in common hours.
Henry David Thoreau

N ow that you have selected three potential careers that you are attracted to and that you feel would be excellent vehicles for pursuing your life's work (see page 277), we invite you to take a screen test. An actor takes a screen test to determine if he is right for the part. Now you can take a screen test to determine if the part (career role) is right for you. This section is an extensive and detailed visualization process designed to help you mentally project yourself into three different ways of fulfilling your life's work. Once you have determined which of these career roles seems best for you, you will have a chance to investigate it further in "Scene II: Reality Testing."

Giving Yourself a Screen Test

Think of
each career option as a
"role" played by you, the main
character. In the exercises that follow,
you will mentally project into the career
roles you have selected. You will begin to get a
sense of which roles might be right for you and to
eliminate inappropriate roles before you go through
the time-intensive "Reality Testing" and "Evaluation:
No or Go?" sections that follow.
    We understand that you may not know all of the
details that some of these questions ask for, and you
haven't yet done the research necessary to answer these questions in a definite way. Still,
you can mentally project yourself into
working in this situation and sort of
feel or intuit the answers for
many of these ques-
tions.

A Day in the Life of Character #1

Answer the following questions as though you were currently doing this work.

What time do you wake up for work? _____

What do you wear to work? _____
_____

Where do you go to work? (Setting? Rural, small town, suburban, or urban area? If indoors, type of building?) _____

Who is the first person you greet (if any)? _____

At what time do you begin your work day? _____

Are you working for yourself, a small firm, large firm, or a branch of the government?
_____

What are the tools you work with? (Paint and brushes? Computer and telephone? Desk? Workbench?) _____
_____

Do you have a boss? What kind of rapport do you have? Do you have subordinates or employees? What do they do? How do you interact?_____
_____

How do you spend the lion's share of your day? (In meetings? Alone? With a team? On the telephone? Making presentations?) _____
_____

Do you work primarily with people inside or outside of your organization? (A manager works more with people on the inside; a sales representative, more with those on the outside.) _____

Where do you have lunch? With whom? _____

At what time do you complete your work day? _____

Do you take your work home? If yes, what kind of work? _____
_____

How much money will you earn at this over the course of one year? _____

I like the dreams of the future better than the history of the past.

Thomas Jefferson

Looking Back on Your Life's Work: Great Moments

Answer the following questions as though you had already successfully completed your life's work.

What was the most important contribution you made through this work?

_____

_____

What was the most exciting aspect of this work? _____

_____

What was your most difficult challenge, and how did you overcome it?

_____

_____

What were you most proud of? What was most rewarding? _____

_____

_____

What were the creative highlights? _____

_____

_____

What skills have you perfected in the course of this work? _____

_____

_____

What did you enjoy most about this work? _____

_____

What did you enjoy least? _____

_____

What awards, commendations, acknowledgements, testimonials, etc., that you received were the most meaningful to you? _____

 Growth is the only evidence of life.
                    Cardinal Newman

Mission Accomplished!

Answer the following questions as though you had already successfully completed your life's work.

How did you fulfill your mission in life through this career? _____
_____
_____
_____
_____
_____

What did you do to eliminate suffering and/or expand joy for your fellow man?
_____
_____
_____
_____
_____
_____

How did your example inspire others to be their best?
_____
_____
_____
_____
_____
_____

What have you left behind as a legacy? _____
_____
_____
_____
_____
_____

Our aspirations are our possibilities.
Robert Browning

Acknowledging the Supporting Cast

Answer the following questions as though you had already successfully completed your life's work.

Whose support was most critical to achieving your success? (If you can't give specific names, perhaps positions, titles, or relationships.)

_____
_____
_____
_____
_____

What role models have influenced you the most?

_____
_____
_____
_____
_____

How did the response and appreciation of the people you were serving inspire you to do and achieve more?

_____
_____
_____
_____
_____

Who else has helped you to succeed, and how have they done so?

_____
_____
_____
_____
_____

Now on separate sheets of paper, apply this same process for career roles number two and number three (from page 277). Once you have completed this process for all three career roles, review them and select your first choice for research and evaluation.

The career role that I will further investigate is: _____

_____

Investigating Career Possibilities

100 Best Careers for Writers and Artists. Field, Sally. New York: Macmillan, 1998.

100 Jobs in the Environment. Quintana, Debra. New York: Macmillan, 1997.

100 Jobs in Social Change. Jebens, Harley. New York: Macmillan, 1997.

Adventure Careers. Hiam, Alexander, and Susan Angle. Franklin Lakes, N. J.: The Career Press, 1995.

Alternative Careers for Lawyers. Mantis, Hillary. New York: Random House, 1997.

Arco College Not Required! 100 Great Careers that Don't Require a College Degree. Corwen, Leonard. New York: Macmillan, 1995.

Alternative Careers in Science: Leaving the Ivory Tower. Robbins-Roth, Cynthia. New York: Academic Press, 1998.

Careers for Animal Lovers and Other Zoological Types. Miller, Louise R. Lincolnwood, Ill.: VGM Career Horizons, 1991.

Careers for Bookworms and Other Literary Types. Eberts, Marjorie, and Margaret Gisler. Lincolnwood, Ill.: VGM Career Horizons, 1995.

Careers for Caring People & Other Sensitive Types. Paradis, Adrian A. Lincolnwood, Ill.: VGM Career Horizons, 1995.

Careers for Computer Buffs & Other Technological Types. Eberts, Marjorie, and Margaret Gisler. Lincolnwood, Ill.: VGM Career Horizons, 1993.

Careers for Culture Lovers & Other Artsy Types. Eberts, Marjorie, and Margaret Gisler. Lincolnwood, Ill.: VGM Career Horizons, 1992.

Careers for Cybersurfers & Other Online Types. Eberts, Marjorie, and Rachel Kelsey. Lincolnwood, Ill.: VGM Career Horizons, 1998.

Careers for Environmental Types & Others Who Respect the Earth. Kinney, Jane, et al. Lincolnwood, Ill.: VGM Career Horizons, 1993.

Careers for Film Buffs and Other Hollywood Types. Greenspon, Jaq. Lincolnwood, Ill.: VGM Career Horizons, 1993.

Careers for Good Samaritans and Other Humanitarian Types. Eberts, Marjorie, and Margaret Gisler. Lincolnwood, Ill.: VGM Career Horizons, 1991.

Careers for Health Nuts & Others Who Like to Stay Fit. Camenson, Blythe. Lincolnwood, Ill.: VGM Career Horizons, 1996.

Careers for History Buffs & Others Who Learn from the Past. Camenson, Blythe. Lincolnwood, Ill.: VGM Career Horizons, 1994.

Careers for Kids at Heart & Others Who Adore Children. Eberts, Marjorie, and Margaret Gisler. Lincolnwood, Ill.: VGM Career Horizons, 1994.

Careers for Nature Lovers and Other Outdoor Types. Miller, Louise R. Lincolnwood, Ill.: VGM Career Horizons, 1992.

Careers for Plant Lovers & Other Green Thumb Types. Camenson, Blythe. Lincolnwood, Ill.: VGM Career Horizons, 1995.

Careers for Self-Starters & Other Entrepreneurial Types. Camenson, Blythe. Lincolnwood, Ill.: VGM Career Horizons, 1997.

Careers for Shutterbugs and Other Candid Types. McLean, Cheryl. Lincolnwood, Ill.: VGM Career Horizons, 1994.

Careers for Sports Nuts & Other Athletic Types. Heitzmann, William Ray. Lincolnwood, Ill.: VGM Career Horizons, 1997.

Careers for the Stagestruck & Other Dramatic Types. Mauro Lucia. Lincolnwood, Ill.: VGM Career Horizons, 1997.

Career Opportunities for Writers. Guiley, Rosemary Ellen. New York: Facts on File, 1996.

Career Paths in Psychology: Where Your Degree Can Take You. Sternberg, Robert J., ed. Washington, D.C.: American Psychological Association, 1997.

Childbirth Instructor Magazine's Guide to Careers in Birth: How to Find a Fulfilling Job in Pregnancy, Labor and Parenting Support without a Medical Degree. Robotti, Suzanne, and Margaret Inman. New York: John Wiley & Sons, 1998.

Create the Job You Love and Still Make Plenty of Money: More Than 550 Ways to Escape the 8 to 5 Grind. Witcher, Barbara Johnson. Rocklin, Calif.: Prima Publishing, 1997.

Education and Career Opportunities in Alternative Medicine. Jones, Rosemary. Rocklin, Calif.: Prima Publishing, 1998.

The Environmental Career Guide: Job Opportunities with the Earth in Mind. Basta, Nicholas. New York: John Wiley & Sons, Inc., 1991.

Full Disclosure: Do You Really Want To Be a Lawyer? Bell, Susan. Princeton: Peterson's Guides, 1992.

Green at Work: Finding a Business Career That Works for the Environment. Cohn, Susan, and Horst Rechelbacher. Washington, D.C.: Island Press, 1995.

Guide to Your Career: How to Turn Your Interest into a Career You Love. Bernstein, Alan, and Nicholas Schaffzin. New York: Princeton Review Press. Published annually.

Student's Guide to Career Exploration on the Internet. Jist Works, with Elisabeth Oakes, ed. Chicago: Ferguson Publishing Co., 1998.

Vital Signs: Working Doctors Tell the Real Story Behind Medical School and Practice. Bernal, Deborah L., M.D. Princeton: Peterson's Guides, 1994.

What Can You Do with a Law Degree? A Lawyers Guide to Career Alternatives Inside, Outside and Around the Law. Arron, Deborah. Portland, Ore.: Miche Press, 1997.

Reality Testing

You should investigate something to see its benefit or harm, examine whether it is appropriate and suitable or not; then after that you may carry it out.

Caotang

You began "Act II" by imagining yourself in several different career roles. When you did this, the actual knowledge you had about these careers may have been somewhat superficial. Your visualization may have been something akin to what we see in a popular Hollywood movie. You need more accurate information. In this section, you will have the opportunity to test your imagined sense of a given career against the reality of it.

Think of the way careers are portrayed in Hollywood. The actor is playing a part—a doctor, a lawyer, a banker, whatever. The role is indicated with a very few actions, words, props, or costume elements. A professional in this field can look at these representations and see that they are often kind of silly. Yet for the general public, it's convincing. We accept (at least for entertainment purposes) that this person is indeed a lawyer, a detective, a brain surgeon, a banker, or whatever. We accept this because enough of the image is there to fit the popular conception.

Unless you've had reason to have more specific knowledge, your first imaginings of your new career were most likely from the "pop culture" understanding of what this field is and what a person in this field does. These images may be accurate or filled with misconceptions. You need to find out.

The next step is to go out and collect data. As you gather information, you will get a clearer understanding of what an individual in this field does, how they spend their days, what their problems are, what issues they face, how they interact with people, and the like. You'll move out of the movie image into a more practical understanding of what it would really be like to work in this role. In the process, you will collect a wealth of information that will prove useful later on, should you decide to go ahead and pursue this career. In "Scene III" of this unit, you will have a chance to evaluate all you have learned about this career role and to decide if it's really right for you.

The "Reality Testing" process involves a good deal of work. You may be tempted to skip over it. We strongly recommend that you do not. The investment of time and energy that you make at this point can save you a great deal of time, money, and heartache later on. For example, if you were to begin retraining for a new career without having done the necessary research, you might find that you had wasted thousands of dollars and many precious years of your life preparing for a career that was not appropriate for you. This can be easily averted by doing adequate research in advance.

You may discover in the course of your research that the career role you were initially attracted to is not appropriate and should be discarded. If that is the case, begin again with your second career choice (see page 277). You might discover that, while your first choice is the best vehicle through which to express your life's work, it will take considerably more work than you first planned. In that case, don't get discouraged. Continue to pursue your life's work, keeping in mind your vision of your best work and your desire to manifest it.

Determining whether a career is truly inappropriate or simply a lot of work is sometimes difficult. It's a judgment you will have to make for yourself. The important thing to remember throughout this process is: Do not compromise your creative visions of your best work. *There is a way, and you will find it if you persist.* It may take a good deal of thought, creativity, and effort, but there is a way. After all, you would not have the deep desire for this work without also having the ability to achieve it.

The "Reality Testing" Process in a Nutshell

Step 1:   Get on the Internet or go to the library.

Step 2:   Conduct interviews.

Step 3:   Get firsthand experience.

Step 4:   Make a skills master list.

Step 5:   Identify necessary credentials.

Research Questions List

The following is a list of research questions, the answers to which will begin to put the career role you are considering into focus. Read these questions now; then refer to them throughout the course of your research. *Do not attempt to write final answers to these questions until you have done the Internet/library, interview, and firsthand experience sections that follow.*

Does the career role you have imagined already exist in the real world? _____

If the answer is yes, proceed to the next question. If the answer is no, what career roles are closest to the one you have envisioned? Pick one.

_____

How well will this career fit with your mission and work purpose statements? That is, at what level of depth and breadth will it allow you to pursue your life's work?

_____
_____
_____
_____

Who do people in this field serve on a day to day basis?

_____
_____

How well do your talents and interests match with what's required in this field?

_____
_____

What values do people in this field generally adhere to? How well do they match with yours?

_____
_____
_____
_____

What do people in this career role actually do in the course of a day?

_____
_____
_____
_____

What skills do they rely upon most?

_____

_____

_____

_____

What generally are their working conditions? (environment, independence, etc.)

_____

_____

What kind of training is required to work in this field?

_____

_____

What additional credentials enhance a person's credibility in this field?

_____

_____

Is there any area of the country where people who do this are especially concentrated? Where is that? (For example: movies and popular music/Los Angeles; theater, dance, music/New York; national politics/Washington, D.C.) Are you prepared to move there?

_____

_____

Who are the leading figures, companies, organizations and/or institutions in this field?

_____

_____

How much do people in this field generally earn?

Entry level _____   Intermediate or average_____   Top level_____

What professional, trade, union, or other organizations do people in this field generally belong to?

_____

_____

Generally, what is the social status of people who are involved in this field? How are they viewed by others in the community?

_____

_____

What are the positive aspects of how these individuals are perceived?

_____

_____

What are the negative aspects?

_____

_____

What kind of lifestyle do people in this profession generally uphold? (Journalists travel and drink a lot. New York executives are traditional and formal; California executives, more casual.)

_____

_____

What is the current market demand for this career? What are its prospects for the future? (Latin teachers are no longer in high demand.)

_____

_____

What hours, generally, do people in this field work? (It's not uncommon for people in high levels of government to work seventy-hour weeks or for beginning entrepreneurs to work fifty, sixty, or more.)

_____

What personal and family sacrifices do people in this field generally make? (For example: Most women executives are not married.)

_____

_____

How is the game played in this field, that is, what does it take to get to the top of it?

_____

_____

Review this list carefully, and write down any additional questions that seem important to you. These additional questions may occur to you immediately, while you are engaged in the process of doing your research, or once you have completed your initial research. If the question is important to you, write it down and find out the answer!

_____

_____

_____

_____

_____

Get on the Internet or Go to the Library

Now that you have your research list in hand, it's time to get on the Internet or go to your local library and begin to get some answers.

Career Research Web Sites

At this writing, there are four excellent sites you can use to research specific career fields. Visits to these sites can answer a great many questions in short order.

StudentCenter.com About Work

www.aboutwork.com/career/
alphasearch.html

This site is probably the best place to begin your search. It is written in a more humane and down-to-earth style than the government sites listed below (though it lists fewer careers). For each career listed you will find: a general description of the work involved, a review of training and educational requirements, a discussion of related careers, a section describing trends in the field, and a "Quality of Life" section that details what you can expect in terms of salary and responsibilities two, five, and ten years out. The site includes "Professional Profiles," detailing general salary ranges, the number of people working in the field, and so on. It also lists trade journals, major employers, and associations in the field.

Occupational Outlook Handbook

www.bls.gov/ocohome.htm

This site is hosted by the Bureau of Labor Statistics. This is an extremely comprehensive site, with many careers listed. Each career listing includes: descriptions of the nature of work, working conditions, the number of people employed in the field, training requirements, job outlook, earn-ings, and related occupations. This site also includes addresses of professional associations in the field that you can contact for additional information.

California Occupational Guides

www.calmis.cahnet.gov/htmlfile/
subject/guide.htm

Sponsored by the California Employment Development Department, this site has an extensive list of careers. The site includes: job descriptions; working conditions; employment outlook; wages, hours and benefits; training and entrance requirements; as well as addresses of professional associations in the field.

JobSmart

http://jobsmart.org/tools/career/
spec-car.htm

This site has links to other sites that give specific information in a number of career areas. A good site with excellent information, it covers fewer careers than the sites listed above.

Career Library Reference Works

Your library contains a wealth of information you can use to test potential career roles. The following are some resources you may want to investigate. If your public library does not contain the source materials listed below, you may be able to find them at your local college or university library or career center.

The American Almanac of Jobs and Salaries. Wright, John. New York: Avon Books. Published biennially in October. Lists job descriptions and annual earning information." ...a comprehensive survey of hundreds of occupations and their pay rates in a wide variety of industries and business organizations." Relatively simple and easy to use.

The Dictionary of Occupational Titles. U.S. Department of Labor. Indianapolis: Jist Works, 1998. This comprehensive guide details what people in various careers actually do and gives you an idea of the skills and training required.

The Encyclopedia of Careers and Vocational Guidance, Vols I-III. Hopke, William E. Chicago: Ferguson Publishers, 1997. Volume I provides general information on career development and a general survey of various fields rather than occupations. Volumes II and III are similar to the *Occupational Outlook Handbook* in format, though somewhat more comprehensive in presentation.

National Business Employment Weekly Jobs Rated Almanac. Krantz, Les. New York: John Wiley & Sons. Published annually. Rates jobs by environment, income, outlook, physical demand, stress, security, benefits, and other features. Easy-to-use information at a glance.

The Occupational Outlook Handbook. Bureau of Labor Statistics. Indianapolis: Jist Works. Published biennially in March. Provides a good introduction to the field. It provides general information about what people in this field do, what they earn, and what the demand outlook is.

Trade Magazines and Newsletters

Virtually every field has trade magazines and newsletters geared toward those already working in the field. Reviewing the trade magazines in your field will give you a feeling for the attitudes, concerns, and interests of people within the field, and will provide you with information about the current topics in the field. Often these journals include job listings. To find trade journals in the fields you are interested in, see:

Gale Directory of Publications and Broadcast Media. Fischer, Carolyn A., ed. Detroit: Gale Research, Inc. Published annually in November.

Scientific and Technical Books and Serials in Print (1995). New York: Bowker, 1994.

Standard Periodical Directory, The. New York: Oxbridge Communications, Inc. Published annually in December.

Check *The Reader's Guide to Periodical Literature*

Look in the guide under your subject area for articles about your field. This is an especially good source for obtaining general information about trends in your field of interest, the field's relationship to the broader community, information about notables in the field, and new developments and breakthroughs.

General Books in the Field

Check the card catalog subject file for books in your field of interest. A good way of researching books in your potential career area is to check out one or two general surveys of the field, as well as several more specialized books that appeal to you.

Books on Playing the Game

Every field has a game. If you're in broadcasting, you need to learn how to be a good broadcaster, but you also need to know how to negotiate, how the rating game works, etc. There are general books on playing the game. Stephen R. Covey's *The 7 Habits of Highly Effective People* and Adele Scheele's *Skills for Success* are just a few of the many books on the subject (see the bibliography on page 304). There are also books on playing the game in specific career fields. Ask your librarian for assistance.

Conduct Interviews

The library is a great place to start. It's a good orienting point from which to begin your search, but there ain't nothin' like hearing it from the horse's mouth. If you want to learn how to do something, talk to people who are doing it. We recommend that you interview at least three individuals who are well respected within the field you are considering. You may not want to stop there, the more information, the better. However, usually after three interviews, you get a good idea of what the work involves and if you really want to do it.

Many people are timid about approaching someone who is experienced in a field unfamiliar to them. Don't let pride or fear keep you from learning vital information. Remember, when you're calling for an interview you are flattering that person by soliciting their "expert" opinions. For the sake of motivation, you might imagine yourself as a reporter for *The Daily Planet*. You have just got to get this scoop. Now get out there!

How to Do an Informational Interview

Setting up the Interview

If you know competent people in this field, call them and set up appointments. If you don't, ask people you do know to refer you. Take advantage of your existing networks. Perhaps a member of an organization you belong to is working in this field. Even if they don't know you personally, they are likely to respond favorably when ap-proached by a member of their organization. If no one in this field belongs to any of your organizations, ask other members to suggest someone. Use the name of the person who gave you the referral to gain access to the person in the field. When you can, call and say John or Mary Doe (whom they know and respect) suggested that they were an outstanding person in their field whom you should talk to, chances are good they will be accommodating.

If all else fails, check your telephone directory and cold call. Expect rejection and persist. When you call, explain what you are doing, and ask if you could get together for a brief interview. Set a time and meeting place for the appointment. We suggest that you invite them to lunch. This is for two reasons:

1. Their time is valuable. If you interview them at their place of work, you're more apt to be taking them away from their duties and thus to meet with resistance.

2. It's good form. You're asking them to give you something (information). It's only right that you give them something (lunch). Consider it a token of your appreciation for their valuable time and vital information.

If the interviewee would prefer to meet you in his or her office, comply with this request and ask for a time that would be relatively free of interruptions.

Another technique is to use the phone book to locate people you're interested in meeting. Then show up there dressed appropriately and ask to see the individual you want to interview. You may be surprised at how open they are to seeing you, especially when you're there in person.

 No man is more miserable than he that hath no adversity.

Jeremy Taylor

Doing the Interview

Be prompt to your meeting. Prepare your questions in advance. (See the list of suggested questions below.) Keep the interview brief and to the point. You may want to tape record the session, provided the other party is comfortable with this. This will help insure that you get an accurate record of the encounter and will free you from taking notes. Thank the interviewee at the close of the interview.

If the interview is going especially well and you feel it appropriate, ask if you might be a silent observer at the interviewee's place of work. Stress your interest in the field and your appreciation for their time. Convince them that you will be an innocuous, silent watcher who will not keep them from the performance of their duties, and that you will be ready to leave at any point they feel it appropriate. (See "Be an Observer" in the "Get Firsthand Experience" section, page 297.)

Interview Questions

Here are some questions you might want to ask:

1. In what ways do you find meaning and fulfillment in this profession?

2. What do you like most about your work?

3. What do you like least?

4. How did you first get involved in this work?

5. What was your training and background coming into this field?

6. Knowing what you know now, how would you have approached this career differently?

7. What would you recommend as the best course of action for someone who wanted to begin in this field?

8. What talents or skills do you feel are most important in this work?

9. What attitudes or values do you view as most important in this work?

10. What do you see as the future of this kind of work? Where is your field heading?

11. What is your typical day like?

12. What hours do you work? What were your hours like when you first started in this field?

13. How is the game played in this field? How do you get to the top?

Make your own list using these and/or other questions that are important to you.

 The real object of education is to have a man in the condition of continually asking questions.
Bishop Creighton

After the Interview

After the interview, send the interviewee a thank-you card expressing your appreciation. If you are especially impressed with their company, you may want to send along a résumé. You might even call and tell them that you were so impressed by what they shared in the interview that you would like to work for their company. Ask them to refer you to their personnel department. Remember when conducting the interview that these individuals are potential contacts for future employment. Treat them accordingly.

Interview Profiles

In the space below, briefly summarize the key points of what you learned in your interviews.

Interview #1: _____
_____
_____
_____
_____
_____

Interview #2: _____
_____
_____
_____
_____
_____

Interview #3: _____
_____
_____
_____
_____
_____

> *Without work, all life goes rotten. But when work is soulless, life stifles and dies.*
> *Albert Camus*

Get Firsthand Experience

In conducting your research, libraries are good, interviews are better, and firsthand experience is best. An interview is not an entirely natural situation. People are more candid in a less formal setting, and there is nothing like seeing them in action. The following are some of the ways you can gain some firsthand experience in your career area.

Short-Term

Be an Observer: In the informational interview section, we recommended asking the interviewee to allow you to observe them at work. If you did not feel it was appropriate to ask for this while conducting the interview, it may be appropriate to do so after you have completed the interview and they have received your thank-you note. Give them a call, and ask if you could be a silent observer for a day. Getting people to agree to let you watch is sometimes difficult, but the payoff is well worth the effort. It's an excellent way to learn a great deal of practical information in a short time.

Meeting Places: You can get to know individuals socially in your career area by frequenting their favorite restaurants, bars, and health clubs. For example, Spago's in Los Angeles is a favorite for hollywood actors, screenwriters, and directors. The Tune Inn in Washington, D.C. is a favorite for congressional staff people. The Four Seasons Restaurant in New York is a favorite for publishers and authors. Also in the Big Apple is Sardi's, the place to be for the Broadway set. Entertainers, lawyers, doctors, etc. frequently congregate in a favorite bar, restaurant, or health club.

Find out where these places are in your community, and be there. You may make contacts that will be invaluable to your career. If you have an outgoing personality (and if you don't, fake it), you can learn a lot in a very short time. One reason is that individuals in these settings are much more relaxed and, therefore, more candid (especially after a few drinks).

Association Meetings: Get yourself invited as a guest to association or trade meetings. Again, you can make contacts and friends and gain a great deal of information. Because these meetings are more formal, don't expect people at them to be as candid as they are at the watering hole or in the gym.

Conventions and Trade Shows: Nowadays most fields hold annual (or more frequent) conventions or trade shows. Many are open to the public. For those that are not, you'll need a guest pass. For your research purposes, these gatherings are somewhere in between the watering hole and the association or the service club meeting. They have the feeling of the association meeting by day and of the watering hole by night.

Long-Term

Part-Time Work: By working part-time in the new career area, you can "learn by doing" in a way that will not force you to give up your current position. This is not always appropriate or applicable, but if it is in your case, you may want to pursue it. It gets you hands-on experience, which, by the way, you might be able to parlay into full-time employment.

 What you see is what you get.
Flip Wilson

Volunteer Work: Benefits are similar to part-time work and some internships, with added flexibility and objectivity on the upside, but no pay on the downside. (See appendix B, "Volunteering," pages 600–607.)

Internships: Similar to part-time and volunteer work in benefits. You will receive training in lieu of pay or in addition to nominal payment.

Internship Sources

America's Top Internships. Oldman, Mark and Sarner Harnadeh. New York: Princeton Review Publishing. Updated regularly.

The Back Door Guide to Short-Term Job Adventures: Internships, Extraordinary Experiences, Seasonal Jobs, Volunteering, Work Abroad. Landes, Michael. Berkeley: Ten Speed Press, 1997.

The Internship Bible. Oldman, Mark and Sarner Harnadeh. New York: Princeton Review Publishing. Published annually.

Internships: 38,000 On-the-Job Training Opportunities for All Types of Careers. Jobst, Katherine. Cincinnati: Writer's Digest Books. Published annually.

Internship Success: Real World Step-by-Step Advice on Getting the Most Out of Internships. Green, Maryanne Ehrlich. Lincolnwood, Ill.: VGM Career Horizons, 1977.

Internship Internet Resources

National Internships
www.internships.com

Lists internships in the government, nonprofit, and private sectors.

Princeton Review Online
www.review.com/career

Provides a search engine that targets listings by state, field of interest, and weekly compensation.

Rising Star Internships
www.rsinternships.com

Lists internships in over a hundred fields.

Intern-NET™
www.vicon.net/~internnet

Lists internships in the fields of sports and fitness, parks and recreation, and hospitality.

The Washington Intern Foundation
http://interns.org

Lists internships on Capitol Hill and in the Washington, D.C. area.

Environmental Career Organization
www.eco.org

Lists hundreds of paid internships in the environmental field.

 He conquers who endures.
Persius

Make a Skills Master List

From your (library, interview, and firsthand) research, make a list of the skills required to move into your new career. The reference works on pages 292-293 can be of great help in completing this process. Also, a list of skills is provided on the next page.

List the skills that you would employ in doing this work.

1. _____
2. _____
3. _____
4. _____
5. _____
6. _____
7. _____
8. _____
9. _____
10. _____
11. _____
12. _____
13. _____
14. _____
15. _____
16. _____
17. _____
18. _____
19. _____
20. _____

Trifles make perfection, and perfection is no trifle.

Michelangelo

Skill T.I.P. List

Things	Ideas	People
1. Setting up	1. Synthesizing	1. Mentoring
2. Adjusting	2. Developing concepts	2. Advising
3. Precision working	3. Coordinating	3. Counseling
4. Controlling/operating	4. Executing	4. Guiding
5. Driving/operating	5. Reporting	5. Negotiating
6. Manipulating	6. Analyzing	6. Debating
7. Tending	7. Examining	7. Arguing
8. Feeding	8. Evaluating	8. Exchanging ideas
9. Inserting	9. Adapting	9. Selling
10. Throwing	10. Compiling	10. Instructing
11. Placing	11. Gathering	11. Teaching
12. Handling	12. Collating	12. Training
13. Lifting	13. Classifying	13. Demonstrating
14. Cutting	14. Computing	14. Supervising
15. Fitting	15. Copying	15. Organizing
16. Pressing	16. Transcribing	16. Managing
17. Cleaning	17. Entering	17. Delegating
18. Arranging	18. Posting	18. Motivating
19. Assembling	19. Comparing	19. Entertaining
20. Installing	20. Budgeting	20. Performing
21. Repairing	21. Purchasing	21. Persuading
22. Typing	22. Composing	22. Influencing
23. Operating a computer	23. Proofreading	23. Speaking
24. Ploughing	24. Studying	24. Directing
25. Drilling	25. Classifying	25. Attending
26. Planting	26. Testing	26. Helping
27. Harvesting	27. Visualizing	27. Taking instructions
28. Massaging	28. Writing	28. Making recommendations

You are what you do.
Anonymous

Playing-the-Game Skills List

In the space below, list all the skills necessary to playing the game in this career. Draw upon your library work, interviews, and firsthand experience. You may want to consult the list and sources that follow on the next two pages.

Playing-the-Game Skills (the auxiliary skills necessary to maintain and enhance your acceptance in this profession)

1. _____
2. _____
3. _____
4. _____
5. _____
6. _____
7. _____
8. _____
9. _____
10. _____
11. _____
12. _____
13. _____
14. _____
15. _____
16. _____
17. _____
18. _____
19. _____
20. _____

Playing-the-Game Skills: Some Examples

The following is a list of a few of the skills involved in playing the game.

Things

1. How to select a winning wardrobe
2. How to coordinate your wardrobe
3. How to select and collect things that will improve your image
4. How to buy appropriate gifts
5. How to invest your money
6. How to manage your money
7. How to have good posture
8. How to move your body in a manner that commands attention and respect
9. How to play appropriate sports
10. How to manipulate objects at table
11. How to make professional presentations of your written materials

Ideas

1. How to organize and prepare written materials
2. How to develop a powerful vocabulary
3. How to keep abreast of current topics of interest to those in your field or those who interact with the people in your field
4. How to do research on people so that you have information about them before you meet them
5. How to predict cycles and trends in your field
6. How to use metaphors to communicate your ideas
7. How to extract the essentials from large bodies of written material in a short amount of time
8. How to create systems for organizing information
9. How to ask intelligent questions in areas you know nothing about
10. How to translate technical or advanced concepts into simple language that the layman can understand
11. How to plan strategy
12. How to prove an idea through logic

13. How to explain a difficult concept in simple, successive steps

14. How to sort peripherals from essentials in any body of information

15. How to make complicated ideas seem simple

16. How to make simple ideas seem complicated

People

1. How to get noticed in a favorable way by your superiors

2. How to know where the power is in your organization (It's probably not represented in the organizational chart.)

3. How to tell the difference between a real promotion and a symbolic one

4. How to ask for a promotion or a raise

5. How to listen effectively

6. How to know what to do if you're asked to relocate

7. How to handle difficult people within your organization

8. How to sell effectively (This is important even if you're not in sales.)

9. How to deal with enemies within your organization

10. How to be emotionally detached

11. How to make yourself look good at meetings

12. How to know whom to trust and how much

13. How to avoid office romances

14. How to know what the boss really means

15. How to handle criticism well

16. How to read body language

17. How to motivate your team

18. How to delegate effectively

19. How to understand the real motives of your clients or coworkers

20. How to deal effectively with authority

21. How to assume authority in an effective manner

22. How to fit in and show that you belong

23. How to develop networks

24. How to conduct an interview

25. How to build a team and get the most out of it

26. How to project a pleasing personality

27. How to make whatever you're doing sound fascinating

"Playing the Game" Sources

The 7 Habits of Highly Effective People: Powerful Lessons in Personal Change. Covey, Stephen R. New York: Fireside, 1990.

7 Survival Skills for a Re-engineered World. Yeomans, William N. New York: Penguin USA, 1998.

1000 Things You Never Learned in Business School: How to Manage Your Fast-Track Career. Yeomans, William N. New York: New American Library, 1990.

Career Intelligence: Mastering the New Work and Personal Realities. Moses, Barbara. Toronto, Canada: Stoddart Publishing Co., 1997.

Career Power! : 12 Winning Habits to Get You from Where You Are to Where You Want to Be. Koonce, Richard H. New York: Amacom, 1994.

Career Survival: Strategic Job and Role Planning. Schein, Edgar H. San Diego, Calif.: Pfeiffer and Co., 1994.

Credibility: How Leaders Gain and Lose It, Why People Demand It. Kouzes, James S., Barry Z. Posner, and Tom Peters. San Francisco: Jossey-Bass, 1995.

Empowering Yourself: The Organizational Game Revealed. Coleman, Harvey J. Dubuque, Iowa: Kendall/Hunt Publishing Co., 1996.

Games Mother Never Taught You: Corporate Gamesmanship for Women. Harragan, Betty Lehan. New York: Warner, 1987.

The Popcorn Report. Popcorn, Faith. New York: HarperBusiness, 1992.

Roger's Rules for Success: Tips That Will Take You to the Top by One of America's Foremost Public Relations Experts. Rogers, Henry C. New York: St. Martin's Press, Inc., 1986.

Skills for Success: A Guide to the Top. Scheele, Adele M. New York: Ballantine, 1981.

Welcome to the Real World: You've Got an Education, Now Get a Life! Kravetz, Stacy. New York: W.W. Norton & Company, 1997.

What They Don't Teach You at Harvard Business School: Notes from a Street-Smart Executive. McCormack, Mark H. New York: Bantam, 1988.

> There is no great thought that has become an impelling power in history which has not been espoused at its origin by men willing to put all their physical and spiritual powers entirely at its service.
>
> Louis Ginzberg

You May Have More Skills Than You Realize

When reflecting upon your skill development, it's worthwhile to recall that, for the average adult, skill is a matter of degree. For example, Harold Figler, in his book, *The Complete Job Search Handbook* (an excellent primer on the skills necessary to the job seeker), lists what he calls the "Ten Hottest Transferable Skills." These are:

1. Budget Management
2. Supervising
3. Public Relations
4. Coping with Deadline Pressure
5. Negotiating/Arbitrating
6. Speaking
7. Writing
8. Organizing/Managing/Coordinating
9. Interviewing
10. Teaching/Instructing

Anyone who ever had an allowance as a child, or any money, for that matter, has engaged in *budget management*. Everyone who has ever babysat, looked after a younger sibling, or been a parent has engaged in *supervising*. If, on a date, you made an effort to make a favorable impression, you have engaged in *public relations* work. If you have filed an income tax form, you have dealt with *deadline pressure*. We all *negotiate* every day in our relationships. Have you ever answered a question in class? If so, you've engaged in *public speaking*. Anyone who has *written* the famous "What I Did Last Summer" paper in school has engaged in *writing*. Life in every household requires the skills of *organizing*, *managing,* and *coordinating*, for example, coordinating who uses the bathroom when. If you've ever asked for directions, you have conducted an *interview*. Every parent, sibling, or friend has done his or her share of *teaching* and *instructing*.

Of course, managing a multimillion dollar budget requires a greater degree of skill than balancing a personal checkbook, and supervising a staff of hundreds requires more sophistication than babysitting the familial brood. Still, recognizing that you already possess these skills gives you the confidence to expand upon your current ability in that skill area.

Rate the Career Game

Below is a list of career-game variables. Rate the career you have selected according to the variables below. Indicate where the career you are considering stands in relation to each of these variables (one low, ten high). Next, review your assessment and ask yourself: Am I willing to agree with this game? Can I get into playing this game?

	1	2	3	4	5	6	7	8	9	10
1. Stress level										
2. Variability of tasks										
3. Flexibility of hours										
4. Physically demanding										
5. Emotionally demanding										
6. Mentally demanding										
7. Formality of dress										
8. Formality of language										
9. Formality of ethical code										
10. Opportunities for advancement										
11. Independence of work selection										

	1	2	3	4	5	6	7	8	9	10
12. Opportunities for creative thinking										
13. Degree of physical mobility										
14. Degree of social interaction within the organization										
15. Degree of social interaction outside of the organization										
16. Degree of competitiveness within the field										
17. Degree to which your personal life affects your career advancement										
18. Degree of participation of rank-and-file in management decisions										
19. Number of "off duty" hours you are expected to work or engage in work-related activities										
20. Importance of volunteer and community activities to career advancement										

Identify Necessary Credentials

In the space below, list the legal, *de facto*, and optional credentials necessary to begin work in this field.

1. Legal requirements for participation in this career (degrees, certifications, licensing required by the state or federal government, inspection standards, or updates in training).

    _____
    _____
    _____
    _____
    _____

2. Non-legal but *de facto* necessary credentials (e.g., for job seekers: inside connections, physical capacities; for entrepreneurs: an office or store, association memberships, etc.).

    _____
    _____
    _____
    _____
    _____

3. Optional enhancing credentials (i.e., publishing books, articles, getting media attention, winning awards, etc.).

    _____
    _____
    _____
    _____
    _____

As every divided kingdom falls, so every mind divided between many studies confounds and saps itself.   Leonardo da Vinci

Evaluation:
No or Go?

We are free up to the point of choice. Then the choice controls the chooser.

Mary Crowley

We assume that you have completed the "Reality Testing" section. If so, now is the time to reassess the career role that you chose at the beginning of "Act II." Since you now know what it takes, you are ready to determine whether or not this career role is right for you. If, after careful examination, you determine that it is, proceed to "Act III: The Battle for Life's Work." If not, go back to step one of "Act II: The Game of Life's Work," and start over again, this time working with the second career role you selected on page 277.

The Evaluation Process in a Nutshell

Step 1:   Skills Evaluation: How do you measure up?

Step 2:   Mission Match: Does this career provide the best way of pursuing your mission in life?

Step 3:   Personal Motivation: How much are you into this career?

Step 4:   Self-Esteem: Do you believe you can do it?

Step 5:   Sacrifices: What will it cost you?

Step 6:   Benefits: What will you gain?

Step 7:   Financial Factors: What about money?

Step 8:   Demand: How much will they want you?

Skills Evaluation: How Do You Measure Up?

The first step in your evaluation process is to assess your skills in light of those needed for the career role you are considering. You will determine which of the necessary skills you already possess and which you have yet to acquire. Next, you will indicate the relative difficulty of each of these skills. Finally, you will determine whether the skills involved are primarily concerned with things, ideas, or people.

The end product is a "Skills Map" that will tell you at a glance how ready you are to pursue this career at this time and what areas to concentrate on in developing greater ability. You can think of your "Skills Map" as the universe of skills necessary to pursuing this career. In "Act IV: The School of Life's Work," you'll have an opportunity to develop a strategy for acquiring the additional skills you need.

Note: The exercises that immediately follow require subjective self-assessment. You may feel as though you can't give exact answers. Don't be concerned about this. Simply rate each as well as you can. This exercise is but one component of the evaluation process through which you will determine whether or not you want to pursue your life's work through the career role you first imagined.

 He who has a why can endure any how.
Friedrich Nietzsche

Part I
Skills: What You've Got, What You Need to Get

Enter the skills from your "Skills Master List" (on page 299) in the column provided. Rate your skill level on a scale of one to ten (one low, ten high), and plot your answer on the graph to the right. Finally, in the spaces to the right of the graph, indicate which of the skills you are already competent in and which you still need work in. All the skills you rated with scores of six or more, mark in the AC (Already Competent) column, and those less than six, in the NW (Needs Work) column.

Necessary Skills	Needs Work					Already Competent						
	1	2	3	4	5	6	7	8	9	10	NW	AC
1.												
2.												
3.												
4.												
5.												
6.												
7.												
8.												
9.												
10.												
11.												
12.												
13.												
14.												
15.												
Example: Public Speaking			✔								✔	

Note: It is important that each skill be recorded in the same order throughout the skill assessment process.

Part II
Skills: Some Come Easy, Some Don't

The purpose of this exercise is to help you to estimate the amount of time it may take you to acquire the various skills, based upon their relative difficulty for you. Rate each of the skills from your "Skills Master List" according to the length of time required to master it. If you already possess the skill, did the acquisition of that skill take a few weeks, or did it take years to master? If you have yet to acquire the skill, do you anticipate the acquisition of that skill taking a relatively short time or significantly longer? Use the key below to assist you in selecting the appropriate space: A, B, C, D.

Key	
A	1–3 Months
B	3 Months–1 Year
C	1–3 Years
D	3+ Years

Necessary Skills

1._____A( )B( )C( )D( )
2._____A( )B( )C( )D( )
3._____A( )B( )C( )D( )
4._____A( )B( )C( )D( )
5._____A( )B( )C( )D( )
6._____A( )B( )C( )D( )
7._____A( )B( )C( )D( )
8._____A( )B( )C( )D( )
9._____A( )B( )C( )D( )
10._____A( )B( )C( )D( )
11._____A( )B( )C( )D( )
12._____A( )B( )C( )D( )
13._____A( )B( )C( )D( )
14._____A( )B( )C( )D( )
15._____A( )B( )C( )D( )
Example: Public Speaking_____A( )B( )C(✓)D( )

Note: It is important that each skill be recorded in the same order throughout the skill assessment process.

Part III
Skills: Getting Some T.I.P.s as to Content

The purpose of this exercise is to help you to determine whether this career role primarily involves working with things, ideas, or people. This exercise can help you to clarify the actual content of the work and how that fits with your personality. If you are having difficulty determining whether a particular skill is primarily concerned with things, ideas, or people, refer to the "Skill T.I.P. List" on page 300.

Key

T . . . . Things
I . . . . Ideas
P . . . . People

Necessary Skills

1._____T( )I( )P( )
2._____T( )I( )P( )
3._____T( )I( )P( )
4._____T( )I( )P( )
5._____T( )I( )P( )
6._____T( )I( )P( )
7._____T( )I( )P( )
8._____T( )I( )P( )
9._____T( )I( )P( )
10._____T( )I( )P( )
11._____T( )I( )P( )
12._____T( )I( )P( )
13._____T( )I( )P( )
14._____T( )I( )P( )
15._____T( )I( )P( )
Example: Public Speaking _____T( )I( )P(✓)

Note: It is important that each skill be recorded in the same order throughout the skill assessment process.

Charting Your Skills Map

Now refer to the three skill exercises you have just completed. Use the data from these to help you plot out your "Skills Map." Notice that your skills map has a line through the center of it. The left-hand side of the map represents the skills you are already competent in. The right-hand side of the map represents the skills you need to improve in, in order to work in your new career. The concentric circles represent the relative difficulty of each skill for you. The three pie slice sections in both the left and right hemispheres indicate whether the skill primarily involves things, ideas, or people.

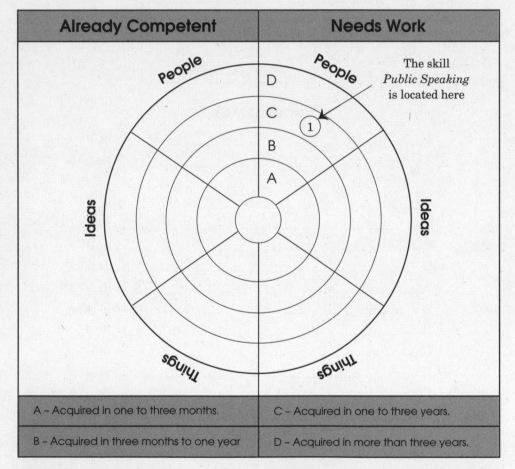

Already Competent	Needs Work
A – Acquired in one to three months.	C – Acquired in one to three years.
B – Acquired in three months to one year	D – Acquired in more than three years.

Example: Public Speaking—I=NW, II=C, III=P. Let's say that you had "Public Speaking" in position number 1. This is a skill which you rated as "Needing Work," so you will enter it in the right hemisphere of your "Skills Map." It primarily involves people, so it will appear in the "People" pie slice. You estimate that it will take you one to three years to master and, therefore, corresponds to the C sphere. So skill number 1, Public Speaking, appears in the right hemisphere, in the second concentric circle of the "People" pie slice as indicated above. Chart your "Skills Map" on the next page.

My Skills Map

Career _____

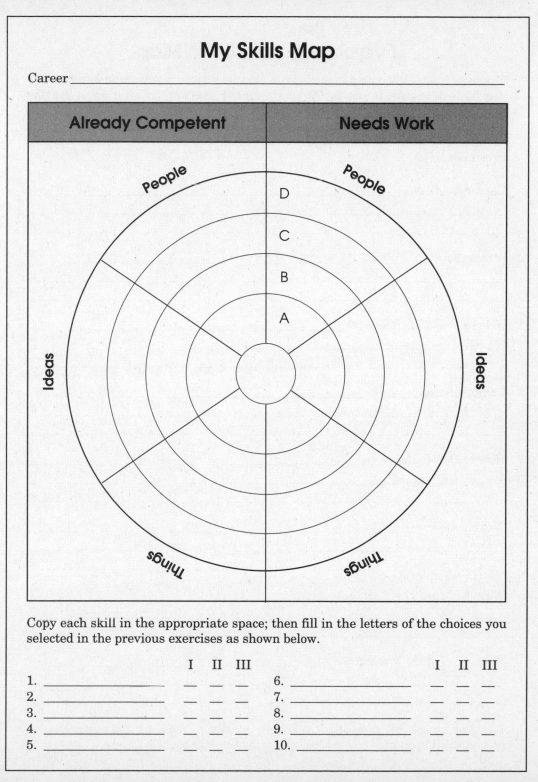

Already Competent	Needs Work

Copy each skill in the appropriate space; then fill in the letters of the choices you selected in the previous exercises as shown below.

	I	II	III		I	II	III
1. _____	__	__	__	6. _____	__	__	__
2. _____	__	__	__	7. _____	__	__	__
3. _____	__	__	__	8. _____	__	__	__
4. _____	__	__	__	9. _____	__	__	__
5. _____	__	__	__	10. _____	__	__	__

Evaluating Your Skills Map

Examine your skills map and make an evaluation of where you stand in relation to the skills necessary to the career role you have selected. In what areas are you already strong? In what areas are you competent? And in what areas are you weakest? Next, indicate how you can take full advantage of the areas you excel in, develop areas where you are conpetent, and bring the areas where you are weak up to competency.

Career Objective: _____

_____

_____

Strengths: _____

_____

_____

How to Maximize These: _____

_____

_____

Competencies: _____

_____

_____

How to Develop These: _____

_____

_____

Weaknesses: _____

_____

_____

Ways to Bring Them up to Adequacy: _____

_____

_____

Ways around the Weakness: _____

_____

_____

Based on your evaluation of your skills in relation to those needed to pursue this career, would you give it a "no" or "go"at this time? (No___Go___)

Mission Match:
Does This Career Provide the Best Way of Pursuing Your Mission in Life?

If you are absolutely certain that this career is the best way of pursuing your "mission" or life vocation, you may determine that you must pursue it at all costs. On the other hand, even if you have the necessary skills, a given career may not be the best way of pursuing your life's work and, therefore, would not be an appropriate choice. After all, the simple fact that you are able to do something does not necessarily imply that it is the right thing for you to do.

Can you do this kind of work and remain true to yourself and your mission? (Refer to page 196.) What makes you think so?

_____

_____

_____

_____

Does it allow you to make the statement you want to make? How so?

_____

_____

_____

_____

_____

Does it allow you to serve the people you want to serve? In what ways?

_____

_____

_____

_____

_____

Based on your evaluation of how well this career choice will enable you to fulfill your mission, would you give it a "no" or a "go" at this time? (No___ Go___)

 Obstacles will look large or small to you according to whether you are large or small.
Orison Swett Marden

Personal Motivation:
How Much Are You into This Career?

In order to do the work to establish yourself in a new career, it is essential that your motivation level be and remain high. The questions that immediately follow will help you to evaluate the strength of your desire to make this new career yours.

Are you making this choice freely? _____
_____
_____

Are you enthusiastic when you talk about it? _____
_____
_____

When you talk about it, do you feel defensive? _____
_____
_____

Is there anything you want more? _____
_____
_____

Do you want it for yourself? _____
_____
_____

Do you want it enough to do whatever it takes?_____
_____
_____

Based on your evaluation of your motivation for wanting to pursue this career, would you give it a "no" or a "go" at this time? (No___Go___)

 Isn't the fulfillment of our duty towards our neighbor an expression of deepest desire?
Dag Hammarskjold

Self-Esteem: Do You Believe You Can Do It?

Considering your skills and motivation may not be enough to make an adequate evaluation of the likelihood of success in this field. You also need to know how your self-esteem compares with that of people already in the field. Some individuals are qualified for a given field (for example, starting their own business) and are even ready to make the necessary sacrifices, but they don't believe that they can do it. They lack the self-esteem necessary to make their dreams become reality.

In evaluating your self-esteem, consider how self-esteem works together with skills and experience. If you currently possess relatively few of the requisite skills, but you are willing to take the necessary steps to acquire them and your self-esteem is such that you believe that you will be ultimately successful, you might decide on a "go" decision, even though your skills are relatively few. However, if your skills and self-esteem are both relatively low, you might choose an intermediate career, while building your skills and confidence.

Do you believe you can do this? _____

Generally, how does your self-esteem compare with that of people already in this field? _____

If there is a significant gap, is it a gap you can close easily within the time you have allowed? _____

Do you believe you can grow, learn, and change for the better? Write down examples of how you have grown as a person. List some of the new things you have learned.

_____

_____

Are you willing to test your belief in yourself by trying new things? _____

Are your self-esteem reserves ample enough for you to risk a little by possibly failing, or are they so small that you feel you can't risk it?

_____

All in all, given your self-esteem reserves at this time, do you *feel* to give this career move a "no" or a "go?" (No ___ Go___)

 A strong passion . . . will insure success, for the desire of the end will point out the means.
William Hazlitt

Sacrifices: What Will It Cost You?

One way or another, everything has a price. This process provides you with the opportunity to think in advance about the likely sacrifices you'll need to make in terms of time, money, and your personal life in order to succeed in your new career.

Time

From your research, how many years or months of training do people in this field have? Will you need this much or perhaps more, or less? Is the amount that is required acceptable to you? _____

_____

What hours do people in this field work? (Remember to include "playing the game" time. These are hours put into activities that may not be part of your job description but are necessary to excel in this work.) Are these hours acceptable to you?

_____

_____

Given your current skill level, how long do you estimate it will be before you can begin in this new career? Is this acceptable to you? Why do you think so? Is there any way that you could significantly shorten this time? _____

_____

Once in this career, how long does it generally take people to hit their stride? Is this time acceptable for you? Is there any way you can significantly reduce this time? How?

_____

Personal

What personal activities or interests might you have to sacrifice for a time or altogether in pursuing this career role? Are these trade-offs acceptable to you?

_____

What sacrifices are you likely to have to make in the way you relate to your family, friends, or other loved ones in order to pursue this career? Are these sacrifices acceptable to you? _____

_____

All in all, based on the sacrifices you will have to make, do you *feel* to give this career role a "no" or "go" at this time? Check one. (No___ Go___)

 Wisdom begins with sacrifice of immediate pleasures for long-range purposes.
Louis Finkelstein

Benefits: What Will You Gain?

Okay, so you've taken a good look at what your new career endeavor is going to cost you. Now it's time to examine the benefits you can expect to enjoy. Among these are the increased contributions you can make, improvements in your finances, family life, and in your psychological and physical health.

What impact are you likely to make with your new career? How will the world be better for your efforts?

_____

_____

What psychological benefits are you likely to derive? (For example, feeling more worthwhile, having higher self-esteem, knowing that you are making the world a better place.)

_____

_____

How will this career change improve your family life? (For example, your increased self-esteem improves your relationships with your mate and children. Your example of giving your best inspires your children to pursue theirs. Your courage to pursue your work puts your family in contact with interesting people and places. Your increased status in the community reflects well on your family. Your increased earnings make for a better lifestyle.)

_____

_____

What benefits to your health are you likely to derive from your pursuit of this career?

_____

_____

What material benefits will you derive from pursuing your new career? (For example, increases in income, and the kinds of improvements that income may make possible.)

_____

_____

All in all, based on the benefits you will receive as a result of this career move, do you *feel* to give the move a "no" or a "go" at this time? (No___Go___)

 Desire creates the power.
Raymond Hollingwell

Financial Factors: What about Money?

How much do people in this career role earn? _____

At entry level?_____

At top level? _____

Are these earnings acceptable to you? _____

Is there any way that you can significantly increase the money you'd make through spin-offs, related products and services, etc.? Are you willing to do this?

_____

_____

_____

How much money must you make in order to maintain a lifestyle that is acceptable to you? Can you do it working in this field?

_____

_____

_____

Estimate approximately how much it will cost you to train for this field. Is this amount acceptable to you?

_____

_____

_____

Are you likely to lose additional money in the transition? For example, in addition to the money that you spend on training, there is the amount of income lost while devoting yourself to training. Also, if you are at a high level in your current career, you may be starting at a lower level in your new work. If these sacrifices apply in your case, how great are they? Are you willing to make them?

_____

_____

_____

All in all, based on financial considerations, do you *feel* to give this career a "no" or "go" at this time? Check one. (No___Go___)

 The chief value of money lies in the fact that one lives in a world in which it is overestimated.
H. L. Mencken

Demand: How Much Will They Want You?

In choosing your new career, it's wise to assess the current and future market demands for your products or services.

How much in demand are people in your career role? In other words, how hard will you have to work at marketing yourself at this? Is this amount of work acceptable to you?

_____

_____

_____

_____

_____

_____

_____

_____

How strong are your marketing skills? If you plan to work for someone else—job-hunting skills. If you plan to work for yourself—entrepreneurial and, especially, marketing and sales skills. If your career choice is a new field, do you have a good idea of how to market yourself at this and what it's going to take to do it? You will have a chance to examine these issues in more depth in "Act III."

_____

_____

_____

_____

_____

_____

_____

_____

Given the demand for the product or service you will be providing, do you _feel_ it is best to proceed with your career choice at this time? (No___ Go___)

 Every individual has a place to fill in the world and is important in some respect, whether he chooses to be so or not. Nathaniel Hawthorne

Evaluation Checklist

The following checklist summarizes the evaluation process that you have just completed. Answer the questions below with a yes or no for an overview of your work. If you were too lazy to complete the evaluation process, this checklist will give you some idea of whether the career you have selected is right for you.

Y/N

1. Would this career role allow you to pursue your life's work effectively?   _____

2. Would it make the best use of your talents?   _____

3. Would it provide you with opportunities for continued development and growth?   _____

4. Do you now possess the skills necessary to work in this field?   _____

5. (Answer only if you answered no to question four.) Is the amount of training that would be required to gain the skills necessary to assume this role acceptable to you?   _____

6. Would it give you a work environment that you could excel in?   _____

7. Would it allow for the maximum expression of your creativity?   _____

8. Would you actually be serving the people whom you most want to help?   _____

9. Would you be working with the kind of people who would stimulate, challenge, and support you?   _____

10. Would you earn an acceptable amount of money in this career role?   _____

11. Are the likely trade-offs and sacrifices that you would have to make acceptable to you?   _____

12. Would your self-esteem and self-image allow you to achieve this goal?   _____

13. If the answer is no, is there ample time to improve your self-esteem sufficiently, within the required time, to make it work?   _____

14. How long do you perceive it will be before you are actually doing this work?_____

15. Given everything you have considered, is this career role right for you?   _____

Nothing is more difficult, and therefore more precious, than to be able to decide.
Napoleon I

Act II Review

Briefly describe your #1 career role. Why did you choose this role? *(page 277)*

Summarize the key points of what you learned during your interviews with professionals in this field.   *(page 296)*

Of the skills needed to succeed in this career, list those that you are already competent in and those that need work.   *(page 315)*

Describe how this career provides the best way to fulfill your mission in life.   *(page 317)*

List the sacrifices you'll need to make in terms of: *(page 320)*

Time:

Personal Life:

What benefits will you gain from succeeding in this career?   *(page 321)*

Describe the financial factors relevant to this field.   *(page 322)*

The Battle for Life's Work

Wherein our hero selects a marketing strategy

Choose always the way that seems the best, however rough it may be. Custom will soon render it easy and agreeable.

Pythagoras

This unit is about power. We have spent a good deal of time talking about a loving motive and the wisdom to consider one's actions in light of personal integrity and social good. Further, we have considered the "game" aspects of career and role. All of this is well and good, yet without the power of will and a knowledge of the marketplace and how to be effective in it, we may abandon our grand intentions to the realm of mere dreams. Whether you choose to work for yourself or to take a job within an existing organization, you will have to market yourself and your work. "Act III: The Battle for Life's Work" is designed to arm you with what you need to "take it to the street." In addition to providing you with specific information about creating your own business, working as a freelance, starting a nonprofit organization, and landing the right job, we will consider, in the section entitled "Street Smarts," a number of general marketing skills with applications in virtually any field.

*Note: If additional training is required before you can pursue the career you identified in "Act II," you may want to go directly to "Act IV: The School of Life's Work."

Winning in the Marketplace;

or, How to Kick Butt Without Being a Total Jerk

Everybody lives by selling something.
Robert Louis Stevenson

There is a war going on. Like it or not, you're on the battlefield. Now, as we discussed earlier, the really important battles are the ones within yourself, but that does not negate the fact that there is an outer war happening as well. This war is a battle for power and control. It is played out in the economic sphere. In the battlefield of the economy, the large corporations are the superpowers. Superpowers get even bigger by gobbling up the midsized companies. So the giant fish eat the large and medium-sized fish. And what do the medium-sized fish eat? Why, the biggest little fish, of course. A fish can only get so big without being noticed by a hungry bigger fish. Giant fish are too large to bother little fish, and medium-sized fish are too large to notice tiny fish.

The tiny fish are, of course, the countless small businesses and freelancers that provide a myriad of services we all use and enjoy every day. These small fry get away only because they aren't really interesting to bigger fish. Tiny fish companies are what Gerald Michaelson (see highlight on page 331) and others have termed "guerillas." Their survival depends on their ability to attract the attention of customers, clients, investors, benefactors, etc., without doing this so well that they attract a hungry bigger fish.

Guerillas, including small business people, nonprofit operators, and freelancers, must have the market savvy to survive in a big-gun environment. Except for occasional strikes, guerillas don't take on large armies in their strongholds—they hold rugged terrain and rely on the support of the local people. They go under, around, and behind the big armies but almost never meet them head-on.

Appear where they cannot go, head for where they expect you least.

Sun Tzu

Although most people report that they would like to work for themselves, few do. Many who are unhappy working for someone else could make the transition if they had the necessary confidence and marketing skill. We can't do much about the confidence part (see "Act IV, Scene III"), but we would certainly encourage you to gain the marketing skill necessary to make it as a guerilla. Throughout this "Act," you will find a good deal of specific information as well as a preliminary planning process for thinking through your new enterprise. We will also direct you to a wide variety of additional sources.

Instead of working for ourselves, most of us have jobs. No doubt, this is partly because we understand that there is a war going on, and a lot of gung-ho guerillas come back as casualties. We attempt to join forces with large organizations, figuring there is strength in numbers, or because in our field, a job is the best or only vehicle for achieving the results we want. Yet even within the belly of a whale, the market sea can be a dangerous place, with shifting currents and raging winds. There is always the chance of the whale running aground.

Recognize that as an employee, your efforts and talents will be used for whatever ends your employer has in mind. For this reason, it's imperative that you understand the purpose of any organization you plan to work for and that you choose one whose purpose is congruent with your own, or at least tolerant of it (see highlight on page 439). You probably are not going to single-handedly reform

Only a life lived for others is a life worthwhile.

Albert Einstein

Bravery never goes out of style.

William M. Thackeray

organizations (especially large ones), so stay with organizations where you can, in good conscience, go with the flow. Landing the jobs you really want (you can easily have a dozen or more in your work life) requires the necessary self-marketing, or job-hunting skills. As much as the guerilla entrepreneur (though in different ways), the job-seeker must be a marketing warrior. (We direct you to the "Landing the Right Job" scenario, beginning on page 429.)

The conflict in "The Battle for Life's Work" arises from the tension between the way things are now and the way they could be. This gives your marketing adventure its inherent drama. You want to sell more of your products or services, spread your message, provide greater community service, or get a job that allows you to share more of your abilities, etc. You want something. You may or may not get it—that's exciting. You will have to fight against your own fear and laziness, as well as outside barriers—that's character building. Marketing—character building?

I can hear it, rolling around not too far in the back of some of your minds, a philosophical debate centered on the question, "Can one be intelligent, moral, *and* successful?" Much of modern literature tells us that we cannot. Novel after nauseating novel has given us images of the defeated hero, or anti-hero—the intelligent, moral man as the proverbial outsider. Implied is the notion that all successful, self-confident people must be fools or crooks—"not deep" or "not decent." This is bunk. If by success you mean achieving what you, in your heart, want—not somebody else's idea—then of course, you can and should be successful. If your success or some part of it requires winning in the marketplace—go for it.

Zen will have nothing to do with defeat, self-pity, or retreating to The Ivory Tower of Should Be. It adapts to circumstance. In India and China, Buddhism had a legacy of nonviolence. In Japan, Zen embraced the *samurai* tradition and refined it—bringing a code of acceptable martial conduct. Zen was not squeamish about the martial arts, and it needn't be squeamish about the marketing arts—today's equivalent. Zen brings its energy, detachment, self-discipline, humor, and grace wherever it goes. Even when, like the little piggy, it goes to market.

East and West (around the world, for that matter), there is a tradition of the noble warrior. Martial skill without self-discipline and restraint was recognized as a danger to the community. (Today, the same may be said of marketing skill.) Codes of martial conduct were established to check the potential abuses of this power. Andrea Hopkins, in her wonderful book, *Knights,* states that the distinguishing characteristics of the true medieval knight were *bravery, skill in combat,* and *integrity*.[1] These can provide a basis for a code of conduct for today's marketing warrior. He or she

The Marketing Battlefield

The following, from Gerald A. Michaelson's *Winning the Marketing War: A Field Manual for Business Leaders*, is a concise description of current battlefield positions and strategies. (Abt Books, Lanham, Md., 1987.) Reprinted with the permission of the publishers.

The Marketing Battlefield

The big ones own the strongest positions.

Positions on the Battlefield

The marketplace is much like the political geography of the Cold War.

1. The big ones—always in control.
2. The secondary powers— squeezed in the middle.
3. Everyone else—fighting like guerrillas.

The Super Powers

They own the territory.

1. Their best defense is an active offensive.
2. They should allow no one to camp on their battlefield.
3. When the super powers don't protect their armies, they lose their position.

Secondary Powers

They are in the dangerous middle ground.

1. They must get bigger so that they don't get smaller.
2. They don't attack the major powers.
3. They get their territory from the smaller companies.

The Guerrillas

Everyone else with a small market share.

1. Their struggle is for survival.
2. Survivors keep a watchful eye on the super powers.

needs the *bravery* to go into the marketing battle, the *marketing skill* to be masterful, and the *integrity* to remain true to principle throughout. (If today's battleground is the marketplace, then skill in combat means marketing skill.)

Bravery Is a Battle You Can Win or Lose: Overcoming Fear

Within the marketing context, bravery means simply that you believe in what you are doing enough to fight for it, to enter the fray, to risk getting roughed up a bit. If you're looking for a job, go for the one you really want—don't settle for less. If you want to start your own business, get out there and mix it up with the competition. If you want to start a nonprofit organization, drum up support for your ideas, solicit from potential donors, organize events to fund your efforts, hassle with the paperwork, etc. Fight for what you believe in.

A warrior must only take care that his spirit is never broken.

Shissai

To be a warrior is to learn to be genuine in every moment of your life.

Chögyam Trungpa

A poet once said, "Only the gentle are brave." Gandhi repeatedly instructed that the "nonviolence" of the weak is not nonviolence but cowardice and that only the strong can be nonviolent. The person who stays in a job he hates and condemns others for being "too materialistic" is a hypocrite. Poverty, of itself, is no virtue. Self-denial out of cowardice is a waste, not a gift. Your bravery as a marketing warrior comes from your caring, your compassion, your commitment to the vision you hold. The words *valor* and *value* come from the same Latin root, *valere,* meaning "to be strong."[2] The person with the conviction of their values has the strength to initiate, endure, and ultimately, triumph (see "Zen and the Art of Marketing," page 352).

Integrity Is a Battle You Can Win or Lose: Overcoming Laziness and Greed

It's natural for us to think of greed as compromising integrity—just as often, the culprit is laziness. Selling out is easy. Standing up for what you want and believe in takes a lot of energy. At every step along the way, you will meet with the temptation to compromise your integrity for the sake of ease, financial reward, recognition, understanding, acceptance, etc. In the employment sector, you may be offered a lucrative position doing work that violates your principles or work that, while not ethically or morally repugnant, isn't what you know in your heart you want.

> *First see to it that you, yourself, are all right, then think of defeating an opponent.*
> *The Way of the Spear*

In business, tests of integrity come into play in the way you conduct yourself with your employees, customers, suppliers, other businesses, and the general public. In the nonprofit sector, you may be asked to abandon controversial programs in order to receive funding from governments and corporations. These are just a few of the integrity issues that may arise. We will discuss these issues in greater depth within each of the four organizational "scenarios." The remainder of the present discussion concentrates on marketing skill and the attitudes that support it.

Marketing Skill Is a Battle You Can Win or Lose: Developing Resourcefulness

In Japanese martial arts, there is a saying: "Zen seven, *ken* three." *Ken* refers to the sword. The meaning of the saying is that success in swordsmanship is seven parts Zen, or inner approach, and three parts *ken*, or technical ability with the sword. We have already given the metaphor of the marketplace as a battlefield. Within this context, the saying "Zen seven, *ken* three" applies equally well with the English meaning of the word *ken*. In English, *ken* means "to know"(*v.*) or "range of knowledge"(*n.*).[3] What you know about the marketplace and the range of knowledge you have about effective market strategies can spell the difference between success and failure. Yet your attitude, your Zen, is always the single most important factor. Developing a positive image of the creative use of aggressive energy can take you a long way.

> *We can see unmistakeably that there is an inner relationship between Zen and the warrior's life.*
> *D. T. Suzuki*

No doubt, some of you are still having difficulty with the warrior metaphor. The word *warrior* may conjure images of war, brutality, death, and destruction. As we use the term, *warrior* isn't limited to combat veterans but applies to anyone who uses their aggressive energy in a disciplined, focused way. Aggressive energy is a part of life. There is no getting around it. It can be used creatively, or it can be used destructively, but it cannot be eliminated. But what about nonviolence? You say—"I believe in nonviolence."

Nonviolence is the creative use of aggression—not its negation. But don't take my word for it; listen to the world's foremost nonviolence practitioner, Mahatma Gandhi: "I have learned through bitter experience the one supreme lesson to conserve my anger, and as heat conserved is transmuted into energy, even so anger controlled can be transmuted into an energy which can move the world."[4]

When you reach real ability you will be able to become one with the enemy. Entering his heart you will see that he is not your enemy after all.
Tsuji (Japanese sword master)

Joy lies in the fight . . .

Mahatma Gandhi

How can we learn to "control" our aggressive energy—and in so doing tap the benefits of its power? When you get behind the wheel of an automobile, you respect its power—or pay the price. You know that, depending on how well it is controlled, your car can be a means of locomotion or of destruction. Similarly, your aggressive energy can work for or against you. It *will* find expression—either in creativity and initiative or in negativity and self-sabotage. Determine to respect this energy and make it work for you. In Tibetan Buddhism, the adept is said to "turn round" the energy of anger (sometimes called stubbornness) into tenacity or "immovable" determination. Controlled, aggression becomes the force of tenacious concentration—the key discipline of the warrior, the source of her power.

In the Western tradition, we find the same understanding in the lore of knights. To this day, the most famous and prestigious order of knights is the Order of the Garter. It was originally called the Order of St. George. (He is still its patron saint.) One of the great icons of Western history is the image of St. George the dragon-slayer (sometimes shown as St. Michael). If you look closely, you will notice that St. George does not actually kill the dragon (symbol of the aggressive energy); he keeps his sword at its throat. He does not destroy his aggressive energy; he keeps it under his control. A knight uses his aggression in a disciplined way. He does not waste this energy but concentrates it into an immovable determination to accomplish his objectives.

Another objection that sometimes arises to the warrior metaphor is this nonsense that women can't relate to being warriors. Suffice to say that anyone who makes this claim can take a few lessons from world history, mythology, and current events. Throughout history, scores of women have marched into battle with their menfolk; various cultures produced whole battalions of female warriors, for example, the African Dahomeyan.[5] There have been numerous warrior queens. Mythology abounds with legends of female warriors and warrior goddesses, recognizing the warrior energy within the feminine psychology. In today's marketing wars, most of the new guerillas (entrepreneurs) are women.

Of course, smart marketing warriors do a lot better than naive ones. They know that without the right attitudes and the right information, they are going to get slaughtered in the marketing wars. To be successful in your marketing efforts, you must project confidence. In the long run, confidence can't be faked. You must develop the attitudes and knowledge that breed confidence. Below are a few attitudes that smart marketing warriors adopt.

*In walking, just walk.
In sitting, just sit.
Above all,
don't wobble.*

Yun-men

1. Know there is a way.

2. Find a way.

3. Take action on the basis of the knowledge that you find.

4. Keep at it.

Know There Is a Way

Marketing warriors *never* doubt what they want. That is why we asked you to take the time to identify exactly what you want in your life's work. When you run up against an obstacle, there is a big difference between saying, "I don't know if I really want this after all" and saying, "This is a damn difficult obstacle." Many people abandon the ship of their dreams as soon as they run into the first strong wind. Marketing warriors don't retreat from their goals. They have the understanding and the detachment to seek creative strategies. They put the full force of their creative energy into finding a way.

Some view marketing as a boring activity. This is a mistake. To think of anything as boring makes it so. It matters less how exciting *things are*; it matters more how much excitment *we bring* to them. Some people have boring sex! There is nothing so intrinsically

*They conquer who
believe they can.*

Emerson

thrilling that it can't seem boring when approached in a half-hearted
or distracted manner. On the other hand, there is nothing we can't
experience in the heightened state of full attention and awareness.
We get out of our marketing efforts what we put into them.

> *Go to the battlefield firmly confident of victory and
> you come home with no wounds whatsoever.*
> Kenshin Uesugi (Samurai general)

By now, you have definite goals. Start with the conviction that
you are going to achieve them. Affirm that there is a way. In a sense,
every marketing problem is simply a lack of knowledge. Understanding this gives a direction for your efforts—get the knowledge
and skill you need to succeed. Nothing can stop a person with
initiative and drive, one who keeps looking for a way and never
gives up.

Find a Way

These days, one has to be very careful about saying that something
can't be done. In fact, 99 percent of the time, there is someone doing
that very thing right now, in equally difficult or more adverse
circumstances. Marketing warriors take the attitude, "I know there
is a way, and I'm going to find it. How am I going to find it? Well, first
and foremost, I'm going to keep looking until I do."

> *You must push yourself beyond your limits, all the
> time.*
> Carlos Castaneda (Don Juan)

Looking *is* looking, not ruminating on the problem. Many people
confuse idle conversation with the action of finding a way. They
seem to believe that a little fairy godmother is going to hear their
complaints and magically solve all of their problems. Their approach is: "Well, here is my problem; I want you to listen to me recite
my litany of weaknesses and disabilities and all the reasons why it
won't work." Of course, we can always do this (and we may do it
more than we care to admit), but when we are done complaining,
our situation will not have improved.

You'd be better off to take the time spent in idle complaint and
go out and learn something. Get knowledge—it's power. Weakness

is a lack of knowledge. Gain knowledge until you are clear about what to do. Determine that you are going to keep looking until you find a way—until the light bulbs go off. When you don't find a way right away, don't conclude that there *is* no way. Take the approach, "I haven't found a way yet, but I know there is one, and I'm still looking." This is the time to redouble your efforts—get more information. Avoid complaining and negative talk of all kinds. Unless your conversation is a matter of seeking information from a more knowledgeable source or bouncing off a sounding board you know you can trust—clam up.

People will tell you that there is no way before they have done any research to find out. They picture mental "Road Closed" signs where none exist. They allow fear of failure to stop them in their tracks. If you want to be successful, don't worry about failure. All failure is simply a failure to *concentrate*. Fear of failure distracts your attention from the search for a way to make it work. In this way, *the fear of* failure actually helps to create it. There is a way. Keep looking. If you don't see it right away, persist. Go back and affirm that there is a way. Stay with the search like a leopard on the hunt. Know what you want to do, and concentrate on finding a way to make it work.

---

*With enough knowledge and self-confidence,
you can do anything.*

All the things you want to do will fall into one of two categories. Either it has been done before, but not by you, or it has never been done. In either case, *finding the way is a matter of inner listening (intuition) and outer research*. In proper combination, these are an unbeatable tandem.

It Has Been Done before, but Not by You: If the thing you want to do has been done before, but not by you, your emphasis will be on outer research. You need to find a good model and follow it. The model will provide the primary guiding force. Of course, you will want to adapt the model to fit your unique situation by listening to your intuition, or gut feelings, and by keeping an awareness of relevant environmental factors.

The process, though more complicated in practice, is not unlike that of assembling a bicycle or a piece of furniture that you buy ready-made in the box. All of the necessary steps have been laid out for you; if you simply follow the instructions, you'll get results. You don't have to be Einstein and invent something that doesn't exist. Just go out there, get good information, and follow instructions.

*Whatever is worth
doing at all, is worth
doing well.*

Phillip Stanhope

There is a wealth of information available today for improving your marketing skill. If you are seeking employment, developing your job-hunting skills can give you the power to choose the position you really want. You don't have to settle for less—not if you have the power of knowledge working for you. You can select the organizations you want to work for and aggressively go after them. You put the power in your hands.

Action is doing *something,* reacting *is having it* happen.

Syd Field

Those of you interested in starting your own businesses will need to know about markets and management, accounting and advertising, sales and red tape, capital acquisition and business planning, and more. All of this is in addition to the knowledge specific to operating your particular business. If you want to start a nonprofit organization, you will need to know about the legalities of incorporation and tax-exempt status; legal restrictions on officers, directors, and programs; fundraising; publicity; proposal writing; strategic planning; management; evaluation; record keeping; and more. Again, all of this is in addition to the specific knowledges necessary to providing the services which your organization offers.

In the military, information about the enemy is referred to as "intelligence." If you have sufficient intelligence on the enemy, you can develop an effective campaign for achieving your objectives. Marketing warriors understand that their biggest enemy is their own lack of knowledge. Know your enemy. Identify the specific knowledges you need to acquire and attack them with relentless intensity. Conquer them. Make them yield before you.

Marketing warriors understand that their biggest enemy is their own lack of knowledge.

Be strategic in the use of your energy resources. Identify the knowledges you require. Select which you will focus on first. (Don't try to learn everything at once.) Next, get general information (read general surveys) on the subject. This gives you an overview of this mental battlefield and a strategic approach to knowledge acquisition. Once you have a strategy, you can select the tactics (the specific learning options, see page 560) you will use to master this knowledge. When you are clear on your strategy and tactics, you are ready to move in for the kill.

Remember, it's important to know where you are. If the thing you want to do has been done before, you needn't start from scratch, and you shouldn't. Find good models and follow instructions, adapted, of course, to your particular situation. People often try to invent at the stage where they would be better off copying; that's a mistake. Every artist has to learn how to copy before he can invent. Every warrior has to go into training before she is ready for battle.

He who can copy can do.
Leonardo da Vinci

It Has Never Been Done Before: If the thing you want to do has never been done before, your emphasis will be on inner listening (intuition), with adaptations based upon your outer research. In this case, the primary guiding force will be your own inner promptings and creative ideas. These, of course, must be grounded and adapted to the practical realities of the environments you want to work in. In this case, your research gives you the knowledge necessary to bridge the intuition with the physical world. In addition to research to find links with the old, you will use reason to present your intuition in a logical way that people can understand. Research and reason, then, are the structural supports of intuition and are necessary to bridging the old with the new.

The Creative Bridge

Intuition

Old   New

Research   Reason

The ability to find a way is one anyone can develop with practice. As you gain in confidence, you will be ready to take on bigger and bigger tasks. You can magnify this ability such that you spend the lion's share of your time looking for ways for your society, nation, or planet. You can keep looking and looking until you find better ways, then share the wonderful gifts or inventions you find.

Think first, then do.

Albert Schweitzer

Take Action on the Basis of the Knowledge that You Find

As we have said, marketing warriors don't waste time trying to reinvent the wheel. They have the self-confidence and humility necessary to follow instructions. *People who can't follow instructions can't direct the course of their own lives.* The self-directed individual selects what she wants (or needs) to learn and do and sets about following the models necessary to learning and doing it.

In order to arrive at what you do not know
You must go by the way which is the way of
ignorance.

T. S. Eliot

When an experienced, knowledgeable person says, "This is the way to do it," accept that that is the way to do it, at least until you know enough to find a better way. Act! Don't allow intervening thoughts such as, Oh, but can I do it? or, I don't know if I'm cut out for this, or, Am I doing it wrong? to distract your mind. Concentrate on what you need to do. Do what the model says—Do step one. Begin!

That's the important thing—Did you do step one? Did you actually do it? If you did, you're on your way to achieving your result. Now do step two. This entire discussion seems almost ridiculously obvious, but I am continually struck by how often people tend to focus on tangential issues of self-evaluation (Can I? Can't I? Am I doing it right or wrong?) rather than taking the action that gets the results. Do step three. Do step four. Do what the model tells you. It's not a matter of "Can you do it?" If you do it, you're doing it.

It is necessary to any originality to have the courage to be an amateur.

Wallace Stevens

Expect nothing; be prepared for anything.
Samurai saying

Just follow instructions! This gets all the personal angst out of it. If you approach each action with the idea that it's going to make you great (or justify your existence), you'll get so tense that you can't act. It will become such a big deal in your mind that you will be effectively paralyzed from taking action. Instead, concentrate on taking action—step one, step two, step three. Act through from beginning to end. Focus on the model and you stay objective.

Action is character, right? What a person does is what he is, not what he says.

Syd Field

Now, is this action going to prove that you are a more worthwhile human being or redeem your sins? No, nothing of the kind. It's just going to demonstrate that you can do step one—whatever that is. Does that make you better than anyone else? No, it just means you're getting closer to getting the result you want. Does it mean you're a worse human being if you don't do it? No, it just means you won't get the result associated with that series of steps. Don't take the whole thing personally; just get good information (from intuition and research), and follow instructions.

Another really obvious but often overlooked point is that a process is a series of steps. For example, if you want to start your own business, there is a series of steps you must take before your idea can become a reality. If you do step one really well and quit, you're not going to get the result. You must do all of the steps and in appropriate sequence.

To take a simple example, let's say the action you are taking involves mailing a letter. The last step of putting the stamp on the letter and sending it in, though almost inanely simple, is as important to the total process of mailing the letter as the more involved steps of thinking about and actually writing the letter. It doesn't matter how many minutes you spent thinking about the letter if you didn't write it. It doesn't matter how much effort you put into writing it if you didn't send it. Follow step one, step two, step three. Don't skip any step, no matter how difficult or easy.

When you read the book, attend the seminar, or listen to the mentor and they tell you to do A, B, and C, go out and do A, B, and C. Get the result, and see how that feels. Do it again and again, and you may start to think there is nothing you can't learn, digest, and apply in action. If you can follow instructions, this is an incredible time to be alive. Today there is a wealth of organized information on virtually every subject.

If one source says to do it one way, and a second suggests another way, and a third offers still another way, feel your way to which is best. Most likely, a synthesis will be best. For this reason (the superiority of the synthesis), you should almost always (always when dealing with written material alone) seek out more than one source of information. A synthesis of several sources is helpful, but don't let confusion stop you from acting. Any one way is better than none. Act!

Whether you think you can or you can't— you are right.

Henry Ford

Keep at It

Think not so much of what thou hast not, as of what thou hast.

Marcus Aurelius

Don't worry about what you don't have; use what you do. This point is so important that it can't be overstated. Begin where you are. Act into your goals. When you are hiking cross-country, it is often necessary to get to the top of one hill or plateau before you can see the next peak. From the starting point, you couldn't have seen the peak that now stands before you. You had to get on the trail first. Always go as far as you can, based upon your current understanding. This creates a positive force of momentum. The more invested you are in the outcome, the less likely you are to turn back when the going gets rough. Go to the highest peak you can, and see what you can see from there.

A journey of a thousand miles is many thousand steps.

When we are stuck, it's simply because we can't see what to do next. Sometimes we can't see because we aren't looking, that is, we are looking at all that needs to be done instead of what needs to be done next. You can only take one step at a time. You don't look at a pizza and say, "I can't eat it; it's too big to fit into my mouth." No, you slice it into pieces and eat it one bite at a time. Go back to your model; see where you are in the process, and do the next step. If you start worrying that you will never get there, stop and look at your map (your model), and see how far you have come.

Have you ever asked yourself, "What is worry?" Isn't worry just the misuse of imagination? When we are exercising our imaginations properly, we are using them to go before us, to mentally see a way to do the things we want to do before we actually do them. When we are worrying, we are allowing our imaginations to picture negative results.

Guard your imagination. Be careful of what you mentally associate with your goals. Let's say you want to develop skill in public speaking. If, when you think of this goal, your imagination conjures up pictures of negative results like embarrassment or ridicule, you will experience the associated feelings of pain. Out of self-protection, your subconscious mind will move you away from

To worry is to pre-pare for failure.

situations where you might experience the painful results you have envisioned. This puts you in a state of struggle; consciously you are trying to move forward (toward the action of public speaking); subconsciously you are moving away. Unite the subconscious imaginative energy with your conscious intention, and you magnify your capacity for constructive action. Our subconscious minds work on a kind of pleasure principle. They naturally move us toward pleasure and away from pain. If you hold only positive pictures (pleasure-producing) in association with your goals, you will move easily toward them.

> *Approach the moment with the idea that you're in the fight to the finish.*
>
> *Mataemon Iso*

If it seems that you can only associate negative pictures with your goals, it may be because you lack the information necessary to construct positive ones. Think of the children's game of making so many things (e.g., a tree, a house, a man) out of toothpicks. Certainly one can make more arrangements out of fifteen toothpicks than she can out of three and more out of thirty-five than fifteen. Think of each toothpick as a set of knowledge. We can, of course, be more or less creative with any number of toothpicks, but certain arrangements will be impossible with only a few. We might think a teacher cruel who instructed her young students to construct an elaborate barnyard scene, complete with buildings and animals, but provided them with only three toothpicks. Yet, if she gave them several boxes of toothpicks, we know they could do it. The more knowledge you have, the greater the opportunities for creative arrangements. If you are stuck, you may be asking your mind to build a picture without enough toothpicks—get more information.

Again, you can't force yourself to move into a situation that you envision with negative (pain-producing) pictures. If you find yourself worrying or procrastinating, check your imagination. Make the change directly in your imagination or with the aid of new information. These really go hand in hand. Use both aspects of mind, the rational side to select the behaviors that are going to move you forward and the imaginative side to associate these behaviors with positive (pleasure-producing) pictures. Hold only positive (pleasure-producing) pictures of the things you want, and you are sure to move into the actions that will bring them to you.

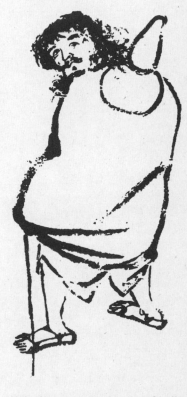

It is the greatest of all mistakes to do nothing because you can only do a little. Do what you can.

Sidney Smith

Value Progress; or,
Those Beautiful Shades of Gray

Look at a Zen *suiboku* (ink-monochrome) painting. It has no color. Yet all subtlety and suggestion is there in the beautiful shades of gray. Space, depth, infinity itself appear in the beautiful shades of gray. There is a lesson here. We can learn to see and love the many shades of gray in our own lives. There are dangers to living in a world without gray—to viewing things in terms of sharp contrasts between black and white. On the one hand, we may whitewash the world and ourselves and miss important "darker" information that we need to be aware of. On the other hand, we may become submerged in a black pit from which we can see no light.

1. Whitewash: The Avoidance Factor. The black/white construction blocks our openness to feedback: feedback from life, feedback from others, even feedback from ourselves. The need to have everything be all white means you may block out knowledge about yourself or things that you are doing that aren't working. The rationale, if you can call it that, goes something like this: "If I allow myself to be aware of this personality fault or this ineffective way of doing things, it will mean that I am bad, hopeless, a born loser, or some such. If there are things about me or what I am doing that are imperfect, then I must be all wrong, bad, or dark." Instead of seizing on important information they require to be more effective, people with the whitewash syndrome tend to avoid anything that they perceive as putting them in a dark light. They also dismiss unfavorable news from the marketing battlefield—information they may need to make shifts in strategy or tactics.

2. Black Pit: The Baby with the Bath Syndrome. Where the "whitewash" involves the tendency to avoid negative or unpleasant information, the "black pit" is the tendency to get overwhelmed by it. While in the "black pit," all seems black, as though one mistake or failure means one is forever doomed. One tends to fixate one's attention on the failure and block out all intelligent thought of course correction. In the black pit, one rejects and condemns oneself (I'm no good), the objective standard one had been striving to reach (I didn't really want to do it anyway), or the source of the feedback (It's not fair, they're wrong). In the black pit, one misses, not only the shades of white in the black, but also the idea that one might ever be capable of change. After all, black is black, and white is white. Clearly, we can see that we cannot steadily grow until we learn to see the beautiful shades of gray.

Discriminate grays *and* appreciate the ground you've already walked on the journey toward your goals. Take an objective standard as your guiding light, and work steadily toward it. You may make mistakes; no doubt, you will, but don't exaggerate their importance. Reject neither the standards of excellence nor yourself in the process of learning. Instead, focus on your successes and the steps you can take toward further improvement. This gives you a sense of momentum, a forward thrust into your full creative expression.

What's Ahead in Act III

In **"Scene I: Taking It to the Street: Choosing Your Marketing Strategy,"** you will have the opportunity to select an organizational form for your new career endeavor. You may choose to create your own business or nonprofit organization, work as a freelance, or land the right job.

"Scene II, Scenario I: Sailing the Entrepreneurship" is devoted to starting your own business. The entrepreneurial sector is the fastest growing part of the American economy. Increasingly, individuals are ready to strike out on their own and take a shot at calling their own shots. The essay "Sailing the Entrepreneurship" gives a brief overview of the challenges and opportunities that face today's new entrepreneurs. Detailed worksheets will help you plot out the basic framework of your new business. Also included are over fifty references to help you pursue areas of special interest in greater depth.

"Scene II, Scenario II: Wielding the Freelance" is designed for those of you who are looking for maximum freedom in your work environment and who are comfortable with a minimum of structure. Artists, musicians, craftspeople, and those with highly specialized technical skills, such as pilots or computer programmers, are often good candidates for the freelance option. It offers the greatest control over one's work, with the least bureaucratic and organizational hassle. We will discuss the three essentials of a freelance business: marketing, negotiation, and administration. Since freelance businesses often require aggressive marketing, you will find a section designed to help you overcome self-marketing barriers. Also included is a section on designing and using promotional pieces.

In **"Scene II, Scenario III: Crafting the Nonprofit Foundation,"** you will explore some of the major advantages and disadvantages of starting a nonprofit corporation. Though in many ways similar to for-profit businesses, the nonprofit foundation presents some unique management challenges including: defining the purpose of the organization, agreeing upon effective strategies for achieving this purpose, determining objectives, making planning decisions, and measuring the success of your efforts. At the end of this section, you will find a helpful worksheet for clarifying your purpose, strategies, and primary objectives. You will learn how to fund your nonprofit corporation. Finally, you will find a resource list of over fifty relevant publications for further research.

"Scene II, Scenario IV: Landing the Right Job" is designed to help you locate the organization and the position within the organization where you can best put your talents to work in the pursuit of your purpose. You'll have a chance to map out a job-hunting strategy, zeroing in on the organizations you want to work for and the people within them who have the power to hire you. (We'll introduce you to over forty references to help you locate these.) Then we'll discuss eight different methods you can use for landing interviews, the all-important key to getting the job you want. Next, we will discuss over twenty-five key techniques that you can use before, during, and after your interview to make sure it's a success. Finally, we include over fifty additional sources to help you sharpen your job-hunting skills.

"Scene III: Street Smarts" covers the essentials of networking, generating publicity for your work, writing grant proposals, and negotiation. With these invaluable tools at your command, you'll be ready to take it to the street.

Detour #3: The Availability Trap

The detour of availability comes into play when we look casually over the work landscape and decide that what we want is not available. You may find a little gold on the surface, but the rich veins are deep inside the earth. You have to dig to find them. So it is with putting yourself to work. You may find some opportunities on the surface, but you usually have to dig for the real treasures. The availability trap takes the form of "Can't Find It" or "Can't Make It," depending upon whether you want to work for an existing organization or start your own.

Can't Find It: If you can't find the job you are looking for (and are qualified for), there are only a few possibilities: It doesn't exist, you don't know how to find it, or you have given up too soon. While it's possible that the job you want really does not exist, it generally takes a good deal of research to be sure of that. Some people try a few places, decide it's impossible, and give up. Keep looking! The next thing that could keep you from finding a job is not knowing how to. We have included a section to help you, but you will probably want more detail. Consult the bibliographies at the end of this unit for further reading.

If you don't learn well from books or are confused by what you read, you may want professional assistance. The primary job-hunting skills are learning how to target organizations, land interviews, and succeed in the interview process. While the process is basically simple, there are hundreds of techniques that can help you improve your effectiveness. Keep looking and learning. Don't give up until you get what you want.

Can't Make It: If, after careful consideration, you have decided to create your own organization, don't let the "can't make it bug" get you down. "Can't Make It" takes two forms: "I haven't done it before," or "It hasn't been done before."

If it's been done, but not by you, other people's experience can help see you through. Go after it through books, classes, seminars, workshops, friends, and mentors. Aggressively seek out all you need to know. Assemble a capable team of people committed to the purpose and vision of your organization. Hire outside experts when you are stuck, but never, never give up.

If what you are considering has never been done before, the task ahead of you presents a great challenge. It takes a special kind of person to pull this off. You must be able to see your vision as clear as a bell and communicate it to people who don't see it so well. Even after the prototype's a hit, there will be doubters, but don't quit. All the while, you will be asking people to invest their time, energy, and money into something that doesn't yet exist. It's difficult, but not impossible, if your belief in your vision is unstoppable.

What to Look for in an Existing Organization

Shared Vision/Purpose: Choose an organization whose purpose matches yours, one that you can wholeheartedly and enthusiastically take responsibility for. This is the most important criteria for full involvement and satisfaction in your work.

Purpose-Focused Management: Purpose-focused management means that the leadership of the organization frames and makes important the question: What's right? They don't get bogged down in peripherals or in personality (Who's right?). Where the leadership of an organization is focused on peripherals and personalities, the atmosphere will be one of aimlessness and negativity. Where the leadership is focused on purpose, the entire work force comes to understand that it is their purposeful action that is rewarded and given attention. People's advancement within the organization is based upon their ability to advance the organization's goals, not upon personal favoritism or other considerations.

Encourages Full Participation of Its Employees: Choose an organization that encourages the full participation of its employees, an organization that wants thinking people. Select organizations that won't treat you as a body or even as a cluster of skills. Choose one that wants your ideas, that gives you the freedom to do your work in the way that works best for you. This relates to the previous point. If an organization is purpose based, then its interest is in getting quality work done. It doesn't get bogged down with rules and regulations for their own sake. You need to be able to control your work, to have authority that matches your responsibility, and to possess the freedom to innovate when you discover a better way.

An Emphasis on Ongoing Learning and Development: Choose an organization that emphasizes ongoing learning and development, both as an organization and for the people within the organization. Times change. Situations change. Successful organizations are able to adapt to changes because they make ongoing learning and development a part of their practice. They are able to capitalize on opportunities, take advantage of emerging trends, and ensure that they do not become obsolete or get left behind. Additionally, these kinds of organizations encourage and facilitate the development of their work force. They help individuals to discover what they need to learn in order to be more effective, and they encourage them to learn it. They are concerned with the individual as a whole person and help him to understand what he must learn in order to advance.

Why Start Your Own Organization?

You have a vision. You have in mind a genuine innovation. By innovation we simply mean: you want to do something that is currently going undone, or you see a better way of doing something that is already being done. Innovations come in all shapes and sizes. Your innovation may be a new idea or invention. It may be the application of an existing technology to a new area or purpose. Your innovation could be a combination of existing factors that you organize in a new way. Your innovation should be well thought out and tested. It must be clearly understood by yourself and the members of the team you assemble. An organization without vision and purpose is more likely to drown in run-around than endure in the long run.

You desire greater control than you can find within an existing organization. As we will discuss later, entrepreneurial freedom may be something of a myth, but entrepreneurial control is a fact of life. You believe that you could do a better job as captain of your own ship than as first or second mate of someone else's. You want creative or managerial control that you can't get within an existing framework. You enjoy having the rewards for efforts directly tied to your performance and decisions.

You have or are ready to acquire management knowledge and experience. There is not much sense in starting an organization only to watch it fail. You, of course, want to succeed. Success will require effective management. Hit and miss is more often a miss than a hit. If you lack management knowledge and experience, you must be prepared to acquire or hire it.

You enjoy making decisions. As leader of your new organization, the ball will be in your court. You will bear the responsibility for and consequences of your decisions. You must not only enjoy making decisions, but you must also make good ones. A combination of intuition and intelligent analysis generally yields the best results.

The Power of Team Working

Never doubt that a small group of thoughtful, committed citizens
can change the world. Indeed it is the only thing that ever has.
Margaret Mead

Together: **The Strength of a Common Purpose.** Shared vision and purpose collects and focuses energy. A team can draw upon the experience, talents, knowledge, skills, and contacts of all its members. They share in a common struggle and adventure that promotes endurance and gives meaning and purpose to their actions. Members of a team combine and share their spiritual and emotional strength. The example of one individual or segment of the team spurs others on to their best. Even peer pressure can have positive influence in enhancing individual and team performance. Committed team members develop strong relationships built on loyalty and trust. The mutual understanding, love, and respect they share provides the emotional support necessary to persevere in the face of great difficulties.

Each: **Commitment to Team Motivates Each to Excel and Grow.** The sense of shared vision and personal loyalty prompts each individual to go the extra mile—not only to continue beyond where he would normally give up but to make excellence a consistent value. Within the environment of a supportive team, the individual feels safe to explore new ideas, test new skills, and try out new modes of self-expression. Individuals who have been members of teams involved in extremely difficult undertakings often discover within themselves more strength and ability than they ever knew they had. The group benefits from their efforts and they, as individuals, have tapped into a deep reservoir of strength and confidence that they will carry with them for the rest of their lives. Having been tested in the fire, these individuals are less likely to get rattled by the slings and arrows of outrageous fortune that attend life, generally.

Accomplishes: **A Team Is Organized for Action.** A well-organized team is an efficient vehicle for advancing an agreed-upon purpose through the achievement of definite objectives. It avoids the wastes of duplication of effort or misappropriation of resources. It organizes and divides labor so as to take full advantage of individual strengths and abilities. The shared goals of the team are measured and assessed by feedback systems that help to keep everyone moving in the same direction. A committed team develops a learning curve of experience. In the process of creating projects and meeting challenges, a team develops effective policies and standard operating procedures that enable it to handle reoccurring situations with maximum efficiency and ease. A team may even evolve effective ways of dealing with entirely new situations in an optimal manner.

More: **The Whole Is Greater Than the Sum of Its Parts.** A committed team has, as well as the efficiency of planned action, the indefinable power of synergistic action. As a team develops its own rhythm and harmony, it moves beyond mere rational thought into a realm of intuitive group action. Things happen that never could have been planned or predicted. The dynamic force released when divergent energies become focused around common objectives is truly awesome in its power to generate ideas, attract opportunities, and execute action. Team works!

Taking It to the Street: Choosing Your Marketing Strategy

Take time to deliberate; but when the time for action arrives, stop thinking and go in.

Andrew Jackson

The purpose of this section is to help you select the way (or ways) you intend to market yourself and your work. We will start with a general discussion of marketing. Whether you intend to start your own business, go freelance, get a job, or create a nonprofit organization, we think you will find it valuable. Immediately following "Scene I," we will present in-depth information on four marketing scenarios. In this section, we briefly sketch the advantages and disadvantages of each of these options, and we present some questions and checklists to help those of you who are undecided make the right choice.

Zen and the Art of Marketing

The purpose of the discussion that follows is to consider something like a Zen of marketing. We will explore how we can approach our marketing efforts with attitudes favorable to success. We will consider traditional marketing functions, or variables, from a perspective appropriate to this book. Indicated in the subheadings below are the marketing variables relevant to each section. These are: the product, the package, the price, the promotion, and the delivery.

Marketing Is a Fact of Life: The Product

As Robert Louis Stevenson said, "Everybody lives by selling something." Even the Buddhist monk going door to door with his begging bowl is selling a blessing and a chance to accrue karmic benefit by giving alms. The chart below is overly simple but makes the point—no matter what you choose to do, you are going to be selling something. Of course, you will be selling *yourself* in any case, yet if you choose to work at a job, you are *all* you will be selling.

For reasons that are rather self-evident, marketing has traditionally been important to entrepreneurs and freelancers. Yet recent trends in the job market and in the nonprofit sector have made marketing increasingly important for folks who work in these areas as well. In the old days, it was not uncommon for an individual to hold a job for twenty or thirty years. Most men—and in those days, most people in the work force were men—looked forward to retiring from the company they were working for for many years. They might have had two or three jobs in their entire lives. Developing a streetwise marketing sense was not as important for them as it is for today's working women and men.

In today's shifting economy, everyone is self-employed. Today, people have more *careers* in the course of their lives than they had *jobs* thirty years ago. Competition is fierce, and knowledge of effective self-marketing (or job-hunting) techniques can mean the difference between getting what you want and settling for less. Even if you plan on working for large, existing organizations for the rest of your life, you had better know a good deal about self-marketing.

Some years ago, nonprofits were relatively isolated from the demands of the marketplace. Today the situation has changed. Declining private contributions and cutbacks in federal and state grants and programs have forced many nonprofits to come up with new ways of garnering financial support, including cooperative ventures with the corporate sector and profit-making ventures under the nonprofit umbrella. Many nonprofits are selling subscriptions to newsletters or magazines or putting out catalogues of books and merchandise. Some contract out services for profit. Many have become extremely sophisticated in using direct mail and telemarketing techniques. If they want to give their organizations a fighting chance, today's nonprofit managers require an understanding of effective marketing techniques.

The Product: What Are You Selling, Anyway?

Business	Freelance	Nonprofit	Job
a product or service, an organization, and you	creative work or service, and you	a message, an organization, and you	you

---

The point of all we have said so far is simply this—no matter which way you go, you are going to be marketing something. Accepting this as a fact of life makes it easier to deal with. Be clear on what you are selling.

Marketing Is a Matter of Image and Perception: The Package

Everyone knows that a business, let's say a bank, that is *perceived* as being in trouble (even when it isn't) soon becomes so *in fact*. Wall Street is notorious for its reliance on perception. A company can be "hot," selling at an inflated price one month—and bottom out the next. Global and national economies rise and fall, to a great extent, on the basis of perception. Terms like "consumer confidence" and "investor confidence" reflect the economic power of perception. Perceptions of economic strength or weakness affect practical decisions, which, in turn, affect still more perceptions and practical decisions. Nowhere in the marketplace can we altogether separate perception from fact. Even at the level of the individual seeking a job, the person currently employed typically has an easier time finding the next job than one who is unemployed. This, again, is a matter of the perception of success.

> *Nothing succeeds like the appearance of success.*
> *Christopher Lasch*

Part of the sense of falseness or charade in the world of business comes from the fact that everyone is trying to project success. It isn't just business. Politicians, hospitals, universities, and all kinds of nonprofits are in on the act, and as you know, when you look for a job, you are in on it too.

Many people find the perception game and the need to constantly project success a bit nauseating and dishonest. Yet the truth is, most people don't see you; they see what you look like. They see your image. You really can't judge a book by its cover—but most people do. Studies have shown that people size you up and form a first (and somewhat lasting) impression in the first thirty seconds.[1] The same is true of the product or message you are promoting. People will judge these on the basis of what they (and you) look like before they ever find out what the product can do or what the point of your message is.

Effective marketing requires that we play the image game. Honesty and integrity demand that we have confidence in what we are selling—confidence in its value and confidence that it can deliver what we say it can. Part of the repulsion many have to playing the image (marketing) game is the fact that so much worthless junk is hyped from morning 'til night over radio and television. Yet if you have confidence in the value of what you are selling—be it a product, a service, a creative work, a message, or your own talent and energy, and you don't make the effort to create the appropriate image, you risk doing a disservice to these. You wouldn't present a diamond ring in a smelly old sock. A beautiful package or wrapping is appropriate to a beautiful gift, and a strong image can enhance the perceived and even the real value of what you are selling.

Below are a few image variables. Some we call left-brain—appealing to the sense of logos or logic; some, right-brain—appealing to the sense of pathos or feeling. We can think of a continuum running from, say, aloof to folksy, or from traditional to "hot," and so on. Consider what image works best for you, based on what you are selling, who you are selling it to, and what you feel comfortable with.

Left-Brain	Right-Brain
Respectable	Friendly
Traditional	"Hot"
Stable	Cutting Edge
Established	Growing
Aloof (snobbish)	Folksy

Marketing Is a Matter of Negotiation: The Price

You must determine a fair price for what you are selling. For example, if you are seeking a job, your price is your salary. We will discuss the specifics of negotiation as it relates to the various marketing strategies when we get to them. We also have a general discussion of negotiating principles in the "Street Smarts" section. We only mention it here to alert you to the fact that it is one of the important marketing variables.

Marketing Is a Matter of Personality: The Promotion: Part I

In his autobiography, philosopher and Zen writer Alan Watts wrote that "no one can succeed as an independent author, or as a teacher or minister, [let alone a business-woman or man] without a flair for drama and for coming on strongly as a personality, and by success I mean, not only financial reward, but also effective communication."[2] It's not true that nice guys always finish last—but it's certainly true that weak personalities do.

On the other hand, as Watts points out, "strength of personality—even though you know very well that it is a big act—is always taken for an 'ego-trip'..."[3] Many of us, certainly most from the middle and lower classes, were taught to downplay ourselves and our strengths. Those of us who do project ourselves in a strong and dynamic way risk being labeled "ego-maniacs" or worse. Part of the reaction comes from the violation of the norm itself, a kind of "shame on you." Part of it is jealousy. After all, it is easy to see that those who project themselves well are having fun doing it. Those who feel constrained by the norm from getting in on the fun often resent those who enjoy expressing themselves. The more repressed project an attitude of "Who do you think *you* are?" onto the less inhibited. The implication is that if you were someone else—say someone rich, famous, or powerful—this behavior would be acceptable.

Everyone on this earth is wearing an ego or *persona* mask of some kind and, in some way or another, projecting through it. Watts points out that the "enlightened ones" he knew all projected strong personalities. Look at the images of the Zen masters scattered throughout these pages—strong personality comes through every one. Modern-day saints like Gandhi, Schweitzer, and Mother Teresa all had strong personalities. Incidentally, these three were extremely effective promoters (or marketers) of their beliefs. All wrote books and toured the world speaking on behalf of their causes.

Where, then, do we get the idea that projecting a strong personality is "unspiritual"? Much of the popular religion in the West teaches false humility, a sort of psychological self-flagellation. We have been taught that a weak, self-deprecating personality is good (acceptable) and a strong personality is bad (threatening). Putting oneself down or hiding in the crowd is not humility. Humility comes of itself when we have no desire to be better than anyone else. When we let go of this craving, we simultaneously let go of the shame of being worse than anyone. We realize that at the deepest levels, we are no better, no worse, and no different.

The only difference between a wise man and a fool is that the wise man knows he's playing.
Fritz Perls

We all are on an "ego trip," journeying through time and space, projecting to one another through personality masks—egos. The so-called "enlightened ones" realize that this "ego trip" is going nowhere, has of itself no particular point or purpose, but is rather more like theater-in-the-round. They put on their masks, play in the theater, go on the ego trip—remaining all the while at home—perfectly at rest within themselves. The point of the drama *is* the drama, the expression of Infinite Compassion and Bliss in a seemingly endless variety of forms. As Shakespeare said, "The play's the thing."

Projecting a strong personality—essential to marketing success in any arena—is no more or less egotistical than projecting a weak one. Whatever the image portrayed on it, a mask *is* a mask. The kid wearing the Alfred E. Neuman mask on Halloween night is in costume as much as the kid wearing the Clark Gable mask.

Zen would say that both a *strong persona* and a *weak persona* are masks—both are equally fictitious. Neither is any better or worse than the other. Buddhism, however, does give the notion of *upaya* or "skillful means." If you want to succeed at marketing, the adoption of a strong, dynamic personality is a more skillful choice. Any other choice would make for added struggle, tension, and frustration and would therefore be a less skillful, more clumsy choice. One does not use a cross-country ski for water skiing or a weak personality for marketing. Whether we are taking a job interview or advocating a particular cause, promoting a business or book, a strong personality helps.

No matter which marketing strategy you choose, you will find a number of ways of marketing yourself within "Act III." All require a strong personality to gain maximum benefit from them. If you don't already have a strong personality, we suggest that you work on developing one—or more accurately, on letting it out. Everyone has a little ham in him or her. Ham it up, toot your own horn. Just remember that it is all, as Alan Watts says, a "big act."

Marketing Is a Matter of Circulation: The Promotion: Part II

We spent a good deal of time discussing a strong personality because, without it, you will probably have a hard time getting into circulation. Circulation is the name of the game in marketing—getting into and staying in circulation. Getting out and meeting people is circulating. Circulating flyers, circulating direct mail pieces, making the talk show rounds, speaking tours—all types of advertising and publicity expand your circulation. Think of what you are selling and how you can increase its circulation. The means you employ will vary, depending on what you are selling, but the principle of circulation applies across the board. When you come to the marketing party, be ready to circulate.

Our word *circulation* comes from a Latin root meaning "to form a circle."[4] View your marketing strength in terms of the circles you have formed and the circles you intend to form: circles of friends, circles of acquaintances, circles of contacts, circles of leads, circles of clients or customers, circles of investors, circles of like-minded individuals. Make a graphic representation of these, perhaps on a poster board. Maintaining and expanding these circles opens doors to new opportunities. *Remember, the wealth of the universe comes to you through people. No matter what kind of work you do, you are in the people business.*

To make more sales, inform more people of your cause, or create more or better job opportunities—increase your circulation. There are many ways of doing this. What's best for you will depend on your situation. We have included specific information within each of the four marketing "scenarios" that follow. We also have included sections on networking and generating publicity in the "Street Smarts" section of "Act III." We encourage you to use these tools to increase your circulation.

Marketing Is a Matter of Organization: "The Delivery"

We will approach the way you organize the delivery of your work in the most general terms by considering the advantages and disadvantages of four broad organizational choices. These are: starting your own business, working freelance, founding a nonprofit organization, and getting a job working for an existing organization.

Scenario I:
Sailing the Entrepreneurship

If you're a self-reliant, self-motivated person who enjoys taking responsibility and making decisions, starting your own business may be your next step. Do you have an idea for a new product or service that you can't wait to take to market? Have you thought of a genuine innovation on an existing product or service? Ideas like these are often the first steps to creating a successful business. The entrepreneur must be passionately committed to her vision and willing to take risks to make it happen. She must be resourceful and able to motivate others—a take-charge kind of person who enjoys challenge and hard work.

Advantages: Starting your own business offers you the freedom to control and market your product or service as you see fit. You enjoy the responsibilities of being your own boss, creating a crack team, and deciding who gets to play. You are able to use your talents to come up with a new and innovative approach to your product or service, and you reap the financial profits that result from your efforts.

Disadvantages: If your business fails, you may be held liable for some or all of its debts. (See page 376.) The success or failure of your new endeavor is all in your hands—including all the management and financial hassles. Running your own business usually entails very long hours and lots of hard work, especially in the beginning.

Scenario II:
Wielding the Freelance

If freedom, flexibility, and creative control over your work are strong values for you, you may want to consider working as a freelance. Many writers, craftsmen, musicians, and artists of all kinds find a freelance structure the most conducive to creative work. It takes a self-disciplined, passionate, and committed person to make it as a freelance. You must believe in yourself and your work enough to survive some rejection, especially in the beginning stages. If you do, you will enjoy the freedom to live your life as you see fit, while building a successful career doing what you enjoy most.

Advantages: The freelance option offers the most freedom to create and control your work. You choose your own hours and work environments. This option also tends to minimize the hassles you'll get from others, since a freelance often spends much of her working time alone. You are free to capitalize on your talents and abilities in the way you see fit.

Disadvantages: Your income as a freelance may be unstable, especially in the beginning. You may have to contend with long periods of reduced income or unemployment. You will not have the security of benefits or retirement plans. Also, the freelance option offers less opportunity for teamwork and the feedback of others on a daily basis.

 Therefore the considerations of the intelligent always include both benefit and harm. As they consider benefit, their work can expand; as they consider harm, their troubles can be resolved.

— Sun Tzu

Scenario III: Crafting the Nonprofit Foundation

If you are committed to working on a particular social, cultural, or environmental issue, you may want to consider founding a nonprofit organization. Building a successful nonprofit organization can be an exciting challenge. It takes vision, creativity, resourcefulness, and strong "people skills." Since nonprofits are cause-driven organizations, formed to benefit others, they provide excellent opportunities for meaningful and rewarding work.

Advantages: Nonprofits often attract committed people who are dedicated to social or cultural change. Working together with those who share a common altruistic purpose offers unparalleled opportunities to experience genuine teamwork and cooperation in the workplace. Creating a nonprofit allows you to follow your purpose-based agenda and to craft solutions for issues that matter to you. You can solicit contributions and enjoy the tax advantages and increased credibility that accrues to nonprofits. People will know that you're not just "in it for the buck."

Disadvantages: You'll put in a lot of time and effort, without making a lot of money (at least in the beginning). You will probably endure some frustration with the apparent insignificance of your efforts. There's lots of rules and regs in the nonprofit sector—you may have to climb a mountain of paperwork to get anything done. You will need to go through the hassle of getting most of your actions approved by your board of directors.

Scenario IV: Landing the Right Job

If you enjoy working in a structured environment and being a team player, if security and stability are important factors in your work life—you are sure to find some challenging opportunities in the job market, provided you are willing to aggressively look until you do.

Advantages: You will enjoy opportunities for advancement within the organization as you "learn the ropes," and you may get a chance to benefit from the training and skill of fellow employees. You'll get a secure paycheck (which definitely makes it easier to budget), and you may get medical and retirement benefits as well.

Disadvantages: You'll have to subordinate a measure of your freedom to the needs of the organization. You'll have to follow someone else's schedule and, usually, answer to a boss. You may not experience much input in the decision-making process involved with your work. You may have to do things that are counter to your purposes or values in order to keep your job.

Note: The pages that follow outline in greater detail the four options of creating your own business, wielding the freelance, creating a nonprofit organization, and getting a job. This will help you get a clearer sense of what avenues are best suited to you at this time.

Success on any major scale requires you to accept responsibility. . . In the final analysis, the one quality that all successful people have . . . is the ability to take on responsibility.
Michael Korda

Getting Organized: Which Way to Go

In considering which of the four options you would like to pursue at this time, the questions that follow may be of assistance to you. Examine the four sets of statements below. If the statement fits you, check "Yes." If it does not, answer "No." Answer as honestly and objectively as possible. See scoring instructions on page 359.

Scenario I—Entrepreneurs

Y/N

1. Having the freedom to create my own work is extremely important to me. _____

2. When I have an idea that I'm excited about, I get everybody around me excited about it too. _____

3. I enjoy aggressively going after what I want. _____

4. When I take on a project, I'm practically married to it until it's done. _____

5. I trust my instincts, and I am able to act decisively. _____

6. I thrive on challenge. _____

7. It's okay with me if people think I'm a little crazy, as long as I believe in what I'm doing. _____

8. I'd say that a natural ability to lead is one of my strongest talents. _____

9. I am prepared to work more than forty hours a week. _____

10. I never let it stop me if I don't know how to do something. I just jump in the middle of it, and pretty soon, I've got it figured out. _____

Scenario II—Freelancers

Y/N

1. The freedom to follow my creative instincts is extremely important to me. _____

2. I do my work because I enjoy it. I'd probably do it whether I was getting paid or not. _____

3. I enjoy working alone—in fact, I thrive on solitude. _____

4. If I'm doing what I love best, I can easily adjust to fluctuations in income. _____

5. It's very important to me to live by my own schedule. _____

6. I have little patience for bureaucracy and red tape. _____

7. I make most of my business decisions intuitively, independent of the feedback of others. _____

8. I don't want to be tied down to any one location. _____

9. I'd say that I possess a good deal of self-discipline. _____

10. I don't want the responsibility or the hassle of managing an organization. _____

 The difficulty in life is the choice.
George Moore

Scenario III—Nonprofit Founders

Y/N

1. Although I am a strong leader, I enjoy teamwork and cooperative decision-making. _____

2. I am able to work cooperatively with a board of directors, staff, and volunteers in order to accomplish my organization's objectives. _____

3. Economic profit is not as important to me as working at something I believe in. _____

4. I have the willingness and the patience to put up with a lot of red tape. _____

5. I am able to work effectively with a variety of viewpoints and agendas while sticking to my organization's purpose and long-term goals. _____

6. Making a difference for others is a very strong value for me. _____

7. I enjoy finding creative ways to fund my organization, and I am willing to do so indefinitely. _____

8. I am able to delegate responsibility in order to accomplish a variety of tasks. _____

9. I enjoy getting people motivated around an idea. _____

10. I am willing to speak out in public for my beliefs and for my organization and to attract media and community attention when necessary to accomplish my goals. _____

Scenario IV—Job Seekers

Y/N

1. The only way I can do my work is as an employee of an existing organization. _____

2. I believe there are organizations already in existence where I could pursue my work purpose in alignment with the company's objectives. _____

3. I like the predictability of a large organization—its policies and opportunities for advancement. _____

4. I believe I could benefit from the training and experience that I would receive by working at a job in my field. _____

5. I do not want to enter into any kind of financial venture that might threaten my ability to maintain my present standard of living. _____

6. I do my best work as a member of a team. _____

7. One of my strongest talents is an ability to be reliable and consistent. _____

8. I like work in which my responsibilities are clearly spelled out for me. _____

9. I want to create a steady, reliable income to support myself while I am training for my chosen field. _____

10. I like to leave work at work. I try to keep my work life and my personal life separate. _____

Now check over your answers, and tally up the number of "Yes" responses in each scenario. If most of your "Yes" answers were in the first scenario, you may prefer to create your own business now or later. If you had more "Yes" responses in the second scenario, you may want to try working as a freelance. If most of your "Yes" answers were in scenario III, you may want to begin your own nonprofit organization. If you had more "Yes" answers in scenario IV, you will probably want to work for an organization that fits your goals.

Personality/Organizational Match

Qualities Important for Individuals Who Want to Start Their Own Business

1. Self-reliant
2. Self-motivated
3. Committed
4. Persuasive
5. Decisive
6. Adventurous
7. Able to motivate others
8. Risk-takers
9. Innovative
10. Quick learners

Qualities Important for Freelancers

1. Creative
2. Intuitive
3. Like to work alone
4. Flexible
5. Independent
6. Self-disciplined
7. Respond well to change
8. Ability to create and market their work
9. Prefer unstructured work environments
10. Acknowledge their own efforts

Qualities Important for Individuals Who Want to Start Nonprofit Organizations

1. Service-oriented
2. Committed
3. Resourceful
4. Persistent
5. Team Players
6. Passionate
7. Patient
8. Good at both long and short-term planning
9. Focused
10. Tolerant

Qualities Important for Individuals Who Want to Work within Existing Organizations

1. Reliable
2. Cooperative
3. Cautious
4. Analytical
5. Well-organized
6. Objective
7. Other-directed
8. Preference for structure
9. Responsive to feedback
10. Steady

 Blessed is he who has found his work. Let him ask no other blessing.

Thomas Carlyle

Your Organization:
To Find It or to Found It

It is a good idea to decide at the outset whether you want to work for yourself or someone else. If you choose to work for someone else, plan on developing your job-hunting skills, not simply as an obligatory nuisance for landing your next job, but as part of a long-term strategy for achieving your life's work. If you plan to work for yourself, start perfecting the entrepreneurial skills you'll need over the course of your work life. It helps in either case to see the development of these skills as part of a long-term process for improving career effectiveness.

The chart on the following page depicts various types of organizational structures and compares them on four key variables: *Independence, Structure, Benefits,* and *Rewards/Performance Measure. Independence* refers to the individual's ability to choose his hours, the kind and quantity of work he will do, the setting that the work is done in, etc. *Structure* refers to the extent to which the organization has formal organizational structure, rules, regulations, policies, etc. *Benefits* refers to those extra-income renumerations, such as sick leave, paid vacations, health care, life insurance, pension plans, vacation, travel, etc. By *Rewards/Performance Measure* (R.P.M.), we mean the degree to which the rewards one experiences (be they monetary or others) are related to their efforts.

Note: The relative rankings given each of the organizational categories are general composite ratings. For particular organizations within the categories, different circumstances may apply. Obviously, for this chart to be entirely accurate, it would have to consider these variables for each organization individually. Take these ratings, then, as general guides to broad organizational categories. You will want to research these variables (and others that are important to you) for specific organizations you are considering.

Man finds the meaning of his human existence in his capacity for decision, in his freedom of choice. It is a dreadful freedom, for it also means responsibility, but without it man would be as nothing.

Will Herberg

Organizational Comparison Chart

	Type of Organization	✓	Primary Market Skill Group	Independence	Structure	Benefits	R.P.M.
Create Your Team	Sole Proprietorship		Entrepreneurial Skills	♦♦♦♦♦	♦	♦	♦♦♦♦♦
	Partnership		Entrepreneurial Skills	♦♦♦♦	♦♦	♦	♦♦♦♦
	Corporation		Entrepreneurial Skills	♦♦♦♦	♦♦♦	♦♦	♦♦♦♦♦
	Nonprofit Corporation		Entrepreneurial Skills	♦♦♦	♦♦♦	♦♦	♦♦♦
	Franchise		Entrepreneurial Skills	♦♦	♦♦♦♦	♦♦♦	♦♦♦♦
Find Your Team	**Commercial Sector**						
	Large		Job-Hunting Skills	♦♦	♦♦♦♦♦	♦♦♦♦	♦♦
	Medium		Job-Hunting Skills	♦♦	♦♦♦♦	♦♦♦	♦♦♦
	Small		Job-Hunting Skills	♦♦♦	♦♦♦	♦♦	♦♦♦
	Public Sector						
	Local		Job-Hunting Skills	♦♦	♦♦♦	♦♦♦	♦♦
	State		Job-Hunting Skills	♦	♦♦♦♦	♦♦♦♦	♦
	National		Job-Hunting Skills	♦	♦♦♦♦♦	♦♦♦♦	♦
	Nonprofit Sector						
	Nonprofit Corporation		Job-Hunting Skills	♦♦♦	♦♦♦	♦♦♦♦	♦♦

Final Selection _____

Starting Your Own Organization

1. **Sole Proprietorship:**   One individual owns and operates the business and has unlimited personal liability for taxes, debts, and legal damages in case of a lawsuit.

2. **Partnership:**   Two or more individuals own and operate the business, dividing all profits and dividing the personal responsibility for all taxes, debts, and legal damages in case of a lawsuit. A general partner(s) may take on a limited partner who does not participate in the business operations but who may invest money in the business and has only limited liability for the business, up to the amount of money he invests.

3. **Corporation:**   A corporation is a legal entity that pays taxes and is liable for its own debts and legal damages, apart from the people who own and operate it.

4. **Nonprofit Corporation:**   A nonprofit corporation is a legal entity, subject to state and federal laws. Some are tax exempt.

5. **Franchise:**   A franchise is typically a business that is owned by an individual but operated as a part of a large chain, with standardized products, services, advertising, trademarks, store appearance, etc.

Working for an Existing Organization

Commercial/Private Sector: A business that is privately (as opposed to governmentally) owned and run for a profit.

1. **Large:** A business with over 2,000 employees.
2. **Medium:** A business with 400 to 2,000 employees.
3. **Small:** A business with less than 400 employees.

Public Sector: An organization that is owned and run by the government.

1. **Local:** An organization run by the city or county government.
2. **State:** An organization run by the state government.
3. **National:** An organization run by the federal government.

Nonprofit Corporation: See point 4 above.

Your Life's Work: Step by Step

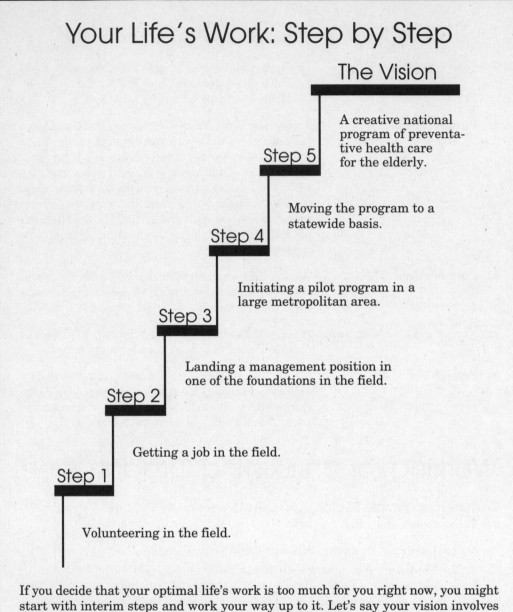

The Vision

Step 5 — A creative national program of preventative health care for the elderly.

Step 4 — Moving the program to a statewide basis.

Step 3 — Initiating a pilot program in a large metropolitan area.

Step 2 — Landing a management position in one of the foundations in the field.

Step 1 — Getting a job in the field.

Volunteering in the field.

If you decide that your optimal life's work is too much for you right now, you might start with interim steps and work your way up to it. Let's say your vision involves a creative approach to health care for the elderly, which you want to introduce on a nationwide basis. Interim-step 1 might be familiarizing yourself with the field through volunteer work. Interim-step 2 might be getting a job working for what you consider to be a state-of-the-art organization in your field. For interim-step 3, you might take a management position in one of the leading foundations in your field. Interim-step 4 might be starting a pilot program in a large metropolitan city. Interim-step 5 might be expanding your program to encompass an entire state. Not giving up, you work on the intermediate steps while keeping your eye on your optimal vision.

Social Change and Organizations

Individuals and organizations are both creators and products of the society in which they operate. Even as the already existing house you move into is probably not the house you would design from scratch, so the society you are born into is probably not your idea of utopia. In an already existing society or house, you must acknowledge the structural limitations of the existing framework. You can redecorate, remodel, add on, adapt, or even abandon the structure. Still, you must in some way reckon with things as they are, even while you are creating changes.

If one does not confront the fact that he is a creator of society, he risks alienation, boredom, and emptiness. On the other hand, if one does not confront the fact that he is a product of society, he risks getting clobbered by it. As a practical matter, we have to deal with many aspects of society that may not be to our liking. For example, like it or not, we live in a money economy. This has far-reaching consequences, many of which the individual cannot directly control. As for organizations, those of any size frequently require other people's money to start and maintain themselves. Little money comes without strings attached. The goals and values of the organization will be influenced to a greater or lesser extent by those from whom it receives money.

Who gives the bread lays down the law.
Spanish Proverb

Efforts to effect (social or technological) change always face the tension between the need to enlist the support of the status quo and the danger of being co-opted by it. Here is the dilemma that all who would innovate must face: on the one hand, to remain true to one's ideals and, on the other hand, to be "relatable" enough to the mainstream that one can have an impact on it. One does not want to be so extreme that he has no influence, nor so relatable that he has nothing new to offer. It helps to have either an intuitive or a cultivated understanding of the existing psycho-techno-culture and its likely evolutionary directions.

For those interested in social change, it is important to realize that the more fundamental the social change your organization proposes, the less likely it is to adopt values that will make it effective within the context of the mainstream culture. To be an effective agent of social change, you have to be in the middle of the field; yet to get in the middle of it, you have to adopt many values of the larger society. There are no easy answers to these problems. Every organization must strike its own balance. The question is really: What are the essentials to cling to, and what are more peripheral matters you can yield on?

The larger your organization becomes, the more likely it is to become like what already exists. In our culture, we tend to think bigger is better. Yet when it comes to social change, bigger is not necessarily more effective. Margaret Mead has remarked: "Never doubt that a small group of thoughtful, committed citizens can change the world. Indeed, it's the only thing that ever has." The analysis of historian Michael H. Hart in *The 100: A Ranking of the Most Influential Persons in History*[5] seems to confirm this observation. Five of his top ten most influential persons made their mark as individuals, not as members or leaders of any groups. These were inventors, explorers, and theorists. The other five were spiritual leaders. Only three of the ten, Mohammed, Buddha, and St. Paul, could be said to be leaders of large organizations, and each of these began with a handfull of followers.

More important than the size of a group is its dedication, or commitment, to purpose. As Louis Ginzberg has put it, "There is no great thought that has become an impelling power in history which has not been espoused at its origin by men [or women] willing to put all their physical and spiritual powers entirely at its service." This is the kind of commitment that catches fire. We tend to forget that political changes like the American Revolution, technological changes like the personal computer, and social changes like the abolition of slavery or women's suffrage began with a relatively few dedicated individuals.

While an organization is relatively small, it can create its own subculture. The larger it gets, the more heavily it becomes influenced by the broader society, and so, the more like it it becomes. The artist often faces the choice between going commercial, i.e., appealing to a wider audience, or developing in such a way that her work is appreciated only by an esoteric few. Similarly, an organization, in moving to a larger size, may risk the very principles and ideals upon which it was founded. This is simply because, as it grows, it becomes increasingly plugged into what already exists. Dynamic organizations tend over time to become sluggish. They tend to lose their original purpose, not to mention spark, and become self-perpetuating bureaucracies.

Walking the line between the ideals that give birth to an organization and the values of the existing psycho-culture affects decisions at every point in the development of an organization. For example, take a business. When it comes to product development, the creator holds certain values with reference to the quality of the product and the need it is intended to serve. Additionally, there are considerations as to how widely the product will sell. These values are often in conflict. Soul searching and thought must be ongoing.

Sailing the Entrepreneurship

Perfect freedom is reserved for the man who lives by his own work and in that work does what he wants to do.
R. G. Collingwood

There is a perception among some that business—any kind of business—is by definition immoral, materialistic, and otherwise "uncool." This conception is probably a holdover from the sixties, when the term "business" came to be synonymous with "selling out." Of course, this is far too simplistic. Many engage in business without selling out, and many more sell out without becoming entrepreneurs. If we accept that "selling out" means forsaking one's integrity and convictions for some apparent short-term gain, it is easy to see that there are many ways to sell out quite apart from business. In this section, we briefly consider the value of the entrepreneur option and what it takes to play. We also provide a series of worksheets to help you think through the preliminary planning work necessary to setting up your new business.

*A true definition of an entre-
preneur comes closer to: A
poet, visionary, or packager
of social change.*
                    Robert Schwartz

To be sure, the business world *does* provide plenty of opportunities for "character
tests." Yet when the character of the
businessperson fails, the fault lies, not with
business per se, but with the individual's
own greed, thirst for power, inhumanity, or
any of a number of other personality flaws.
Business may exaggerate existing flaws,
but it does not create them. If your heart is
true and your principles solid, you needn't
worry that business will corrupt you. In a
sense, you are already "in business."

When we get right down to it, business or
"commerce" means "trade." Of course, you
can trade fairly, or you can cheat. You can
trade quality goods or shoddy goods. You can
trade good service or poor service. You just
can't get away from trading. The products
we need and enjoy come to us by way of
trade, from food and clothing to shelter and
entertainment. Everyone who works for
someone else is in the business of trading
labor for wages. Yet the entrepreneur exercises far greater control than the employee
over what his business does, how it treats its
staff and customers, and the role that it
plays in the community. Many today are
seeking the greater opportunities for service, creativity, and control that going into
business for themselves offers.

In fact, the small business sector is the
most dynamic and fastest growing sector of
the American economy. Small business has
been responsible for creating more than
two-thirds of the new jobs in America over
the last two decades. More than seven hundred thousand new businesses are started
each year. Two-thirds of the new businesses
are owned by women. Clearly, from the
standpoint of economic growth, small busi-

ness is where the action is. In the words of
noted management consultant Peter
Drucker, "The old job creators have actually
lost jobs in these last twenty years." In
Fortune 500 companies and government, at
universities and even hospitals, there are
fewer jobs today. Drucker concludes that
most of the "new jobs must have been created by . . . small and medium-sized businesses, and a great many of them, if not the
majority, *new* businesses that did not even
exist twenty years ago."[1]

What is motivating all of these people to
start their own businesses? For many, opening their own business means a chance to
escape the conventional nine-to-five job rut.
In *Re-Inventing the Corporation,* John
Naisbitt writes: **"The unspoken factor
behind the entrepreneurial boom is
that working for most companies is so
demeaning to the human spirit that
many talented people are forced out
the door.** The only way to have a nurturing
work environment, they reason, is to create
it themselves."[2] (Bold type in original)

In *Growing a Business*, Paul Hawken
concurs, "This movement toward new enterprise must reflect a certain amount of
alienation of the work force from the conditions of their jobs."[3] People who strike out on
their own often find working for themselves
to be more rewarding and meaningful than
the jobs they left behind.

While some few may be motivated by
simple greed, most of today's new entrepreneurs have more interesting reasons for
setting up shop. Small business owners enjoy the satisfaction of offering products and
services they genuinely believe in. They enjoy shaping their businesses to reflect their
social and personal values, setting a tone or
atmosphere for their work lives that they feel
comfortable with. They enjoy making the
decisions about the direction of their businesses and seeing the results of their efforts.

They enjoy the creative opportunities to
experiment, to try out new ideas without
needing bureaucratic approval. These
people are working to be themselves, not to

fit into some giant bureaucracy or to gain the approval of a boss. In addition to providing valuable services, an increasing number of today's new entrepreneurs donate some portion of their profits to charities or causes they believe in. Given all these reasons (and others we haven't the space to discuss), it is not surprising that job satisfaction surveys consistently find that the self-employed are the most likely of any group to report that they are *very happy* in their work.

In the marketplace, new small businesses often have advantages over the larger, well-established corporate institutions. Think of the difference between a fleet of giant luxury liners and a speedboat. When it comes to making a change, the smaller, more maneuverable speedboat has the edge. Like a speedboat, a small business can easily maneuver around the huge corporate boats. It doesn't require the deep waters of enormous capital investment necessary to launch the giant corporate fleets. It can play in the shallow waters of innovation. Consequently, small businesses often discover and develop ideas that larger corporations won't even touch until there is a "proven market."

While the huge corporations battle it out for the deep water of proven markets, small business is creating new ones close to the shore. From this special vantage point, the entrepreneur can feel the pulse of the people and respond more quickly to their special needs, aspirations, and concerns. Large corporations seldom lead the way to innovation, as a General Electric vice president observed: "I know of no original product invention, not even electric shavers or heating pads, made by any of the giant laboratories or corporations . . . The record of the giants is one of moving in, buying out, and absorbing the small creators."[4]

Time and again, small business has brought innovation and invention. Many small businesses have begun as a response to a particular need that was going unmet. The entrepreneur senses a need in the community or nation that no one else sees, or if they do, they lack the creativity and initiative to come up with a way of serving it. Sometimes a small business begins when an individual desires a product or service that no one is providing. She says in effect, "Wouldn't it be great if there was . . . ?" And then she goes on to provide that product or service for others to enjoy.

Today's new entrepreneurs are no stuffed shirts; they are dynamic social innovators living exciting lives on the cutting edge of social and technological transformation. Below you find a list of qualities that make a New Entrepreneur. See if they fit you.

What Makes a New Entrepreneur

Sensitivity To perceive what is needed.

Creativity To conceive of a way of providing it.

Courage To try something new, perhaps even something no one has tried before.

Initiative To act and act and act.

Grit To stick with it when all the people who don't have the above qualities tell you it can't be done.

Magazines and Periodicals of Interest to Entrepreneurs

You may want to subscribe to one or more magazines or periodicals of interest to entrepreneurs. Choose from among:

Business Edge
215 W. Harrison
Seattle, WA 98119

Business Ethics
52 S. 10th St. Ste. 110
Minneapolis, MN 55403

Business Ideas
1051 Bloomfield Ave.
Clifton, NJ 07012

Business Opportunities Journal
P.O. Box 60762
San Diego, CA 92166

Business Week
1221 Avenue of the Americas
New York, MY 10020
www.businessweek.com

Entrepreneur Magazine
P.O. Box 50368
Boulder, CO 80323-0368
www.entrepreneurmag.com

Fortune Magazine
P.O. Box 61490
Tampa, FL 33661-1490
www.fortune.com

Inc.
Subscription Serice Dept.
P.O. Box 51534
Boulder, CO 80323-1534
www.inc.com

Minority Business Entrepreneur
3528 Torrance Blvd. Ste. 101
Torrance, CA 90503

Opportunity
P.O. Box 420199
Palm Coast, FL 32142-9115

Self-Employed Professional
P.O. Box 11668
Riverton, NJ 08076-7268

Selling Magazine
477 Madison Ave.
New York, NY 10022

Small Business Computing
P.O. Box 54756
Boulder, CO 80323-4756

Small Business Journal
407 Vine St. Dept. 189
Cincinnati, OH 45202
www.tsbj.com

Small Business Opportunities
Harris Publications Inc.
1115 Broadway
New York, NY 10160-0397

Success Magazine
P.O. Box 3038
Harlan, IA 51537
www.successmagazine.com

Working Woman
P.O. Box 3276
Harlan, IA 51593-2456

The Ten-Step Business Builder

What follows on the next several pages is a ten-step formula that will help you begin to sharpen your vision of your new business. While this process should not be confused with a formal business plan (see page 384), completing it will begin to put your new business into focus and give you a good idea of what it will take to get it started. Many have found this to be an extremely valuable exercise.

Step 1.   Outline your business: Decide on the products and/or services your new business will offer. What benefits will others derive from these products or services? How will they use them? What are the unique features of your product or service? Who will be your major competitors, and how will you distinguish yourself from them?

Step 2.   Know your market: Zero in on exactly who your potential clients or customers are. Define your market by demographics, geography, and lifestyle interests.

Step 3.   Determine how to reach your market: Next, determine how you will reach your market. In what ways will you advertise and promote your business? Will you advertise in newspapers or use direct mail marketing? How will you deliver your products or services? For example, will you establish a retail store or work from a home office?

Step 4.   Assemble a team: Will you have employees? If so, at what levels of responsibility? What qualities and skills will you want from them? What outside professionals will you want on your team (for example, lawyers, accountants, advertising agencies, and so on)?

Step 5.   Decide on a legal structure: Determine what kind of legal entity your business will be. Will it be a sole proprietorship, partnership, or corporation?

Step 6.   Determine the cost of doing business: Next, assess the one-time costs associated with the start-up of your business as well as its regular monthly operating expenses.

Step 7.   Raise money: Develop strategies for obtaining the necessary financial resources to launch your business and keep it afloat through the difficult early years. Will you be looking for loans, partners, or equity investors?

Step 8.   Establish a system to monitor your dough: Determine how you will keep track of your money. What inventory, accounting, or bookkeeping procedures will you employ?

Step 9.   Cut through the red tape jungle: Make sure that your new business will be on solid legal footing with all the appropriate government regulatory and tax agencies.

Step 10. Concentrate your energy and resources: Finally, consider how you see your business growing over the years. What specific objectives would you like to accomplish in the first year? In the first three years? And so on.

Step One: Outline Your Business

1. What products or services do you want to offer? _____
   _____

2. What benefits do your products or services offer? _____
   _____

3. How will your product or service be used? _____

4. When (from the customer's point of view) will the product or service be used?
   _____
   _____

5. What unique features can you bring to the design, delivery, or marketing of this
   product or service? _____
   _____

6. Who will be your major competition? _____
   _____

7. What are their strengths? _____
   _____

8. What are their weaknesses? _____
   _____

9. How will you distinguish yourself from the competition? _____
   _____

10. If product, will you manufacture it yourself? How? Will you buy ready-made
    products from suppliers? Who? Where? _____
    _____

The empires of the future are empires of the mind.

Winston Churchill

Step Two: Know Your Market

Who Is Your Market?

Identify potential buyers of your product or service according to the following criteria:

Demographics

Age	_____	Ethnicity	_____
Sex	_____	Family size	_____
Socio-economic level	_____	Marital status	_____
Education	_____	Profession	_____
Religion	_____	Income	_____

Geography

Neighborhoods	_____	Regional	_____
Segments of cities	_____	Multistate	_____
Citywide	_____	Nationwide	_____
Countywide	_____	Multinational	_____
Segments of states	_____	Global	_____
Statewide	_____	By climate	_____
Bicoastal	_____	By terrain	_____

Lifestyle

Activities	_____	Interests	_____
Values	_____	Opinions	_____

Using the variables above (or any others pertinent to your ends), identify your market.

_____

_____

_____

_____

_____

 The difference between intelligence and education is this: Intelligence will make you a good living.
                                        Charles Kettering

Step Three:
Determine How to Reach Your Market

Promotion: How will you get the attention of your market? Check the applicable methods:

_____ Word of mouth	_____ Flyers
_____ Newspapers	_____ Brochures
_____ Magazines	_____ Promotional speeches
_____ Television	_____ Demonstrations
_____ Radio	_____ Introductory seminars
_____ Trade publications	_____ Writing books and
_____ Outside advertising	publications
(Signs, billboards, etc.)	_____ Direct mail
_____ Trade shows	_____ Telephone directories
_____ Publicity	_____ Internet

Delivery: How will you distribute your product or service to the market? Check the applicable methods:

_____ Retail	_____ Trade shows
_____ Wholesale	_____ Field sales force
_____ Mail order	_____ Manufacturing representatives
_____ Multilevel marketing	_____ Independent agents
_____ Franchising	_____ Sell to manufacturer
_____ Telemarketing	_____ Web site

 A wise man will make more opportunities than he finds.

Francis Bacon

Step Four: Assemble a Team

Put together a team of committed, competent people who agree on the purpose of the organization. Listed below are important qualities to look for in building your team.

Management Team

1. Agreement on purpose
2. Complementary skills
3. Complementary personalities
4. Highly motivated/dedicated
5. Willing to risk getting less in the beginning for more in the end

Professional Support Team

1. Credibility
2. Professional standing
3. Personal rapport
4. Prestige in the community
5. Support for your objectives

Staff Team

1. Able to cooperate
2. Self-reliant
3. Positive
4. Growth-oriented
5. Willing to work long hours

In your view, what is important that members of your team understand to be the purpose of your organization? _____
_____

What undeveloped skills can you compensate for by having an individual on your team who is strong in that area? _____
_____

What weaknesses in your personality can you compensate for by having an individual on your team who is strong in that area? _____
_____

What is it about the concept and purpose of your organization that will attract highly dedicated individuals? _____
_____

What is it that you can offer the people on your team that will entice them to want to give their all (e.g., the opportunity to make a significant contribution, challenge, training and skill development, a financial stake in the organization, the opportunity to work with the very best, camaraderie, etc.)?

_____

 Your associates can be priceless.
Napoleon Hill

What will be the initial size of your team? _____

How many individuals will you require at each of the following levels?

_____ Ownership   _____ Supervisory   _____ Management   _____ Workers

Professional Support Team

Identify the following:

Accountant   _____

Advertising Agent   _____

Attorney   _____

Banker   _____

Business Consultant   _____

Insurance Agent   _____

Other   _____

Step Five: Decide on a Legal Structure

1. Sole Proprietorship

Pros: You have total control over it. Simple and very easy to start. Doesn't need to be registered with the state.

Cons: Personal liability. Limits access to capital.

2. Partnership

Pros: Simple, relatively easy to start. Doesn't need to be registered with the state. (You will probably want a partnership agreement prepared by an attorney.) Greater access to capital than with a sole proprietorship.

Cons: You are personally liable and may be vulnerable to lawsuits. A partnership usually terminates when one of the partners dies. Potential for conflict. (Don't start a partnership unless you really know and trust the individual(s) involved.)

3. Corporation

Pros: Limited liability for debts, taxes, and litigation. Continuous existence.

Cons: More difficult to start. Many corporate actions must be formalized by the board of directors. Legal fees involved. Must be registered with the state.

Investigate further; then determine the type of legal structure you would like to use.

Note: Be advised that tax consequences of the various legal structures are significant and should play a role in your decision. See a Certified Public Accountant for up-to-date details.

Step Six: Determine the Cost of Doing Business

One-Time Start-Up Costs

Equipment _____

Furnishings _____

Renovations _____

Licenses, Permits, Fees _____

Professional Services _____

Start-Up Inventory _____

Rent Prepayments _____

Insurance Prepayments _____

Special Advertising or Promotion _____

Printing Stationery, Forms, etc. _____

Utility Deposits and Installation _____

Start-Up Cash _____

Other _____ _____

Other _____ _____

Other _____ _____

Total _____

Monthly Operating Costs

Rent _____ Postage and Freight _____

Utilities _____ Insurance _____

Advertising/Promotion _____ Loan Payments _____

Professional Fees _____ Monthly Payments _____

Wage/Salaries _____ Bad Debts _____

Employee Benefits _____ Transportation _____

Taxes _____ Printing _____

Inventory _____ Other _____ _____

Supplies _____ Other _____ _____

Total _____

Step Seven: Raise Money

Where to Get the Money

1. Start on a shoestring and slowly build.
2. Acquire a business on a no-cash basis.
3. Friends and family
4. Banks
5. Savings and loans companies
6. The SBA (Small Business Administration)
7. Venture capitalists
8. Silent partnerships
9. Organize a syndication
10. Small business investment corporations
11. State development commissions
12. Credit unions
13. Investment consultants (can help you find investors)
14. Suppliers (can give you credit)
15. Foundations

Approaching Potential Investors

The first step to approaching potential investors is to decide what kind of investment you want: a security-based investment, an equity-based investment, or a purpose-based investment. Your process will vary according to the avenues you choose.

Security-Based Investments: A security-based investment is essentially a loan. The prime consideration for this type of lender is security. Your task is to demonstrate that loaning you money is a safe proposition. Do this by convincing them that:

1. Your venture is based on solid planning, will be well managed, and has a high probability of success, in other words, that it makes economic sense. Be well prepared. Go with your business plan in hand, and make sure that all of the marketing and financial projections are realistic and solid. Bring along other important financial data, for example, recent balance sheets, profit/loss statements, etc.

2. You have sufficient collateral in case the unforeseen occurs. Some common security-based investors include: banks, savings and loans, credit unions, thrifts, small business investment corporations, friends and family. (Be clear and be careful!)

Equity-Based Investments: Equity-based investors want a piece of the action. They become part owners of your business, for example, as general or limited partners or corporate shareholders. The equity investor incurs greater risk than the debt investor, with the prospect of realizing greater profit when the business succeeds. Understand their point of view. First convince them, if you honestly can, that they have little or nothing to lose. Then convince them how much they have to gain. (Again, approach with a realistic and well-prepared business plan.) Your task with the equity investor is to convince him that your idea is viable, marketable, and will realize sizeable profits for him. Some examples are: venture capitalists, silent partnerships, syndications, small business investment corporations, friends, and family. (Be clear and be careful!)

Purpose-Based Investments: Private foundations, public agencies, and individual philanthropists invest in projects that reflect their purposes, values, and objectives. These investments can take the form of no-strings grants, low interest loans, free services, or other assistance. Some organizations and individuals will invest directly in a profit-making business without giving prime consideration to either security or equity. Others will only invest in a charitable or nonprofit enterprise. You may still be able to obtain monies from these investors by gaining the sponsorship of a nonprofit organization that receives the money on your behalf. They then pass the money along to you for a nominal service charge. Your primary task is to convince these investors that what you are planning to do furthers their purpose-based investment objectives and that your organization is a credible and responsible one that will reflect well on them. Foundations, individual philanthropists, the SBA (Small Business Administration), State Development Commissions, and a host of other government agencies are potential sources. Additional sources might include churches, universities, friends, and family.

Now indicate the funding vehicles you plan to employ: _____

_____

_____

_____

_____

Whom will you approach?   By when?

_____   _____

_____   _____

_____   _____

_____   _____

"Raise Money" Sources

Check out the Small Business Administration website (www.sbaonline.sba.gov), a fabulous resource for anyone interested in starting and funding their own business. It has information, loan applications, and more.

Financing Your Business Dreams with Other People's Money: How and Where to Find Money for Start-Up and Growing Businesses. Lacy, Harold. Traverse City, Mich.: Rhodes and Easton, 1998.

Guerilla Financing: Alternatives to Finance Any Small Business. Blechman, Bruce Jan, and Jay Conrad Levinsen. Boston: Houghton Mifflin, 1992.

Starting on a Shoestring: Building a Business without a Bank Roll. Goldstein, Arnold S. New York: John Wiley & Sons, 1995.

Step Eight:
Establish a System to Monitor Your Dough

Here is a simple system for keeping track of your money when you're first starting your business. (Adapted from *The Small Time Operator* by Bernard Kamoroff.[5])

1. Open a business bank account.

2. Deposit all of your income. That way you'll know exactly how much money you're taking in.

3. Pay all bills by check. That way you'll know exactly what your expenditures are.

4. Never use the business account for anything else. That way you'll be able to keep track of your business income and expenditures.

5. Decide whether you want to use a cash or accrual accounting system. If you use a cash accounting system, you record income when you receive payments and expenditures when you make payments. In an accrual accounting system, you record income and expenses at the time of the transaction, whether or not money has physically changed hands. Though a cash accounting system is simpler, the accrual system gives you a more complete picture of your finances. See an accountant for advice on your accounting system.

Additional Financial Sources

201 Great Ideas for Your Small Business. Applegate, Jane. Princeton: Bloomberg Press, 1998.

Accounting and Recordkeeping Made Easy for the Self-Employed. Fox, Jack. New York: John Wiley & Sons, 1994.

Accounting for the New Business: The Strategies and Practices You Need to Account for Your Success. Malburg, Christopher R. Holbrook, Mass.: Adams Media Corporation, 1997.

Basic Accounting for the Small Business. Cornish, Clive G. Bellingham, Wash.: Self-Council Press Inc., 1992.

Getting Yours: The Complete Guide to Government Money. Lesko, Matthew. New York: Penguin, 1987.

Pratt's Guide to Venture Capital Sources. Daniel Bokser, ed. Wellesley Hills, Mass.: Capital Publishing. Published annually.

The Small Time Operator. Kamoroff, Bernard. Laytonville, Calif.: Bell Springs Publishing, 1997.

Step Nine: Cut Through the Red Tape Jungle

There may be a red tape jungle separating you from what you want to do. Think of it as an obstacle course set up to test the intensity of your desire and your willingness to go the extra mile to make your work happen. Here are just a few of the red tape items you may want to consider.

Business Identity: Almost without exception, you will need to obtain a business license from the city and/or county in which you intend to run your organization. You will need to file for an employer ID number or tax ID number from the IRS in order to open a bank account for your organization. Articles of incorporation will need to be filed for profit and nonprofit corporations. You will need to file a fictitious name statement if you call your business by a name other than your own surname. After completing the necessary research, indicate the red tape obstacles you need to overcome to establish your business identity.

_____

_____

_____

Regulations: You will need to check with your city, county, state, and federal governments to make certain that your organization complies with all of their regulations. Some of these may include: zoning regulations, building codes, health codes, land use restrictions, and special licenses and permits which your state and/or federal government may require that are unique to the product or service you are providing. After completing the necessary research, indicate the steps you need to take to ensure that you are in compliance with all pertinent laws and regulations.

_____

_____

_____

Taxes: Consult a tax accountant and make sure that you are aware of and pay all necessary local, state, and federal taxes. These include, but are not limited to: income tax, self-employment tax, sales tax, property tax, payroll tax, federal unemployment tax, state unemployment tax, social security, federal excise taxes, etc. After completing the necessary research, indicate the red tape obstacles you need to overcome to ensure that you are paying all relevant taxes and paying no more than your fair share. _____

_____

_____

 The art of living is more like wrestling than dancing.

Marcus Aurelius

Insurance: Consult an independent professional insurance consultant who will go over with you what insurance coverage is mandatory and what is highly advisable for your particular needs. Armed with this information, you are then ready to approach an insurance agent to purchase the insurance you need. After completing the necessary research, indicate the steps you need to take to ensure that you are properly insured. _____

_____

_____

_____

Employees: As soon as you hire your first employee (or in the case of a corporation, if you are an employee), you geometrically increase the amount of red tape you will need to wade through. Some areas to be aware of include: social security tax and federal income tax withholding, payroll tax, state and federal unemployment tax, workman's compensation insurance, federal OSHA (Occupational Safety and Health Act of 1970) record-keeping requirements, as well as pension plans, welfare plans, federal wage and hour laws, and fair employment practices. Once again, we urge you to seek the help of a qualified professional in determining how best to meet these requirements. After completing the necessary research, indicate the steps you need to take to ensure that you are complying with all existing laws and regulations with regard to employees.

_____

_____

_____

_____

Miscellaneous Red Tape: Include any additional action steps necessary to be on top of any red tape requirements not listed above.

_____

_____

_____

_____

 The entrepreneur is essentially a visualizer and an actualizer. He can visualize something, and when he visualizes it he sees exactly how to make it happen.

Robert Schwartz

Step Ten:
Concentrate Your Energy and Resources

Grow at a pace you're comfortable with. Seize opportunities while operating from a solid base. Understand that there are advantages to starting small. It allows you to perfect your product or service and your delivery systems before you try to market them on a wide scale. Determine realistic growth projections for the next five years.

Where I want my business to be in one year:

_____

_____

_____

Where I want my business to be in two years:

_____

_____

_____

Where I want my business to be in three years:

_____

_____

_____

Where I want my business to be in four years:

_____

_____

_____

Where I want my business to be in five years:

_____

_____

_____

 To climb steep hills requires a slow pace at first.
Shakespeare

Create a Business Plan

Why Do You Need a Business Plan?

1. A business plan helps you clarify the exact nature of your business and how you plan to develop it. It is a road map from where you are now to where you want to be—in business. It helps you mark out your objectives and stay on course as you move toward them.

2. A business plan is a tool to attract investors. Your well-thought-out business plan can stimulate potential investors to provide you with the seed money you may need to launch your business.

What Is in a Business Plan?

While business plans vary in format, the four parts below are basic to all.

Summary: The first part of a business plan summarizes the three parts that are to follow, namely: the business (operations), the marketing plan, and relevant financial data. It gives the reader "the plan in a capsule."

The Business: This section describes your business operations, including: the goods and/or services you will provide, the legal entity (sole proprietorship, partnership, corporation, etc.), the management team, (including résumés of the key players), your staffing plan, your professional support team, the physical facilities of your business, the process and procedures by which your business will run, and an overall scheme of your goals and objectives.

The Market: This section contains your marketing plan, the most essential part of your business plan. Your marketing plan will include a description of the market (what's out there) and your place in it, observable trends in the market, forecasts for the future, and the specific individuals, groups, or organizations that you intend to sell to (your target markets). Additionally, you will describe pricing policies, sales terms, customer service policies, methods of sales and distribution, advertising and promotional strategies, and all other relevant marketing data.

Finances: This section includes a budget for implementing the plans you have made in your business and marketing sections. It details where you expect to get your money from, how much you expect to make, where the proceeds of your business will go, and how much your business would need to make in order to break even. This section will also include a proposal to your investors: What you want from them, what they can expect to gain, and exactly where they would fit into your plans.

Writing Your Business Plan

We recommend that you read several books on writing a business plan before you attempt to write one. You may want to seek the help of professional business consultants, lawyers, tax accountants, and market research firms in the preparation of your plan. If you can't afford professional assistance, contact the Service Corps of Retired Executives (SCORE) through your local Small Business Administration office or via their Web site (www.score.org). While it is helpful to consult experts, we recommend that you do the bulk of the work yourself. That way you will get full value out of your plan, both as a road map for action and as an investment tool. The effort you put into making your business plan the best it can be will pay off both when you approach potential investors and when you finally get down to business.

"Sailing the Entrepreneurship" Sources

Business Plan

Anatomy of a Business Plan. Pinson, Linda, and Jerry Jinnett. Chicago: Upstart Publishing Co., 1996.

The Business Planning Guide. Bangs, David H. Chicago: Upstart Publishing Co., 1996.

The Complete Book of Business Plans. Covello, Joseph A., and Brian J. Hazelgren. Naperville, Ill.: Sourcebooks Trade, 1994.

The Ernst and Young Business Plan Guide. Seigel, Eric S., Brian R. Ford, and Jay M. Bornstein. New York: John Wiley & Sons, 1993.

How to Prepare and Present a Business Plan. Mancuso, Joseph R. Englewood Cliffs, N.J.: Prentice-Hall, 1992.

Entrepreneurship

101 Successful Businesses You Can Start on the Internet. Janal, Daniel S. New York: John Wiley & Sons, 1997.

199 Great Home Businesses You Can Start (And Succeed in for Under $1,000). Hicks, Tyler Gregory. Rocklin, Calif.: Prima Publications, 1992.

1001 Ways to Market Yourself and Your Small Business. Shaw, Lisa. New York: Perigee Books, 1997.

Adams Streetwise Small Business Start-Up. Adams, Bob. Holbrook, Mass.: Adams Media Corp, 1996.

Disclosing New Worlds: Entrepreneurship, Democratic Action, and the Cultivation of Solidarity. Spinosa, Charles, Fernando Flores, and Hubert L. Dreyfus. New York: John Wiley & Sons, 1997.

The E-Myth Revisited: Why Most Small Businesses Don't Work and What to Do About It. Gerber, Michael E. New York: HarperCollins Publishers, 1995.

Encyclopedia of Entrepreneurs. Hallett, Anthony, and Diane Hallett. New York: John Wiley & Sons, 1997. Inspiring stories of entrepreneurial success.

Entrepreneuring: The 10 Commandments for Building a Growth Company. Brandt, Steven C. Friday Harbor, Wash.: Archipelago Publishers, 1997.

Growing a Business. Hawken, Paul. New York: Simon & Schuster, 1987.

Inc. Yourself: How to Profit By Setting Up Your Own Corporation. McQuown, Judith H. New York: HarperBusiness, 1995.

Innovation and Entrepreneurship. Drucker, Peter F. New York: HarperBusiness, 1993.

Kiss Off Corporate America: A Young Professional's Guide to Independence. Kivirist, Lisa. Kansas City, Mo.: Andrews & McMeel Publishing, 1998.

Making a Living without a Job: Winning Ways for Creating Work that You Love. Winter, Barbara J. New York: Bantam, 1993.

Running a One Person Business. Whitmeyer, Claude, and Salli Rasberry. Berkeley: Ten Speed Press, 1994.

Secrets of Self-Employment. Edwards, Paul, and Sarah Edwards. New York: Putnam, 1996.

Sister CEO: The Black Woman's Guide to Starting Her Own Business. Broussard, Cheryl D. New York: Viking Books, 1997.

Small Business Sourcebook. Detroit: Gale Research Co. Published annually in October.

Visionary Business. Allen, Marc. Novato, Calif.: New World Library, 1997.

The Way of the Guerilla. Levinson, Jay Conrad. Boston: Houghton Mifflin Co., 1997.

Working Free: Practical Alternatives to the Nine to Five Job. Applegath, John. New York: Amacom, 1982.

Legal

155 Legal Do's (and Dont's) for the Small Business. Adame, Paul. James E. Gray & Associates, 1996.

How to Form Your Own Corporation without a Lawyer for Under $75.00. Nicholas, Ted. Chicago: Upstart Publishing Co., 1996.

Management

Enlightened Leadership. Oakley, Ed, and Doug Krug. New York: Fireside, 1994.

The Fifth Discipline: The Art and Practice of the Learning Organization. Senge, Peter M. New York: Doubleday, 1994.

In Search of Excellence. Peters, Thomas J., and Robert H. Waterman, Jr. New York: Warner Books, 1988.

Leader's: The Strategies for Taking Charge. Bennis, Warren, and Burt Nanus. New York: HarperBusiness, 1997.

Management: Tasks, Responsibilities, Principles. Drucker, Peter F. New York: HarperBusiness, 1993.

Principle Centered Leadership. Covey, Stephen R. New York: Fireside, 1992.

Synchronicity: The Inner Path of Leadership. Jawarski, Joseph, and Betty S. Flowers. San Francisco: Berrett-Koehler Publishers, 1998.

Marketing

10 Secrets of Marketing Success. Crandell, Rick, ed. Corte Madera, Calif.: Select Press, 1997.

301 Do-It-Yourself Marketing Ideas. Decker, Sam, ed. Boston: Inc. Publishing, 1997.

 Experience is the best of school masters, only the school fees are heavy.

Thomas Carlyle

The Advertising Handbook for Small Business. Dennison, Dell. Bellingham, Wash.: Self Counsel Press Inc., 1994.

AMA Complete Guide to Small Business Marketing. Cook, Kenneth J. Lincolnwood, Ill.: NTC Business Books, 1994.

Guerrilla Marketing: Secrets for Making Big Profits in Your Small Business. Levinson, Jay Conrad. Boston: Houghton Mifflin Co., 1993.

Marketing without Advertising. Phillips, Michael, and Robert Rasberry. Berkeley: Nolo Press, 1997.

Positioning: The Battle for Your Mind. Ries, Al, and Jack Trout. New York: Warner, 1996.

Sales Sources

The Greatest Salesman in the World. Mandino, Og. New York: Bantam, 1987.

How I Raised Myself from Failure to Success in Selling. Bettger, Frank. Englewood Cliffs, N.J.: Prentice-Hall, 1992.

How to Master the Art of Selling. Hopkins, Tom. New York: Warner Books, 1994.

Non-Manipulative Selling. Alessandra, Anthony J. et al. New York: Fireside, 1992.

The One-Minute Sales Person. Johnson, Spencer. New York: Avon, 1991.

Sales Magic: Revolutionary New Techniques that will Double Your Sales Volume in 21 Days. Johnson, Kerry L. New York: Quill, 1995.

Sales Negotiation Skills That Sell. Kellar, Robert E. New York: Amacom, 1996.

Sales Power: The Silva Mind Method for Sales Professionals. Silva, Jose. New York: Berkeley Publishing Group, 1994.

Selling for People Who Hate to Sell. Massie, Brigid McGrath. Rocklin, Calif.: Prima Publications, 1996.

Selling the Dream: How to Promote Your Product, Company, or Ideas—And Make a Difference—Using Everyday Evangelism. Kawasaki, Guy. New York: HarperBusiness, 1992.

Selling the Invisible: A Field Guide to Modern Marketing. Beckwith, Harry. New York: Warner Books, 1998.

Zig Ziglar's Secrets of Closing the Sale. Ziglar, Zig. New York: Berkeley Publishing Group, 1987.

 Our greatest glory is not in never falling, but in rising every time we fall.
Confucius

Internet Resources for Small Business

Small Business Focus (Search Engine)   www.sbfocus.com

This unique and powerful search engine links to hundreds of Web sites of relevance to entrepreneurs (and would-be entrepreneurs). You can bring direction and focus to your research efforts by making this search engine your first stop for business information. From business plans to advertising, marketing to accounting—a wealth of information is at your fingertips.

U. S. Small Business Administration   www.sbaonline.sba.gov

At this Web site, you can tap into the vast and varied resources of the U.S. Small Business Administration, a government agency created by Congress in 1953 to promote the success of America's entrepreneurs and small business enterprises. This site offers general information on starting and running a business, as well as detailed information on an array of programs offered by the SBA. You can locate regional offices throughout the U.S. and its territories or even fill out a loan application online. This site also links to special sub-offices within the SBA.

The Entrepreneurial Edge Online   www.edgeonline.com

Well-rounded and user-friendly, this Web site is chock full of helpful news, facts, information, and advice—business resources of all kinds. One terrific feature is its "Business Toolbox," in which you'll find training modules that take you step by step through the procedures of marketing, managing, promoting, and expanding your business—in addition to self-calculating financial management and assessment worksheets. True to its name, this site really can give your business an edge. Great links!

National Association for the Self-Employed   www.membership.com/nase

The National Association for the Self-Employed (NASE) was founded in 1981 when a group of small-business owners banded together to form a trade association that could wield the purchasing power of a large corporation. Now the largest association of its kind, NASE is able to provide an impressive list of benefits to its members in addition to advocating legislation favorable to small enterprise. (Membership fees are currently less than one hundred dollars a year.) This site includes a business reference area, updates on pending legislation affecting small business, a library of news releases on issues impacting small business, a small-business showcase, an online edition of their magazine *Self-Employed America*, and a comprehensive directory of links to small-business Web sites.

The Entrepreneur's Corner Office   http://catalog.com/corner

No need to go it alone. Visit this informal chat room when you want to meet with other entrepreneurs to brainstorm or exchange ideas.

SHBBL:
Small and Home Based Business Links   www.bizoffice.com

This site offers a number of opportunities for the self-employed or potentially self-employed through links to various franchises, business opportunities, multi-level marketing programs, business services, and marketing sites. It has its own "library" with dozens of business-related articles as well as a "Talkboard" for the exchange of information and ideas. It also provides links to business-related news groups and to general information and reference sites to assist you in your research.

The Business Forum Online™   www.businessforum.com

This Web site provides information and resources of specific interest to small companies, start-ups, and entrepreneurs. Their "Internal Index" offers a collection of articles directed to and concerning entrepreneurs and owner/managers of emerging businesses. The "External Index" links to informational and professional resources throughout the world.

National Small Business Development Center www.smallbiz.suny.edu

This office provides research support to the Small Business Administration's network of Small Business Development Centers throughout the United States and its territories. By contacting the Small Business Development Center in your community, you can utilize this formidable information clearinghouse to find the answers to your most difficult, complicated, or obscure questions relating to small business—for free.

Price Waterhouse National Venture Capital Survey   www.pw.com/vc

The Price Waterhouse Survey Research Center gathers and analyzes investment data from venture capital firms throughout the U.S. and publicizes the results in a quarterly study. You can review the results of their studies on this Web site. Good research site for information on venture capital sources you want to approach.

Research Institute for Small & Emerging Business   www.riseb.org

The Research Institute for Small and Emerging Business is a nonprofit research and educational organization that disseminates information pertaining to small business to policy makers, the media, and various groups and individuals working to promote the interests of the entrepreneurial segment. In addition to conducting research and publicizing their findings, this organization provides technical assistance to small business owners through seminars, publications, hotlines, research, and other services.

Small Business Advancement National Center   www.sbaer.uca.edu

The Small Business Advancement National Center assists entrepreneurs and small business owners through business counseling, training, and education via:

the Internet, conferences, distance learning, newsletters, seminars, camps, internships, and international exchanges. The Small Business Advancement Electronic Resource serves as a link among small business owners, entrepreneurs, foundations, educational institutions, associations, international partners, and local, state, and federal government. It also houses an extensive database of up-to-date information and research pertinent to small business and entrepreneurship.

MIT Enterprise Forum   http://web.mit.edu/entforum/www

The MIT Enterprise Forum supports the formation and growth of technology-based companies through educational programs and networking opportunities. This site includes articles on a variety of topics of interest to small business owners. It also includes online links to eighteen local chapters around the country.

**SBA Office of Women's
Business Ownership**   www.sba.gov/womeninbusiness

A branch of the Small Business Administration, this office administers an array of services and resources for women who own or would like to start small business ventures. Their Web site features a directory of Women's Business Centers throughout the United States that offer financial, management, marketing, and technical assistance to female business owners. It also links to the Online Women's Business Center, which provides training, advice, and counseling as well as a comprehensive database with information on business principles and practices, management, marketing, public relations, finance, technological tools, procurement, mentoring, networking, and more. This site also has links to lending programs and venture capital resources, as well as to a number of related SBA services.

SCORE   www.score.org

SCORE—the Service Corps of Retired Executives—is a nonprofit association working in conjunction with the SBA to provide education and resources to promote the formation, growth, and success of small business nationwide. Working and retired executives and business owners donate their time and expertise to provide free counseling and low-cost workshops via local chapters throughout the United States and its territories. This Web site assists you in finding the SCORE chapter nearest you. The SCORE CyberChapter lets you establish a confidential e-mail dialog with a SCORE business counselor anywhere in the country.

Business Resource Center   www.morebusiness.com

This online small business consulting office publishes daily business news as well as tips for starting and running your business. It also includes templates and worksheets for business plans, marketing plans, business checklists, press releases, and business agreements. It provides opportunities for interaction through discussion groups, a free e-mail newsletter, a Q & A feature, and links to other business sites.

Self-Employment and the Jeffersonian Ideal

America at its inception—Hamilton and Jefferson debate the future of the new nation. Hamilton wants an urban country with a strong centralized government, a sort of aristocracy of the merchant class. Jefferson wants a land of independent farmers. The farmers would control property, and with it, the means of subsistence. They would be free of the need to sell their labor for wages. Their political strength would come from their economic independence. Of course, our country has evolved along the Hamiltonian model. We are an urban nation with a strong central government. While as late as 1900, 60 percent of the nation's population were living an agrarian lifestyle, today less than 3 percent are independent farmers.

Yesterday's independent farmer has hired himself out to earn his keep and buy his consumer goods. Today his wife is selling her services as well. The landholding farmer is already quaint history in the developed world and is becoming rarer and rarer in the undeveloped world in its rush to modernize. Today's closest facsimile to the Jeffersonian free man is the self-employed individual. Of course, he (or she—today most new businesses are started by women) still has to deal with the bureaucratic red tape, but he is free to choose his work and make the decisions that affect it.

When men and women are asked to indicate the career roles they find most attractive, they come up with very different choices—except, that is, for the number one position. Both men and women choose working for themselves as the most attractive career option. Apparently, this is with good reason. In a recent Gallup poll, 58 percent of all people who work for themselves reported that they are "very happy" in their work, while only 35 percent of those who worked for others gave a similar response.

Still, it would be wrong to think of self-employment as a panacea or an escape from discipline. To give up the discipline of the time clock is to assume the discipline of capital acquisition, of government red tape, of client needs, of operational expenses, of management. To escape the trials of having a boss is to embrace the trials of being a boss or of experimenting with co-operative management styles.

It would probably be a mistake to think of self-employment as working for oneself. One is working for clients or customers, for the government, for the bank, for the respect and acceptance of the community. Much of the freedom of self-employment is theoretical. Theoretically, the self-employed person can choose not to show up for work, but in all likelihood, he will be working harder and longer than when he was employed by others. Only if his business is very small or very large can he expect greater leisure time. While the self-employed person may not enjoy a great deal more free time, he does have a great deal more control over his destiny. He controls the purpose, objectives, and performance of his company. With control comes the responsibility for making decisions and for enjoying their consequences. In other words, the freedom to live life as you choose.

Over 200 Businesses You Can Start with Little or No Money

Below is a list of ideas for starting businesses or freelance operations with little or no money. Many are ideas for interim ways of making money while you train and prepare for the work you truly want to do. Some have long-term career potential.

1. Abstract or technical writing
2. Ad agency
3. Aerobic instructor
4. Air conditioning and heating repair services
5. Aquarium service
6. Astrology
7. Auctioneer
8. Auto detailing
9. Balloon design and delivery
10. Basket weaving
11. Bed and breakfast reservation service
12. Bicycle repair and sales
13. Bicycle touring
14. Blind cleaning
15. Boat maintenance
16. Boat painting
17. Bridal consulting
18. Burglar alarm sales and installation
19. Business consulting
20. Business janitorial services
21. Cake delivery
22. Car alarm installer
23. Care of horses and other animals
24. Care of the disabled
25. Care of the elderly
26. Career counselor
27. Caricaturist
28. Carpet cleaning
29. Cartoon map publishing
30. Catering truck
31. Catering
32. Ceiling cleaning
33. Child care
34. Child-care referral and consulting
35. Children's party planning
36. Chimney sweep
37. Christmas lighting design, installation and removal
38. Christmas tree lot
39. Clown
40. Collection agency
41. College campus tours
42. Commercial freelance writing
43. Companion to the elderly or disabled
44. Computer consultant
45. Computer disk repair
46. Consignment store
47. Consumer research and protection service
48. Cooking classes
49. Costume rentals
50. Costume sales
51. Crafts businesses
52. Dance instructor
53. Dating service
54. Desktop publishing service
55. Dog grooming
56. Dog training
57. Drafting and blueprint making
58. Drapery cleaning
59. Drywaller
60. Editing and proofreading service
61. Embroidery

62. Errand service
63. Etiquette training
64. Event planning
65. Financial planning services
66. Finder's fee service
67. First aid instructor
68. Flea market sales
69. Flower stands
70. Foreign language instruction
71. Fundraising consultant
72. Furniture refinishing
73. Furniture repair
74. Garage sale organizer
75. Gardener
76. Gift basket maker
77. Glass tinters
78. Grant writing consultant
79. Graphic design services
80. Greeting card sending service
81. Gutter cleaning
82. Handyman referral service
83. Handyman
84. Herb farming
85. Home inspection service
86. House cleaning
87. House painting
88. Housesitting
89. Ice cream truck
90. Image consultant
91. Import products
92. In-home child care and daycare
93. In-home electronics assembly
94. Indexing
95. Information and research services
96. Information brokering
97. Innsitting service
98. Interior decorating
99. Interior painting
100. Jewelry design
101. Jewelry repair

102. Juggler
103. Knife sharpening
104. Knitting
105. Landscaping
106. Lawn care
107. Letter writing service
108. Limo service
109. Literary agent
110. Loan consultant
111. Local tours (walking, bike, car)
112. Lunch delivery service
113. Macramé
114. Mail order
115. Manicurist
116. Marketing consultant
117. Massage
118. Meal delivery
119. Medical claims processing service
120. Meeting planner
121. Message answering service
122. Message delivery (bike)
123. Mime
124. Mobile disc jockey
125. Mobile hair cutting service
126. Mobile home repair
127. Mobile home washing
128. Mobile locksmith service
129. Mobile tune-up service
130. Mobile television and appliance repair
131. Mobile window screen repair
132. Monogramming service
133. Multilevel marketing
134. Musical instructor
135. Musical instrument maker
136. Musician
137. Nail salon
138. Nanny placement service
139. Newsletters
140. Novelty sign rental

141. Novelty telegrams
142. Organizational consultant
143. Outdoor guide
144. Outdoor maintenance
145. Packaging and shipping store
146. Party services
147. Personal cook
148. Personalized children's book publishing
149. Pest removal
150. Pet grooming
151. Pet sitting
152. Pet taxi service
153. Piano tuner
154. Picture framing services
155. Plant maintenance
156. Plasterer
157. Pool service
158. Portrait artist
159. Pottery
160. Prepared foods service
161. Pretzel stands
162. Private investigating
163. Process servers
164. Publicist/Agent
165. Puppeteer
166. Radon detection service
167. Real estate investor
168. Recycling service
169. Relocation service
170. Remodeling planning
171. Rental finding service
172. Restaurant delivery service
173. Résumé writing
174. Retailing by kiosk and cart
175. Reunion planning
176. Roof restoration
177. Sandwich stands
178. Self-publishing
179. Seminar production
180. Seminar promotion
181. Sewing school
182. Shoe repair
183. Shopping service
184. Small business consultant
185. Snowplowing service
186. Specialty advertising brokerage
187. Specialty gardening/ sprout growing
188. Sports camp service
189. Square dance caller
190. Stand-up comedian
191. Surfboard maker
192. Tax preparation service
193. Teaching crafts classes
194. Teaching English to foreign students
195. Telecommunications consultant
196. Temporary help service
197. Thrift store
198. Translation service
199. Truck and car washing
200. Tutoring
201. Typing service
202. Upholstery cleaning
203. Upholstery repair
204. Used bookstore owner
205. Used car inspections
206. Used car assessment
207. Used clothing sales
208. VCR installation and training
209. Vehicle moving service
210. Vending machine service
211. Videotaping service
212. Wedding planner
213. Wallpaper hanging
214. Window cleaning
215. Windshield repair service
216. Word processing service
217. Yoga instructor

Wielding the Freelance

The people who get on in this world are the people who get up and look for the circumstances they want, and, if they can't find them, make them.
George Bernard Shaw

The term *freelance* has come down to us from medieval times, when knights independent of any lord roamed the countryside in search of adventure. Because they were unattached, they were known as "free lances." Today, a freelance has come to mean "a person who acts according to his principles and is not influenced by any group; an independent."[1] In the *I Ching,* we find a description that fits both the medieval and modern sense of a freelance: "one who does not serve either a king or a feudal lord, but in a lofty spirit values his own affairs."[2] Modern day freelances can include: artists, writers, musicians, actors, journalists, photographers, inventors, consultants of any kind, commercial artists, editors, and more. In this section, we will outline important issues you may want to consider in setting yourself up as a freelance. (Much of the process work on pages 372–383 applies to the freelance. We encourage the would-be freelance to examine it.)

Of course, in a certain sense, a freelance is really operating a small business. The basic difference is this: a freelance is not interested in starting an organization. For our purposes, a restaurant is a small business (even if it only has two employees), but an inventor who sells her ideas to industry is a freelance. As an up-and-coming young country and western singer, Dolly Parton was a freelance, but as an executive of Dollywood, she is running a not-so-small business. Freelancing has nothing to do with how much money you make. A professional sports figure or entertainer may make big bucks as a freelance or may, like Oprah Winfrey, start her own production organization. Successful freelancers don't usually want to run organizations, though many of them could.

Freelancers want the relative freedom and control of managing their own business, without the responsibility of running a company. The freelance has an even greater freedom in how he structures and uses his time than the small business owner. Most businesses have to keep regular hours (at least if they want to stay in business), but freelancers might start their day at two p.m. and work late into the night, or they may work intensively on a project for six months and take six months off. As a freelance, you can take advantage of your natural life rhythms and work at those times when you feel most creative and have the most energy. You are running your schedule; your schedule is not running you. As with time, so with space, you are free to create. The freelance can work at home in her underwear. I know one who does. Today, the computer and modem make home work possible in many more fields.

Many personal and informational services that are commonly run as small businesses can easily be adapted to a freelance format. People who enjoy working primarily with ideas or information (e.g., journalists) or those with a great deal of highly specific skills (e.g., pilots) or specialized knowledge (e.g., engineers) are good freelance candidates. Creative artists often freelance, whether by choice or necessity.

Many former executives find that the knowledge, skill, and experience they acquired in the corporate world can be applied in ways that better reflect their current values by taking advantage of the freelance option. For example, a former management executive for a large defense contractor became an organizational consultant for nonprofits. What he learned about effective management and organization he now shares with nonprofits, helping them to better organize their efforts. He gains satisfaction working for people and causes that more adequately reflect his values. On the other hand, some former executives find they want a minimum of time constraints and organizational hassles. They want to focus on spiritual or psychological growth, which they may have neglected while climbing the ladder of success. These folks often have highly marketable skills that can provide them a comfortable living with a minimum of hassles.

Of course, a freelance may be one by temperament or by necessity. Certain fields require a freelance status, especially in the early stages of a career. You may be a dancer with a dream of starting your own dance troupe, but you will probably have to spend many years as a freelance (and a very exceptional one at that) before you will have the credibility and visibility to gain the necessary financial and audience backing for your organization.

Freelancers are ready to trade security for freedom. There are no gold watches, pensions, HMOs, or yearly cost-of-living adjustments waiting for the freelance—unless, of course, they create these for themselves. Some do, but even with these, the freelance life is a bit on the edge. You must like or at least be comfortable with this. Many freelancers spend a good portion of their work days alone. Ask yourself if this works for you. There are, of course, ways of minimizing one's sense of isolation.

Joining a local club or guild (for example, a writer's or artist's guild, a songwriter's or actor's club, a speaker's or self-publisher's association, etc.) can provide, especially the beginning freelancer, with much-needed balance, knowledge, and support. Membership is usually a matter of a nominal yearly fee. Joining a club gives you a chance to get out and meet with other folks in your field. In addition to providing the emotional support of others who share common experiences (and frustrations), these groups offer the individual a chance to exchange ideas and learn from more experienced colleagues. Clubs provide information about opportunities for jobs and late-breaking trends in the field. Besides offering talks and forums by successful individuals in the field, most clubs conduct seminars and workshops on subjects including the legal, marketing, and accounting aspects of their profession.

Freelancers often hold jobs but of short duration. An actor working on a film; a dancer performing in a show; a consultant working for a particular company, non-profit, or government agency for several months at a stretch; a photographer making a big shoot for a catalogue or magazine—all have jobs, but they know these jobs aren't going to last. Successful freelances have the confidence, connections, and skill to keep creating work. They know how to take care of business, or they hire people who do.

Taking Care of Business

As a freelance, the business end of your work is likely to be a matter of making contacts, negotiating contracts, and handling paperwork—in other words, marketing, negotiation, and administration. There are, of course, professionals skilled in all of these areas whom you can hire to do most or all of your business work. Should you choose to seek professional help, it is a good idea to stay involved and informed. If you are going to do most of the work yourself, the most essential skills you will need are marketing and negotiation. If you are successful at these, you can hire someone to do your paperwork, record-keeping, and accounting—otherwise, guess who must do it?

Get Yourself Some Hired Guns: Agents, Marketing Consultants, Lawyers, and Accountants

Agents: People who are looking to sell their creative work or talent may be able to profit from the services of an agent. There are agents for authors, artists, musicians, entertainers of all kinds, and professional sportspeople, among others. Agents are professionals who handle the business end of creative work for a percentage fee. Agents are in the business of contacts, making them and keeping them. They endeavor to connect the creative artist or their work with opportunities for exposure, negotiate deals, protect the artist's work from infringement, or promote the artist's name or reputation. Of course, before an agent will agree to take you on as a client, he or she must be convinced that his efforts at promoting you will be worthwhile for him. In other words, they have to know that you will be marketable and that they stand to earn enough on the 10 to 20 percent they get from the sale of your work to make it work for them.

Marketing Consultants: There are marketing consultants who specialize in working with small business and even with freelancers. They can create and design a complete marketing program for you. They can help you develop a marketing strategy, target specific markets, design promotional and advertising materials, get publicity, and more. Marketing consultants often work for a flat fee or on a retainer basis. If you can afford it and it is appropriate to your field, hiring a professional in the beginning is usually a good idea. Later on, we will discuss how to create the promotional materials that will help you let people know about what you are doing. A marketing consultant can greatly assist you in developing these. For many freelancers, this is often the best way to utilize the services of a marketing consultant—come to them with specific requests—for example, to design specific promotional materials.

Lawyers: Even if you decide you don't need or you can't get an agent or marketing consultant, you should have a good attorney. This is for the simple reason that contracts can be a boon or bane for the freelance, and a good lawyer can make the difference. From authors to artists, from songwriters to consultants, from inventors to speakers, contracts are basic to doing business in a freelance way. In some fields, you may be able to have an attorney draw up a standard contract (or several) that you can use over and over with slight alterations (like varying the numbers). Lawyers can also help you deal with issues like copyrights, trademarks, patents, and their protection. They can tell you what to do if someone is infringing on you and/or your work.

Accountants: You should avail yourself of the advice of a good accountant, preferably one who specializes in working with people in your field. Special tax considerations can apply to independent contractors, artists, authors, actors, and others. These frequently change. It is your accountant's job to stay on top of these and help you get the best breaks.

Do It Yourself: Give Yourself a Promotion

In many fields, hiring an agent doesn't apply. Even in those where it does, there are circumstances where you may not want or be able to get an agent. Similarly, you may not be able to afford or you may not want to work with a marketing consultant. In that case, you are on your own. Fortunately, there are many good books on the subject. (See pages 386–387.) On the road to freelance freedom, there are several barriers, which the beginner must overcome. The way you deal with these barriers can mean the difference between making it as a freelance and returning to the job market.

Break Through Self-Marketing Barriers

Anti-Marketing Bias: If you have a job, you try to do good work and hope that someone will notice and promote you. If you work for yourself, you have the opportunity or the obligation to promote yourself. Whether you view it as an opportunity or an obligation could spell the difference between success or failure in your marketing attempts. If you resent having to market yourself—the time that it takes away from other activities, the sometimes silly hornblowing, the ingratiating inanities—you will probably be ineffective. If Zen can be Zen chopping wood and carrying water, then Zen can be Zen through the marketing drama—a modern-day equivalent. Understand that this whole business of ego is a show, and you can drop any hang-ups about being a showman or show-woman.

Embarrassment: If you feel too shy or embarrassed to promote yourself, this could stop you in your tracks. Get a friend to help you, one who can see you objectively and help you to accent your strengths and minimize your weaknesses. The real marketing geniuses turn weaknesses into strengths. Even if you are able to get others to assist you in your efforts, you will need to think through your strategy and be able to look at your image with a degree of objectivity. Believe in you and in what you do. After all, it's your life. Have fun promoting yourself.

Perfectionism: The perfect has been called "the enemy of the good." The good you can enjoy today is often better than the perfection you might have someday. Somedays have a way of never coming. Eventually, you just have to do it.

Lack of Persistence: To be successful, you generally must accept self-marketing as an essential, ongoing part of your business. If you land one big account, you have to maintain it and get the next one. If you complete one project, no matter how well you did it, there's always the next. If you write one book, paint one painting, or compose one piece of music, there's always the next, no matter how good the last one was. It's easy to rest on your laurels and coast on your last success, but if you're going to make it as a freelance, you have to keep at it. The promotion you do today will pay off later on.

Lack of Knowledge: We assume you have the specialized knowledge necessary to do your work. (If not, see "Act IV, Scene II.") Beyond this, you will need marketing knowledge, including how to create an effective marketing strategy, find the specific markets in your field, assemble relevant marketing pieces, network, negotiate, and more. Be willing to learn.

Take Action

Research Your Markets: Artists need to make connections with dealers, actors with producers or studios, writers with publishers, songwriters with music publishers or recording companies. There are publications such as *Writer's Market, Artist's and Graphic Designer's Market, Songwriter's Market, Photographer's Market* (all published by Writer's Digest), which will help you make your connections on a kind of do-it-yourself basis. You may want to work as a professional speaker; there are speaker's bureaus you should know about. You may have inventions to market; you should know how to submit these products to industry. We won't say a whole lot more about researching your markets here in this general discussion. Recognize it as an important

first step. Find out where you will be able to market your work. (See examples on pages 411 and 412.)

Shake the Grant Tree: There are many grants available for the freelance. Special grants exist for writers, artists, dancers, theater directors, musicians, researchers, analysts, and many others. You can apply directly, through organizations such as National Endowment for the Arts, 1100 Pennsylvania Avenue, NW, Washington, DC 20506. They have grants available in areas including: opera, theater, music, visual arts, film, radio, television, dance, literature, design arts, folk arts, museums, etc. It helps if you know how to write a good proposal. For a brief sketch of the process and a list of books that you may want to consult, see pages 491-494. Many grants can only be given to tax-deductible nonprofit organizations. You may be able to receive a grant that "flows through" one of these organizations. They receive the money from a donor you have selected and pass it on to you. The organization will usually charge you a fee for this service (around 10 percent).

Develop a Self-Promotional Orientation and Network: Get aggressive about promoting what you do. Use the promotional pieces and tips on publicity that appear below. If appropriate, carry samples of your work with you. Pass your business cards out to people you meet. Develop networking skills. See the networking and association sections on pages 477–486.

Sharpen Your Image: Like it or not, people judge you by the way you look. It's their first impression of you and often the strongest. Choose your image with care, because it is following you everywhere. Most freelancers do not have to conform to the standard business dress code, thank God. Whatever look you choose, make sure that it is well put together. Be aware that people are attracted to success. Of course, the way that an author or an artist looks successful may be different from the way a business consultant does; still, no matter your profession, look like you're making it. Finally, recognize that if your appearance runs to the unconventional, you could be getting yourself into a box. If you always dress like a Guatemalan peasant or a cowboy, people will think that's what you are.

Negotiate

There are dozens of books today on the subject of negotiating. A few of the better ones are included in the bibliography. We also have included some general tips on negotiation, which you will find on pages 495-497. Beyond this, we will simply restate that it's a good idea to have your lawyer examine any contracts before you sign. There are also books on understanding legal contracts such as: *Sign Here: How to Understand Any Contract Before You Sign,* by Mari Privette Ulmer.[3] Even if you learn how to write your own contracts, you should probably have them reviewed by an attorney. Beginners in fields such as songwriting and screenwriting have been taken to the cleaners, so beware. A few hundred dollars in attorney's fees up front could save many thousands later on.

By All Accounts: The Paper Work

If you don't already have one, we recommend that you buy a personal computer to help you get a handle on the paper end of your business. A personal computer and printer will cost you anywhere from $1,500-$5,000, or more, depending upon the setup you require. It is well worth the investment. You can save thousands of dollars a year for the services of a secretary, a graphic designer, a typographer, a research assistant, a bookkeeper, and a file clerk by doing the routine work yourself, with the help of a personal computer. More than money, your computer will save you valuable time.

You'll have more time to concentrate on doing your work and promoting it, which is, after all, what keeps you in business.

No need to get buried in paper or spend long hours filing, sorting, or looking for your important papers. You have all of your business records, billing information, invoices, mailing lists, and letters organized for easy access. With a graphics software program, you can even design and store your own promotional pieces. The addition of a modem enables you to subscribe to electronic mail services, data banks, and networks. You can even shop, pay your bills, and catch up on the latest news by computer. New software and services are coming on line all of the time to make your life easier and save you valuable time.

It pays to do some research before you go into the store. There are various books and magazines available to help you understand and compare what various machines and programs can do for you. You may want to hire an independent computer consultant who can help you select the right software and hardware for your needs. Once you have at least a basic idea of what you want, look in the yellow pages for computer stores in your area. Make appointments to meet with sales representatives to see demonstrations of various models. Let them know what your budget is and what uses you have in mind. Shop around and compare prices. Ask about service contracts. These can cost as little as ten to twenty dollars a month and are well worth it.

No matter how much you rely on a computer, you will probably never completely eliminate the need for paper. One key to keeping your paperwork under control is to make certain you have plenty of ways to "receive" your paper—these include file folders, filing cabinets, notebooks, index cards, index files, paper trays, paperclips, labels, etc. Where you see a workspace piled with disorderly papers, you will almost always find a lack of these important supplies (or their effective use).

Put It in Writing and Get the Word Out

One vital thing to understand about our society is that it runs on paper. Many people think that if it isn't on paper, it can't be real. On the other hand, the written word carries a kind of mystique. Perhaps this goes back to ancient times when priests or magicians were the only ones who could read and write. Whatever the origin of our fascination with the written word, it is definitely something to be aware of and to take advantage of. Additionally, studies have shown that most people process information visually—show beats tell every time. Keep these points in mind when creating and designing your promotional materials.

Many beginning freelancers don't like to deal with creating promotion pieces, but sooner or later, most professionals come around to seeing their importance. You save time, hassle, and lost business by doing it right from the start. Begin by thinking through the image you want to present to the public (see page 552). You will most likely want to take advantage of the promotional pieces below:

Logo: It may be worth your while to hire a professional graphic designer to create a logo for your business. For some freelance businesses, a logo is practically mandatory; for others, it's not important. A logo is especially useful if you use a business name other than your own name. Once you have the logo, you can use it on all of your promotional pieces, e.g., business cards, stationery, brochures, flyers, advertisements, etc. If you are going to use a logo, take the time to create one you will be comfortable with for years to come. In marketing, it is important to be consistent—it helps you build name recognition over time.

Business Cards: By all means, get yourself a business or, if you prefer, calling card, and take the time, thought, and care to do it right. For the freelance, using your own name for your business name is often best. Even if you decide to incorporate, you can still be Susan Smith, Ltd. With a business card, you can promote your business and give your address and phone number—all in one shot. For many freelancers, it is a good idea to put additional information on the card. You can use your card as a mini-advertisement to list services or to give a tag line that tells how your work is different.

Make sure your card looks professional. Choose high quality paper. Cheap cards are almost as bad as no cards. If you have a logo, use it. Look at other cards to get ideas. Be appropriate to your field. A computer or business consultant's card should probably be rather conventional, saying, "I'm competent and reliable." The same card design for a photographer, artist, or jewelry designer would be a mistake. Their cards should say, "I create." Also, buy a card organizer, and collect the cards of others. They provide a ready reference for contacts, leads, and clients; you'll have an instant Rolodex.®

Stationery and Envelopes: Everything that applies to business cards goes for your stationery. It should be professional, appropriate, high quality, and "you." Again, if you have a logo, use it.

Portfolio: Every freelance should have a portfolio. One of the most common mistakes that beginning freelances make is failing to document in words and pictures exactly what it is that they do. A portfolio is good for your self-confidence. It helps you to see where you have come from and stimulates you to grow. Most importantly, it shows people what you can do by showing what you have done. Obviously, the ingredients in the portfolio of a fine artist and computer consultant are going to vary greatly, but every freelance needs a portfolio. Select a high quality binder that commands respect. Use clear plastic page coverings. As to the contents of your portfolio, choose from the list below. Create a showcase that fits your particular field and image, one that highlights your best work.

Résumé
Examples of work
Photos
Letters of recommendation
Testimonials

Brochures: If you can afford to hire someone to design, write, photograph, and print a glossy four-color brochure, that's great. (In quantities of a few thousand, they could easily cost you a dollar apiece or more for the printing alone.) If not, it doesn't mean you can't create an effective, inexpensive brochure that will get people excited about what you are doing. Inexpensive—yes, but not cheap. All of your marketing materials should have the look and feel of professional work. Better a small, high quality black-and-white brochure than a large, cheap looking four-color job.

The simplest brochure is an $8^{1}/_{2}$ x 11 sheet of paper folded in three to produce six panels. (An $8^{1}/_{2}$ x 14 sheet is often folded in four to produce eight panels.) What goes on your brochure will, of course, depend on what you do. Remember the value of pictures—try to include some photographs of your work (high quality black and white is fine). Also, since most freelancers are offering personal services or their own creative work, it's a good idea to include a photograph of yourself. If you write the copy yourself, remember not to get too wordy. More is often less in promotional materials. A few clear ideas well communicated in words and pictures can make a strong impression. You may want to include testimonials from satisfied clients. Look at other brochures to get ideas.

Flyers: Flyers are one of the most inexpensive ways of getting the word out about your offerings. Make a simple but attractive flyer describing what you do. Then get them photocopied or printed and post them around town. Many communities have kiosks in areas with a high volume of pedestrian traffic. Retail store windows and bulletin boards in local libraries, colleges and universities, laundromats and employee lounges are good places to post your flyers. Some people hand them out on busy street corners or go door-to-door with them. Some even put them on car windshields, as you have probably noticed.

Advertising: Get the biggest bang for your advertising buck. Newspaper and magazine space and classified ads, telephone directories, radio and television spots, buses and billboards are just a few of the ways you can advertise. You don't need to spend a great deal of money to make effective use of advertising. Some freelancers do very well by simply running classified ads in magazines. These ads alert the public to what they have to offer and help develop a mailing list of interested leads. These "leads" can then be sent brochures or letters detailing the benefits of their products or services.

Direct Mail: Direct mail is one of the best marketing techniques for freelancers. The concept of direct mail is extremely simple. It consists of a mailing list, a marketing package, and postage. Professionals in direct marketing will tell you that success is all in the list, that is, in getting a highly targeted and current list of names of people who want what you've got. There are professional services that sell mailing lists. Check your yellow pages. Keep a list of people you do business with who might like to know about future offerings. There are books available on how to write effective copy that will pull. Also read your own junk mail and get ideas. The standard direct-mail package includes:

a brochure or flyer,
a letter,
a return card (a postcard with your
    name and address printed on it).

Experiment and find what works best for you and your budget. Your package may be as simple as a letter with an enclosed business card. Don't write off direct mail until you are absolutely sure it can't work for you. If you find that the postage is too expensive, you may be able to do a cooperative mailing with others—share the costs and everyone benefits.

Promotional Video: For performers such as speakers, musicians, comedians, actors, dancers, etc., a promotional video helps people to see what you can do before they make the decision to meet with you and discuss working with you. Many agencies and would-be employers are requiring them today. Again, make it a professional presentation—hire a pro. Send your homemade video to *America's Funniest Home Videos*.

Contracting Your Services

You may choose to operate as an independent professional who contracts services to existing organizations. As an independent contractor, you maintain the independence of being your own boss and choosing your clients. Yet since your relationship with these types of clients is generally sustained over a long period of time, you may have greater security than you would in other freelance endeavors.

General Steps to Contracting Your Services

1. Identify organizations that are fulfilling purposes you support or that might be persuaded to pursue purposes that you support.

2. Prioritize these based upon your desire to work with them.

3. Research these organizations. Understand their relative strengths and weaknesses. What problems do they have that you can help solve? What areas are they neglecting that you could help put into focus? Find out.

4. Identify the individual or individuals who have the authority to hire you.

5. Develop a proposal that demonstrates your credibility and how you can benefit their organization.

6. Approach these organizations with your proposal.

Note: Be advised that there are legal questions about exactly what constitutes an independent contractor versus what constitutes an employee. The IRS says if you act like an employee, you are an employee as far as they are concerned. Check with a competent tax attorney or the IRS for updated details.

Taking It All Home:
A Look at Home Business

More and more are people are discovering the home-based business as an effective alternative to the traditional nine-to-five job. In fact, not since the days of the cottage industries that helped launch the Industrial Revolution in the late eighteenth and early nineteenth centuries has such a large portion of the population worked from home in non-agrarian activities. Today, there are over thirty million home businesses. Each day more than 8,000 new ones are born—about one every ten seconds. According to Larry Brockman, President of the American Home Business Association, by the year 2001, 50 percent of all American households will be engaged in some sort of home-based business enterprise.[4] Home-based businesses are not only numerous, they are also highly profitable. According to *Entrepreneur* magazine, income from home-based business averages over $50,000 per year, and more than 1.7 million home businesses have annual incomes in excess of $100,000.

In addition to significant income potential, working at home offers a variety of attractive features that are fueling this boom. First, overhead expenses (and, therefore, capital risks) are low. This undoubtedly helps to account for the much higher success rate that home-based businesses enjoy when compared to other kinds of small business. Fully 85 percent of non-home small businesses will be out of business within three years of opening up shop. On the other hand, 85 percent of home-based businesses will still be going strong three years after they are born.[5]

When you work at home, you do away with the daily commute. Rush hours and traffic jams and the stress and wasted time that go with them become a thing of the past. The rigidity of the time clock and the absurdity of office politics fade into distant memory. When you work at home, you can structure your work life to harmonize with your own natural energy cycles. You dress in a way that suits you rather than your employer. Most importantly, you can build a life around your most cherished values and take advantage of your real talents and strengths. What's more, many people find that working at home affords them the opportunity to spend more time with the people they love.

When you work at home, you get to be your own boss, but then, of course, you have to *be* the boss. Without the pressures of a time clock or the physical presence of a supervisor, you are free to work at your own pace in accord with your natural rhythms. You are also free to procrastinate or avoid working altogether. It's easy to spend too much time reading newspapers or magazines, to turn on the television, putter in the garden, yack away on the telephone, surf the Internet, or otherwise avoid getting down to work. On the other hand, if you are a workaholic who can't seem to "call it a day" after eight or ten hours at the office, you might find your life getting even more out of balance when home *is* the office.

In addition to a structured work environment, jobs typically provide opportunities for social interaction. When you leave behind the traditional nine-to-five work setting to work at home, you will probably also be leaving behind a significant part of your social life. Many new to working at home are surprised at the loneliness and isolation they feel after the initial excitement of starting out on their own wears off.

While working at home can add comfort and convenience to your work routine, it can also confound it with interruptions and distractions. The same features that make working at home so appealing—freedom, flexibility, independence, and increased family contact—can limit your effectiveness when not carefully planned for. Below are some tips for making a success of your at-home business:

How to Make Working at Home Work

1. **Minimize Your Risk:** Every new business venture entails an element of risk. Put the odds in your favor by devoting ample time and attention to planning before you launch your new home business. While you may not need a formal business plan, you should address yourself to each of the elements that comprise one (see pages 371-384). It's usually best to begin in a field you already know. Taking advantage of the expertise and networks you have already developed is less risky than plunging headlong into a brand new field. If you do want to try your hand at something entirely new, you may want to reduce the financial pressure by holding onto your current job. Work part time at your new home business. Then, when your home business really starts taking off, you can let go of your regular job. Many people begin planning for a new home business when they suspect their jobs might be in jeopardy or when they feel burned out in their current positions. This allows them to ease into the new venture before it becomes an urgent necessity to do so.

2. **Schedule Your Work:** Make a daily schedule and stick to it. Determine the number of hours you need to work each week, and schedule your time accordingly. If you are a night owl (and your kind of work allows it), schedule your work for late evenings. If you are an early bird, begin your day at the crack of dawn, and call it quits by mid-afternoon. If your

business involves working on long projects, break them up into smaller units and assign intermediate deadlines for each. Trying to cram at the end is no way to run a business, and it isn't worth the added stress. A schedule serves not only as a prod to the would-be procrastinator but also as a balancing tool for the overachiever. Many successful home business owners find it useful to set appointments with themselves for exercise, family outings, community involvement, and so on. Balance work with time for play and fun. Of course, you can and should be flexible with your schedule, altering it with the ups and downs of your workload and adjusting it as your business grows and evolves. It's all right to deviate from your schedule from time to time. Just make sure you have one!

3. **Designate a Place for Your Business:** If at all possible, designate an entire room (with a door that closes) as the site for your home business. Closing the door will help filter out sounds from pets, children, the garbage disposal, and so on. It also reinforces the feeling that you are now in your "work mode" and should not be interrupted or disturbed. This not only sends a message to members of your family but, just as importantly, helps keep *you* focused. What's more, it closes off your work when it's time to walk away from it. A separate outside entrance is ideal if you will be receiving clients in your home office. Check with the city or county for local zoning ordinances. These may impose limitations on foot traffic, parking, the number of employees you can have working in your home at any given time, and so on.

Make sure you have a comfortable chair and a roomy desk—these items are *not* the place to cut corners. Equip your home office with the technology you need: computers, printers, additional phone lines, fax machines, and so on. Also, be sure to check out the tax laws for home office deductions. You will probably qualify for some significant tax breaks.

4. **Pay Attention to Your Image:** Just because you work at home is no reason to have anything less than a professional image. For example, make sure all the written materials representing your business (stationery, business cards, brochures, etc.) are high quality and attractive (see pages 401–402). Similarly, written correspondences with clients should be well written, neat, and free of typos. Have checks printed with your business name and logo.

Where once others in the business community tended to look with suspicion at those working from home, the sheer number of people doing business this way today is rapidly eliminating this prejudice. Nevertheless, you may want to project the illusion of having an outside office or of being a larger organization than you really are. Certainly you will want at least one phone line designated exclusively to your business. Instruct children not to answer this phone. Equip your primary business line with voice mail; its popularity in the corporate world means those calling will have no idea you are at home (or that you are changing diapers) while their call is coming in. You might want to use a mailbox service for your correspondence. This can give your stationery a downtown street address and "suite number." If you can't afford the time and expense of creating a full-blown Web site, you will certainly want an e-mail address.

For most home businesses, the telephone is the primary sales tool. Some people find it helpful to get dressed as though they were going to work in a corporate office before they make their calls. It helps put them in a confident and down-to-business mode. If you bring clients to your home office, keep it clean and professional in appearance. If you don't have a separate entrance to your office, make sure your house is neat and presentable and that your clients won't be tripping over children's toys on their way to closing a deal.

5. **Build and Strengthen Your Networks:** Networking is especially important for the home-based business person (see pages 477-486). It gives you an inexpensive way to develop contacts for your business, while helping to alleviate the sense of isolation that can come with spending so much time alone at home. You may want to join leads clubs, service clubs, or trade groups or to volunteer in your community. You might even want to start a networking group of your own.

6. **Join Trade Associations:** Whatever your specific field, if there is a "National Association for_____"—join it! There are also a number of trade associations that address the needs of home-based business owners in a more generic fashion. These generally publish newsletters and provide seminars and other educational resources of interest to the home-based business person. Some lobby Congress for legislative changes to benefit home-based and small businesses.

Membership in a home-based business trade association can give you the buying clout of a large organization. With a trade association membership (some costing as little as $50.00 annually), you can get discounts in a number of areas, including: business and personal insurance, financial services (tax and legal assistance, investment opportunities, and the ability to accept credit cards from your customers), communications (long-distance rates, discounts on access to the Internet, etc.), and a diverse variety of products and services (travel, car rentals, business products, copying services, etc.).

Working at home provides real opportunities for generating a strong income while creating a balanced and healthy lifestyle. With careful planning, a little ingenuity, and determined effort, the freedom, flexibility, and profitability of a home-based business can be yours.

Home-Based Business Sources

101 Best Home Businesses. Ramsey, Dan. Franklin Lakes, N.J.: The Career Press, 1997.

121 Internet Businesses You Can Start from Home. Gielgun, Ron E. Brooklyn: Actium Publishing, Inc., 1997.

The Best Home Businesses for the 90s. Edwards, Paul, and Sarah Edwards. New York: Jeremy P. Tarcher/Putnam, 1994.

The Complete Idiot's Guide™ to Starting a Home-Based Business. Weltman, Barbara. New York: Alpha Books, 1997.

Going Solo: Developing a Home-Based Consulting Business from the Ground Up. Bond, William J. New York: McGraw-Hill, 1997.

Guerilla Marketing for the Home-Based Business. Levinson, Jay Conrad, and Seth Godin. Boston: Houghton Mifflin Co., 1995.

Home Business, Big Business. Cook, Mel. New York: Macmillan, 1998.

Home Business Made Easy. Hanania, David. Grants Pass, Ore.: The Oasis Press, 1998.

The Home Office and Small Business Answer Book. Attard, Janet. New York: Henry Holt & Co., 1993.

Making Money with Your Computer at Home. Edwards, Paul, and Sarah Edwards. New York: G.P. Putnam & Sons, 1997.

Moneymaking Moms: How Work at Home Can Work for You. Hull, Caroline, and Tonya Wallace. Secaucus, N.J.: Citadel Press, 1998.

Moonlighting for a Second Income at Home. Mueller, Jo. Grants Pass, Ore.: The Oasis Press, 1997.

The Work-at-Home Sourcebook. Arden, Lynie. Boulder: Live Oak Publications, 1996.

Turn Your Talents into Profits: 100+ Terrific Ideas for Starting Your Own Home-Based Microbusiness. Saunders, Darcie, and Martha M. Bullen. New York: Pocket Books, 1998.

Working from Home. Edwards, Paul, and Sarah Edwards. New York: Putnam Publishing Group, 1994.

Magazines

Home Business® Magazine
Publisher's Creative Systems
PO Box 469052
Escondido, CA 92046-9052

Home Office Computing Magazine
www.smalloffice.com

Work@Home Magazine
P.O. Box 676285
Rancho Santa Fe, CA 92067-9972

Trade Associations

American Association of Home Based Business
1 (800) 447-9710
www.aahbb.org

American Home Business Association
1 (800) 664-2422
www.homebusiness.com

Home Office Association of America (HOAA)
1 (800) 809-4622
www.hoaa.com

National Association for the Self-Employed (NASE)
1 (800) 232-NASE
www.membership.com/nase/
default.html

Small Office Home Office Association (SOHOA)
1 (888) SOHOA11
www.sohoa.com

Home-Based Business Internet Sites

Mothers' Home Business Network
www.homeworkingmom.com

Work from Home
www.ivillage.com/work

For Information in Specific Freelance Fields, Contact:

American Dance Guild
31 W. 21st St., 3rd Floor
New York, NY 10018

American Federation of Musicians of the United States and Canada
Paramount Bldg.
1501 Broadway Ste. 600
New York, NY 10036
www.afm.org

Associated Actors and Artistes of America
165 W. 46th St.
New York, NY 10036

American Federation of Television and Radio Artists (AFTRA)
260 Madison Ave.
New York, NY 10016
www.aftra.org/home.html

Independent Computer Consultants Association
11131 South Towne Square, Ste. F
St. Louis, MO 63123
www.icca.org

National Arts Education Assn. (NAEA)
1916 Association Dr.
Reston, VA 20191
www.naea-reston.org

National Speaker's Assn.
1500 S. Priest Dr.
Tempe, AZ 85281
www.nsaspeaker.org

Professional Photographers of America
57 Forsyth St. NW, Ste. 1600
Atlanta, GA 30303
www.ppa-world.org

Writer's Guild of America, East
555 W. 57th St.
New York, NY 10019
www.wga.org

Writer's Guild of America, West
7000 West Third St.
Los Angeles, CA 90048

Freelance Sources

100 Best Freelance Careers. Reno, Kelly. New York: Arco Publishing, 1998.

Adams Streetwise Guide to Consulting. Kintler, David. Boston: Bob Adams, 1997.

Business Plan Guide for Independent Consultants. Holtz, Herman R. New York: John Wiley & Sons, 1994.

The Complete Idiot's Guide to Making Money in Freelancing. Rozakis, Laurie E., and David Rye. New York: MacMillan, 1998.

The Computer Consultant's Guide: Real-Life Strategies for Building a Successful Consulting Career. Ruhl, Janet. New York: John Wiley & Sons, 1997.

Consulting on the Side: How to Start a Part-Time Consulting Business While Still Working at Your Full-Time Job. Cook, Mary F. New York: John Wiley & Sons, 1996.

Freelance Photographer's Handbook. Bodin, Frederik D. Curtin & London Inc., 1981.

Freelance Writing for Magazines and Newspapers. Yudkin, Marcia. New York: HarperCollins, 1993.

Getting Started as a Freelance Illustrator or Designer. Fleishman, Michael. Cincinnati: North Light Books, 1990.

How to Be a Successful Internet Consultant. Keyes, Jessica. New York: McGraw-Hill, 1996.

How to Start and Run a Successful Consulting Business. Kishel, Gregory, and Patricia. New York: John Wiley & Sons, 1996.

How to Survive & Prosper as an Artist: Selling Yourself without Selling Your Soul. Michels, Carroll. New York: Henry Holt & Company, 1997.

Marketing Your Consulting and Professional Services. Korlson, David. Menlo Park, Calif.: Crisp Publications, 1988.

Power Freelancing: Home Based Careers for Writers, Designers and Consultants. Sorenson, George. Minneapolis: Mid-List Press, 1995.

Secrets of a Freelance Writer: How to Make $85,000 a Year. Bly, Robert W. New York: Henry Holt, 1997.

Solo Success: 100 Tips $100,000 a Year Freelancer. Perlstein, David. New York: Three Rivers Press, 1998.

The Streetwise Guide to Freelance Design and Illustration. Williams, Theo Stephan. Cincinnati: Writer's Digest Books, 1998.

Successful Freelancing: The Complete Guide to Establishing and Running Any Kind of Freelance Business. Faux, Marian. New York: St. Martins Press, 1997.

Writer's Digest Handbook of Making Money Freelance Writing. Boyd, Amanda, and Thomas Clark, eds. Cincinnati: Writer's Digest Books, 1997.

Selling Information by Mail

Selling information by mail gives you the opportunity to share what you know with others while earning income independent of your job or primary business. It may even become your primary business. Choose practical subjects you have a special knowledge of or interest in. How-to books, source lists, newsletters, and catalogues—these are just a few examples of possible formats. You can write the material yourself or with the help of friends or a professional writer. Make your product attractive, but remember, when buying by mail, people are more interested in the information than the package.

Producing Your Product: Print or photocopy your product. Ask your printer to help you choose appropriate paper and binding. Get quotes from several printers.

Pricing Your Product: Even dollar amounts are best for items under ten dollars. For higher priced items, end your price with $.95. For example, $30.00 becomes $29.95.

Mailing Costs: The postal service's Fourth Class Book Rate can significantly reduce your mailing costs. Call the postal service for information on current regulations and costs.

Advertising: There are three traditional advertising options for those interested in selling information by mail: classified ads, large or small display ads, and direct-mail packages. *Classified advertising* is great for beginners. Write an ad of twenty words or less. Check your local library for the addresses of relevant publications. Write and ask for their media kits (includes circulation, demographics, ad costs, etc.). *Display ads* are more costly and, therefore, more risky. An effective display ad should include a headline, subhead, benefits list and a money-back guarantee. *Direct mail* targets your market with carefully selected mailing lists. Buy a list with a good track record. (Look in the yellow pages under "Mailing Lists" for companies selling lists.) The standard mailing package includes a letter, a circular or brochure, an order card, and a reply envelope.

Writing Your Ad: Know your buyer and offer the benefits he desires. Watch for similar products from your competition to see what sells. Have a punchy headline. Make each word count. Experiment with different ads. Track their performance and go with those that pull the best.

Mail Order Sources

How You Too Can Make at Least $1,000,000 (but Probably Much More) in the Mail-Order Business. Joffe, Heraldo. New York: HarperCollins, 1979.

Mail Order Moonlighting. Hoge, Cecil C. Berkeley: Ten Speed Press, 1988.

Money in Your Mailbox: How to Start and Operate a Mail Order Business. Wilbur, L. Perry. New York: John Wiley & Sons, 1992.

412 ACT III • THE BATTLE FOR LIFE'S WORK

Where Do Artists Sell Their Work?

Do you have a body of work you would like to show? Are you ready to get feedback on it? Are you willing to spend the time, energy, and money to get your work out there? If you answered yes to the above questions, you may be ready to begin marketing your work. Check out:

Galleries: Research the galleries that you are most interested in. Check them out with the Better Business Bureau, and ask other artists who have used them for their feedback. When you've finished your research, make a list of the galleries that you are most interested in. Call them and set up as many appointments as possible.

Studio Viewings: Studio viewings provide a good opportunity for a curator or collector to see all of your work, and you don't have to schlep it.

Studio Shows: Studio shows provide you with an opportunity to show your work to many in an atmosphere of fun and play. Hold a reception with drink and food, and get them in a cheery mood—to buy.

Cooperative Galleries: Because cooperative galleries are run by artists, they may allow you to show works commercial galleries would not touch. Also, you can network with and learn from other artists.

Commissions: A commissioned work is one you are paid to make from scratch. Commissions might come from record or publishing companies, city airports, corporations, or city government—even friends and aquaintances.

Sidewalk Shows: Sidewalk shows represent artists of all levels who show and sell their work. You don't have to be a pro to show your art here. Contact your local artist's association to find out about shows in your area.

Art Fairs: Art fairs are similar to sidewalk shows, except that they are jurored events. In many cases, prizes are awarded. Entering these exhibitions can open up doors to other opportunities. Often dealers and collectors go to shows, seeking out new talent. You can contact your city's parks and recreation department for a schedule of such shows.

Artist's Sources

The Art Business Encyclopedia. Duboff, Leonard. New York: Allworth Press, 1994.

Artist's and Graphic Designer's Market. Mary Cox, ed. Cincinnati: Writer's Digest. Published annually.

The Business of Art. Caplin, Lee, ed. Englewood Cliffs, N.J.: Prentice-Hall, 1989.

Crafting the Nonprofit Foundation

Such gardens are not made
By Singing:". . .Oh, how beautiful" and
Sitting in the shade.

Rudyard Kipling

L et's say you have a vision in mind of a particular good you'd like to accomplish, one requiring the efforts of several people, at least. Let's further say the nature of this effort rules out forming a profit-based company and that there is no existing nonprofit already doing what you would like to do or doing it in the way you would like to do it. You may want to consider starting a nonprofit corporation of your own. This section will help you to determine if this option is right for you.

A nonprofit corporation is a legally chartered state corporation. Establishing such a corporation is not a particularly difficult procedure, though you generally must follow specific instructions about how your organization is formed and how its business is to be conducted. These procedures vary from state to state. More complicated and often more difficult to meet are the requirements for tax-exempt status, which, of course, most potential nonprofit organizations would like to get.

The variance from state to state of incorporation and other regulations and the possibility of continued changes in federal tax law make it difficult to say much in detail about the legal aspects of nonprofit corporations. If you are really serious about forming a tax-exempt nonprofit corporation, you should consult a qualified attorney who works in this field.

If the nonprofit form of organization is best for you, don't be intimidated by the procedures or paperwork. Remember, thousands of others have started nonprofits, which today are actively providing many valuable services to their communities and the world that never would have happened had they been unwilling to deal with the red tape.

Apart from legal considerations, nonprofit corporations have their own unique set of problems and opportunities. Below, we discuss some of the major advantages and disadvantages of beginning a nonprofit corporation, as well as some of the major challenges faced by those interested in running this kind of organization.

Advantages

Credibility: People are more likely to trust you when they know that your organization has met certain legal requirements for operation and that you are not "just in it for the buck." In this world, where it often seems that everyone is trying to sell you something, the fact that your organization was set up for altruistic purposes carries considerable weight with the general public. People will be more likely to listen to your message and publicize or participate in your activities if you carry nonprofit status. Of course, your organization's continued credibility depends first and foremost on the quality of its performance.

Access: In order for your organization to work in certain fields, you simply must have nonprofit tax-exempt status. It's the law, and again, it varies from state to state. In other cases, the increased credibility of nonprofit status helps to open doors that otherwise might be closed to you. If you're interested in working in or with certain types of organizations (for example, elementary or secondary schools, colleges and universities, hospitals, prisons, the armed forces, state or national legislatures, churches, etc.) or with certain types of individuals (for example, veterans, runaways, the handicapped, the mentally retarded, the elderly, etc.), your opportunities for access are greatly enhanced when you make your approach as a representative of a nonprofit organization.

Publicity: People love to hear about good things that are happening in their community and the world at large. Consequently, your nonprofit organization may enjoy enhanced opportunities for free media attention. Newspapers and magazines are often very receptive to doing stories on nonprofit activities, as are local television and radio stations. Local and national radio and television talk shows are constantly looking for credible and interesting guests and often invite controversial and issue-oriented speakers. Additionally, radio and television stations are obliged to grant free air time for public service announcements. You can take advantage of these to get your message out, enlist volunteer support, or announce your upcoming fundraising events and opportunities.

Funding: Nonprofit tax-exempt status can help you obtain grants from federal and state governments, private foundations, corporations, and individuals. In some fields (for example, the arts), the special prestige that accrues to those who give large-scale support tends to loosen their purse strings. Nonprofit tax-exempt status may also increase the possibility of obtaining gifts, low-interest loans, or donated products and services. You can cut costs with volunteers, interns, nonprofit mail privileges, and by buying products and services at a discount. Members and subscribers can provide continuing support. You can solicit funds through direct-mail campaigns or get local or national celebrities to put on benefits on your organization's behalf. These are just a few of the many funding possibilities available to nonprofit organizations, many of which simply don't apply to other types of organizations.

Volunteers: As a nonprofit corporation, you can attract an army of committed individuals to further your organization's mission. Each year, thousands of Americans and people around the world donate their time and effort to working for causes they believe in. A certain percentage of these become extremely dedicated to particular organizations. As your organization grows, you may want to select from these individuals when filling permanent positions. You know their commitment, and they know your organization—its goals and needs, its opportunities and challenges. In addition to free help from volunteers, many organizations take advantage of the efforts of interns who, in exchange for learning and training, work for nominal wages.

Disadvantages

Cost: Launching a nonprofit corporation can be a considerable expense. Legal and consulting fees and research-and-development costs add up. Your start-up team may be able to do some or all of the non-legal work itself or with the help of other volunteers. You might even find a lawyer willing to donate his services. (But don't count on it.) Even if you can't find an obliging, qualified lawyer,

you may—depending on the type of organization you want to start and the availability of good self-help materials in your state—be able to do much or all of the legal work yourself. In California, Nolo Press provides excellent legal materials for the self-starter. (See page 421 for contact information.)

Complexity: Nonprofits are somewhat complicated to begin and maintain. Starting your nonprofit corporation includes writing articles of incorporation and bylaws (spelling out the purpose of your organization and the way its business is to be conducted) and filing a number of forms with various agencies, including the Internal Revenue Service. Following the proper start-up procedure is only the beginning of many requirements set by state and federal government agencies with which you must comply.

Again, the rules and regulations vary from state to state and tend to be somewhat involved. Failure to comply can result in the loss of your nonprofit standing or in even more severe penalties. Be sure that your board of directors and all officers and employees know exactly what the law requires of them. Again, if you are serious about starting a nonprofit organization, qualified legal and accounting professional help is a must—and be sure you understand the information or advice they give.

Paper Jungle: You can expect to file a steady stream of paper, not only with various governmental agencies, but with members and contributors, as well as contractors (those who hire your organization) and others, all of which someone must write. Minutes, reports, proposals, never-ending government forms and filings, balance sheets, mailings, newsletters, public service announcements—nonprofits can seem awash in a sea of paper. The larger your organization gets, the more administrative mumbo-jumbo it will have to deal with. Of course, this can and does take time and energy away from fulfilling the purpose for which your organization was founded. It's not a perfect world we live in and, like it or not, red tape is a fact of life.

Limited Financial Compensation: While you can eventually earn a comfortable living, recognize that no one ever got rich in the nonprofit sector. Especially in the beginning, you can expect to work long, hard hours for a modest salary. Still, if you have gotten this far into the process of discovering and realizing your life's work, it is safe to assume that you are committed to values and a vision that mean more to you than a profit motive and that the experience of giving your gifts to mankind means more to you than getting rich.

Management Challenges

In many respects, managing a nonprofit organization is similar to managing a business or any other type of organization. You start with your vision and state your purpose for existence. Next, you shape broad strategies for the fulfillment of that purpose. Then you step those strategies down into specific objectives and plan exactly how you will achieve these goals. Finally, you evaluate the results of your efforts in light of your original vision and purpose.

Though in many ways similar to other types of organizational management, the nonprofit organization presents managers with unique opportunities and challenges. Here's an advance look at a few of the special management challenges you can expect to face should you decide to build your own nonprofit organization.

1. The challenge of defining the purpose or mission of the organization.

2. The challenge of determining and agreeing upon effective strategies to achieving the organization's mission.

3. The challenge of determining objectives for achieving agreed-upon strategies.

4. The challenge of making planning decisions and allocating resources to achieve agreed-upon objectives.

5. The challenge of measuring the effectiveness of efforts to achieve objectives.

Defining Mission: Nonprofits differ from for-profit organizations in that their missions are usually more difficult to define and their performance in fulfilling these missions, more difficult to measure.

The for-profit corporation's main purpose is to make money. A nonprofit organization's purpose may be as open-ended as promoting world peace or protecting the environment, advancing education or promoting volunteerism. These kinds of purposes are less clear-cut than the simple "make profit." The first step, then, for your start-up team will be to define as clearly as possible the purpose of your nonprofit organization.

Selecting Strategies: Let's say you all agree that the purpose of your organization will be to promote world peace. How will you do it? What will be your strategies? Will you focus on education? If so, will you try to educate the young (the future generation) or world leaders? Will you attempt to limit nuclear proliferation or promote international understanding, or will you try to work on root causes of greed and violence—or some combination? These are just a few of the possibilities you might come up with.

One difficulty that nonprofit planners face is the dilemma between long-term and short-term strategies for action. Will your foundation focus most of its energy on long-term change or short-term solutions? Short-term solutions often seem more attractive because:

a) *Your staff will receive more recognition and feedback and receive it more quickly for short-term solutions.* Efforts at short-term solutions have dramatic and immediate impacts, both on their recipients and on those providing the service. It feels good to see your efforts result in immediate improvements in the quality of the lives of those you work with. Tackling long-term objectives may be more frustrating. (Examples: Distributing food and blankets to the homeless vs. working to alleviate the underlying causes of homelessness. Providing famine relief to hungry children vs. building irrigation systems or promoting farming practices that may prevent future famines from occurring.)

b) *It is often easier to raise funds and enlist support for dramatic short-term solutions.* For example, in recent years, extensive droughts in sub-Saharan Africa brought massive emergency relief from around the world. Yet though there were effective strategies for establishing long-term self-sufficiency, the influx of support began to dry up as soon as the immediate crisis was alleviated—leaving the seeds of another crisis. When a problem has reached crisis proportions, it seems more "real" to people. The image of famine communicated the need in a dramatic and powerful way. When the need you want to serve is less immediately dramatic, it may require more creativity and effort to communicate it effectively to your would-be supporters.

Long-term strategies often involve fundamental changes, including changes in basic values, long ingrained customs or procedures, and calcified thinking. The more fundamental the changes you are proposing, the greater resistance you are likely encounter.

In addition to consideration of long- vs. short-term efforts, you must determine the scope your organization will work at. Will it work primarily on a local, state, national, or global scale—or some mix? Who in particular will your organization focus on serving?

Whatever mix your organization comes up with in selecting strategies for action, it is important that it reach a consensus. Coming to consensus can be a time-consuming and even divisive process. Yet it is vital that members of your organization agree on its

strategies if they are to work effectively and harmoniously toward achieving them. Whatever strategies you choose, keep moving forward, step by step, holding to your purpose while remaining flexible in your response to changing times and circumstances.

Determining Goals: Picking up on the earlier example, let's say that your organization has chosen to fulfill its purpose of promoting world peace through the strategy of education. Even though all of the key members of your organization have agreed upon the organization's purpose and strategies, there may be as many ideas on how to actually implement these strategies as there are participants in your organization.

For example, Tom wants to teach elementary school children about sharing and the value of caring for others. Judy has just come back from a seminar on "conflict mediation" and believes that teaching these skills is, without a doubt, the quickest and surest road to world peace. Roger is convinced that international exchange-student programs at the college level should be the organization's primary focus. Carlotta wants to produce a peace play, featuring an international cast of children, and take it on a global tour. And the list goes on.

All of these objectives and others could further the organization's mission of furthering world peace through education. The point is simply that choices must be made.

Allocating Resources: What weight will various objectives be given within the organization? How do projects and programs stack up against administrative and fundraising efforts in terms of the share of available time and money resources? These are difficult questions that provide the possibility of ongoing friction and tension within the organization.

Various members of your organization may have their own pet projects. Each wants the greatest possible allocation of financial and personnel resources for his or her favorite. In addition to potential conflict over which programs will get what piece of the allocation pie, there are questions about the balance between the activities that further an organization's mission and those that pay for them.

How much emphasis should be placed on raising funds, and how much on the pure pursuit of the organization's mission? When does the organization risk compromising its principles in furthering its pocketbook? Do environmental groups, for example, accept large contributions from oil companies or industrial polluters? Many will say no. Others will say the good the organization can do with the money outweighs the potential harm to credibility and morale.

Every organization has to find its own balance and ethics. If an organization concerns itself too much with fundraising, it may become distracted from its mission. If, on the other hand, the foundation devalues the fundraising process, it may soon find its power to serve greatly reduced or eliminated entirely. This is a tightrope that every nonprofit foundation must walk: to generate enough income to keep itself viable, without becoming consumed by fundraising and administrative functions.

Whenever possible, try to combine fundraising activities with direct action on your mission objectives. (For example, organizing a benefit concert or event performs the dual functions of publicizing your cause and generating income.)

Assessing Feedback: Another striking difference between profit and nonprofit companies comes in evaluating performance. Management consultants have long known that clear feedback on performance is one of the strongest motivations for sustained action. Yet for many nonprofit enterprises, it is often difficult to measure exactly how effective the organization's efforts are.

For profit-based companies, measures set up to evaluate the company's performance are rather clear-cut—quarterly sales figures, cost per unit, market share, balance sheet, net worth, etc. The profit-based corporation is, after all, dealing with quantities—numbers related to money. Measuring nonprofit performance often does not lend itself to reduction to numbers. Issues of quality—the kind of things you just can't put a number on—are often more important than issues of quantity. For example, efforts in public education, or "consciousness raising," while important, are difficult to measure.

Another difficulty with a nonprofit corporation is knowing when it has outlived its usefulness. Let's say you begin an organization to stop development on a local mountain. You found a nonprofit organization called "The Coalition to Save Mt. X." After many years of struggle, and much to your delight, Congress passes a special bill naming this mountain off limits to future development. The purpose of the organization has now been achieved. But by this time you have a well-trained staff, a long list of subscribers, and a dependable mailing list. The question now becomes: Do you disband or become "The Coalition to Save Mt. Y"? Or perhaps expand the purpose of your organization to include more far-reaching objectives, such as slowing global deforestation?

After thinking through the factors discussed above, you can begin to get a sense of whether creating a nonprofit foundation is the best way for you to accomplish your mission objectives. If you feel that it might be, by all means, do more research. The annotated bibliography on pages 425–427 will help you get started.

I was made to work; if you are equally industrious, you will be equally successful.
Johann Sebastian Bach

Starting Your Nonprofit Organization

State Your Purpose

The mission of the _____ organization is:

_____

_____

Determine Effective Strategies

The most effective strategies for achieving the mission of the organization include:

_____

_____

_____

State Prime Objectives

The primary objectives of strategy number one, for the period from _____
to _____ include: _____

_____

_____

The primary objectives of strategy number one, for the period from _____
to _____ include: _____

_____

_____

The primary objectives of strategy number one, for the period from _____
to _____ include: _____

_____

_____

The primary objectives of strategy number one, for the period from _____
to _____ include: _____

_____

_____

The primary objectives of strategy number one, for the period from _____
to _____ include: _____

_____

_____

Funding Your Nonprofit Corporation

Clarify Your Vision: Clarify on paper the goals and objectives of your program or organization. What do you want to accomplish? Whom do you want to serve? How do you plan to accomplish these objectives? How much money do you need? How will you document your results? Think it through; getting absolutely clear on what you want and why you want it is the first and most vital step to obtaining the results you desire.

Research: The purpose of the research process is to target those funding sources that most appropriately fit your specific needs. This may be the most time-consuming (and often the most tedious) part of the funding process. Hang in there. Time spent in careful research is time that will pay off in a greater percentage of successfully funded proposals. There are six factors involved in choosing your potential funding sources:

1. **Field of interest:** Many funding sources only give grants in specific fields. Target those awarding grants in your field.

2. **Geographic limitations:** Many foundations only fund projects within a given locale or region.

3. **Type of support needed:** Determine exactly what kind of assistance your project needs (seed money, equipment, building funds, etc.).

4. **Type of recipient:** Find out who your potential funding source gives to (nonprofit organizations, individuals, schools, hospitals, youth groups, etc.).

5. **Amount requested:** Make sure the amount you requested in your proposal is consistent with the amounts this funder has granted before.

6. **Application process:** Find out how this funder prefers to receive proposals and whether their funding cycle is consistent with your needs.

Write Your Proposal: Stress the benefits your project will provide. Tailor your proposal to the goals and objectives of your funding source. Keep it short and to the point. Include any information that enhances your credibility. Convince them you have the credentials and the experience necessary to successfully complete your project. Make sure to include a carefully thought out, itemized budget. Mention any other sources or donations you've received, and include financial projections for the future of your project or program. For additional information on how to write a proposal, see pages 491–494.

Follow Through: Find out the name of and get background information on the person(s) who make(s) final funding decisions. Call to set up an appointment to discuss your proposal. Come well prepared. First impressions are essential. If your proposal is rejected, find out why and keep in contact. You may want to send another proposal in the next funding cycle. Persist until you succeed. Consider these potential sources of funding: local foundations, statewide and national foundations, government grants, grants to individuals, corporate philanthropic programs.

INCORPORATION CHECKLIST

Chapter	Step	Page	New• Groups	Existing• Groups	Optional••	Step Name	My Group	Done
6	1	6/2	✓	✓		Choose a Corporate Name		
	2	6/12	✓	✓		Prepare Articles of Incorporation		
	3	16/22		✓	✓	Prepare Articles for Unincorporated Association		
	4	6/25	✓	✓	✓	File Articles Early		
	5	6/25	✓	✓		Prepare Bylaws		
7	6	7/2	✓	✓		Prepare State Tax Exemption Application		
8	7	8/2	✓	✓		Consolidate Paperwork		
	8	8/2	✓	✓		Make Copies		
	9	8/3	✓	✓		File State Tax Exemption and Articles		
9	10	9/2	✓	✓		Prepare and File Federal Tax Exemption Application		
10	11	10/2	✓	✓		Mail IRS Letter to Franchise Tax Board		
	12	10/2	✓	✓		Set Up Corporate Records Book		
	13	10/5		✓	✓	Prepare Offer to Transfer Assets		
	14	10/11		✓		Prepare Minutes of First Board Meeting		
	15	10/19	✓	✓		Place Minutes and Attachments in Corporate Records		
	16	10/19		✓	✓	Comply with Bulk Sales Law		
	17	10/20		✓	✓	Prepare Bill of Sale for Assets		
	18	10/23		✓	✓	Prepare Assignments of Leases and Deeds		
	19	10/23		✓	✓	File Final Papers for Prior Organization		
	20	10/23		✓	✓	Notify Creditors of Prior Organization		
	21	10/24	✓	✓	✓	File Fictitious Business Name Statement		
	22	10/24	✓	✓	✓	Apply for Nonprofit Mailing Permit		
	23	10/25	✓	✓	✓	Apply for Property Tax Exemption		
	24	10/25	✓	✓		File Domestic Corporation Statement		
	25	10/27	✓	✓	✓	Register with Attorney General (Public Benefit Corps)		
	26	10/28	✓	✓	✓	Issue Membership Certificates		
	27	10/28		✓	✓	File Articles with County Recorder		
	28	10/29	✓	✓	✓	Register with Fair Political Practices Commission		

• **New** = Groups starting operations as a newly-formed corporation.

• **Existing** = Groups in operation prior to incorporation.

•• **Optional** = 1) optional step may be elected by new or existing groups or

2) step must be followed by some (but not all) new or existing groups to which step applies.

from *The California Nonprofit Corporation Handbook*
Copyright © 1989-1992 by Anthony Mancuso
Published by Nolo Press, Berkeley, CA (415) 549-1976

Three Vital Aspects of Nonprofits

One: *The nonprofit sector is an important part of the U.S. economy.*

The contribution to our well-being of the traditional for-profit sector and the government sector of our economy is obvious. But no less important to the fulfillment of our purpose as a nation is the nonprofit sector, which pays the wages of the eight million people (approximately 10 percent of our workforce) who comfort, feed, house, protect, inform, educate, and uplift each and every one of us at one or more times in our lives. The people involved in the nonprofit sector pay special attention to those who cannot get by without help, for a little while, or for a long time. By expressing compassion in their wise acts, the many people who work in the nonprofit sector demonstrate their knowledge of the fact that what happens to the least of us, happens to the whole of us.

Two: *The nonprofit sector is cause driven.*

The nonprofit sector defines a mission—like helping disaster victims—and boldly asks us to help. And we do. It has been estimated that 92 million Americans give some sort of volunteer service on a regular basis. A nonprofit organization can have a paid staff of two and have 2,500 volunteers working for free, working for the sheer greatness of the cause.

Some of the current activities of people working in the nonprofit sector…

Discovering the truth:

- Researching the causes of cancer
- Studying the distribution of wealth
- Uncovering side effects of industrial processes

Sharing interests:

- Supporting members of a group that have similar concerns or objectives
- Promoting new ideas that benefit a profession
- Forming societies to discuss ideas
- Banding together to create greater strength as a group

Great Careers: The Fourth of July Guide to Careers, Internships and Volunteer Opportunities in the Nonprofit Sector.
Copyright © 1991 by Devon Smith, Published by Garrett Park Press, Garrett Park, Maryland.
Reprinted by permission.

Protecting the earth:

• Controlling pollution
• Guarding the sanctity of wildlands
• Banning nuclear weapons
• Promoting gentle treatment of other creatures
• Teaching appreciation

Uplifting humanity:

• Supporting the arts
• Recognizing the value of other cultures
• Promoting self-determination and grassroots development
• Housing the homeless
• Protecting the abused
• Feeding the hungry
• Establishing peace

The nonprofit sector, being cause driven, provides channels for the caring and creative people of our society. The organizations are specific, targeted, and formed to benefit others. There is a large voluntary dimension to much of the work, and it tends to attract those whose reasons for involvement are value centered. The essential motivation is often kindness toward others and this good will manifests through whatever skill the person has, whether scientific, mathematical, interpersonal, administrative, artistic, or legal. Another name for the nonprofit sector is the philanthropic sector. The nonprofit strives to embody our highest values for the benefit of all, not for financial gain.

Three: *The nonprofit sector is idealistic.*

The nonprofit sector developed through the power of great ideas....
And though the formulations vary from tradition to tradition, all the world's great religions and philosophic traditions hold in common that certain fundamental and inspiring principles underlie the type of activity that is embodied in today's nonprofit sector. One formulation of these principles is shown in the following chart.

Twelve Principles that Motivate
the Creation of Nonprofit Organizations

VISION
Inspired action
based on a vision of the Good.
Self-motivating

HARMONY
Balanced feelings; accord; shared
responsibilities; cooperation.
Cooperating

POWER
Providing resources
the authority to act.
Establishing

PURIFICATION
Seeking out hidden problems to
effect transformation.
Transforming

TRUTH
Knowledge of
the incontrovertible.
Educating

LAW
Principles on which
shared ethics are based.
Leading

LOVE
Fidelity to the
principle of benevolence.
Sharing

FOUNDATION
Forms which support
the function of institutions.
Structuring

WISDOM
Expressing intelligence in life.
Creating

VIRTUE
Evolving life through practical
adherence to ideals.
Refining

COMPASSION
Serving others; providing
for basic life needs.
Serving

SUSTAINMENT
Preservation of the
social, conceptual, and artistic
institutions of society.
Protecting

Nonprofit Foundation Sources

The Art of Asking. Schneiter, Paul. Amber, Pa.: Fund-Raising Institute, 1985.

Beyond Fund Raising: New Strategies for Nonprofit Innovation and Investment. Grace, Kay Sprinkel. New York: John Wiley & Sons, 1997.

The Board Member's Guide to Strategic Planning: A Practical Approach to Strengthening Nonprofit Organizations. Howe, Fisher, and Alan Shrader. San Francisco: Jossey-Bass Publishers, 1997.

The California Nonprofit Corporation Handbook. Mancuso, Anthony, and Barbara Kate Repa. Berkeley: Nolo Press, 1996. Guides you step by step through the process of forming a nonprofit corporation in California.

Catalog of Federal Domestic Assistance. Washington, D.C.: Claitors Publishing Division. Published annually in February.

Changing By Design: A Practical Approach to Leading Innovation in Nonprofit Organizations. Eadie, Douglas E. San Francisco: Jossey-Bass Publishers, 1997.

Corporate Five Hundred: Directory of Corporate Philanthropy. Public Management Institute. San Francisco. Published annually.

Corporate Foundation Profiles. New York: The Foundation Center, 1998.

Critical Issues in Fund Raising. Burlingame, Dwight, F. New York: John Wiley & Sons, 1997.

Cumulative List of Organizations, 2 vols. U.S. Government Staff. Washington, D.C.: Claitors, 1997.

Discretionary Grants Administration Manual. U.S. Department of Health and Human Services, Washington, D.C., 1987. Sets forth applicable administrative policies and procedures to recipients of discretionary federal grants.

Directory of Financial Aids for Women. Schlacter, Gail Ann. Redwood City, Calif.: Reference Service Press. Published biennially. A listing of scholarships, fellowships, loans, grants, awards, and internships designed primarily or exclusively for women.

Directory of New and Emerging Foundations. New York: The Foundation Center. Published annually. Lists and describes over 2,900 recently incorporated independent, community and corporate foundations.

Doing Good Better! Stoesz, Edgar, and Chester Raber. Intercourse, Pa.: Good Books, 1997.

Financial Empowerment: More Money for Mission. Brinckerhoff, Peter C. New York: John Wiley & Sons, 1998.

Financial Planning for Nonprofit Organizations. Blazek, Jody. New York: John Wiley & Sons, 1996.

The Five Most Important Questions You Will Ever Ask about Your Nonprofit: Participant's Workbook. Drucker, Peter. San Francisco: Jossey-Bass Publishers, 1994.

The Foundation Center's Guide to Grant Seeking on the Web. The Foundation Center. New York: The Foundation Center, 1998.

Foundation Fundamentals. New York: The Foundation Center, 1994. Contains a simple four-point strategy for assisting beginning fundraisers in generating national foundation funding.

The Foundation Grants Index. The Foundation Center. New York. Published annually. Offers information on recent grant awards to assist grant seekers in determining foundation's future funding priorities. Includes over 68,000 new grant descriptions.

Foundation Grants to Individuals. Hall, L. Victoria, and Phyllis Edelson, eds. New York: The Foundation Center, 1997. The most comprehensive listing available of private U.S. foundations which provide financial assistance to individuals, containing information on over 3,000 foundations.

Foundation Trusteeship: Service in the Public Interest. Nason, John W. New York: The Foundation Center, 1989. Contains up to date information on the roles and responsibilities of foundation trusteeship, and the mechanics of operating a nonprofit foundation.

Fundraising for Nonprofits. Keegan, P. Burke. New York: HarperCollins, 1994.

Fundraising: Hands-On Tactics for Nonprofit Groups. Edles, Peter L. New York: McGraw-Hill, 1995.

Fundraising on the Internet: Recruiting and Renewing Donors Online. Allen, Nick., Mal Marwick, and Michael Stein, eds. Berkeley: Strathmoor Press, 1997.

Grant Seekers Guide: Foundations that Support Social and Economic Justice. Morris, James McGrath, and Laura Adler, eds. Mt. Kisco, N.Y.: Moyer Bell, Ltd., 1996.

How to Form a Nonprofit Corporation. Mancuso, Anthony. Berkeley: Nolo Press, 1998.

In Search of America's Best Nonprofits. Steckel, Richard, Jennifer Lehman, and Alan Shrader. San Francisco: Jossey-Bass, 1997.

The Jossey-Bass Handbook of Nonprofit Leadership and Management. Herman, Robert D. San Francisco: Jossey-Bass, 1994.

Leadership Skills: Developing Volunteers for Organizational Success. Morrison, Emily Kittle. Tuscon: Fisher Books, 1994.

Loans and Grants from Uncle Sam: Am I Eligible and for How Much? Alexandria, Va.: Octameron Associates. Updated regularly.

Making the News: A Guide for Nonprofits and Activists. Salzman, Jason. Boulder, Colo.: Westview Press, a division of HarperCollins, 1998.

Managing the Nonprofit Organization: Principles and Practices. Peter F. Drucker. New York: HarperBusiness, 1992.

Mapping the Third Sector. Van Til, Jon. New York: The Foundation Center, 1988. Analyzes the role of volunteerism in today's changing social economy.

Marketing for Nonprofit Organizations. Rados, David L. Dover, Mass.: Auburn House Publishing Company, Inc., 1996.

Nonprofits & Education Job Finder. Lauber, Daniel. River Forest, Ill.: Planning Communications, 1997.

Nonprofit Enterprise: Law and Taxation. Phelan, Marilyn E. Deerfield, Ill.: Clark, Boardman and Callaghan, 1990. Contains current cases and rulings, and changes in the nonprofit law and taxation.

The Nonprofit Entrepreneur: Creating Ventures to Earn Income. Skloot, Edward, ed. New York: The Foundation Center, 1988. A guide to entrepreneurial business enterprises and money-making ventures for nonprofit organizations.

The Nonprofit Guide to the Internet. Zeff, Robbin Lee. New York: John Wiley & Sons, 1996.

The Nonprofit Management Handbook: Operating Policies and Procedures. Connors, Tracy Daniel, ed. New York: John Wiley & Sons, 1995.

Nonprofit Organization Operating Manual: Planning for Survival and Growth. Olenick, Arnold J., and Phillip R. Olinick. New York: The Foundation Center, 1991. A primer for people in nonprofit organizations who want to increase their understanding of the administrative skills necessary to successfully operate a nonprofit organization.

Philanthropy and Voluntarism, an Annotated Bibliography. Layton, Daphne Niobe. New York: The Foundation Center, 1987.

Promoting Issues and Ideas: A Guide to Public Relations for Nonprofit Organizations. M. Booth Inc. Associates. New York: The Foundation Center, 1995.

Securing Your Organization's Future: A Complete Guide to Fundraising Strategies. Seltzer, Michael. New York: The Foundation Center, 1987. A handbook and reference work designed for leaders of existing nonprofit organizations.

Starting and Running a Nonprofit Organization. Hummel, Joan M. Minneapolis: University of Minnesota Press, 1996.

Strategic Planning Workbook for Nonprofit Organizations. Barry, Bryan. St. Paul: Amherst H. Wilder Foundation, 1997.

The Taft Foundation Reporter. Washington, D.C.: The Taft Group, 1990.

Update to the Catalog of Federal Domestic Assistance. Office of Management and Budget. Washington, D.C.: U.S. Government Printing Office, 1988. Lists and describes 1,117 federal assistance programs in the areas of agriculture, AIDS, community development, education, environment, health care and services, housing and rural development.

Also check "Taking It for Granted; or, Proposal Writing at a Glance" on pages 491–492 for additional bibliographical entries.

Nonprofit Internet Web Sites

Internet Nonprofit Center   www.nonprofits.org

This is a good first-stop site for those who want to familiarize themselves with what is going on in the nonprofit sector. It claims to have information on more nonprofits than any other site in the world. It features a nonprofit locator, which will help you find any tax-exempt nonprofit in the U.S., as well as the "heliport," which links you to resources of special interest to volunteers and donors. Also check out their library, loaded with valuable information on the nonprofit sector, or the "parlour" where, in addition to volunteer opportunity listings, you can get information on starting your own Web site. The "gallery" offers links to various nonprofit organizations.

Foundation Center Online   http://fdncenter.org

The Foundation Center describes its mission as fostering "public understanding of the foundation field by collecting, organizing, analyzing and disseminating information on foundations, corporate giving, and related subjects." The Foundation Center issues more than sixty informational publications each year. They're some of the best in the field. Check them out on their site. Also find out about trainings and seminars the Center offers. This site has an online library as well as articles from *The Philanthropy News Digest,* the Center's newsletter. The Foundation Center maintains five libraries around the country. The site will tell you where they are and how to use them.

The Grantsmanship Center   www.tgci.com

The Grantsmanship Center offers training around the country in grant-writing and other topics of interest to those who are or who want to become involved in the nonprofit sector. This site has information on their training programs (including schedules and locations around the country), online excerpts from their magazine, nonprofit resources, publications, and more.

Center for Excellence in Nonprofits   www.cen.org

The Center for Excellence in Nonprofits focuses on improving leadership and management in the nonprofit community. Its Web site outlines the management consulting, seminar, and workshop services that the Center offers. Also, find articles, book reviews, and an online edition of *The Connection*, the Center's print newsletter. This site also has excellent links to organizations that deal with management and technical issues that confront nonprofits.

The great use of life is to spend it for something that will outlast it.

William James

Landing the Right Job

God gives every bird its food,
but He doesn't throw it in the nest.
J. G. Holland

This section begins with a brief overview of the job landscape, then focuses specifically on the corporate, government, nonprofit, and small-business sectors. Next, we outline a complete program for conducting an aggressive job search. From identifying your goals, targeting potential employers, and landing and taking job interviews, all the way through salary negotiation—the material that follows will guide you every step of the way. The efforts you put into researching the jobs you really want, into aggressively seeking out potential employers, and into making sure that you really stand out at interview time—all will pay off in the long run. In fact, they could spell the difference between starting each day excited about the work in front of you or dreading that alarm clock because it signals the start of another dreary day of meaningless or monotonous routine.

Why Aren't There More Good Jobs?

In little over a hundred years, we have gone from an agrarian to an urban society. It is hard to believe that as late as the 1880s, most Americans grew their own food, made their own clothes, built their own homes, even made their own soap. Today, few of us do any of these things for ourselves. Beyond this, the number of "necessary" consumer products has exploded. As a result, most of us are, or believe we are, in need of jobs, not only to satisfy our desire to contribute to society but simply to survive.

Have you ever asked yourself: Why aren't there more good jobs? By "good jobs" we mean jobs that challenge, jobs that inspire, jobs that encourage maximum self-development and allow one to make a meaningful contribution. This is not to say that these jobs do not exist (and we encourage those of you seeking jobs to find them). It is simply to ask: Why aren't there more? Below we will briefly consider how work is organized today and see if we can't, perhaps, discover an answer to this question.

Large organizations are a fact of modern life. In the words of famed management consultant Peter Drucker: "Our society has become, within an incredibly short fifty years, a society of institutions. It has become a pluralist society in which every major social task has been entrusted to large organizations—from producing economic goods and services to health care, from social security and welfare to education, from the search for new knowledge to the protection of the natural environment."[1]

The major employers are the corporations, government, and the nonprofit sector. Government (local, state, and federal) directly employs about eighteen million (one in seven in the work force) and another eight million indirectly through federal contracts. Nonprofit corporations employ approximately 11 percent, or one in nine American workers. The largest single employer is, by far, the corporate sector—large, midsize, and small corporations. Roughly one in eight of all working Americans work for a *Fortune* 500 company. Of course, there are a great many large corporations that are not in the exclusive *Fortune* 500 club. While it is true that there has been a steady trend (as we discussed in the entrepreneur section) in recent years toward smaller organizations, the simple fact is that most people who work for someone else work for fairly large organizations.

Corporations are the dominant organizational form today and not simply in business. A host of commentators, including Buckminster Fuller,[2] Richard J. Barnet,[3] and Michael Parenti,[4] have suggested that governments are dominated to a great extent by the large corporations. The large corporations likewise exercise a good deal of control over the nonprofit sector through the awarding of grants, sponsorships, and the sharing of board members. Further, the large corporations exercise influence over small business through their ownership of banks and thrifts. Small business needs money to grow, and since the large corporations control the lion's share of the capital fund, they can greatly influence the visions and values that small businesses are likely to actualize.

In our highly institutionalized and organized society, massive amounts of capital are required to establish and maintain large organizations. Most large nongovernmental organizations are corporations, for the simple reason that this is how they are financed (through the sale of shares of corporate stock) and further, because the existing legal framework favors incorporation. *The larger the organization, the greater the probability that it will be a corporation, because that is how most large (nongovernmental) organizations are structured and financed.*

The most important power that the corporations wield is the power to employ people—to employ, not simply their labor, but their knowledge and intelligence toward ends that the corporations deem worthy. Remember, every existing job reflects visions and values that someone deems worthy of support. The large corporations determine, to a great extent, the visions and values that society reflects through the work they set for millions to do.

Clearly, if we are to understand how work is organized, we must understand something of the role that the large corporations play. For anyone interested in an in-depth consideration of this subject, we recommend *When Corporations Rule the World,* by David C. Korten.[5] Large corporations have certain characteristics that shape their social role: Corporations are profit-driven organizations that limit personal responsibility and tend to consolidate wealth and power.

Profit-Driven: Profits are the primary value of the corporation. They are its discipline, the basis upon which decisions are made. "[Profits are] the immediate, unique, unifying, quantitative aim of corporate success."[6] People invest their money in corporations because they want more money. Corporate game players keep score on the basis of profits alone. All other values are subordinated.

Short-term return on capital investment takes precedence over the well-being of the environment, work force, consumers, or the general public. Corporations are interested in the well-being of their employees to the extent that "a happy worker is a productive worker," one who is likely to produce more profit for the corporation. The worker (white collar or blue) is, first and foremost, a means to profit. Corporations are interested in the well-being of the environment or the general public to the degree that there is profit potential in servicing them. This service may generate profit directly, through the sale of goods and services, or indirectly, through an enhanced public image. Of course, an emphasis on profit applies to all business, from the medieval town fair to the mom-and-pop grocery.

Yet there are certain aspects of corporations that make their profit orientation especially severe in application.

First, corporations have great influence over the other sectors of society (government, nonprofit, small business). To a great extent, the corporations set the agenda for the work that gets done in our society. For example, it is clearly essential for life on this planet that we develop clean, safe, renewable energy. Yet we are told the profit incentive just isn't there. No one doubts, however, that there is plenty of profit in the dirty, dangerous, and nonreplenishable energy we currently rely on. Government is reticent to do anything (e.g., fund research or mandate tough standards) that might interfere with the profits of the large corporations.

Second, corporations are not interested in working in areas without profit potential. For example, while there may be profit in providing nursing-home care (and therefore, corporate involvement), there is not the same interest in providing care for the homeless. Additionally, the quality of care that corporate nursing homes provide is likely to be dictated by profit considerations at every turn. This doesn't necessarily mean the service provided will be shoddy. Nursing homes for the well-to-do are likely to provide excellent service because there is greater profit potential in doing so. The point is simply that the basic question asked is not, "How do we provide the best care?" but, "How do we make the most profit?"

Third, the larger the corporation, the more removed the decision-makers are likely to be from the human implications of their decisions. Small businesses (from mom and pop operations to small corporations) are more likely to include other value considerations when making decisions—they are more likely to view the people they interact with as human beings rather than simply as customers, clients, employees, etc. Small-time operators are more likely to meet and know the people whom their decisions affect, while corporate managers frequently set company policy in a vacuum. They never see, feel, or in any way directly experience the effects their decisions have on customers, employees, the general public, or the environment.

Corporate decision-makers are often insulated and isolated high atop great glass towers, where they make their decisions with a cool eye to the bottom line. The exclusive emphasis on profit performance gives them a kind of tunnel vision. They are focused on how their decisions affect numbers, not people. Indeed, survival in management positions often depends upon having such tunnel vision. Corporate managers are likely to have "their feet held to the fire" for their numbers, not for their humanity.

Limited Responsibility: A corporation is a fictional person without personal responsibility. Indeed, corporations were created to limit personal responsibility. Personal responsibility is limited by law in terms of financial debt and liability and by practice in terms of accountability for values beyond profit making. Again, corporations are not expected to be interested in anything that will not produce profit. A corporate manager who attempts to make decisions on the basis of other considerations is likely to be replaced by one who "knows the value of the bottom line." Today, even managers who base their decisions on profit considerations but are perceived as taking a too long view are likely to be replaced. In this sense, there are no people running corporations. They are run, instead, by the drive to maximize short-term profits.

Monopolistic: In practice, this tends to make the large corporations rather like hungry ghosts which roam the earth devouring natural resources, human labor, knowledge, and culture, and even other corporations in an attempt to satisfy an insatiable appetite for growth. The corporate logic of "eat or be eaten" demands sustained growth. Grow or die is the corporate battle cry. This growth tends to be malignant to life. Large corporations feed on the real wealth of life, labor, and knowledge to produce an abstraction called "economic profit."

This drive for growth tends to consolidate wealth in monopolies controlled by a relative few. Since corporate interests tend to dominate governments, they can, through legal metaphysics such as banking, inheritance, trusts, and holding companies, insure progressively greater consolidation of wealth. In fact, this is the case. Relatively few individuals control a large percentage of the abstract wealth called "capital assets," and through it, the real wealth of knowledge, labor, and resources.

The nature of the large corporations, with their single-minded focus on profits, means that they provide relatively few job opportunities for those interested in exciting challenges in personal growth, creative expression, and direct human service—the kind of jobs readers of this book are likely to be interested in. Of course, there are many exceptions, but the exceptions prove the rule.

Make It Count

"My employer uses twenty-six years of my life for every year I get to keep. And what do I get in return for the enormous thing I am giving? What do I get in return for my *life*?"

Michael Ventura,
L.A. Weekly

Who Is Responsible?

But if you do not have the Tao yourself, what business have you spending your time in vain efforts to bring corrupt politicians into the right path?
Confucius

We cannot discuss, even briefly, the social responsibility of large organizations, especially the corporations, without discussing the social responsibility of the individual. It is the individual's responsibility to choose work that expresses the values he considers most worthy of being supported by his time and energy. Those who offer money for work and those who offer their talents, skills, and energy for hire share responsibility for the world they create. The argument that the corporation must be socially irresponsible to make a profit is no more or less spurious than the argument that the individual must join an organization whose goals he does not believe in, simply to survive.

Organizations can (and many do) profit quite nicely by doing socially useful things. Many organizations profiting from less noble pursuits could redirect their efforts toward more socially valuable efforts if they had the will to do so. Similarly, many individuals work within organizations whose purposes they genuinely agree with and deem useful and as contributing to the greater good. Many individuals who do not could do so if they had the will to continue their search until they found such organizations.

The large organizations that control the capital fund have a responsibility for the use of the natural resources, human knowledge, and labor that it represents. (Again, enormous capital assets do not just fall from the sky; they represent an accumulation of the labor, knowledge, skill, and intelligence of thousands of individuals, not to mention the beneficence of the planet, its living and mineral resources.) Each of us is, likewise, responsible for how we use our talent, knowledge, skill, intelligence, labor, time, and energy.

Take, for example, the knowledge you possess. Knowledge is, as Francis Bacon said, power. Today, that power is truly enormous. Consider the power that practitioners of physics, chemistry, genetics, and engineering wield today. Yet all one has to do to gain initiation into these powerful knowledges is to go to any university in the land. No attempt will be made to measure one's wisdom or character before he is initiated into these fantastic powers. He will not even be admonished that the power he controls (through his knowledge) is extraordinary and should be used with great care. He need only be clever and have money for school.

Many times a day I realize how much my own outer and inner life is built upon the labors of my fellow men, both living and dead, and how earnestly I must exert myself in order to give in return as much as I have received.
Albert Einstein

Knowledge, which is an accumulation of centuries of human endeavor, is taken by him to be his personal property. Since he believes that he owns this knowledge, he deems it his right to sell it to the highest bidder, regardless of the purpose the bidder has in mind. Then, he takes the cloak of scientific respectability as his defense and says, "Well, I'm just 'doing science.' (Or, I just work here.) It is not my responsibility how my work will be used." Of course, there are exceptions, but this kind of attitude is rampant, not only in science, but in many of the professions.

When you go to a university and learn physics or genetics, chemistry or computer science, engineering or architecture, or any science or art, for that matter, what you learn represents thousands of years of intellectual accumulation and millions of years of human evolution. The notion that each of us ought to do with this planetary accumulation whatever he or she pleases, without a sense of social responsibility or obligation, is a prescription for global disaster. A society of hired guns, selling off planetary accumulation for personal profit, without consideration of the use to which that accumulation is put, can only turn our beautiful blue planet into a nightmare world.

I understood . . . that those who desired salvation should act like the trustee who, though having control over great possessions, regards not an iota of them as his own.

Gandhi

Of course, everything we have said with respect to responsibility for how you use your knowledge applies equally to your talents, skill, time, and energy. When you join your efforts to any organization, consider how this organization is likely to use your assets. Your sense of obligation to the past and responsibility for the future will naturally move you toward an organization whose purpose is a humane one.

Working the Corporate Scene

What we have said above should not be taken as a wholesale indictment of corporations or of corporate employment. It is, rather, our intent to indicate structural dynamics of corporations, which tend to limit their capacity to provide fulfilling life work.

Still, there are thousands of worthwhile jobs within the corporate sector. Those interested in jobs in this sector are encouraged to take advantage of the resources below. You should be able to find most of these in your public library or college or university career center. You will find additional sources on pages 444–446.

Corporate Sector Sources

The 100 Best Companies for Gay Men and Lesbians. Mickens, Ed. New York: Pocket Books, 1994.

The 100 Best Companies to Work for in America. Levering, Robert, and Milton Moskowitz. New York: Plume, 1994.

The 150 Best Companies for Liberal Arts Graduates: Where to Get a Winning Job in Tough Times. Woodruff, Cheryl. New York: John Wiley & Sons, 1992.

A Great Place to Work: What Makes Some Employers So Good (And Most So Bad). Levering, Robert. New York: Avon Books, 1990.

Adams Job Almanac. The editors of Adams Media Corp. Holbrook, Mass.: Adams Media Corp. Published annually.

Hoover's Top 2,500 Employers. Hoover's Inc. Austin, Tex.: Hoover's Business Press, 1996.

The Job Vault. Harnadeh, Sarner, and Mark Oldman. Boston: Houghton Mifflin Co., 1997.

The World Almanac Job Finder's Guide. Krantz, Les. New York: St. Martin's Press. Published annually.

Working for the "Gov."

When you think of government jobs, you probably think of postal clerks or bureaucratic office workers. Fortunately, these are not the only jobs available within the government sector. Government jobs vary as much as those in the private sector—ranging from baker to typist, nurse to zoologist, accountant to physical therapist, radio operator to community planner, lawyer to economist. There are more than nine hundred job classifications within the federal government, and many more at state, county, and city levels. At this writing, nearly half of all U.S. government workers are employed by the Department of Defense. The rest work in a wide range of other capacities.

Whatever your field of interest, opportunities exist to serve the public good by working within the government. Those interested in public action may want to explore programs within the Departments of: Housing and Urban Development, Labor, Education, or Health and Human Services. If you are interested in environmental issues, you may want to consider programs within the Department of the Interior or the Environmental Protection Agency. Those interested in civil rights might consider the Justice Department; in international relations, the State Department. State and local governments often develop innovative programs designed to address specific needs. For example, the state of California developed a statewide program to enhance the self-esteem of school children. Washington state developed an innovative program to assist welfare recipients in starting their own small businesses.

Each year, the federal government hires over three hundred thousand new employees. Only 14 percent of these work in the Washington, D.C. area. Behind these statistics lie a lot of boring, and a few really great, jobs. (A great service opportunity for someone would be to select out those better jobs and make them known through a newsletter or similar type of service.) You will probably have to sift through a lot of chaff to find the wheat. Keep your ear to the ground; read newspapers and listen to radio and television to find out about interesting programs, and then pursue them. There are a number of excellent resources that can assist you in finding out about good government jobs. Some of these appear below.

Applying for Federal Jobs: You can obtain general information about federal job openings by contacting the Federal Job Information Center in your area. To find the one nearest you, look in the federal government listings of your phone book under the Office of Personnel Management. For most positions, you will need to take a written exam; for others, you can rely upon your experience and training. The application form for federal jobs is the Standard Form 171. This four-page form serves the same purpose that a résumé does in the private sector. It provides the hiring agency with your qualifications, experience, references, etc. Fill it out carefully, and tailor each application to the particular job you are applying for. Long application procedures and mumbo jumbo jargon take patience to wade through—so get out your hip boots.

The Federal Vacancy Announcement: If you're interested in a specific job, try to get hold of its Federal Vacancy Announcement prior to filling out your Standard Form 171. It provides you with a thorough description of the vacancy: its title, job requirements, salary, growth potential, geographic location, description of duties, and posting and closing dates. Take note of the "Quality Ranking Factors" section. It describes the specific skills, knowledge, and abilities you will need for the position, stating the criteria that will be used in scoring your application.

Your local employment office has a Federal Job Opportunity Listing (FJOL), which is a computerized listing of current federal job openings. You can also contact the hiring agency directly. Visit the local offices of agencies you are interested in working for.

There you will find posted official Federal Vacancy Announcements. Take note of the staffing specialist (contact person) listed on the announcement—this is the only person authorized to give you specific information about the position.

Additional Sources of Federal Job Listings: Your local library is an additional source of job information. Look for the *Federal Jobs Digest* (310 N. Highland Avenue, Ossining, NY 10562). The Federal Research Service in Virginia publishes *Federal Career Opportunities,* a magazine that lists current jobs available with the federal government. If your library doesn't carry it, you can write to Federal Research Service Inc., 243 Church St. NW, Vienna, VA 22180. Libraries also have other nongovernmental newsletters that have federal job vacancy listings. Ask your reference librarian for assistance. Many high-paying professional jobs in government are listed in the business section of your local newspaper (especially the Sunday edition).

If you are a student within nine months of graduation from college, a recent college graduate, or seeking an entry-level job, contact the Administrative Career with America program. They fill jobs in over a hundred fields. For more information, call the Career America College Hotline at 1-900-990-9200 or contact your local Federal Job Information Center.

City, State, and County Employment Opportunities: Your local employment office has information about government jobs at the city, county, and state levels. Some states have state job information telephone numbers, which are similar to the Federal Job Information Centers in the service they provide, except of course, they list state jobs. Most states have Career Information Delivery Systems (CIDS)—computerized job information systems available at libraries, job training sites, employment service centers, colleges, and universities. You can also contact your local city or county personnel office directly.

Government Jobs Sources

America's Federal Jobs: A Complete Directory of Federal Career Opportunities. Rutsohn, Rita, ed. Indianapolis: Jist Works, 1991.

Careers In Government. Pitz, Mary Elizabeth. Lincolnwood, Ill.: VGM Career Horizons, 1994.

The Complete Guide to Public Employment. Krannich, Ronald L., and Caryl Rae Krannich. Manassas, Va.: Impact Publications, 1995.

The Directory of Federal Jobs and Employers. Krannich, Ronald L., and Caryl Rae Krannich. Manassas, Va.: Impact Publications, 1996.

Federal Career Opportunities. Federal Research Service, Inc. Vienna, Va.: Federal Research Service, Inc. Updated regularly.

Federal Résumé Guidebook. Troutman, Katherine K. Indianapolis: Jist Works, Inc., 1997.

Federal Yellow Book. Washington, D.C.: Leadership Directories, Inc. Published quarterly.

Finding a Federal Job: How to Cut the Red Tape and Get Hired. Krannich, Ronald L., and Caryl Rae Krannich. Woodbridge, Va.: Impact Publications, 1995.

Government Job Finder. Lauber, Daniel. River Forest, Ill.: Planning Communications, 1997.

Real People Working In the Government. Camenson, Blythe. Lincolnwood, Ill.: VGM Career Horizons, 1998.

Working in the Nonprofit Sector

If teamwork, challenge, and a service motivation interest you, the nonprofit sector is likely to offer excellent employment opportunities. If you are interested in starting your own nonprofit organization, you will find working for a nonprofit already established in your field to be an invaluable source of experience.

Commitment to Service: Generally, work in the nonprofit sector provides an opportunity for service to others. People enjoy the opportunity to work with colleagues who share a similar commitment and vision. Motive counts in the nonprofit sector. Most employees enjoy the sense of purpose, commitment, and integrity that comes from believing in what they're doing. Many people who work in the nonprofit sector start out as volunteers and end up filling paid positions.

Comraderie: Nonprofits generally offer a less competitive and more harmonious work environment than corporations. Many nonprofits operate on a consensus basis and value each individual's input in decision-making. While building consensus takes considerably more time, people tend to be more committed to successfully implementing resulting decisions.

Freedom to Initiate: Individuals who succeed in the nonprofit sector are generally self-motivated and desire the freedom and flexibility to design programs and solutions to problems as they see fit. They often enjoy greater autonomy and challenge than in similar business or government jobs.

Organizational Structure: Nonprofits tend to be somewhat looser in structure than business or government organizations. The average nonprofit is a smaller organization with a more varied workload. For this reason, many nonprofits can be flexible in responding quickly to changes and developments in their field. Nonprofits can often be quickly and effectively organized to deal with local or short-term issues.

Stress Level in Work: Nonprofit workers experience a different type of stress than their counterparts in business or government. There is less high-pressure stress than in the corporate world, but there may be more immediate contact with human suffering. This can take an emotional toll. Further, many nonprofits, for example, in the arts, continually face funding crises and the associated stress.

Earnings and Benefits: Although pay in the nonprofit sector is usually lower than in business, the gap has been steadily closing. A good nonprofit manager can expect to earn almost as much as his corporate counterpart. In addition, nonprofit workers usually enjoy greater flexibility in hours. Medical coverage, working conditions, and fringe benefits vary greatly from organization to organization.

Note: Do careful research on each organization you are considering. If possible, talk to the people who work there. We recommend that you check out the source books listed on the next page.

Of all the infirmities we have, the most savage is to despise our being.

Montaigne

Nonprofit Sector Job Sources

100 Best Nonprofits to Work For: Find Your Dream Job—And Launch a Rewarding Career Doing Good! Hamilton, Leslie, and Robert Tragent. New York: Macmillan Reference USA, 1998.

Careers for Dreamers and Doers: A Guide to Management Careers in the Nonprofit Sector. Cohen, Lilly, and Dennis Young. New York: The Foundation Center, 1989.

Good Works: A Guide to Careers in Social Change. Colvin, Donna, and Ralph Nader. New York: Barracade Books, Inc., 1994.

Magazines

Community Jobs
Networking in the Public Interest
1001 Connecticut Ave., NW
Washington, DC 20036

Foundation News and Commentary
Council on Foundations, Inc.
1828 L St. NW Ste. 300
Washington, DC 20036-5104
www.cof.org

Nonprofit World
Society for Nonprofit Organizations
6314 Odana Rd., Ste. 1
Madison, WI 53719-1141
www.cpn.org/sections/
affiliates/society_
nonprofitorgs.html

Working for Small Business

The small-business sector is the fastest growing segment of the American economy. By the year 2000, 85 percent of the U.S. labor force will be working for firms employing fewer than 200 people.[7] Over 600 thousand new businesses are created each year in the United States. This booming sector offers many exciting job opportunities, especially for aggressive, self-motivated individuals.

The small-business sector (as we define it) includes organizations with annual sales of under ten million dollars. Typically, small businesses are less structured than larger firms, with more creative work environments that offer greater opportunities to learn new skills and take on new responsibilities. Small businesses are often looking for dedicated people who are willing to go above and beyond the call of duty. Start-up businesses are often run by individuals with a kind of missionary zeal for their enterprises. While they often expect more of their employees (e.g., greater loyalty, longer hours, fewer benefits and vacations), entrepreneurs offer greater opportunities to become involved in the equity side of the business—to own a piece of the action. Additionally, if you become involved in a rapidly growing business and show real leadership ability, you may have unique opportunities for rapid advancement. Finally, small businesses often provide opportunities for deeper personal relationships than larger firms—a chance to feel like you are part of a team or even a family. To find small businesses in your area that you might like to work for, check your local telephone directory or visit your local Chamber of Commerce.

 Hold yourself responsible for a higher standard than anyone else expects of you. Never excuse yourself.   Henry Ward Beecher

The Secrets to Finding the Right Organization

Famed management consultant and writer Peter Drucker has discussed motivation in work, noting changes in today's workers from previous generations. He has concluded that the stick (fear) no longer motivates, except in rare instances. Neither does the carrot (material rewards)—not, at least, with any degree of consistency. This, Drucker explains, is for the simple reason that the more we get, the more we want. He suggests that embracing responsibility for the organization and its contribution to the larger society is the best long-term motivator. (See *Management: Tasks, Responsibilities, Practices,* by Peter Drucker, New York: HarperBusiness, 1993.)

Choose an Organization You Can Take Responsibility For: Here, then, is a key to continued motivation in the workplace, but also, and more importantly, a key to selecting the organizations you choose to work for. It is imperative that you select an organization for which you can actively and wholeheartedly take responsibility. Any other choice will, eventually, lead to motivational problems and their attendant side effects: apathy, depression, poor performance, and the like. *Remember, only if you can take full responsibility for the organization you are working for and for its contribution can you do your best work.* You must agree with and support the organization's purpose.

Look for Agreement and Commitment: In addition to choosing an organization for which you can take responsibility, look for an organization that has strong agreement among its members as to purpose. This will help ensure that the work environment will be productive and harmonious. In "Act II," we discussed the axiom: *Peripherals move in to fill the void left by lack of purpose.* Peripherals in the work environment can take the shape of pointless bickering, useless rivalries, distracting preoccupations, routine redundancies, or endless delays. They drain you emotionally and leave little energy for the important work. People who have only worked in this type of work environment come to believe that all work is draining and exhausting. In fact, purposeful work replenishes and renews; it gives as much energy as it takes. It is working on peripherals that is exhausting, and all the more so, because one recognizes that they are such a waste. Choose, then, an organization you can take responsibility for and one with an energetic *esprit de corps.*

 There are three essentials to leadership: humility, clarity and courage.

Fuchan Yuan

Aggressive Job-Search Strategies

The competitive demands of the marketplace and the desire to realize your own best work require that you take an aggressive approach to the job-hunting process. Whether you choose to work for a large or small business, in government or the nonprofit sector, the dynamics of an aggressive job search are essentially the same. The first step is to specify exactly what you want from a potential employer. Next, thoroughly research organizations in your field and determine the ones you most want to work for. Make contact with these organizations and set up interviews. (We will show you a number of ways to do this.) Then prepare for and take the interviews and, when all goes well, negotiate salary and other considerations. Before we get into more detail, we will briefly contrast aggressive job-search strategies with more conventional approaches.

The Hit-and-Miss Approach: The hit-and-miss approach is the most common job-search strategy. It involves responding to newspaper ads and going to private employment agencies and state employment offices. (See page 458.)

Attitude: Passive selection. "I'll leave it to employers to tell me what positions they have available and hope they offer one that matches what I want to do."

Weakness: Limited selection (only 20 percent of all jobs are advertised) and lack of control in the selection (many of the best jobs are never advertised).

The Broadcast Approach: This approach involves sending a barrage of résumés or applications to as many potential employers as possible in the hope of eliciting a few requests for interviews.

Attitude: Send and wait. "I will barrage employers with hundreds of résumés and hope that a few will want me and that those who do can give me a match with what I want to do."

Weakness: You are depending on a piece of paper, a résumé, to find you a job. This is a mistake for two reasons: (1) No résumé can represent you as well as you can. (People hire people, not paper qualifications.) (2) The personnel departments of large organizations are inundated with résumés. Yours simply becomes one more in the stack. In a small organization without a personnel department, the individual you are soliciting is most likely swamped with routine paperwork. Expecting him to even read your résumé (let alone respond to it) may be asking too much, especially if the position you are seeking has not been advertised. You are expecting too much of others and too little of yourself.

The Laser-Focused Approach: This approach involves determining in advance the organizations you would like to work for and arranging, through a variety of means, to set up interviews.

Attitude: Take charge of the process from beginning to end. "I will select the organizations I want to work for and will creatively and consistently go after them until I get the position I want."

Weaknesses: Only the limits of your creativity, effort, and persistence.

The Laser-Focused Job Search

We will concentrate on the laser-focused approach. We assume you already know how the others work and that you see advantages to a more aggressive approach. Aggressiveness is critical in two key areas: in researching organizations and in approaching them. You've had the courage to think differently, to plan your career on the basis of your vision, values, ideals, and talents. Now, make it pay off by employing aggressive job search strategies to land the job you really want. It will take planning, research, and effort. It will take undaunted persistence and courage. A winning attitude is a must.

P. T. Barnum said that a sucker is born every minute. Suckers get beat in the job market game. Suckers focus on their weaknesses rather than concentrating on the value of what they have to give. You're no sucker if you know you have the power to win. Power *is* a matter of perception. It is important that you perceive yourself as powerful. If you think you have no power in looking for a job, you'll get clobbered, knocked over by a lob (of rejection). On the other hand, if you take command of the process, you'll be the one hitting the grand slams. Raise your aspirations, up your expectations, and you'll get more of what you want. You'll never get more by settling for less.

Recognize that the process of landing a job is a negotiation and that the first person you're negotiating with is yourself. If you lose this negotiation and settle for less than what you really want, you're beaten before you've even started. Be in your own corner and commit yourself to aggressively going after what you want.

"Aggressive Job-Search Strategies" in a Nutshell

Step 1: Decide: Identify what you want from an organization.

Step 2: Research: Know your market. Research organizations.

Step 3: Select: Target the organizations you want to work for. Identify the exact position you want and the person with the power to hire you.

Step 4: Solicit: Get your foot in the door—set up interviews.

Step 5: Prepare: Prepare for interviews.

Step 6: Communicate: Conduct successful interviews.

Step 7: Celebrate: Get the job you want.

Getting into the Right Position

1. Throughout all your efforts, take the attitude that you are self-employed. You are hiring yourself an employer.

2. Be selective. Be selective. Be selective. Target. Target. Target. There is nothing more frustrating or demeaning than working your tail off to get a job you don't really want.

3. Master self-marketing and job-hunting skills to give yourself more freedom. Many people report staying in jobs they can't stand, simply because they dread the "hunting" process so much.

4. If the freedom argument doesn't get you, the security one will. On the average, people change companies or positions within companies every two and a half years. The old notion of a secure job is increasingly a thing of the past. To keep pace, you must learn to sell yourself.

5. Networking is key. The more people you know, the more ways you have to go, the more room you have to grow. This applies after you get your next position, as well as before.

6. You are seeking membership in an organization—of people. Play with paper as required (résumés, cover letters, applications, etc.), but remember, people ask *people* to join their organizations.

7. Remember—in all forms of marketing, nothing succeeds like the appearance of success.

8. Project a strong personality. Confidence counts.

Step One–Decide: Identify What You Want from an Organization

Take creative control of the job-hunting process. Begin by establishing criteria for potential employers. First, they have to pass your test; later, you will have to pass theirs.

What type of organization do you want? e.g., government agency, nonprofit, small-business, etc. _____

The Big Picture

What kind of values or philosophy must this organization reflect? _____
_____

What goals or objectives must this organization have? _____
_____

What kind of people do you want to work with? _____
_____

What level of responsibility do you seek within this organization?
_____
_____

How much do you want to earn working for this organization?
_____
_____

The Details

Assuming that two or more organizations offer similar opportunities to satisfy your big-picture work goals, which of these additional factors are most important to you?

1. Schedule flexibility _____	8. Opportunities for advancement _____	
2. Creative environment _____		
3. Attractive work setting _____	9. Prestige _____	
4. Job security _____	10. Day-care facilities _____	
5. Convenience from your home _____	11. Opportunities for additional training _____	
6. Health and dental _____		
7. Pensions _____	12. Other_____ _____	

Establish Criteria for Your Employer

In the space below, prioritize your employment needs using the following three criteria. An example appears at the bottom of the page.

1. Bottom-line needs: These conditions must be met by an employer before you give them any consideration. They are non-negotiable.

2. Priority needs: These are important (more important at the top of the list, less important as you descend) but not absolutely essential.

3. Extras: These are benefits that exceed your bottom line and priority needs.

Bottom-line Needs	Priority Needs	Extras
1.	1.	1.
2.	2.	2.
3.	3.	3.
4.	4.	4.
5.	5.	5.
6.	6.	6.
7.	7.	7.
8.	8.	8.
9.	9.	9.
10.	10.	10.
11.	11.	11.
12.	12.	12.

Bottom-line Needs	Priority Needs	Extras
1. Common purpose	1. Health and dental insurance	1. Convenient location
2. Harmonious relationships	2. Pension plan	2. Attractive environment
3. Advancement opportunities	3. Profit-sharing	3. Travel opportunities
4. Career development opps.	4. Flexible hours	4. Bonuses
5. Income $55,000–$60,000	5. Day care	5. Company car

Step Two–Research Organizations: Know Your Market

Once you have identified what you're looking for in an organization, the next step is to research existing organizations and find those best suited to you. In many ways, this is the most important part of the job-hunting process. The more information you have, the more options you have and the better the choices you can make. You wouldn't think of opening a business without conducting market research, and you ought not think of taking a job without conducting a thorough search for the right organization. Below is a list of sources to help you identify organizations that meet the criteria you outlined in the previous step. Keep track of what you learn. Take notes and organize the information on three-by-five cards. You can review these cards before taking interviews. Also, refer to sources listed on pages 434, 436, and 438.

Name of Organization:		
Address		
City	State	Zip
Telephone Number		
Comments:		

Research Organizations Sources

Career Employment Opportunities Directory: A Guide to Career Employment Opportunities, Volume 1: Liberal Arts and Social Sciences, Volume 2: Business Administration, Volume 3: Engineering and Computer Science, Volume 4: Sciences. Renetzky, Alvin, ed. Santa Monica, Calif.: Ready Reference Press, 1985.

Career Guide to Professional Associations: A Directory of Organizations by Occupational Field, Second Edition. Staff of Carroll Press. Cranston, R.I.: Carroll Press, 1980.

Community Jobs: The National Employment Newspaper for the Non-profit Sector. A monthly publication providing a monthly listing of socially responsible jobs and internships. Available from Networking in the Public Interest, 1001 Connecticut Ave., NW, Washington, DC 20036. (212) 785-4233.

Company Information: A Model Investigation. Washington, D.C.: Washington Researchers Publications, 1983.

Directories in Print. Desjardins, Dawn Conzett. Detroit: Gale Research Co. Published annually in January.

The Directory of Business Information Resources: Associations, Newsletters, Magazines, Trade Shows, Directories, Databases. MacKenzie, Leslie. Lakeville, Conn.: Grey House Publishing, 1998.

Encyclopedia of Business Information Sources. Woy, James. Detroit: Gale Research, Co. Published biennially in November.

The Foundation Directory. Tuller, Michael, ed. New York: The Foundation Center. Published biennially in March.

Guide to Careers in World Affairs. Foreign Policy Association, ed. Manassas, Va.: Impact Publications, 1993.

How to Find Information about Private Companies. Washington Researchers Publishing. Washington, D.C.: Washington Researchers Publications. Published annually in March.

Information U.S.A. Lesko, Matthew, and Sharon Zarozny. New York: Penguin USA, 1986.

International Employment Hotline. A monthly survey of the international job market, listing international job openings available to U.S. citizens. Published by Direct Communications, 24 Wales Street, PO Box 6628, Rutland, VT 05702-6628. (802) 747-3376. E-mail: info@direct-com.com.

Jobs '98. Petras, Kathryn, and Ross Petras. New York: Fireside, 1996.

National Trade and Professional Associations of the United States. Downs, Buck, R., Wilson Hardy, and Nathan L. Cantor, eds. Washington, D.C.: Columbia Books, Inc. Published annually in March.

Peterson's Job Opportunities for Engineering and Computer Science Majors. Peterson's Guides. Princeton: Peterson's Guides. Published annually in August.

Places Rated Almanac. Savageau, David, and Geoffrey Loftus. New York: Macmillan, 1997.

The future belongs to those who believe in the beauty of their dreams.
Eleanor Roosevelt

The Service Edge: 101 Companies that Profit from Customer Care. Zemke, Ron. New York: New American Library, 1990.

Taft Foundation Reporter. Yvette, Henry, ed. Washington, D.C.: The Taft Group, 1990.

Business Reference Works

1. *Annual Reports of Corporations.* Ask your reference librarian for access to these reports. You may find more complete information in a business library than a regular public library. All the business and finance libraries in the United States are listed in: *Subject Directory of Special Libraries and Information Centers, Vol. I, Business and Law Libraries.* Labash-Young, Margaret, et al., eds. Detroit: Gale Research Co. Published annually in November.

2. *Dun & Bradstreet Million Dollar Directory.* New York: Dun & Bradstreet. Published annually in February/March.

3. *MacRae's Blue Book.* Deydo, Harry P., ed. New York. Published annually in March/April.

4. *Moody's Manuals.* New York: Moody's Investor's Service, Inc. Published annually.

5. *Poor's Register of Corporations, Directories and Executives.* New York: Standard and Poor's, Subsidiary of McGraw-Hill. Published annually in January.

6. *Thomas Register of American Manufacturers.* New York: Thomas Publishing Company. Published annually.

7. *Ward's Directory.* Detroit: Gale Research Co. Published annually.

Individuals and Organizations

1. Current employees (best source, take these folks to lunch)
2. Former employees
3. Competitors
4. Clients
5. Community leaders
6. Suppliers
7. Chamber of Commerce
8. Better Business Bureau
9. Professional associations in the field
10. University professors in the field

Company Information Online

Annual Reports: Many companies post their annual reports on the Internet. Go to the home pages of the companies you are interested in working for and click "investor relations" or use search engines such as **Investor Relations Information Network:** www.irin.com

10-K Filings: You can also use the Internet to search for companies' 10-K filings with the SEC. Especially note the "Competition" and "Outlook" sections. These will give you insights into companies' vulnerable areas, stress points, and growth opportunities. A review of this material will help you better understand the companies you are investigating and provide important information you can use later in your job interviews. To search for 10-K filings, visit **InvestQuest:** www.investquest.com

Step Three–Select the Organizations You Want to Work for and the Position(s) You Want

Based upon your initial research, list the organizations you are most interested in working for.

1. Organization: _____
   Position: _____

2. Organization: _____
   Position: _____

3. Organization: _____
   Position: _____

4. Organization: _____
   Position: _____

5. Organization: _____
   Position: _____

6. Organization: _____
   Position: _____

7. Organization: _____
   Position: _____

8. Organization: _____
   Position: _____

9. Organization: _____
   Position: _____

10. Organization: _____
    Position: _____

 There is nothing which persevering effort and unceasing and diligent care can not accomplish.   Seneca

Create a Job Where There Is None

When looking for a job, you are not limited to existing positions. You can help an employer create a position for you. The following are a few of the common situations that provide opportunities for creating jobs:

1. **They are aware of the need but haven't filled it.** They know that they need help, but they haven't gotten around to advertising a position. You remind them of the obvious need and demonstrate how you are the person best qualified to fill it.

2. **They're not aware of the need.** You make them aware. They're having chronic problems in a specific area where you have expertise. They don't understand the problem, either because they lack the expertise or because they are too busy focusing on other things. You identify the problem, point out how much it's costing them, and indicate how you can help solve it. On the other hand, you might show them how they are missing opportunities to grow or expand into new areas or markets. You demonstrate how hiring you will help them take advantage of these opportunities.

3. **Consolidate and streamline what they have.** They may be currently paying several people to do the work that you, because of your special talents and abilities, could do more efficiently on your own (or with a smaller team). You demonstrate how, by reorganizing and hiring you, they will be more effective in achieving their goals.

4. **Start at another position and gradually assume the responsibilities of the position you want.** You create the new position *after* you make it into the organization. This takes patience and a clear idea of your ultimate goal.

Below, indicate organizations for which one of these job-creating strategies might be appropriate and how you can convince the employer to give you a job.

Organization	Position to Create	Strategy of Approach
_____	_____	_____
_____	_____	_____
_____	_____	_____
_____	_____	_____
_____	_____	_____

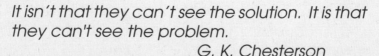

It isn't that they can't see the solution. It is that they can't see the problem.

G. K. Chesterson

Step Four–Solicit: Get Your Foot in the Door

In business, there is an old saying: Nothing happens until you've made the sale. In looking for a job, nothing happens until you "get your foot in the door," that is, until you get an interview. This section is about how to get interviews with the people who can help make your dreams come true.

The Mechanics

Before we get into strategies you can use to get your foot in the door, let's consider a few mechanics that will facilitate getting the most from your efforts.

1. **Set a schedule.** If you're out of a job and looking for work full time, then do it full time. That doesn't mean send out 800 résumés every month. It means try to schedule two interviews a day, four days a week, perhaps, Tuesday through Friday. Take Mondays (and Saturdays if necessary) for research and preparation.

   If you are currently employed, set a regular schedule and follow it. Perhaps you can take one day a month off for interviews or arrange to take a number of interviews during your vacation. If you have a flexible job schedule, you may be able to get away for a couple of hours; if not, arrange interviews for early mornings or after regular office hours. Whatever type of arrangement works best for you, create a schedule and stick to it until you get what you want.

2. **Establish a base of operation, a regular workplace.** Here, you can be set up with a desk or table and a telephone. Have all relevant reading material handy, as well as your appointment book, calendar, and perhaps a copy of this book. Make sure this is a place where you can work in an uninterrupted and undistracted way. From here, you can also write thank-you notes to people who give you leads and help, and thank-you letters to those with whom you have had interviews.

3. **Enlist the support of your family.** Unemployed people frequently spend a lot of their time answering phones, running errands, babysitting, and the like. Tell your family that you are looking for a job on a full-time basis and that you will need their cooperation in allowing you to work uninterrupted during this time. Get someone to answer the phone for you and take messages when you are not in. You might get a family member to type résumés, letters, and proposals for you.

4. **Assemble letters of recommendation, personal and professional references.** Develop and have on hand copies of letters of recommendation and personal and professional references.

Strategies for Soliciting Employers

Choose the strategies for "getting your foot in the door" that are best suited to your personality and career objectives. We will consider each of these methods in greater depth in the pages following.

Strategy 1: **Résumé/Follow-Up Call.** This is a solid method. You send out your résumé and cover letter and then follow up with a phone call to set up an interview. You could try calling cold (without sending a résumé or coming by referral), but this is tough—not recommended unless you have strong sales skills.

Strategy 2: **Working Your Network.** This increasingly popular method utilizes your personal and professional contacts to help you set up interviews with potential employers who might otherwise be difficult to get to. Highly recommended.

Strategy 3: **Direct Mail.** In this method, you contact by mail the people who have the power to hire you at the organizations you want to work for. Write each a personal letter, follow up with a phone call, and arrange to meet in person. A good method that is often overlooked.

Strategy 4: **Parlay Your Way.** This is the practice of taking advantage of employment opportunities that result from informational interviews, volunteer work, internships, and the like.

Strategy 5: **Walk-Ins.** Not for the faint hearted. This method involves walking in off the street, making your way to the person who has the power to hire you, and setting up an interview on the spot.

Strategy 6: **Executive Search Firms** ("Headhunters"). These firms specialize in locating executives for client companies.

Strategy 7: **Unconventional Approaches.** These involve putting yourself right in the middle of the action and making it pay off for you.

Strategy 8: **Traditional Approaches.** These include answering newspaper want ads and utilizing private and state employment agencies.

 It's the constant and determined effort that breaks down all resistance, sweeps away all obstacles.

Claude M. Bristol

Strategy 1:
Résumé/Follow-Up Call

The Résumé

Résumés are not all they're cracked up to be. They're certainly not worth getting anxious over. There are about as many different approaches to this subject as there are experts on it. Some say, "Forget about résumés." Others would call that blasphemy. Your purpose in sending out résumés is to get interviews. This seldom happens without a follow-up call. While it's true that nobody gets hired because of a terrific résumé, a good résumé can help you get an interview, and interviews get you hired.

There are basically two kinds of résumés. Other variations exist, but we will limit our discussion to these two. (Those seeking more detailed information can consult one of the many fine books on résumés listed in the bibliography.) The first and most traditional is the chronological résumé. The second is the functional résumé. A chronological résumé usually works best when you want to continue working in the same field. A functional résumé is often the best choice for the career changer, the first-time job-seeker, and those who have been long absent from the workplace. The difference comes into play in the way you demonstrate how your experience qualifies you for the position you are seeking. (See point 3 below.) Whether you write a chronological or a functional résumé, it should include the following, and usually in this order:

A "Formula" for a Two-Page Résumé

1. Personal information: Be sure to include name, address, and phone number. Beyond this, everything is optional. Health information and military record are examples of things you might include.

2. Education: Start with your most advanced degrees. If you have post-graduate

degrees, list those and then your undergraduate college work. If you graduated from a university, you don't need to put down your high school. Include non-degree educational training pertinent to the position you are seeking.

3. Work experience or accomplishments: This will vary according to whether you are using a chronological or a functional résumé.

Chronological: Put your most recent work experience at the bottom of the first page. Go into what you did quite extensively—your position, responsibilities, salary, and accomplishments. Be sure to include the name and address of your employer and the name and number of your immediate supervisor. Continue on the next page (in most cases, your résumé should not be more than two pages) to list additional work experience. A good rule of thumb is to allow each entry of previous work experience one half the space of the one that preceded it. In other words, if the first entry of work experience requires ten lines, give the second five, and the third, two and a half. The employer is more interested in what you have done recently, less interested in your distant past.

Functional: The functional résumé is organized around your skills and abilities rather than your work history. This gives you the opportunity to anticipate what your potential employer is looking for and to convince him that you are the best qualified for the job. Identify the skills and abilities required for the position you are seeking. Then look over your experience and describe the things you have achieved or accomplished that best demonstrate that you possess the requisite skill.

Note: Your personal information, education, accomplishments and/or work experience represent the meat of your résumé. Include the information that follows only as space permits.

4. Community involvement: Includes any community service involvement or leadership that indicates how you are an asset to your community and, by extension, how hiring you will reflect well on the company that you are asking to hire you.

5. Special interests: If there is space remaining, you might include hobbies, special interests, etc. This is less important than other entries.

6. Personal references: If you have remaining space (this will probably only apply to people new in the world of work), include personal references. Otherwise simply state: "References available upon request."

Additional Points about Résumés

If you're applying for employment with a large organization, private or public, be aware that your résumé may only get ten to fifteen second's attention. You can increase the odds that your résumé will be noticed by:

1. The paper that you select. (High quality linen is best. Stay away from colored paper or from cheap typing paper.)

2. Paying special attention to your use of language. Make every word count.

3. Keeping your résumé under two pages.

4. Using a good quality typewriter or computer printer or paying someone to type for you. Photocopied résumés are usually fine. Cover letters should be freshly typed.

5. Of course, spelling and punctuation are important. Additionally, the layout of the material on the page ought to give an attractive, neat appearance that is well balanced and proportioned.

When to Use a Cover Letter

A cover letter briefly describes who you are, the position you're seeking, and the contribution you feel you can make. Use a cover letter when: (1) You know the exact position you are applying for, and (2) You know the name of the person doing the hiring. (If you don't know, do more research.)

Key Points for an Effective Cover Letter

1. Address it to the specific individual who has the capacity to hire you.

2. State the position that you are seeking.

3. Highlight important features of your qualifications and how you will help their organization achieve their goals.

4. Ask for an interview. Indicate that you will call to set up a time.

5. Keep your letter short (two or three short paragraphs).

6. Make it interesting, clear, and well written. Try to distinguish your letter from the others on his or her desk.

7. Type each one fresh, no photocopies.

 Whatever we conceive well we express clearly.
Nicolas Boileau-Despréaux

The Follow-Up Call

You've already sent a résumé and a cover letter, which gives you a reason (or an excuse) to follow up with a call. Call in the mornings. (People are generally sharper and more responsive in the morning.) You'll either be talking to a secretary/receptionist or with the individual who will be conducting the interview. If you are talking to the secretary, understand that it is her job to get rid of you. It is your job to see that she doesn't (politely). Once you have the person you want the interview with on the line, your conversation might go something like this:

Caller: Hello Mr._____, this is Ms. _____calling.

Potential Employer: Yes, how can I help you?

Caller: Last week I sent you my résumé and a letter outlining ways that I feel I could contribute to your organization. Have you had a chance to look at it?

Potential Employer: No. (Chances are good that they haven't.)

Caller: I know, Mr._____, that you're a busy man and that your time is valuable. That's why I'd like to come in and discuss with you how I can be an asset to your company.

Potential Employer: We really don't have a position available right now.

Caller: I understand that within the context of the usual way of looking at things, you don't have any openings available right now. Still, I've been studying your organization, and I have some exciting ideas that I'd like to discuss with you about how we can work together.

Potential Employer: You'll probably be wasting your time, Ms._____.

Caller: I can understand how you might feel that way, especially since you haven't had a chance to look over my proposal. I value my time and yours. I wouldn't ask for an appointment unless I felt it was going to be a valuable use of time for both of us.

Potential Employer: Well, Ms._____ , you are persistent; I must say that.

Caller: Thank you. I'd like to get together with you next week and discuss this with you in person. How about Tuesday at 9:00 a.m.?

Potential Employer: Well, 10:00 would be better for me.

Caller: Very well, 10:00 it is.

In the space below, list the important points you'd like to get across in your phone conversation.

1. _____
2. _____
3. _____
4. _____
5. _____
6. _____
7. _____

Now list possible objections that the potential employer may have to meeting with you, and ways that you might overcome them.

1. Objection: _____
Solution: _____
_____
_____
_____
_____

2. Objection: _____
Solution: _____
_____
_____
_____
_____

3. Objection: _____
Solution: _____
_____
_____
_____
_____

> *Either do not attempt at all or go through with it.*
>
> Ovid

Strategy 2: Working Your Network

The old saying, "It's not what you know, it's who you know" is more true than many would care to admit. Developing effective networking skills is your key to increased opportunity. (See "Turning on Your Networks," page 477.) Take advantage of opportunities (obvious, and not-so-obvious) to develop new contacts. In the meantime, work your existing network. You may know people right now who can put you in touch with potential employers or whose names you could use to open doors that might otherwise be closed. Don't be embarrassed to ask for help.

Put your network to work by:

1. Getting them to set up an interview (not always appropriate).

2. Getting them to speak to the party and obtain their agreement to meet with you. You call and confirm.

3. Getting them to write a letter of introduction or recommendation that you can send along with your résumé.

4. Getting their permission to use their name when you call to set up an interview.

Perseverance Furthers

Strategy 3: Direct Mail

In direct mail to employers, as in any type of direct-mail advertising, three factors are critical to success. The first is reaching your target market. Make sure your promotional piece reaches the person who has the power to hire you. (You can send your letter to their home or office.) The second is quality promotional materials—in this case, a letter advertising you. The third is follow-up—in this case, converting contacts into interviews.

The method is as follows: Send a cover letter along with your résumé, or skip the résumé and write a personal letter. Your letter briefly describes what you have to offer. Make it dynamic. Let the would-be employer know there is a real person on the other end of the letter. Include a brief statement of your past accomplishments, your skills, and the kind of results you are likely to produce for them. Indicate that you have some ideas on how to help their organization better achieve its goals. Don't oversell or make exaggerated promises.

Expect anywhere from between 1 percent and 10 percent response requesting an interview. (The range will depend upon target selection, the quality of your materials, and, of course, what you have to offer.) When you receive a rejection letter, don't get discouraged; instead, realize that you are one step closer to your goal. You are now *certain* you have the name of the person who has the power to hire you, i.e., the person who sent you the rejection letter. Guess who gets another letter.

Strategy 4: Parlay Your Way

1. **Informational Interviews.** The contacts that you make during informational interviews can assist you in realizing your career objectives. For a review of how this process works, see pages 294–296 in the "Reality Testing" section.

2. Internships. In many fields, especially in the nonprofit and government sectors, you can begin work as an intern. Interns receive nominal pay in exchange for training and experience in the field. Often, interns have the inside track for permanent full-paid positions when they become available.

3. Volunteer Work. Volunteer work is not only an excellent way to make contacts that could lead to jobs; it is also an excellent way to gain knowledge and experience, build up a track record, and test your dream career in the laboratory of reality. Many employers in overcrowded fields have unwritten hiring policies that favor volunteers and interns. It's called "paying your dues."

Strategy 5:
Walk-Ins

1. Walk in to arrange later interview. The purpose of walk-ins of this type is essentially like that of making cold calls on the telephone. The difference is you do it in person. It's generally harder for people to say no in person than on the phone. This technique works best in small organizations without gatekeepers. Where you do encounter them, make it clear that you don't want to see the boss right now, but at a later date, convenient with his or her schedule.

2. Walk in to arrange same day interview. This is not for everyone. It takes a special kind of individual to pull it off. Below are a couple of approaches you might want to employ if you're going to try for a same-day interview and have to get past a gatekeeper.

The Charmer: Walk up to the secretary or receptionist with a warm friendly smile and introduce yourself. Learn her name (about nine out of ten secretaries are women), then use it as you tell her why you came and who you want to see. Kindness and courtesy pave the way. Don't activate her defenses with a lot of manic hype (it is her job to get rid of gooney salespeople) or try to bowl over her (she may make a point of blocking you just to let you know she's no pushover). Do be courteous and genuinely like her, and she may want to help you (no guarantee). If she says no, ask her again and then again. If you are successful, she will use her influence to get you a shot at the decision-maker.

The Outlaster: This is for the tough customer. Forget about charming her. The only time she's impressed with charmin' is when she retires to the ladies' room. Tell her who you want to see, and she'll tell you he's in a meeting. You say, "I'll wait," or more politely, "I'd be happy to wait," and begin to sit down. Some may insist that you leave. If they are really adamant, just leave. Otherwise, pull up a chair or couch and begin the war of nerves. Who gets on whose nerves faster?

She'd like you to just disappear into the woodwork so she can go about her business. You want her to remember that you're there. She's already agreed that you could wait, so she's not going to call security. Now is the time to haul out the old handkerchief and blow like the dickens. If there's a water cooler, get up and (glub, glub) have a few drinks. Interrupt her a few times asking questions. Harmless, even inane questions will do. The object is to get her to want to get rid of you by passing you on to the interviewer.

 The man who makes no mistakes does not usually make anything.

Edward Phelps

Note: Be sure you change your tactics before you see the interviewer or your interview will be a brief one. This method is a big gamble. Some individuals will be impressed by your persistence; others will resent the interruption.

Strategy 6: Executive Search Firms

Executive search firms specialize in locating executives for their client companies. They prefer to hire executives who are currently employed. A few firms will interview people not currently working. If at all possible, don't just send a résumé, get an interview. Consider this a screening interview for your new job. If they agree to work with you, they will arrange interviews with employers who want what you have to offer. Generally, these services are free to the potential employee (the employer pays). There are two primary advantages for using these kinds of firms:

1. They know where the action is, i.e., where the jobs are. It's their business.

2. They have contacts within the company that can hire you. Instead of approaching the company as a stranger, you are approaching them with an inside connection.

Executive Search Firms Sources

The Directory of Executive Recruiters. Kennedy, James H. Fitzwilliam, N.H.: Kennedy and Kennedy Inc. Published annually in December.

The Guide to Executive Recruiters: The Largest and Most Comprehensive Listing of Executive Recruiters. Betrus, Michael. New York: McGraw-Hill, 1997.

You can also identify executive search firms in your area by using your local Yellow Pages.

Strategy 7: Unconventional Approaches

Be on the lookout for unconventional ways of getting to the people that can give you what you want. For example, Aristotle Onassis broke into the big time in the shipping business by waiting for thirty-seven days outside of the office of the man he wanted to talk to. He was prepared, he knew what he wanted, and he was persistent. When the man he was trying to see finally relented, the deal was done in a matter of hours, and Onassis was on his way to a huge fortune. People have landed jobs, negotiated deals, and funded projects because they "just happened" to be staying in the right hotel, drinking in the right lounge, or even riding in the right elevator.

Note: Try to avoid job interviews over lunch. Do this only as a last resort if you're really interested in the company. There are too many distractions at lunch, and you may be judged on factors that have nothing to do with the job (for example, the food you order, or the noise you make when you chew).

 Fortune favors the audacious.
Desiderius Erasmus

Strategy 8: Traditional Approaches

For those who would like to take a shot at the more traditional job-hunting sources, consider the following:

Answering Newspaper Ads: Perhaps the most popular method of finding a job, answering newspaper ads, is by no means the best. If you are going to use this method, keep in mind some of the other techniques we have described above. Also, remember that qualifications are not written in stone. Individuals seeking employment often take themselves out of the running for jobs they would enjoy because they take written statements outlining qualifications as decrees from on high.

If the want ad says, "Must have X degree and five years experience" but you only have a year's experience and you want the job, apply anyway. If they ask you why you applied even though you didn't meet the criteria, tell them, "While I may not meet the exact criteria you've listed, I do feel that I'm qualified for this position, and here's why. . ." and then proceed to tell them why you are the best person for the job. You have nothing to lose, and if you present yourself well, you may have just won yourself a job. Remember, employers hire people, not qualifications. Everything we've said here applies to positions listed on in-house bulletin boards as well as to those advertised in newspapers, magazines, trade journals and newsletters.

Private Employment Agencies: These agencies fill employers' requests for workers with people whose qualifications match those specified for a particular job. Some will charge you an expensive fee, but most are paid by the company looking for employees. It is important that you go in knowing exactly what you want. Remember, they are being paid by the employers, so they will tend to have the employer's interests at heart more than yours. If they do charge a fee, be sure you understand what you are getting yourself into before you sign.

State Employment Offices: If you like drab offices, long lines, and are looking for a low-paying entry-level job, then a state employment office may be a good bet for you. Most employers tend to fill their middle- and upper-level positions through other sources. Even at the entry level, your odds of landing a job through an employment office are not good, as the number of applicants is typically far greater than the number of available openings.

College Placement Offices: College students, go to the career placement office at your school (preferably well before graduation). Get to know the staff and what they have to offer. College placement offices are especially good when you go in knowing what you want instead of expecting them to tell you. Some schools provide training in job-hunting skills. Ask staff members to keep you informed of recruiters from the various companies who visit your school and of other positions they know of through various sources.

Your Plan for Landing the Interview

Name of Organization: _____

Position You Are Seeking: _____

Name of Person Who Can Hire You: _____

Position: _____

How You Will Get to Them: _____

_____

Plan B: _____

_____

Plan C: _____

_____

Name of Organization: _____

Position You Are Seeking: _____

Name of Person Who Can Hire You: _____

Position: _____

How You Will Get to Them: _____

_____

Plan B: _____

_____

Plan C: _____

_____

Name of Organization: _____

Position You Are Seeking: _____

Name of Person Who Can Hire You: _____

Position: _____

How You Will Get to Them: _____

_____

Plan B: _____

_____

Plan C: _____

_____

Step Five–
Prepare for Interviews

Put Yourself in the Interviewer's Shoes

Imagine that you are in charge of hiring employees for a large organization. The future of your organization depends upon your judgment. After all, the quality of its employees, more than any other factor, will affect this organization's ability to achieve its goals. Additionally, at even a modest salary, the organization will be spending several hundred thousand dollars over the course of ten years on each employee. Hiring, then, is one of the most important business transactions any organization undertakes. Given all of this, you might be in a state of mild anxiety as you are faced with deciding the fate of your organization— selecting its employees.

One way that employers attempt to reduce this anxiety is through familiarity, that is, by hiring people they know or hiring people recommended by those they know and trust. From the interviewer's point of view, he's taking a chance in hiring a stranger, a chance that may affect his own standing in the company. He would rather deal with a known commodity than take a risk with an unknown. It is not surprising, then, that 67 percent of all positions filled result from personal and professional contacts. The list opposite suggests some ways you can become familiar to the interviewer and thus reduce his anxiety about hiring you.

Employers want to interview you because they want to see a real person, not a piece of paper. They don't simply want someone who looks good on paper. They want someone who functions well in the work environment. The interviewer is interested in how you look, how you smell, how you respond to difficult questions, how developed your verbal skills are, how well you are likely to get along with other people, how passive or assertive you are, how apathetic or dynamic you are. In short, they want to get to know you. The tips on the next few pages can help you insure that they meet you at your best.

How to Become "Familiar" with the Interviewer

1. Get to know the person doing the hiring through an informational interview or through social or professional contacts.

2. Come recommended by someone within the organization whom they know and trust.

3. Come recommended by someone outside the organization whom they know and trust.

4. Come recommended by someone who has a position of credibility and respect within the field.

5. Come recommended by someone who has a position of high standing and respect within the community.

6. Be persistent in approaching them. Without becoming a nuisance, make sure that they remember you.

Knowledge is power if you know about the right person.

Ethel Mumford

Do Your Homework

Read: Read everything you can get your hands on that has been written by the organization or about the organization (refer to pages 444–446) and about the interviewer. (This will most likely only apply to individuals who are at the upper end of the economic and professional scale.)

Talk to People: Talk to people who know the person who will interview you.

1. Current employees.
2. Former employees.
3. Also-rans (i.e., unsuccessful interviewees)
4. Personnel directors

Practice: Be sure to do a number of practice interviews. (Get a friend to play the interviewer and ask you tough questions.) In your practice interviews (at least for some of them), dress as you would for the real thing. Ask your partner to critique you, not only what you say but in your appearance and nonverbals as well. If possible, videotape the experience. Viewing the tape will give you an excellent feel for how you are coming across. It allows you to see yourself from the interviewer's point of view. Sample interview questions can be found on the following page.

Sources for Information on Interviewers

1. *Who's Who*—General, by region, and by field of interest. New Providence, N.J.: Marquis Who's Who.

2. Newspaper and magazine articles.

3. *American Men and Women of Science.* New Providence, N.J.: R. R. Bowker.

4. *The Address Book: How to Reach Anyone Who's Anyone.* Levine, Michael. New York: Perigee Books. Biennial.

5. *United States Government Manual.* Superintendent of Documents. Washington, D.C.: U.S. Government Printing Office. Published annually in September.

6. *Business Phone Book USA: The National Directory of Addresses and Telephone Numbers.* Detroit: Omnigraphics, Inc. Published annually.

7. **WhoWhere**   `www.whowhere.lycos.com`

   In this site, you can search phone numbers and addresses and also find e-mail addresses. Also links to companies online.

Interview Questions

Here's a brief list of questions that you may encounter in the interview process. We recommend that you practice answering them. For more questions, *Sweaty Palms: The Neglected Art of Being Interviewed,* by Anthony Medley has a very complete list.

1.   Tell me about yourself.

When the interviewer asks this question, they're not interested in your great rock collection or favorite rock 'n' roll band. Remember, they're sizing you up for the position they have in mind. Don't answer the way you would if asked by a blind date.

2.   Why should I hire you?

Now, don't get defensive, intimidated, or hostile. Be cool and state how your skills, attitude, enthusiasm, and experience will contribute to their organization.

3.   What are your career goals? Where do you want to be in five to ten years?

This is a good test question. They want you to sign up for life. You want to move on in a year and a half. Handle this one with deftness and sincerity, but don't make unrealistic promises. Speak in terms of positions you'd like to achieve or things you'd like to accomplish.

4.   Why did you leave your last position?

Don't tell them you hated the job, were bored out of your mind or ready to shoot your boss. Tell them that you'd gone as far as you could go in your previous or current job, and you're looking for the opportunity to work for a growth-oriented and challenging company like theirs. If you have done your research properly, you ought to be able to indicate what attracts you to their organization, and mean it.

5.   Why are you interested in this position?

This question is an exciting, wide-open door. It's your chance to demonstrate all that you know about their company, its history, philosophy, products, and services.

6.   Why did you choose this field of work?

You have a tremendous advantage when answering this question. Assuming you have followed the formula given in this book, you have discovered the work you really love to do. Let that love show through as you clearly articulate your reasons for entering the field.

7.   How much do you expect to earn?

You should know approximately what they're offering and find it acceptable or not waste your time on the interview. Your answer to this question, then, should be within their range, only a tad higher. For example, if their range is $45,000–$50,000 you could suggest $47,000–$52,000 or even $50,000–$55,000. This way, you're more apt to get the high end of their range, and you're letting them know that you expect to be well rewarded.

When asked tough questions, for example, "What are your weaknesses?" avoid being "honest" to a fault: state the weakness so that it sounds like a strength. For example, "If anything, I probably work too hard…" Or else state the weakness as something that was operative in the past, under specific circumstances that no longer apply. For example, "In the past, in a few instances, I would get irritated by customers who were overbearing and rude. I've matured since then and learned to deal with the situation in a way that works well for everyone."

Take a Pre-Interview Inventory

The process of landing a job is a negotiation. In any negotiation, it is important to know what your needs and strengths are. Likewise, it is important that you know the other party's needs and strengths. The key is to match your strengths to their needs and their strengths to your needs. The purpose of the exercise below is to help you identify what you have to offer employers and what they have to offer you. (All potential employers should meet the criteria you established on page 443.)

Name of Organization: _____

Position Sought: _____

Your Employment Strengths: In the space below, list the things that make you desirable to a potential employer.

How do your skills make you a valuable asset to this organization?

_____
_____
_____
_____

In what ways do your experience and knowledge of the field make you an asset to this organization?

_____
_____
_____
_____

How does your knowledge of this organization make you an asset?

_____
_____
_____
_____

Why would you make a good addition to their team? (What makes you a good team player?)

_____
_____
_____
_____

Potential Employer's Needs: In the space below, make a prioritized list of your potential employer's needs or goals and how you can help satisfy or achieve them.

Current Needs and Goals and How You Can Help

1. _____
   _____
2. _____
   _____
3. _____
   _____
4. _____
   _____

Future Needs and Goals and How You Can Help

1. _____
   _____
2. _____
   _____
3. _____
   _____
4. _____
   _____

Potential Employer's Strengths: In the space below, list what you perceive to be your potential employer's current and future strengths. Why is this a good organization to work for now? In the future?

Current Strengths: What They Can Offer You Now

1. _____
   _____
2. _____
   _____
3. _____
   _____
4. _____
   _____

Future Strengths: What They Can Offer Later

1. _____
   _____
2. _____
   _____
3. _____
   _____
4. _____
   _____

Great works are performed not by strength, but by perseverance.

Samuel Johnson

Step Six–Communicate: Conduct Successful Interviews

Setting the Scene

The Prelims: These are screening interviews, designed to sift the wheat from the chaff. They are the most formal and structured of employment interviews. Everything that applies to the "main event" applies to the "prelims," with the following addition: Be a bit more cautious in these interviews—less aggressive and careful not to offend. Your objective in the screening interview is simply to pass the first cut.

The Main Event: Now don't fret, lament, or stick your head in cement. You're ready to stay in control through preparation. You've already done a good deal of research and planning. Now it's time to make sure that you are mentally prepared.

An interview is a high-stress situation. But then, so is a great deal of work in the real world. If you choke under the pressure of the interview, you can't blame the interviewer for generalizing that you will choke under the pressure of the work situation. Similarly, if you handle the interview well, you use it to showcase (though not in a flashy way) your capacity to excel under pressure.

Generally, in today's job market, the interviewer has a host of qualified candidates. He's going to pick the one he likes best, the one who makes the best overall impression. There's nothing terribly objective about this, and it varies from interviewer to interviewer. While there's no magic formula, we can suggest two attitudes that, used in proper balance, will always work to

your advantage. These are *confidence* and *caring,* and they are both linked to preparing. Preparation increases your confidence in yourself and exhibits your caring for your new organization.

Confidence: Confidence increases as you mentally focus on your strengths and diminishes as you focus on your weaknesses. If you go in for an interview while mentally focused on your weaknesses, you'll make a poor impression. People generally focus on their weaknesses, only because they haven't taken the time to identify and practice projecting their strengths. If your confidence is lacking, put more time and effort into preparation.

Confident people tend to be well-prepared, and preparation increases confidence. People sometimes assume that lack of preparation comes from overconfidence. Actually, it demonstrates a lack of confidence—a chronic tendency to focus on weakness (low self-esteem). Low self-esteem can keep you from doing the homework you need to do before the interview and from making your best presentation during the interview. It can also keep you from doing your best once you get the job, and interviewers know that. When you make the effort to identify and focus on your strengths, you may be doing more than preparing for a job interview. You may be giving yourself a permanent self-esteem boost.

Caring: There is an old saying that *people don't care what you know until they know that you care.* This certainly applies to job interviews. When you show a potential employer that you understand their needs and objectives, you demonstrate that you care about their organization. Come well prepared, and they'll be glad that you were the one they snared.

The successful man will profit from his mistakes and try again in a different way.
Dale Carnegie

The Interview

Interviewers are trained to observe you from beginning to end. They are rating you at least as much on how well you project yourself as on what you say. Indeed, one of the best reasons to be well prepared in your answers is so you can concentrate on projecting confidence while answering them.

1. **Groom:** Dress the way that you would dress if you were working for this organization. Make sure your clothes are neatly pressed, your shoes carefully polished, and your hair neatly combed. Don't overdo it with makeup, perfume, cologne, or aftershave.

2. **Right from the Start:** Realize that the interview begins the moment you come into the interviewer's view. Don't wait for the first serious question to begin making a good impression; start immediately. Greet them warmly, with a sincere smile and a handshake. If you can give them a sincere compliment, do so. Many interviewers begin with a little chit-chat. Be graciously engaged, not impatient, antsy, or nervous. Don't worry, you'll get to the serious questions soon enough.

3. **Project Confidence:** Your voice, well used, is one of the surest ways of projecting confidence. Watch the pitch, the tone, the volume, and the speed of your communication. Project self-command, enthusiasm, and dynamic energy. Recognize that your body language is speaking for you. Make sure that it is saying what you want it to say.

4. **Listen:** In most interviews, the interviewer is talking nearly as much as the interviewee. Yet the interviewee is often preoccupied with what he himself is saying and paying too little attention to what the interviewer is saying. This is a big and common mistake. Remember, the interviewer is a person (not a rating machine). Like all people, interviewers want to feel important. One of the best ways of making anyone feel important is by listening to them. Demonstrate alert interest through eye contact, facial gestures, and body language. Answer the questions they are asking. (It is surprising how many people don't.) Active listening is one of the best ways of ensuring that interviewers like you (and whether they admit it or not, interviewers hire people they like).

5. **Tell Stories:** Be sure to include stories that demonstrate the qualities you want to highlight. Telling a story captures the interest of the interviewer. It enhances your credibility by demonstrating that you not only possess a certain skill, attitude, or talent but that you also know how to use it in real life situations that may be similar to those you will encounter in your new position. Most important, people remember stories better than dry facts.

6. **Respond:** Keep it short but not too short. According to Richard Bolles *(What Color Is Your Parachute?),* research has found the ideal response time to interviewer questions to be between twenty seconds and two minutes.

7. **Ask:** Take advantage of your opportunity to ask questions. Be prepared with questions in advance. For example: Whom will I be reporting to? Can you tell me a little something about this person? Develop your own list of questions, and practice asking them. Ask questions when given the opportunity. It shows interest and confidence.

8. **Like:** Make a sincere effort to genuinely like the person who is interviewing you. If you genuinely like them, the chances greatly increase that they will like you, and, again, interviewers hire people they like.

Step Seven–
Celebrate and Analyze

1. **Celebrate:** Preparing for and taking interviews is hard work. When the work is done, it's time to have some fun. Taking time to play afterward will help to keep you fresh and ensure that you maintain your enthusiasm for the search.

2. **Analyze:** Reflect on the interview you have just completed. Where were you strong? How could you improve? You might want to develop a checklist and give yourself points based upon your performance. Interviewing is a game as much as a skill. Unless you are very experienced and/or extremely well prepared, we don't recommend that you start with the organization you most want to work for. Get a few interviews under your belt before you take them on. Practicing with a partner is a valuable part of your preparation, but there's nothing like getting real experience when the pressure's on.

3. **Express appreciation:** Let the interviewer know that you are glad he considered you for the position. Write the interviewer a formal letter thanking him for the opportunity to discuss the position with them. Restate what you consider to be the high points of the interview, for example, your qualifications, personal attributes, or expertise in the field. Indicate that you are looking forward to further association with them, and close formally. Try to send this letter out in the next day's mail. It's an added reminder, not only of your qualifications, but of your conscientiousness, and it comes at the most critical time—while the interviewer is still making up his mind.

4. **Follow through:** It is appropriate to call back and find out if you got the position. If you didn't get it, ask them to tell you why. If they mention factors you know can be improved, thank them for their feedback, and tell them that you intend to work on these. Ask the employer to keep you in mind for any future positions. If it is clear that there is no possibility of working with this organization, you might ask them if they know of opportunities with other organizations.

Evaluate Your Interviews

1. Name of Organization:

_____

Position Sought: _____

Interviewer: _____

What went well during the interview?

_____

_____

What could you have improved?

_____

_____

What steps will you take to follow up?

_____

_____

2. Name of Organization:

_____

Position Sought: _____

Interviewer: _____

What went well during the interview?

_____

_____

What could you have improved?

_____

_____

What steps will you take to follow up?

_____

_____

"Landing the Right Job" Sources

Résumés

100 Winning Resumes for $100,000+ Jobs: Resumes that Can Change Your Life! Enelow, Wendy. Manassas, Va.: Impact Publications, 1997.

175 High Impact Resumes. Beatty, Richard. New York: John Wiley & Sons, 1996.

Cover Letters that Knock 'Em Dead. Yate, Martin John. Holbrook, Mass.: Adams Media Corp., 1997.

Dynamic Cover Letters. Hansen, Katherine et al. Berkeley: Ten Speed Press, 1995.

Dynamite Resumes: 101 Great Examples and Tips for Success. Krannich, Ronald L., and Caryl Krannich. Manassas, Va.: Impact Publications, 1996.

High Impact Résumés and Letters: How to Communicate Your Qualifications to Employers. Krannich, Ronald L., Caryl Krannich, and William J. Banis. Manassas, Va.: Impact Publications, 1998.

How to Write Better Résumés. Lewis, Adele, and Gary Joseph Grappo. Hauppauge, N.Y.: Barron's Educational Series, 1998.

Job Résumés: How to Write Them, How to Present Them, Preparing for Interviews. Biegeleisen, J.I. New York: The Putnam Publishing Group, 1991.

Résumés That Get Jobs. Reed, Jean, and Ray Potter. New York: MacMillan, 1998.

Resumes for the Over-50 Job Hunter. Ray, Samuel N. New York: John Wiley & Sons, 1993.

Throw Away Your Résumé. Hochheiser, Robert M. Hauppauge, N.Y.: Barron's Educational Series, 1995.

Your Résumé: Key to a Better Job. Corwen, Leonard. New York: Arco Publishing, Inc., 1995.

Interviews

101 Dynamite Questions to Ask at Your Job Interview. Fein, Richard. Manassis, Va.: Impact Publications, 1996.

Ask the Headhunter: Reinventing the Interview to Win the Job. Corcodilos, Nick A. New York: Plume Books, 1997.

The Complete Q and A Job Interview Book. Allen, Jeffrey G. New York: John Wiley & Sons, 1997.

Get Hired! Winning Strategies to Ace the Interview. Green, Paul C. Austin, Tex.: Bard Press, 1996.

 If a rich man is proud of his wealth, he should not be praised until it is known how he employs it.   Socrates

How to Turn an Interview into a Job. Allen, Jeffrey G. New York: Simon & Schuster, 1986.

Knock 'Em Dead. Yate, Martin John. Boston: Bob Adams, Inc., Published annually in November.

Negotiating Your Salary: How to Make $1,000 a Minute. Chapman, Jack. Berkeley: Ten Speed Press, 1996.

Power Interviews: Job-Winning Tactics from Fortune 500 Recruiters. Yeager, Neil, and Lee Hough. New York: John Wiley & Sons, 1998.

Selling Yourself Face to Face. Washington, Tom. Bellevue, Wash.: Mt. Vernon Press, 1995.

Sweaty Palms: The Neglected Art of Being Interviewed. Medley, H. Anthony. Berkeley: Ten Speed Press, 1992.

Finding a Job

The Complete Job-Search Handbook: All the Skills You Need to Get Any Job and Have a Good Time Doing It. Figler, Howard. New York: Holt, Henry & Co., 1988.

How to Become Happily Employed: A Step-by-Step Guide to Finding the Job that Is Right for You. Vinitsky, Barbara Bloch, and Janice Yukon Benjamin. Kansas City, Mo.: Career Management Press, 1986.

Job Hunter's Sourcebook: Where to Find Employment Leads and Other Job Search Resources. Lecompte, Michelle. Detroit: Gale Research, Inc., 1996.

The Job Search Handbook. Noble, John H. Boston: Bob Adams, Inc., 1988.

Jobshift: How to Prosper in a Workplace without Jobs. Bridges, William. Reading, Mass.: Addison-Wesley Publishers, 1995.

The National Job Bank. Holbrook, Mass.: Adams Media Corp. Published annually.

The Only Job Hunting Guide You'll Ever Need. Petras, Kathryn, and Ross Petras. New York: Fireside, 1995.

Professional's Job Finder. Lauber, Daniel. River Forest, Ill.: Planning Communications, 1997.

The Rights of Passage at $100,000+: The Insider's Lifetime Guide to Executive Job-Changing and Faster Career Progress. Lucht, John. Viceroy Press, 1993.

What Color Is Your Parachute? Bolles, Richard Nelson. Berkeley: Ten Speed Press. Published annually.

Who's Hiring Who: How to Find that Job Fast. Lathrop, Richard. Berkeley: Ten Speed Press, 1989.

 Men's natures are alike; it is their habits that separate them.

Confucius

Work Your Way Around the World. Griffith, Susan. Princeton: Peterson's Guides, 1997.

Unemployed or About to Be

Career Bounce-Back! The Professionals in Transition™ Guide to Recovery and Re-employment. Birkel, Damian, and Stacey J. Miller. New York: Amacom, 1997.

Finding Work without Losing Heart: Bouncing Back From Mid-Career Job Loss. Byron, William J. Holbrook, Mass.: Adams Media Corp., 1995.

Firing Back: Power Strategies for Cutting the Best Deal When You're About to Lose Your Job. Galos, Jodie-Beth, and Sandy McIntosh, Ph.D. New York: John Wiley & Sons, 1997.

From Fired to Hired: Bounce Back from Losing Your Job and Get Your Career Back on Track. Elkort, Martin L. New York: Arco Publishing, 1997.

How to Hold It All Together When You've Lost Your Job. Albright, Townsend. Lincolnwood, Ill.: VGM Career Horizons, 1995.

Losing Your Job—Reclaiming Your Soul: Stories of Resilience, Renewal, and Hope. Pulley, Mary Lynn. San Francisco: Jossey-Bass Publishers, 1997.

Internet Job-Search Sources

CareerXRoads. Crispin, Gerry, and Mark Mehler. Kendall Park, N.J.: MMC Group. Published annually.

Electronic Resumes: A Complete Guide to Putting Your Resume On-Line. Gonyea, James C., and Wayne M. Gonyea. New York: McGraw-Hill, 1996.

How to Get Your Dream Job Using the Web. Karl, Shannon, and Arthur Karl. Scottsdale, Ariz.: Coriolis Group Books, 1997.

Internet Resumes. Weddle, Peter D. Manassas, Va.: Impact Publications, 1998.

Jobsearch.Net. Straub, Carrie. Menlo Park, Calif.: Crisp Publications, 1998.

Point and Click Jobfinder: How to Get a Great Job Online. Godin, Seth. Chicago: Dearborn Trade, 1996.

Resumes in Cyberspace: Your Complete Guide to a Computerized Job Search. Criscito, Pat. Hauppauge, N.Y.: Barrons Educational Series, 1997.

Using the Internet in Your Job Search: An Easy Guide to Online Job Seeking and Career Information. Jandt, Fred E., and Mary B. Newrich. New York: Jist Works, 1997.

It is easier to go down a hill than up, but the view is from the top.

Arnold Bennett

Internet Job Search

Search Engines: The Best Place to Start Your Search

Most of the major Web search engines maintain excellent career or employment "channels." These channels are a good place to start your job search for two reasons. First, they offer hundreds of annotated sites to choose from. Second, and most importantly, they are constantly being updated. Search-engine career channels will direct you to scores of sites from which you can get information on job-hunting skills and tips, research hundreds of thousands of job listings, post your resume, research companies, and more. For example, from the Excite home page (www. excite.com) click "Careers and Education," then under "Careers," click "Search for Jobs" to see over 100,000 job listings—or "Resume Central" to post your résumé. The search engines listed below currently have excellent career "channels." Go to the search engine and find the "career channel" under the following names.

Infoseek:	`www.infoseek.com`	click "Careers"
Lycos:	`www.lycos.com`	click "Careers"
Excite:	`www.excite.com`	click "Careers and Education"
Webcrawler:	`www.webcrawler.com`	click "Careers and Education"
Search.com:	`www.search.com`	click "Employment"
Snap:	`www.snap.com`	click "Employment" under "Business and Money"
Yahoo:	`www.yahoo.com`	click "Jobs" under "Business and Economy"
AOL Netfind:	`www.aol.com`	click "WorkPlace"

Important Sites of Interest to Job-Seekers

America's Employers   `www.americasemployers.com`

Developed by career outplacement consultants, this well-rounded site offers extensive resources to organize, expand, and refine your job search. A great first stop, the "Job Search Essentials" page on this site provides an overview of the entire job-search process, with valuable tips on setting goals, writing and submitting résumés and cover letters, networking, interviewing, and organizing your job search campaign step by step. A unique feature of this site is an interactive interview chat room, where you can have "live" interviews with potential employers.

America's Job Bank   `www.ajb.dni.us`

The U.S. Department of Labor unites with the state-operated public Employment Service offices nationwide to provide a database of job listings from across the nation, as well as national exposure for your résumé. Combining all the job listings from American's 2,000 or more state employment offices, this site is enormous, boasting more than 400,000 job listings—and it continues to grow.

CareerMosaic   www.careermosaic.com

This award-winning site is one the few major sites that allows free posting as well as free viewing of résumés. It offers a job database with thousands of listings, links to sites around the world, profiles on hundreds of employers, and a database of job opportunities and entry-level positions for college graduates.

CareerPath.com   www.careerpath.com

Using the CareerPath site in your job search gives you the speed and efficiency of reading the Sunday help-wanted ads of more than thirty of the nation's largest newspapers—the day before they appear in print at the newsstand.

CareerWeb   www.careerweb.com

This site specializes in higher salaried professional, technical, and managerial jobs. You can post your résumé and also match it to job listings you are interested in for free. The JobMatch feature on this site will automatically e-mail you about new job listings according to categories, locations, and keywords you specify.

E-span   www.espan.com

E-span offers a unique feature to employers that might well work in your favor. Résumés posted on this site are "pushed," or sorted and e-mailed directly to employers, on a weekly basis. If your résumé matches the profile registered by a prospective employer, it is automatically selected out from countless others and brought directly to his or her attention.

Federal Jobs Digest   www.jobsfed.com

Federal Jobs Digest is a private site that specializes in federal job listings. You can post your résumé for free—a process referred to on this site as "the passive approach," and you can subscribe to a service that e-mails you updated job listings according to your specifications—"the active approach."

The Monster Board   www.monster.com

This lively site brings warmth and levity to your career search with the whimsical monsters that inhabit its pages. Features include: national and international searches by location, category, and keyword; focus sites for honing in on specific careers; access to companies and descriptions of their open positions; and a customized job search, courtesy of a monster job-search agent. Also includes links to sites with nonprofit job listings.

Online Career Center   www.occ.com

The Online Career Center offers information about job fairs, conferences, and colleges, and it features career-related articles from well-known authors. At this writing, over 8,000 employers advertise on this site annually, including 400 of the *Fortune* 500 corporations.

Working For a Nonprofit

If you are interested in working for a nonprofit, the sites listed on page 428 can provide helpful information. For example, the Nonprofit Internet Center has a nonprofit locator database that contains the names and addresses of every tax-exempt nonprofit in the U.S. In addition to the nonprofit job-search sites listed below, be sure to check out the sites of specific organizations you would like to work for.

Philanthropy Journal Online   www.pj.org

This site is a free online newsletter, the fastest growing in the nonprofit sector. The main site has useful information on current issues of interest to those in the nonprofit field. Philanthropy Journal Online is also one of the best sources for nonprofit job listings at all levels. The Nonprofit Jobs Classified section (http://jobs.pj.org) is organized by state as well as by job category. The main site also has links to other sites with searchable employment listings.

Nonprofit Career Network   www.nonprofitcareer.com

At this site, you can post your résumé, research nonprofit job openings, and explore volunteer opportunities. It also has a schedule of job fairs, conferences, and convention sites around the country.

Community Career Center   www.nonprofitjobs.com

This excellent site allows you to search for job listings by employer name, job title, salary level, as well as geographic location.

National Opportunity Nonprofit Classifieds   www.opportunitynocs.org

This site is a terrific resource, with many job listings and links to other sites listing nonprofit job opportunities. Job postings are searchable by keyword and region.

Electronic Résumés

Many of the above sites will allow you to post your résumé, some for free, others for a fee; some can scan from your hard copy; others must be entered online in a keyword format. Unless you are working in a computer-related field, you can't realistically expect to find a job by posting your résumé on the Internet. On the other hand, it probably can't hurt. Be aware though, that in most instances, your posted résumé is not confidential. Also, don't confuse posting your résumé on the Internet with taking real action toward finding the job you want.

Electronic résumés are different in form and character from the traditional hard-copy variety. They rely on keywords, not on writing style, organization, or presentation. For excellent resources on converting your conventional résumé into an electronically friendly format, see *Electronic Resumes* or *Resumes in Cyberspace* (check bibliography on page 470 for complete information on these titles).

A Summary List of Job Sources

a. Traditional Approaches

(This is the way most people look for jobs. These account for about 20 percent of all jobs.)

1. Newspaper ads
2. Employment agencies
3. State employment offices

The other 80 percent are found in different ways. Here are just a few:

b. Personal Connections

1. Family
2. Friends
3. Neighbors
4. Social contacts
5. Mentors

c. Schools

1. College or alumni associates
2. College libraries
3. Teachers
4. Professors
5. Guidance counselors
6. Career centers
7. Placement offices
8. Campus interviews

d. Information Services

1. Search the Internet (see pages 471-473)
2. Phone book/yellow pages
3. Chamber of commerce directories
4. Professional magazines
5. Professional associations
6. Trade journal ads
7. *National Business Employment Weekly*
8. Federal job centers
9. Library career centers
10. Civil Service commissions
11. *Federal Yellow Book*
12. *Congressional Yellow Book*
13. *Encyclopedia of Associations*

e. Direct Approach

1. Unsolicited applications
2. Walk-ins
3. Call-ins
4. Internships
5. Volunteer work

f. Coming in through the Back Door

1. Current employees at the organization where you want to work
2. Former employees who still have contacts
3. In-house bulletin boards
4. Also-rans (unsuccessful interviewees)

Street Smarts

Zen is not some kind of excitement, but concentration on our usual everyday routine.

Shunryu Suzuki

Wise up! If you don't have street smarts, you could be losing battles you might otherwise win. The "Street Smarts" section introduces you to the fundamentals of networking, publicity, grant-proposal writing, and negotiation. Networking expands your options, often in ways you could never have imagined. Publicity gets the word out about you and/ or your organization. Grant-proposal writing can get your projects and ideas funded! Good negotiation skills can move you forward and cover your rear. Think of these as skills to develop over the long run to improve your street savvy. Many, if not all these skills, can be used regardless of whether you choose to work as an entrepreneur, a freelancer, a nonprofit administrator, or as an employee in business or government.

It often takes considerable effort to create opportunities to do the work we really love. Say, for instance, that you are a naturally gifted speaker. Speaking comes easily and effortlessly to you. On those occasions when you have had the opportunity to speak, you have felt, not a tingle, but a tornado run up your spine. You know from the comments of others that you have reached them. So you love to speak, and you have natural talent. You may even be clear on what you want to communicate. Yet you experience difficulty in creating a context that allows you to express this talent as fully or often as you would like. You may lack the persona, the role, the expertise, the image of authority, or other connecting bridges that would draw people to you. A speaker must be able to create an audience.

In creating an audience or market, you may have to do many things that are not as fun or exciting (for you) as the direct expression of your talent. Still, making the effort can often make the difference between fulfillment and might-have-beens. Even when it seems like opportunities fall in your lap, it takes street savvy to recognize and make the most of them.

Opportunities come to all, but only those well prepared take full advantage of them. In the words of Winston Churchill, "To every man there comes in his lifetime that special moment when he is figuratively tapped on the shoulder and offered the chance to do a very special thing, unique to him and fitted to his talents. What a tragedy if that moment finds him unprepared or unqualified for the work which could be his finest hour." Being "street smart" can make all the difference. In the section that follows, we will consider these street-smart skills:

Networking: On one level, you are the star of your life, with others cast in supporting roles. On another level, we are all participants in a grand play—the scope of which we can hardly imagine. Creative engagement requires seeing and making opportunities for synergistic connections with other players, even those in seemingly unrelated fields. We can't simply hope that all of our connections will fall into place; we need to seek out and maintain a strong network of support. In this section, we will consider how to develop and maintain a strong reputation, how to sharpen your networking skills, and how to select and work with associations and organizations that will further your work.

Publicity: Being street smart means you know how to get the word out about the exciting products, services, or events that you or your organization have to offer. You need to know how to work with the various media and take advantage of the assistance they can offer in promoting your work and that of your organization. In this section, we include information on writing news releases, obtaining feature stories, reviews, and interviews. Additionally, we consider how to promote your work by writing your own magazine or newspaper column, as well as a variety of miscellaneous publicity tips. And, of course, we offer additional sources for those who seek more in-depth information.

Negotiation: It has been said that every human interaction is a negotiation. The more skilled you are as a negotiator, the more likely it is that you will be able to achieve your objectives in every area of life. In this section, we briefly outline negotiation strategies and encourage you to think of negotiation as a win-win proposition. Again, we supply sources for those who want more information.

Proposal Writing: There are literally billions of dollars (and a host of services) available from thousands of public and private grant-awarding institutions. Developing the skill of proposal writing can be the key that opens the door to a whole new world of support for your projects. In this section, we offer some basic information about the process of proposal writing and provide you with a list of sources to follow up on.

Turning on Your Networks

The New York Stock Exchange is a formal, organized trading exchange. On the floor of the New York Stock Exchange, stock issues are traded. A network is an informal trading exchange. A network is an exchange that trades in trust. Individuals, through their care, effort, and integrity, build up a certain store of trust and goodwill with people. They then trade portions of this trust in exchange for access to the trust store that others have garnered.

Even as trust is the commodity traded in a network, reputation is the currency of exchange. With a great reputation, you can obtain a good deal of trust and thereby gain access to the networks of others. As long as you act in a manner that maintains your reputation, your access continues to grow. If you have a poor reputation, you will not be able to garner much trust. Your network will be small and unattractive, and you will have little to trade with others whose networks you may want to penetrate. Developing effective networks, then, is not simply a matter of meeting a lot of people. Meeting people is important, but your reputation is more important. That's where we will start.

How to Develop and Maintain Your Reputation

1. Be Sharp: Look your best. It shows that you care about yourself and others. After all, they are the ones who are looking at you. Be alert. Give people your attention, and you will get their respect.

2. Be Prompt: Be on time. If you're too early, you will rush people; if you're too late, they will resent your making them wait.

3. Be Trustworthy: Follow-through separates the men from the boys, the women from the girls. It is easy to break promises and to fail to recognize the importance of the value of agreements you have made. *Though a promise is easy to break, the damage is often difficult to repair.* Failing to keep your promises is a sure way to ruin your reputation and to inflict deep wounds, even fatal blows, to your relationships with others. Keep your promises and you demonstrate to people that they can count on you. You also demonstrate your trustworthiness by keeping confidences and by refraining from speaking negatively about others. After all, if you speak negatively about others to me, I have every right to assume that you are speaking negatively about me when I am not around.

4. Be Honest: Honesty is not simply a matter of not telling lies. It includes the capacity to be precise in your statements and measured in your judgments. If you develop a reputation of being prone to wild exaggeration or distortion, people may not believe you even when you are being careful to state things clearly and precisely. Don't be a know-it-all. Avoid trying to be an "expert" on everything. Be willing to say, "I don't know. That's not my area of expertise." Value the experience of others.

5. Be Responsible: Accept total responsibility for your actions. When you make mistakes, admit them without blame, excuse, or defense. Whenever you enlist the aid of others, maintain responsibility for decision-making and for the consequences. Don't

 No man is an island, entire of itself; every man is a piece of the continent, a part of the main.
John Donne

attempt to dump your problems onto others. Wear your responsibilities well, with competence, confidence, and good cheer.

6. Be Courteous: Show consideration. Politeness and courtesy are always well received. One of the best ways of showing people that you respect them is by respecting the value of their time. Don't impose. Don't overstay your welcome. Don't embarrass people or put them in awkward situations. *Show thoughtfulness.* Remember birthdays, children's names, favorite things, places, and events.

7. Be Prepared: Demonstrate that you value the relationship by giving your best. Show that you care enough to prepare. *Prepare for your time together.* Whether it be a business transaction, a social event, or a day at the beach, preparation can spell the difference between a successful encounter and a disappointing one. Prepare for your outings with others by clearing the decks of possible distractions or interruptions and by anticipating how best to accomplish your common goals. Organize the things you need to bring along as well as notes on subjects you want to discuss.

Prepare when you ask for help. Don't impose on people by asking them to solve problems that you could have solved yourself with a little thought, study, or legwork. If you ask people to help you before you have done your homework, you risk their irritation and displeasure. When you do ask for assistance, be clear on exactly how people can help you *before* you approach them. *Prepare what you have to give.* Don't spill the beans. It is often better to keep an idea to yourself than to bring it up before you are prepared to discuss it fully. Bite your tongue until you are ready to make your best case.

8. Be Appropriate: A sense of appropriateness is critical to successful human relations. Appropriateness is a matter of knowledge, sensitivity, and timing.

Knowledge: There are ways in which certain things are done. These involve issues of protocol and custom: whom to invite to various functions, what gifts to buy for whom, how to address and conduct oneself with various individuals, and so on. Happily, this can all be learned. Mentors help. Books on social and professional etiquette and foreign customs are widely available. *Sensitivity:* A good deal of appropriateness is simply a matter of empathy and common sense. It's sensing when it's appropriate to broach a subject, to give a word of encouragement, or a gentle chide. If we are alert and really listening with all of our senses, we will know what is appropriate and what is not. *Timing:* Recognize that what might be appropriate in one situation could be entirely inappropriate in another. For example, if you have established a friendship with a superior, it may be appropriate for you to call him by his first name and relate to him in an informal manner in his home. However, when you are in the company of subordinates or clients, a more formal interaction is appropriate.

9. Be Discriminating: People with discriminating tastes are held in high regard. It is especially important that you *choose your associates carefully.* Far more than you may realize, you are judged by the company you keep.

10. Be Valuable: Add value to the lives of those you touch. Make their lives better for every encounter they have with you. Increase your value by making a lifelong commitment to learning and growing. The bottom line of a good reputation is that people have good things to say about you. Work on your behavior and demeanor so that's all they have to say. *Your reputation precedes you. It is either paving your way or getting in the way.*

Don't Forget to Smile

Strengthening Your Reputation

Using the list on the previous page and any other factors that are important to you, indicate below how you can improve your reputation by developing in each of the following:

Appearance:_____

_____

Promptness: _____

_____

Trustworthiness: _____

_____

Honesty:_____

_____

Responsibility: _____

_____

Courtesy: _____

_____

Preparedness: _____

_____

Appropriateness: _____

_____

Discrimination: _____

_____

Service: _____

_____

Other: _____

_____

Undertake not what you can not perform, but be careful to keep your promises.
George Washington

Developing Contacts and Relationships

1. Don't miss opportunities to develop contacts. We are virtually surrounded by people who are ready and willing to help us. If we have our eyes and ears open, we will be able to take advantage of many opportunities we might otherwise miss. Be on the lookout for individuals who can help you. Sometimes, opportunity comes in ways you might not expect. Be alert. Don't dismiss opportunities because you don't see exactly how certain people can further your career objectives.

2. Ask for help. Regardless of whether you need information, leads, or referrals, ask for what you need. Express appreciation for the help you receive. Let people know that they are important to you and that you value their contribution.

3. Follow up on information, advice, or leads given you and communicate back. If it turns out that certain leads are not appropriate for you, you will be able to communicate that back to the party who has helped you get together. If you take some action on the advice that people give you and let them know about it, they will be much more likely to help you further. If you do nothing, they may not want to spend their valuable time trying to help you.

4. Develop well-rounded relationships that are not "all business." Obviously, you do not have the time to do this with everyone; however, for the really key members of your networks, it is essential.

5. Give more than you get. Share what you have to give with the members of your network. It may be your knowledge and experience; it may be your encouragement and support; it may be access to important people. You can share current information, perhaps a book or magazine article that members of your network might enjoy or benefit from.

6. Live up to the trust that others place in you. Recognize that when someone shares important contacts with you, they are giving you a vote of confidence and placing their trust in you. Do not violate that trust or fail to appreciate it. When you meet with someone who has been referred or introduced to you by a member of your network, the way that you conduct yourself is going to reflect upon that individual as well as on you. If you present yourself well, the esteem that you garner accrues to the one who sent you. If you present yourself poorly, you reflect badly, not only on yourself, but upon the one who helped you establish the contact.

7. Protect the members of your network. In the same way, those whom you refer go out as your ambassadors as well as their own. Don't refer people who will reflect badly on you and themselves by failing to appreciate the opportunity. Remember, it takes time and energy to cultivate trust, and while trust often takes a long time to develop, it can easily be weakened or destroyed.

8. Identify your social strengths and weaknesses, and develop strategies for improving your effectiveness. In developing a networking strategy, you will want to look at your style of relating to people in various settings. Identify your social strengths and weaknesses (e.g., formal, informal, one-on-one, small groups, large groups, etc.). You might say, "I'm fine one-on-one but feel awkward in small groups," or, "I do well in informal settings but feel uncomfortable in a formal environment." "I feel comfortable with people my own age but have difficulty with those who are much older." Know what your strengths are and, as much as possible, take advantage of them.

Anticipate potential problem areas, and endeavor to strengthen or mitigate weaknesses in advance. Play it out in your mind beforehand. Visualize the scene in advance, and identify exactly what it is that makes you feel uncomfortable. It may be a lack of knowledge. It may be that you are judging yourself or others harshly. It may be that you are recalling some past failure. The important thing in this process is to identify exactly what the problem is and then make the correction. As always, understanding gives you power over fear.

9. Get to know the right people. Recognize that people judge you by who you know as much as by who you are or what you have accomplished. In virtually any endeavor, there are people whom you should know, key people who can help you gain access to others. They may be within your field or simply so influential within your community that their names open doors. Get to know them.

Your Networking Strategy

In the space below, indicate your strategy for developing and maintaining effective relationships with each of the following which are applicable to you:

Mentors: _____

_____

Colleagues/coworkers: _____

_____

Superiors: _____

_____

Subordinates: _____

_____

Miscellaneous

1. Benefactors: _____
2. Investors: _____
3. Clients and customers: _____
4. Suppliers: _____
5. Distributors: _____

 Trust men, and they will be true to you. Treat them greatly, and they will show themselves great.   Ralph Waldo Emerson

Associations: The American Way

Americans of all ages, all conditions and all dispositions constantly form associations. They have not only commercial and manufacturing companies in which all take part but associations of a thousand other kinds: religious, moral, serious, futile, restricted, enormous, or diminutive.

Democracy in America
Alexis de Tocqueville

Associations play as important a role in American society today as they did when Tocqueville wrote this in the early nineteenth century. In many professions, membership is an absolute must. In most any profession, they're a definite plus. Associations serve as places of fellowship and clearinghouses of information. They provide a sense of a common identity to people with common interests. Associations, through the vehicle of peer pressure, attempt to direct the behavior of their membership toward the attainment of certain values, goals, or principles. Joining associations can enhance your prestige and credibility and expand your networks. Identify and join the associations that will enhance your effectiveness in fulfilling your life's work.

Key Points for Association Membership

1. Select organizations you want to develop long-term relationships with. In making your selections, take a long-range view. Select quality organizations with quality people who have a lot to offer.

Be as interested in what you have to give to the organization as you are in what you have to get out of it.

2. Show appreciation for the organization and its leadership. It is important that you show appreciation for the privilege of membership in the organization and respect for its current leadership. (After all, they have usually been elected by the membership and are held in esteem by them.) Validating the group and its leadership is honoring a basic principle of sociology: *Groups give acceptance to those who support the group's social structure.* Some have suggested links between this phenomenon in human behavior and the hierarchical social orders among certain animals, for example, baboons. Whatever its origin, its existence cannot be denied.

Individuals who try to ignore this fact and operate as though their organization were a meritocracy are usually disappointed. They assume that they are being judged on the basis of their work alone. This often leads to frustration as the individual attempts to gain greater recognition and responsibility within the group by working harder. They dismiss other considerations as merely "politics." Often they are disappointed before they come to realize that if you want to "play the game," you have to play politics. *Validate the group and its leadership.*

3. Look for responsibility vacuums and fill them as appropriate. Show your interest in the group by assuming responsibility for areas that are currently being neglected. Look for ways you can help. Be sure, when you do this, that you are operating "within channels." Sometimes "go-getter" types try to assume too much

> *Life is to be fortified by many friendships. To love and to be loved is the greatest happiness.*
> Sydney Smith

responsibility too early, in the hope of ingratiating themselves with the membership. They are just as likely to be viewed as pushy and overbearing as they are to be appreciated for the work they do. This is especially true if they appear arrogant and do not express sincere appreciation for the organization and for the privilege of being a member of it. *Without being pushy, assume as much responsibility as you can.*

4. Develop long-term win-win relationships with members of the organization. Give at every available opportunity to individuals *as* individuals. Recognize that every individual in the association is a representative of a particular network, which they have developed. *If people are thanking you or expressing gratitude when they leave you, you are probably on the right track.*

5. Consider organizations in the following categories:

Professional: e.g., ABA, AMA.

_____

_____

_____

_____

_____

Community Service: United Way, Rotary, Red Cross, Optimists, PTA, etc.

_____

_____

_____

_____

_____

Recreational/Social: Health clubs, sports teams, sailing clubs, community theater, etc.

_____

_____

_____

International/Current Affairs: World Affairs Council, Commonwealth Club.

_____

_____

_____

Special Interest Associations: Sierra Club, League of Women Voters, Audubon.

_____

_____

_____

Religious Associations:

_____

_____

_____

_____

Political Parties and Associations:

_____

_____

_____

Associations Source

Encyclopedia of Associations. Koek, Karin, and Susan Boyles-Martin, eds. Detroit: Gale Research Co, 1992.

The best portion of a good man's life—his little, nameless, unremembered acts of kindness and of love.

William Wordsworth

Your Mission Team Mastermind

Find the key individuals in your life who share your dreams, and assemble them in a team. Give yourself the added benefits of a mastermind team, people who will support your goals and work in a spirit of cooperation. Meet with these individuals for breakfast, or have them over for coffee once a week.

Assemble your mastermind team:

Team member #1: _____

His or her motivation for helping you: _____

Strengths: _____

_____

Team member #2: _____

His or her motivation for helping you: _____

Strengths: _____

_____

Team member #3: _____

His or her motivation for helping you: _____

Strengths: _____

_____

Team member #4: _____

His or her motivation for helping you: _____

Strengths: _____

_____

Team member #5: _____

His or her motivation for helping you: _____

Strengths: _____

_____

The sole meaning of life is to serve humanity.
Leo Tolstoy

Creating Your Mental Mastermind

Libraries are full of great conversations. You can pick up a book and have a conversation with Homer, Plato, or Einstein. In his book, *Think and Grow Rich,* Napoleon Hill describes how he had mental meetings with the greats of history who represented particular virtues he wanted to develop. (*Emerson*—an understanding nature, *Burbank*—a harmonizing nature, *Napoleon*—inspiration, faith, *Paine*— freedom of thought, *Darwin*—patience, *Lincoln*—justice, patience, humor, and tolerance, *Carnegie*—principles of organized effort, *Ford*—persistence, determination, poise, self-confidence, *Edison*—faith.) Take some time to develop your mental mastermind.

Individual	Quality
1. _____	_____
2. _____	_____
3. _____	_____
4. _____	_____
5. _____	_____
6. _____	_____
7. _____	_____
8. _____	_____
9. _____	_____
10. _____	_____

Go into daily (or regular) meditation, and ask these individuals to assist you, to give you ideas, to help you solve problems. Conduct a mental board meeting.

Mastermind Sources

Current Biography Yearbook. Moritz, Charles. Bronx, N.Y.: H.W. Wilson Company, 1995.

Encyclopedia of World Biography. Bourgoin, Suzanne Michele, and Paula K. Byers, eds. Detroit: Gale Research Co., 1998.

Think and Grow Rich. Hill, Napoleon. New York: Ballantine, 1996.

 Man's brain may be compared to an electric battery . . . a group of electric batteries will provide more energy than a single battery.
Napoleon Hill

Networking Objectives

Write your networking goals in the space below. Make them as specific as possible. You may want to include goals about the number and kinds of contacts you want to make, the organizations or associations you want to join, positions you might want to hold within various organizations, the assemblage of your mastermind team, or any other networking goals of importance to you. Be sure to include the date by which you expect to have each goal completed.

Networking Goal 1: _____

_____

_____

Networking Goal 2: _____

_____

_____

Networking Goal 3: _____

_____

_____

Networking Goal 4: _____

_____

_____

Networking Goal 5: _____

_____

_____

Networking Sources

Contact: The First Four Minutes. Zunin, Leonard, M.D., with Natalie Zunin. New York: Ballantine, 1994.

Conversationally Speaking: Tested New Ways to Increase Your Personal and Social Effectiveness. Garner, Alan. Los Angeles: Lowell House, 1997.

The Leader in You: How to Win Friends, Influence People and Succeed in a Changing World. Carnegie, Dale, and Dale Carnegie Associates, Inc. New York: Pocket Books, 1995.

Letitia Baldridge's Complete Guide to the New Manners for the '90s. Baldridge, Letitia. New York: Rawson Associates, 1990.

The Overnight Guide to Public Speaking. Wohlmuth, Ed. New York: Signet, 1993.

Publicity: Working the Media

The purpose of publicity is to enhance public awareness of yourself and your offerings. Think of publicity as free advertising. When planning your publicity strategy, keep in mind the goals of the various media, as well as your own goal (exposure). Generally, the media want to inform, educate, and entertain. If you can help them to do any of these things (and you can), you are helping them to achieve their objectives while meeting yours. Remember, every day throughout the land, the media write thousands of articles and broadcast hundreds of hours of radio and television programming. They need help in finding new stories. That's where you come in.

Look at publicity as a long-term activity. It helps to build from the ground up. For example, even if your goal is to be on *The Oprah Winfrey Show,* you probably will want to start with your local cable access channel and work your way up through local television and radio interviews. Research local media options, and determine which will work best for you.

Start with the easy access media, and move up to the big time as you gain skill, experience, and a publicity track record. Use easy access media as a springboard to gaining access to major market newspapers, radio, and television stations. A man I know, who lives in the San Diego area, promoted his self-published books by starting with articles and reviews in local suburban newspapers. He was able to parlay these into reviews from the *San Diego Union* and then the *L.A. Times.* Below are a few tips on how to let people know about you and your offering.

> *The worst fear is the fear of living.*
> Theodore Roosevelt

Write a News Release

The centerpiece of any publicity campaign is a well-written news release. If you want people to know what you are doing, write a press release, and send it to all the local newspapers, magazines, radio shows, and television stations. Take some time with your news release. The style of a press release is that of a journalistic report. Many beginners make the mistake of writing a press release as though it were advertising copy.

Remember, your press release is the first impression that an editor or interviewer has of you, and it will determine whether or not they are going to be interested in doing a story on or an interview with you. Also, many small newspapers, newsletters, and magazines print press releases as news stories in their publications with little or no editing. Spend some time honing your message. Make sure it communicates accurately the essence of your work.

Use your letterhead stationery. Include the release date, for example, "For Release May 1, 2003," or the words, "For Immediate Release." Also include the name of a contact person and her (day and evening) phone numbers. Type the words "PRESS RELEASE" across the top. Headline your press release with an attention-getting line that encapsulates your message.

There are three parts to a standard news release—the lead, the body, and the conclusion. The *lead* is the first three or four sentences. It gives the essence of what you have to say—in capsule form. Start with an attention grabber. You may want to use a question, quotation, or a bit of humor here to catch the reader's attention. The *body* is three or four paragraphs in length and contains, in descending order of importance, everything you think the reader should know about what you are doing. The *close,* or final paragraph, summarizes your message. Close with something that will stick in the editor's or producer's mind. Follow up your news release with a phone call. Media people are often inundated with paper. Persistence pays.

Ways of Publicity

Here is a list of publicity options that gives you an idea of different access levels.

Easy Access Media

Calendars and Bulletins:

Radio and television bulletin boards
Calendar and event sections of local
    newspapers
Church bulletins
Newsletters

Features and Interviews:

Low wattage college radio programs
Local cable TV programs
Small-town newspapers
Weekly newspapers
Local magazines

Intermediate Access Media

Level A

Features and Interviews:

Public affairs programs
Radio and television talk shows
Features in local radio and television
    news programs
Midsize city newspapers
National trade publications
Association magazines
Professional trade journals

Level B

The same types of avenues, only in major city and regional markets.

"The Big Time"

Major National Newspapers:

The New York Times	*The Washington Post*	*The Wall Street Journal*
U.S.A. Today	*The Boston Globe*	*Chicago Tribune*
L.A. Times	*The Philadelphia Inquirer*	

National Magazines of All Varieties Such As:

Time	*Newsweek*	*People*
Life	*Rolling Stone*	*Atlantic Monthly*
Esquire	*Vanity Fair*	*The New Yorker*

Television Programs:

ABC News Nightline	*Oprah Winfrey*	*This Week*
Good Morning America	*David Letterman*	*Prime Time Live*
60 Minutes	*Larry King Live*	*Meet the Press*
20/20	*The Tonight Show*	*Face the Nation*
The Today Show	*Rivera Live*	*Later*
Dateline	*Charlie Rose*	*Crossfire*

Make a Press Kit

On many occasions, a press release alone won't do—you'll need a press kit. A press kit is a packet of information that offers editors, producers, and interviewers the information they need to know about you. The most important item in your press kit is a carefully written news release. Your kit should also include a one- or two-page "bio," or summary of your educational background, marital and family status, current and prior occupations, professional credentials, local awards, and community service participation.

Write a short cover letter, typed on a single page and directed toward the specific individual who will be making the interviewing decisions. Tell them why you would make a great guest and why their readers, listeners, or viewers will want to hear what you have to say. Include a black-and-white photograph of yourself, either 5 x 7 or 8 x 10. If you have color slides, don't send them, but simply write "Color Slides Available on Request" on your cover letter. Also send along a list of ten to twenty sample interview questions that you would like to be asked. Arrange all of these items in a sturdy, attractive, and fairly conservative looking folder, and you're off to let the public know about you and your gig!

Include in your press kit:

1. *A one- or two-page news release, offset or typeset*
2. *A cover letter*
3. *A one- or two-page biography*
4. *One or two photographs*
5. *A list of "suggested interview questions"*
6. *Sample clippings or quotes from previous interviews or features*
7. *A preprinted Rolodex® card with your contact information*
8. *Your business card*
9. *A folder with your name or your company or organization's name either preprinted or stuck on the cover with a mailing label*

Be the Feature Attraction: Get Them to Do a Feature Article or Story on You

A feature article on you in a local newspaper or a feature story by a radio or television show can get the word out about what you are doing faster and more effectively than paid advertising, and it's free besides. Articles about you and/or about what you do are perhaps the single most effective piece of written publicity. It's more believable than an advertisement because the credibility of the newspaper or magazine accrues to you. Of course, the same applies to television and radio feature stories. A two- to four-minute feature on you is worth a great deal of paid advertising. Again, it's more credible and suggests that you are "hot." Television has the advantage of showing you in action.

Be the Talk of the Town: Get Interviews

Newspapers, radio, and television stations also do interviews. Cable or public access television, local newspapers, and morning radio talk shows are good places for the beginner to start. Approach your interviews with confidence. Focus on the valuable information you have to share and watch nervousness vanish into thin air. Have in mind three or four points you would like your audience to remember, and keep coming back to these. (If people remember this much of what you say, you can consider yourself fortunate.) You may want to rehearse your answers, especially to tough questions. This will help you to stay relaxed. Don't get defensive, even if the interviewer is hostile. Be gracious in manner, measured and precise in speech. Speak with authority and command; after all, you are being interviewed because you're the expert. Television interviews present added dimensions. Make sure your look (dress, posture, gesture, facial expression) effectively conveys the image you want to project. Keep in mind that over 90 percent of all communication is nonverbal.

The "U—Revue:" Get Them to Review Your Work

Writers have books reviewed. Artists have gallery showings reviewed. Musicians and entertainers of all kinds have performances reviewed. Even caterers get reviewed. Be sure that people who write the local reviews are aware of you and your work. Send them a press release and a copy of your work (if appropriate).

The Write Way to Publicity: Write Your Own Article or Column

If you've got something to say that could be of ongoing interest to readers, try writing your own newspaper article or perhaps a column. You can spread your message, showcase your expertise, and offer a service to your audience at the same time. Write some sample columns, and then approach the editor of your local newspaper. The "Lifestyle" section of your newspaper has regular columns on health, entertainment, food and nutrition, astrology, consumer affairs, education, parenting, and many other subjects of general interest. When writing your article, choose your words carefully, and consider how the reader will perceive what you are saying. Anticipate questions, and think your answers through in advance.

Most professions, trades, and special interest groups publish newsletters that offer readers the most current information in their field. Use *Newsletters in Print* at your local library to target newsletters most likely to be read by the people you want to reach, and submit an article. (Or ask them to interview you.) This is an easy way to get publicity that's targeted to a specific audience.

Public Service Announcements

Radio and television stations are required to allot a certain portion of their air time for public service announcements. If you're promoting a free or charity event, or anything that could be defined as a community service, take advantage of these. Call your local radio and television stations, and find out how to get your PSA on the air.

Other Publicity Ideas

1. Write a letter to the editor.
2. Write a book.
3. Give a speech.
4. Sponsor an event.
5. Produce your own cable access show or regular program.
6. List in community calendars
7. Get yourself listed in: *Yearbook of Experts, Authorities, & Spokespersons*. Their Web site is www.yearbook.com

---

Publicity Sources

Getting Publicity: The Very Best Book for Your Small Business. Fletcher, Tana, and Julia Rockler. Bellingham, Wash.: Self-Counsel Press, 1995.

High Visibility. Rein, Irving J., Philip Kotler, and Martin R. Stoller. Lincolnwood, Ill.: NTC Contemporary Publishing Co., 1997.

Your Public Best: The Complete Guide to Making Successful Public Appearances in the Meeting Room, on the Platform, and on T.V. Brown, Lillian. New York: Newmarket Press, 1992.

Presentations Plus: Techniques that Work from the Experts' Expert. Peoples, David A. New York: John Wiley & Sons, 1997.

Taking It for Granted; or, Proposal Writing at a Glance

Developing the skill of proposal writing gives you yet another way of supporting your visions and bringing them into reality. You can join the ranks of thousands who have received assistance from submitting grant proposals. Every year billions of dollars in grants are awarded by private, public, and federal institutions to individuals, nonprofit organizations, and business.

It has been estimated that there are roughly 35,000 independent, privately endowed foundations giving grants. In addition, there are more than 1,000 grant-giving programs administered by the federal government.

Grants are awarded in a variety of areas, including education, research, training, health, performing arts, acquisition of equipment, conferences, travel, or to supplement operating costs. In virtually any area you may be working in, there is the possibility of gaining funding assistance through some type of grant.

Here are just a few examples of grant awards: The Jacob and Annita France Foundation gave $3,500 to the March of Dimes Walk-A-Thon in Baltimore, Maryland; the Herbst Foundation, Inc. gave $4,500 to the Museum of Fine Arts in Boston, Massachusetts; The Helena Rubenstein Foundation awarded the Alvin Ailey American Dance Theater $25,000 to support their Repertory Ensemble; The Joseph P. Kennedy, Jr. Foundation awarded $34,240 to the California Rural Indian Health Board in Sacramento, California to support the Teen Parent Survival Program; the Pew Memorial Trust awarded $100,000 to the Big Brothers/Big Sisters of America in Philadelphia in support of their District Field Service System;

the Kellogg Foundation awarded $206,093 to Youth for Understanding in Washington, D.C. to help them develop and deliver a national intercultural volunteer leadership development program.[1]

Start by developing the general concept of your project; consider the issues you want to address along with the methods you will use in your approach to them. Once you have clarified your project objectives, the keys to receiving a grant to fund your project are three: comprehensive research of appropriate and available grants, the writing of effective proposals, and persistence.

The last point is critical. I know of one case where a man seeking a grant for a unique educational program he had developed received over 300 rejections before his proposal was finally funded. The private foundation that eventually funded his program liked his idea so much they gave him more money than he had originally requested. The last I heard, his program was being taught in hundreds of schools throughout the nation. If you are serious about proposal writing, it's a good idea to develop a thick skin about rejection. At the same time, you will want to develop the skills that will increase your chances of success—selecting the right organizations to approach and writing effective proposals.

Your local library will probably have many of the sources you need to research grant options. When you are seeking a grant, check sources such as *Grant Seeker's Guide, The Taft Foundation Reporter: Comprehensive Profiles and Analyses of America's Private Foundations, The Foundation Grants Index, Foundation Grants to Individuals,* (See bibliography for complete information and additional sources.) These sources will give you a general idea of who is giving grants and for what purposes, along with information on how to contact the grant-giving organizations.

Proposal writing is a skill which, like any other, improves with practice. The information that we can provide in this limited space is necessarily incomplete. We include it to give you a general idea of the process and to stimulate those who are interested to avail yourselves of other resources. We suggest you contact The Grantsmanship Center, 79 5th Ave. New York, NY 10003, (212) 620-4230. Besides providing a wealth of information and sources, The Grantsmanship Center offers seminars and workshops (around the country) that give you a chance to learn directly from those who have had experience and success in grant writing.

There are a number of how-to books on proposal writing. A list of a few of the better ones is provided at the end of this section. (See also the nonprofit bibliography on pages 425–427.) Of course, it helps to examine samples of successful proposals to get a sense of what works. *The Proposal Writer's Swipe File* by Susan Ezell et al., put out by The Taft Group, contains fifteen winning proposals from which you can, as the title suggests, swipe ideas. There are also private grant-writing consultants who specialize in areas such as writing proposals for government agencies. You may want to seek these out.

Government and many of the large private foundations have application checklists or specific guidelines dictating the way a proposal must be submitted. Contact your target organizations, and ask them to send you their guidelines. While you are waiting for these (and many organizations don't have them), write a preliminary or rough-draft proposal. This will assist you in clarifying your own thinking. As Francis Bacon said, ". . . writing [maketh] an exact man [or woman]."[2] Besides clarifying your thinking, writing your rough draft will show you what you know and what you need to find out. On the following two pages, you will find key elements for effective proposals from *Getting Funded: A Complete Guide to Proposal Writing,* by Mary S. Hall (Continuing Education Publications, Portland, Ore., 1988, $19.95).

Grant-Writing Sources

The Complete Guide to Getting a Grant: How to Turn Your Ideas into Dollars. Blum, Laurie. New York: John Wiley & Sons, 1996.

The Foundation Center's Guide to Proposal Writing. Geever, Jane C. et al. New York: The Foundation Center, 1997.

Getting Funded: A Complete Guide to Proposal Writing. Hall, Mary S. Portland, Ore.: Continuing Education Publications, 1988. We highly recommend this book. One of the best step-by-step guides to proposal writing.

Grants for the Arts. White, Virginia. New York: Plenum Press, 1980.

Grassroots Grants: An Activist's Guide to Proposal Writing. Robinson, Andy, and Kim Klein. Berkeley: Chardon Press, 1996.

The 'How To' Grants Manual: Successful Grantseeking Techniques for Obtaining Public and Private Grants. Bauer, David G. Phoenix: Oryx Press, 1995.

Proposal Planning and Writing. Miner, Lynn E., and Jerry Griffith. Phoenix: Oryx Press, 1993.

Secrets of Successful Grantsmanship: A Guerilla Guide to Raising Money. Golden, Susan L., and Alan Shrader. San Francisco: Jossey-Bass Publishers, 1997.

Winning Grants Step by Step. Carlson, Mim. San Francisco: Jossey-Bass Publishers, 1995.

MAJOR COMPONENTS IN A PROPOSAL TO FOUNDATIONS AND CORPORATIONS

ELEMENT	INFORMATION NORMALLY PROVIDED
Title Page	Legal name of applicant organization; name of group to which check is to be made out (if different); address, name, title and telephone number of contact person; title of project; 25-word summary of project; amount requested; statement that project has been approved for submission by the Board of Directors; and, sometimes, statement of assurance of non-discrimination.
Purpose	Goals, objectives and/or expected results of project; description of whom it will serve, their geographic location and number; significance and need for project; comparison with other efforts in the same field and/or geographic area or other documentation of non-duplication of effort; and relevance to the donor's priorities and guidelines.
Approach	Plan of action or sequence of activities to be carried out including staff responsibilities, staff and volunteer training, client selection procedures or policies, major milestones, beginning and ending of project, justification for the approach, specific outcomes anticipated, and method of evaluating and reporting results. This section also usually mentions plans for project dissemination and any recognition to be received by the donor.
Qualifications	General description of the organization's mission, history, major programs or activities and how these relate to the proposed project. Give names and backgrounds of those key to project, including consultants or cooperating agencies (evidence of their willingness to participate should be included). Mention special facilities, equipment or other capabilities to argue for your ability to complete the project.
Budget	Detailed budget for the project; amount to be contributed by applicant (usually distinguished between cash and in-kind); names (and amounts) of funds received from other donors; names (and sometimes amounts) of pending applications; description of how project will be funded after the grant expires; plans for additional fundraising (if needed); overall description of budget, expenses and revenues for the total organization. This last is usually only summarized if an audited financial statement and most recent 990 form are enclosed.
Attachments	Names of board of directors and their major affiliations; copy of IRS determination letter; organization's last annual report; brochure describing organization (optional); and letters of support (optional).

This handout taken from *Getting Funded: A Complete Guide to Proposal Writing* by Mary Hall, 1988. Available from Continuing Education Publications, P.O. Box 1491, Portland, OR 97207.

MAJOR COMPONENTS IN A PROPOSAL TO STATE AND FEDERAL AGENCIES

ELEMENT	INFORMATION TO BE PROVIDED
Title Page(s)	Title of project; name of project director; name, address and telephone number of submitting agency; name of program and organization to which submitted; inclusive dates of project; budget request; signatures of persons authorizing submission; and compliance certifications. A table of contents is usually also supplied.
Abstract	A self-contained, ready-for-publication description of the project covering objectives, need and significance, procedures, evaluation, and dissemination components. Should stress end products or project's advancement of knowledge. Usually 200 to 500 words long.
Purpose	Specific indication of the expected outcomes of the project, usually stated as goals and objectives, hypotheses, and research questions. May explain how project relates to overall goals of a larger program. Should clearly identify both short-term and long-term results expected.
Statement of Need	Well-documented description of the problem to be addressed and why it is important. Should establish significance, timeliness, generalizability, and contribution to related existing knowledge or work in progress.
Procedures	A plan of action for how the purposes will be achieved. In non-research projects, this section usually starts with a description of the overall approach and its relevance or innovativeness and then provides details on methodology, participants, organization, and timeline. In research projects, one usually describes the design, population and sample, instrumentation, data analysis, and time schedule. This may also include a review of related research.
Evaluation*	Details the means by which the local agency and funding source will know that the project has accomplished its purposes. May also describe plans for collecting information or data to improve project operation. States purpose of evaluation, type of information to be collected, details on instruments, data collection, analysis, utilization and how results will be reported.
Dissemination*	Specifies how products and findings will be shared with others. This section may also detail reports to be provided to funding source.
Qualifications	Documents the ability of the sponsoring organization to successfully complete the project, including prior related experience. Outlines facilities and equipment required and how these will be provided. Lists specific personnel who will work on the project and what they will do. Includes résumés (and in research proposals, a list of prior publications). Describes rationale for any consultants to be involved, their role, and background and evidence of their commitment to participate.
Budget	The cost of the project annually and overall. Usually divided into categories such as personnel, supplies and materials, travel, data processing, facilities or equipment and indirect costs. Matching funds to be provided or other funds to be sought should also be specified. Most public sources provide specific budget forms.

* These categories may or may not be included in research proposals, or, if required, can be discussed as elements of the procedures component.

This handout taken from *Getting Funded: A Complete Guide To Proposal Writing* by Mary Hall, 1988. Available from Continuing Education Publications, P.O. Box 1491, Portland, OR 97207.

Negotiation

Whether you're discussing an important contract with a new client, talking to your boss about a raise, or finding the financial support to begin a new business, good negotiating skills are a vital part of your success. There are two basic styles of negotiation: hardball and win-win. We encourage you to use a win-win approach whenever possible.

Hardball Negotiations

In the business world, most people are playing the hardball game. It helps to be aware of this game when you're dealing with someone who insists on being your opponent or is trying to take advantage of you. The object of the hardball game is to make sure one gets what one wants, no matter what happens to the other guy. If you're aware of these tactics, you're less likely to be affected by them. There will also be times when you may need to use them yourself.

The Hardball Game

1. **Whenever possible, take the initiative in the negotiation.** This gives you added power. You increase the likelihood that you will get what you want when you are calling the shots. If you make an outrageous offer, they might just take it. (They might not know about point number four below.)

2. **Be prepared to walk away.** The one who needs the deal the most is at the biggest disadvantage. Everything is negotiable, but you don't *have* to negotiate. Still, *don't make threats unless you're prepared to back them up.* Don't threaten to walk away unless you really mean it, or you will lose credibility fast.

3. **Understand their objectives as well as their weaknesses and vulnerabili-**ties. Do your homework. Smoke out their real bottom line. Get them talking and keep them talking—discover where their soft underbelly is. Many hardballers have a sort of "underbelly" sixth sense. They know how to find it and how to tear into it.

4. **You don't ever have to take the first offer.** You can always try to get a better deal. Sometimes silence helps—if you say nothing, they may start scrambling to offer you something better. In any case, *don't agree to anything right away.* If you're not sure about your decision, give yourself plenty of time to think it over. You can always postpone and set up a later meeting.

5. **Always ask for more than what you really want.** In this way, you can seem to be giving up more than you really are. While you are negotiating away small points, the other side is making real concessions. Get something for everything you give up, even the smallest points. Minimize what they are giving up while maximizing what you are.

6. **Create demand by starting a bidding war.** People want what they think other people want. Create an image of yourself as hot and in demand. Let them know that if they don't take your offer, somebody else will. Remember, there are plenty of fish in the sea.

7. **Always have a back-up plan in mind in case something doesn't work out.** Have a "Plan B." In fact, make "Plan C" and "Plan D" while you're at it. This will help you to keep your cool, no matter what happens. You won't have to cave in out of desperation.

8. **Get your adversary saying "Yes" to you as often as possible.** This will get them into the habit of saying yes when it comes to the final decision.

9. **Get everything in writing.** Whenever possible, have *your* lawyer write the contract. Carefully check out your adversary's credentials. Some people will try to screw you, so protect yourself. Make them put it in writing, and by all means, don't sign anything until you are clear about what it says.

10. **Remember, you don't have to settle for less than what you want**. If you're willing to persist, you can usually get a good deal.

Win-Win Negotiations

Win-win negotiations start with the premise that when the people involved combine creative energies, they most often come up with a better solution than either party originally had in mind. When dealing with people with whom you have a continuing relationship, for instance your spouse or your boss, it is obviously in your best interest to emphasize win-win negotiating strategies. Yet in all you do, you sincerely want people to be happy with the results of the negotiations you enter into. Win-win works best; after all, what goes around comes around.

The Win-Win Game

1. **Think in terms of a long-term relationship.** In hardball negotiations, you might win the battle and lose the war. You might take the guy to the cleaners once, but now you've made an enemy, and he's going to be looking to get you at the first available opportunity. At the very least, he's not going to be very cooperative the next time you need his agreement. Also, you may get a reputation for being a real jerk, in which case, people whom you have never dealt with before may be gunning for you and take satisfaction in nailing "that S.O.B." Trust that if you do right by people, it will come around again and again.

2. **Approach your win-win negotiations with certainty.** Start with the assurance that there is a way for both parties to win. Come in knowing that you will continue to explore ideas and generate options until you find a mutually beneficial solution.

3. **Come prepared.** Before you meet, find out as much as you can about your partner, including his life situation, personality, and interests, as well as his likely attitudes on the issues you will be considering together. Explore all factors relevant to your negotiation. For example, consider how third parties might play a role or how the situation is likely to change or evolve over time. Begin generating mutually beneficial solutions even before you meet for discussion. Be creative.

4. **Be agreeable—view the other party as a partner.** In the hardball game, the other guy is your adversary. It's easier to work with a partner than an adversary. Be friendly. Stay focused on agreement; don't get into hard positions. Remember, agreement is the goal. Genuinely want to help the other party.

5. **Listen.** Although it helps to find out as much as you can in advance, don't come in with set solutions. Take the time to understand the other party's needs, concerns, and desires. Ask questions and really listen. Active listening can help you hear what is not being said, as well as what is. In some situations, it may be necessary to draw the other party out— to help them clarify their needs and desires. To make sure you understand them clearly, feed back what they have shared with you until they indicate that you have got it right.

6. **Be honest about what you want and ask for it.** That means you have to know what you want. State it clearly and be specific. Then show the other party how

they can help you get it. Ask them flat out. Especially in personal relationships, it is important to state exactly what you want. Otherwise, you may frustrate the other party by making yourself impossible to please. They can help you get what you want, but they can't save you from your own moods.

7. **Don't view compromise as loss.** We have been trained to think that we have to win every point or be thought a fool. Pride and self-righteousness can keep us from making compromises that will be better for everyone in the long run. Alexander Hamilton wanted a form of government more closely akin to a monarchy than the representative democracy that the Constitutional Convention decided upon. Still, once the decision had been taken, he supported the Constitution and lobbied hard for it. He saw the country had more to win by his supporting this decision than by taking his marbles and going home. *Win-win players keep a greater good in mind.*

8. **See conflict as opportunity.** An apparent conflict or dispute offers an opportunity for creative solutions. Often conflict comes in when we get into rigid or limited thinking. All that may be needed is to look at the situation from a fresh perspective. Stay detached and objective. Don't take conflict personally or as an affront. Keep the emotional tone from getting overheated—if you need to, take a break.

9. **Remember you are entering into a dynamic creative process.** The spirit of win-win negotiation is creative and playful, fluid and fun. Like a jazz improvisation, it starts to jive when the players are harmonizing and staying loose. The music that you make in these negotiations will surprise and delight. Harmonious playfulness triggers the right-brain holistic and inspirational solutions that you can never get from

scheming or from a defensive adversarial posture. You tap into something beyond the range of critical thought.

10. **Don't settle for less than the right solution for both parties.** If you've tried in every way to come up with a mutually beneficial solution and you find that there really isn't one in this instance—let it go. Don't jeopardize the relationship by trying to make sparks fly from wet sticks. After a time, you'll know if it is not going to click. Part company as friends, and leave the door open to work together again.

Be on the lookout for new opportunities to use a win-win approach. As you develop and practice your win-win negotiation skills, you'll find hundreds of opportunities to apply them, not simply in work, but in every aspect of your life. It gives you an ongoing experience of a world that works for everyone.

Negotiation Sources

The Art of Closing Any Deal: How to Be a Master Closer in Everything You Do. Pickens, James W. New York: Warner Books, 1991.

The Dynamics of Effective Negotiation: A Win Win Approach to Getting What You Want. Sparks, Donald B. Houston: Gulf Publishing Company, 1993.

Getting to Yes: Negotiating Agreement without Giving In. Fisher, Roger, and William Ury, with Bruce Patton, ed. Boston: Houghton Mifflin Co., 1992.

On Negotiating. McCormack, Mark H. Beverly Hills: Dove Books, 1997.

You Can Negotiate Anything. Cohen, Herb. New York: Bantam, 1989.

Ten Keys to Effective Selling

1. **Believe in what you are selling.** When you're totally convinced that your product or service is of genuine benefit to your clients and you sincerely want to provide them with the best, your enthusiasm is irresistible, and your sales will soar!

2. **Project the right image.** Be neat, organized, and professional in your sales presentation. Remember—the first impression you make on a prospective buyer is the most important factor in whether or not you will close the sale. Nonverbals are at least as important as verbals.

3. **Become an expert.** Learn as much as you can about your product or service. Your knowledge and confidence will put your customers at ease and make it easy for them to trust you.

4. **Qualify your prospects.** Make sure you're talking to a qualified buyer who has both the authority and the means to make the final decision. Be aware that qualifying goes both ways. Make sure that what you are selling is really appropriate to your client.

5. **Assess your client's needs.** If possible, do homework on the client before you meet. Learn as much as you can. If you know what they want, it'll be easy to show them how owning and enjoying your product or service will help them get it. Conduct interviews with your clients to help you identify their needs. Let them tell you what they want, and match it to what you've got.

6. **Stress the benefits when making your presentation.** Talk about the benefits that your new client will receive from owning your product or service. Do they want more challenge and excitement in their lives? A greater sense of self-esteem? Do they want to save money or time? People buy for emotional reasons. They buy benefits, not products and services. If you can demonstrate that owning your product or service will help them get what they want, you've made the sale.

7. **Handle their objections.** If they say no, find out why. Get clear on their objections. Once you know what their problems are, you'll be able to solve for them and close the sale. Because you believe in the value of what you are selling and know your client is qualified and will benefit from your product or service, you'll be able to handle any objections with ease and confidence.

8. **Close the sale naturally.** This is the most crucial and most challenging aspect of the sales process. More sales are lost because the salesperson was afraid to ask for the sale than for any other reason. Go ahead—close the sale. Make sure that your buyer gets to enjoy the benefits of your product or service.

9. **Follow through.** Give your client a follow-up call to make sure they're satisfied. If they are, this is a great opportunity to ask for referrals. If not, find out why, and handle the problem right away. Focus on developing long-term business relationships with satisfied customers. Consistent follow-through is the most important key to keeping track of satisfied clients and building your business.

10. **Stay positive.** Every sales presentation is a valuable learning experience. Think about what you did well and what you could improve upon. Find out how many "no's" it takes you to close one sale. Then remind yourself that each "no" brings you one step closer to your next "yes!" Don't get discouraged. An unrelentingly positive attitude is the greatest asset of an effective salesperson. If you persist, you will succeed.

Information, Please

Economists, futurists, social pundits, prognosticators, and experts of every stripe and hue have been telling us for over twenty years now about the movement toward the "information economy." Of course, it isn't just talk. It has been estimated that by the year 2000, 85 percent of the labor force will be working in the service sector, and that the lion's share of these workers will be engaged in information-related industries.[3] Yet despite the facts and all the ink, and the miles of video- and audiotape devoted to feature stories on this subject, there are a lot of us who may not fully understand what this shift means.

Organized information is highly valued in this economy. If you were to view all business as the sale of organized information, you wouldn't be too far off the mark. What is a doctor or lawyer, accountant, engineer, or any professional selling? Information. Even in such labor-intensive and thing-oriented industries as manufacturing and mining, nothing happens unless someone knows what to do with the raw materials and knows something about how to package and market them.

These are key skills, or abilities, for the information economy:

1. The ability to research and collect data
2. The ability to organize information
3. The ability to target specific markets
4. The ability to package information
5. The ability to sell information

The more you can develop these skills, the more valuable you make yourself in this economy. If you don't already have them, develop informational skills. Learn to research, organize, package, and sell information, keeping in mind specific markets all the while. From a long-term perspective, you probably want to be moving toward work that requires imagination, thought, and people skills—things computers or robots aren't very good at.

If what you're doing is not primarily knowledge-based, you might want to start moving in that direction. Think of ways you can turn what you're doing into information. Document and promote your work. Develop seminars, books, audio- and videotapes, newsletters, catalogs, etc. Be prepared to share or teach what you know. When you pass along what you're doing and learning, you multiply your value in the marketplace. Keep in mind what is valued in the new economy; develop your information skills, and you improve your chances for success.

Using the Internet

No matter which of the marketing strategies or scenarios you choose to adopt, the Internet can be a tremendous resource. If you don't own a computer with a modem, get one—now! If you can't afford to get one, get on one. Use a friend's. Go to a local public or college library. The U.S. Office of Education currently has a program to help libraries throughout the nation make free Internet access available to the public. There are even copy stores and Internet cafes that offer access to the Web on an hourly fee basis.

Develop a Strategy

Develop your own strategy for utilizing the Internet, one tailored to your specific goals. Generally speaking, you can use the Internet to research, communicate, and disseminate information; to publicize yourself, your business or nonprofit mission; and to advertise, as well as to buy and sell products and services. Determine which of these general strategies will work best for you and how you can best employ them. Concentrate on high pay-off areas. For example, if you are looking for a job, posting your résumé on a lot of sites is a waste of time (few employers ever visit them). On the other hand, the Internet is one of the best ways to gather information about companies you are considering working for and about the people who may potentially hire you. Though it may be fun, a personal Web page with a résumé and a picture of yourself isn't an effective marketing tool for the typical job hunter. Yet for the small business owner, a full-blown Web site is a virtual must in today's marketplace. In short,

the best ways for you to use the Internet will depend on your goals. Consult the books and magazines listed in the bibliography on the next page for ideas and strategies that will help you maximize your Internet experience.

Stay Focused and In Control

For all the many opportunities it offers, the Internet can also be a huge distraction and a big waste of time. It's easy to be pulled off into tangents or to become overwhelmed by the sheer volume of information. The computer screen has a hypnotic effect on the brain, and hours may go by before you realize what has happened. There is more than one reason they call it "the Web." Don't let yourself get tangled up in it. Of course, there is nothing wrong with endless browsing if that's your intention; just don't let it sneak up on you. It's best to have a clear idea of what you are looking for before you log on—and then stick with it. Set the alarm clock on your computer to go off at intervals. These "checkpoints" will help you stay on track and keep you aware of how much time you are actually spending on the Internet.

Web technology is still in its infancy and will undoubtedly become much faster and more user-friendly in years to come. In the meantime, you may want to avail yourself of the "text only" option on your Web browser to facilitate the more rapid receipt of information. If you take the time to develop your own Internet strategy and determine to stay control, this emerging technology can provide you with an array of communication and information services that are only likely to improve in the coming years.

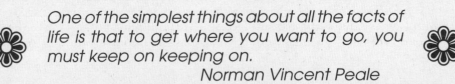

One of the simplest things about all the facts of life is that to get where you want to go, you must keep on keeping on.
Norman Vincent Peale

"Street Smarts" Sources

How the Internet Works. Gralla, Preston, Sarah Ishida, and Mina Reimer. Indianapolis: Ziff Davis Press, 1997.

Internet Research

Official Netscape Guide to Internet Research: For Windows and Macintosh. Calishain, Tara, and Jill Alane Nystrom. Florence, Ky.: International Thomson Publishing, 1998.

Researching on the World Wide Web: Spend More Time Learning, Not Searching. James-Catalano, Cynthia N. Rocklin, Calif.: Prima Publishing, 1996.

Web Search Strategies. Pfaffenberger, Bryan. Foster City, Calif.: IDG Books Worldwide, 1996.

Web Marketing

Advertising on the Internet. Zeff, Robbin Lee, and Brad Aronson. New York: John Wiley & Sons, 1997.

Advertising on the Internet: How to Get Your Message Across on the World Wide Web. Barrett, Neil. Dover, N.H.: Kogan Page Ltd, 1997.

How to Grow Your Business on the Internet. Emery, Vince. Scottsdale, Ariz.: The Coriolis Group, 1997.

The Internet Marketing Plan: A Practical Handbook for Creating, Implementing and Assessing Your Online Presence. Bayne, Kim M. New York: John Wiley & Sons, 1997.

Publicity on the Internet: Creating Successful Publicity Campaigns on the Internet and the Commercial Online Services. O'Keefe, Steve. New York: John Wiley & Sons, 1996.

What Makes People Click: Advertising on the Web. Sterne, Jim. Indianapolis: Que Education & Training, 1997.

Web Page Design

Create Your First Web Page in a Weekend. Callihan, Steven E. Rocklin, Calif.: Prima Publications, 1996.

Creating Web Pages for Dummies. Smith, Bud E., and Arthur Bebak. Foster City, Calif.: IDG Books Worldwide, 1997.

The Non-Designer's Web Book: An Easy Guide to Creating, Designing, and Posting Your Own Web Site. Williams, Robin, and John Tollett. Berkeley: Peacepit Press, 1997.

Magazines

Internet Computing
P.O. Box 55483
Boulder, CO 80323-5483
www.computer.org/internet

Yahoo! Internet Life
P.O. Box 53381
Boulder, CO 80323-3381
www5.zdnet.com/yil

Act III Review

If you've decided to create your own organization, answer the following questions. If you want to work in an already existing organization, turn to page 504.

Sailing the Entrepreneurship

Describe the products and/or services you will provide.   *(page 372)*

Identify the chief markets for your product or service.   *(page 373)*

Briefly, how will you get their attention?   *(page 374)*

How will you distribute your product or service?   *(page 374)*

List the key players on your management team.   *(page 375)*

List the key players on your professional support team.   *(page 376)*

What legal structure will you use (partnership, sole proprietorship, corporation, etc.)?   *(page 376)*

Indicate the funding vehicles you plan to employ.   *(page 379)*

Summarize your strategy for dealing with the "red tape" involved in creating your business.   *(pages 381-382)*

Write a goal for the completion of your business plan here.   *(page 384)*

Wielding the Freelance

The advantages of my freelance option are: *(page 395)*

The top markets for my project are: *(page 399)*

Crafting the Nonprofit Foundation

State the mission of your organization. *(page 419)*

List your top three strategies for achieving this mission. *(page 419)*

List three potential sources of funding below. *(page 420)*

Landing the Right Job

Identify what you want from an organization. *(page 442)*

List your top employment needs. *(page 443)*

Identify the top three organizations you would most like to work for, and the position you want. *(page 447)*

Describe your strategy for landing the interview with employer #1. *(page 459)*

List your employment strengths. *(page 463)*

List your #1 potential employer's needs and how you can help. *(page 464)*

List your #1 potential employer's strengths, including current and future opportunities. *(page 464)*

Street Smarts

My networking strategy will be: *(page 481)*

The media options I will use to promote myself are: *(page 488)*

My ideas for further exploring proposal writing are: *(pages 491-492)*

The negotiation strategy I will emphasize in regard to my current negotiation is: *(pages 496-497)*

The School of Life's Work

Wherein our hero learns to change and grow

One is always seeking the touchstone that will dissolve one's deficiencies as a person and as a craftsman. And one is always bumping up against the fact that there is none except hard work, concentration, and continued application.

Paul Gallico

So far, we have talked about your life's work as an Art, a Quest, a Game, and a Battle. Now we are going to look at it as a School—an ongoing learning process. We started this book with a discussion about recognizing and honoring the timeless in life. We close by honoring the role that time (the learning process) plays in creating and developing a life's work. The nature of *time* is *change;* the two words are virtually synonymous. "Act IV: The School of Life's Work" is about making the changes that will enable you to pursue your life's work. We will consider training and skill development, developing an effective transition strategy, improving your self-image, enlisting support, and getting the most out of what you're doing now. Before we get into these specifics, we will consider lifelong learning in creating—and responding to—change.

Learning to Change:
The Old Boy and the Student-Sage

The only person who is educated is the one who has learned how to learn . . . and change.
Carl Rogers

The following remarks from *Megatrends'* author John Naisbitt help us understand how vital it is that we learn to *create* change and learn to effectively *deal with* the changes we are not directly creating. "In the new information society, where the only constant is change, we can no longer expect to get an education and be done with it. There is no one education, no one skill that lasts a lifetime now. Like it or not, the information society has turned us all into lifelong learners."[1] I would suggest that it makes a difference whether we "like it or not," that our attitudes toward change and learning are critical to our effectiveness.

Change. What does the word conjure up for you? Anticipation? Fear? In anticipation, we look forward to change, demonstrating an inherent trust in our ability to learn and grow and in the basic goodness of life. Fear reflects a lack of trust in ourselves and in life. We can distinguish between the fear of *changing* and the fear of *change*. The fear of changing, of actively initiating change, comes from a lack of confidence in our ability to learn. The fear of change, the fear of the effects of any portion of a generalized "other," (for example, people, circumstances, the weather, God, etc.) comes from the belief that life is basically hostile, that what's coming is likely to be bad. We can say, in the vernacular, that the fear of changing is the fear of screwing up; the fear of change, the fear of getting screwed.

> *Do not cherish the unworthy desire that the changeable might become the unchanging.*
> *Teachings of the Buddha*

Learning plays a part, both in creating change (for example, in retraining and skill development) and in responding or adapting to change (for example, changes in the economy or in specific markets). The Latin origins of two English words long associated with learning suggest approaches for effectively creating and responding to change. Our word *student* comes from *studere*, "to be eager about, to study;" the word *sage*, from *sapere*, "to know, to taste."[2]

The student is eager to learn, to gain knowledge; the sage has the patience to taste wisdom. As students of life, we are eager to learn the new. As would-be sages, we develop the patience and insight to taste, experience, and penetrate into the very essence of change itself. The true student of life has mastered the fear of changing; the true sage, the fear of change.

If ever there was a book designed to illuminate the essence of change, it is the ancient Chinese classic the *I Ching,* or *Book of Changes*. Of course, we can only touch on the profound wisdom in this book, which some claim as the oldest in the world. A lifetime of devoted study will not exhaust its treasures. The *I Ching* reflects the distilled wisdom of the "ancients" and their profound understanding of change. The *I Ching* instructs that "The Creative and the Receptive are the real secret of the Changes."[3]

What we have called "the fear of changing" (indecisiveness) can, from the standpoint of the *I Ching*, be viewed as a blockage of the Creative energy. What we have called "the fear of change" can be conceived of as a deficiency or blockage of the Receptive energy. The following lines from the *Ta Chun (The Great Treatise)* of the *I Ching*

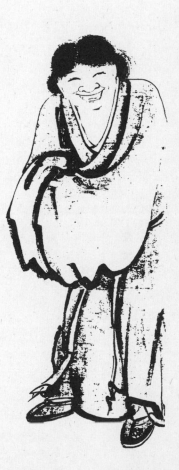

There is no security in life, only opportunity.

Mark Twain

*Learning is
movement
from moment
to moment.*

J. Krishnamurti

give the sense of what is meant by the "Creative" and the "Receptive":

The Creative knows the great beginnings.
The Receptive completes the finished things.
The Creative is decided and therefore shows to men the easy.
The Receptive is yielding and therefore shows to men the simple.[4]

The Creative brings the end of difficulties through the strength of decisive action. In developing a life's work, our creative power is enhanced by learning how to learn. The way of creative change is easy for those who know how to learn. True students of life bring an eagerness, a joyous ease into every circumstance. "Knowing the great beginnings," they easily decide upon a way and set about learning what is required. They create a course of study, learning-practice, and action that brings the desired result.

Thomas Jefferson said, "Nothing is troublesome that we do willingly." We are willing when we are decided. Where we lack ease in our lives, we lack the strength of decisive action. Our word *crisis* comes from the Greek *krinein*, "to decide."[5] *Crisis is what happens when we don't decide.* For example, you know it's time for a career change, but you lack the skills or knowledge necessary to move into the career you desire. If you don't take decisive action and aggressively seek the skills and knowledge you need, you could end up feeling trapped in a dead-end job.

The Receptive brings the end of complications through simplicity of motive. Where there is complexity in our lives, we have too many motives crashing into each other. For example, retraining for a new career might mean the temporary loss of income and status. Unless you are clear about your motive, you may quit before you have achieved your goals. The desire for the approval of others can all at once or bit by bit pull you away from your stated objectives. When we are devoted to our objectives, we can let go of our concern about how we appear to others. We let go the vain attempt to control things that we can't (like the opinions of others) and concentrate on what we can control (our own thoughts, feelings, and actions).

The Receptive aspect of change in developing a life's work demonstrates itself in the flexibility and sensitivity to follow the line of least resistance. Those with the wisdom of the sage know that the plans and intentions of our conscious minds are but a small part of life, so they remain flexible. They realize that success is often a matter of moving with events that are larger than oneself, so they are sensitive to the flow of events. Receptivity doesn't mean abandoning our goals but moving toward them in a way that is as simple and harmonious as possible. A surfer has an aim (toward shore), yet to realize it, he must put himself in accord with the rhythm of the ocean and ride the waves. To be Receptive, we must, like the surfer, expand our attention and trust that the great ocean of life will carry us forward if we are patient enough to catch the right wave and let it do most of the work.

We can think of the Creative as the *will* and the Receptive as the *willingness* of change—the will to transform, the willingness to let go, to receive. As we develop confidence in our ability to learn, we become students of Creative change, confidently creating the transformations (inner and outer) we desire. As we simplify our motives, we become willing to embrace and harmonize with the larger-than-self changes, all the while moving patiently and steadily toward our goals. To be good students of life, we need to retain (or reclaim) the childlike eagerness to learn. Yet too much eagerness leads to frustration and disappointment, and so, like a wise old sage, we must be able to detach—to stand back, look at where we are going, and consider the best way.

> The only way to make sense out of change is to plunge into it, move with it, and join the dance.
> *Alan Watts*

The name of the Taoist sage Lao Tzu has been translated "old boy." We can all learn to be old boys or old girls—eager, playful, and decisive, and yet wise, patient, and enduring. When we are confident in our ability to learn, we can plunge, like a child at play, into the life we have imagined. When we are clear in our motives, we can let go any need to justify or defend ourselves or our actions or to desperately seek approval. Like the wise old sage, we keep our own counsel. Long after others have given up or burned out, we endure—flowing with circumstances while remaining devoted to our ideals. We pace ourselves, like the venerable turtle of Aesop, and win the race through steady application.

Again and again, the *I Ching* instructs on the merits of perseverance and encourages us to take a long view: "The secret of action lies in duration. Good fortune and misfortune are slow in the making."[6] If we are to persevere, we must exercise both the Creative and the Receptive potentials, possessing both the eagerness of the student and the wisdom of the sage. Next, we will consider how we can improve our capacity to learn and, in so doing, enhance our ability for creative, decisive action. Later, we will consider the wisdom of patient, persistent action.

> . . . in the world of the future, the new illiterate will be the person who has not learned how to learn.
>
> *Alvin Toffler*

Learning: The Difference Between Here and There

In a world that is constantly changing, there is no one subject or set of subjects that will serve you for the foreseeable future, let alone for the rest of your life. The most important skill to acquire now is learning how to learn.

John Naisbitt

Through the ages, man has searched for the secret of youth. In the Middle Ages, witches and magicians invoked spirits with spells, potions, and amulets to confer the vigor of youth. Western and Chinese (Taoist) alchemists mixed strange herbal brews and concocted elaborate mineral combinations in the hope of prolonging life. In the eighteenth century, Ponce de Leon traversed vast expanses of the American continent in search of the Fountain of Youth. In the nineteenth century, elixirs were sold from the backs of medicine wagons and at carnival shows. Today health food, nutritional supplements, and regular exercise are touted as the answers. While the efficacy of these methods can be debated, in the end the secret of youth may be found in learning—keeping the fresh perspective that new knowledge and experience bring—keeping an open mind!

Anyone who stops learning is old, whether twenty or eighty. Anyone who keeps learning today is young. The greatest thing in life is to keep your mind young.

Henry Ford

A "well-educated" man once went to a Zen master to acquire understanding of Zen. After greeting him, the master instructed the visitor to be seated and proceeded to pour him a cup of tea. The cup was filled and still he poured. Tea spilled over the sides of the table onto the floor and still the Zen master poured. Finally, the visitor could contain himself no longer, "The cup is already full! It can hold no more!" The Zen master replied, "So it is. Just as you come to me so full of what you know that you can receive nothing new."

Learning requires an empty cup, what some Zen practitioners refer to as "the beginner's mind." The wide-open zest and spontaneity of the child reveal the beginner's mind. Young children learn at a fantastic rate. Pushing this pace is an incessant driving beat of the simple question: Why? Why? Why? Often their questioning outlasts our patience. It threatens our deeply held assumptions and pat answers.

As Mark Twain put it, "The trouble with most of us is that we know too much that ain't so." We've lost the questioning of youth. We settle for answers we don't understand, but, oh well, they sound okay, and who wants to make the effort to look anew? We become mentally old and rigid as we attach ourselves to ignorance. We reclaim the beginner's mind when answering the question *Why?* once more becomes more important to us than protecting any particular point of view.

But what does this have to do with achieving your career goals? Simply this: Every goal requires learning. Were it not so, it would not be a goal but an accomplished fact. Given ample desire (and that's a big "given"), all that stands between you and your new career is ignorance: what you don't know (knowledge and skills) and who you don't know (contacts). The remedy for both is learning.

Self-education is, I firmly believe, the only kind of education there is.

Isaac Asimov

While your understanding is incomplete, you are sure to be frustrated in your efforts to reach your goals. As long as your skill is undeveloped, you'll feel overwhelmed and out of your league. While unable to enlist the help of others, the ship of your dreams is dead in the water. Learning how to learn can help in all these areas.

Learning is also the primary means of improving self-esteem. In his book *Awareness Through Movement*, Moshe Feldenkrais points out that self-image is determined by "[1] physical and genetic heritage, [2] education, and [3] self-education."[7] Over the first, our genetic endowment, we have no control. The second, too, is largely out of our hands; as Feldenkrais puts it, "education makes each of us a member of some definite human society and seeks to make us as like every other member of that society as possible." Then, as Feldenkrais writes, "of the three active areas in the establishment of our self-image, self-education alone is somewhat in our hands."[8] Active engagement in lifelong learning improves one's self-image and, in so doing, not only her ability to achieve, but her sense of

All human beings, by nature, desire to know.

Aristotle

well-being. The steps that follow will help you reclaim the beginner's mind and improve your learning capacity.

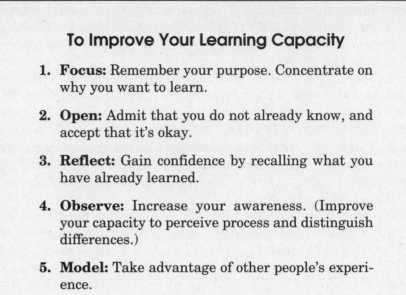

To Improve Your Learning Capacity

1. **Focus:** Remember your purpose. Concentrate on why you want to learn.

2. **Open:** Admit that you do not already know, and accept that it's okay.

3. **Reflect:** Gain confidence by recalling what you have already learned.

4. **Observe:** Increase your awareness. (Improve your capacity to perceive process and distinguish differences.)

5. **Model:** Take advantage of other people's experience.

6. **Act:** Practice, practice, practice.

Remember Your Purpose: Concentrate on Why You Want to Learn

Learning can be defined as the process of remembering what you are interested in.
Richard Saul Wurman

Attention is the key to learning. Anything you can do to increase your attention will increase your capacity to learn. I knew a woman who was an understudy in a play with a city repertory company. She had learned her lines well enough but paid little attention to the subtleties of delivery. Then one night, just before the curtain came up, the lead learned that her mother, who lived on the other side of the country, was seriously ill. She had to return immediately after that night's performance. Suddenly it dawned on the understudy that the next evening she would be playing the part for real. That night she watched and learned as never before.

The story illustrates a simple point: *whenever we increase our intention, we increase our attention, and with it, our ability to learn.* The understudy's intention increased when she had a practical purpose for learning. Think of how many times a child has seen his parents starting and driving the family car. Yet most kids don't really pay attention until they are sixteen or so. Suddenly what they had taken for granted becomes fascinating. This mundane activity now means freedom, dates, social acceptance—and that makes it interesting. Again, a clear purpose brings increased intention and, with it, increased attention and, thereby, accelerates the learning process.

> *The readiness is all.*
> *William Shakespeare*

Learning the mundane aspects of your subject matter (and every subject has them) becomes more interesting when you keep in mind why you want to learn them. What does it mean to you to gain this new knowledge or skill? How will it affect your life? In addition to sharpening your attention, keeping your purpose in mind helps you to prioritize the various elements of your subject matter. Looking at all you need to learn can seem overwhelming or threatening. Focusing on purpose helps you sort out the principal from the peripheral, the essential from the extraneous. You'll be able to plot your course and pursue it without distraction. At every point, you will know why you are doing what you are doing.

George Washington Carver said, "There is nothing that will not reveal its secrets if you love it enough." This statement holds another great key for increasing your attention and, with it, your learning capacity. Learn to pursue knowledge like a lover wooing a would-be sweetheart, and you find great joy in the learning process itself. A lover loves the courting process. Knowledge will flirt with you, tease you, smile on you, run from you, disappoint you, and yet, if you are true to your love, she will at last be won. We trust that each of you who is learning and training for a new career has real love for this area. Keep loving it until you are on intimate terms, until it whispers all its secrets.

Your desire to achieve your goals and your love for your subject give a natural impetus to your learning efforts. Focusing on these will propel you to act, to get out and learn all you require to be successful. Desire always leads to action, unless it is somehow inhibited. What often inhibits our natural desire to learn is judging ourselves for not already knowing.

> *To know that you do not know is the best. To pretend to know when you do not know is a disease.*
>
> *Lao Tzu*

Admit Your Ignorance, and Accept that It's Okay

*Who has no faults?
To err and yet be
able to correct it is
best of all.*

Yuanwu

Let's face it; it's difficult to learn anything while we are trying to prove that we already know it all. None of us likes to admit our ignorance. Yet most of us will admit we don't know everything, which means we are ignorant of something. Once we admit ignorance, we can do something about it. We can take responsibility to learn. Admitting ignorance can come after a long and difficult process or as simply and as innocently as a child asks why.

What is it that makes us think we should have learned something before we have studied it or even thought of studying it? Let's say you go to a party and you meet someone there who is, or appears to be, a genuine expert in his field. You find yourself feeling uncomfortable around this person and intimidated by what he knows. What's happening internally is that you're judging yourself for not knowing what he knows. This is a little silly because you've made no effort to learn this subject, while he has devoted years to it. When you judge yourself for not knowing, you miss the opportunity to learn more by asking questions that further your understanding. This illustrates a principle that operates whenever we are engaged in the process of learning: *When we judge ourselves for not already knowing, we miss the opportunity to learn now.*

What keeps us from admitting our ignorance is a compulsive need to be right, expecting ourselves to know before we have learned. Accepting yourself for not already knowing allows you to keep your attention on what you want to learn. Until we admit our ignorance, part of the attention that we need in order to learn becomes tied up with defending ignorance. These defenses take three forms: denying, blaming, and playing sour grapes.

Everyone is ignorant, only in different subjects.
Will Rogers

By *denying* we mean refusing to admit that what you don't know can hurt you. Joan's career objective requires going into business for herself. Yet she knows very little about administering a business. She says, "I can make the sales; administration isn't important." She's denying that a vital aspect of her business is important, simply because she doesn't know much about it. She feels anxious and uneasy about her goal because she's avoiding an area that is vital to her success. Deep down she knows this, but insecurity prevents her from admitting it. She is blocked from learning until she admits that something she doesn't know is important. As long as she refuses to admit her ignorance, she blocks the perception of potential solutions (for example, taking night classes in business administration, hiring full- or part-time help, reading, etc.) *Remedy: Stop denying and take action!*

By *blaming* we mean directing your attention into building an inpenetrable fortress of excuse rather than channeling it into learning what you must to be successful. The moment we start rehearsing our excuses or pointing the finger of blame, in that moment we are defeated. Jack is blaming his wife and kids for holding him back from getting the retraining he needs to achieve his career objectives. Because his responsibilities and his wife's earning capacity prevent him from pursuing his career objective by going back to school full-time, he is looking at giving up altogether. If he does, he may blame and resent his wife and his children for the rest of his life. As soon as he stops blaming, he can begin to take a realistic look at what he can do to further his training right now. *Remedy: Stop blaming and take action!*

Learning is the very essence of humility. . .
J. Krishnamurti

By *playing sour grapes* we mean pretending that you don't really want what you want because you are not ready to risk what it would take to get it. Eileen had a natural gift for working with people. People often told her she would make a great therapist. She was constantly doing informal therapy with her friends and family, helping them to clarify and express their feelings. With only two years of college training, she felt that the master's degree she would need to become a marriage and family counselor would take too long and was beyond her reach. While a bright woman, Eileen was never strong academically. She feared that she would not be able to complete the necessary academic work to get her credential. Eileen was pretending that she could be satisfied with using this, her strongest talent, in a peripheral way. She was ready to give up on her strongest talent without giving it a fair chance. Once she admitted what she really wanted, she was ready to give it her best shot. *Remedy: Stop pretending you don't want it and take action!*

In every case, the remedy is to take action.
Get clear about exactly what it is that you need to
learn and exactly what you need to do to learn it.
BEING CLEAR KILLS FEAR.

Admit your ignorance, and learning is possible. Deny, blame, pretend, and you are sure to hit a dead end. As we detach ourselves from our shortcomings and begin to look at them objectively, we find new ways of approaching our goals. Accepting ourselves for not knowing allows us to grow and expand. Judgment brings anxiety, tension, and a sense of struggle that inhibits learning. It creates interference. Simply put, judging yourself hurts and keeps you from learning. Self-acceptance fosters learning, and it feels good. Despite what some of us may have been taught at school, learning is fun. The moment of learning is always a moment of exhilaration. It is not necessary to struggle in order to learn. The first step to easy learning is to recall what you have already learned. This gives you the confidence to learn even more.

Recall What You Have Already Learned

Lest you feel overwhelmed as you ponder all you must learn in order to pursue your new career, consider the following: When you were born, you could not walk, talk, write, drive an automobile, comb your hair, go to the bathroom, brush your teeth, or add figures, yet you probably do all of these things every day. But these are simple things, right? Try telling that to a child learning to walk or talk. Few things you will ever learn are as complex as these. Valuing what you have already learned gives you the confidence to learn still more. You may be ignorant of many things, as we all are, but you certainly are not stupid (unable to learn). As a practical matter, *intelligence is simply confidence in your ability to learn.*

Make it thy business to know thyself, which is the most difficult lesson in the world.
                              Miguel de Cervantes

Review all you have learned. You may be surprised. If you think you have difficulty learning, take a look at the evidence. (See the exercise on page 535.) Simply to function in our highly complex society, you have had to learn a great deal already. Say to yourself: If I can learn _____, I can certainly learn _____, and you leverage your learning. Now let's look a little deeper into what learning is.

Increase Your Awareness:
Perceive Process and Distinguish Differences

. . . I found that I was fitted for nothing so well as for the study of truth: as having a mind nimble and versatile enough to catch the resemblances of things (which is the chief point) and at the same time steady enough to fix and distinguish the subtle differences . . .

Francis Bacon

Your capacity to learn is your capacity to perceive process and distinguish differences. We'll start with process. The ability to recognize process—to understand what gives a complex operation or function its fundamental unity, to notice the similarities within and between operations—is a powerful tool for organizing and comprehending vast amounts of information.

The great Confucian scholars referred to this as *ko wu*, "apprehending the principle in things."[9] Jacob Bronowski, in *Science and Human Values*, describes it as the essence of science and art. "All science is the search for unity in hidden likenesses. . . . Science is nothing else than the search to discover unity in a wide variety of nature—or, more exactly, in the variety of our experience. Poetry, painting, the arts are the same search."[10]

In the work of Joseph Campbell, one recognizes a profound understanding of process, the "apprehension of the principle in things." Campbell's greatest contribution was his well-documented presentation of the essential unity of world mythology. By identifying a fundamental and universal symbolic language, Campbell was able to make sense of the various supernatural beings, animals, totems, and archetypal heroes that populate the myths of the world. Through a symbolic understanding, he could see how what was portrayed in one culture's mythology by, say, a buffalo, and in another culture's by a tree, were representations of the same archetypal energy.

If one looked at the material forms, one only saw differences. However, Campbell could see the process and, therefore, recognized the similarity of the function of various forms. His ability to perceive process gave him a tool for organizing vast amounts of information from diverse sources. He could move into an unfamiliar culture, with a totally foreign set of symbols, and make sense of them quickly and accurately because he understood process.

Incidentally, Joseph Campbell said, "Everything I know I've gotten from reading."[11] Neo-Confucians such as Chu Hsi viewed reading as a means of enlightenment. They taught that one could most clearly and easily recognize "the one principle that resides in all things" by reading the Confucian Classics. Having realized it thus, one then could proceed to recognize the one principle within all things. Of course, what Chu Hsi had in mind was not a casual or even a merely intellectual reading. The reading he advocated was a rigorous discipline that required the right subject matter, a reverential and yet critical approach, a calmness of mind enhanced by meditation, tenacious application, and endless patience.[12]

There is then creative reading as well as creative writing.

Emerson

Individuals who are especially adept in a given area communicate about it in a simple language laypeople can understand. An understanding of process makes this possible. People who do not understand process get lost in complexity or simply bore us. As Thoreau put it, "I am put off with a parcel of dry technical language. Anything living is easily and naturally expressed in popular language."

Penetrate to process. Fix in your mind the essence of the particular career you want to pursue. Break it down into process. What are the four or five essential elements of this career? As you move into the complexity of the details, keep in mind the simplicity of process. Concentrating on the essence of your career will not only make you more effective in practicing, it will also help you organize what you need to learn. There may be a host of skills and knowledge that you will need to learn. A focus on process helps you stay on track and move confidently into new areas. An understanding of process brings simplicity, clarity, and breadth to your work, but you also want depth. You want to become a genuine expert in the field of your choice. This brings in the other aspect of learning, i.e., distinguishing differences.

Distinguish Differences

To the uninitiated, computer programming language looks like a mass of incomprehensibility. We lump it all together and say, "It's Greek to me." Yet the trained expert easily perceives the various languages and their applications. Any area of knowledge in which

The chief object of education is not to learn things but to unlearn things.

G. K. Chesterson

you have a high degree of mastery is an area in which you are able to distinguish a high degree of difference. This is true regardless of your field of expertise. It could be gardening, designing aircraft, baking cookies, managing corporations, installing telephone equipment, or administering city governments.

One is an expert because she knows the subtleties of her craft. The uninitiated can enjoy the end products but not all the details that go into creating them. For example, the uninitiated may say, "That was a delicious cookie," or, "This new computer is really incredible," but how the cookie was made or exactly how the computer does what it does, the uninitiated do not know. *The greater knowledge we have in any field, the subtler the degree of difference we can perceive.*

Because the "differences" vary so much from subject to subject, there is little we can say about them generally. One thing we can say: Start with the general and move to the specific; understand the "differences" at each stage along the way. Build on a foundation of understanding. Thoroughly chew each bite of knowledge you take, and minimize the indigestion of confusion. Make sure you understand the vocabulary of your subject area. Don't proceed past words you don't understand.

Take Advantage of Other People's Experience

There is an easy way and a hard way to learn most anything. The hard way is by trial and error; the easy way is by using other people's experience (O.P.E.). Take the attitude, "If I don't know, someone does. It's my responsibility to find out who knows and either hire their experience or learn from them." Where can you find O.P.E.? We live in the midst of an information explosion. Other people's experience is readily available in whatever form suits you best.

> *We can be knowledgeable with another man's knowledge, but we cannot be wise with another man's wisdom.*
>
> Michel de Montaigne

Here are just a few of the ways you can access it: live interviews, conversations, classes, seminars, plays, books, audiotapes, videotapes, films, trade journals, newsletters, magazines, and newspaper articles. All of these methods and more provide you with that most valuable of treasures, other people's experience. We encourage you to seek it out.

By tapping other people's experience, you can internalize a great deal of knowledge in a relatively brief time. For example, it may have taken an individual fifteen years to learn the ins and outs of her business, yet you can learn many of the essential aspects in an eight-hour seminar or by reading a two-hundred-page book. Because she is sharing her hard-won experience, you can spare yourself many of the costly and time-consuming mistakes she has made. Learn as much as you can from everyone. The following are some of the ways you can take full advantage of other people's experience:

Imaginative Projection allows you to take advantage of other people's experience, even when they're not physically present. Through the creative use of imagination, you can gain maximum benefit from learning materials such as the printed page, audio-tapes, videotapes, and so on. As you read (or listen or watch), pause periodically to mentally project yourself into the situations you are learning about. Read, digest, and then build mental images of yourself doing the thing described. This is an extremely effective way of learning from "how-to" books and tapes. What you learn in this fashion is not simply stuff you know but actual experience you can draw upon.

> Accumulate learning by study, understand what you learn by questioning.
>
> Mingjiao

Once you have pre-experienced the content through imaginative projection, you can deal more confidently and effectively with it when you meet it in actual experience. The remaining ways of taking advantage of other people's experience require the physical presence of the person you want to learn from, though in some cases you could use videotapes.

Osmosis involves simply being in the presence of the individual you want to learn from. Getting yourself in his presence and having the intention to learn from him starts things happening. Without effort, you pick up his vibes and attitudes. Your subconscious mind is constantly learning and incorporating ways of being and acting, of carrying and presenting yourself, simply by being in that person's presence.

Observation requires that you deliberately and consciously pay attention to what the individual you want to learn from is doing. Additionally, you're bringing in a critical analysis. Remember, even the best role models can teach what not to do as well as what to do. You want to pick up what they do well, without collecting

Earthly things must be known to be loved: divine things must be loved to be known.

Blaise Pascal

their bad habits. Determine what they are doing that works well, and zero in on the step-by-step process of doing it. Likewise, as you encounter practices and procedures (or the lack of them) that aren't working quite so well, make note of these. You may want to observe a better role model for that particular aspect or devise your own method.

Modeling is similar to observation, except instead of making notes about what you will apply later, you are going one step further to actually imitate, or copy, what the individual is doing as they are doing it. This is a natural process in learning. It's sometimes referred to as "monkey see, monkey do." It brings the learning all the way into your body. It's the way the great masters of art taught their students. Children do this all the time, quite spontaneously. They see someone making cookies and want to jump in the batter. The monkey business of modeling plays a big part in the speed with which children learn.

As adults, we don't imitate because we want to be original, "different," and unique. We miss out on tremendous opportunities to accelerate learning when we refuse to copy, or model, behavior. Of course, once you gain mastery, you can bring in your own touch, but you can usually learn the basics much more quickly if you're willing to imitate.

One of the first behaviors that was systematically modeled was skiing. Observers carefully analyzed films of expert skiers and broke down the process into small components that could be easily duplicated. Then they simply had to teach the various components in succession, and the complex set of skills necessary for skiing could be learned easily and rapidly by virtually anyone. Study how people who are expert in your field approach their work. How do they prepare themselves? How do they execute? Break it down into steps you can apply. Make their skill your own.

Is there anyone so wise as to learn by the experience of others?

Voltaire

Seek out Mentors

One of the most effective ways of tapping other people's experience is working with a mentor. When you are entering a new environment, you need a guide or guides. Mentors play the role of guides. They have learned their way and can show you around. Take advantage of their experience. A good mentor provides you with a total learning experience. The mentor shows you what he is doing; he tells you about what he is doing, and you get a feel for it. After a short time with a mentor, you will know whether or not the mentor's work is something you want to pursue.

Often what blocks us from learning is being too proud or too shy to ask people who know. This comes from failing to perceive the difference between ignorance and stupidity. I have never met a man or woman who isn't ignorant (about something) nor yet met anyone who is inherently stupid (unable to learn). If you find yourself failing to avail yourself of the help you might receive by asking others, ask yourself if it is because:

- You won't admit your ignorance.
- You have a compulsive need to be right.
- You lack confidence in your ability to learn.
- You are too emotionally attached to "getting it."
- You fear the other party may reject you.
- You are afraid they may ask you to work too hard.

Practice

The final step to learning is to practice, practice, practice. Actors in Broadway plays average about three months of rehearsal before a new production. Olympic athletes train for years. Great speakers practice their speeches. Comedians practice their jokes. You will want to practice the skills that you require to achieve your objectives. Be willing to make mistakes. Refrain from making the ridiculous demand of yourself that you must be able to do something perfectly before you'll do it at all. Anything worth doing is worth doing poorly at first. Practice makes perfect.

> *Tell me, I'll forget. Show me, I may remember. But involve me and I'll understand.*
> *Chinese Proverb*

Let Go: Detach and Learn

Detachment can be seen as the essence of Zen. From the Buddhist perspective, attachment is the source of suffering. Attachment to "having it my way" binds us to ignorance and the suffering it fosters. Before we can overcome ignorance, we must detach from automatic emotional reactions to events. Only then are we free to embrace all of our experience and learn from it.

Trying too hard can actually keep us from learning. One reason young children learn so rapidly is that they've yet to develop any emotional hang-ups about learning. They can stay relaxed and present. As adults, we often burden ourselves with performance anxiety and negative memories. We are not interested in learning for its own sake but as a means of justifying or proving ourselves. If you are having difficulty learning anything, take your emotional temperature before you decide that it's too hard or you are "too stupid." You may just be too emotionally involved. Let go of the emotional charge, and you may discover you were pretty bright all along.

In antiquity men studied for their own sake; nowadays men study for the sake of (impressing) others.

Confucius

Before the transmission of your car can go from reverse to forward, it must pass through neutral. When you are learning, your life is going forward. When you are emotionally reacting, you are going in reverse. To get things moving forward again, shift into the neutral gear of detachment. Humor helps. When you laugh at your emotional attachment and drama, you release your hold on ignorance and pass into neutral. Now you are ready to go full speed ahead toward your objectives. Don't take yourself too seriously. The joke may be on you.

On average, an infant laughs nearly two hundred times a day; an adult, only twelve. Maybe they are laughing so much because they are looking at us.

Learning Summary

In review, the attitudes best suited for creative learning can be verbalized as follows: "I have a strong desire to learn. I know what I want to learn and why. Instead of wasting my energy by judging myself for not already knowing, I will keep my attention fixed on my objectives. I can detach emotionally and penetrate to process and distinguish differences. I will seek out knowledge and those who know. I will practice and practice and keep a sense of humor."

I love laughing.

William Blake

Dancing through the Changes

I once knew a Zen teacher whose favorite saying was: "One by one. Day by day." He often repeated this expression to his too eager students. Impatient with daily application, they demanded instant results and wondered out loud if they would *ever* "get it." The wisdom he shared reflected the patience that comes with age and experience. Youth is eager and enthusiastic, yet tends to be impetuous and easily frustrated. The wisdom of age brings a long-view perspective, one that knows that nothing of lasting value was ever accomplished without long and patient effort. So far, we have discussed how we can improve our capacity to learn to effectively and deliberately create change. Now, we will consider how we can foster the staying power to go the distance by learning how to respond well to changes we are not directly intending.

> To be able to preserve joyousness of heart and yet to be concerned in thought: in this way we can determine good fortune and misfortune on earth, and bring to perfection everything on earth.
> *I Ching*

In *creating* change, we are acting intentionally. In *responding to* change, we act best when we act receptively. Many of the changes we must respond to are beyond our direct control, changes that result from the actions of others or from "acts of God." Sometimes, however, the changes we are responding to are, in fact, our own creations, though not fully intended. If we think of our lives as whole systems, we can easily understand that significant change in any one part of the system will bring considerable change to other aspects of the system. Some of these changes may be anticipated, some even intended, but many will be neither intended nor anticipated. (Of course, it is best to anticipate as much as possible. The exercises that follow are designed to assist you in doing just that.) How well we respond to these unintended, peripheral changes is as much a part of our success as our ability to initiate and effect intentional change.

The process of creation is, after all, a rather messy business. Look at a painter or sculptor at work. While creating order on the canvas or the stone, he is making a mess of his clothes and studio. Writers, scholars, and research scientists, who may be extremely precise, neat, and orderly in their work, are notorious for having chaotic offices piled high with books, files, and scraps of paper, particularly while in the white heat of a creative flow. Some peripheral disorder always attends the process of creating a new order.

The work of art is above all a process of creation, it is never experienced as a mere product.
Paul Klee

The movement to create a truer manifestation of your life's work is an attempt to bring a greater order into your life. By integrating more fully your visions, values, and talents into daily expression, you are creating a more ordered (harmonious) life. In the process, you can expect to generate a good deal of peripheral disorder. The first step to dealing effectively with the increased disorder is accepting it as a sign that you are making progress.

Before you can better order your closet, you first make a bigger mess of the room it's in. If you focus on the mess, it seems that you are getting nowhere and that things are actually getting worse. Of course, with the simple task of cleaning a closet (which may take a few hours), you understand and accept the temporary chaos as part of the process of creating a new order. However, when you are dealing with the much larger task of creating a fulfilling life's work (a process which may take many years), the resulting temporary disorder can seem overwhelming.

This is especially true if moving toward your new career requires major lifestyle changes. Changes such as going back to college, letting go of a financially secure and steady job, or moving to another city, can be very disruptive. The additional demands on your time can put a strain on your relationships and other aspects of your life. If you lose sight of purpose, these additional demands may seem like more than you can bear.

Simplify!
Henry David Thoreau

A strong sense of purpose enables you to respond positively to the inevitable difficulties, annoyances, and inconveniences of life in general and change in particular. Your sense of purpose brings both meaning and direction to the problems associated with change. This is one reason why we have emphasized the importance of purpose throughout. It will provide you with the motivation, not only to move ahead, but also to deal with some of the waves which that forward movement makes.

Dealing with Disorder

There are three things we can do with disorder. First, we can learn to live with it and do nothing about it. Second, we can decide to leave it alone for now. Third, we can deal with it immediately. While disorder doesn't always need to be dealt with or dealt with right away, it does need to be confronted. What we are not aware of can, and usually does, hurt us. Being aware of something and deciding to leave it alone is not the same as avoiding it.

Some disorder can be dealt with on a systematic basis. You may want to establish a regular time to review your disorder. In household or support team meetings, assign priority ratings to various areas. Determine whether to learn to live with it, leave it alone for now, or deal with it immediately. Of course, your decisions may change as your decision-making criteria or the circumstances of your life change.

Everything is in flux.
Heraclitus

While some kinds of disorder can be dealt with systematically, other kinds of disorder come more immediately into our experience. Here again, the key is to be aware of it and consciously decide to accept it as it is, leave it alone for now, or deal with it.

While on a backpacking trip, I was awakened in the middle of the night by my companion. He informed me with some alarm that there was a "bunch of bears" nosing around near our camp site (a disorderly situation). I told him that was nice and attempted to go back to sleep. (I was deciding to accept the bears.) He was not interested in rest right then and asked me what we should do. I told him "nothing," which he wasn't quite ready to accept. So I told him to stay awake and keep an eye on them, and if they got any closer or started pawing on his sleeping bag, to wake me. (In other words, I told him to leave it alone for now.) This he could accept, though it didn't help him get much sleep.

Much of our disorder is simply bears in the night. We can accept them or leave them alone for now. Had these bears been known for feasting on human flesh, I would have, no doubt, made a different decision. The bears that are ready to eat us must be dealt with now.

Learn to Live with It: You can't do everything. If you start going back to school and your house gets a little messier (and you can't enlist someone to help you), learn to live with it. Don't judge yourself. The important thing is that you do the important things.

Leave It Alone for Now: Many of our problems will resolve themselves simply by leaving them alone (as any good doctor or psychologist will tell you). The American sage, Mark Twain, remarked on how he had dealt with a lot of trouble in his life, most of which never happened. In addition to the fears that never manifest, there are the situations that we eventually will want to deal with but, for whatever reason, now is not the time.

Deal with It Now: Things that are critical to your purpose and well-being must be dealt with right away. To delay here is dangerous. It might cost you a missed opportunity or put you in needless jeopardy. There is an old Czech folk saying: "Trouble comes in a door left open." The door is a hole in your awareness. Fortunately, most of your opportunities and potential pitfalls come with repeated advance notice. You can usually see them coming and have plenty of time to respond. They do, however, reach a critical stage where action is a must.

Everything flows on and on like this river, without pause, day and night.
                              Confucius

It may not be necessary to totally handle a situation that must be dealt with now. Some circumstances lend themselves to a partial disposement. A partial disposement could take the form of putting a fence around a problem or achieving limited objectives that leave a need for later mopping up. Remember, containing the potentially dangerous aspects of a situation or achieving only limited objectives generally requires that you get back to the issue. Only take this option if you are certain that it is not better to totally handle the situation now. Much time is lost in getting back to problems or opportunities we have taken our attention off of.

The Simple Power of Purpose

When we are clear on our purpose, we simply act. We put an end to the complexity of the better/worse game of comparisons and competitiveness, of looking over our shoulder to see what the other fellow is doing. We accept that we cannot be all things to all people and concentrate on doing our best to achieve our purpose. Purpose provides an organizing principle to our lives, bringing greater order and a higher degree of synthesis and integration. As we have seen, acting on purpose can bring with it a certain degree of temporary disorder, yet purpose provides us with an indispensable guidepost for effective decision-making.

This is true regardless of the level of decision under consideration. Of course, when making major decisions, we want to keep in mind our purpose in life. But purpose can also help us as we approach specific, even routine, tasks. Ask yourself, "What is the purpose of this task?" Your answer will tell you, not only how much energy a particular task deserves, i.e., its relative importance, but also where to concentrate your energy to effect the best result. In other words, purpose helps you establish priorities among competing tasks, as well as within a task or set of tasks.

State Your Purpose and Stay with It

Many people become a bit compulsive about what they are doing and lose sight of their original purpose. One way that you can help yourself to stay on purpose is to write down your objective and how long you think it will take you to complete it. This will help you to stay on track and make sure that the activities you undertake are the result of a conscious decision. Energy has momentum. It can take on a force of its own, and you can quickly become involved in peripheral pursuits.

It is not enough to be busy, so are the ants. The question is, what are we busy about?
Henry David Thoreau

For example, one day you decide to clean out a shelf in your garage so that you can save time finding certain tools. Your purpose was to organize the shelf, and you imagined it would take you about an hour to complete the task. Once you get involved, you find yourself cleaning out the entire garage. The afternoon has passed, and things are still in disorder. Your one-hour task has already taken four, and it's going to take another hour to put all this stuff away. Of course, there is nothing wrong with cleaning out the entire garage, but that was not your purpose. What is true for simple tasks like this goes double for more complex operations. Clearly stating your purpose in advance helps you stay on track.

We can get confused with ideas and with people as easily as we can with things. Let's say you have a report to write. Clearly stating your purpose in advance with a time estimate will help you stay on track. Periodically check yourself to make sure that what you're doing is pertinent to your original purpose. This will keep you from

Make your work to be in keeping with your purpose.

Leonardo da Vinci

getting lost in tangents and will stimulate additional thoughts relevant to the report.

We've all had the professor or teacher who enjoys telling his stories so much that he forgets what his original point was. He starts out dutifully with his lecture notes in hand, but soon he is rambling on and on. He becomes so fascinated with the sound of his own voice that, before you know it, the bell has rung and, "We'll talk about that next time." State your purpose and stay on track.

Establish Completion Criteria

Of course, nothing we do is perfect, so completion is, in a sense, arbitrary. It's up to each of us to determine what completion means by establishing criteria for the task. For example, in making a transition into a new career, when do you know enough to jump into a new field? Of course, if you don't jump in, you'll never get wet. Knowing when you are ready can make the difference between a belly flop and a triple somersault. Establish criteria in advance so you will know when the time has come. Some of these criteria are external (completing degree requirements, passing the bar, or obtaining a license), but many are internal, subjective perceptions of readiness.

Completion and the Energy of Success

There is great satisfaction in the completion of a task well done. It is an exhilarating and energizing experience. This energy provides the force and momentum to make the large change that a transition into a new career represents. Making your transition in discreet, quantifiable steps keeps you from getting overwhelmed in the process and energizes you along the way. Spell out the major action steps to your transition as well as the sub-points that comprise them. Value each step you take.

The Receptive completes the finished things.
I Ching

The satisfaction and energy that you feel from the completion of any task is proportional to the amount of energy and concentration you have put into it. For example, it's energizing and satisfying to wash and clean your car. It's more satisfying to graduate from high school. The students who have been most purposeful and have put the most energy into their work will feel the greatest sense of satisfaction and energy from their completion (graduation).

This is true so long as the individual actually experiences completion. If, for example, the student is ruminating after the fact about how he should have gotten an "A" rather than a "B+" in chemistry class, his mental energy is still involved in pre-graduation activity. In his mind, he has not completed. In order to be able to tap into the wellspring of energy that completion brings, we must know when something is complete—when it is time to let it go.

A Final Word

Persistence: Your persistence level is a function of your emotional investment in your purpose and your belief in your ability to accomplish that purpose. Persistent application toward the realization of a given purpose is the result of a burning desire to see it manifest. Don't give up. Believe in yourself and your purpose. Everyone who takes a risk, tries new things, does things in new ways will fail from time to time. Success is not about going through life without making mistakes. Rather, it has to do with a determined effort to see it through. Learn from your mistakes, and stay on track. Remember, as the *I Ching* says: "Perseverance furthers."

'Tis a lesson you should heed: Try, try again. If at first you don't succeed, try, try again.

William Hickson

What's Ahead in Act IV

Think of the transition between where you are now and where you want to be as a journey to a new life. "Act IV" is about planning the journey to make sure that it is as smooth, pleasurable, and exciting as possible. You have the opportunity to express the eager movement into change of the student and the sage-like patience to endure.

Transformations: Creating Changes (Eagerness)

"Scene I: Getting There: Transition Strategies." When you plan a trip, you start by identifying your destination; this you have already done in your previous work in this book. You have determined where you want to go and what you have to do to get there. Now you need to determine how fast you will travel. Will you travel by supersonic Concord, bullet train, or compact car? These decisions involve considerations of time, money, and other responsibilities.

"Scene II: Training Thrills: Knowledge and Skills." In this section, you will have a chance to formulate a strategy for the acquisition of the additional skills and knowledge you will require to move into your new career. You will differentiate between the training you require to improve your ability, your credibility, and your marketability. This will help you to keep your purpose in mind throughout your training. You will examine the most effective ways to go about learning what you need to learn. Then you will research the best places to go to learn it.

Acceptance: Adapting to Changes (Patience)

"Scene III: Creating the Self-Image You Need to Succeed." This section provides you with specific methods for improving your subconscious image of yourself. You will learn to apply techniques of visualization, affirmation, and behavior modification to reshape your old self-image into a new one that allows you to express your best.

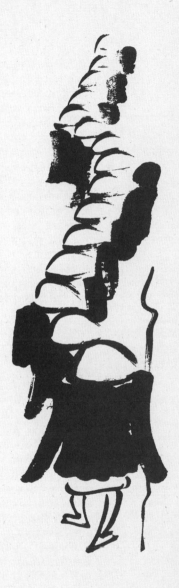

"Scene IV: Help!: Enlisting Support." We are so tied to our families and immediate friends that a major change for us is a significant change for them. Simply because they are so closely related to us, they're going on the journey with us, whether they know it or not, whether they like it or not. How well we manage to enlist the support of our friends and family may well determine how successful we will be in making the change to a new life, as well as how enjoyable the process will be.

"Scene V: Loving What You Do ('Til You Are Doing What You Love)." No matter how great your destination or how beautiful the scenery along the way, if you have a bad attitude, you're probably not going to enjoy the trip. In the same way, you need a constructive attitude while making the journey to your new life's work. That's what this section is about.

Detour #4: The Lack of Self-Confidence Trap

Lack of self-confidence is, more often than not, simple laziness. We feel confused and uncertain because we do not know. But instead of making the effort to investigate, we procrastinate and worry. We tell ourselves we can't instead of learning how we can. If we used the mental energy we expend in worry and fear to get out and find out about what we do not know, we would see our self-confidence grow. Lack of self-confidence is not overcome by faith but by action. It is a lack, not of certainty, but of effort. Too often we are certain that we can't before we give ourselves a fair chance.

Act on the impulse that says, "I want to know. I want to find out." If you "know" you don't have time to take a certain class or are "sure" you couldn't pass it, find out about it anyway. Start taking action. Move in the direction of your desire, and watch your confidence increase. Let your sense of duty to purpose and to the potential that lives within you propel you to act. Remember, taking it personally causes delay. Focusing on purpose smooths the way. The first thing to learn is what you need to learn. Next, how and where you can best learn it. Beware these hang-ups: "Don't Investigate" and "Don't Act."

Don't Investigate: Assuming you've gotten past laziness and you're ready to act, it helps if you know how to organize information so that it doesn't overwhelm you. Learn to approach a new subject by first understanding its general principles and practices. Outline them. Next, go to more specialized information within the general headings. Of course, we were all taught to do this at school, but it is surprising how many people do not seem to know how to research or investigate new subject matter. Even if you approach the subject in a systematic and organized fashion, you still may become confused, especially if you don't understand the "language of the field." Learn the requisite terms, and persevere until the light goes on in your head.

Don't Act: Some of us have no difficulty investigating all the ways to learn about a new subject. We buy books we never read, tapes we never listen to. We collect brochures on every training, seminar, and workshop from here to China and back, but we never act. Others of us will take the class, read the book, but as soon as the bell rings or the cover is closed, we forget all we "learned." When it comes to skill, it takes application; you learn by doing. You have learned, not what you can remember, but what you can apply. Take action! Read the book, attend the meeting, approach a mentor, watch a videotape, practice what you know, learn about it now—it's not too late. Every piece of knowledge leads to the next. Move aggressively and persistently toward the knowledge you desire.

Recall What You Have Learned

Make a list of at least thirty things you have learned to do. Be sure to include things that may be obvious, things you may discount as insignificant but which, in fact, are important, e.g., learning to walk, learning to talk, learning to drive a car, learning to read, etc.

1. Write everything you have learned in the last five years.

    _____

    _____

    _____

    _____

    _____

    _____

    _____

    _____

    _____

2. Write everything you have learned in the previous ten years (five to fifteen years ago).

    _____

    _____

    _____

    _____

    _____

    _____

    _____

    _____

    _____

3. Write everything you have learned prior to this (from birth to fifteen years ago).

    _____

    _____

    _____

    _____

    _____

    _____

    _____

    _____

    _____

The School of Life's Work Affirmations

1. I am confident in my ability to learn all I need to excel in my new career.

2. I now see the easiest, best, and most credible ways of learning all I need to realize my life's work.

3. I am now developing a definite strategy for acquiring the skills and knowledge I need to succeed in my new career.

4. My desire to achieve my life's work and my belief in myself attract all those who can help me to realize my dreams for myself and humanity.

5. I am now attracting people who are helping me to achieve success in all areas of my life.

6. Because I want to help others, I know that others want to help me. I easily accept their help and support.

7. I never feel ashamed or embarrassed for not knowing the skills, knowledge, or people that I need to know in order to succeed. I accept myself and take the action that moves me ever closer to my life's work.

8. I love and accept myself, therefore, I easily admit what I do not know and take the necessary steps to acquire additional understanding and skill.

9. Since my desire is to serve others, I know that the money I require for training in my new career is available and is coming quickly to me now.

10. There is more than enough love, support, time, energy, and money for me to acquire all I need to fulfill my destiny.

Getting There:
Transition Strategies

We must ask where we are and whither we are tending.
Abraham Lincoln

The purpose of this brief section is to help you design a program for moving into your new career as quickly as possible. You'll determine whether you are ready to leave your current position or if you will need to continue in your current work while developing yourself for your new career. If you require retraining, you'll have a chance to evaluate how much time and energy you can devote to it. We will consider training in depth in "Scene II, Training Thrills: Knowledge and Skills."

Our purpose in pointing out a number of transition strategies is to suggest that there is more than one way to make it work. Perhaps you can't devote yourself to full-time retraining, and you're not prepared to begin your new career right away. This doesn't mean you have to abandon your dreams. You can still find a way to make it work. In the discussion that follows, we have divided six transition strategies into two broad categories: transitions that involve immediately quitting your current position and transitions predicated on maintaining your current position for a time.

Quit Your Current Position

1. Quick Shift: The quick shift is for individuals who are ready to quit their current work and move immediately into new careers. If, after careful research, you have determined that: (1) you currently have the necessary skill and knowledge for your new career and (2) you have a realistic strategy for marketing yourself in this field, you're ready for a quick shift. Quick shift candidates would include individuals ready to begin practice as independent consultants in fields they've worked in for some time or individuals who have worked in a given field for some time and are ready to go into business for themselves.

2. Full-Time Training: Full-time training is for those with the financial wherewithal to devote themselves full time to learning what they need to pursue their new careers. This strategy is also appropriate for those who are willing to sacrifice their current lifestyle for the sake of training for a new career. (You may have to rely on student financial aid.)

3. Interim Job and Part-Time Training: This strategy is for those who want an immediate change but are not yet prepared to begin working in the career role they have envisioned. Perhaps you feel as though you have gone as far as you can go in the job you now hold. You know you need a change—

and quick. The challenge and excitement have gone out of what you're doing. Still, you're not ready to begin work in the new field, at least not at the level that you ultimately desire. You might be able to take an interim job that allows you to pick up additional training, experience, contacts, and self-confidence. This will enable you to move toward your new career at a deliberate pace, even if you haven't the time or money for full-time retraining. There are several ways you can approach this:

• *You could work in your new field at a lower level of responsibility.* For example, let's say you're interested in starting a nonprofit organization. You might work for an existing one in your field. In this way, you gain on-the-job training that will come in handy when you start your own organization. You could augment this with additional training through classes, seminars, and independent reading.

If you want to start your own business, you might work for someone else in the same business and learn as much as you can from them. You would endeavor to assume as much responsibility as possible, keeping in mind that one day very soon, you will be doing all of this for yourself. Practical training of this kind is far more useful than anything you can get from educational institutions. You learn how things actually work, not how they're supposed to work. After a time of doing this kind of work for someone else, it will become clear to you whether or not you want to make a career of it. Meanwhile, you will be making contacts who can help you later.

• *You could work in a different field at a position that would give you an opportunity to develop needed skill.* Again, let's say you want to start a nonprofit foundation. You recognize that you currently lack the necessary management skills to be effective at this. You could gain valuable management experience working in business or in government. Meanwhile, you might take some of the evening classes in nonprofit administration offered by many universities in major metropolitan areas.

Maintain Your Current Position

1. Part-Time Training: You've decided that you want to stay where you are while training for your new career. Evenings and weekends are devoted to training. Perhaps you can negotiate more flexible hours in your current position that will allow you to get daytime training. You may even be able to arrange for your current employer to give you additional training or to pay for it.

2. Part-Time New Work: This strategy is similar to part-time retraining, except that instead of spending your spare time in retraining, you spend it in working at your new career. You are ready to begin, even if you can't make a full-time living from your new business. You might, for example, start a business working part time out of your home. This strategy especially applies to those who are interested in working freelance or creating their own organizations.

3. Part-Time Training and Part-Time New Work: This strategy is for those who want to move quickly into their new career but don't have the financial resources for full-time training or sufficient skills to make the quick shift. People using this strategy might start businesses from their homes and begin taking business classes at night school, all the while maintaining their current employment. This path requires a lot of forethought and planning and is generally best for people who do not have a lot of additional responsibilities (for example, raising a family).

"Making the Transition" Sources

The 10 Natural Laws of Successful Time and Life Management. Smith, Hyrum W. New York: Warner Books, 1995.

Balancing Work and Family. Lizotte, Ken, and Barbara A. Litwak. New York: Amacom, 1995.

The Career Decisions Planner: When to Move, When to Stay, and When to Go Out on Your Own. Lloyd, Joan. New York: John Wiley & Sons, 1992.

Career Shifting: Starting Over in a Changing Economy. Sharlan, William. Holbrook, Mass.: Adams Media Corp., 1993.

Getting Your Act Together. Morrisey, George L. New York: John Wiley & Sons, 1980.

How to Get Control of Your Time and Your Life. Lakein, Alan. New York: New American Library, 1996.

In Transition. Burton, Mary Lindley, and Richard A. Wedemeyer. New York: HarperBusiness, 1992.

The Management of Time. McCay, James T., Richard Ward, and Laurie Blanch Ward. Englewood Cliffs, N.J.: Prentice-Hall, 1995.

Managing Transitions. Bridges, William. San Francisco: Perseus Press, 1991.

 The present is great with the future.
Gottfried Leibnitz

Transition Strategy

1. What transition strategy have you chosen? Check one.

Quit Current Position	Maintain Current Position
❑ 1. Quick Shift	❑ 1. Part-Time Training
❑ 2. Full-Time Training	❑ 2. Part-Time New Work
❑ 3. Interim Job and Part-Time Training	❑ 3. Part-Time Training and Part-Time New Work

2. Why do you feel this is the best choice for you? _____
   _____
   _____
   _____

   What are the benefits of this approach? _____
   _____
   _____
   _____

   What are the potential risks, costs, and sacrifices to this approach? _____
   _____
   _____
   _____

   Are they acceptable to you? _____

3. What steps do you need to take to implement this strategy?

   Date

   Step One: _____ _____
   Step Two: _____ _____
   Step Three: _____ _____
   Step Four: _____ _____
   Step Five: _____ _____

4. When do you plan to be fully engaged in your new career?*(Give specific dates.)*
   _____
   _____
   _____

Living the Dream

Remember when you were a child? Do you remember how your parents talked about what they did? Was there anything they ever talked about doing that they never did? And I don't mean failed at. I mean never really worked at. Do you remember what that did for your belief in yourself, for your understanding about life, and for your expectations of it? Do you want to do that to your children? Or do you want to show by example what they can do when they trust themselves and make the commitment to follow their hearts? Do you want to give your children a world where people are divorced from themselves, alienated from their own desires, or a world where people dare to express themselves fully in making this world the best it can be?

Nothing has a stronger influence psychologically on their environment, and especially on their children, than the unlived life of their parents.
Carl Jung

Isn't alienation at the root of so many of our problems? Alienated individuals make an alienated society. And we are that—alienated from nature, from the Great Spirit of life, from our own souls and their gifts, and from each other. Isn't there at the base of apathy, at the root of every mean and violent act, an alienated individual who feels powerless and adrift? Isn't so much of the hostility we see reflected in our youth today simply a cry, a scream that says, "I can't do it. I can't express. I can't make a constructive difference"? Perhaps as a society, we are better to encourage and develop the good within young people than to concentrate on answering their cries with greater punishment. People are good and will do good if they think they can. Youth look to their elders for the way, but they will not be deceived. There is no substitute for authentic examples.

Life is not simply a process of disillusionment, where childhood fantasies are crushed and ground to dust by the heavy "you can't do it" wheel. Life is a growth of competency, an expansion in love, in which one's desire to give propels one into new universes, new interests, new skills. When you doubt whether or not you can live your dreams, remember, someone is counting on you.

It's Never Too Late to Change Your Career

Many people believe that because they have trained in one field, they are stuck with it for the rest of their lives. If the people below had stuck with their original work, none of us would ever have heard of them. Sometimes formal retraining is required, as in the case of Dr. Albert Schweitzer. However, all of the others on our list made the transition to new or auxiliary careers without formal retraining.

Mohandas K. Gandhi was trained as a lawyer and became a spiritual leader who developed effective principles of nonviolent resistance and was instrumental in liberating his country.

Michael Faraday trained as a book binder and made important contributions to physics.

Vincent van Gogh studied for the ministry and became a great artist.

Mother Teresa was a nun who worked as a school teacher and principal before she began her missionary work with the Sisters of Charity.

Nicolaus Copernicus studied law and medicine and was a part-time astronomer.

Dr. Martin Luther King was a Baptist minister who left his mark as a civil rights leader.

Medical missionary **Dr. Albert Schweitzer** originally trained as a musician and theologian.

Benjamin Franklin was trained as a printer and left his mark in science and technology, government and diplomacy.

Thomas Jefferson was a gentleman farmer who trained as a lawyer. He made significant contributions as a political theorist and writer, an architect, a botanist, an educator, a diplomat, and a president.

Playwright and poet **William Shakespeare** was trained as an actor.

Gregor Mendel (Mendel's laws of heredity) was an Austrian monk and an amateur scientist.

Poet **Wallace Stevens** was a practicing lawyer.

Philosopher and art critic **Ananda K. Coomaraswamy** originally trained as a geologist.

Zen art historian **Yasuichi Awakawa** was trained as an economist.

Of course, many not-so-famous people have made equally dramatic career changes, often well into midlife. It's never too late to follow your dreams. Even if you can't or don't want to take formal retraining, recognize that avocations often turn out to be vocations.

Training Thrills:
Knowledge and Skills

I'm a great believer in luck, and I find that the harder I work, the more I have of it.

Thomas Jefferson

Now that you have determined how much time you have to devote to your training efforts, we encourage you to think of how you can acquire the skill and knowledge you need to succeed—as quickly and painlessly as possible. That's what this section is about—developing an effective strategy for skill and knowledge acquisition. We'll start by sorting out the different functions of training to help you clarify and accelerate the process. We'll ask you to differentiate between training designed to enhance your ability, credibility, and marketability. Unless a particular degree or credential is mandated by state (or, in some cases, federal) law in your field, it's probably best to look for alternatives to traditional academic course work. Alternative methods can often help you learn exactly what you need in less time and at less expense.

For the most part, universities and colleges don't do a very good job of teaching new skills (some specific vocational training programs excepted). As a career changer, you've been around for awhile. You've probably learned most of the *skills* that college work has to teach you—for example, writing, research, study, listening, note taking, etc. What you *can* learn in college is specialized knowledge, but even this can often be learned more quickly and effectively through self-directed study.

Assuming you have the initiative and discipline, self-directed study has a lot to offer. First, it puts you in control. You learn what you want to learn, when you want to learn it, *because* you want to learn it. It sparks creative synthesis and enhances retention because you learn with an eye toward applying what you learn.

Self-directed study, especially when combined with some form of apprenticeship, is often superior to the formal lecture/exam mode of training. (See *The Independent Scholar's Handbook: How to Turn Your Interest in Any Subject into Expertise* for tips on making the most of your self-directed learning excursions.) Where you need new skills, try to get into a program where you can actually practice what you learn.

Skills are best learned through practice. Even when you are seeking specialized knowledge, stay away from relying entirely upon books. As much as possible, learn from people who are doing what you want to do. On page 555, we list a number of learning resources. Select those that are right for you in constructing your self-directed program.

When degrees are mandated by law or where they are *de facto* requirements, look for alternative university and college programs. These programs may allow you to take advantage of previous work experience, participate in selecting your curriculum, develop flexible hours that fit your schedule, and save money. See *Bear's Guide to Earning College Degrees Nontraditionally*.

Why Go Back to College?

1. You have to. It's the law in your field.

2. It will significantly improve your credibility.

3. The school you are considering has an outstanding program in your field, with individuals who have real experience in it.

4. You lack the discipline necessary for self-directed study, and you like the learning environment.

5. You've never been before, and you want to check out the experience.

6. You're looking to date people half your age.

Why Not Go to College?

1. A degree is no guarantee of a job; you'd still have to market yourself after you got it.

2. You may be bored with work not specifically related to your interest.

3. It will take your precious time.

4. It costs a lot of money and keeps you from making any.

5. You may have more life experience than your professors.

6. You'll be the oldest kid in the class.

"Training Thrills" in a Nutshell

Step 1: Identify what you need to learn and your purpose for learning it. From the research you did in "Act II: The Game of Life's Work," indicate what you need to learn in each of three categories: ability, credibility, and marketability. See pages 545–554.

Step 2: Select the ways you want to learn. See the "Learning Resources" list on page 555.

Step 3: Conduct research and identify specific learning options. See pages 556–558.

Step 4: Analyze learning options. Compare the benefits of various learning options in terms of the cost, the time it's going to take, and the relative pay-off from each of these training options. See page 560.

Step 5: Develop a training strategy and schedule. See pages 561–564.

Step One–Identify What You Need to Learn and Your Purpose for Learning It

Now it's time to develop your training strategy. The first step is to determine your purpose for learning. Do you need training in terms of your ability to actually do the job? Do you need training so that you can be more credible in this work? Do you need training in marketability, in your ability to market yourself in this career role? Perhaps you require training in all three or some combination? Let's look at a few examples of what we mean by *ability*, *credibility*, and *marketability*.

Ability

Jennie, who was trained as a geologist, has worked in other fields for many years. She now wants to pursue a career in a specific branch of geology related to environmental concerns. Though she has a Ph.D. in geology, she hasn't worked in this field in nearly fifteen years. Her *ability* is lacking.

She's had little practical experience and has forgotten much of what she learned in school. Going back to school for another Ph.D. would not be an effective training strategy for her. She is better off concentrating on raising her ability by brushing up on general material on her own, taking classes in her specialization, and working with people in her new field.

Jennie's Strategy: *Focus on ability by working as an apprentice, studying on her own, and taking targeted classes.*

 If there is anything education does not lack today it is critics.

Nathan M. Pusey

Credibility

Tom worked as an accountant in a large metropolitan area. His dream was to open his own accounting firm, specializing in service to nonprofit corporations. He felt that he could make a meaningful contribution by offering his services to organizations that he recognized as special assets to the community and nation. He had worked for a C.P.A. for many years, and though he essentially did the C.P.A.'s work, he himself was not a C.P.A. He did the work, and his boss signed the papers and enjoyed the status, income, and independence of a C.P.A.

Tom had the ability (he could, in fact, do the work), still he was not allowed to start his own practice because the law stipulates that only a C.P.A. can do certain kinds of work. He lacked a college degree, and his state required such a degree before he could take the Uniform C.P.A. Examination. In his training, the essential point was to focus on getting the credential, which would enable him to do this kind of work more effectively and at a higher level of contribution, satisfaction, income, and status.

Tom's Strategy: *Focus on credibility by going to the local university (evenings as much as possible), acquiring his degree, and passing the Uniform C.P.A. Exam.*

Marketability

Monica deeply values physical health and well-being. She wants to work as a massage therapist. She has the ability—plenty of training and hands-on experience. Additionally, she has the essential credential (she is certified by the state of California). She lacks the marketing skill necessary to practice her trade on a full-time basis as an entrepreneur. She has worked in hotels, resorts, and health spas but has found this unsatisfactory and would prefer to work on her own. In looking at the training necessary to pursue her career the way she wants

to, she recognizes she needs to concentrate on developing marketing skills.

Monica's Strategy: *Monica focuses on marketability by taking seminars on marketing techniques for small businesses and by arranging to exchange professional advertising, graphic design, and marketing services for massage therapy. She reads books such as* **Guerilla Marketing** *by J. Conrad Levinson.*

Of course, you may need to develop yourself in all three areas. The purpose of the exercises that follow is to help you ascertain exactly what you need to learn and develop a strategy for learning it. The definitions below may help to clarify the differences between ability, credibility, and marketability.

Ability: that combination of skill and knowledge necessary to execute the particular work you are pursuing. This includes: formal training, previous work experience, apprenticeships, internships, independent training, or scholarship.

Credibility: that which is legally required or that which makes you appear to be especially qualified or outstanding in your field. This includes: previous work experience, degrees, titles, awards, the quality or prestige of the companies or clients you have worked for, endorsements, testimonials, associations, certifications, affiliations, publications, media attention.

Marketability: that group of self-presentation skills (be they in the area of job-hunting and career development or entrepreneurial skills) that enhance your standing in the marketplace. These include: job-hunting skills, sales skills, entrepreneurial skills, grantsmanship skills, promotion and advertising skills, negotiating skills, and human relations skills.

Variables to Consider in Training

It is important to specify the exact nature of the training you need because training (or retraining, as the case may be) can be an expensive and time-consuming proposition. You want to make your investment of time, money, and energy pay off. Toward this end, we ask you to rate yourself on the variables of: **ability**, **credibility**, and **marketability**. Give yourself a percentage score between one and one hundred. For example, if you have eighty percent of the skills necessary to do the job, give yourself eighty percent in the area of ability and so on. If you don't feel confident filling in the chart below at this time, complete the chart *after* you have completed the exercises that follow.

Ability	Credibility	Marketability
_____%	_____%	_____%
Skill: What additional skills will you need to learn and practice? _____ _____ _____ _____ _____ _____ _____	**Requisite Credentials:** Requisite credentials are those needed to legally operate in your career role. (For example, a lawyer must pass a state bar in order to practice law; a realtor must pass a licensing exam, etc.) What requisite credentials will you need? _____ _____ _____	**Image:** How can you improve or clarify your image? _____ _____ _____ _____ _____ _____ _____
Specialized Knowledge: What information will make you more effective in the performance of your new career role? _____ _____ _____ _____ _____ _____	**Additional:** Additional credentials refer to anything that improves your credibility that is not mandated by law. What additional credentials do you need? _____ _____ _____ _____	**Projection:** How can you better project your image in the marketplace? _____ _____ _____ _____ _____ _____

Ability Training

While every career requires different skills and abilities, there are certain general abilities that apply to many fields. We have included two lists of these skills. You may want to take them into consideration when developing your training strategy. The first list contains factors that were rated most important by employers when selecting college candidates for positions in their organizations. The study was conducted by Michigan University Placement Services. This data was compiled from a survey of five hundred employers throughout the United States.

Skills Most Sought After by Employers

1. Ability to get things done
2. Common sense
3. Honesty/Integrity
4. Dependability
5. Initiative
6. Well-developed work habits
7. Reliability
8. Interpersonal skills
9. Enthusiasm
10. Judgment skills
11. Motivation to achieve
12. Adaptability
13. Intelligence
14. Decision-making skills
15. Oral communication skills
16. Energy level
17. Problem-solving abilities
18. Attitude toward work ethic
19. Mental alertness
20. Emotional control

Here is a list of the ten hottest transferable skills compiled by Harold Figler, and found in *The Complete Job Search Handbook*,[1] an excellent primer on the skills necessary to the job seeker.

Ten Hottest Transferable Skills

1. Budget management
2. Supervising
3. Public relations
4. Coping with deadline pressure
5. Negotiating/Arbitrating
6. Speaking
7. Writing
8. Organizing/Managing/Coordinating
9. Interviewing
10. Teaching/Instructing

Skills Transfer More Readily Than Specialized Knowledge

It is not unusual for individuals in top level management to move from field to seemingly unrelated field. For example, John W. Gardener served as Secretary of Health, Education, and Welfare. He then became chairman of the National Urban Coalition. Later he founded the public interest group Common Cause. Then he founded a new organization called "Independent Sector" to increase the strength and effectiveness of America's volunteer sector. In addition, he was a distinguished editor and author. Although these positions spanned a great variety of fields and endeavors, he used many of the same skills in each position. (Note how many of the skills listed above Gardener used in all four positions.)

 Every man takes the limits of his field of vision for the limits of the world.
Arthur Schopenhauer

Ability Training Worksheet

This process summarizes for easy reference the work you did in "Act II" on identifying skills and specialized knowledge.

Doing-the-Work Skills: What skills do you most need to acquire to do this work effectively? Refer to "My Skills Map" on page 315.

1. _____
2. _____
3. _____
4. _____
5. _____
6. _____
7. _____
8. _____
9. _____
10. _____

Playing-the-Game Skills: These are the auxiliary skills necessary to maintain and enhance your acceptance in this profession. Refer to "Playing-the-Game Skills: Some Examples" on pages 302–303.

1. _____
2. _____
3. _____
4. _____
5. _____
6. _____
7. _____
8. _____
9. _____
10. _____

Try to know everything of something and something of everything.
Lord Brougham

Credibility Training: Requisite Credentials

Check with the proper agencies in your state (see source below), and determine which of the following (if any) you will need to operate legally in your state. Next, indicate what you need to do to acquire the credentials in question.

Entrance Requirements	✓	What Do I Need to Do?
Boards (State)		
Degrees		
Certification (State)		
Licenses (Federal and State)		
Bonding and Insurance		
Fees		
Mandatory Monitoring	**✓**	**What Do I Need to Do?**
Inspection		
Updates		
Standards		
Ongoing Review		
Renewals		
Others		

Issuing and Oversight Agencies: List the relevant agencies you will be dealing with:

_____

_____

 One learns through the heart, not the eyes or the intellect.

Mark Twain

Additional Ways to Enhance Your Credibility

	✓	What?	Where?	How?
Degrees				
Titles				
Certifications				
Endorsements				
Registers				
Testimonials				
Letters of Recommendation				
Join Associations				
Participate in Affiliations				
Join Service and Social Clubs				
Get Media Attention (Articles, Interviews, etc.)				
Write Books				
Produce Audio or Videotapes				
Conduct Seminars				
Write Articles				
Do Public Speaking				
Other_____				

Marketability Training

Whether you're thinking of creating your own organization or working for an existing one, the way you present yourself can spell the difference between success and failure, recognition and anonymity. Employers report that the single most important factor to the success of an employment interview is the first impression the interviewee makes. Making the right impression can be even more important for people who own their own business. We have included an image and projection section under "Marketability" because these factors apply to both the job seeker and the entrepreneur. For more specific information on the mechanics of marketing yourself, and resources for doing so, refer to "Act III: The Battle for Life's Work."

Image

The following are examples of certain qualities that make up the images of various companies and individuals.

Microsoft: Dominant, innovative, aggressive.

Nike: Hip, outrageous, energetic.

B.M.W.:   Performance, engineering, quality.

McDonald's: Inexpensive, fast, clean, family.

David Letterman: Cynical, witty, obnoxious.

Now write no more than five key qualities that you want to project as part of your image.

1._____
_____
2._____
_____
3._____
_____
4._____
_____
5._____
_____

If you are planning to create your own organization, write the key points of the image you want it to project:

1._____
_____
2._____
_____
3._____
_____
4._____
_____
5._____
_____

In matters of principle, stand like a rock; in matters of taste, swim with the current.
Thomas Jefferson

Projecting Your Image

Now that you have determined the image you want to project, consider how you can systematically and consistently build and project this image. Some vehicles for accomplishing this are: dress, language, voice, posture, body language, stories of past experience, résumés, brochures, business cards, stationery, etc. Indicate below how you will project each of the main points of your image.

Quality #1: _____

How you will project it: _____

_____

_____

_____

Quality #2: _____

How you will project it: _____

_____

_____

_____

Quality #3: _____

How you will project it: _____

_____

_____

_____

Quality #4: _____

How you will project it: _____

_____

_____

_____

Quality #5: _____

How you will project it: _____

_____

_____

_____

Image Sources

Change Your Voice, Change Your Life: A Quick, Simple Plan for Finding and Using Your Natural Dynamic Voice. Cooper, Morton. North Hollywood, Calif.: Wilshire Book Co., 1996.

Conversationally Speaking: Tested New Ways to Increase Your Personal and Social Effectiveness. Garner, Alan. Los Angeles: Lowell House, 1997.

The First Five Minutes: How to Make a Great First Impression in Any Business Situation. Mitchell, Mary, with John Corr. New York: John Wiley & Sons, 1998.

John T. Molloy's New Dress for Success. Molloy, John T. New York: Warner, 1988.

The New Professional Image: From Business Casual to the Ultimate Power Look. Bixler, Susan. Holbrook, Mass.: Adams Media Corp., 1997.

New Woman's Dress for Success. Molloy, John T. New York: Warner, 1996.

Power Presentations: How to Connect with Your Audience and Sell Your Ideas. Brody, Marjorie, and Shawn Kent. New York: John Wiley & Sons, 1992.

Talk to Win: Six Steps to a Successful Vocal Image. Glass, Lillian. New York: Putnam Publishing Group, 1988.

Let It Out!

You'll never have all the pieces. You'll never have all the parts. Don't wait to be perfect before you start. Walt Whitman said to himself, "Walt, you contain enough, Why don't you let it out then?"[2] You are a dynamic life force full of mystery and wonder, not a machine to which all the parts can be added and properly arranged. Building your skills and resources is important and helpful to the extent that it is moving you forward; don't let it become a trap. Don't let it become an excuse for inaction. *Remember, focus on the value of what you have to give, not on your weakness—and act.*

Thousands of people have talent. I might as well congratulate you for having eyes in your head. The one and only thing that counts is: Do you have staying power?

Noel Coward

Step Two– Select the Ways You Want to Learn

Learning Resources: Skill Blocks. After reviewing your answers on the previous pages, enter (in the spaces provided at the top of the diagram) the skills you want to learn. Next, check the ways that you will go about learning these.

List Skills
Public Speaking

Ways to Learn	Example	Skill #1	Skill #2	Skill #3	Skill #4	Skill #5	Skill #6	Skill #7	Skill #8	Skill #9
Formal Training										
Classes	✓									
Seminars	✓									
Home Study Courses										
Direct Observation	✓									
Mentors	✓									
Internships										
Volunteer Work										
Books	✓									
Audio and Videotapes	✓									
Informational Interviews										
Films	✓									
Trade Journals										
Newsletters	✓									
Magazines										
Newspapers										
Other: _____										

Step Three– Conduct Research and Identify Specific Learning Options

In "Act II," you identified the skills and knowledge you must acquire before working in your new career. The next step is to conduct research and specify exactly how you will acquire these. Below are a few places you can do research and a number of sources to check.

Places to Do Research

- Career centers
- Libraries
- Adult education centers
- Community colleges
- University extension offices
- Bookstores

Sources to Investigate

The 100 Best Colleges for African American Students. Wilson, Erlene B. New York: Plume, 1998.

America's 100 Best College Buys. Institutional Research, Inc. Camden, S.C.: John Culler & Sons. Pulished annually.

America's Best College Scholarships. Camden, S.C.: John Culler & Sons. Published annually.

Bears' Guide to Earning College Degrees Nontraditionally. Bear, John, and Mariah P. Bear. Berkeley: Ten Speed Press, 1995.

Been There, Should've Done That: 505 Tips for Making the Most Out of College. Tyler, Suzette. Lansing, Mich.: Front Porch Press, 1997.

But What If I Don't Want to Go to College?: A Guide to Success Through Alternative Education. Unger, Harlow G. New York: Facts on File, 1998.

Campus-Free College Degrees. Thorson, Marcie Kisner. Tulsa, Okla.: Thorson Guides, 1998.

The College Handbook. The College Board Staff. New York: College Board. Published annually in August.

College Online: How to Take College Courses without Leaving Home. Duffy, James P. New York: John Wiley & Sons, 1997.

Distance Degrees. Wilson, Mark V. Sutherlin, Ore.: Umpqua Education Research Alliance, 1997.

Earn College Credit for What You Know. Lamdin, Lois S., and Susan Simosko. Dubuque, Iowa: Kendall/Hunt Publishing Co., 1997.

 Education can train, but cannot create intelligence.

Edward McChesney Sait

Education for the Earth: The College Guide for Careers in the Environment. Princeton, N.J.: Peterson's Guides, 1997.

The Evelyn Wood 7 Day Speed Reading and Learning Program: Remember Everything You Read. Frank, Stanley D. New York: Avon, 1992.

Government Reference Books: A Biennial Guide to U.S. Government Publications. Schwarzkopf, LeRoy C., compiler. Littleton, Colo.: Libraries Unlimited, Inc. Published biennially.

The Guide to Correspondence Study. New York: Macmillan. Published biennially in September.

Guide to Popular U.S. Government Publications. Schwarzkopf, Leroy C. Littleton, Colo.: Libraries Unlimited, Inc., 1992.

Handbook of Alternative Education. Mintz, Jerry. New York: Macmillan, 1994.

How to Get a College Degree Via the Internet. Atich, Sam. Rocklin, Calif.: Prima Publishing, 1998.

How to Get into Your Dream College Using the Web. Karl, Arthur, and Shannon Karl. Scottsdale, Ariz.: Coriolis Group Books, 1997.

The Independent Scholar's Handbook. Gross, Ronald. Berkeley: Ten Speed Press, 1993.

MacMillan Guide to Correspondence Study. Modoc Press, Inc., compiler. New York: Macmillan Publishing Co., Inc., 1996.

Mentoring: The Tao of Giving and Receiving Wisdom. Huang, Chungliang Al, and Jerry Lynch. New York: HarperCollins, 1995.

Peterson's Guide to Nursing Programs: Baccalaureate and Graduate Nursing Programs in the U.S. and Canada. Princeton, N.J.: Peterson's Guides. Published biennially.

Planning Your Career in Alternative Medicine: A Guide to Degree and Certificate Programs in Alternative Healthcare. Lyons, Dianne J. B. Albuquerque, N.Mex.: Avery Publishing Group, 1997.

The Prelaw Handbook: Official Guide to U.S. Law Schools. Law School Admission Council. Newton, Pa.: Law School Admission Services. Published annually.

Private Independent Schools. Wallingford, Conn.: Bunting & Lyon, Inc. Published annually in March.

Self-Help: 1,400 Best Books on Personal Growth. Katz, Bill, and Linda Sternberg-Katz. New York: R.R. Bowker, 1985.

Training and Development Organizations Directory. McLean, Janice. Detroit: Gale Research Co., 1994.

The World of Learning. London, England: Europa Publications Ltd., Taylor & Francis. Published annually in January.

Your Hidden Credentials. Smith, Peter, ed. Washington, D.C.: Acropolis Books, Ltd., 1986.

Associations: You can phone or write these organizations for additional information. Most publish directories of member organizations and their services.

American Association of Community and Junior Colleges
1 Dupont Circle NW, Ste. 410
Washington, DC 20036-1176
(202) 728-0200

American Association for Adult and Continuing Education
1200 19th Street NW, Ste. 300
Washington, DC 20036
(202) 429-5131

American Library Association Adult Services Division
50 E. Heron St.
Chicago, IL 60611
(312) 944-6780

Cooperative Education Assn.
8640 Guilford Rd. Ste. 215
Columbia, MD 21046
(410) 290-3666

Corporation for Public Broadcasting
(Learn through public television programs.)
901 E. St. NW
Washington, DC 20004-2037
(202) 897-9600

The National Homestudy Council
1601 18th St. NW
Washington, DC 20009
(202) 234-5100

The National Association for Trade and Industrial Education
P.O. Box 1665
Leesburg, VA 20177
(703) 777-1746

When I consider the desires of countless millions of men and women down through the ages, my own desires seem as nothing.

Financial Aid

At this writing, over $55 billion in financial aid is available annually in the U.S.[3] If you're female, have a low income, are a member of a racial or ethnic minority, if you are handicapped or disabled, if you are a veteran, or if you have a parent belonging to any of the above groups, you may qualify for special financial assistance programs. Organizations centered around specific vocations (e.g., health care, agriculture, or teaching) often provide financial assistance to students pursuing careers in these fields. The best way to find out is to visit a financial-aid counselor, either at the school you plan to attend or at your local community college or career center. Religious or community service organizations are also potential sources of financial aid. Additionally, many employers offer financial assistance to employees who wish to attend college. Research all of the above in your search for funding. You may also wish to explore the following sources:

Financial Aid Sources

The College Blue Book. New York: MacMillan Publishing Co. Published biennially in October.

College Cost and Financial Aid Handbook. College Scholarship Service. New York: College Board of Publications. Published annually in August.

Directory of Financial Aids for Women. Schlacter, Gail Ann. Redwood City, Calif.: Reference Service Press. Biennial.

Financial Aid for Veterans, Military Personnel and Their Dependents. Schlacter, Gail Ann, and David R. Weber. Redwood City, Calif.: Reference Service Press. Published biennially in February. (Includes scholarships, fellowships, loans, grants, awards, and internships.)

How to Find Out about Financial Aid. Schlacter, Gail Ann. Redwood City, Calif.: Reference Service Press. Updated regularly. (A guide to over seven hundred directories listing scholarships, fellowships, loans, grants, awards and internships.)

Money for College: Everything You Need to Know to Get Financial Aid. Rae, Gail. Research & Education Association, 1998.

Peterson's Scholarships, Grants and Prizes: The Most Comprehensive Guide to College Financial Aid from Private Sources. Princeton, N.J.: Peterson's Guides. Published annually in September. (A complete guide to scholarships, costs, and financial aid at U.S. colleges, including athletic and merit awards, special aids, grants, and tuition plans.)

The Scholarship Book. Cassidy, Daniel J. Englewood Cliffs, N.J.: Prentice-Hall, 1998. (A complete guide to private-sector scholarships, grants, and loans for undergraduates.)

Step Four–Analyze Learning Options

Now that you have clearly identified the skills necessary to your success and have researched how you might go about acquiring these, it's time to assess the relative merits of the various kinds of training. Evaluate each of the training options you are considering according to the criteria below. Remember, employers and clients are concerned with what you can do and what you know. How you came to the ability is of less importance than the fact that you possess it.

Skill or Specialized Knowledge #1	Quality of Instruction	Cost	Time Required
Learning Option #1_____			
Learning Option #2_____			
Learning Option #3_____			
Learning Option #4_____			
Skill or Specialized Knowledge #2	**Quality of Instruction**	**Cost**	**Time Required**
Learning Option #1_____			
Learning Option #2_____			
Learning Option #3_____			
Learning Option #4_____			
Skill or Specialized Knowledge #3	**Quality of Instruction**	**Cost**	**Time Required**
Learning Option #1_____			
Learning Option #2_____			
Learning Option #3_____			
Learning Option #4_____			

Step Five–
Develop a Training Strategy and Schedule

Training Strategy 1: Ability		
Skills to Acquire	**How?**	**By When?**
Specialized Knowledge to Acquire	**How?**	**By When?**

 A little learning is a dangerous thing; drink deep or taste not the Pierian spring.
Alexander Pope

Training Strategy 2: Credibility

Requisite Credentials to Acquire	How?	By When?
Additional Credentials to Acquire	**How?**	**By When?**

For every credibility gap there is a gullibility fill.
Richard Clopton

Training Strategy 3: Marketability

Marketing Skill to Acquire	How?	By When?

Marketing Knowledge to Acquire	How?	By When?

The superior man understands what is right; the inferior understands what will sell.
                                                        Confucius

Training Summary

Review your answers on the three previous pages and indicate your training strategy below.

One Year	Three Year	Five Year
Over the next year, my training objectives in priority order are:	Over the next three years, my training objectives in priority order are:	Over the next five years, my training objectives in priority order are:
1	1	1
2	2	2
3	3	3
4	4	4
5	5	5
6	6	6
7	7	7
8	8	8
9	9	9
10	10	10

 My strength lies solely in my tenacity.
Louis Pasteur

Creating the Self-Image You Need to Succeed

Every man has three characters: That which he exhibits, that which he has, and that which he thinks he has.
Alphonse Karr

The most important factor to your total success in life is your self-image. It's more important than your IQ, family background, place of birth, education, or training. Your self-image determines your ability to motivate yourself to get going on your new career objectives. It determines the respect you receive from others, which in turn largely affects your ability to accomplish your goals. In the words of Moshe Feldenkrais: "Each of us speaks, moves, thinks, and feels in a different way, each according to the image of himself that he has built up over the years. In order to change our mode of action, we must change the image of ourselves that we carry within us."[1]

Your self-image is constructed of mental pictures of yourself in the past. These mental pictures may not reflect you at your best. Fortunately, you can change your self-image for the better. When you expose the negative pictures that linger in the dark corners of your subconscious past to the present light of conscious awareness, you strike a mortal blow to the bondage these negative pictures have held you in. In this section, you will meet powerful tools for changing your self-image for the better. The first step in this process is to take a self-image inventory, identifying the problem areas of your self-image and the changes you would like to make (see next page).

"Creating the Self-Image You Need to Succeed" in a Nutshell

Once you know the specific self-image changes that you would like to make, the next step is to begin creating these changes. To do this we suggest that you do the following:

Step 1: Take a self-image inventory.

Step 2: Visualize your success.

Step 3: Affirm your success.

Step 4: Reinforce: stroke your way to success.

All of the significant battles are waged within the self.

Sheldon Kopp

Take a Self-Image Inventory

In the column marked "Old Negative Image," list all of the aspects of your self-image that might limit success in your new career role. Next, under the heading "My New Image," write the opposite of the negative traits you listed. For example, the opposite of "sloppy" might be "organized"; the opposite of "awkward" might be "at ease," and so on.

Old Negative Image	My New Image
1.	1.
2.	2.
3.	3.
4.	4.
5.	5.
6.	6.
7.	7.
8.	8.
9.	9.
10.	10.
11.	11.
12.	12.
13.	13.
14.	14.
15.	15.
16.	16.
17.	17.
18.	18.
19.	19.
20.	20.
21.	21.
22.	22.
23.	23.
24.	24.
25.	25.

Now use the traits you listed under "My New Image" to help you in the visualization and affirmation processes that follow.

Visualization:
What You See Is What You Get

Visualization is a powerful technique, both for achieving specific goals and for improving your self-image. We are all constantly visualizing. However, most of our visualizations are subconscious, and many times, they are actually destructive to our success. For many years, athletes, entertainers, and successful people from all walks of life have understood and used the power of consciously directed visualization. Below is a simple, easy-to-use formula for effective visualization.

Visualization in Seven Steps

1. **Deserve:** Know that you can have what you repeatedly see. Be willing to create the picture exactly as you want it.

2. **Intend:** Direct the picture; concentrate your mind. See the picture and hold it. Don't let your mind wander.

3. **Ease:** Relax, don't tense or strain. You may want to do muscle relaxation exercises first.

4. **Intensity:** Pour your feelings into the image. Let yourself feel an intense longing, or desire, for what you see.

5. **Detail:** Step into your picture and see the detail. See the grain in the wood, the dew in the grass.

6. **Include:** If you want the object of your visualization, be sure to include yourself in the picture.

7. **Enjoy:** Feel good about what you see. Express gratitude for receiving it. Let it go. Know that it *is* done.

Visualization Sources

Creative Visualization. Gawain, Shakti. Novato, Calif.: New World Library, 1995.

Mental Training for Peak Performance: Top Athletes Reveal the Mind Exercises They Use to Excel. Ungerleider, Steven. Emmaus, Pa.: Rodale Press, 1996.

Psycho-Pictography: The New Way to Use the Miracle Power of Your Mind. Howard, Vernon. Englewood Cliffs, N.J.: Prentice-Hall, 1996.

 When the task is done beforehand, then it is easy.

Yuantong

Seeing Success Scenarios

Visualize yourself in various scenarios related to your new career. Describe these in the space below. What are you doing? What are the surroundings? What are you feeling? Note: It is important that you go into as much detail as possible. If there is not sufficient space below, write your scenarios on a separate piece of paper.

Scenario 1: _____

_____

_____

_____

_____

_____

Scenario 2: _____

_____

_____

_____

_____

_____

Scenario 3: _____

_____

_____

_____

_____

_____

You may want to make an audiotape. An audiotape can assist you in maintaining a regular routine of visualization, and thus, maximize the creative benefits of this process. On this tape, give yourself instructions to relax, to feel deeply calm and at peace. Next, instruct yourself to visualize one of the scenarios you have written above. Allow a thirty-second to one-minute pause on the tape to visualize the scenario. Repeat this process for as many scenarios as you like. It's best to do your visualizations every night just before you retire. If this is not practical for you, do them as often as possible.

Building a Vision

You can translate your goals into positive images of success. Make a scrapbook. Fill it with vivid images of you successfully doing your life's work. Draw them. Cut pictures out of a magazine. Take photographs and paste them in. Be creative and have fun. Get out your scissors, drawing pencils, glue, tape, and paints. Work in whatever medium most appeals to you. Write captions beneath your illustrations, referring to them as if they have already occurred.

Affirmation: The Power of Positive Belief

Changing careers can be a difficult process. There are plenty of opportunities for doubts to arise. You may doubt your ability. You may doubt whether there is sufficient demand in the marketplace for what you want to give. You may doubt your ultimate success. In addition to your own doubts, you are surrounded by the doubts of others. You must believe in yourself and in the course you have chosen. Recognize that *you believe what you hear repeated*, and most of all, what you repeat to yourself. Repetition opens the doors to your subconscious mind. Think of how a song sticks in your mind after repeated hearings.

The subconscious mind works like a computer. If you try to execute a function on your computer that the program you are running is not designed to handle (e.g., sophisticated graphics on a word processing program), you have no luck. Yet if you take out that program and put in the proper one, you can do it easily. It works the same way with your mind. If you put in programming that says you can, you'll be able to do things you could never do with the old program.

One way to enter a new program is through a process called "affirmation." The most powerful way to use affirmation is to say *"I am"* before that which you want to be, do, or have. The words *I am* form the primary link to your self-image. Therefore, they should be used with the greatest of care. Remember, *I am* makes a strong impression. Be careful not to link negative thoughts with the words *I am, I, me,* or *mine,* or these negative thoughts will attach to your self-image. Always affirm something positive and beneficial.

Now write positive statements that will reflect the kind of progress you want to make. Here are a few examples:

I love my work. It energizes me and challenges me to give my very best. Excellence is my goal and my reality.

I am a positive, productive, and happy person. I'm glad to be alive, and I'm glad to be who I am.

I always do what I know is right, easily and without delay.

I am confident of my ability to get the job done and done right.

_____

_____

_____

 Speak the affirmative; emphasize your choice by utterly ignoring all that you reject.
Ralph Waldo Emerson

Behavior Modification:
Stroke Your Way to Success

It may be some time before you are actually doing your life's work. You will need to maintain your interest, concentration, and enthusiasm along the way if you are to make steady progress toward your goals. Reinforce your progress by giving yourself positive strokes along the way. Your heart has its desires, to give, to share, to make a constructive contribution. Your ego also has desires. The ego wants stimulation and attention. Get the ego on board. The ego's desire for attention is not necessarily in conflict with the heart's desire to express its love. However, you may want to look at how you can get them working together right from the start.

Indicate your career goals below, then write down when you plan to complete them and what positive strokes you may want to give yourself along the way. These goals might include: acquiring necessary training, landing your first position, or achieving a particular objective in your career.

Career Goal #1: _____

_____

Estimated Arrival Time: _____

Positive Strokes Along the Way: _____

_____

Career Goal #2: _____

_____

Estimated Arrival Time: _____

Positive Strokes Along the Way: _____

_____

Career Goal #3: _____

_____

Estimated Arrival Time: _____

Positive Strokes Along the Way: _____

_____

Behavior Modification Sources

The Miracle of Mind Dynamics. Murphy, James F. Englewood Cliffs, N.J.: Prentice-Hall, 1980.

Psycho-Cybernetics. Maltz, Maxwell. Englewood Cliffs, N.J.: Prentice-Hall, 1987.

Get An Act-As-If Degree

Act as if. Beware the voice that tells you you can't, the one that tells you you have to get permission or that you must have a title, a degree, or certification. Your desire and willingness to act the part are all you need to start. The fact that Ezra Cornell never graduated from any school didn't stop him from founding Cornell University. The fact that Thomas Edison had three weeks of formal education didn't keep him from making scores of historic inventions. The fact that George Bernard Shaw had but five years of schooling didn't keep him from acting like a great intellectual. The fact that Grandma Moses never had a painting lesson didn't keep her from acting the part and receiving critical acclaim for doing it.

There is education by degrees. You are no doubt familiar with these: B.A., B.S., M.A., M.S., Ph.D., L.L.D., etc. Then there are degrees of education by experience. You gain experience by acting the part. Go ahead and start. Don't let the lack of formal education stop you from doing what you want. If you want additional formal training or really think you need it, go for it, but don't let it stop you from acting as if in the meantime. After all, by the time you get your degree, you may have four (or more) years of practical experience under your belt. Start doing what you want to do in your spare time. Get into the feeling of it. Try it on for size.

For those of you who feel bad about not having a degree or diploma, you will find one on page 574 (suitable for framing). While it is true that this degree is not accredited by any university, you must remember that neither was the scarecrow's, and that didn't keep him from using his brain. Anyone outrageous enough to post this degree publicly has already earned it.

> *The great end of education is to discipline rather than to furnish the mind; to train it to the use of its own powers, rather than fill it with the accumulation of others.*
>
> *Tryon Edwards*

Self-Educated Greats

All the greats below were entirely, or in respects important to their contributions, self-educated.

Abraham Lincoln
Eric Hoffer
Thomas Edison
Charles Dickens
Alan Watts
Walt Whitman
William Blake
Vincent van Gogh
William Shakespeare
George Bernard Shaw

> *The true perfection of man lies not in what man has, but in what man is.*
> Oscar Wilde

Doctor of Audacity

This certifies that on this date _____,
the bearer _____ *has been conferred a*
Doctor of Audacity Degree (Ad.D.)
for _____.

Count Von Suksiss
PRESIDENT EMERITUS AND MOST EXALTED EXCELLENCY

Keith D. Fayth
SECRETARY AND HIGH COUNSELOR

Royal Order of the Bold and Audacious

Help!:
Enlisting Support

If you want to get the best out of a man, you must look for the best that is in him.
                                        Bernard Haldane

In this section we'll explore how you can garner the support you need to achieve your goals. We will start by looking at how to make sure you have your own support. Next, we will examine how you can gain the support of your family. Finally, we will look to the particular issues of relationships and how these impact on life's work.

Enlisting Your Own Support:
Getting Past Guilt and the Need to Blame

Before you go looking for support from others, make sure you have your own. Remember, no matter what you are doing: *The desire to make it work is the most important factor to your success.* Begin by making sure that you are not burdened by guilt. It could rob you of the energy you need to succeed. Many people were told as children that they were the reason why their parents were unable to pursue their dreams. The implication is that if the child had not been born, the parent would have gone on to do great things. Children who accept this often become adults who are burdened with guilt. Guilt, in turn, saps them of the strength they need to tackle their life's work.

Implicit in guilt is a perceived need for punishment. In order to relieve the sense of guilt that the individual feels, she may create circumstances that allow her to feel that what she "did to her parents" is being "done to her." That is, just as she held her parents back, someone (her children, her mate, etc.) is now holding her back. The release from all of this comes in the realization that each individual is responsible for his or her own life and the choices that he or she makes. Recognizing that you are not now, and never were, responsible for your parents' achievements reclaims the energy tied up in guilt and allows you to put it to good use.

It's easy to support someone who knows what they want and where they are going. Instead of needing others to make you feel okay in spite of your guilt (a hopeless task),

you can suggest specific things they can do to see you through. Below are a few pointers for enlisting the support of your family once you are sure you have your own.

Enlisting Support from Your Family

1. Let them know that you are committed to your objectives, and ask for their support.

2. Give them your support in the things they care about.

3. Give them specific ways of helping you.

4. Set clear, definite boundaries that enable you to carry on your work.

5. Delegate areas of responsibility to each family member, and instill a sense of pride in each person for their area.

6. Schedule a meeting time to organize, plan, and coordinate efforts.

7. Express gratitude and appreciation for their help.

8. Share your achievements with them. Give them generous credit for their part in your accomplishments.

9. Keep the lines of communication open.

 We are born for love. It is the principle of existence, and its only end.
Benjamin Disraeli

Relationships That Work

Below we discuss three kinds of partner relationships and how they impact upon the pursuit of a life's work.

The Growth-Based Relationship

Growth-based relationships are mutually supporting. They are entered into by mature, self-reliant individuals who take responsibility for their lives as individuals and as partners in a relationship. Each is dedicated to the growth of the other as well as to his or her own. Growth-based relationships don't just happen. They are created by people who know themselves and what they want. Being in touch with their own desire to express their best, each partner recognizes and supports that desire in their mate. Because they themselves are risk takers, they are supportive of the risks their partners take and understand the vulnerability of the creative life. These individuals are working on themselves as whole people, not halves of a relationship. They know that $\frac{1}{2} \times \frac{1}{2} = \frac{1}{4}$, not one.

The Need-Based Relationship

Often relationships are based, not on growth, but on need. The premise is that each individual is too weak to make it on his or her own, so they need to be together. This we might call a distractive-destructive relationship. It distracts the individuals, through diversion or mutual resignation, from devoting themselves to being the best they can be. It destroys the opportunity for both of the individuals to achieve their best as long as they are tied to this kind of relationship. Individuals in these types of relationships for many years tend to blur their identities. John and Mary become "we this" and "we that."

In order to achieve your life's work, you must grow. As you grow, you are moving away from where you have been. If your partner is not willing to move with you to a new level of strength and ability, he will tend to perceive you as moving away from him. He will tend to resist your forward progress because he perceives you, not as growing toward your best, but as moving away from him. His need has blinded him. He cannot see you as an individual but only as an object who either satisfies or frustrates his need. Occasionally, need-based relationships masquerade as growth-based ones. If you have any doubt about whether you are in a growth-based or need-based relationship, it will certainly show when you take a major step to grow.

When one person in a need-based relationship starts to grow, she needs the other less. She has less need for excuses, less need to reinforce her weakness, less need to attack those who try and those who succeed. Consequently, the one "less needed" feels the relationship threatened. This is a real threat. The old need relationship is in jeopardy. Since it was mutual need that formed the relationship and mutual need that sustained it, when need diminishes on one end, the balance of power in the relationship, and ultimately the relationship itself, is in jeopardy.

Individuals in need-based relationships are very aware of each other's faults. They are often taken aback when one party no longer believes in a limitation he has been holding on to for years. *As long as the relationship remains based upon need, the party who is not growing must subconsciously thwart the progress of the other.* If you recognize that you are in a need-based relationship, you needn't feel guilty, hopeless, or bitter. First realize that your awareness is your best friend and will help you through the tests that lie ahead. Next, recognize that there are three basic options.

1. You continue to grow and your partner grows along with you. (We discuss this option below under "The Transforming Relationship.")

2. You continue to grow, and you sever your destructive relationship. This is a painful and difficult decision, to be sure, but sometimes it is the only viable option. Surely, every effort should be made to move into a new growth-based relationship. However, if your partner refuses to grow, and by extension, refuses to support your growth, you may, at last, be faced with this choice. Recognize that if you make a break, you may feel a bit vulnerable and shaky for a time. Stand strong in your intention to give and be your best, and you will go on to better days.

3. You give up your efforts to grow, and maintain your relationship (with added bitterness and/or depression). This is the least desirable and most painful of the alternatives. You may end up hating yourself and your partner.

The Transforming Relationship

The transforming relationship is one in the process of moving from a need-based relationship into a growth-based one. A pivotal turning point is reached when both individuals recognize that, while they no longer need each other, they love and respect one another and want to grow together as individuals. A "want to" that is free of need is an exhilarating feeling. Though one party in the relationship may initiate the process of transforming the relationship, it will ultimately take the desire of both parties to make it work. Often the best thing for the relationship is to focus, not on the relationship, but on the individuals in it.

How does one transform a need-based relationship into a growth-based one? You must discover this for yourself. Here are a few suggestions that might prove helpful.

1. Admit the need of the past. Communicate openly and freely. Admit the pain that the need-based relationship has fostered. Ask the other party to share his hurts as well. While sharing, avoid blaming each other. Recognize that it was the premise of the relationship that was wrong, not the individuals in it.

2. Discuss what a growth-based relationship means to you. Discuss your goals and dreams. List ways in which each of you could be more supportive of the other. Compare notes.

3. Communicate clearly and emphatically that you are dedicated to being your best and that you are going to do it with or without him. You love him and want his support. You admit that in the past you let fear rule you and hold you back. But no more! You will not be stopped. To try to stop you is futile!

4. Let your partner know you support his best, and encourage him to grow into it. Tell him that you realize you could have been more supportive in the past and that now you are ready to be so.

5. If your partner is willing to take a risk that will test his belief in himself, encourage him to do so and be supportive of the process.

6. The more you can get your partner focused on his own life and working to make it the best it can be, the more supportive and less resistant he will be to your growth.

 May you live all the days of your life.
Jonathan Swift

Loving What You Do ('Til You Are Doing What You Love)

The power of man's virtue should not be measured by his special efforts, but by his ordinary doings.
Blaise Pascal

We've talked a great deal about the value of planning for the future and about developing a strategy for achieving your goals. Still, many of us are not in a position to quit our current jobs immediately and begin pursuing our new career objectives. The question then becomes: How do we do our work in the meantime? What kind of attitudes do we take to work with us every day? If we view our current jobs negatively, we will rob ourselves of the energy we need to go beyond them. Throughout this book, we have emphasized the importance of identifying clear objectives and working toward them. You will have far more success if you view your new work as something you are moving toward, than if you view your old work as something to get away from.

Frustration with your current work has served you well. It helped motivate you to discover and develop a plan for achieving your life's work. Now it's time to put frustration aside. Redirect the energy that once went into frustration into developing yourself for your new career. Put it into working at your current job in such a way as to glean from it all you can. Put it into making the greatest contribution you can through your current work. Don't let negative emotions get the best of you. Stop and objectively consider what works and what doesn't.

What Doesn't Work

1. Being discouraged, reactive, and depressed.

2. Hating your job and doing it poorly.

3. Hoping it will get better and fearing it won't.

4. Complaining, blaming, or procrastinating and staying where you are.

5. Feeling inferior because you lack training, experience, or connections—and doing nothing.

What Works

1. Staying positive, objective, and motivated.

2. Loving what you're doing and putting your best into it.

3. Having a plan and making it work.

4. Accepting responsibility for where you are now and for putting yourself where you want to be.

5. Believing in yourself and doing what it takes.

Basically, what it comes down to is this: Work as though you are working for yourself, even though you're not. Work as though you're doing your ultimate life's work, even while you aren't. Work with the same commitment to excellence, the same intensity that you will put into your ultimate work. This gives you the confidence to conceive of yourself doing more. If you think, "Well, this is just a dumb job, it's not important," you won't totally put yourself in. If you don't totally put yourself in, you will lose self-respect. Any kind of work can be done with dignity, pride, and self-respect. Every day you are developing habits. You're either developing good habits that will serve you later on or poor ones that will frustrate your future plans.

While writing this book, I was working one evening at a local coffee shop. The waitress asked me what I was doing, and I told her that I was writing a book on career planning and fulfilling life's work. She said, "Oh, I really need that." She then went on to discount her work as a waitress, to lament what a meaningless and nothing job it was. Not suprisingly, she was not a very competent waitress. While she professed to want something better, she was acting in a way that locked her into work far below her potential. Hating your current job, complaining, and hoping that it will get better without taking constructive action are all prescriptions for failure. In Communist Poland, the workers had a saying: "We pretend to work and they pretend to pay us." That kind of attitude is a prescription for failure and low self-esteem.

If you give your all to a position that is below your capacity, you will outgrow it. If, on the other hand, you do poor quality work or work that you know is less than your best, you will begin to lose confidence in yourself. You start out thinking, "I could do better, but I won't." But after a while, you end up wondering, "Could I do better, even if I wanted to?" Value what you're doing. Treat it with respect. Learn everything it has to teach you. You might learn practical skills that you can transfer to later work. Even if you don't learn any skills or knowledge that you can directly apply later (and this is highly unlikely), you can still develop attitudes and work habits that will stand you in good stead for the rest of your life. Recognize that there is something to learn from everything, and determine to learn it.

Loving what you do will give you the confidence you need to do what you love, if you understand that expressing your best in your current work is your ticket out of it, not a sign of resignation to it. The person who is resigned to less than his best holds back. The person who is determined to fulfill his life's work gives their all to everyone they work for. It's a matter of honor, integrity, and decency. Should you become an employer, you will, in turn, expect the best of others. You'll know what it takes to do quality work, and you'll know that it's good for people to do it—good for their self-respect. You cheat people far more by expecting too little out of them than by expecting them to give their best. This goes double for yourself. Focus on the value of what you have to give, and do your best work. Channel frustration with your current circumstance into constructive action.

Love It and Leave It

1. Staying positive, objective, and motivated.
   How am I doing? _____
   How can I improve? _____

2. Loving what you're doing and putting your best into it.
   How am I doing? _____
   How can I improve? _____

3. Having a plan and making it work.
   How am I doing? _____
   How can I improve? _____

4. Accepting responsibility for where you are now and for putting yourself where you want to be.
   How am I doing? _____
   How can I improve? _____

5. Believing in yourself and doing what it takes.
   How am I doing? _____
   How can I improve? _____

 The best preparation for good work tomorrow is to do good work today.
Elbert Hubbard

Act IV Review

In the space below, write the transition strategy you've chosen. Why is this the most effective strategy for you? *(page 540)*

Summarize your plan for developing yourself in your career in terms of:

    a. Ability *(pages 545–553)*

    b. Credibility

    c. Marketability

List the top three qualities you want to project as part of your new image and how you plan to do this. *(page 552)*

Briefly describe your positive visions of your new career in the space below. *(page 569)*

Write below three affirmations that reflect the growth you want to see in your new career. *(page 571)*

How will you give your ego some positive strokes along the way? *(page 572)*

List several ways you could improve on loving what you are doing until you are doing what you love. *(page 581)*

A Final Note

Milder Gradients to Life's Work

We have suggested throughout this book that you approach your life's work from the standpoint of your values and the broad issues that face us all in the world today. We recognize that this is a difficult and demanding task. Fortunately, it does not have to be all or nothing, and it doesn't have to be all right now. If this seems like too steep a gradient for you right now, you might want to consider the alternatives suggested below. In any case, we encourage you to act.

Alternatives

1. **Become involved.** In "Act I" we discussed discovering your purpose in life. Even if you don't know exactly what your purpose is, get involved in something you can believe in.

2. **Part-time work.** In "Act II" we discussed shaping your work purpose into career roles. If you cannot (for whatever reason) or are not ready to dedicate yourself to make a career of it, take some action part time in an area of interest to you.

3. **Support or volunteer or recruit for an existing organization.** In "Act III" we discussed finding a job or creating your own organization. We discussed the importance of organized effort and teamwork in making a difference. If you're not ready to either take a job in the field or create your own organization, you can still take advantage of organized effort by becoming a member of groups or organizations that are interested in your area of focus. (See appendix B.)

4. **Do the best you can with what you already have and continue to develop yourself.** In "Act IV" we discussed creating a strategy for developing your knowledge, skill, and contacts. If you are not ready to go after these in a concerted fashion, make the most of the skills and resources you already possess. In addition, we discussed making the transition from your current work into your new role. If you're not ready to do this at this time, we suggest that you periodically review your situation and determine if, perhaps, some day in the future, you might be ready to do so. Commit yourself to continued learning and development.

 Never give in, never give in, never, never, never, never. . .

Winston Churchill

Economics: Scar-city or Mutual Support System?

The ideas by which people . . . interpret their existence and in measure guide their behavior, were not forged in a world of wealth.

John Kenneth Galbraith

We can hardly leave the subject of work without at least a brief consideration of economics. Modern economics is based upon two major assumptions: the scarcity of physical nature and the avariciousness of human nature. As we will see, these assumptions have, over the last hundred years, been called into question. Today, we have the benefit of knowledge that early economists understandably lacked. First, while they posited physical nature as scarce, we now have evidence that our planetary life-support system is incredibly abundant. Second, cross-cultural studies have demonstrated the great variety of human experience. Today, we recognize the early economists' views of human nature as outgrowths of a peculiar historical and cultural perspective (some would say bias), not as definitive truths. Starting from a recognition of the abundance of physical nature and the malleability of "human nature," postmodern economics will move from notions of scarcity and greed toward an understanding of the earth and all of its life as a mutual support system.

Scarcity: The Basis of Modern Economics

For many today, the subject of economics, and particularly economic theory, is a baffling and confusing one. Still, it is one that affects us all in ways we hardly realize. As the most influential economist of the twentieth century, John Maynard Keynes, wrote: "The ideas of economists and political philosophers, both when they are right and when they are wrong, are more powerful than commonly understood. Indeed the world is ruled by little else. Practical men who believe themselves to be quite exempt from intellectual influences are usually the slaves of some defunct economist."[1]

Perhaps, then, it is worth our while to see if we can't get behind all of the charts, graphs, and forecasts, all the figures related to money supply and GNP and see if we can't understand what—at the most fundamental level—economics really is. Exactly what is economics? A recent economics textbook defines it this way: "Economics is a science concerned with choosing among alternatives involving scarce resources."[2] Modern economics is, then, inexorably linked to the notion of scarcity. In *The Making of Economic Society,* economist Robert Heilbroner is emphatic on this point: "If there were no scarcity . . . economics . . . would cease to exist as a social preoccupation."[3]

In the discussion that follows, we will briefly trace how the assumption of physical scarcity and its corollary of human acquisitiveness have shaped economic thinking over the last two centuries and continue to influence us to this day. These assumptions were implicit (and often explicit) in the economic theories of Adam Smith and David Ricardo whose work we consider below. After briefly demonstrating their importance to modern economics, we will examine these assumptions in some detail in light of our current understanding of the world. We will then consider alternative assumptions and the role these might play in transforming our experience of economic reality.

Adam Smith's Marketplace

Adam Smith is generally recognized as the father of modern economics. To give you some idea of how the world has changed since Smith's time: when he was born, the people in his Scottish town were still using nails for money. Smith's most important work, *The Wealth of Nations,* was first published in 1776. The two elements of Smith's economic theory that have had the greatest impact on the modern world are: the virtues of the pursuit of self-interest and the glories of free enterprise.

The Virtues of Self-Interest: Adam Smith saw the driving force in human nature as "the propensity to truck, barter, and exchange one thing for another." He believed that, when left alone, human beings naturally do what brings them economic gain or helps them to avoid economic loss. Smith thought that if everyone followed their own economic self-interest, they would benefit society, almost in spite of themselves. As he put it, man, "by pursuing his own interest . . . frequently promotes that of the society more effectively than when he intends to promote it."[4] This is his famous "invisible hand" at work.

Self-interest and freedom of enterprise were a secular faith in the old world. In the new world, they emerged as religion.

John Kenneth Galbraith

For Smith, the self-interested, if not selfish, streak in man is really a kind of virtue, since it becomes channeled into ever greater production, which, in turn, helps to ameliorate the big problem of economics—scarcity. While exercising his *right* to pursue economic self-interest, the individual is fulfilling his *duty* to society in helping it conquer scarcity. Produce more and more, and you ameliorate the problem of scarcity and overcome nature's stinginess. Yet Smith believed that the pursuit of economic self-interest could only work its social magic if allowed to operate unchecked in a free-market economy.

The Glories of Free Enterprise: Smith thought that the free practice of trade should not be interfered with, either by government or by corporations, which were then called "joint-stock companies." His view was that joint-stock companies "without an exclusive privilege have commonly mismanaged the trade. With an exclusive privilege they have both mismanaged and confined it . . . Such exclusive companies, therefore, are nuisances in every respect . . ."[5] Of course, the "Adam Smithers" of today seldom mention Smith's aversion to monopolistic control. They, rather, focus on his disdain for government regulation.

The difficulty in assessing Smith's theory is that it has never had a chance to operate (although, as we will see, he, like most modern economists, started with flawed assumptions). Even in his own day, giant monopolies and government regulation made the "free market" an ideal only. (In fact, 1776, the year his *Wealth of Nations* was first published, saw the start of a famous revolution caused in part by government regulation and monopolistic limitations on trade.) We should recognize that monopolies have been around for a long time. Already in the sixteenth century, Jean Bodin was complaining that monopolies were one of the major causes of high prices in his day.[6] Governments have had their very visible hands in the market at least since the days of Babylon. Today's government regulation and the monopolist influence in the now global marketplace make the restriction of trade in Adam Smith's day seem minor in comparison.

Still, we hear echoes of Adam Smith's free market in our contemporary economic debate. Ironically, the most lavish praise for "the free-market system" often comes from those in the employ of the kind of monopolistic organizations that Smith himself viewed as an interference to free trade. The modern notion of a "free-market system" favors both government "deregulation" and government subsidy of large, private cartels (for example, in the banking, agribusiness, transportation, and defense monopolies). Governments allow monopolies to operate with minimal regulation but stand ready to bail them out when they get into trouble. This having-your-cake-and-eating-it-too brand of "free-market system" is popular today throughout the Western world. It is not what Adam Smith had in mind.

Of course, monopolies monopolize, not only natural resources and consumer markets, but opportunities for employment. By artificially inflating the price of entering the marketplace, monopolies tend to increase workers' dependence on wage positions. For example, the very existence of giant supermarket and convenience store monopolies (not to mention banking, utility, and trucking monopolies) means that it costs more to open a mom-and-pop grocery or a health-food store than it otherwise would. Surveys of small business failures consistently indicate that lack of capital is the primary reason new businesses close up shop. No doubt, it is also a principal reason why many would-be businesses never open their doors in the first place.

The large amounts of capital needed for the formation of new business helps to ensure large numbers of individuals ready to accept wage positions, while at the same time limiting the number of available jobs. For the past several decades, small business has created virtually all of the new jobs in the private sector. Yet large capital requirements limit small-business start-ups. Again, while government regulation is often cited by "free-traders" as a limit on small business (and no doubt, it is), the role of monopolies in inflating the cost of doing business is hardly mentioned. We are told that the economies of scale, which monopolies offer, make for cheaper consumer products; if this is true, they also tend to limit new business formation and, with it, the additional employment opportunities that new businesses create. It also should be noted that economies of scale, especially in service industries, tend to limit human interaction. (For example, chain stores in shopping malls offer fewer opportunities to form relationships than locally owned retail stores.)

From the standpoint of the individual, it can be in her economic self-interest to accept a job working for an organization whose net effect on the society is an indifferent or negative one. Moreover, economic self-interest (combined with restricted opportunities to enter the market directly) drives many to seek employment destructive to their own spiritual, psychological, or even physical health. Today, economic self-interest and lopsided free enterprise are clearly not producing the social benefit Smith envisioned.

> That soul-destroying, meaningless, mechanical, moronic work is an insult to human nature which must necessarily and inevitably produce either escapism or aggression, and that no amount of 'bread and circuses' can compensate for the damage done—these are facts which are neither denied nor acknowledged but are met with an unbreakable conspiracy of silence—because to deny them would be too obviously absurd and to acknowledge them would condemn the central preoccupation of modern society as a crime against humanity.   E. F. Schumacher[7]

Ricardo: Poverty Is Inevitable

While Adam Smith viewed the joint-stock companies (corporations) as "a nuisance in every respect," David Ricardo, the next major economist, was himself a stockbroker. Ricardo held that workers would receive the minimum wage necessary to subsist, and no more. This was an "iron law of wages" that could not be changed. If you were successful in bettering the lot of the poor, they would simply breed more of themselves until, with a surplus of labor, wages would again fall. In the words of John Kenneth Galbraith, this type of thinking "led, among other things, to the conclusion that not only was compassion wasted on the working man, but it was damaging."[8]

In Ricardo's view, the world was a naturally cruel place—one simply had to face facts. Poverty had to be accepted as inevitable. For Ricardo, the only way to increase profits was to reduce wages. Profits and wages were irreconcilably at odds. This type of thinking justified pitiful wages, on the one hand, and spurred Marx and his followers to view "class conflict" as fundamental and inevitable on the other. Monopolists could claim (and still do) that the only way

It is only when the maker of things is a maker of things by vocation, and not merely holding down a job, that the price of things is approximate to their real value . . .

Ananda K. Coomaraswamy

they could remain competitive (with other monopolies) was to keep wages low. Some attempted to adapt the discoveries of Charles Darwin to social and economic theory—justifying economic inequality as a fundamental law of nature. In the words of John D. Rockefeller, "[survival of the fittest] is not an evil tendency in business. It is merely the working of a law of nature and a law of God."[9] Ricardo's friend, Thomas Malthus, hammered home the inevitability of poverty with his theory that while population increased geometrically, food supply could only increase arithmetically.

Rethinking Economic Assumptions

From its fledgling beginnings with Adam Smith and David Ricardo (there were, of course, other lesser figures before them), economics has grown into a respectable "science." Today this "science" depends as much as ever on the assumption of scarcity. Noted economist Robert Heilbroner writes: "To be sure, the economic problem itself—that is, the need to struggle for existence—derives ultimately from *the scarcity of nature.*" (Emphasis added.) But he quickly goes on to say that "scarcity is . . . not attributable to nature alone but to 'human nature' as well . . ." He suggests, then, both physical and psychological components to the problem of economics. The physical component of scarcity assumes the "stinginess of the physical environment." The psychological component of scarcity assumes the insatiable "appetite of the human temperament."[10]

The first question to ask in addressing economics is, Are its assumptions correct? Is the physical environment of planet Earth stingy? Second, is "human nature" fundamentally greedy and acquisitive?

The World of Nature: Abundant or Stingy

In the course of a long and extremely productive life, Buckminster Fuller made important contributions to a number of fields, including architecture, engineering, mathematics, and poetry. In the area of economics, his most important contribution was the demonstration that the fundamental premise of economics, the very foundation on which it stands, is false. *The notion of physical scarcity is a lie!* Remember, our textbook defined economics as "choosing among alternatives involving scarce resources." This particular text is hardly alone; every major economic theory, from Smith to Marx, from Mill to Keynes, has assumed scarcity. This assumption came in part from their definitions of wealth.

Fuller begins with a conception of wealth fundamentally different from those of earlier economic theorists. The first economists were called the *physiocrats*. They viewed land as the basis of wealth. Land provides sustenance and even an abundance of food to exchange for other items. The mercantilists found the basis of real wealth in gold and silver. This concept of wealth spurred European exploration and colonial expansion resulting in what remains to this day a worldwide cultural (if not political) hegemony by the West. Ricardians and Marxists viewed labor as the basis of wealth. Early industrial development required vast numbers of "cheap" unskilled laborers. Generally, the more people one employed, the richer he became. All of these definitions of "wealth" (land, gold, and labor) are based on limited, that is, scarce resources.

For Buckminster Fuller, "wealth consists of physical energy (as matter or radiation) combined with metaphysical know-what and know-how." (This and all the Buckminster Fuller quotes following are from *Critical Path*.)[11] This conception of wealth (as all energy available to planet earth and ever-growing-human-knowledge) makes us all, as he puts it, "billionaires." This is so since physical energy, as we know from physics, is always conserved and since the application of knowledge brings ever greater knowledge. "Metaphysical know-what and know-how" are always expanding. From Fuller's conception, then, the basis of wealth is virtually infinite.

After extensive study of world resources and technologies, Fuller concluded that "humanity can carry on handsomely and adequately when advantaged of only its daily energy income from the Sun-gravity system" and that "we can take care of all of our food needs." We haven't the space here for extended discussion of how Fuller arrived at his conclusions (see *Earth, Energy and Everyone* and *Hoping: Food for Everyone,* both by Fuller's protégé, Medard Gabel). In any case, this is not the central point. More important than his data (which is impressive and convincing) is his conception of wealth.

Even a brief look at history reveals that as people's ideas about wealth changed, so did their experience of economic reality. For example, while the conception of wealth as precious metals fostered the European Age of Exploration, the conception of wealth as labor was central to industrial development (hence, child labor on one side and labor movements on the other) and lay just beneath the surface of many of the geo-political conflicts of the twentieth century. On the face of it, Fuller's notion of wealth (as energy and knowledge) is at least as plausible as the others we have considered (land, precious metals, labor) and, if enough of us accept it, it will produce a fundamentally different experience of the world. We have believed in scarcity because we have equated wealth with scarce resources. (For example, gold is valuable *because* it is scarce.)

There is no economic problem and, in a sense, there never has been.

E. F. Schumacher

We think of energy as scarce because we confuse all energy available for planet earth as supported by the limited quantities of stored energy. For Fuller, resources such as fossil fuels and atomic energy constitute a "planetary savings account." Economist E. F. Schumacher referred to them as "planetary capital." Both writers distinguish between these resources and "planetary energy income." While the planet's energy savings account is finite and scarce, its energy income is freely available for the life of the sun and is incredibly abundant. Fuller notes that "the quantity of physical, cosmic energy wealth arriving aboard planet Earth each minute is greater than all the energy used annually by humanity."[12]

Fuller and others, including Schumacher, have noted the failure of modern accounting systems to reflect the true costs of using non-replenishable resources. For example, geologist Francois de Chadenedes calculated the cost of oil at well over a million dollars a gallon, if one factors in the cost of the energy (heat and pressure) required to turn vegetation into oil at New York's Con Edison retail rates.

Fuller suggests that instead of continuing to deplete our planetary savings account, we are better advised to use the energy income available from what he calls "the Sun-gravity system." "Everyone knows we should live on our (energy) income and not our savings account." The fossil fuel savings account is a collective wealth of the planet and is "not to be stolen by exploiters."

To accomplish the switch from eating up our energy savings to utilizing our energy income, Fuller advocates what he calls a "design revolution." He writes: "This is a new kind of revolution; it is one that, instead of revengefully pulling down the fortunate top few, will elevate all the heretofore unfortunates and the fortunates alike to new and sustainable heights of realized life far superior to those previously tenuously attained by the most privileged few." Fuller assures that "this can be done using only the already proven technology and with the already mined, refined and in-recirculating technologies."[13] (For some, a fantastic assertion, but one that deserves further investigation before being dismissed.)

This seems so eminently sensible that one immediately asks why it is not practice. Here again, Fuller offers insight: "Big government can see no way to collect taxes to run its bureaucracy if people are served directly and individually by daily cosmic-energy-wealth income. Money-makers cannot find a way of putting meters between people and the wind, Sun, waves, etc."[14] It is not in the "economic self-interest" of either big business or big government to move away from dipping into the planetary savings account and toward developing the use of planetary energy income.

The Psychology of Scarcity

If we are all, as Buckminster Fuller puts it, billionaires, how come it doesn't seem that way? Why do we experience scarcity, or lack? Perhaps it is because we accept the conventional notions of the psychology of scarcity. The psychology of scarcity relies upon wide acceptance of the fallacious notion of physical scarcity. Certain interests have a stake in perpetuating this view. As Fuller puts it, "With their game of making money with money, the money-makers and their economists continue to exploit the general political and religious world's assumptions that a fundamental inadequacy of human life support exists around our planet."[15]

A world view of scarcity generates conflict. From physical scarcity, we get the notion that someone has to win and someone has to lose. In the era of colonial economics, winning meant winning in the game called "balance of trade"—that when all the trading (and colony exploiting and pirating) was done, your country ended up with more gold and silver than theirs. Colonial powers took what they wanted from their colonies (mostly raw materials). They then sold the colonists finished goods at high prices, with taxes thrown in for good measure. In the colonial era, there were relatively few nations participating in the international trade game. There were, too, far fewer people on the earth, and most of these lived a simple agrarian existence that required far less energy than today's urban lifestyles demand.

Today, the international trade game is viewed as a battle between "have" and "have-not" nations. Yesterday's colonies are, of course, today's new nations, the Third World. In the half-century since World War II, the number of nations has risen from 72 to 172 (at last count). Most of these 100 new countries are former colonies. Today, the new nations want to have their own industrial revolutions. They are desperately trying to develop and oil their own industrial machines.

While economics was originally conceived of as a battle for balance of trade supremacy waged by large nation-states, with the rise of industry and corporate power, it soon came to be conceived of as a battle between wage earners and profit makers. Remember that, according to Ricardo's theory, wages and profits are inevitably at odds. The only way profits can increase is if wages decrease. After a brief period dominated by more liberal economic theories, Ricardo's view regained popularity in the 1980s. (The liberal theories consider it in the interest of business to pay higher wages so that the laborer-consumers can buy more.) In any case, the notion of physical scarcity creates a dualistic, conflict-generating psychology (win/lose, have/have-not, labor/capital, etc.).

If the only prayer you say in your whole life is "thank you," that would suffice.

Meister Eckhart

The Psychology of Plenty

Earth provides enough to satisfy every man's need, but not every man's greed.

Mahatma Gandhi

Assuming that there is, in principle, enough for everyone, there remains the issue of the psychological component of economics. Where Buckminster Fuller concentrated on the capacities of a design revolution to facilitate sustainable prosperity, economist E. F. Schumacher focused on the human dimensions of economics. He concentrated on the need for what might be called an ethical, metaphysical, or spiritual revolution. Schumacher held that without internalizing values that favor an experience of prosperity, even enough is not enough. There is no purely objective measure of "enough." The subjective component is a function of the individual's state of mind—his thoughts and feelings. The unhappy individual, craving more, *feels* lack, even in the most opulent environment.

Modern economics assumes that human nature is fundamentally selfish and greedy, that human beings will never be content with their material circumstance and will always crave more. Remember Heilbroner's "Scarcity is . . . not attributable to nature alone but to 'human nature' as well." The modern notion of human nature was shaped to a great extent by the writings of the political (or, as they called themselves, "moral") philosophers of the seventeenth and eighteenth centuries. Men such as Hobbes, Locke, and Smith viewed drives for power and security as the prime motives of human nature. If these are the core of human nature, then it is wrong to expect that human beings would ever feel they had enough. (One could conceivably always acquire more power and security.)

Today, we have come to recognize these views as reflections of a peculiar cultural bias, not as final statements about human nature. Since the time of Hobbes and Smith, literally thousands of cultures have been studied. It is clear that, in many traditional cultures, a psychology of plenty, of interdependence and cooperation was just as naturally viewed as the state of "human nature."

Today, most cultural anthropologists reject the notion of a fixed human nature. Fair-minded individuals who study the range of human diversity represented by different cultural groups will have to concur that human nature, if we can accept the concept at all, is very malleable stuff, indeed. It can, no doubt, take the shape of selfishness and greed, but it can also express in love, harmony, and cooperation. If we were to postulate a reason for the Western view of human nature, we would suggest that it has to do with a sense of alienation from nature itself. (See the introduction and the first chapter of this book.)

To better understand how we might approach a psychology of plenty, of sustainable and harmonious relationships with the earth, its creatures, and the human family, we can draw on the metaphysical treasures of Native American culture. The Native American view of life considered nature, not as a wilderness to be conquered, but as a supportive environment filled with wonderful gifts. It was populated by plants and animals, sky, sun, earth, and water, freely giving of themselves for the benefit of all. The Native American did not see his animal prey as an enemy to dominate and conquer. Rather, he felt that the animal he killed had given its life for the benefit of the hunter, his family, and people. Hunted and hunter were partners in a sacred relationship.

Similarly, within Native American society, each individual was viewed as having come to life bearing gifts to share with the community. Their approach to life was one of constant thanksgiving. One gave thanks to the trees for shade, fruit, and nut. One gave thanks to the sun for warmth and light, to the sky for winds and rains, to the earth for providing the platform upon which all living things could live, grow, and enjoy life. In this way, people lived for thousands of years in harmony and accord with nature. Living as part of nature, they cherished its gifts and protected its resources.

The earth does not belong to man, man belongs to the earth.

Chief Seattle

Native Americans, and many other peoples from traditional cultures, did not conceive of nature as something to be owned. It seems that implicit in the idea of ownership of nature is the psychology of scarcity and poverty. To think that we own nature makes us think we are owed something from it. If you "own land" and your crop yields are off from your calculations, you are disappointed. You feel cheated—like you are owed something you haven't got. If, on the other hand, you view the earth as a living being, you are able to appreciate and receive its fruits as gifts. The conception "own" sets up the feeling "due." A sacred relationship of mutual respect sets up a feeling of "thanks."

For whatever reason, Western people tend to feel owed. Life owes us, nature owes us, society owes us, our parents or children owe us, our mates owe us. It is difficult for us, then, to feel real joy, for we cannot simply receive. If you think you are owed and you receive, it is only the fulfillment of an obligation, and if you don't get what you think you are owed, you feel cheated. When we view life itself as a gift, we are free to receive all of the gifts of nature, of family, friends, and community, and of our own talents and abili-

Never say there is nothing beautiful in the world any more. There is always something to make you wonder, in the shape of a leaf, the trembling of a tree.

Albert Schweitzer

ties, with genuine joy and appreciation. We are free to move in a world of plenty, with a spirit of thanksgiving.

As we can see, the psychology of plenty differs fundamentally from the psychology of scarcity. Where the psychology of scarcity is based upon fear and fosters conflict, struggle, poverty, and oppression, the psychology of plenty is based upon love and fosters thanksgiving, cooperation, abundance, and reverance for life. It recognizes life as a gift to be enjoyed rather than as an account to be settled. If I view my life as a struggle to sustain my existence in an unfriendly world, then intimidation, competitiveness, and greed make sense. If I view life itself as a gift, attitudes of praise, thanksgiving, and responsibility naturally follow.

Where the psychology of scarcity produces feelings of guilt and obligation, the psychology of plenty is based upon an understanding of mutual support and responsibility. Where the psychology of scarcity produces aggression and defensiveness—the aggressive hoarding of scarce material resources and the defense against others who might take them—the psychology of plenty embraces the gifts of life, of nature, and of one's own talents and abilities and seeks to steward these gifts in ways that support life.

The psychology of scarcity distrusts life, things, and others. It produces the feeling that there is never enough, that I am not good enough, that my material station is not good enough, that others are withholding from me the emotional support I need, etc. The psychology of plenty receives the gift of life, of material things, and of the support of others and so experiences a fullness and abundance.

While no individual can single-handedly change the global economic system we all live in, he can change his own experience—his own economic reality. By changing his outlook, he changes his experience. Where once he saw lack, debt, and conflict, he can begin to see gifts, opportunities, and mutual support. While you may be interested in changing the overall economic system, you needn't make your own experience of prosperity conditional to that change. To view the economic system as an enemy that must be changed before you can be prosperous, happy, and free is to put yourself in a position of powerlessness, frustration, and resentment.

We have tried, in this brief discussion, to demonstrate that the starting place of modern economic theory—what it takes as incontrovertible facts—are not facts at all, but metaphysics, beliefs about nature and human nature. It is not a fact to say that there isn't (in principle) enough for everyone, but a metaphysic, a belief. It is not a fact that people are naturally and inevitably greedy and acquisitive, but again, a belief. To say that these are beliefs and not facts in no way invalidates their importance; to the contrary, as

We didn't inherit the land from our fathers. We are borrowing it from our children.

Amish Saying

Carl Menninger said, "Attitudes are more important than facts." We can underscore this by harkening back to Keynes' quote at the beginning of this paper—ideas, "both when they are right and when they are wrong," make all the difference in the practical affairs of humanity. We make the world with our beliefs.

We can look at it one way and see plenty and look at it another way and see only lack. In principle, there is planetary abundance, yet many live in horrible poverty. Again, we can look at human behavior and see instances where people clearly are motivated by greed and a thirst for power, yet we can also see people motivated by love, brotherhood, and service. In our experience of the world as individuals, it will make all the difference whether we approach it from the metaphysics of scarcity and greed or plenty and love. Because the assumptions of scarcity and greed are so widely accepted, we have been trained to look for evidence that supports these beliefs. It is our habit to do so.

If we are to change our experience, we must deliberately cultivate new beliefs and train our minds to look for evidence supportive of them. In our own minds, we can counter belief in physical scarcity with the belief: There is enough for everyone, including me. We can counter our sense of feeling owed with praise and thanksgiving— fully appreciating the blessings we now receive. One meaning of the word "appreciation" is "an increase in value," as in the appreciation of an investment. When we appreciate the blessings we now enjoy, we add to their value and attract still more.

The mutual support philosophy of economics assumes individual responsibility—that is, that each individual's experience of wealth or lack is his or her responsibility. Wealth comes in many forms and is not limited to greenbacks or the numbers in a bank account. Health is wealth. The love and support of friends and family is wealth. Knowledge is wealth. Food is wealth. Beauty is wealth. Peace is wealth. The services that others offer, the products we use—all are forms of wealth. Defining our wealth on the basis of bank account numbers alone creates an artificial experience of poverty. It is artificial because every day one lives and is supported by the universe. This is cause for thanksgiving.

There is a saying: If you are happy with what you have, you are rich, and if you are dissatisfied with what you have, you are poor. This is the difference between the psychology of scarcity and the psychology of plenty. The individual of relatively modest means who is content and happy with what he has enjoys a richer experience of life than the man who has a large bank balance and many possessions but feels owed, bitter, and resentful.

This is not to suggest that the desire to improve our material circumstances is "wrong" but rather that we recognize that true

All that we behold is full of blessings.

Wordsworth

wealth begins within. Starting from a consciousness of plenty and thanksgiving, we naturally expand into ever greater abundance in all areas of our lives. This is an altogether different experience from seeing ourselves as poor and unhappy, struggling for "a better life." Of course, this we can do, and in so doing, if we concentrate and obsess on money, we can add to our bank accounts and acquire the possessions we covet; yet psychologically, we remain poor. The means are the ends—to start from lack always leads us back to lack. The only way to grow in wealth is to come from wealth, that is, to recognize and appreciate the gifts of life, of nature, of our own talents, and of the love and support of others.

Starting from wealth, we can expand by opening to the recognition that mutual support is the reality of our lives. Every day, we enjoy the gifts of nature and of other people's talents and energies. Even our clothes, food, and shelter are not the products of our own hands but the gifts of nature and of other people and, if one sees it, of a Great Spirit in life. As we recognize mutual support, we open ourselves to the full joy of living in giving and receiving.

We have been brought up with the idea that you should "do it for yourself," "stand on your own two feet," but the truth is, we are all interdependent. Few of us are the self-made, rugged individualists we might pretend to be. If we do achieve material wealth through obsessing and out of a consciousness of lack, then we, rather than acknowledge the support we have received, hold on to the notion, "By God, I earned every bit of this, and I'm not going to share. I did it all on my own, and they can do it all on their own." This kind of thinking is poverty thinking and produces walled estates, barbed-wire fences, guard dogs, and armored patrols. It is foolish to think of this as real wealth.

To *brace* ourselves against the natural world and our fellow man as enemies is to be poor. To *embrace* the gifts of a friendly universe in a spirit of thanksgiving is to enjoy real wealth. We can transform our experience of economic reality by adopting the *thought* of plenty (based on a more open-ended definition of wealth) and the *feeling* of gratitude. In this way, we can celebrate our mutual support system and enjoy a life of harmonious cooperation with the natural world and our fellow man.

> When you're both alive and dead,
> Thoroughly dead to yourself,
> How superb the smallest pleasure!
> Bunan

Love Makes a
World of Difference

Love conquers all things; let us too surrender to Love.
Virgil

The Spirit of Buddha is that of great loving kindness and
compassion.
(The Teachings of the Buddha)

He that dwelleth in love dwelleth in God, and God in him.
I John 4:16

Virtue is to love men.
Confucius

The highest wisdom is loving kindness.
(The Talmud)

Accustomed long to contemplating Love and Compassion,
I have forgotten all difference between myself and others.
Milarepa

We are all born for love. . . . It is the principle of existence
and its only end.
Disraeli

Take away love and our earth is a tomb.
Robert Browning

Volunteering

I am only one, but still I am one; I cannot do everything, but still I can do something; I will not refuse to do the something I can do.

Helen Keller

Volunteer service activities provide opportunities to explore potential new careers and gain valuable experience. You can learn how other people live, experience new environments, and learn useful new skills. You may even gain new insights into yourself. Service work can put us in touch with qualities within ourselves we have ignored or with latent talents and abilities. For example, a successful, hard-driving entrepreneur may find that he has the patience and sensitivity to work in a warm and intimate way with children or the elderly. An individual who has always had a quiet or shy personality may discover that she has, all the while, possessed powerful leadership abilities that only a deep sense of commitment and responsibility could bring to the surface. Most of all, volunteer service gives you the satisfaction of helping people, of making an immediate impact on your world and community. A few hours of your time can make a tremendous difference in the lives of many.

Recent surveys indicate that over half of all adult Americans engage in some kind of volunteer service. The profile of today's volunteer differs greatly from the traditional image of the housewife "with extra time on her hands." Today, two-thirds of all volunteers work outside the home. Men and women are almost equally represented; only 2 percent more women than men work as volunteers. Single parents, high school and college students, the home-bound and disabled are well-represented in the volunteer sector. Increasingly, whole families are getting involved in volunteer service. Improved familial relations, team spirit, as well as the transmission of values (like caring and service) to one's children are just a few of the side benefits of volunteering.

The first step is to establish your goals for working in the volunteer sector. Basically, these goals will fall into one of three major categories:

- To make an immediate impact in areas that may not have any career applications but which are simply areas you want to serve in.

- To investigate or gain experience working in areas you consider potential career fields.

- To "find yourself," taking time out from the conventional work world and devoting yourself to volunteer service.

Make an Immediate Impact

Perhaps you recognize it will be some time before you will be able to move into your life's work on a full-time basis. You may need additional training or experience before you'll be ready or qualified to work in this area. Still, you have a desire to serve and make an immediate impact. Right now, without any further training, knowledge, or experience, you can take effective action to make a positive difference in the world you live in. Find an immediate outlet in your community for your desire to share your talents, skills, and love. You can get involved in doing direct, hands-on service, anything from child care to serving food at a community shelter or mission, from working at a recycling center to tutoring. You may want to serve on a steering committee —from planning to publicity, public education to fund-raising or finance. You might choose to become a member of the board of directors and take responsibility for policy-making and providing leadership to the nonprofit organization.

People often find that the best way to help themselves is to get involved in serving others. Those who have experienced personal tragedy, loss, or abuse in their own lives often find that they can heal their own pain by serving others in similar situations. For example, one concerned mother started Mothers Against Drunk Driving (MADD) after her child was killed by a drunk driver. The awareness-raising and pressure that her organization was able to bring to politicians have dramatically impacted state penalties for drunk drivers throughout the country. Getting involved in community service can help you through a period of personal difficulty or transition: losing a job, a divorce, the death of a family member or friend, children leaving the nest, retirement, moving to a new town. While serving others, we tend to forget our own troubles.

Service helps break rigid patterns of relating and teaches new ways of give and take with other people. Volunteers consistently report improved friendships and better relationships within their families.

John and Eleanor Raynolds

Even after you have arranged your life so that you are concentrating full time on areas that you feel to be your life's work, you still may want to work as a volunteer. Such service will enable you to express different aspects of yourself and/or to interact with different kinds of people or in different settings from what you are accustomed to. The variety helps keep you fresh and feeling that all the important aspects of yourself are being expressed.

Explore and Gain Experience in Areas with Career Potential

Volunteering can provide an exciting avenue for you to explore a variety of career options. You can develop a network of contacts and friends in your field, learn new skills, and gather valuable information, as well as get the inside scoop on many upcoming career opportunities by working as a volunteer. You get a chance to see the way things really work in your field, to feel the pressures and stresses associated with certain kinds of work. If nursing interests you, you can spend a few hours a week working in hospitals, geriatric institutions, hospices, or birthing centers. Some people find that working around sick and/or emotionally distressed people makes them feel depressed. If this is your case, you want to find this out *before* you spend many years and thousands of dollars going through a nursing program.

In some fields, volunteer or intern experience is virtually a requirement for career employment. For example, in the popular field of outdoor recreation education, new hires come almost exclusively from the ranks of volunteers. Even in areas where volunteer service is not a critical requirement, it will definitely be a plus on your résumé. Those who can site volunteer or internship experience in the field have a definite edge. Further, most jobs are inside affairs, that is, only 20 percent of all jobs are listed publically through newspapers, em-

ployment offices, etc. The other 80 percent are filled by promoting within organizations or by people hiring people they know or people their employees, coworkers, clients, friends, relatives, etc. know. When you're on the inside, you'll not only know about job opportunities that those on the outside will never hear of, but there's also a good chance you'll get to know people who are doing the hiring or people who have influence with them.

Take Some Time to Find Yourself While Working As a Volunteer

Many people find that taking time for volunteer service in between school and work, or when they reach a career turning point, gives them an opportunity to see and experience life in an entirely new way, while making a meaningful contribution.

Some people, for example, find working for a few years in the **Peace Corps** gives them a break from the urban rat race while they assist people in the Third World (and Eastern Europe—over eighty countries in all), with needs at very basic levels. The mission of the Peace Corps is to "promote world peace and friendship, to help other countries in meeting their needs for trained manpower, and to help promote understanding between the American people and other peoples served by the Peace Corps." The pay, of course, is meager, a living allowance for basic necessities (and a small readjustment allowance), but the rewards in character-building, friendships, and inner satisfaction can be well worth it. In fact, according to the Peace Corps, "Despite the rigors of Peace Corps service, more than nine out of ten volunteers say they would do it again." You must be a U.S. citizen, at least eighteen, meet medical and legal requirements, and have skills requested by the host country. The Peace Corps rarely accepts volunteers with dependents. The service term is for two years. Write to **Peace Corps of the United States,** 1990 K Street, NW,

Washington, DC 20526, or visit their Web site at www.peacecorps.gov.

Americorps*VISTA offers a host of full-time volunteer opportunities throughout the United States. Settings can range from inner-city neighborhoods to Native American reservations. Projects can range from revamping broken-down buildings, to working with drug and alcohol abuse, to dealing with issues of hunger or employment. Like the Peace Corps, the pay is a minimal allowance. You must commit yourself to at least one full year of service. Write to Americorps*VISTA, 1201 New York Ave. NW 4th Floor, Washington, DC 20525, or visit their Web site at www.cns.gov/americorps/ac_vista.html.

You might want to work a stint as an intern for a nonprofit organization. Again, if you get paid at all, you can expect a minimal salary. Some internships may develop into full-time jobs, but many won't. (See pages 298 and 456.)

Where to Find Information on Volunteer Options

Many communities have volunteer bureaus or clearinghouses. If you can't find one in your phone book, write **United Way of America**, 701 N. Fairfax St., Alexandria, VA 22314-2045 or visit their Web site at www.unitedway.org. They will be able to give you information on your local United Way, as well as on other agencies they support. Ask for their *Agency Directory*. It's free and can be a big help. In many communities, the Chamber of Commerce can provide you with a list of local nonprofit organizations that are seeking volunteer assistance—schools, hospitals, churches, food banks, homes for the aged, libraries, political, governmental, and civic organizations, to name a few.

You can also find out about volunteer opportunities through your local public library, college and university libraries, or career centers. Among the sources you may

want to explore, two of the better general directories are *Volunteer: The Comprehensive Guide to Voluntary Service in the U.S. and Abroad* and *Volunteerism: The Directory of Organizations, Training Programs, and Publications*. Ask your librarian about these. The best widely available book (one you can probably find in your local bookstore) on volunteer options is *Volunteer America*, by Harriet Clyde Kipps. Nationally recognized as the foremost authority on volunteerism, her comprehensive book lists over 1,450 organizations, including: organizational mission statement and objectives, services provided, contact person, and publications.

These are all great places to start if you know you want to "do something" but you don't know what. Sources for volunteering opportunities in specific areas abound. A few are listed below and in the bibliography at the end of this section. (Of course, if you know you want to work with a particular organization, contact them directly.)

If you want to work with the homeless, contact **Volunteers of America**, 110 South Union St., Alexandria, VA 22314, (703) 548-2288, or visit their Web site at www.voa.org. Volunteers of America provides programs for the homeless, as well as children, the elderly, and families. They can give you information on service options in your community. If you want to work with children, you can contact your local **Head Start** office. They have many volunteer opportunities for people of all ages. Perhaps you would like to develop a long-term relationship with a child who needs your love and support. Contact your local office of **Big Brothers** or **Big Sisters of America**. Perhaps you would like to work on the problem of illiteracy. Contact your local library, or write **Reading Is Fundamental, Inc.**, 600 Maryland Ave. SW, Suite 600, Washington, DC 20024. Perhaps you are interested in issues related to the environment. Depending on the specific issues you are interested in, you can contact your local office of the **Sierra Club** or visit their Web site at www.sierraclub.org or the **Rainforest Action Network** at 221 Pine St. Suite 500, San Francisco, CA 94104 or visit their Web site at www.ran.org, or any of a host of other organizations.

Know What You Have to Offer: Take a Self-Inventory

Once you've determined your general volunteer goals and focused in on a specific field you would like to work in, take an inventory of your skills, contacts, personality, and time and financial resources. This will help you to decide how you can be most effective in your volunteer activities.

Skills: Take an inventory of your skills. Perhaps you are a lawyer who is interested in the issue of homelessness. As a trial lawyer, you have developed an ability to speak convincingly and argue forcefully for your point of view. Put it to work; become a spokesperson. Your knowledge of the law is a skill, which, together with your contacts, will allow you to approach the problem from the political arena. You can push for legislation. You can put legal pressure on local, state, and federal government agencies to make sure they are fulfilling their commitment under the law. The important point is that you use the highest level of skill that you have. If you can inspire large donations or influence policy at a high level, you would probably do greater good for a greater number doing that than washing dishes at the local church feeding program. Ask yourself: how can I use my current skills in the most effective way?

Contacts: To understand the principle of multiplication of effort is to know that when you can get other people working on a problem, you can do a great deal more than you could ever do yourself. Talk about what you believe in to your friends, family, and co-workers. When people are interested, get them involved. Especially important are high level, influential contacts. They have the resources and connections necessary to make things happen. You may already have such contacts, which you could use more effectively. You might want to assemble an action team of friends and acquaintances who are interested in the project. Ask yourself: How could I take advantage of the contacts I have to further my volunteer service?

Personality: What is it about your personality that sets you apart? Perhaps it's your charisma. Maybe it's your sense of humor. Maybe it's your warmth and gentleness, your easy and relaxed manner, your keen intellect, your vivacious smile and exuberant energy. Get to know your strengths and lead with them. Are you a leader who can motivate a group of people? Take charge. Are your talents artistic? Put them to use. Intellectual? Go to it. Are you good on camera? Become a spokesperson. How do you work best? Are you the kind of person that works best alone, one on one, in small groups, or with large groups of people? When are you naturally most creative and productive? Some people work best in the early morning, just after waking; others are night owls and prefer the late night quietude; still others reach their creative zenith in the late afternoon.

In addition to your strengths, it pays to know your weaknesses. How well do you handle pressure? Does a deadline give you a rash? Does working under a supervisor get you climbing up the walls? Does the idea of speaking before a group make your stomach do backflips? Does the prospect of being judged or evaluated by others make you see red? Whatever your personality strengths and weaknesses, it's important that you become aware of them and consider how your personality fits the context you will be serving in and the people you will be serving with. Ask yourself: What aspects of my personality can be of greatest service in furthering my volunteer efforts?

Money: Perhaps you can make a substantial financial contribution or raise a large amount of money for the cause you want to serve. Maybe you have the know-how to secure grants from foundations or philanthropists. Put it to work. Perhaps you have business and marketing abilities that you can use to create support for the service you want to give. Ask yourself: How can I contribute financially or help others to do so?

Time: As important as the quantity of time that you invest is, the quality is even more important. Time managers use the 80/20 principle. Usually, 20 percent of what we do is really effective, 80 percent isn't. Through thoughtfulness, organization, and concentration, you can make even a small amount of time yield significant results. Remember, no matter how busy you are, you can do something, even if it's just motivating your friends or writing your congressman. Everyone can do something. Ask yourself: What would be the most effective appropriation of my time to further my service?

Develop Your Plan of Action

You've had a chance to consider the needs you want to serve. You know where to find the organizations that are serving this need. You have examined your resources and have a sense of what you have to offer. Now it's time to develop a plan for immediate action.

1. Identify approximately how many hours a week you have to give to this service. How regular are these hours? It will make a difference in the kind of service you can do.

2. Based upon your understanding of the area of service you have selected and the resources at your disposal, identify what your top priority service activities will be. What activities and responsibilities do you want to tackle? Once you have identified what you want to do, start thinking about where you want to do it. You might want to work with a single organization or a number of organizations. You might develop your own independent approach to solving the problem which you work on solely or in conjunction with other organizations. The point is, based on the need and your resources, put yourself to work in a way that maximizes your effectiveness.

3. Next, schedule time for your high priority activities.

4. Take action.

Volunteering Sources

A Student's Guide to Volunteering. De Geronimo, Theresa. Franklin Lakes, N.J.: The Career Press, 1995.

Golden Opportunities: A Volunteer Guide for Americans Over 50. Carroll, Andrew. Princeton: Peterson's Guides, 1994.

Grassroots: How Ordinary People are Changing America. Adams, Tom. New York: Citadel Press, 1991.

The Halo Effect: How Volunteering to Help Others Can Lead To a Better Career and a More Fulfilling Life. Reynolds, John F., and Gene Stone. New York: Golden Books Publishing Co., 1998.

1994 Helping Out in the Outdoors: A Directory of Volunteer Work and Internships on America's Public Land. Washington, D.C.: American Hiking Association, 1993.

How to Make the World a Better Place: 116 Ways You Can Make a Difference. Hollender, Jeffrey, and Linda Catling. New York: W. W. Norton & Company, 1995.

The International Directory of Voluntary Work. Pybus, Victoria, ed. Princeton: Peterson's Guides, 1997.

In the Tiger's Mouth: An Empowerment Guide to Social Action. Shields, Katrina, and Phil Somerville. New Haven, Conn.: New Society Publishers, 1993.

Universal Benefits of Volunteering: A Practical Workbook for Nonprofit Organizations, Volunteers, and Corporations. Pidgeon, Walter. New York: John Wiley & Sons, 1977.

Voices from the Heart: A Celebration of America's Volunteers. O'Connell, Brian. New York: The Foundation Center, 1998.

Volunteer America. Kipps, Harriet Clyde. Chicago: Ferguson Publishing Co., 1997.

Volunteering: 101 Ways You Can Improve the World and Your Life. Lawson, Douglas M. Poway, Calif.: Alti Publishing Co., 1998

Volunteers. Lauffer, Armand, and Sarah Gorodenzky. Beverly Hills: Sage Publications, 1977.

Volunteers in Action. O'Connell, Brian, and Ann Brown. New York: The Foundation Center, 1989.

Volunteers in Public Schools. Bernard, Michael, ed. Washington, D.C.: National Academy Press, 1990.

Volunteer Vacations: Short-Term Adventures that will Benefit You and Others. McMillon, Bill. Chicago: Chicago Review Press, 1997.

You Can Make a Difference! Helping Others and Yourself Through Volunteering. Wilson, Marlene. Boulder, Colo.: Volunteer Management Associates, 1990.

 Real generosity toward the future consists in giving all to what is present.
Albert Camus

Afterword

There are a number of lessons I've learned in the process of making this book that are illustrative of the creative process in general. I refer to a few of these below in the hope that they may be of help to you.

First and foremost—begin! Too often we wait for "perfect" circumstances to begin work on something we are inspired to do, or we wait for permission or acknowledgment. Given the unorthodox nature of this book and its length, few publishers would have wanted to touch it as a proposal, especially one from an unknown first-time author. Self-publishing offered a way to get the word out immediately. Yet at the time, I knew next to nothing about the self-publishing process. You too may have to learn new skills and acquire new knowledge to bring your vision to life.

The fact that the book already existed (the design for the book you are reading is essentially the same as in the original self-published edition) made it more attractive to major publishers. Often, we want others to help us with our projects or ventures before we have done our homework or in some way made tangible the vision we see. If you want people to get excited about your ideas, build some kind of a model that they can see, feel, and touch.

The marriage of a spiritual/artistic perspective with the practical mechanics of career development had not been attempted before. Many of you may have visions of things that have never been done before in the way you are inspired to do them. Don't give up your vision simply because there is no clear model to follow. Trust yourself and the vision that inspires you. It may be your work to chart new ground.

This book was over four years in the making, yet I was only able to concentrate on it full time for one of those years. Many of you may have to work part time through a period of transition into a new career or on a project you love. Don't think that because you can't do it all at once, you can't do it at all. Do what you can step by step and stay with it. The universe has a way of responding to those who won't give up!

One day, I encountered an acquaintance while I was having lunch at a local restaurant and feverishly rewriting text. "Are you *still* working on that book?" he asked. "Aren't you afraid that you will waste a year of your life working on something that no one will want?" I told him that, no, I wasn't concerned. Whatever the outcome, this was something I wanted to do and indeed felt I had to do. Don't listen to voices of doubt, be they in the outside world or inside your own head. Do what *your* heart dictates and trust that you and the universe are one and the same.

CHAPTER NOTES

Preface

1. Kakuzo Okakura, *The Book of Tea* (Tokyo: Kodansha International, 1989), 70.
2. D. T. Suzuki, *Zen and Japanese Culture* (Princeton: Princeton University Press, 1959), 63.

Doing the Work You Love: A Social Movement for the 21st Century

1. In 1997, Microsoft had a worldwide total of approximately 1,115 full-time employees engaged in manufacturing and distribution—this for a company with annual revenues in excess of 11 billion dollars. Source: Microsoft Corp. 10-K filing with the U.S. Securities and Exchange Commission, September 29, 1997.
2. Lawrence Mishel, Jared Bernstein, and John Schmitt *The State of Working America 1996-1997* (Armonk, N.Y.: M. E. Sharpe Inc., 1997).
3. Juliet B. Schor, *The Overworked American: The Unexpected Decline of Leisure* (New York: HarperCollins, 1991).
4. Ibid. Median family income is less today in real dollars than it was in 1974.
5. Ann Kathleen Bradley, "Is Less More?" *New Age Journal* (July/August 1997): 86-146.
6. Sources: E-mail figures: Forrester Research, Inc. online; Estimated commercial use of internet: GartnerGroup as reported in *Time* magazine (July 20, 1998).

Introduction: The Grail Quest or the Bourgeois Nest?

1. *Webster's New Twentieth Century Dictionary,* 2d ed., s.v. "leisure."
2. Erich Fromm, *The Art of Loving: An Enquiry into the Nature of Love* (New York: Harper & Row, 1956), 72.
3. Quoted by Dudley Lynch and Paul L. Kordis, *Strategy of the Dolphin* (New York: Ballantine, 1988), 131.
4. Joseph Campbell, *The Power of Myth* (New York: Doubleday, 1988), 41.
5. Colin Wilson, *The Craft of the Novel* (Bath, Great Britain: Ashgrove Press Limited, 1990), 233.
6. For a general introduction to Jung, see: Carl G. Jung, *Man and His Symbols* (New York: Dell Publishing, 1964); Carl G. Jung, *The Portable Jung,* ed. Joseph Campbell, trans. R.F.C. Mull (New York: Penguin, 1976); Harry A. Wilmen, M.D., *Practical Jung: Nuts and Bolts of Jungian Psychotherapy* (Wilmette, Ill.: Chiron Publications, 1987).
7. Joseph Campbell, *The Hero with a Thousand Faces* (Princeton: Princeton University Press, l949), 229.
8. Ann M. Lindbergh, *Gift from the Sea* (New York: Vintage, 1955), 57.
9. Quoted by Jack Meadows, *The Great Scientists* (New York: Oxford University Press, 1987).
10. Freud referred to love and work as, "the parents of civilization." See Sigmund Freud, *Civilization and Its Discontents*, ed. and trans. James Strachey (New York: Norton, 1961).
11. Ananda K. Coomaraswamy, "Art and Craftmanship," in *Reflections on Art,* ed. Susanne Langer (New York: Oxford University Press, 1961), 241.
12. Ananda K. Coomaraswamy, *Christian & Oriental Philosophy of Art* (New York: Dover Publications, Inc., 1956), 18.
13. Quoted in D. T. Suzuki, *Zen and Japanese Culture* (Princeton: Princeton University Press, 1959), 16.
14. William Blake, *The Portable Blake,* ed. Alfred Kazin (New York: Viking Press, 1946), 499.
15. Coomaraswamy, *Christian & Oriental Philosophy of Art,* 72.
16. Coomaraswamy, "Art and Craftmanship," in *Reflections on Art,* 242.
17. Ellen Dooling Draper, "Focus," *Parabola* 17(1992): 2.

18.   *Webster's New Twentieth Century Dictionary,* 2d ed., s.v. "culture."

19.   Coomaraswamy, "Art and Craftmanship," in *Reflections on Art,* 240.

20.   Joseph Campbell, *The Way of Art* (New York: Mystic Fire Audio, 1990). Audiocassette.

21.   For discussion of the limits of logic to prove or disprove God, see: Immanuel Kant, *Critique of Pure Reason,* trans. Norman Kemp Smith (New York: St. Martin's Press, 1929).

22. Aldous Huxley, Introduction to *The Song of God: Bhagavad-Gita,* trans. Swami Prabhavananda and Christopher Isherwood (New York: Mentor Books, 1951), 13.

23. Campbell, *The Power of Myth*, 117.

24. Arthur Schopenhauer, *Foundations of Morality*, Quoted by Joseph Campbell in *Transformations of Myth Through Time* (New York: Harper & Row, 1990).

25. Quoted by Joseph Campbell, *The Flight of the Wild Gander* (New York: HarperCollins 1990), 45.

26. *Webster's New Twentieth Century Dictionary,* 2d ed., s.v. "conscience."

27. Miguel Serrano, *Carl G. Jung and Herman Hesse: A Record of Two Friendships*, trans. Frank MacShane (New York: Schocken Books, 1968), 42.

28. R. Buckminster Fuller and E. J. Applewhite, *Synergetics* (New York: Macmillan, 1982), XXVII.

29. Campbell, *The Power of Myth*, 99.

30. Jan Halper, Ph.D., *Quiet Desperation: The Truth about Successful Men* (New York: Warner Books, 1989).

31.   E. F. Schumacher, *A Guide for the Perplexed* (New York: Harper & Row, 1977), 138.

32.   Coomaraswamy, *Christian & Oriental Philosophy of Art.*

Prologue: The Art of Life's Work

Chapter One

1. For an introduction to Taoist thought see Lao Tzu, *The Way of Life*, trans. R. B. Blakney (New York: Mentor Books, 1955); Alan Watts, *Tao: The Watercourse Way* (New York: Pantheon Books, 1975); Herrlee G. Creel, *What Is Taoism?* (Chicago: University of Chicago Press, 1970); Chang Chung-yuan, *Creativity and Taoism* (New York: Harper & Row, 1963).

2. For a simple introduction to the uncertainty principle, see Gary Zukav, *The Dancing Wu Li Masters* (New York: Bantam, 1979), 111–114.

3. Rollo May, *The Courage to Create* (New York: Bantam, 1975), 44–45.

4. *Webster's New Twentieth Century Dictionary,* 2d ed., s.v. "job."

5. Ralph Waldo Emerson, *Ralph Waldo Emerson: Selected Prose and Poetry,* ed. Reginald L. Cook (New York: Holt, Rinehart & Winston, 1963).

6. Thomas Mann as quoted by Joseph Campbell in: Stephen and Robin Larsen, *Fire in the Mind* (New York: Doubleday, 1991), 250.

7. Leonardo da Vinci, *The Notebooks of Leonardo da Vinci,* ed. Irma A. Richter (New York: Oxford University Press, 1982).

8. Swami Prabhavananda and Christopher Isherwood, trans. *The Song of God: Bhagavad-Gita* (New York: Mentor Books, 1951).

Chapter Two

1. The Zen master Tosu reportedly gave just this answer:
   Monk, "What is Zen?"
   Tosu, "Zen."
   Quoted by D. T. Suzuki, *Zen and Japanese Culture,* (Princeton: Princeton University Press, 1959), 34.

2. David Ben-Gurion, *The Jews in Their Land,* trans. Madechai Nurock, and Misha Louvish (New York: Doubleday, 1974), 79.

3. Paul Williams, *Mahayana Buddhism: The Doctrinal Foundations* (Routeledge: Chapman Hall, 1989).

4. Aldous Huxley, Introduction to *The Song of God: Bhagavad-Gita,* trans. Swami Prabhavananda and Christopher Isherwood (New York: Mentor Books, 1951), 12.

5. Troy Wilson Organ, *Hinduism: Its Historical Development* (Woodbury, N.Y.: Barron's Educational Series, 1974), 57.

6. *Webster's New Twentieth Century Dictionary,* 2d ed., s.v. "poet."

7. Quoted by Whitall N. Perry, *A Treasury of Traditional Wisdom* (San Francisco: Harper & Row, 1971), 336.

8. George Bernard Shaw, *Man and Superman* (New York: Airmont Publishing, 1965), 27.

9. Lao Tzu quoted in Alan Watts, *The Way of Zen* (New York: Vintage, 1957), xii.

10. *Karuna* (Sanskrit), literally "compassion." *Karuna* is one of the two principle virtues of Mahayana Buddhism, the other being *prajna* (Sanskrit), literally, "consciousness," or "wisdom." *Ananda* is a Sanskrit word meaning literally "bliss," or "absolute joy." *Ananda* is one of the three properties of the *Atman—sat* (being, or existence), *chit* (consciousness), and *ananda* (bliss).

11. Phil Cousineau, *The Hero's Journey: The World of Joseph Campbell* (New York: Harper & Row, 1990), 65.

12. *Webster's New Twentieth Century Dictionary,* 2d ed., s.v. "art."

13. Ibid., s.v. "sacrifice."

14. From the Greek, *theoritica,* literally "a look at." *Webster's New Twentieth Century Dictionary,* 2d ed., s.v. "theory."

15. Herbert Read, *The Meaning of Art* (London: Faber & Faber, 1931), 18.

16. James Joyce, *The Portable James Joyce,* ed. Harry Levin (New York: Penguin, 1976).

17. See D.T. Suzuki, *The Zen Doctrine of No Mind* (York Beach, Minn.: Samuel Weiser, 1972).

18. Joyce, *The Portable James Joyce.*

19. While it is clear that the word *Zen* comes from the Indian *dhyana* by way of the Chinese *ch'an* (or *ch'an-na*), there is some dispute as to whether "Zen" is a shortening of *Zazen* (i.e., sitting meditation), or simply of *Zenna* (meditation). This may seem a small point, but the difference in emphasis which each gives reflects a long-standing dispute within the Zen community as to the exigency of sitting meditation to ultimate Zen realization.

20. Arthur Schopenhauer, "On Aesthetics" in *Essays and Aphorisms* (New York: Penguin Classics, 1986), 159.

21. Lao Tzu quoted in *The Secret of the Golden Flower,* trans. Richard Wilhelm (New York: Harcourt, Brace & World, 1962), 21.

22. Quoted by Ananda K. Coomaraswamy, *Christian & Oriental Philosophy of Art* (New York: Dover Publications, Inc. 1956).

23. Joseph Campbell, *The Way of Art* (New York: Mystic Fire Audio, 1990). Audiocassette.

24. Quoted by Ananda K. Coomaraswamy, *The Dance of Shiva* (New York: Noonday Press, 1957), 179.

25. Quoted in Cousineau, *The Hero's Journey: The World of Joseph Campbell,* 32.

26. Quoted by Coomaraswamy, *Christian & Oriental Philosophy of Art.*

27. Quoted by Coomaraswamy, *The Dance of Shiva,* 179.

28. Gottfried von Strassburg, *Tristan* (New York: Penguin, 1960), 41.

29. *Webster's New Twentieth Century Dictionary,* 2d ed., s.v. "design."

30. Joseph Campbell, *The Power of Myth* (New York: Doubleday, 1988), 150–151.

31. William Blake, *The Portable Blake,* ed. Alfred Kazin (New York: Viking Press, 1946), 253.

32. Roy Harris, *The Bases of Artistic Creation* (New Brunswick, N.J.: Rutgers University Press, 1942).

33. Suzuki, *Zen and Japanese Culture,* 84.

34. Coomaraswamy, *Christian & Oriental Philosophy of Art,* 65.

35. Jacob Bronowski (condensed from a speech to the American Academy of Arts and Letters).

Chapter Three

1. Phil Cousineau, *The Hero's Journey: The World of Joseph Campbell* (New York: Harper & Row, 1990), 40. Campbell says he got the term "transparent to transcendence" from Karlfreid Graf Dürkheim.

2. Joseph Campbell, *The Hero with a Thousand Faces* (Princeton: Princeton University Press, l949), 3.

3. Carl G. Jung, *On the Nature of the Psyche,* Bollingen Ser., vol. 20 (Princeton: Princeton University Press, 1969).

4. Carl G. Jung, *Symbols of Transformation*, Bollingen Ser., vol. 5 (Collected Works) (Princeton: Princeton University Press, 1956).

5. Carl G. Jung, *Man and His Symbols* (New York: Dell Publishing, 1964).

6. Isshu Miura and Ruth Fuller Sasaki, *The Zen Koan* (New York: Harcourt, Brace & World, 1965), 66.

7. Jung, *Man and His Symbols*.

8. The word *Maya*, as well as *illusion*, means magic, art, and that which we create with.

9. *Webster's New Twentieth Century Dictionary,* 2d ed., s.v. "illusion."

10. The reference here is to a passage quoted on page 226 of this work taken from Alan Watts, *The Way of Zen* (New York: Vintage, 1957), 125.

11. Steven Ungerleider, *Mental Training for Peak Performance: Top Athletes Reveal the Mind Exercises They Use to Excel* (Emmaus, Pa.: Rodale Press, 1996).

12. Bernie Siegal, *Love, Medicine and Miracles* (New York: Harper & Row, 1986).

13. *Bushido* has been translated "the way of the Warrior" and is a developed code of conduct for the Japanese Samurai warrior. The "Luke" referred to here is Luke Skywalker, a *jedi* knight or warrior, from the fictional film trilogy *Star Wars*, *The Empire Strikes Back*, and *Return of the Jedi*.

14. Lao Tzu, *The Way of Life*, trans. R. B. Blakney (New York: Mentor Books, 1964), 62.

15. Ajit Mookerjee and Madhu Khanna, *The Tantric Way* (New York: Little Brown & Company, 1977), 45.

16. Joseph Caster, *Putnam's Concise Mythological Dictionary* (New York: G. P. Putnam's Sons, 1980), 89.

17. Michael Harner, *The Way of the Shaman* (New York: Mentor Books, 1964).

18. Quoted in *The Spirit of Shamanism* (Los Angeles: Jeremy P. Tharcher, Inc., 1990), 141.

19. Quoted by Whitall N. Perry, *A Treasury of Traditional Wisdom* (San Francisco: Harper & Row, 1971), 206.

20. Frances Gies, *The Knight in History* (New York: Harper & Row, 1984).

21. I saw this on American television (PBS), but have been unable to track the title.

22. Chu Hsi, *Learning to Be a Sage*, trans. Daniel K. Gardner (Berkeley & Los Angeles: University of California Press, 1990).

23. Lu Chi, *The Art of Writing*, trans. Sam Hamill (Minneapolis: Milkweed Editions, 1991), 29–30.

24. Quoted by Ananda K. Coomaraswamy, *Christian & Oriental Philosophy of Art* (New York: Dover Publications, Inc. 1956).

25. Jung, *Man and His Symbols*, 87.

26. Joseph Campbell, *The Power of Myth* (New York: Doubleday, 1988), 4.

27. Jung, *Man and His Symbols*.

Chapter Four

1. Albert Camus, *The Myth of Sisyphus*, trans. Justin O'Brien (New York: Vintage, 1955), 3.

2. George Bernard Shaw, *Man and Superman* (New York: Airmont Publishing, 1965), 27.

3. *Mother Teresa* (Petrie Productions, Inc., Home Today Entertainment, 1986). Videocassette.

4. Albert Einstein, *The World as I See It* (Secaucus, N.J.: Citadel Press, 1979), 21.

5. From the Greek, *katharsis*, purification. *Webster's New Twentieth Century Dictionary,* 2d ed., s.v. "catharsis."

6. William Blake, *The Portable Blake,* ed. Alfred Kazin (New York: Viking Press, 1946).

Act I: The Quest for Life's Work

The Quest for Your Best

1. Joseph Campbell, *Transformations of Myth Through Time* (New York: Harper & Row, 1990), 211.

2. *Webster's New Twentieth Century Dictionary,* 2d ed., s.v. "heretic."

3. Joseph Campbell, *The Hero with a Thousand Faces* (Princeton: Princeton University Press, 1949), 78.

4. John Matthews, *The Elements of the Grail Tradition* (Longmead, Shaftesbury, Dorset, Great Britain: Element Books Limited, 1990).

5. Colin Wilson, *The Craft of the Novel* (Bath, Great Britain: Ashgrove Press Limited, 1990), 20.

6. Leonardo da Vinci, *The Notebooks of Leonardo da Vinci,* ed. Irma A. Richter (New York: Oxford University Press, 1982).

7. Wilson, *The Craft of the Novel*, 151–152.

8. Ibid., 87.

9. Quoted by Ibid., 28.

10. Wilson, *The Craft of the Novel*.

11. Ralph Waldo Emerson, *Ralph Waldo Emerson: Selected Prose and Poetry,* ed. Reginald L. Cook (New York: Holt, Rinehart & Winston, 1963), 168.

12. Heinrich Dumoulin, *Zen Enlightenment* (New York: Weatherhill, 1979, 1983), 73.

13. Isshu Miura and Ruth Fuller Sasaki, *The Zen Koan* (New York: Harcourt, Brace & World, 1965), 42–43.

14. Wolfram von Eschenbach, *Parzival* (New York: Penguin,1980).

15. Ibid., 75.

16. Dag Hammarskjold, *Markings*, trans. Leif Sjoberg and W.H. Auden from the Swedish (New York: Alfred A. Knopf, 1970).

17. Eschenbach, *Parzival*, 15.

18. Ibid., 131.

19. Ibid., 135.

20. Ibid., 396.

21. Chretien de Troyes, *Perceval: The Story of the Grail,* (including "The Three Continuations") trans. N. Briant (D. S. Brewer, 1982).

22. Eknath Easwaran, *Gandhi the Man* (Petaluma, Calif.: Nilgiri Press, 1973), 29.

23. Edmund Burke, *On the Sublime and Beautiful* (New York: P. F. Collier & Son Corporation, 1937, 1969), 35.

24. Leo Tolstoy, *War and Peace* (New York: The Modern Library, 1931), 1039.

25. Ibid., 1060.

26. Mary Harrington Hall, "A Conversation with Peter Drucker," *Psychology Today,* (March 1968): 21 ff.

27. Campbell, *The Hero with a Thousand Faces,* 59.

28. Dumoulin, *Zen Enlightenment,* 72.

29. George Herbert, *The Complete Works in Verse and Prose of George Herbert*, 3 vols. (New York: AMS Press, Inc., Reprint of 1874 ed.).

30. Harold C. Schonberg, *The Lives of Great Composers* (New York: W. W. Norton & Company, 1981, 1970), 99.

31. This painting was thirty years in the planning. Theodore Rousseau, Jr., *Cezanne* (New York: Pocket Books, 1953), plate 25.

32. Oxford University Press has recently put out an excellent biography: *Goethe: The Poet and the Age* in two volumes. Nicholas Bayle, *Goethe: The Poet and the Age,* 2 vols. (New York: Oxford University Press, 1991).

Scene I: Vision Questing

1. A. R. Lacey, *Dictionary of Philosophy* (New York: Macmillan, 1977), 319.

2. *Webster's New Twentieth Century Dictionary,* 2d ed., s.v. "sacred."

3. Fritjof Capra, *The Tao of Physics* (New York: Bantam, 1977).

4. Erica Anderson, additional text by Albert Schweitzer, *The Schweitzer Album* (New York: Harper & Row, 1965), 47.

5. Albert Einstein, *The World as I See It* (Secaucus, N.J.: Citadel Press, 1979), 29.

6. Ibid.

7. E. F. Schumacher, *Small Is Beautiful: Economics As If People Mattered* (New York: Harper & Row, 1975). Schumacher may have got this from Ananda K. Coomaraswamy. He says something remarkably similar in *Christian & Oriental Philosophy of Art* (New York: Dover Publications, Inc., 1956), 62.

8. Eknath Easwaran, *Gandhi the Man* (Petaluma, Calif.: Nilgiri Press, 1973), 75.

9. Peter Tompkins and Christopher Bird, *Secret Life of Plants: A Fascinating Account of the Physical, Emotional, & Spiritual Relations between Plants and Man* (New York: Harper & Row, 1984).

10. Diane Sukiennik, Lisa Raufman, and William Bendat, *The Career Fitness Program: Exercising Your Career Options* (Scottsdale, Ariz.: Gorsuch Scarisbrick, Publishers, 1986), 13.

11. See L. Reti, *The Unknown Leonardo* (New York: McGraw-Hill, 1974).

12. R. Buckminster Fuller, *Critical Path* (New York: St. Martin's Press, 1981), 125.

13. Leonardo da Vinci, *The Notebooks of Leonardo da Vinci,* ed. Irma A. Richter (New York: Oxford University Press, 1982).

14. Fuller, *Critical Path*, 217.

15. Accounts of the life of the Buddha may be found in: Edwin Arnold, *The Light of Asia* (Boston: Robert Brother's, 1887); *Life and Teachings of the Buddha* (Mt. Vernon, N.Y.: Peter Pauper Press, n.d.); Paul Carus, *Gospel of the Buddha: According to Old Records* (Tuscon, Ariz.: Omen Publications, 1972).

16. William Blake, *The Portable Blake,* ed. Alfred Kazin (New York: Viking Press, 1946).

17. Ibid, 97.

18. Gautama Buddha, *Dhammapada*, trans. Irving Babbitt (New York: New Directions, 1965).

19. *Webster's New Twentieth Century Dictionary,* 2d ed., s.v. "imagination."

20. Quoted in Miyamoto Mushaski, *Book of Five Rings*, trans. Victor Harris (Woodstock, N.Y.: Overlook Press, 1982), 39.

21. Confucius, *Wisdom of Confucius*, ed. Lin Yutang (New York: Random House, 1938).

22. Voltaire, *The Portable Voltaire*, ed. Ben R. Redman (New York: Penguin, 1977).

23. Ken Keyes, *The Hundredth Monkey* (Coos Bay, Ore.: Living Love, 1984).

24. Henry David Thoreau, *The Portable Thoreau,* ed. Carl Bode (New York: Penguin, 1977).

25. Walt Whitman, "Leaves of Grass" in *Leaves of Grass and Selected Prose* (New York: Holt, Rinehart & Winston, 1949), 41.

26. Einstein, *The World as I See It,* 8.

Scene II: Clarifying Values

1. Thomas Jefferson, *Complete Jefferson*, facs ed., ed. Saul K. Pandover (Salem, N.H.: Ayer Co. Pubs., Inc., 1943).

2. D. T. Suzuki, *Zen and Japanese Culture* (Princeton: Princeton University Press, 1959), 41–57.

3. Confucius, *Wisdom of Confucius*, ed. Lin Yutang (New York: Random House, 1938).

4. See Idries Shah, *The Sufis* (London: Octagon Press, 1964).

5. Oswald Spengler, *The Decline of the West* (New York: Modern Library, 1965).

6. William Blake, *The Portable Blake,* ed. Alfred Kazin (New York: Viking Press, 1946), 540.

7. Quoted by Joseph Campbell in *The Inner Reaches of Outer Space: Metaphor as Myth and as Religion* (New York: Harper & Row, 1988), 53.

Scene III: Pointing to Purpose

1. Maxwell Anderson et al., *The Bases of Artistic Creation* (New Brunswick, N.J.: Rutgers University Press, 1942).

2. Joseph Campbell, *The Power of Myth* (New York: Doubleday, 1988), 123.

3. Ibid., 126.

4. Thomas Cleary, trans. *Zen Lessons*, (Boston and Shaftesbury: Shambhala, 1989), 34.

Scene IV: Targeting Talents

1. John Addington Symonds, *The Life of Michelangelo* (New York: Carlton House, n.d.), 46–47.

2. Matt. 25:14–30.

3. Quoted by Ananda K. Coomaraswamy in *The Dance of Shiva* (New York: Noonday Press, 1957), 144.

Act II: The Game of Life's Work

Playing the Game: Winners, Losers, and Choosers

1. For popular books on this subject, see: Patricia Garfield, *Creative Dreaming* (New York: Ballantine, 1976), and Stephen LaBerge, *Lucid Dreaming* (New York: Ballantine, 1986).

2. William James, *Varieties of Religious Experience*, ed. Martin Marty (New York: Penguin, 1982).

3. Henry Grady Weaver, *The Mainspring of Human Progress* (Irvington-on-Hudson, N.Y.: Talbot Books, 1947), 105–106.

4. Joseph Campbell, *The Power of Myth* (New York: Doubleday, 1988), 130.

5. Francis Bacon, *Essays,* ed. John Pitcher (New York: Penguin, 1986), 196.

6. Erich Fromm, *The Art of Loving: An Enquiry into the Nature of Love* (New York: Harper & Row, 1956), 72.

Act III: The Battle for Life's Work

Winning in the Marketplace

1. Andrea Hopkins, *Knights* (New York: Quarto Publishing, 1990).

2. *Webster's New Twentieth Century Dictionary,* 2d ed., s.v. "valor," "value."

3. Ibid, s.v. "ken."

4. Eknath Easwaran, *Gandhi the Man* (Petaluma, Calif.: Nilgiri Press, 1973).

5. Tim Newark, *Women Warlords: An Illustrated Military History of Female Warriors* (London: Blandford, 1989), 40–52.

Scene I: Taking It to the Street: Choosing Your Marketing Strategy

1. Leonard Zunin with Natalie Zunin, *Contact: The First Four Minutes* (New York: Ballantine, 1972).

2. Alan Watts, *In My Own Way: An Autobiography* (New York: Pantheon Books, A Division of Random House, 1972), 278.

3. Ibid.

4. *Webster's New Twentieth Century Dictionary,* 2d ed., s.v. "circulation."

5. Michael H. Hart, *The One Hundred: A Ranking of the Most Influential Persons in History* (New York: Beaufort Books, 1985).

Scene II: Scenario I: Sailing the Entrepreneurship

1. Peter F. Drucker, *Innovation and Entrepreneurship: Practice and Principles* (New York: Harper & Row, 1986), 2–3.

2. John Naisbitt and Patricia Aburdene, *Re-Inventing the Corporation* (New York: Warner Books, 1985), 95.

3. Paul Hawken, *Growing a Business* (New York: Fireside, 1987), 13.

4. John Molloy, *Molloy's Live for Success* (New York: Bantam, 1983).

5. Bernard Kamoroff, *The Small Time Operator* (Laytonville, Calif.: Bell Springs Publishing, 1988).

Scene II: Scenario II: Wielding the Freelance

1. *Webster's New Twentieth Century Dictionary,* 2d ed., s.v. "freelance."

2. Richard Wilhelm and Cary F. Baynes, trans. *The I Ching* (Princeton: Princeton University Press, 1967).

3. Mari Privette Ulmer, *Sign Here: How to Understand Any Contract Before You Sign* (Angel Fire, N.Mex.: Intrigue Press, a division of Columbine Publishing Group, Inc., 1998).

4. Larry Brockman, "Letter from the President." From the web site of the *American Home Business Association* (March 1998).

5. Barbara Weltman, *The Complete Idiot's Guide to Starting a Home-Based Business* (New York: Alpha Books, 1997), 5–6.

Scene II: Scenario IV: Landing the Right Job

1. Peter F. Drucker, *Management: Tasks, Practices, Responsibilities* (New York: HarperCollins, 1974).
2. R. Buckminster Fuller, *Critical Path* (New York: St. Martin's Press, 1981).
3. Fuller, *Critical Path*, 379.
4. Ibid.
5. Richard J. Barnet and Ronald E. Müller, *Global Reach: The Power of the Multinational Corporations* (New York: Simon & Schuster, 1974).
6. Paul Baran and Paul Sweezy, *Monopoly Capital* (New York: Monthly Review Press, 1968).
7. James E. Person, Jr., ed. and Sean R. Pollock, associate ed., *Statistical Forecasts of the United States* (Detroit: Gale Research, Inc., 1993), 439.

Scene III: Street Smarts

1. The Taft Group, *Taft Foundation Reporter: Comprehensive Profiles and Analyses of America's Private Foundations* (Washington D.C.: The Taft Group, 1987).
2. Francis Bacon, *The Essays or Councils, Civil and Moral, of Francis Ld. Verulan* (Mt. Vernon, N.Y.: Peter Pauper Press, n.d.).
3. James E. Person, Jr., ed. and Sean R. Pollock, associate ed., *Statistical Forecasts of the United States* (Detroit: Gale Research, Inc., 1993), 438.

Act IV: The School of Life's Work

Learning to Change: The Old Boy and the Student-Sage

1. John Naisbitt, *Megatrends: Ten New Directions Transforming Our Lives* (New York: Warner Books, 1983).
2. *Webster's New Twentieth Century Dictionary*, 2d ed., s.v. "student," "sage."
3. Richard Wilhelm and Cary F. Baynes, trans. *The I Ching* (Princeton: Princeton University Press, 1967), 322.
4. Ibid, 227.
5. *Webster's New Twentieth Century Dictionary*, 2d ed., s.v., "crisis."
6. Wilhelm and Baynes, trans. *The I Ching*, 326.
7. Moshe Feldenkrais, *Awareness Through Movement* (San Francisco: HarperCollins, 1972, 1977), 3.
8. Ibid., 4.
9. Chu Hsi, *Learning to Be a Sage*, trans. Daniel K. Gardner (Berkeley & Los Angeles: University of California Press, 1990).
10. Jacob Bronowski, *Science and Human Values* (New York: Harper & Row, 1972).
11. Joseph Campbell, *The World of Joseph Campbell: In Search of the Holy Grail: The Parzival Legend* (NP:Mythology Limited, 1989). Audiocassette.
12. Chu Hsi, *Learning to Be a Sage*.
13. Henry David Thoreau, *The Portable Thoreau,* ed. Carl Bode (New York: Penguin, 1977).

Scene II: Training Thrills: Knowledge and Skills

1. Harold Figler, *The Complete Job Search Handbook* (New York: H. Holt & Company, 1980).
2. Walt Whitman, *Leaves of Grass and Selected Prose* (New York: Holt, Rinehart & Winston, 1949), 46.
3. *College Money Handbook* (Princeton: Peterson's Guides, 1998).

Scene III: Creating the Self-Image You Need to Succeed

1. Moshe Feldenkrais, *Awareness Through Movement* (San Francisco: HarperCollins, 1972, 1977), 10.

Appendix

Appendix A: Economics: Scar-city or Mutual Support System

1. John Maynard Keynes, *The General Theory of Employment, Interest, and Money* (San Diego, Calif.: Harcourt, Brace and Janovich, 1936, 1965), chapter 24.

2. Lila and Dale Truett, *Economics* (St. Paul: West Publishing Company, 1982), 6.

3. Robert Heilbroner, *The Making of Economic Society* (Englewood Cliffs, N.J.: Prentice Hall, 1962), 5.

4. Adam Smith, *Wealth of Nations*, vol. 1 (London: Methuen & Company, 1950).

5. Ibid., 8.

6. Esmond Wright, ed., *History of the World: The Last Five Hundred Years* (Middlesex, England: Bonanza Books, 1984), 14.

7. E. F. Schumacher, *Small is Beautiful: Economics As If People Mattered* (New York: Harper & Row, 1975), 35.

8. John Kenneth Galbraith, *The Age of Uncertainty* (Boston: Houghton Mifflin Company, 1977), 35.

9. John D. Rockefeller quoted in John Kenneth Galbraith, *The Age of Uncertainty*, 48.

10. Heilbroner, *The Making of Economic Society*, 5.

11. R. Buckminster Fuller, *Critical Path* (New York: St. Martin's Press, 1981), 198.

12. Ibid., 199.

13. Ibid., 200.

14. Ibid., 198.

15. Ibid.

BIBLIOGRAPHY

Prologue: The Art of Life's Work

Introduction to Zen

Suzuki, Daisetz, T., and Carl Gustav Jung. *Introduction to Zen Buddhism*. New York: Grove Press, 1991.

Suzuki, Shunryu. *Zen Mind, Beginner's Mind*. Ed. Trudy Dixon. New York: Weatherhill, Inc., 1972.

Watts, Alan W. *The Way of Zen*. New York: Vintage Books, 1989.

Stories, Koans, Poems

Blyth, R. H. *Zen in English Literature and Oriental Classics*. Tokyo: Dutton Paperback, Heian International, 1942.

Cleary, Thomas, trans. *The Book of Serenity: One Hundred Zen Dialogues*. Boston: Shambhala Publications, 1998.

_____. *Zen Lessons: The Art of Leadership*. Boston: Shambhala Publications, 1993.

Miura, Isshu, and Ruth Fuller Sasaki. *The Zen Koan*. New York: Harcourt, Brace and Janovich, 1989.

Reps, Paul, ed., with Nyogen Senzaki. *Zen Flesh, Zen Bones: A Collection of Zen and Pre-Zen Writings*. Boston: Shambhala Publications, 1994.

Stryk, Lucien, and Takashi Ikemoto, eds. and trans. *The Penguin Book of Zen Poetry*. New York: Penguin USA, 1988.

_____, trans. *Zen: Poems, Prayers, Sermons, Anecdotes, Interviews*. Ohio University Press, 1982.

_____, trans. *Zen Poems of China and Japan: The Crane's Bill*. New York: Grove Press, 1988.

Sohl, Robert, and Audrey Carr. *Games Zen Masters Play: The Writings of R.H. Blyth*. New York: New American Library, 1976.

Tze-Chiang, Chao. *A Chinese Garden of Serenity: Reflections of a Zen Buddhist*. Mt. Vernon, N.Y.: Peter Pauper Press, 1959.

Zen, History, Art, and Culture

Addiss, Stephen. *The Art of Zen: Paintings and Calligraphy by Japanese Monks, 1600-1925*. New York: Harry N. Abrams, 1998.

Dumoulin, Heinrich. *Zen Buddhism: A History, Volume 1: India and China with a New Supplement on the Northern School of Chinese Zen*. New York: Macmillan Publishing Co., 1989.

_____. *Zen Buddhism: A History, Volume 2: Japan*. New York: Macmillan Publishing Co., 1989.

Fontein, Jan, and Money L. Hickman. *Zen Painting and Calligraphy*. Boston: Boston Museum of Fine Arts, 1970.

Suzuki, D.T. *Zen and Japanese Culture*. New York: Fine Communications, 1997.

Act I: The Quest for Life's Work

Grail Sources

Jung, Emma, and Marie-Louise Von Franz. *The Grail Legend*. Boston: Sigo Press, 1986.

Matthews, John. *The Elements of the Grail Tradition*. Shaftesbury, Great Britian: Element Books, 1997.

Ravenscroft, Trevor. *The Cup of Destiny*. New York: Samuel Weiser, 1995.

Von Eschenbach, Wolfram. *Parzival of Wolfram Von Eschenbach*. New York: Penguin Classic, 1980.

Your World Needs Your Love Sources

Barnet, Richard J. *Global Dreams: Imperial Corporations in the New World Order*. New York: Simon & Schuster, 1995.

Benjamin, Medea, and Miya Rodolfo-Sioson. *The Peace Corps and More: 175 Ways to Work, Study and Travel at Home and Abroad*. Santa Ana, Calif.: Seven Locks Press, 1997.

Block, Peter. *Stewardship: Choosing Service Over Self-Interest*. San Francisco: Berrett-Koehler Publishers, Inc., 1996.

Brown, Lester R. *State of the World: A Worldwatch Institute Report on Progress Toward a Sustainable Society*. New York: W.W. Norton & Co. Published annually in January.

Brown, Lester R., Michael Renner, Christopher Flavin, and Linda Starke. *Vital Signs: The Environmental Trends That Are Shaping Our Future*. New York: W.W. Norton and Company, 1997.

Council on Environmental Quality Staff. *The Global 2000 Report to the President: Entering the Twenty-First Century, Vol. I*. New York: Penguin, 1982.

Daly, Herman E. *Beyond Growth: The Economics of Sustainable Development*. Boston: Beacon Press, 1997.

Daly, Herman E., and John B. Cobb, Jr. *For the Common Good: Redirecting the Economy Toward Community, the Environment, and a Sustainable Future*. Boston: Beacon Press, 1994.

Ekins, Paul et al. *Gaia Atlas of Green Economics*. New York: Anchor Books, 1992.

Eppsteiner, Fred. *Path of Compassion: Writings on Socially Engaged Buddhism*. Berkeley: Parallax Press, 1988.

Ferencz, Benjamin B., Ken Keyes Jr., and Robert Muller. *Planethood: The Key to Your Future*. Coos Bay, Ore.: Love Line Books, 1991.

Frankel, Carl. *In Earth's Company: Business, Environment, and the Challenge of Sustainability*. New Haven, Conn.: New Society Publishers, 1998.

Gale Research Staff. *Newsletters in Print*. Detroit: Gale Research Co. Published annually.

Greider, William. *One World, Ready or Not: The Manic Logic of Global Capitalism*. New York: Touchstone Books, 1998.

Hammond Incorporated. *Hammond Atlas of the World*. New York: Random House. Updated Reglarly.

Henderson, Hazel. *Building a Win-Win World: Life Beyond Global Economic Warfare*. San Francisco: Berrett-Koehler Publishers, Inc., 1996.

Karliner, Joshua. *The Corporate Planet: Ecology and Politics in the Age of Globalization*. San Francisco: Sierra Club Books, 1997.

Kidron, Michael, and Ronald Segal. *What You Need to Know about Business, Money, and Power*. New York: Simon & Schuster, 1987.

Kidron, Michael, Ronald Segal, and Angela Wilson. *Political, Economic and Social Trends*. New York: Penguin USA, 1995.

Korten, David C. *When Corporations Rule the World*. San Francisco: Berrett-Koehler Publishers/Kumarian Press, 1996.

Krieger, David, and Frank Kelly, eds. *Waging Peace II: Vision and Hope for the 21st Century*. San Bernardino, Calif.: Noble Press, 1988.

Kurian, George T. *The Illustrated Book of World Rankings*. Armonk, N.Y.: M.E. Sharpe, 1996.

_____. *The New Book of World Rankings*. New York: Facts on File. Published annually in September.

Myers, Norman, and Nancy J. Myers. *Gaia: An Atlas of Planet Management*. New York: Anchor Press, Doubleday, 1993.

Richards, Dick. *Artful Work: Awakening Joy, Meaning, and Commitment in the Workplace*. New York: Berkeley Books, 1997.

Rosenbaum, Robert A. *The Public Issues Handbook: A Guide for the Concerned Citizen*. Westport, Conn.: Greenwood Press, Inc., 1983.

Schumacher, E. F. *Small Is Beautiful: Economics as if People Mattered*. New York: HarperCollins, 1989.

Testemale, Phil. *Our Ecological Footprint: Reducing Human Impact on the Earth*. New Haven, Conn.: New Society Publishers, 1995.

Weisman, Alan. *Gaviotas: A Village to Reinvent the World*. White River Junction, Vt.: Chelsea Green Publishers, 1998.

The World Bank. *World Development Report*. New York: Oxford University Press. Published annually in July.

Act II: The Game of Life's Work

Investigating Career Possibilities

Arron, Deborah. *What Can You Do with a Law Degree? A Lawyers Guide to Career Alternatives Inside, Outside and Around the Law*. Portland, Ore.: Miche Press, 1997.

Basta, Nicholas. *The Environmental Career Guide: Job Opportunities with the Earth in Mind*. John Wiley & Sons, Inc., 1991.

Bell, Susan. *Full Disclosure: Do You Really Want to Be a Lawyer?* Princeton: Peterson's Guides, 1992.

Bernal, Deborah L., M.D. *Vital Signs: Working Doctors Tell the Real Story Behind Medical School and Practice*. Princeton: Peterson's Guides, 1994.

Bernstein, Alan, and Nicholas Schaffzin. *Guide to Your Career: How to Turn Your Interest into a Career You Love*. New York: Princeton Review Press. Published annually.

Camenson, Blythe. *Careers for Health Nuts & Others Who Like to Stay Fit.* Lincolnwood, Ill.: VGM Career Horizons, 1996.

_____. *Careers for History Buffs & Others Who Learn from the Past.* Lincolnwood, Ill.: VGM Career Horizons, 1994.

_____. *Careers for Plant Lovers & Other Green Thumb Types.* Lincolnwood, Ill.: VGM Career Horizons, 1995.

_____. *Careers for Self-Starters & Other Entrepreneurial Types.* Lincolnwood, Ill.: VGM Career Horizons, 1997.

Cohn, Susan, and Horst Rechelbacher. *Green at Work: Finding a Business Career That Works for the Environment.* Washington, D.C.: Island Press, 1995.

Corwen, Leonard. *Arco's College Not Required! 100 Great Careers that Don't Require a College Degree.* New York: Macmillan, 1995.

Eberts, Marjorie, and Margaret Gisler. *Careers for Bookworms and Other Literary Types.* Lincolnwood, Ill.: VGM Career Horizons, 1995.

_____. *Careers for Computer Buffs & Other Technological Types.* Lincolnwood, Ill.: VGM Career Horizons, 1993.

_____. *Careers for Culture Lovers & Other Artsy Types.* Lincolnwood, Ill.: VGM Career Horizons, 1992.

_____. *Careers for Good Samaritans and Other Humanitarian Types.* Lincolnwood, Ill.: VGM Career Horizons, 1991.

_____. *Careers for Kids at Heart & Others Who Adore Children.* Lincolnwood, Ill.: VGM Career Horizons, 1994.

Eberts, Marjorie, and Rachel Kelsey. *Careers for Cybersurfers & Other Online Types.* Lincolnwood, Ill.: VGM Career Horizons, 1998.

Field, Sally. *100 Best Careers for Writers and Artists.* New York: Macmillan, 1998.

Greenspon, Jaq. *Careers for Film Buffs and Other Hollywood Types.* Lincolnwood, Ill.: VGM Career Horizons, 1993.

Guiley, Rosemary Ellen. *Career Opportunities for Writers.* New York: Facts on File, 1996.

Heitzmann, William Ray. *Careers for Sports Nuts & Other Athletic Types.* Lincolnwood, Ill.: VGM Career Horizons, 1997.

Hiam, Alexander, and Susan Angle. *Adventure Careers.* Franklin Lakes, N.J.: The Career Press, 1995.

Jebens, Harley. *100 Jobs in Social Change.* New York: Macmillan, 1997.

Jist Works with Elisabeth Oakes, ed. *Student's Guide to Career Exploration on the Internet.* Chicago: Ferguson Publishing Co., 1998.

Jones, Rosemary. *Education and Career Opportunities in Alternative Medicine.* Rocklin, Calif.: Prima Publishing, 1998.

Kinney, Jane et al. *Careers for Environmental Types & Others Who Respect the Earth.* Lincolnwood, Ill.: VGM Career Horizons, 1993.

Mantis, Hillary. *Alternative Careers for Lawyers.* New York: Random House, 1997.

Mauro Lucia. *Careers for the Stagestruck & Other Dramatic Types.* Lincolnwood, Ill.: VGM Career Horizons, 1997.

McLean, Cheryl. *Careers for Shutterbugs and Other Candid Types.* Lincolnwood, Ill.: VGM Career Horizons, 1994.

Miller, Louise R. *Careers for Animal Lovers and Other Zoological Types.* Lincolnwood, Ill.: VGM Career Horizons, 1991.

_____. *Careers for Nature Lovers and Other Outdoor Types.* Lincolnwood, Ill.: VGM Career Horizons, 1992.

Paradis, Adrian A. *Careers for Caring People & Other Sensitive Types.* Lincolnwood, Ill.: VGM Career Horizons, 1995.

Quintana, Debra. *100 Jobs in the Environment.* New York: Macmillan, 1997.

Robbins-Roth, Cynthia. *Alternative Careers in Science: Leaving the Ivory Tower.* New York: Academic Press, 1998.

Robotti, Suzanne, and Margaret Inman. *Childbirth Instructor Magazine's Guide to Careers in Birth: How to Find a Fulfilling Job in Pregnancy, Labor and Parenting Support without a Medical Degree.* New York: John Wiley & Sons, 1998.

Sternberg, Robert J., ed. *Career Paths in Psychology: Where Your Degree Can Take You.* Washington, D.C.: American Psychological Association, 1997.

Witcher, Barbara Johnson. *Create the Job You Love and Still Make Plenty of Money: More Than 550 Ways to Escape the 8 to 5 Grind.* Rocklin, Calif.: Prima Publishing, 1997.

Career Reference Works

Hopke, William E. *The Encyclopedia of Careers and Vocational Guidance, Vols I-III.* Chicago: Ferguson Publishers, 1997.

Krantz, Les. *National Business Employment Weekly Jobs Rated Almanac.* New York: John Wiley & Sons. Published annually.

Bureau of Labor Statistics. *The Occupational Outlook Handbook*. Indianapolis: Jist Works. Published biennially in March.

U.S. Department of Labor. *The O*Net Dictionary of Occupational Titles*. Indianapolis: Jist Works, 1998.

Editors of VGM in conjunction with the U.S. Department of Labor. *The Big Book of Jobs*. Lincolnwood, Ill.: VGM Career Horizons, 1996.

Wright, John. *The American Almanac of Jobs and Salaries*. New York: Avon Books. Published biennially in October.

Trade Journals and Magazines

Fischer, Carolyn A., ed. *Gale Directory of Publications and Broadcast Media*. Detroit: Gale Research, Inc. Published annually in November.

Scientific and Technical Books and Serials in Print (1995). New York: Bowker, 1994.

Standard Periodical Directory, The. New York: Oxbridge Communications, Inc. Published annually in December.

Internship Sources

Green, Maryanne Ehrlich. *Internship Success: Real World Step-by-Step Advice on Getting the Most Out of Internships*. Lincolnwood, Ill.: VGM Career Horizons, 1977.

Jobst, Katherine. *Internships: 38,000 On-the-Job Training Opportunities for All Types of Careers*. Cincinnati: Writer's Digest Books. Published annually.

Landes, Michael. *The Back Door Guide to Short-Term Job Adventures: Internships, Extraordinary Experiences, Seasonal Jobs, Volunteering, Work Abroad*. Berkeley: Ten Speed Press, 1997.

Oldman, Mark, and Sarner Harnadeh. *America's Top Internships*. New York: Princeton Review Publishing. Updated regularly.

———. *The Internship Bible*. New York: Princeton Review Publishing. Published annually.

Playing the Game Sources

Coleman, Harvey J. *Empowering Yourself: The Organizational Game Revealed*. Dubuque, Iowa: Kendall/Hunt Publishing Co., 1996.

Covey, Stephen R. *The 7 Habits of Highly Effective People: Powerful Lessons in Personal Change*. New York: Fireside, 1990.

Harragan, Betty Lehan. *Games Mother Never Taught You: Corporate Gamesmanship for Women*. New York: Warner, 1987.

Koonce, Richard H. *Career Power!: 12 Winning Habits to Get You from Where You Are to Where You Want to Be*. New York: Amacom, 1994.

Kouzes, James S., Barry Z. Posner, and Tom Peters. *Credibility: How Leaders Gain and Lose It, Why People Demand It*. San Francisco: Jossey-Bass, 1995.

Kravetz, Stacy. *Welcome to the Real World: You've Got an Education, Now Get a Life!* New York: W.W. Norton & Company, 1997.

McCormack, Mark H. *What They Don't Teach You at Harvard Business School: Notes from a Street-Smart Executive*. New York: Bantam, 1988.

Moses, Barbara. *Career Intelligence: Mastering the New Work and Personal Realities*. Toronto, Canada: Stoddart Publishing Co., 1997.

Popcorn, Faith. *The Popcorn Report*. New York: HarperBusiness, 1992.

Rogers, Henry C. *Roger's Rules for Success: Tips That Will Take You to the Top by One of America's Foremost Public Relations Experts*. New York: St. Martin's Press, 1986.

Scheele, Adele M. *Skills for Success: A Guide to the Top*. New York: Ballantine, 1981.

Schein, Edgar H. *Career Survival: Strategic Job and Role Planning*. San Diego: Pfeiffer and Co., 1994.

Yeomans, William N. *1000 Things You Never Learned in Business School*. New York: New American Library, 1990.

———. *7 Survival Skills for a Reengineered World*. New York: Penguin USA, 1998.

ACT III: The Battle for Life's Work

Raise Money Sources

Blechman, Bruce Jan, and Jay Conrad Levinsen. *Guerilla Financing: Alternatives to Finance Any Small Business*. Boston: Houghton Mifflin, 1992.

Goldstein, Arnold S. *Starting on a Shoestring: Building a Business without a Bank Roll*. New York: John Wiley & Sons, 1995.

Lacy, Harold. *Financing Your Business Dreams with Other People's Money: How and Where to Find Money for Start-Up and Growing Businesses*. Traverse City, Mich.: Rhodes and Easton, 1998.

Additional Financial Sources

Applegate, Jane. *201 Great Ideas for Your Small Business.* Princeton: Bloomberg Press, 1998.

Cornish, Clive G. *Basic Accounting for the Small Business.* Bellingham, Wash.: Self-Council Press Inc., 1992.

Daniel Bokser, ed. *Pratt's Guide to Venture Capital Sources.* Wellesley Hills, Mass.: Capital Publishing. Published annually.

Fox, Jack. *Accounting and Recordkeeping Made Easy for the Self-Employed.* New York: John Wiley & Sons, 1994.

Kamoroff, Bernard. *The Small Time Operator.* Laytonville, Calif.: Bell Springs Publishing, 1997.

Lesko, Matthew. *Getting Yours: The Complete Guide to Government Money.* New York: Penguin, 1987.

Malburg, Christopher R. *Accounting for the New Business.* Holbrook, Mass.: Adams Media Corporation, 1997.

Sailing the Entrepreneurship Sources

BUSINESS PLAN

Bangs, David H. *The Business Planning Guide.* Chicago: Upstart Publishing Co., 1996.

Covello, Joseph A. and Brian J. Hazelgren. *The Complete Book of Business Plans.* Naperville, Ill.: Sourcebooks Trade, 1994.

Mancuso, Joseph R. *How to Prepare and Present a Business Plan.* Englewood Cliffs, N.J.: Prentice-Hall, 1992.

Pinson, Linda, and Jerry Jinnett. *Anatomy of a Business Plan.* Chicago: Upstart Publishing Co., 1996.

Seigel, Eric S., Brian R. Ford and Jay M. Bornstein. *The Ernst and Young Business Plan Guide.* New York: John Wiley & Sons, 1993.

ENTREPRENEURSHIP

Adams, Bob. *Adam's Streetwise Small Business Start-Up.* Holbrook, Mass.: Adams Media Corp, 1996.

Allen, Marc. *Visionary Business.* Novato, Calif.: New World Library, 1997.

Applegath, John. *Working Free: Practical Alternatives to the Nine to Five Job.* New York: Amacom, 1982.

Brandt, Steven C. *Entrepreneuring: The 10 Commandments for Building a Growth Company.* Friday Harbor, Wash.: Archipelago, Pubs., 1997.

Broussard, Cheryl D. *Sister CEO: The Black Woman's Guide to Starting Her Own Business.* New York: Viking Books, 1997.

Drucker, Peter F. *Innovation and Entrepreneurship.* New York: HarperBusiness, 1993.

Edwards, Paul, and Sarah Edwards. *Secrets of Self-Employment.* New York: Putnam, 1996.

Gale Research Co. *Small Business Sourcebook.* Detroit: Gale Research Co. Published annually in October.

Gerber, Michael E. *The E-Myth Revisited: Why Most Small Businesses Don't Work and What to Do About It.* New York: HarperCollins Publishers, 1995.

Hallett, Anthony, and Diane Hallett. *Encyclopedia of Entrepreneurs.* New York: John Wiley & Sons, 1997. Inspiring stories of entrepreneurial success.

Hawken, Paul. *Growing a Business.* New York: Simon & Schuster, 1987.

Hicks, Tyler Gregory. *199 Great Home Businesses You Can Start (And Succeed in for Under $1,000).* Rocklin, Calif.: Prima Publications, 1992.

Janal, Daniel S. *101 Successful Businesses You Can Start on the Internet.* New York: John Wiley & Sons, 1997.

Kivirist, Lisa. *Kiss Off Corporate America: A Young Professional's Guide to Independence.* Kansas City, Mo.: Andrews and McMeel Publishing, 1998.

Levinson, Jay Conrad. *The Way of the Guerilla.* Boston: Houghton Mifflin Co., 1997.

McQuown, Judith H. *Inc. Yourself: How to Profit By Setting Up Your Own Corporation.* New York: HarperBusiness, 1995.

Shaw, Lisa. *1001 Ways to Market Yourself and Your Small Business.* New York: Perigee Books, 1997.

Spinosa, Charles, Fernando Flores, and Hubert L. Dreyfus. *Disclosing New Worlds: Entrepreneurship, Democratic Action, and the Cultivation of Solidarity.* New York: John Wiley & Sons, 1997.

Whitmeyer, Claude, and Salli Rasberry. *Running a One Person Business.* Berkeley: Ten Speed Press, 1994.

Winter, Barbara J. *Making a Living without a Job: Winning Ways for Creating Work that You Love.* New York: Bantam, 1993.

LEGAL

Adams, Paul. *155 Legal Do's (and Dont's) for the Small Business.* James E. Gray & Associates, 1996.

Nicholas, Ted. *How to Form Your Own Corporation without a Lawyer for Under $75.00.* Chicago: Upstart Publishing Co., 1996.

MANAGEMENT

Bennis, Warren, and Burt Nanus. *Leaders: The Strategies for Taking Charge.* New York: HarperBusiness, 1997.

Covey, Stephen R. *Principle Centered Leadership.* New York: Fireside, 1992.

Drucker, Peter F. *Management: Tasks, Responsibilities, Principles.* New York: HarperBusiness, 1993.

Jawarski, Joseph, and Betty S. Flowers. *Synchronicity: The Inner Path of Leadership.* San Francisco: Berrett-Koehler Publishers, 1998.

Oakley, Ed, and Doug Krug. *Enlightened Leadership.* New York: Fireside, 1994.

Peters, Thomas J., and Robert H. Waterman, Jr. *In Search of Excellence.* New York: Warner Books, 1988.

Senge, Peter M. *The Fifth Discipline: The Art and Practice of the Learning Organization.* New York: Doubleday, 1994.

MARKETING

Cook, Kenneth J. *AMA Complete Guide to Small Business Marketing.* Lincolnwood, Ill.: NTC Business Books, 1994.

Crandell, Rick, ed. *10 Secrets of Marketing Success.* Corte Madera, Calif.: Select Press, 1997.

Decker, Sam, ed. *301 Do-It-Yourself Marketing Ideas.* Boston: Inc. Publishing, 1997.

Dennison, Dell. *The Advertising Handbook for Small Business.* Bellingham, Wash.: Self Counsel Press Inc., 1994.

Levinson, Jay Conrad. *Guerrilla Marketing: Secrets for Making Big Profits in Your Small Business.* Boston: Houghton Mifflin Co., 1993.

Phillips, Michael, and Robert Rasberry. *Marketing without Advertising.* Berkeley: Nolo Press, 1997.

Ries, Al, and Jack Trout. *Positioning: The Battle for Your Mind.* New York: Warner, 1996.

SALES

Alessandra, Anthony J. et al. *Non-Manipulative Selling.* New York: Fireside, 1992.

Beckwith, Harry. *Selling the Invisible: A Field Guide to Modern Marketing.* New York: Warner Books, 1998.

Bettger, Frank. *How I Raised Myself from Failure to Success in Selling.* Englewood Cliffs, N.J.: Prentice-Hall, 1992.

Hopkins, Tom. *How to Master the Art of Selling.* New York: Warner Books, 1994.

Johnson, Kerry L. *Sales Magic: Revolutionary New Techniques that will Double Your Sales Volume in 21 Days.* New York: Quill, 1995.

Johnson, Spencer. *The One-Minute Sales Person.* New York: Avon, 1991.

Kawasaki, Guy. *Selling the Dream: How to Promote Your Product, Company, or Ideas—Using Everyday Evangelism.* New York: HarperBusiness, 1992.

Kellar, Robert E. *Sales Negotiation Skills That Sell.* New York: Amacom, 1996.

Mandino, Og. *The Greatest Salesman in the World.* New York: Bantam, 1987.

Massie, Brigid McGrath. *Selling for People Who Hate to Sell.* Rocklin, Calif.: Prima Publications, 1996.

Silva, Jose. *Sales Power: The Silva Mind Method for Sales Professionals.* New York: Berkeley Publishing Group, 1994.

Ziglar, Zig. *Zig Ziglar's Secrets of Closing the Sale.* New York: Berkeley Publishing Group, 1987.

Home-Based Business Sources

Arden, Lynie. *The Work-at-Home Sourcebook.* Boulder: Live Oak Publications, 1996.

Attard, Janet. *The Home Office and Small Business Answer Book.* New York: Henry Holt and Co., 1993.

Bond, William J. *Going Solo: Developing a Home-Based Consulting Business from the Ground Up.* New York: McGraw-Hill, 1997.

Cook, Mel. *Home Business, Big Business.* New York: Macmillan, 1998.

Edwards, Paul, and Sarah Edwards. *The Best Home Businesses for the 90s.* New York: Jeremy P. Tarcher/Putnam, 1994.

———. *Making Money with Your Computer at Home.* New York: G.P. Putnam and Sons, 1997.

———. *Working from Home.* New York: Putnam Publishing Group, 1994.

Gielgun, Ron E. *121 Internet Businesses You Can Start from Home.* Brooklyn, N.Y.: Actium Publishing, Inc., 1997.

Hanania, David. *Home Business Made Easy.* Grants Pass, Ore.: The Oasis Press, 1998.

Hull, Caroline, and Tonya Wallace. *Moneymaking Moms: How Work at Home Can Work for You.* Secaucus, N.J.: Citadel Press, 1998.

Levinson, Jay Conrad, and Seth Godin. *Guerilla Marketing for the Home-Based Business.* Boston: Houghton Mifflin Co., 1995.

Mueller, Jo. *Moonlighting for a Second Income at Home.* Grants Pass, Ore.: The Oasis Press, 1997.

Ramsey, Dan. *101 Best Home Businesses.* Franklin Lakes, N.J.: The Career Press, 1997.

Saunders, Darcie, and Martha M. Bullen. *Turn Your Talents into Profits: 100+ Terrific Ideas for Starting Your Own Home-Based Micro-business.* New York: Pocket Books, 1998.

Weltman, Barbara. *The Complete Idiot's Guide™ to Starting a Home-Based Business.* New York: Alpha Books, 1997.

Freelance Sources

Bly, Robert W. *Secrets of a Freelance Writer: How to Make $85,000 a Year.* New York: Henry Holt, 1997.

Bodin, Frederik D. *Freelance Photographer's Handbook.* Curtin & London Inc., 1981.

Boyd, Amanda, and Thomas Clark, eds. *Writer's Digest Handbook of Making Money Freelance Writing.* Cincinnati: Writer's Digest Books, 1997.

Cook, Mary F. *Consulting on the Side: How to Start a Part-Time Consulting Business While Still Working at Your Full-Time Job.* New York: John Wiley & Sons, 1996.

Faux, Marian. *Successful Freelancing: The Complete Guide to Establishing and Running Any Kind of Freelance Business.* New York: St. Martins Press, 1997.

Fleishman, Michael. *Getting Started as a Freelance Illustrator or Designer.* Cincinnati: North Light Books, 1990.

Holtz, Herman R. *Business Plan Guide for Independent Consultants.* New York: John Wiley & Sons, 1994.

Keyes, Jessica. *How to Be a Successful Internet Consultant.* New York: McGraw-Hill, 1996.

Kintler, David. *Adam's Streetwise Guide to Consulting.* Boston: Bob Adams, 1997.

Kishel, Gregory, and Patricia Kishel. *How to Start and Run a Successful Consulting Business.* New York: John Wiley & Sons, 1996.

Korlson, David. *Marketing Your Consulting and Professional Services.* Menlo Park, Calif.: Crisp Publications, 1988.

Michels, Carroll. *How to Survive & Prosper as an Artist: Selling Yourself without Selling Your Soul.* New York: Henry Holt and Company, Inc., 1997.

Perlstein, David. *Solo Success: 100 Tips $100,000 a Year Freelancer.* New York: Three Rivers Press, 1998.

Reno, Kelly. *100 Best Freelance Careers.* New York: Arco Publishing, 1998.

Rozakis, Laurie E., and David Rye. *The Complete Idiot's Guide to Making Money in Freelancing.* New York: MacMillan, 1998.

Ruhl, Janet. *The Computer Consultant's Guide: Real-Life Strategies for Building a Successful Consulting Career.* New York: John Wiley & Sons, 1997.

Sorenson, George. *Power Freelancing: Home Based Careers for Writers, Designers and Consultants.* Minneapolis: Mid-List Press, 1995.

Williams, Theo Stephan. *The Streetwise Guide to Freelance Design and Illustration.* Cincinnati: Writer's Digest, 1998.

Yudkin, Marcia. *Freelance Writing for Magazines and Newspapers.* New York: HarperCollins, 1993.

Mail Order Sources

Hoge, Cecil C. *Mail Order Moonlighting.* Berkeley: Ten Speed Press, 1988.

Joffe, Heraldo. *How You Too Can Make at Least $1,000,000. (but Probably Much More) in the Mail-Order Business.* New York: HarperCollins, 1979.

Wilbur, L. Perry. *Money in Your Mailbox: How to Start and Operate a Mail Order Business.* New York: John Wiley & Sons, 1992.

Artist's Sources

Caplin, Lee, ed. *The Business of Art.* Englewood Cliffs, N.J.: Prentice-Hall, 1989.

Duboff, Leonard. *The Art Business Encyclopedia.* New York: Allworth Press, 1994.

Mary Cox, ed. *Artist's and Graphic Designer's Market.* Cincinnati: Writer's Digest. Published annually.

Nonprofit Foundation Sources

Allen, Nick., Mal Marwick, and Michael Stein, eds. *Fundraising on the Internet: Recruiting and Renewing Donors Online.* Berkeley: Strathmoor Press, 1997.

Barry, Bryan. *Strategic Planning Workbook for Nonprofit Organizations.* St. Paul: Amherst H. Wilder Foundation, 1997.

Blazek, Jody. *Financial Planning for Nonprofit Organizations.* New York: John Wiley & Sons, 1996.

Brinckerhoff, Peter C. *Financial Empowerment: More Money for Mission.* New York: John Wiley & Sons, 1998.

Burlingame, Dwight, F. *Critical Issues in Fund Raising*. New York: John Wiley & Sons, 1997.

Claitors. *Catalog of Federal Domestic Assistance*. Washington, D.C.: Claitors Publishing Division. Published annually.

Connors, Tracy Daniel, ed. *The Nonprofit Management Handbook: Operating Policies and Procedures*. New York: John Wiley & Sons, 1995.

Drucker, Peter. *The Five Most Important Questions You Will Ever Ask about Your Nonprofit: Participant's Workbook*. San Francisco: Jossey-Bass Publishers, 1994.

Eadie, Douglas E. *Changing By Design: A Practical Approach to Leading Innovation in Nonprofit Organizations*. San Francisco: Jossey-Bass Publishers, 1997.

Edles, Peter L. *Fundraising: Hands-On Tactics for Nonprofit Groups*. New York: McGraw-Hill, 1995.

Grace, Kay Sprinkel. *Beyond Fund Raising: New Strategies for Nonprofit Innovation and Investment*. New York: John Wiley & Sons, 1997.

Hall, L. Victoria, and Phyllis Edelson, eds. *Foundation Grants to Individuals*. New York: The Foundation Center, 1997.

Herman, Robert D. *The Jossey-Bass Handbook of Nonprofit Leadership and Management*. San Francisco: Jossey-Bass, 1994.

Howe, Fisher, and Alan Shrader. *The Board Member's Guide to Strategic Planning: A Practical Approach to Strengthening Nonprofit Organizations*. San Francisco: Jossey-Bass Publishers, 1997.

Hummel, Joan M. *Starting and Running a Nonprofit Organization*. Minneapolis: University of Minnesota Press, 1996.

Keegan, P. Burke. *Fundraising for Nonprofits*. New York: HarperCollins, 1994.

Lauber, Daniel. *Nonprofits & Education Job Finder*. River Forest, Ill.: Planning Communications, 1997.

Layton, Daphne Niobe. *Philanthropy and Voluntarism, an Annotated Bibliography*. New York: The Foundation Center, 1987.

M. Booth, Inc. Associates. *Promoting Issues and Ideas: A Guide to Public Relations for Nonprofit Organizations*. New York: The Foundation Center, 1995.

Mancuso, Anthony. *How to Form a Nonprofit Corporation*. Berkeley: Nolo Press, 1998.

Mancuso, Anthony, and Barbara Kate Repa. *The California Nonprofit Corporation Handbook*. Berkeley: Nolo Press, 1996.

Morris, James McGrath, and Laura Adler, eds. *Grant Seekers Guide: Foundations that Support Social and Economic Justice*. Mt. Kisco, N.Y.: Moyer Bell, Ltd., 1996.

Morrison, Emily Kittle. *Leadership Skills: Developing Volunteers for Organizational Success*. Tuscon, Ariz.: Fisher Books, 1994.

Nason, John W. *Foundation Trusteeship: Service in the Public Interest*. New York: The Foundation Center, 1989.

Octameron Associates. *Loans and Grants from Uncle Sam: Am I Eligible and for How Much?* Alexandria, Va.: Octameron Associates. Updated regularly.

Office of Management and Budget. *Update to the Catalog of Federal Domestic Assistance*. Washington, D.C.: U.S. Government Printing Office, 1988.

Olenick, Arnold J., and Phillip R. Olenick. *Nonprofit Organization Operating Manual: Planning for Survival and Growth*. New York: The Foundation Center, 1991.

Peter F. Drucker. *Managing the Nonprofit Organization: Principles and Practices*. New York: HarperBusiness, 1992.

Phelan, Marilyn E. *Nonprofit Enterprise: Law and Taxation*. Deerfield, Ill.: Clark, Boardman and Callaghan, 1990.

Public Management Institute. *Corporate Five Hundred: Directory of Corporate Philanthropy*. San Francisco. Published annually.

Rados, David L. *Marketing for Nonprofit Organizations*. Dover, Mass.: Auburn House Publishing Company, Inc., 1996.

Salzman, Jason. *Making the News: A Guide for Nonprofits and Activists*. Boulder: Westview Press, a division of HarperCollins, 1998.

Schlacter, Gail Ann. *Directory of Financial Aids for Women*. Redwood City, Calif.: Reference Service Press. Published biennially.

Schneiter, Paul. *The Art of Asking*. Amber, Pa.: Fund-Raising Institute, 1985.

Seltzer, Michael. *Securing Your Organization's Future: A Complete Guide to Fundraising Strategies*. New York: The Foundation Center, 1987.

Skloot, Edward, ed. *The Nonprofit Entrepreneur: Creating Ventures to Earn Income*. New York: The Foundation Center, 1988.

Steckel, Richard, Jennifer Lehman, and Alan Shrader. *In Search of America's Best Nonprofits*. San Francisco: Jossey-Bass, 1997.

Stoesz, Edgar, and Chester Raber. *Doing Good Better!* Intercourse, Pa.: Good Books, 1997.

The Foundation Center. *Corporate Foundation Profiles*. New York: The Foundation Center, 1998.

_____. *Directory of New and Emerging Foundations.* New York: The Foundation Center. Published annually.

_____. *Foundation Fundamentals.* New York: The Foundation Center, 1994.

_____. *The Foundation Center's Guide to Grant Seeking on the Web.* The Foundation Center. New York: The Foundation Center, 1998.

_____. *The Foundation Grants Index.* The Foundation Center. New York. Published annually.

The Taft Group. *The Taft Foundation Reporter.* Washington, D.C.: The Taft Group, 1990.

U.S. Department of Health and Human Services. *Discretionary Grants Administration Manual.* Washington, D.C., 1987.

U.S. Government Staff. *Cumulative List of Organizations, 2 vols.* Washington, D.C.: Claitors, 1997.

Van Til, Jon. *Mapping the Third Sector.* New York: The Foundation Center, 1988.

Zeff, Robbin Lee. *The Nonprofit Guide to the Internet.* New York: John Wiley & Sons, 1996.

Corporate Sector Sources

The editors of Adams Media Corp. *Adams' Job Almanac.* Holbrook, Mass.: Adams Media Corp. Published annually.

Harnadeh, Sarner, and Mark Oldman. *The Job Vault.* Boston: Houghton Mifflin Co., 1997.

Hoover's Inc. *Hoover's Top 2,500 Employers.* Austin: Hoover's Business Press, 1996.

Krantz, Les. *The World Almanac Job Finder's Guide.* New York: St. Martin's Press. Published annually.

Levering, Robert. *A Great Place to Work: What Makes Some Employers So Good (And Most So Bad).* New York: Avon Books, 1990.

Levering, Robert, and Milton Moskowitz. *The 100 Best Companies to Work for in America.* New York: Plume, 1994.

Mickens, Ed. *The 100 Best Companies for Gay Men and Lesbians.* New York: Pocket Books, 1994.

Woodruff, Cheryl. *The 150 Best Companies for Liberal Arts Graduates: Where to Get a Winning Job in Tough Times.* New York: John Wiley & Sons, 1992.

Government Jobs Sources

Camenson, Blythe. *Real People Working in the Government.* Lincolnwood, Ill.: VGM Career Horizons, 1998.

Federal Research Service, Inc. *Federal Career Opportunities.* Vienna, Va.: Federal Research Service, Inc. Updated regularly.

Krannich, Ronald L., and Caryl Rae Krannich. *Finding a Federal Job: How to Cut the Red Tape and Get Hired.* Woodbridge, Va.: Impact Publications, 1995.

_____. *The Complete Guide to Public Employment.* Manassas, Va.: Impact Publications, 1995.

_____. *The Directory of Federal Jobs and Employers.* Manassas, Va.: Impact Publications, 1996.

Lauber, Daniel. *Government Job Finder.* River Forest, Ill.: Planning Communications, 1997.

Leadership Directories, Inc. *Federal Yellow Book.* Washington, D.C.: Leadership Directories, Inc. Published quarterly.

Pitz, Mary Elizabeth. *Careers in Government.* Lincolnwood, Ill.: VGM Career Horizons, 1994.

Rutsohn, Rita, ed. *America's Federal Jobs: A Complete Directory of Federal Career Opportunities.* Indianapolis: Jist Works, 1991.

Troutman, Katherine K. *Federal Résumé Guidebook.* Indianapolis: Jist Works, Inc., 1997.

Nonprofit Sector Job Sources

Cohen, Lilly, and Dennis Young. *Careers for Dreamers and Doers: A Guide to Management Careers in the Nonprofit Sector.* New York: The Foundation Center, 1989.

Colvin, Donna, and Ralph Nader. *Good Works: A Guide to Careers in Social Change.* New York: Barracade Books, Inc., 1994.

Hamilton, Leslie, and Robert Tragent. *100 Best Nonprofits to Work For: Find Your Dream Job—And Launch a Rewarding Career Doing Good!* New York: Macmillan Reference USA, 1998.

Research Organizations Sources

Staff of Carroll Press. *Career Guide to Professional Associations: A Directory of Organizations by Occupational Field, Second Edition.* Cranston, R.I.: Carroll Press, 1980.

Desjardins, Dawn Conzett. *Directories in Print.* Detroit: Gale Research Co. Published annually in January.

Direct Communications. *International Employment Hotline.* Rutland, Vt.: Direct Communications. Updated monthly.

Downs, Buck, R., Wilson Hardy, and Nathan L. Cantor, eds. *National Trade and Professional Associations of the United States.* Washington, D.C.: Columbia Books, Inc. Published annually in March.

Foreign Policy Association, ed. *Guide to Careers in World Affairs.* Manassas, Va.: Impact Publications, 1993.

Lesko, Matthew, and Sharon Zarozny. *Information U.S.A.* New York: Penguin USA, 1986.

MacKenzie, Leslie. *The Directory of Business Information Resources: Associations, Newsletters, Magazines, Trade Shows, Directories, Databases.* Lakeville, Conn.: Grey House Publishing, 1998.

Networking in the Public Interest. *Community Jobs: The National Employment Newspaper for the Non-profit Sector.* Washington, D.C.: Networking in the Public Interest. Published monthly.

Peterson's Guides. *Peterson's Job Opportunities for Engineering and Computer Science Majors.* Princeton: Peterson's Guides. Published annually in August.

Petras, Kathryn, and Ross Petras. *Jobs '98.* New York: Fireside, 1996.

Renetzky, Alvin, ed. *Career Employment Opportunities Directory: A Guide to Career Employment Opportunities, 4 Volumes.* Santa Monica, Calif.: Ready Reference Press, 1985.

Savageau, David, and Geoffrey Loftus. *Places Rated Almanac.* New York: Macmillan, 1997.

Tuller, Michael, ed. *The Foundation Directory.* New York: The Foundation Center. Published biennially.

Washington Researchers Publications. *Company Information: A Model Investigation.* Washington, D.C.: Washington Researchers Publishing, 1983.

_____. *How to Find Information about Private Companies.* Washington, D.C.: Washington Researchers Publications. Published annually in March.

Woy, James. *Encyclopedia of Business Information Sources.* Detroit: Gale Research, Co. Published biennially.

Yvette, Henry, ed. *Taft Foundation Reporter.* Washington, D.C.: The Taft Group, 1990.

Zemke, Ron. *The Service Edge: 101 Companies that Profit from Customer Care.* New York: New American Library, 1990.

Business Reference Works

Deydo Harry P., ed. *MacRae's Blue Book.* New York. Published annually in March/April.

Dun & Bradstreet. *Dun & Bradstreet Million Dollar Directory.* New York: Dun & Bradstreet. Published annually in February/March.

Gale Research Co. *Ward's Directory.* Detroit: Gale Research Co. Published annually.

Labash-Young, Margaret, et al., eds. *Subject Directory of Special Libraries and Information Centers, Vol. I, Business and Law Libraries.* Detroit: Gale Research Co. Published annually in November.

Moody's Investor's Service, Inc. *Moody's Manuals.* New York: Moody's Investor's Service, Inc. Published annually.

Standard and Poor's. *Poor's Register of Corporations, Directories and Executives.* New York: Standard and Poor's, Subsidiary of McGraw-Hill. Published annually.

Thomas Publishing Company. *Thomas Register of American Manufacturers.* New York: Thomas Publishing Company. Published annually.

Sources for Information on Interviewers

Levine, Michael. *The Address Book: How to Reach Anyone Who's Anyone.* New York: Perigee Books. Biennial.

Marquis Who's Who. *Who's Who.* New Providence, N.J.: Marquis Who's Who. Published annually.

Omnigraphics, Inc. *Business Phone Book USA: The National Directory of Addresses and Telephone Numbers.* Detroit: Omnigraphics. Published annually.

R. R. Bowker. *American Men and Women of Science.* New Providence, N.J.: R. R. Bowker.

Superintendent of Documents. *United States Government Manual.* Washington, D.C.: U.S. Government Printing Office. Published annually in September.

Landing the Right Job Sources

RÉSUMÉS

Beatty, Richard. *175 High Impact Resumes.* New York: John Wiley & Sons, 1996.

Biegeleisen, J.I. *Job Résumés: How to Write Them, How to Present Them, Preparing for Interviews.* New York: The Putnam Publishing Group, 1991.

Corwen, Leonard. *Your Résumé: Key to a Better Job.* New York: Arco Publishing, Inc., 1995.

Enelow, Wendy. *100 Winning Resumes for $100,000+ Jobs: Resumes that Can Change Your Life!* Manassas, Va.: Impact Publications, 1997.

Hansen, Katherine et al. *Dynamic Cover Letters.* Berkeley: Ten Speed Press, 1995.

Hochheiser, Robert M. *Throw Away Your Résumé.* Hauppauge, N.Y.: Barron's Educational Series, 1995.

Krannich, Ronald L., Caryl Krannich. *Dynamite Resumes: 101 Great Examples and Tips for Success.* Manassas, Va.: Impact Publications, 1996.

Krannich, Ronald L., Caryl Krannich, and William J. Banis. *High Impact Résumés and Letters: How to Communicate Your Qualifications to Employers.* Manassas, Va.: Impact Publications, 1998.

Lewis, Adele, and Gary Joseph Grappo. *How to Write Better Résumés.* Hauppauge, N.Y.: Barron's Educational Series, 1998.

Ray, Samuel N. *Resumes for the Over-50 Job Hunter.* New York: John Wiley & Sons, 1993.

Reed, Jean, and Ray Potter. *Résumés That Get Jobs.* New York: MacMillan, 1998.

Yate, Martin John. *Cover Letters that Knock 'Em Dead.* Holbrook, Mass.: Adams Media Corp., 1997.

INTERVIEWS

Allen, Jeffrey G. *How to Turn an Interview into a Job.* New York: Simon & Schuster, 1986.

_____. *The Complete Q and A Job Interview Book.* New York: John Wiley & Sons, 1997.

Chapman, Jack. *Negotiating Your Salary: How to Make $1,000 a Minute.* Berkeley: Ten Speed Press, 1996.

Corcodilos, Nick A. *Ask the Headhunter: Reinventing the Interview to Win the Job.* New York: Plume Books, 1997.

Fein, Richard. *101 Dynamite Questions to Ask at Your Job Interview.* Manassis, Va.: Impact Publications, 1996.

Green, Paul C. *Get Hired! Winning Strategies to Ace the Interview.* Austin: Bard Press, 1996.

Medley, H. Anthony. *Sweaty Palms: The Neglected Art of Being Interviewed.* Berkeley: Ten Speed Press, 1992.

Washington, Tom. *Selling Yourself Face to Face.* Bellevue, Wash.: Mt. Vernon Press, 1995.

Yate, Martin John. *Knock 'Em Dead.* Boston: Bob Adams, Inc., Published annually in November.

Yeager, Neil, and Lee Hough. *Power Interviews: Job-Winning Tactics from Fortune 500 Recruiters.* New York: John Wiley & Sons, 1998.

FINDING A JOB

Adams Media Corp. *The National Job Bank.* Holbrook, Mass.: Adams Media Corp. Published annually.

Bolles, Richard Nelson. *What Color Is Your Parachute?* Berkeley: Ten Speed Press. Published annually.

Bridges, William. *Jobshift: How to Prosper in a Workplace without Jobs.* Reading, Mass.: Addison-Wesley Publishers, 1995.

Figler, Howard. *The Complete Job-Search Handbook: All the Skills You Need to Get Any Job and Have a Good Time Doing It.* New York: Henry Holt & Co., 1988.

Griffith, Susan. *Work Your Way Around the World.* Princeton: Peterson's Guides, 1997.

Lathrop, Richard. *Who's Hiring Who: How to Find that Job Fast.* Berkeley: Ten Speed Press, 1989.

Lauber, Daniel. *Professional's Job Finder.* River Forest, Ill.: Planning Communications, 1997.

Lecompte, Michelle. *Job Hunter's Sourcebook: Where to Find Employment Leads and Other Job Search Resources.* Detroit: Gale Research, Inc., 1996.

Lucht, John. *The Rights of Passage at $100,000+: The Insider's Lifetime Guide to Executive Job-Changing and Faster Career Progress.* Viceroy Press, 1993.

Noble, John H. *The Job Search Handbook.* Boston: Bob Adams, Inc., 1988.

Petras, Kathryn, and Ross Petras. *The Only Job Hunting Guide You'll Ever Need.* New York: Fireside, 1995.

Vinitsky, Barbara Bloch, and Janice Yukon Benjamin. *How to Become Happily Employed: A Step-by-Step Guide to Finding the Job that Is Right for You.* Kansas City, Mo.: Career Management Press, 1986.

UNEMPLOYED OR ABOUT TO BE

Albright, Townsend. *How to Hold It All Together When You've Lost Your Job.* Lincolnwood, Ill.: VGM Career Horizons, 1995.

Birkel, Damian, and Stacey J. Miller. *Career Bounce-Back! The Professionals in Transition™ Guide to Recovery and Reemployment.* New York: Amacom, 1997.

Byron, William J. *Finding Work without Losing Heart: Bouncing Back From Mid-Career Job Loss.* Holbrook, Mass.: Adams Media Corp., 1995.

Elkort, Martin L. *From Fired to Hired: Bounce Back from Losing Your Job and Get Your Career Back on Track.* New York: Arco Publishing, 1997.

Galos, Jodie-Beth, and Sandy McIntosh, Ph.D. *Firing Back: Power Strategies for Cutting the Best Deal When You're About to Lose Your Job.* New York: John Wiley & Sons, 1997.

Pulley, Mary Lynn. *Losing Your Job—Reclaiming Your Soul: Stories of Resilience, Renewal, and Hope.* San Francisco: Jossey-Bass Publishers, 1997.

INTERNET JOB SEARCH SOURCES

Criscito, Pat. *Resumes in Cyberspace*. Hauppauge, N.Y.: Barrons Educational Series, 1997.

Crispin, Gerry, and Mark Mehler. *CareerXRoads*. Kendall Park, N.J.: MMC Group. Published annually.

Godin, Seth. *Point and Click Jobfinder: How to Get a Great Job Online*. Chicago: Dearborn Trade, 1996.

Gonyea, James C., and Wayne M. Gonyea. *Electronic Resumes*. New York: McGraw-Hill, 1996.

Jandt, Fred E., and Mary B. Newrich. *Using the Internet in Your Job Search*. New York: Jist Works, 1997.

Karl, Shannon, and Arthur Karl. *How to Get Your Dream Job Using the Web*. Scottsdale: Coriolis Group Books, 1997.

Straub, Carrie. *Jobsearch.Net*. Menlo Park, Calif.: Crisp Publications, 1998.

Weddle, Peter D. *Internet Resumes*. Manassas, Va.: Impact Publications, 1998.

Associations Source

Koek, Karin, and Susan Boyles-Martin, eds. *Encyclopedia of Associations*. Detroit: Gale Research Co, 1992.

Mastermind Sources

Bourgoin, Suzanne Michele, and Paula K. Byers, eds. *Encyclopedia of World Biography*. Detroit: Gale research Co., 1998.

Hill, Napoleon. *Think and Grow Rich*. New York: Ballantine, 1996.

Moritz, Charles. *Current Biography Yearbook*. Bronx, N.Y.: H.W. Wilson Company, 1995.

Networking Sources

Baldridge, Letitia. *Letitia Baldridge's Complete Guide to the New Manners for the '90s*. New York: Rawson Associates, 1990.

Carnegie, Dale, and Dale Carnegie Associates, Inc. *The Leader in You: How to Win Friends, Influence People and Succeed in a Changing World*. New York: Pocket Books, 1995.

Garner, Alan. *Conversationally Speaking: Tested New Ways to Increase Your Personal and Social Effectiveness*. Los Angeles: Lowell House, 1997.

Wohlmuth, Ed. *The Overnight Guide to Public Speaking*. New York: Signet, 1993.

Zunin, Leonard, M.D., with Natalie Zunin. *Contact: The First Four Minutes*. New York: Ballantine, 1994.

Publicity Sources

Brown, Lillian. *Your Public Best: The Complete Guide to Making Successful Public Appearances in the Meeting Room, on the Platform, and on T.V.* New York: Newmarket Press, 1992.

Fletcher, Tana, and Julia Rockler. *Getting Publicity: The Very Best Book for Your Small Business*. Bellingham, Wash.: Self-Counsel Press, 1995.

Peoples, David A. *Presentations Plus: Techniques that Work from the Experts' Expert*. New York: John Wiley & Sons, 1997.

Rein, Irving J., Philip Kotler, and Martin R. Stoller. *High Visibility*. Lincolnwood, Ill.: NTC Contemporary Publishing Co., 1997.

Grant Writing Sources

Bauer, David G. *The 'How To' Grants Manual: Successful Grantseeking Techniques for Obtaining Public and Private Grants*. Phoenix, Ariz.: Oryx Press, 1995.

Blum, Laurie. *The Complete Guide to Getting a Grant: How to Turn Your Ideas into Dollars*. New York: John Wiley & Sons, 1996.

Carlson, Mim. *Winning Grants Step by Step*. San Francisco: Jossey-Bass Publishers, 1995.

Geever, Jane C. et al. *The Foundation Center's Guide to Proposal Writing*. New York: The Foundation Center, 1997.

Golden, Susan L., and Alan Shrader. *Secrets of Successful Grantsmanship: A Guerilla Guide to Raising Money*. San Francisco: Jossey-Bass Publishers, 1997.

Hall, Mary S. *Getting Funded: A Complete Guide to Proposal Writing*. Portland, Ore.: Continuing Education Publications, 1988.

Miner, Lynn E., and Jerry Griffith. *Proposal Planning and Writing*. Phoenix, Ariz.: Oryx Press, 1993.

Robinson, Andy, and Kim Klein. *Grassroots Grants: An Activist's Guide to Proposal Writing*. Berkeley: Chardon Press, 1996.

White, Virginia. *Grants for the Arts*. New York: Plenum Press, 1980.

Negotiation Sources

Cohen, Herb. *You Can Negotiate Anything*. New York: Bantam, 1989.

Fisher, Roger, and William Ury. *Getting to Yes: Negotiating Agreement without Giving In*. with Bruce Patton, ed. Boston: Houghton Mifflin Co., 1992.

McCormack, Mark H. *On Negotiating*. Beverly Hills: Dove Books, 1997.

Pickens, James W. *The Art of Closing Any Deal: How to Be a Master Closer in Everything You Do.* New York: Warner Books, 1991.

Sparks, Donald B. *The Dynamics of Effective Negotiation: A Win-Win Approach to Getting What You Want.* Houston: Gulf Publishing Company, 1993.

Street Smarts Sources

Gralla, Preston, Sarah Ishida, and Mina Reimer. *How the Internet Works (Special Edition).* Indianapolis: Ziff Davis Press, 1997.

INTERNET RESEARCH

Calishain, Tara, and Jill Alane Nystrom. *Official Netscape Guide to Internet Research: For Windows and Macintosh.* Florence, Ky.: International Thomson Publishing, 1998.

James-Catalano, Cynthia N. *Researching on the World Wide Web: Spend More Time Learning, Not Searching.* Rocklin, Calif.: Prima Publishing, 1996.

Pfaffenberger, Bryan. *Web Search Strategies.* Foster City, Calif.: IDG Books Worldwide, 1996.

WEB MARKETING

Barrett, Neil. *Advertising on the Internet.* Dover, N.H.: Kogan Page Ltd, 1997.

Bayne, Kim M. *The Internet Marketing Plan: A Practical Handbook for Creating, Implementing and Assessing Your Online Presence.* New York: John Wiley & Sons, 1997.

Emery, Vince. *How to Grow Your Business on the Internet.* Scottsdale, Ariz.: The Coriolis Group, 1997.

O'Keefe, Steve. *Publicity on the Internet.* New York: John Wiley & Sons, 1996.

Sterne, Jim. *What Makes People Click: Advertising on the Web.* Indianapolis: Que Education & Training, 1997.

Zeff, Robbin Lee, and Brad Aronson. *Advertising on the Internet.* New York: John Wiley & Sons, 1997.

WEB PAGE DESIGN

Callihan, Steven E. *Create Your First Web Page in a Weekend.* Rocklin, Calif.: Prima Publications, 1996.

Smith, Bud E., and Arthur Bebak. *Creating Web Pages for Dummies.* Foster City, Calif.: IDG Books Worldwide, 1997.

Williams, Robin, and John Tollett. *The Non-Designer's Web Book: An Easy Guide to Creating, Designing, and Posting Your Own Web Site.* Berkeley: Peacepit Press, 1997.

ACT IV: The School of Life's Work

Making the Transition Sources

Bridges, William. *Managing Transitions.* San Francisco: Perseus Press, 1991.

Burton, Mary Lindley, and Richard A. Wedemeyer. *In Transition.* New York: HarperBusiness, 1992.

Lakein, Alan. *How to Get Control of Your Time and Your Life.* New York: New American Library, 1996.

Lizotte, Ken, and Barbara A. Litwak. *Balancing Work and Family.* New York: Amacom, 1995.

Lloyd, Joan. *The Career Decisions Planner: When to Move, When to Stay, and When to Go Out on Your Own.* New York: John Wiley & Sons, 1992.

McCay, James T., Richard Ward, and Laurie Blanch Ward. *The Management of Time.* Englewood Cliffs, N.J.: Prentice-Hall, 1995.

Morrisey, George L. *Getting Your Act Together.* New York: John Wiley & Sons, 1980.

Sharlan, William. *Career Shifting: Starting Over in a Changing Economy.* Holbrook, Mass.: Adams Media Corp., 1993.

Smith, Hyrum W. *The 10 Natural Laws of Successful Time and Life Management.* New York: Warner Books, 1995.

Image Sources

Bixler, Susan. *The New Professional Image: From Business Casual to the Ultimate Power Look.* Holbrook, Mass.: Adams Media Corp., 1997.

Brody, Marjorie, and Shawn Kent. *Power Presentations: How to Connect with Your Audience and Sell Your Ideas.* New York: John Wiley & Sons, 1992.

Cooper, Morton. *Change Your Voice, Change Your Life: A Quick, Simple Plan for Finding and Using Your Natural Dynamic Voice.* North Hollywood: Wilshire Book Co., 1996.

Garner, Alan. *Conversationally Speaking: Tested New Ways to Increase Your Personal and Social Effectiveness.* Los Angeles: Lowell House, 1997.

Glass, Lillian. *Talk to Win: Six Steps to a Successful Vocal Image.* New York: Putnam Publishing Group, 1988.

Mitchell, Mary, with John Corr. *The First Five Minutes: How to Make a Great First Impression in Any Business Situation.* New York: John Wiley & Sons, 1998.

Molloy, John T. *John T. Molloy's New Dress for Success.* New York: Warner, 1988.

_____. *New Woman's Dress for Success.* New York: Warner, 1996.

Sources to Investigate

Atich, Sam. *How to Get a College Degree Via the Internet.* Rocklin, Calif.: Prima Publishing, 1998.

Bear, John, and Mariah P. Bear. *Bears' Guide to Earning College Degrees Nontraditionally.* Berkeley: Ten Speed Press, 1995.

Bunting & Lyon, Inc. *Private Independent Schools.* Wallingford, Conn.: Bunting & Lyon, Inc. Published annually in March.

The College Board Staff. *The College Handbook.* New York: College Board. Published annually in August.

Duffy, James P. *College Online: How to Take College Courses without Leaving Home.* New York: John Wiley & Sons, 1997.

Education for the Earth: The College Guide for Careers in the Environment. Princeton: Peterson's Guides, 1997.

Frank, Stanley D. *The Evelyn Wood 7 Day Speed Reading and Learning Program: Remember Everything You Read.* New York: Avon, 1992.

Gross, Ronald. *The Independent Scholar's Handbook.* Berkeley: Ten Speed Press, 1993.

The Guide to Correspondence Study. New York: Macmillan. Published biennially in September.

Huang, Chungliang Al, and Jerry Lynch. *Mentoring: The Tao of Giving and Receiving Wisdom.* New York: HarperCollins, 1995.

Institutional Research, Inc. *America's 100 Best College Buys.* Camden, S.C.: John Culler & Sons. Published annually.

_____. *America's Best College Scholarships.* Camden, S.C.: John Culler & Sons. Published annually.

Karl, Arthur, and Shannon Karl. *How to Get into Your Dream College Using the Web.* Scottsdale, Ariz.: Coriolis Group Books, 1997.

Katz, Bill, and Linda Sternberg-Katz. *Self-Help: 1,400 Best Books on Personal Growth.* New York: R. R. Bowker, 1985.

Lamdin, Lois S., and Susan Simosko. *Earn College Credit for What You Know.* Dubuque, Iowa: Kendall/Hunt Publishing Co., 1997.

Law School Admission Council. *The Prelaw Handbook: Official Guide to U.S. Law Schools.* Newton, Pa.: Law School Admission Services. Published annually.

Lyons, Dianne J. B. *Planning Your Career in Alternative Medicine: A Guide to Degree and Certificate Programs in Alternative Healthcare.* Albuquerque, N.Mex.: Avery Publishing Group, 1997.

McLean, Janice. *Training and Development Organizations Directory.* Detroit: Gale Research Co., 1994.

Mintz, Jerry. *Handbook of Alternative Education.* New York: Macmillan, 1994.

Modoc Press, Inc., compiler. *MacMillan Guide to Correspondence Study.* New York: Macmillan Publishing Co., Inc., 1996.

Peterson's Guide to Nursing Programs: Baccalaureate and Graduate Nursing Programs in the U.S. and Canada. Princeton: Peterson's Guides. Published biennially.

Schwarzkopf, Leroy C. *Guide to Popular U.S. Government Publications.* Littleton, Colo.: Libraries Unlimited, 1992.

_____. *Government Reference Books: A Biennial Guide to U.S. Government Publications.* Littleton, Colo.: Libraries Unlimited, Inc. Published biennially.

Smith, Peter, ed. *Your Hidden Credentials.* Washington, D.C.: Acropolis Books, Ltd., 1986.

Thorson, Marcie Kisner. *Campus-Free College Degrees.* Tulsa, Okla.: Thorson Guides, 1998.

Tyler, Suzette. *Been There, Should've Done That: 505 Tips for Making the Most Out of College.* Lansing, Mich.: Front Porch Press, 1997.

Unger, Harlow G. *But What If I Don't Want to Go to College?: A Guide to Success Through Alternative Education.* New York: Facts on File, 1998.

Wilson, Erlene B. *The 100 Best Colleges for African American Students.* New York: Plume, 1998.

Wilson, Mark V. *Distance Degrees.* Sutherlin, Ore.: Umpqua Education Research Alliance, 1997.

The World of Learning. London, England: Europa Publications Ltd., Taylor & Francis. Published annually.

Financial Aid Sources

Cassidy, Daniel J. *The Scholarship Book.* Englewood Cliffs, N.J.: Prentice-Hall, 1998.

College Scholarship Service. *College Cost and Financial Aid Handbook.* New York: College Board of Publications. Published annually in August.

_____. *Finding Financial Resources for Adult Learners*. New York: College Board of Publications, 1985.

MacMillan Publishing Co. *The College Blue Book*. New York: MacMillan Publishing Co. Published biennially in October.

Peterson's Scholarships, Grants and Prizes: The Most Comprehensive Guide to College Financial Aid from Private Sources. Princeton: Peterson's Guides. Published annually in September.

Rae, Gail. *Money for College: Everything You Need to Know to Get Financial Aid*. Research & Education Association, 1998.

Schlacter, Gail Ann. *Directory of Financial Aids for Women*. Redwood City, Calif.: Reference Service Press. Biennial.

_____. *How to Find Out about Financial Aid*. Redwood City, Calif.: Reference Service Press. Updated regularly.

Schlacter, Gail Ann, and David R. Weber. *Financial Aid for Veterans, Military Personnel and Their Dependents*. Redwood City, Calif.: Reference Service Press. Published biennially in February.

Visualization Sources

Gawain, Shakti. *Creative Visualization*. Novato, Calif.: New World Library, a subsidiary of Whatever Publishing, Inc., 1995.

Howard, Vernon. *Psycho-Pictography: The New Way to Use the Miracle Power of Your Mind*. Englewood Cliffs, N.J.: Prentice-Hall, 1996.

Ungerleider, Steven. *Mental Training for Peak Performance: Top Athletes Reveal the Mind Exercises They Use to Excel*. Emmaus, Pa.: Rodale Press, 1996.

Behavior Modification Sources

Maltz, Maxwell. *Psycho-Cybernetics*. Englewood Cliffs, N.J.: Prentice-Hall, 1987.

Murphy, James F. *The Miracle of Mind Dynamics*. Englewood Cliffs, N.J.: Prentice-Hall, 1980.

Appendix B: Volunteering

Volunteering Sources

Adams, Tom. *Grassroots: How Ordinary People are Changing America*. New York: Citadel Press, 1991.

American Hiking Association. *1994 Helping Out in the Outdoors: A Directory of Volunteer Work and Internships on America's Public Land*. Washington, D.C.: American Hiking Association, 1993.

Bernard, Michael, ed. *Volunteers in Public Schools*. Washington, D.C.: National Academy Press, 1990.

_____. *Golden Opportunities: A Volunteer Guide for Americans Over 50*. Princeton: Peterson's Guides, 1994.

De Geronimo, Theresa. *A Student's Guide to Volunteering*. Franklin Lakes, N.J.: The Career Press, 1995.

Hollender, Jeffrey, and Linda Catling. *How to Make the World a Better Place: 116 Ways You Can Make a Difference*. New York: W. W. Norton & Company, 1995.

Kipps, Harriet Clyde. *Volunteer America*. Chicago: Ferguson Publishing Co., 1997.

Lauffer, Armand, and Sarah Gorodenzky. *Volunteers*. Beverly Hills: Sage Publications, 1977.

Lawson, Douglas M. *Volunteering: 101 Ways You Can Improve the World and Your Life*. Poway, Calif.: Alti Publishing Co., 1998

McMillon, Bill. *Volunteer Vacations: Short-Term Adventures that will Benefit You and Others*. Chicago: Chicago Review Press, 1997.

O'Connell, Brian. *Voices from the Heart: A Celebration of America's Volunteers*. New York: The Foundation Center, 1998.

O'Connell, Brian, and Ann Brown. *Volunteers in Action*. New York: The Foundation Center, 1989.

Pidgeon, Walter. *Universal Benefits of Volunteering: A Practical Workbook for Nonprofit Organizations, Volunteers, and Corporations*. New York: John Wiley & Sons, 1977.

Pybus, Victoria, ed. *The International Directory of Voluntary Work*. Princeton: Peterson's Guides, 1997.

Raynolds, John F., and Gene Stone. *The Halo Effect: How Volunteering to Help Others Can Lead to a Better Career and a More Fulfilling Life*. New York: Golden Books Publishing Co., 1998.

Shields, Katrina, and Phil Somerville. *In the Tiger's Mouth: An Empowerment Guide to Social Action*. New Haven, Conn.: New Society Publishers, 1993.

Wilson, Marlene. *You Can Make a Difference! Helping Others and Yourself Through Volunteering*. Boulder: Volunteer Management Associates, 1990.

INDEX

—THE END—

Everything must end;
meanwhile we must
amuse ourselves.
Voltaire

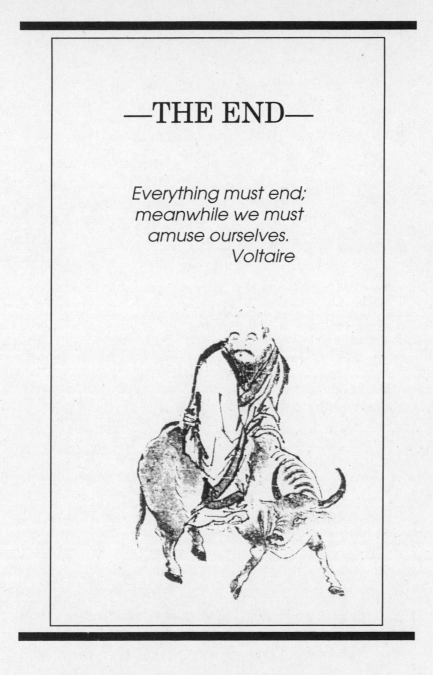

Visit The Center for Creative Empowerment at:

www.empoweryou.com

for career information, resources, links and more.

FOR THE BEST IN PAPERBACKS, LOOK FOR THE 🐧

Available from Laurence G. Boldt and Penguin Arkana

ZEN AND THE ART OF MAKING A LIVING—Expanded and Updated Edition
A Practical Guide to Creative Career Design

This life-changing book helped revolutionize the career planning field by offering a new vision of work. This new edition has been updated throughout with up-to-the-minute contact information and Internet job resources.

"Work is more than a matter of keeping busy all day. It must feed the soul as well. Laurence Boldt has done a splendid job of explaining this truth. I commend this book to all thoughtful readers and seekers."   —Richard N. Bolles, author of *What Color Is Your Parachute?*
ISBN 0-14-019599-8

HOW TO FIND THE WORK YOU LOVE

In today's work environment, doing the work you love is *the* critical factor in personal fulfillment and economic success. Laurence Boldt leads readers toward a breakthrough understanding of what they could and should do with their lives.   *ISBN 0-14-019524-6*

• ALSO AVAILABLE ON AUDIOCASSETTE FROM PENGUIN AUDIOBOOKS

ZEN SOUP
Tasty Morsels of Wisdom from Great Minds East & West

This book of inspirational quotations illuminates the essential qualities associated with Zen. You'll find Lao Tzu on courage, Mahatma Gandhi on responsibility, and Colette on joy—an invaluable source of wisdom for anyone looking for meaning in this world.   *ISBN 0-14-019560-2*

And don't miss Laurence Boldt's upcoming book,
The Tao of Abundance (Fall 1999).

Using eight guiding principles from Taoist philosophy, Boldt presents new definitions of success and new attitudes toward material ambition—proving that real abundance is about much more than money and careers.